# JavaScript™

## THIRD EDITION

*R. Allen Wyke, et al.*

A Division of Macmillan USA
201 West 103rd Street
Indianapolis, Indiana 46290

# Unleashed

# JavaScript™ Unleashed, Third Edition

## Copyright© 2000 by Sams

International Standard Book Number: 0-672-31763-X

Library of Congress Catalog Card Number: 99-63993

Printed in the United States of America

First Printing: June 2000

02    01    00         4    3    2    1

## Trademarks

## Warning and Disclaimer

**ASSOCIATE PUBLISHER**
*Michael Stephens*

**EXECUTIVE EDITOR**
*Rosemarie Graham*

**ACQUISITIONS EDITOR**
*Shelley Johnston*

**DEVELOPMENT EDITOR**
*Robyn Thomas*

**MANAGING EDITOR**
*Matt Purcell*

**PROJECT EDITOR**
*George E. Nedeff*

**COPY EDITOR**
*Gene Redding*

**INDEXER**
*Sandra Henselmeier*
*Deborah Hittel*
*Kevin Kent*

**PROOFREADERS**
*Candice Hightower*
*Linda Seifert*
*Matt Wynalda*

**TECHNICAL EDITOR**
*Jason Wright*

**TEAM COORDINATOR**
*Pamalee Nelson*

**MEDIA DEVELOPER**
*Maggie Molloy*

**INTERIOR DESIGNER**
*Gary Adair*

**COVER DESIGNER**
*Aren Howell*

**COPYWRITER**
*Eric Borgert*

**3B2 PRODUCTION**
*Brad Lenser*

F. Schmidt

# Contents at a Glance

# Contents

## 25 Interacting with Other Technologies 673

## PART V Essential Programming Techniques 703

## 26 Guaranteeing Your Scripts Work in Netscape and Microsoft Browsers 705

## 27 Browser Detection Techniques 737

# About the Authors

## Lead Author

**R. Allen Wyke**, of Durham, North Carolina, is the Director of Product Technology at Engage Technologies. At Engage he works with many of the leading Internet properties to implement advertising and profiling solutions. He has also developed intranet Web pages for a leading networking company and has worked on several Internet sites. He has programmed in everything from C++, Java, Perl, Visual Basic, and JavaScript to Lingo.

Allen's writing credentials include co-authoring *Pure JavaScript*, *The Perl 5 Programmer's Reference*, *The Official Netscape Navigator 4 Book*, and an Internet resource book for college graduates. He also contributed to two other titles on the topic of Web development—*HTML Publishing on the Internet, Second Edition* and *The HTML 4 Programmer's Reference*, and in his spare time writes the monthly "Webmaster" column for *SunWorld* and a weekly article, "Windows and UNIX Integration," for ITworld.com.

## Contributing Authors

**Richard Wagner** is Vice President of Product Development for Acadia Software and was the chief architect of Acadia Infuse, a visual editor for JavaScript that was sold to NetObjects. In addition to being an experienced author in the computer industry, he has considerable development experience in both Web and client/server applications. Wagner is a contributing editor for *Delphi Informant,* in which he has a monthly column called "File|New," which focuses on trends in software development. Wagner wrote *Inside Paradox for Windows* (three editions), *CompuServe Internet Tour Guide,* and *Inside CompuServe* (three editions). He co-wrote *Ultimate Windows 3.1, Inside Windows NT, Inside Microsoft Access, Inside dBASE for Windows,* and *Integrating Windows Applications*. He has a B.A. in political science from Taylor University and pursued a graduate degree at American University. He welcomes your comments at rwagner@acadians.com.

**Jason D. Gilliam**, a software engineer at KOZ.com in the Research Triangle Park, NC, has developed many intranet Web pages as well as numerous C++ and Web-based GUI applications and database connectivity programs. He has been programming since age 13 and is the co-author of the book *Pure JavaScript*. He holds a bachelor's degree in Computer Engineering from North Carolina State University. When he is not at work programming, he creates Windows-based audio programs and composes original music using PCs.

**Francis Botto** was born in Swansea (Wales, UK). He has primarily been a writer and researcher specializing in new technologies since the mid-1980s when he began a pioneering and prolific output of notable articles and enduring books that he wrote in the UK and more recently in Australia. The context of his work shifts between usage, development issues, and conceptual designs, and the range of his writing spans from early works about CAD and multimedia to the modern Internet with all its new, exciting, and radical paradigm shifts. He brings this wealth of experience to his contributions to *JavaScript Unleashed, Third Edition*.

# Dedication

This one is for Matt, Jeff, and Greg. You guys are not only good friends, but also the greatest brother-in-laws that my sisters could have found.

—R. Allen Wyke

# Acknowledgments

First, I would like to thank Bob Kern of TIPS Publishing and my co-authors, Richard, Jason, and Francis, for their professionalism, hard work, and overall support in the writing of this book. I would also like to thank Shelley Johnston, who has been nothing short of an absolutely fabulous Acquisitions Editor and a great pleasure to work with, and Robyn Thomas, who had very encouraging comments, developed the book, and helped keep us focused. Additionally, I would like to thank Jason Wright, Mike Walker, George Nedeff, Gene Redding, and everyone else behind the scenes at Sams who worked on the book and helped make sure it was the best it could be.

Finally, I would like to thank Kimo "King" Kong for allowing me the flexibility and opportunity to write during my duties at Engage.

&mdash;R. Allen Wyke

# Tell Us What You Think!

As the reader of this book, *you* are our most important critic and commentator. We value your opinion and want to know what we're doing right, what we could do better, what areas you'd like to see us publish in, and any other words of wisdom you're willing to pass our way.

As a Publisher for Sams Publishing, I welcome your comments. You can fax, email, or write me directly to let me know what you did or didn't like about this book—as well as what we can do to make our books stronger.

*Please note that I cannot help you with technical problems related to the topic of this book, and that due to the high volume of mail I receive, I might not be able to reply to every message.*

When you write, please be sure to include this book's title and author as well as your name and phone or fax number. I will carefully review your comments and share them with the author and editors who worked on the book.

| | |
|---|---|
| Fax: | 317-581-4770 |
| Email: | java@mcp.com |
| Mail: | Michael Stephens |
| | Associate Publisher |
| | Sams Publishing |
| | 201 West 103rd Street |
| | Indianapolis, IN 46290 USA |

# Introduction

JavaScript has quickly emerged as a significant tool for Web development, whether for simple enhancements to HTML pages or full-fledged Web-based applications. But because its *raison d' être* is not as glamorous, JavaScript will perhaps never be as popular as Java or even HTML. Having said that, JavaScript does something none of the others can do: It makes divergent technologies work together seamlessly. Indeed, the jack-of-all-trades nature of JavaScript is perhaps what gives this language its staying power.

Most people probably see JavaScript as a client-side language. That it is—and much of this book focuses on how to embed JavaScript into HTML to run under supporting browsers. However, JavaScript is also emerging as a server-side scripting language. Netscape's Server-Side JavaScript (SSJS) and Microsoft's Active Server Pages (ASP) were among the first of many products to use JavaScript as their Web scripting language.

I am a developer by trade, and the more I use JavaScript, the more I see its wide-ranging applicability in the applications my company develops. It is my hope that JavaScript's capability to handle a wide variety of tasks will become evident as you read this book. Here are a few of the many questions this book will answer:

- What is the relationship between JavaScript and HTML?

- What is the difference between JavaScript and JScript?

- Are there any compatibility issues surrounding the many versions of JavaScript and JScript?

- How can you create special effects with JavaScript?

- How can you create smart frames with JavaScript?

- What are the core JavaScript objects?

- Where does ECMAScript fit?

- How does JavaScript integrate with ActiveX controls, plug-ins, and Java applets?

- How does JavaScript handle state maintenance?

- How can I use JavaScript on my Web server?

- How does JavaScript compare to Java?

- How can I connect to my SQL database using JavaScript?

# Who Should Read This Book?

Because of its status as the primary Web scripting language, JavaScript is used for all sorts of tasks. Those who use it include

- Webmasters

- HTML authors and designers

- Java developers

- Database application developers

- Power users

I believe that readers in each of these categories will appreciate this book. I assume that you have basic Web and HTML knowledge. You don't need JavaScript experience, but you should have some programming experience in a scripting or full language. If you've never programmed before, this doesn't mean that this book isn't for you. But this book doesn't offer much instruction in beginner programming issues that aren't germane to JavaScript. In the advanced server- and database-related chapters, some server and database experience is required.

# System Requirements

In order to use JavaScript, you need a capable computer that has access to the Web. The authors of this book primarily used Windows (98, 2000, and NT), but the same JavaScript code will work in Netscape Navigator, Internet Explorer, Sun HotJava, and Opera versions for Macintosh, UNIX, and other supported platforms (except where noted).

# How This Book Is Organized

*JavaScript Unleashed, Third Edition* provides a whole-hog look at JavaScript and related technologies. It's divided into six parts, each of which is summarized in the following sections.

## Part I    Getting Started with JavaScript

Part I is a complete introduction to JavaScript and JavaScript tools. Chapter 1 takes a unique look at JavaScript, focusing on how and where it fits into the Web application development framework. You will also see how it relates to other Web technologies, on both the client side and the server side. In Chapter 2, you will learn about the relationship between JavaScript and HTML and how the browser interprets your code at runtime. Chapter 3 looks at the software tools you need to develop in JavaScript, and Chapter 4 steps you through the entire process of writing your first script.

## Part II    The Core JavaScript Language

Part II presents a thorough look at the JavaScript language. In Chapters 5 through 12, you will learn about language basics, operators, control structures, functions, and objects (core, client-side, server-side, and custom).

## Part III    Scripting the Document Object Model

Part III dives into the heart of the Document Object Model with Chapter 13, "Fundamentals of the Document Object Model (DOM)." You will be introduced to this method of referencing elements on a page, as well as how to handle events in Chapter 14. The final part of this section, Chapters 15 through 19, include chapters on the Window, Document, Form, and Frame objects and other DOM objects as well.

## Part IV    Dynamic HTML Programming Techniques

Part IV focuses on some of the things people are doing with JavaScript on the Web. Chapter 20, which shows you how to do rollovers, and moves into Chapter 21 where it looks at how you can create animations, banners, and other special effects in JavaScript—without using any Java applets. Chapter 22 brings you up to speed with cascading style sheets, and Chapter 23 concentrates on the implementation of "layers" introduced in the version 4 browsers. Chapter 24 then pulls all of this together to show you how to build Dynamic HTML menus and toolbars, and Chapter 25 finishes off Part IV by showing you how JavaScript can interact with other technologies, such as Java and ActiveX.

## Part V    Essential Programming Techniques

Part V builds on much of what you have learned by looking at specific areas of interest to JavaScript developers. Chapter 26 shows you how to create scripts that work in Navigator and Internet Explorer browsers, Chapter 27 teaches you about browser detection, and Chapter 28 discusses how you can use JavaScript to make your Web site easier to navigate.

Chapter 29 explores how to enhance HTML forms with JavaScript, such as by providing client-side data validation. Chapter 30 discusses how to build dynamic and personalized pages through the use of cookies and other techniques for handling and maintaining state, Chapter 31 introduces regular expression pattern matching, and Chapter 32 teaches data techniques. Finally, Chapter 33 dives into error-handling, Chapter 34 gives tips on debugging JavaScript applications, and the book concludes with Chapter 35, which discusses security within JavaScript.

## Part VI   Appendix

Appendix A lists online JavaScript resources. It provides URLs to popular and useful sites to help you take your JavaScript knowledge to the next level.

# Conventions Used in This Book

This book uses certain conventions to help make the book more readable and helpful:

- JavaScript code listings, JavaScript method names, and screen messages or displays appear in a special `monospace` font.

- Placeholders (words that are substitutes for what you actually type) appear in *`monospace italic`*.

- Terms being introduced or defined appear in *italic*.

- Menu selections are separated with a comma. For example, "Select File, Open" means that you pull down the File menu and choose the Open option.

- Sometimes a line of JavaScript code is unable to fit on a single line of this book. When this happens, the line is broken and continued on the next line, preceded by a ➥ character.

In addition, this book uses special sidebars that are set apart from the rest of the text. These sidebars include Notes, Tips, Cautions, Warnings, Resources, and Reminders.

# Getting Started with JavaScript

# PART

# I

## IN THIS PART

# CHAPTER 1

# JavaScript and the World Wide Web

## IN THIS CHAPTER

As most of you know, the going rate for an Internet year is equal to about three calendar months. With that in mind, I recommend the best way to learn JavaScript is to jump in headfirst. Sure, you can play with it a little here or a little there, but to get a firm grasp on how it works and operates, you need to embrace it. And like any other project, you should put forth a solid effort to digest the information and expose yourself to examples and projects.

But before diving into the nuts and bolts of creating JavaScript code, it's important to look at the purpose of JavaScript. JavaScript has grown outside its initial browser boundaries and can now be found on the server side and within the most recent release of the Windows operating system. On the browser side, JavaScript by itself has limitations, like other Web technologies such as HTML, Java, CSS (cascading style sheets), and plug-ins. JavaScript emerges as a powerful tool as you begin using it with other technologies to provide effective and deliberate solutions.

In this chapter, I provide an overview of JavaScript and look at JavaScript within the context of the Web application framework. After that, I'll look at the major uses of JavaScript today, current browsers' support for JavaScript, and some distinctions between JavaScript and VBScript.

# Introducing JavaScript

Like everything else connected to the Web, JavaScript is a new technology—even newer than Java itself. JavaScript was initially developed by Netscape under the name of LiveScript. This scripting language was intended to extend the capabilities of basic HTML and provide a partial alternative to using a large number of CGI scripts to process form information and add dynamics to a user's page. After the release of Java, however, Netscape began to work with Sun to provide a scripting language whose syntax and semantics were closely linked to Java—hence the name change to JavaScript. Both Netscape and Sun jointly released the language, once it was complete.

One of the motivations behind JavaScript was the recognition of a need for logic and intelligence to exist on the client, not simply on the server. With all logic on the server side, all processing is forced to go to the server, even for simple tasks such as data validation. In fact, with no logic on the front end, the Web environment falls into the outdated terminal-to-host architecture that was replaced with the PC revolution in the 1980s. Providing logic within the browser would empower the client and make the relationship a true client/server arrangement.

Java was a step in that direction, but it was implemented as an adjunct to HTML itself and was not intended to be integrated from a language standpoint. Also, as a strongly typed language, Java isn't optimal for gluing together the many technologies that Webmasters need in creating their pages. Furthermore, Java requires low-level programming skills, something that most HTML developers would rather not exercise solely to provide some logic behind form elements. A higher-level, client-side scripting language seemed like a natural missing piece in the Web development tool arena.

Since its rollout in December 1995, JavaScript has drawn support from the major industry vendors, including Apple, Borland, Sybase, Informix, Oracle, Digital, HP, and IBM. It has continued to grow by gaining support not only in the most current browsers of today, but also in other applications that these and other companies have released.

The plot thickened, however, when Microsoft entered the equation. Realizing the importance of Web scripting, Microsoft wanted to provide support for JavaScript as well. However, when Netscape would only license the technology to Microsoft rather than give it away, Redmond reverse-engineered JavaScript, based on the public documentation, to create its own implementation, JScript, which is supported in Microsoft Internet Explorer versions 3.0 and higher. JScript 1.0 is roughly compatible with JavaScript 1.1, which is supported in Netscape Navigator 3.0 and higher browsers. However, the myriad of JavaScript versions and various platform-specific quirks have left Web developers with headaches when they try to deploy JavaScript-enabled Web sites. (See Chapter 26, "Guaranteeing Your Scripts Work in Netscape and Microsoft Browsers," and Chapter 27, "Browser Detection Techniques," for more information on working with the various JavaScript versions.)

Fortunately, help was on the way for frustrated JavaScripters. Netscape, Microsoft, and other vendors agreed to turn over the language to an international standards body named ECMA. Since that time ECMA has finalized a language specification, known as ECMAScript, that all vendors can support in unity. Although the ECMA standard helps, both Netscape and Microsoft have their respective implementations of the language (JavaScript and JScript) and continue to extend the language beyond the basic standard.

In addition to JScript, Microsoft has its own competitor to JavaScript called VBScript, which was built to ease current VB developers onto the Web. VBScript is essentially a subset of the Visual Basic language. Because Netscape isn't supporting VBScript, its primary uses are for intranets (or Internet sites) that have a high concentration of Microsoft Internet Explorer users.

Even considering VBScript, JavaScript has emerged as the standard Web scripting language. As vendors produce Web development tools that require a scripting language, JavaScript often is used for that purpose. Netscape uses the language referred to as Server-Side JavaScript (SSJS) on the server side as well. This is something you will dive into later, in Chapter 12, "Server-Side JavaScript."

Of course Microsoft was not far behind, and when it released its Active Server Pages (ASP) technology, it included support for its JScript engine.

# Ten JavaScript Facts Every Scripter Should Know

Trying to learn a new tool such as JavaScript can be challenging, because it can be difficult to understand how it's used and how it fits into the general picture. I have boiled down the basics of JavaScript to 10 facts that will help you as you begin to work with it. Study them before you continue, because you will want to apply this knowledge to your understanding of the language and any projects you do.

## JavaScript Can Be Embedded into HTML

Perhaps the most important JavaScript event was its early marriage with HTML. If you deal with JavaScript on the client side, there is hardly any separation of the two. JavaScript code is usually housed in HTML documents and executed within them. Most JavaScript objects have HTML tags they represent, so the code is included at the core client-side level of the language. If you have little background in HTML, you will discover that, to be an effective JavaScript developer, you also need to learn the ins and outs of HTML.

JavaScript uses HTML as a means of jumping into what I call the *Web application framework*. It also extends the normal capabilities of HTML by providing events to HTML tags and allowing this event-driven code to execute within it.

Although I'll wait for future chapters to explain JavaScript, Listing 1.1 provides an example of how JavaScript code is embedded in HTML source code. The text in bold represents the JavaScript-specific code in the document. Everything else is plain HTML.

**LISTING 1.1**    JavaScript Embedded in an HTML File

```
<html>
<head>
    <title>Status Bar</title>
    <script type="text/javascript">
    <!--
```

LISTING 1.1    continued

```
        window.defaultStatus = "Welcome to the large URL page."

        function changeStatus() {
          window.status = "Click me to go to the Unleashed
➡            home page."
        }

        function changeDefaultStatus() {
          window.defaultStatus = window.document.statusForm.messageList.
➡            options[window.document.statusForm.messageList.
➡            selectedIndex].text
        }
      //-->
      </script>
</head>

<body>
  <p> </p>
  <p> </p>
  <p align="center">
    <font size="7" color="#008040">
      <strong>http://www.samspublishing.com</strong>
    </font>
  </p>
  <p align="center">
    <a href="http://www.samspublishing.com" onmouseover="changeStatus()
➡      ;return true">Go...</a>
  </p>
  <p align=center>
    <font size="1">
      To change the default status bar message, select a message from the
      list below and click the Change button.
    </font>
  </p>
  <form name="statusForm" method="POST">

    <select name="messageList" size="1">
      <option selected>Welcome to the large URL page.</option>
      <option>On route to Sams Publishing</option>
      <option>This page intentionally left (nearly) blank.</option>
      <option>An exciting example of changing status bar text.</option>
    </select>
```

**LISTING 1.1** continued

```
    <input type="button" name="Change" value="Change"
➡    onclick="changeDefaultStatus()">
  </form>
</body>
</html>
```

> **Note**
>
> I bet you noticed the `type="text/javascript"` here, didn't you? Well, it is true—the new HTML standard and the corresponding XHTML standard have deprecated the language attribute of the `<script>` tag in favor of this format. Don't worry for now—we will talk more about this in the next chapter.

## JavaScript Is Environment Dependent

JavaScript is a scripting language, not a tool in and of itself. The software that actually runs the JavaScript code you write is the interpreting engine within the environment—whether it's Netscape Navigator, Microsoft Internet Explorer, or one of the server-side engines. When included in an HTML document, JavaScript depends on the browser to support it, as shown in Figure 1.1. If the browser doesn't support it, your code will be ignored. Even worse, if you don't account for unsupported browsers, the JavaScript code itself may be displayed as text on your page, as shown in Figure 1.2. (See Chapter 2, "How JavaScript and HTML Work Together," for details on how to prevent your code from being displayed.)

It's critical to remember this dependence as you decide when and where to use JavaScript in your applications. Will you require a browser that supports JavaScript? If so, how should you notify users who use an unsupporting browser? Will you create a non-JavaScript solution as well? You need to answer all these questions as you develop your JavaScript applications.

**FIGURE 1.1**
*Microsoft Internet Explorer 4.5 supports JavaScript.*

**FIGURE 1.2**
*Mosaic doesn't support JavaScript.*

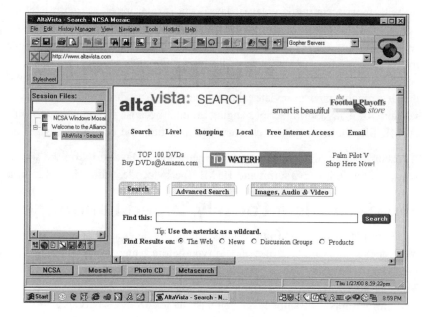

---

**Note**

When they were first released, frames were an innovative solution but could be viewed only if you had Netscape Navigator 2.0. HTML authors had to decide when to use frames and what to do when a browser didn't support them. With the continued popularity of Netscape and Microsoft's support for them in Internet Explorer 3.0, frames have become part of the HTML 4 Recommendation (standard). In fact, the unspoken assumption of many is that if you're "with it," you already have a browser that supports frames.

Fortunately for JavaScript developers, it's likely that the same will hold true for JavaScript support. Netscape Navigator 2.x and above, Microsoft Internet Explorer 3.x and above, Opera 3.x and above, HotJava 3.x and above—the browsers with some 95% of the market—do provide JavaScript support. If these trends continue, browser dependence will become less of an issue.

## JavaScript Is an Interpreted Language

As with most scripting languages, JavaScript is interpreted at runtime by the browser before it's executed. JavaScript isn't compiled into an actual binary—like an EXE file—but remains part of the HTML document to which it is attached. The disadvantage of an interpreted language is that it takes longer for the code to execute, because the browser compiles the instructions at runtime just before executing them. However, the advantage is that it's much easier to update your source code. You don't have to worry about old versions of a JavaScript script hanging around, because if you change it in your source HTML file, the new code is executed the next time the user accesses the document.

It is worth noting that Netscape's implementation of JavaScript on the server side requires you to compile all JavaScript and HTML file bytecode, which is stored in a `.web` file.

## JavaScript Is a Loosely Typed Language

JavaScript is far different from strongly typed languages such as Java or C++, in which you must declare all variables of a certain type before using them. In contrast, JavaScript is much more flexible. You can declare variables of a specific type, but you don't have to. You can also work with a variable when you might not know the specific type before runtime. A short code snippet can demonstrate this. Suppose you want to declare a variable called `myVal`, assign a string value to it, and then display it in a message box. You could use the following code:

```
function flexible() {
    var myVal    // declare variable myVal
```

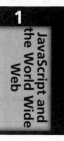

```
   mVal = "Pi"  // assign value to myVal
   alert(myVal) // use it
}
```

Although it's generally a good practice to declare your variables explicitly, you aren't required to do so. The following code, perfectly valid in JavaScript, would be unthinkable in a strongly typed language:

```
function flexible() {
   mVal = "Pi"  // assign value to an undeclared variable myVal
   alert(myVal) // use it
}
```

To further illustrate JavaScript's flexibility, you can change the type of value the variable represents as well. For example, the myVal variable changes from a string to a number value during the course of the function's execution:

```
function flexible() {
   var myVal = "Pi"
   alert(myVal)
   myVal = 3.14159
   alert(myVal)
}
```

## JavaScript Is an Object-Based Language

You might see JavaScript referred to as an object-oriented programming (OOP) language by Netscape and others, but this is actually a stretch of the true meaning of OOP. As you will learn in Chapter 9, "Client-Side Objects," JavaScript is really an *object-based* language.

You work with objects that encapsulate data (properties) and behavior (methods). (If you've used dot notation—in Visual Basic, Java, or Delphi—you will find JavaScript easy to pick up.) However, although you can work with objects, you can't subclass them. The JavaScript object model is instance based, not inheritance based.

# JavaScript Is Event Driven

Much of the JavaScript code you write will be in response to events generated by the user or the system. The JavaScript language itself is equipped to handle events. HTML objects, such as buttons or text fields, are enhanced to support event handlers. If you're coming from a Java or Visual Basic background, this event-driven environment is second nature. If you come from a procedural, top-down language environment, the event-driven nature of JavaScript might require some study. Chapter 14, "Handling Events," provides a complete look at JavaScript events.

# JavaScript Is Not Java

As you surf the Web, you may run into a phrase on some JavaScript-related Web sites: *JavaScript is not Java*. As discussed previously, Java and JavaScript were created by two different companies, and the primary reason for the name similarity is purely for marketing purposes. We will perform a more in-depth comparison between JavaScript and Java in Chapter 5, "Fundamentals of the JavaScript Language," but it might be helpful to mention briefly some of the differences (and similarities) that exist between them in this context as well.

First, although JavaScript is tightly integrated into HTML, a Java applet is simply connected to an HTML document through the `<applet>` tag. The applet itself is stored in another file, which is downloaded from the server.

Second, with strong typing, true object-orientation, and a compiler, Java is a more robust and complete language. Keep in mind that Java is for applets or complete applications; JavaScript is primarily for scripts.

If you look at the language itself, JavaScript's syntax resembles Java. If you get used to the JavaScript control structures, you could use that as a head start to learning Java itself.

# JavaScript Is Multifunctional

JavaScript is multifaceted and can be used in a variety of contexts to provide a solution to a Web-based problem. Later in this chapter, I'll discuss the variety of uses for JavaScript. Some of the primary purposes include the following:

- Enhance and liven static HTML pages through special effects, animations, and banners.
- Validate data without passing everything to the server.
- Serve as a building block for client/server Web applications.
- Develop client-side applications.

- Serve as client-side glue between HTML objects, Java applets, ActiveX controls, and Netscape plug-ins.

- Serve as an extension to a Web server.

- Simulate database connectivity without using CGI.

## JavaScript Is Evolving

Earlier in this chapter, I discussed how new JavaScript is as a technology. If you add that fact to the rapid rate of change on the Web, it's easy to recognize that JavaScript itself continues to evolve as a language. As you develop JavaScript applications, not only do you need to consider whether the browser supports JavaScript, but also which iteration of JavaScript (or JScript) it supports. With six JavaScript versions (1.0 through 1.5) and the many JScript versions (1.0 through 5.5 and several incremental versions), it can become maddening trying to deal with the variations.

**Resource**

Visit Netscape's DevEdge page at `http://developer.netscape.com` or Mozilla.org (the Open Source area for Netscape's browser tools that is currently driving JavaScript direction) at `http://www.mozilla.com` for information on future enhancements to JavaScript. For JScript enhancements, visit Microsoft at `http://msdn.microsoft.com/scripting`.

## JavaScript Spans Contexts

To repeat something mentioned earlier in this chapter: JavaScript is a language, not a tool. As a scripting language, it can be useful in a variety of contexts. Much of the focus on JavaScript by Web developers (and this book) is for client-side scripting. You can also use it on the server side in the Netscape Enterprise Server and Microsoft's Active Server Pages framework. It is used as the native language for Web development tools, such as Borland's IntraBuilder and Macromedia's Dreamweaver (version 2 and higher). When you think of JavaScript, don't think of it exclusively as a client-side scripting language. Moreover, recent versions of Microsoft Windows support JavaScript on the desktop with their Windows Script Host (WSH) environment.

# The Four Phases of the World Wide Web

The revolutionary changes in Web technology over the past six years have made the Web a constantly moving target. Before I discuss Web applications, it will be helpful to review the evolution of the Web from its humble beginnings as an extension of the Internet into a culture that is changing technology today. You can view this transformation as four distinct phases of the Web.

## Phase I: Character-Based Hypertext

The Web was a text-based hypertext system when it started in 1989. This limitation was primarily because the computers that accessed the Web had no good way of displaying graphics. In the Web's early days, users were forced to type in a number representing the page they wanted to access. In time, you could select highlighted text and then move to the associated page. For the Web's scientific and academic uses, the hypertext nature of the Web was revolutionary.

## Phase II: Graphical-Based Static HTML Documents

The second phase of the Web began in 1993 with the release of the first graphical Web browser, called NCSA Mosaic. Mosaic was co-developed by undergraduate student and future Netscape co-founder Marc Andreessen for the National Center for Supercomputing Applications (NCSA). Although the concept of the Web was already proving useful for the scientific and academic communities, a graphical browser suddenly harnessed the raw power of the Internet and made it easy to navigate. At the same time, graphical environments were becoming more popular than character-based systems on the desktop. Microsoft was winning the desktop war with Windows 3.1x.

Adding a graphical browser on top of the graphical desktop environment proved to be the "killer" application that the media were looking for. In just a matter of months, a frenzy of activity emerged from the media, computer companies, and corporations racing to provide content or services on the Web.

The Web itself remained static, as shown in Figure 1.3. Its content consisted of text or graphic documents and little else. Perhaps a page contained a sound or video file, but you would typically download the file and then play it using an external application.

**FIGURE 1.3**
*A static HTML page.*

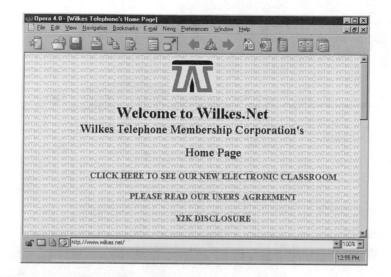

## Phase III: Dynamic HTML Documents

During Phases I and II, Web pages were created using an HTML text editor and placed on a Web server. Once they were placed on the server, most pages remained static until the author modified them. Static pages are satisfactory for some Web uses but not for others. To meet the need for dynamically generated HTML documents, Web developers started using common gateway interface (CGI) scripts on the Web server to generate HTML documents on-the-fly. This provided the first level of interaction with the user on the Web. With this enhancement, the Web could be the platform for hypertext documents but also serve as a distinct application environment. The FedEx Web site, shown in Figure 1.4, was one of the first Web applications that demonstrated the power of the Web.

## Phase IV: Active HTML Documents

The fourth phase of the Web began slowly in 1995 with the use of plug-ins in Netscape Navigator and rose to prominence with support from Java. The major focus of this phase has been to empower the client and not rely exclusively on the server to either run the application or process information entered by the user.

The hype surrounding Java is due primarily to the fact that the Web is no longer simply a collection of HTML documents but can be a true client/server environment in which the client has some independence from the server. This is where JavaScript fits in. With JavaScript, Java, ActiveX, and other client extensions, the browser can become a powerful operating environment in which to run Web applications.

FIGURE 1.4
*FedEx offered
one of the first
compelling Web
applications.*

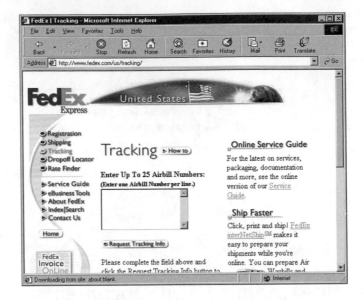

# The Web Application Framework

Using the Web as a development environment is a relatively new phenomenon. With the advent of Java, JavaScript, ActiveX, and other technologies, the idea of developing Web-centric applications has many attractive qualities.

The Web as a development environment can seem rather confusing. Because of the distributed nature of the Web, a Web application can be composed of many parts, using a variety of technologies.

In a typical LAN-based client/server architecture, you might have a client-based application attached to a database server on the network. You would often develop the client application using a single tool such as Delphi or Visual Basic. The server side of the application is typically developed and maintained using SQL Server's administrative tools.

Figure 1.5 shows the various parts that make up the application framework. The next sections examine each of those parts.

The Web development framework is truly an example of the sum being greater than the parts. By themselves, each of these technologies is limited and rather narrow in scope. When combined into cohesive applications, they provide an effective means of developing Internet and intranet solutions.

**FIGURE 1.5**
*A Web application framework.*

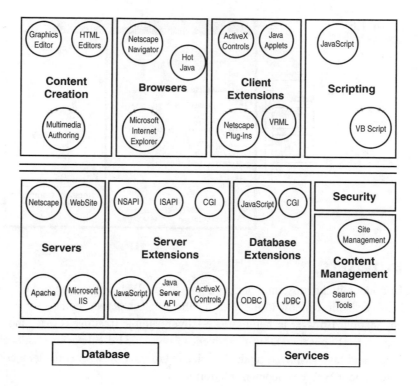

# Client Side

The client side of the Web application framework consists of four building blocks:

- Browsers
- HTML (Hypertext Markup Language)
- Client-Side Extensions (Java applets, ActiveX controls, and Netscape plug-ins)
- Scripting Languages (JavaScript and VBScript)

This section examines each of these technologies and how they work together. Figure 1.6 shows their interrelationships.

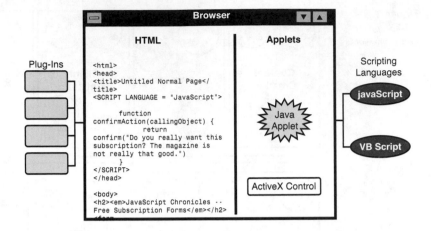

**FIGURE 1.6**
*A client-side framework.*

# Browsers

Undoubtedly the most important component of a Web application is the browser itself. The browser is the window to the Web for the user and serves as the user interface for your application. Browser technology is relatively simple (reading HTML and displaying it appropriately onscreen), but the advent of nonstandard enhancements, such as Netscape layers and JavaScript, has made the selection of your browser software a critical one as you determine a Web development platform.

If you're creating an intranet application, you can probably ensure that all users are using a standard Web browser. You can then make certain assumptions when you develop your application. However, if you're creating an Internet application that the world will use, your application design decisions become more complicated, continuously weighing features against compatibility.

Table 1.1 highlights the two major browsers today and notes the versions that support the specified client-side technologies.

**TABLE 1.1**   Browser Support of Client-Side Technologies

|  | *Netscape Navigator* | *Microsoft Internet Explorer* |
| --- | --- | --- |
| JavaScript/JScript support | 2.0+ | 3.0+ |
| VBScript support | None | 3.0+ |
| Java support | 2.0+ (3.0+ for Mac) | 3.0+ |
| ActiveX support | 3.0+(plug-in) | 3.0+ |
| Netscape plug-ins | 2.0+ | 3.0+ |

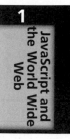

# HTML

HTML is obviously one of the primary technologies upon which the Web is built. HTML is a markup language that is used to provide structure and formatting to a plain text file. As a "technology," it's rather mundane—some would say outdated. Nonetheless, the commonness of the language gives it its power.

Although the browser provides the window for displaying Web-based content to the user, the content itself comes in the form of HTML text. It doesn't matter if you're presenting static documents, returning a query result, providing a feedback form, or displaying a JavaScript-based application. Regardless of the means of obtaining this data, it is ultimately converted into HTML tags for presentation.

# Client Extensions

As the need for active Web pages increased, simply beefing up Web browsers wasn't considered the best solution. Some extensions were third-party add-ons to the browser software to make it more powerful. However, there was also the need to work with *executable content* within the browser. Although the browser needed to support the technology, it didn't need to be tied to the browser to run.

Three separate client-side extensions are emerging today. They have similarities, but each has a distinct identity. They are

- Java applets
- ActiveX controls
- Netscape plug-ins

## Java Applets

If you've never heard of the Java programming language, one could call you Rip Van Winkle. After all, Java has been hyped like no other programming language before. I want to back up and discuss it within the context of the Web application framework.

### Resource

For information on Java, go to the main Java site at Sun at http://java.sun.com.

Java is a platform-independent programming language developed by Sun Microsystems. The reason for all the hype is Java's capability to create content that can be executed on a multitude of platforms.

Within the browser environment, Java programs are called *applets*. The applet is linked via an <applet> tag in the HTML document and can be downloaded onto the client computer. The applet comes to the browser in *bytecode*. If a browser supports Java, it interprets this bytecode and executes it on the client machine. The Java applet reference is ignored in browsers that aren't Java enabled.

Java applets have several uses and, as the language itself matures, the uses grow more sophisticated as well. Figures 1.7 and 1.8 provide two examples of uses of Java.

**FIGURE 1.7**
*A Java applet moves the plane across the screen.*

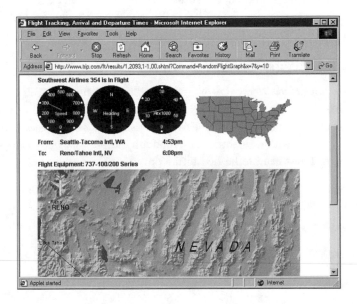

## ActiveX Controls

Formerly known as OCXs, ActiveX controls are Microsoft's answer to Java applets. They are similar to Java applets in that you can use them as a means of providing executable content across the Web, as shown in the spreadsheet in Figure 1.9. Unlike Java, ActiveX controls are currently limited to the Microsoft Windows operating environment.

Although ActiveX controls are limited to running in a single operating environment, they aren't necessarily limited to Web applications. For example, you can use the same ActiveX control in a Web application with an ActiveX-enabled browser and with a Windows programming tool such as Delphi or Visual Basic.

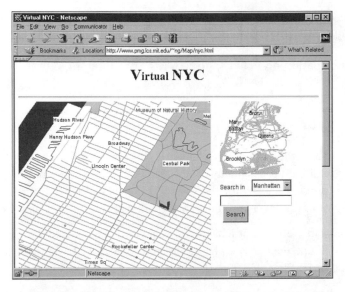

**FIGURE 1.8**
*An interactive
Java map.*

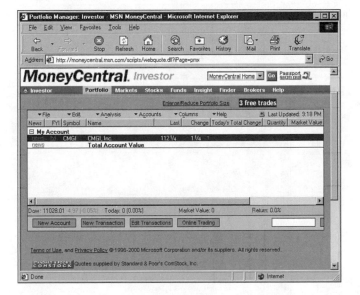

**FIGURE 1.9**
*Is it a Java applet
or an ActiveX
control?*

The jury is still out on whether Java or ActiveX will become the applet standard as the Web development environment matures, but at this point it definitely seems to be leaning toward Java (mostly due to the recent virus scares that are possible via ActiveX controls). Both have strengths and weaknesses. Fortunately for you as a JavaScript developer, your programs can interact with both of these technologies. Chapter 25, "Interacting with Other Technologies," discusses how JavaScript and ActiveX controls work together.

**Resource**

For information on ActiveX, go to Microsoft's Internet Center at `http://www.microsoft.com/com`.

## Netscape Plug-Ins

Plug-ins are a slightly different technology, but they're still a client-side extension of the Web browser. Plug-ins essentially extend the normal capabilities of the Netscape Navigator browser to provide support for additional data types and other features. Specifically, you use a plug-in to display a specific MIME (multipurpose Internet mail extension) type file.

When you start Netscape, it looks in its `program\plugins` folder for any plug-ins to register. Netscape then calls a plug-in on an "as-needed" basis when it comes across a matching MIME file type.

Once installed, plug-ins become added modules on the browser and don't require any user interaction to start. They are proving especially useful for multimedia data, such as sound, video, and graphics. Figure 1.10 demonstrates the use of a plug-in that lets you view Adobe Acrobat files within Netscape.

**FIGURE 1.10**
*Viewing a PDF file using a plug-in.*

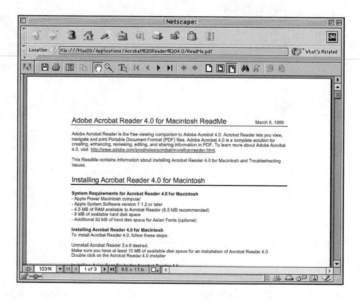

You can use JavaScript to communicate with plug-ins. Chapter 25 explores this subject in detail.

## Client Scripting Languages

The final pieces of the puzzle on the client side are the client scripting languages. JavaScript is the leading scripting language today, but Microsoft is now promoting VBScript as an alternative. Because of the millions of Visual Basic developers, it's likely that VBScript will also prove popular for this community. Near the end of this chapter there is a section on "Comparing JavaScript with VBScript," which compares and contrasts JavaScript and VBScript.

# Server Side

The server side of the Web application framework consists of the Web server itself, along with extensions to the server software. As you will learn, these extensions can take various forms and can be employed with a variety of technologies. Figure 1.11 shows the relationships of the server-side framework.

**FIGURE 1.11**
*A server-side framework.*

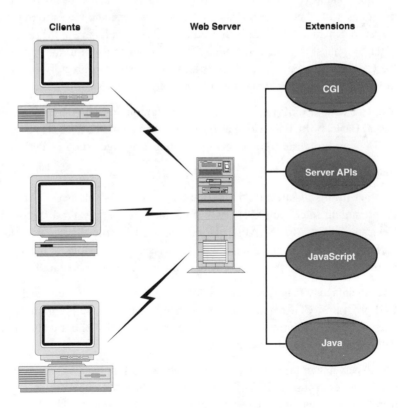

## Servers

The Web server is charged with handling requests for HTML documents from the client and returning them for viewing. The server software is an application that runs on a TCP/IP-enabled machine. Popular servers today include Netscape Enterprise Server (NES), Microsoft Internet Information Server (IIS), and Apache.

## Server Extensions

By itself, the Web server provides static HTML pages to the client when requested and performs a variety of other functions. However, several extensions to servers provide capabilities that the server itself doesn't support. These include CGI, server APIs, JavaScript, and Java.

### CGI

Common gateway interface (CGI) is the *de facto* standard means of interfacing external programs with Web servers. Using CGI, you can execute CGI programs or scripts on the server to generate dynamically created content for displaying to the user. A typical scenario is that a request is generated from an HTML form and sent to the server. The request runs the CGI program or script, which is located in a special directory on the server. The CGI program processes the request and then returns an HTML document with the result.

You can write a CGI program using any programming language—such as Java, C++, Visual Basic, or PHP—as long as it can be executed on the Web server. It is common in the UNIX world to write CGI scripts in scripting languages such as Perl or in a UNIX shell.

### Server APIs

Another means of integration with the server is through its native Application Programming Interface (API). Two of the most commonly used Web server APIs are the Netscape Server API (NSAPI) and the Microsoft Internet Server API (ISAPI). Using the APIs provides tighter integration with the server. For example, in the Windows world, you would create a DLL that is accessed by the server, not a separate EXE.

The advantage to using these server APIs is that the processes are much more efficient than CGI programs. CGI requires that a separate instance of the program be executed for each client request or submittal. Not only is this more expensive, but it also limits the amount of data sharing that can be performed.

The disadvantage to using a proprietary server API is that your solution is specific to that single server. Your ISAPI DLL won't work with a Netscape server. If you're working primarily with one of these servers, then the negative aspect of this limitation is minimized.

### Server-Side JavaScript

Much of the attention given to JavaScript to date has been because of its capabilities on the client side. However, you can use JavaScript as a server-side scripting tool as well. The first such environment out the door is, as you would expect, Netscape.

Netscape's Server-Side JavaScript (SSJS) environment allows you to use scripts to build Web-based applications that are controlled by the Netscape server. There are several server-side extensions to the JavaScript language that provide the additional capabilities of generating dynamic HTML, communicating with the client, accessing external files on the server, and connecting to SQL databases (LiveWire).

Additionally, Microsoft is supporting JScript in its Active Server Pages framework as a server-side scripting language.

### Java

In recent months, we have seen Java on the server side really take off. Sun has released a technology it calls JavaServer Pages (JSP). As you might imagine, this is a competitor to ASP and SSJS. Now that Sun and Netscape have formed an alliance, called iPlanet, it is possible that JSP and SSJS will be rolled into one super-powerful technology environment.

Additionally, you may have heard of Java Servlets. Servlets are small components, much like ActiveX controls in the ASP environment, that are invoked as pages are being built *or* to build pages. This allows developers to apply their knowledge of the Java language, which is easier to learn than C, to build fast, reliable, platform-independent components to create pages.

# What Can You Do with JavaScript?

Now that you have surveyed the technologies that make up Web applications, you can look at the role that client-side JavaScript can play in developing Web applications.

## Client-Side Applications

You can use JavaScript to develop entire client-side applications. Although JavaScript isn't an all-encompassing language like Java, it does provide rather substantial capabilities when it comes to working with HTML tags and associated objects. One of the best known JavaScript applications is hIdaho Design's ColorCenter (`http://www.hidaho.com/c3`), shown in Figure 1.12. You can use this JavaScript application to select browser-related colors and preview them in a separate frame. Trying to design such an application using Java would be much more complex because of the interaction that is required with HTML. For certain cases, JavaScript provides the ideal programming backbone on which to develop the application.

**FIGURE 1.12**
*hIdaho Design's
ColorCenter.*

## Data Validation

JavaScript gives you, as a Web developer, a basic means of validating data from the user without hitting the server. Within your JavaScript code, you can determine whether values entered by the user are valid or fit the correct format. JavaScript is a much more efficient validation method than throwing unqualified values to a server process. Not only is the process more efficient for the user entering the data, but it's better for the server as well. By the time data is transferred to the server for processing, you can be assured the data has been qualified in a proper state for submission.

## Creating Interactive Forms

Another common use of JavaScript is to liven up HTML forms. Part of this task might include validating data. It can also include additional features that are unavailable with straight HTML, such as providing information to the user on the status bar, opening a second browser window for help information, and so on.

## Client-Side Lookup Tables

Besides including data validation, another means of minimizing the need to access the server is to employ JavaScript to generate and maintain client-side lookup tables. The data must be embedded in the HTML document itself, however, so you will want to limit your use of lookup tables to small, read-only databases of information.

## State Maintenance

In the stateless environment of the Web, you can use JavaScript to help maintain state in exchanges between the client and the server. The main use of state maintenance is with cookies (information stored by the browser on the client). JavaScript provides a means for you to store and retrieve cookies on the client. See Chapter 30, "Personalization and Dynamic Pages," for more information on working with cookies in JavaScript.

## Working with Java Applets, ActiveX Controls, and Plug-Ins

As the JavaScript language is enhanced, it continues to have increased capabilities in working with client-side extensions, including Java applets, ActiveX controls, and Netscape plug-ins. You can access a Java or ActiveX object's properties and execute its methods. You can also determine whether a plug-in is installed. As this capability is enhanced, JavaScript will become the glue that holds together HTML, applets, and client-side extensions.

# Browser Support for JavaScript

Compared to other applications, browsers are relatively simple pieces of software, but they are evolving into more powerful applications as Web technology matures. A browser is your window into the Web; therefore, no matter what JavaScript's potential is, it does no good if a browser doesn't support it. This section examines the browsers available today and their support for JavaScript.

Because JavaScript is an interpreted language and is embedded in HTML documents, it's entirely dependent on the browser software to work. If you use an old browser, it won't know what to do with the code and will ignore it.

## Netscape Navigator

During the mid-1990s, Netscape became perhaps the single most important player in the Web industry. Not only was it the first to market many important technological breakthroughs, but it also teamed up with other industry leaders—such as Sun—to push the technology envelope on many fronts on the Web.

Obviously, because Netscape developed JavaScript, you would expect its phenomenally successful Navigator browser to support the scripting language. Navigator 2.0 was the first browser to support JavaScript. Later versions provide important enhancements to the language itself. Now that Navigator has been turned over to Mozilla.org, the Open Source area of Netscape, we are sure that developers around the world will continue to make it the most successful implementation. Figure 1.13 shows a beta of Mozilla (Netscape Navigator 5) displaying the Mozilla.org home page.

**FIGURE 1.13**
*Mozilla/Netscape Navigator 5.*

## Microsoft Internet Explorer

Microsoft Internet Explorer 3.0 was the first non-Netscape browser to support JavaScript. Older versions of Internet Explorer do not support JScript, Microsoft's implementation of JavaScript.

## Other Browsers

At the time this chapter is being written, there are only three other major browsers that provide support for JavaScript. Sun's HotJava 3.0 (JavaScript 1.4), Opera (JavaScript 1.1), and Be's NetPositive 2.1 (experimental version).

# Comparing JavaScript with VBScript

As mentioned, JavaScript is not the only Web scripting language available. This arena currently has two players—JavaScript/JScript and VBScript. Although these languages have moved almost completely away from really competing (it seems that they complement each other more these days), it is helpful to look at VBScript and compare its strengths and weaknesses with JavaScript. In this section, I discuss what VBScript is, contrast it with JavaScript, and provide a sample VBScript application for you to examine.

> **Note**
>
> Current research reveals that the number of sites using VBScript on the Web is a small fraction of the total sites supporting JavaScript.

## What Is VBScript?

VBScript, a Web scripting language developed by Microsoft, directly parallels JavaScript. VBScript's legacy is much different from that of JavaScript. Whereas JavaScript was essentially created from scratch and based loosely on C++ and Java, VBScript is a part of the Visual Basic family of languages. Other family members include Visual Basic—the ubiquitous Windows programming language—and Visual Basic for Applications—a macro language for Microsoft Office and other applications. If you've ever developed software using Visual Basic, you'll be able to pick up VBScript much quicker than you would otherwise.

> **Note**
>
> Look for the latest VBScript information online on Microsoft's site at `http://msdn.microsoft.com/scripting`.

## Embedded HTML Language

Like JavaScript, VBScript is a scripting language embedded in an HTML file. VBScript uses the `<script>` tag in the same way as JavaScript, using `"text/vbscript"` as the type attribute value. For example, the following script shows an alert dialog box when the page is loaded:

```html
<html>
  <head>
    <script type="text/vbscript">
      alert("Is this JavaScript or VBScript?")
    </script>
  </head>
</html>
```

Interestingly, for an example as basic as an alert dialog box, the syntax of the two languages is the same. If you change the `type` parameter to `"text/javascript"`, the same process is performed.

## Object Model

Perhaps the single most important factor when comparing JavaScript and VBScript is that they use the same basic object hierarchy, although various versions of each may reveal minor differences. To a Web developer who might need to use both languages on occasion, this is a major coup; dealing with language syntax differences is much easier than working with two completely different programming paradigms. If you ever need to convert JavaScript code to VBScript or vice versa, your conversion typically will be a line-by-line process.

Not only is the language object model identical for both scripting languages, but the way in which you work with HTML objects is the same as well. Just as JavaScript can react to events triggered by an event handler of an HTML object, so can VBScript. For example, in the following JavaScript code sample (Listing 1.2), the text entered in the `myText` field is converted to uppercase when the user clicks the Convert button:

**LISTING 1.2**   JavaScript Example

```html
<html>
<head>
  <script type="text/javascript">
  <!--
    function convertText() {
      document.SampleForm.myText.value = document.
➥       SampleForm.myText.value.toUpperCase()
   }
  -->
  </script>
</head>
```

LISTING 1.2    continued

```
<body>
  <form name="SampleForm">
    <input type="text" name="myText">
    <input type="button" value="Convert" onclick="convertText()">
  </form>
</body>
</html>
```

If you perform the same process using VBScript, the code resembles that in Listing 1.3:

LISTING 1.3    A VBScript Example

```
<html>
<head>
  <script type="text/vbscript">
  <!--
    Sub convertText()
      document.SampleForm.myText.value =
➥       UCase(document.SampleForm.myText.value)
    End Sub
  -->
  </script>
</head>

<body>
  <form name="SampleForm">
    <input type="text" name="myText">
    <input type="button" value="Convert" onclick="convertText()">
  </form>
</body>
</html>
```

## More Complex Data Types

On the surface, VBScript appears to be very limited in its capability to work with data types. VBScript has this appearance because it has only one data type, `variant`. However, on closer inspection, you will notice that VBScript actually has more power in handling data types than JavaScript does. The `variant` type contains information about the value it's working with at the time and can determine the data type it's being asked to handle in a variety of situations. In other words, if you're using a `variant` variable in the context of a string, as in the following example, VBScript treats `myVar` as a string value:

```
myVar = "String1" + "String2"
```

In the same way, if you're working with numbers as in the following example, VBScript treats the variable as a numeric value:

```
myVar = 1 + 2
```

Strings and numbers are treated as subtypes within the `variant` type. Table 1.2 shows VBScript's numerous subtypes.

**TABLE 1.2  Subtypes of VBScript's `variant` Type**

| Subtype | Description |
| --- | --- |
| String | A variable-length string (a maximum length of some 2 billion characters). |
| Byte | An integer between 0 and 255. |
| Integer | An integer between -32,768 and 32,767. |
| Long | An integer between -2,147,483,648 and 2,147,483,647. |
| Single | A single-precision, floating-point number between -3.402823E38 and -1.401298E-45 for negative values and between 1.401298E-45 and 3.402823E38 for positive values. |
| Double | A double-precision, floating-point number between -1.79769313486232E308 and -4.94065645841247E-324 for negative values and between 4.94065645841247E-324 and 1.79769313486232E308 for positive values. |
| Date (Time) | A number that represents a date between 1/1/100 and 12/31/9999. |
| Boolean | A logical value (`True` or `False`). |
| Empty | An uninitialized variable. The value is `0` for numeric variables or an empty string (`""`) for string variables. |
| Null | The variant contains no valid data (different from `Empty`). |
| Object | An ActiveX object. |
| Error | A VBScript error number. |

VBScript has a set of conversion functions that go beyond JavaScript's `parseFloat` and `parseInt` built-in methods.

> **Note**
>
> VBScript is a loosely typed language like JavaScript.

## Different Procedure Types

VBScript has two different types of procedures: subroutines and functions. A subroutine—denoted using `Sub...End Sub`—is a procedure that doesn't return a value, whereas a function—denoted by `Function...End Function`—is a procedure that does return a value. For example, the following subroutine, when called, assigns the string literal `"See Spot Run"` to the `TextField` text object but doesn't return a value to the calling procedure:

```
<script type="text/vbscript">
  Sub convertText()
    document.MyForm.TextField.value = "See Spot Run."
  End Sub
</script>
```

For an example of a VBScript function, look at the following code. The `showText()` subroutine calls the `getText()` function, which returns the value of the `TextField` text object:

```
<script type="text/vbscript">
  Function getText()
    getText = document.MyForm.TextField.value
  End Function

  Sub showText()
    alert(getText())
  EndSub
</script>
```

In contrast, JavaScript has a single procedure type—`method` (also called `function`)—that uses the `function` keyword regardless of whether a value is returned to the calling procedure.

# Programming in VBScript

To give you a glimpse of programming in VBScript, I will show you a rudimentary example. In Listing 1.4, VBScript multiplies two values entered by the user and displays the result in an alert message box:

**LISTING 1.4**   A More Complex VBScript Example

```
<html>
<head>
  <title>Wizard</title>
  <script type="text/vbscript">
```

**LISTING 1.4**   continued

```
    Sub calculateValues()
      Dim num1, num2, greaterNum, totalVal
      num1 = document.form1.Number1.value
      num2 = document.form1.Number2.value
      totalVal = num1*num2
      alert(totalVal)
    End Sub
  </script>
</head>
<body>
  <h1>Stump the Wizard</h1>
  <p>
    Without connecting to a backend server or using a Java applet, the
    Browser Wizard will multiply the two numbers...
  </p>
  <form name="form1" method="POST">
    <pre>
      First Number:  <input type="text" size="5" maxlength="5" name="Number1">
    </pre>
    <pre>
      Second Number: <input type="text" size="5" maxlength="5" name="Number2">
    </pre>
    <p>
      <input type=button name="WizButton" value="Multiply"
➥         onclick="calculateValues()">
    </p>
  </form>
</body>
</html>
```

Figure 1.14 shows the result of running this script in Internet Explorer 5.

The equivalent JavaScript code, in Listing 1.5, is shown to provide a source of comparison:

FIGURE **1.14**
*The result message box.*

LISTING **1.5** The JavaScript Version

```
<html>
<head>
  <title>Wizard</title>
  <script type="text/javascript">
  <!--
    function calculateValues() {
      num1 = parseFloat(document.forms[0].Number1.value)
      num2 = parseFloat(document.forms[0].Number2.value)
      result = num1 * num2
      alert(result);
    }
  //-->
  </script>
</head>
<body>
  <h1>Stump the Wizard</h1>
  <p>
    Without connecting to a backend server or using a Java applet, the
    Browser Wizard will multiply the two numbers...
  </p>
  <form name="form1" method="POST">
    <pre>
      First Number:  <input type="text" size="5" maxlength="5" name="Number1">
    </pre>
```

Listing 1.5    continued

```
<pre>
  Second Number: <input type="text" size="5" maxlength="5" name="Number2">
</pre>
<p>
  <input type="button" name="WizButton" value="Multiply"
➥     onclick="calculateValues()">
</p>
</form>
</body>
</html>
```

# Summary

This chapter looked at the Web application framework and how the pieces of Web technology fit together. JavaScript is an important tool in a Web developer's toolkit. As you learned in this chapter, JavaScript serves many important functions within the Web application framework, and it's becoming more of a standard in the Web development marketplace. Because JavaScript is a language and not a tool itself, it's dependent on browser software to execute. Since Netscape Navigator and Microsoft Internet Explorer own the lion's share of the marketplace, JavaScript support is very dependable.

Now that you have a solid foundation on which to look at JavaScript, you can begin in the next chapter to look at the details of how JavaScript interacts with HTML.

# CHAPTER 2

# How JavaScript and HTML Work Together

HTML gives you the capability to create remarkable static Web pages. Although these documents can be creative, interesting, and by all means useful, JavaScript gives you the capability to make these static pages interactive and more responsive to user actions and input. Extending your HTML pages with JavaScript gives your page more power and gives your HTML more flexibility.

JavaScript lets the Web developer create more dynamic pages by embedding a script in the existing HTML structure. You can now put processes behind buttons, run calculations on form-entered data, or perform actions when the user moves the mouse cursor over an HTML element or Document object. In general, you get more bang for your HTML buck.

JavaScript offers advantages over server-based interactive documents such as CGI (common gateway interface), because JavaScript-based documents are generally not dependent on server-side processing, so they are quicker to respond to user interactions and requests.

To get a good understanding of how JavaScript works within the HTML world, we are going to take a quick look at HTML and how it pertains to this scripting language. By developing a solid base of HTML knowledge, the developer can more fully implement JavaScript and other interactive and high-level HTML functionality.

# Introducing the Fundamentals of HTML

Although developing simple HTML documents, tags, and basic form design is easy, the advantage of using HTML is that you also can create more complex documents by building on the simple ones. If you use the more complex tags and the attributes associated with them, your documents will grow in complexity and usability with only minor research and trial and error.

## The Current Situation

Standards of HTML are changing constantly. The current Recommendation (*aka* standard) is for HTML 4.01; however, the next generation of HTML is XHTML. Currently XHTML 1.0 is a Proposed Recommendation awaiting acceptance from the World Wide Web Consortium (W3C) and is based on the HTML 4.01 Recommendation.

XHTML is HTML as an application of XML. When XHTML is implemented, it will be possible for other XML applications to process the data in XHTML documents. Those who follow XML will find that XHTML also allows you to include other dialects (such as MathML) in documents. In either case, these technologies are evolving with new elements as well as new and refined attributes for elements.

---

**Resource**

XHTML is beyond the scope of this book. However, if you would like more information about it, you can visit W3C at http://www.w3.org.

---

By keeping up-to-date on the latest releases of the popular browsers, an HTML designer can keep abreast of these enhancements and implement them as they become available to the general public. Luckily, for the most part, enhancements included in HTML 4.01/ XHTML 1.0 and the newest browser releases aren't problematic when displayed in older browsers. However, you should always test your document in older browsers to ensure that the new tags and custom tags you design with don't have a negative effect on older browsers.

However, there are tags out there that are not part of the standard or are not implemented across all browsers. An example is the <marquee> tag, which works with Internet Explorer but not Navigator, which displays straight document text. From the other side, Navigator supports <layer> and <ilayer> tags, which are not implemented by Internet Explorer.

These examples provide an important reason to write a well-defined and segmented document and to account for multiple browsers as you design.

# HTML Basics

Because client-side JavaScript works so closely with HTML, before you write any scripts, you must first know the basics of HTML document structure and document tags. Writing Web pages is fairly straightforward if you know the HTML basics. A Web page is made up of page text, tags, and sometimes comments.

Text is easy to comprehend. You write text, and it appears on the Web page. The part of Web page design that needs more description is the use of tags, which always begin with the < symbol and end with a >. Tags tell your page how to behave, tell your text how to appear, and let you write complex documents for a Web browser.

A tag can be a single marker, as in <hr> for a horizontal rule or <br> for a line break, which are also defined as empty tags. Empty tags do not necessarily apply any formatting to surrounding text, although they can adjust the overall layout and design of an HTML document.

The `<td>` tag, on the other hand, isn't an empty tag. You use it to specify that the text following the tag is to be displayed in a table cell. Tags such as this require an end tag to tell them where to terminate. These tags are called *container tags* because they always contain information (normally text) between the start and end tags. In the following example, note that the end tag has a / before the tag name:

```
<b>Make this text bold</b>
```

An end tag is identical to its start tag except that it contains the additional character.

More complex tags also can have attributes to tell the tag how to behave. If a tag has attributes associated with it, some attributes may be required for the tag to perform as requested. `<table width="3">`, for example, defines a table with a width of 3.

Tag location within a document is sometimes very important. Certain tags must be placed inside other tags. For example, the `<input>` tag must be inside the `<form>` tag. However, some tags can contain other tags but are not required to (the `<head>` tag, for example).

As for comments, these are nothing more than your own document notes that are not supposed to be displayed in the browser. HTML comments begin with `<!--` and end with `-->`. The following is an example of an HTML comment:

```
<!-- here is a comment -->
```

## HTML Document Structure

Structure can be very important. Incorrect placement of tags can cause unwanted and unexpected effects. In the basic HTML document shown in Listing 2.1, the document always starts with `<html>` and ends with `</html>`, as you can see in Figure 2.1. The two main tags inside these tags are `<head>` and `<body>`. You also can place tags inside each of these tags.

**FIGURE 2.1**

*The basic HTML document generated from Listing 2.1 in Navigator 4.7.*

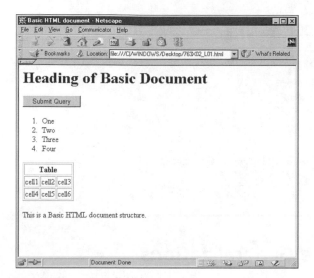

**LISTING 2.1**   A Basic HTML Page

```html
<html>
  <head>
    <title>Basic HTML document</title>
    <script type="text/javascript"></script>
  </head>
<body>
  <h1>Heading of Basic Document</h1>
  <form>
    <input name="EnterBtn" type="SUBMIT">
  </form>
  <ol type=1>
    <li>One</li>
    <li>Two</li>
    <li>Three</li>
    <li>Four</li>
  </ol>
  <table width="3" height="3" border>
    <tr>
      <th colspan="3">Table</th>
    </tr>
    <tr>
      <td>cell1</td>
      <td>cell2</td>
      <td>cell3</td>
    </tr>
```

LISTING 2.1    continued

```
    <tr>
      <td>cell4</td>
      <td>cell5</td>
      <td>cell6</td>
    </tr>
  </table>
  <P>
    This is a Basic HTML document structure.
  </p>
</body>
</html>
```

## Attribute Generalizations

As mentioned previously, many tags have attributes. These attributes are used to modify how the tag is rendered or operates. Not all tags have attributes, and some tags have attributes of the same name. The attributes in Table 2.1 are used in numerous HTML tags. They have the same functionality for each tag that uses them.

**TABLE 2.1    Attributes Used in Multiple Tags**

| Attribute | Description |
| --- | --- |
| class | Specifies the class to which the HTML tag belongs. |
| id | Defines a unique value for an element in reference to the entire document. |
| name | Used to name an instance of a tag. This name is often used by JavaScript to reference particular elements, or by anchor tags, <a>, for internal document links. |
| style | Specifies the style information. |

# Embedding JavaScript in HTML

JavaScript scripts are integrated into an HTML document using the <script> and </script> tag pair. An HTML document can contain multiple <script> pairs, and each pair may enclose more than one set of JavaScript statements. Both tags are required for <script>. The type attribute is used to specify the scripting language in which the script is written, and the src attribute is used to specify the filename of external source JavaScript files.

# Understanding the Attributes of the `<script>` Tag

To better understand how the `<script>` tag works, let's take a quick look at the various attributes associated with it, in Table 2.2. The sections following this table will provide more detail on each of the attributes.

**TABLE 2.2**   Attributes of the `<script>` Tag

| Attribute | Description |
|-----------|-------------|
| defer | This is a Boolean attribute that is used to tell the browser if the script in this section generates any content. |
| language | Deprecated attribute that was used to specify the language and version being used inside the tags. |
| src | Attribute that specifies the URL location of an external source JavaScript file. |
| type | Attribute that replaced the `language` attribute and tells the browser what language is being used inside of the tags. |

## defer

The `defer` attribute is a simple attribute that tells the browser if the code between the beginning and ending `<script>` tags generates any content—in other words, whether the `document.write()` method is used. A sample is as follows:

```
<script type="text/javascript" defer>
<!--
// Just declaring a variable, not writing to a page
var myVar = 500;
//-->
</script>
```

## language

The `language` attribute hasbeen deprecated in the most recent release of the HTML and XHTML languages. Traditionally, it was used to specify the language name and version JavaScript included between the `<script>` tags. The format of this tag is as follows:

```
<script language="JavaScript">
```

This tells the browser to run the script in JavaScript 1.0—compliant browsers. For other JavaScript versions, such as 1.1, you would use the following:

```
<script language="JavaScript1.1">
```

Table 2.3 shows the values you should use with the `language` attribute. It also points out which browsers will interpret which values.

**TABLE 2.3** Current Values of the `language` Attribute

| Language Value | Description |
| --- | --- |
| JavaScript | Represents JavaScript 1.0 and is interpreted by Navigator 2+ and Internet Explorer 3+ browsers. |
| JavaScript1.1 | Represents JavaScript 1.1 and is interpreted by Navigator 3+ and Internet Explorer 3+ browsers. |
| JavaScript1.2 | Represents JavaScript 1.2 and is interpreted by Navigator 4+ and Internet Explorer 4+ browsers. Specifying 1.2 rather than 1.1 changes how Navigator handles some of its equality operators. |
| JavaScript1.3 | Represents JavaScript 1.3 and is interpreted by Navigator 4.05+ and Internet Explorer 5+ browsers. |
| JavaScript1.4 | Represents JavaScript 1.4 and is interpreted by HotJava 3+ and some very early alpha versions (pre-M12) of Mozilla/ Navigator 5. |
| JavaScript1.5 | Represents JavaScript 1.5 and is interpreted by the Mozilla/ Navigator beta 1.0 (M12+) browser. |

**Tip**

If the `language` attribute isn't defined, browsers will assume JavaScript 1.0. Additionally, the current Opera browser release seems to ignore this attribute altogether, due to its deprecation.

By using this attribute, you are able to define multiple sets of JavaScript functions. Browsers that support JavaScript 1.1 can take advantage of newer functions, which are hidden from older versions of browsers. The simplest method to take advantage of these options is shown in Listing 2.2.

**LISTING 2.2** Using Multiple Versions of JavaScript with the `language` Attribute

```
<html>
<head>
  <title>JavaScript version test page</title>
</head>
<body>
<script language="JavaScript">
  //Only JavaScript 1.0 browsers read in this section
```

**LISTING 2.2**  continued

```
    document.write('This browser supports JavaScript 1.0<br>');
</script>

<script language="JavaScript1.1">
  //Only JavaScript 1.1 browsers read in this section

    document.write('This browser supports JavaScript 1.1<br>');
</script>
<script language="JavaScript1.2">
  //Only JavaScript 1.2 browsers read in this section
    document.write('This browser supports JavaScript 1.2<br>');
</script>
<script language="JavaScript1.3">
  //Only JavaScript 1.3 browsers read in this section
    document.write('This browser supports JavaScript 1.3<br>');
</script>
<script language="JavaScript1.4">
  //Only JavaScript 1.4 browsers read in this section
    document.write('This browser supports JavaScript 1.4<br>');
</script>
<script language="JavaScript1.5">
  //Only JavaScript 1.5 browsers read in this section
    document.write('This browser supports JavaScript 1.5<br>');
</script>
</body>
</html>
```

### src

You have two options when integrating JavaScript statements into your HTML document. The method that you choose depends on your requirements when viewing and modifying code. The first option lets you view all your codes simultaneously and involves writing JavaScript statements directly into your HTML document. All your statements are embedded in your HTML page between the `<script>` tags—these are *inline* scripts. The other option, available only in JavaScript 1.1 and higher, is to include your JavaScript code in a separate .js file. That allows you to call the file from within your HTML on the first `<script>` tag line.

Here is the first option for embedding JavaScript in your HTML:

```
<script type="text/javascript">
  function options() {
```

```
    document.write("embedding the code");
  }
</script>
```

Here is the second option, including the script in external files:

```
<script src="/jscripts/myscript.js"></script>
```

In the second option, you will create a file called `myscript.js`, which will have one line of code:

```
document.write("calling from a separate file")
```

Using this option, you may want to include a single statement between the `<script>` tags to give feedback to the user if the `.js` file is incorrect or not available. Otherwise, the user might see incorrect page behavior and not know why.

When you load the script from another file, the `language` attribute is not necessary as long as you use the `.js` extension. Using this methodology, you can modify your JavaScript code without ever opening and risking unwanted changes to your HTML pages. Thus, your code is more modular and portable for use without HTML documents.

A downside to this method is that you might have to modify two sets of code, depending on your JavaScript changes. For example, if you change the name of a function in your JavaScript code, you will also have to remember to change the name in the function call in the HTML code. Another downside is that external JavaScript files can't contain HTML tags; they can contain only JavaScript-specific statements.

## type

Some of you that have written code in JavaScript before may be saying "what the heck is the `type` attribute? I thought the attribute I was suppose to use was `language`." Well, you are partially correct.

`language` was the original attribute that was used to not only define the language used with the `<script>` tag, such as `javascript` or `vbscript`, but also the version, as in `javascript1.1` or `javascript1.5`. If you read through the current HTML Recommendation or the XHTML Proposed Recommendation, you will find that the `language` attribute has been deprecated in favor of the `type` attribute. The value of this new attribute closely resembles the content type of an external source JavaScript (`.js`) file. So for JavaScript you would use `type="text/javascript"`, and for VBScript you would use `type="text/vbscript"`. Here is how it works.

The HTML 4.01 Recommendation says that you should put a `<meta>` tag in the `<head>` portion of your documents that specifies the default language used in all of your scripts. This looks like the following:

```
<meta http-equiv="Content-Script-Type" content="text/javascript">
```

You can replace `text/javascript` with `text/vbscript` or whatever language you are using. If this setting is not there, the browser should check for a `Content-Script-Type` entry in the header of the HTTP request. The format for this would be

```
Content-Script-Type: text/javascript
```

Again, you can replace `text/javascript` with the correct content type of the language that should be the default for that page.

Now that you have these set, the `type` attribute is used to override the default. This makes it possible to have multiple scripting languages in the same document. For instance, you may set `Content-Script-Type` to `text/javascript`, but then set `type="text/vbscript"` in a specific instance of a `<script>` tag that uses VBScript as its language.

Obviously, only the newer browsers will even consider looking at this attribute, so you should take care in using it. Give it another couple of years, and all should be fine—the majority of the browsers out there will support this new method. Until then, however, I would recommend that you use both the `type` and `language` attributes in conjunction with the `<script>` tag.

## Viewing JavaScript Code

Because you can write JavaScript code inline with your HTML code, you can easily view and edit it. By now, you should be familiar with the Document Source menu option that is available in your browser to view the source code of an HTML page (it's usually under the View menu).

When you view the source of the document, you can also view the JavaScript code that is included in the document, as shown in Figure 2.2. (This is obviously not the case when your JavaScript statements are called from the `.js` file instead of written into the document. All you will see is the call to the `.js` file in the `<script>` tag.) JavaScript doesn't need a special viewer and, because it is just interpreted code and not compiled, it appears in your document source by default.

> **Note**
>
> Some browsers, especially Navigator 4, will display only the executed results of JavaScript when you select View Source. In these instances, I recommend you use the Netscape JavaScript Debugger, which is discussed in Chapter 34, "Debugging," to view and step through the execution of these scripts.

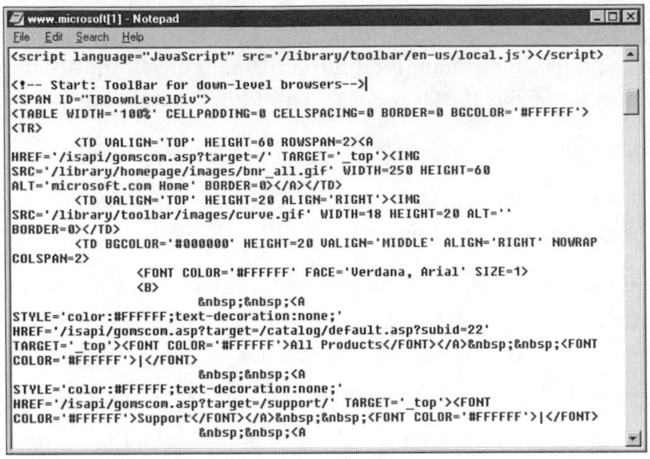

FIGURE 2.2
*Viewing
JavaScript code.*

```
www.microsoft[1] - Notepad                                    _ □ ×
File  Edit  Search  Help
<script language="JavaScript" src='/library/toolbar/en-us/local.js'></script>

<!-- Start: ToolBar for down-level browsers-->
<SPAN ID="TBDownLevelDiv">
<TABLE WIDTH='100%' CELLPADDING=0 CELLSPACING=0 BORDER=0 BGCOLOR='#FFFFFF'>
<TR>
        <TD VALIGN='TOP' HEIGHT=60 ROWSPAN=2><A
HREF='/isapi/gomscom.asp?target=/' TARGET='_top'><IMG
SRC='/library/homepage/images/bnr_all.gif' WIDTH=250 HEIGHT=60
ALT='microsoft.com Home' BORDER=0></A></TD>
        <TD VALIGN='TOP' HEIGHT=20 ALIGN='RIGHT'><IMG
SRC='/library/toolbar/images/curve.gif' WIDTH=18 HEIGHT=20 ALT=''
BORDER=0></TD>
        <TD BGCOLOR='#000000' HEIGHT=20 VALIGN='MIDDLE' ALIGN='RIGHT' NOWRAP
COLSPAN=2>
                <FONT COLOR='#FFFFFF' FACE='Verdana, Arial' SIZE=1>
                <B>
                  <A
STYLE='color:#FFFFFF;text-decoration:none;'
HREF='/isapi/gomscom.asp?target=/catalog/default.asp?subid=22'
TARGET='_top'><FONT COLOR='#FFFFFF'>All Products</FONT></A>  <FONT
COLOR='#FFFFFF'>|</FONT>
                  <A
STYLE='color:#FFFFFF;text-decoration:none;'
HREF='/isapi/gomscom.asp?target=/support/' TARGET='_top'><FONT
COLOR='#FFFFFF'>Support</FONT></A>  <FONT COLOR='#FFFFFF'>|</FONT>
                  <A
```

# Creating JavaScript Code

The basics behind creating JavaScript code are simple. Create your basic HTML page or edit an existing one, and then insert your <script> tags in the <head> or <body> section of the document. Functions and other items that should apply to the entire page are best kept in the <head> of the document. If you need to generate text for the page using JavaScript, this is done or at least called within the <body>.

## Executing Scripts

JavaScript execution begins at different times, depending on how it is written. If the script affects the content on the page, such as with the use of the document.write() method, the script is executed as it is encountered. There is also an event handler, onLoad, that is executed only after the HTML document has completely loaded into the browser.

If your JavaScript scripts are stored in a separate file, they are also evaluated when the page loads and before any script actions take place.

All JavaScript statements that are contained within a function block are interpreted, and execution does not occur until the function is called from a JavaScript event. JavaScript statements that are not within a function block are executed after the document loads into the browser, but as it is being actually rendered. The execution result of the latter will be apparent to users when they first view the page.

## Loading a Page

JavaScript statements that require immediate processing are executed as the page is loaded but before it is displayed in the browser. Listing 2.3 demonstrates the display of an alert dialog as the document is opened. No function is called—JavaScript statements are simply processed in order as the page has loaded.

**LISTING 2.3**   Calling to Display the Alert Dialog Directly

```html
<html>
<head>
  <title>Dialog Test</title>
  <script type="text/javascript">
  <!--
    alert("Dialog called");
  // -->
  </script>
</head>
<body>
  <b>
    Test page of default JavaScript call
  </b>
</body>
</html>
```

The onLoad function appears to be an exception to the rule. In this case, the onLoad function is called not by a user-triggered event but by the event of the document itself loading into the browser. In this instance, the alert dialog will again appear immediately upon the loading of the page, as shown in Figure 2.3, even though it isn't called directly. Listing 2.4 demonstrates a function named opendoc(), called by the document itself after its Load event is fired. You will have the same result in both of these Listings (2.3 and 2.4), but it is achieved through two scripting methodologies.

**LISTING 2.4**   Calling to Display the Alert Dialog onLoad

```html
<html>
<head>
  <title>Dialog from onLoad</title>
  <script type="text/javascript">
  <!--
    function opendoc(){
      alert("Dialog called ")
    }
```

**LISTING 2.4**    continued

```
  // -->
  </script>
</head>
<body onload="opendoc()">
  <b>
    Test page of onLoad JavaScript call
  </b>
</body>
</html>
```

**FIGURE 2.3**

*The alert dialog in Navigator 4.7 called directly from JavaScript.*

## User Action

The second process by which JavaScript statements are executed is through function calls. Any statement contained within a function won't be executed until a JavaScript event calls the function. JavaScript events can be triggered in numerous ways on an HTML page, including user action and explicit event calls from within the script itself. User actions on your document might trigger JavaScript events in many instances when you're unaware they could happen. Fully test your JavaScript statements to be sure that user interaction with your page doesn't cause unnecessary or unwanted events to occur.

Chapter 14, "Handling Events," provides a more detailed explanation of JavaScript events and how they're implemented and incorporated into your HTML.

In Listing 2.5, the dialog appears when the pushbutton is clicked.

**LISTING 2.5**   Calling a Function to Display the Alert Dialog

```html
<html>
<head>
  <title>Dialog from function call</title>
  <script type="text/javascript">
  <!--
    function opendoc(){
      alert("Dialog called by Push Button");
    }
  // -->
  </script>
</head>
<body>
  <b>
    Test page of function called from Push Button
  </b>
  <form method="POST">
    <input type="Button" name="BUTTON1" value="PUSH" onclick="opendoc()">
  </form>
</body>
</html>
```

Figure 2.4 shows the results of the function call.

User actions or explicit event calls are the more frequent methods by which JavaScript is executed. One key advantage of JavaScript is that it can increase the amount of user interaction with your HTML document by providing you with a way to process and evaluate user input in a timely manner.

# Accommodating Unsupported Browsers

The quick pace of changes in HTML and JavaScript makes it necessary to be wary of browsers that don't support the documents you're creating. Not all browsers will be current with the newest HTML enhancements, and you, as the programmer, must make your documents as user friendly as possible for all browsers and environments.

**FIGURE 2.4**

*The alert dialog in Internet Explorer 5 called from the* submit *event.*

---

### Tip

Testing your HTML and JavaScript in as many browser environments as possible will give your documents better stability and usability.

---

Although using JavaScript can allow you to provide HTML enhancements for your users, you must always remember that many older browsers might not be able to make full use of the JavaScript code you have written. By surrounding all statements that are inside the `<script>` and `</script>` tags with HTML comment tags, you will enable users with older browsers to view your page but not display the JavaScript code. They won't get the full effect of your page, but at least they won't see unwanted text in the browser. The format for using these comments is as follows:

```
<script type="text/javascript">
<!-- hide your code from older browsers
// code goes here
// stop JavaScript code hiding -->
</script>
```

Listing 2.6 shows how to hide JavaScript code from older browsers. Note the use of the two following HTML comment statements in Listing 2.6 and how they enclose the lines of JavaScript code.

**LISTING 2.6**   Hiding Scripts from Older Browsers

```
<html>
<head>
  <title>Hide From Browser</title>
  <script type="text/javascript">
  <!-- Hide
    document.write("I can view JavaScript code")
  // End hide -->
</head>
<body>
Content goes here.
</body>
</html>
```

The use of the JavaScript comment tag, //, in the last HTML comment line keeps JavaScript from interpreting this statement during processing. Without these comment markers, JavaScript will attempt to process the statement, and you will receive a JavaScript error upon evaluation.

Listing 2.7 shows a basic page that you can start from. Note the normal HTML tags with the <script> tags defined in the <head> section of the document.

**LISTING 2.7**   A Basic JavaScript Starter Document

```
<html>
<head>
  <title>My first HTML page</title>
  <script type="text/javascript">
  <!-- Hide

    //Your code will go here

  // End hide-->
  </script>
</head>
<body>
  <!-- Your page content will go here -->
</body>
</html>
```

The beginning <script> tag should include the type attribute to specify that the script enclosed in the tags is in fact JavaScript. Remember that for now you may want to use the `language` attribute as well, until the HTML 4.01/XHTML 1.0 Recommendations are fully implemented in the most common browsers.

# Writing the Code

As with any other programming language, JavaScript statements can be implemented using various methodologies. I have found that the practice of defining JavaScript functions in the `<head>` section and then calling these functions within the HTML `<body>` is the best way to take advantage of the object-based JavaScript language.

The JavaScript language itself isn't difficult and, for developers with an object-based background, the hurdles are few. Once you grasp the concepts of object-based development, the creation of JavaScript functions becomes fairly straightforward. Note the following example:

```
document.write("I can view JavaScript code");
```

In plain English, the `document.write()` method statement says, "On my document, write the following text."

> **Note**
>
> Although HTML statements aren't case sensitive (although the XHTML Proposed Recommendation requires it), JavaScript statements are. Be sure you always check the case of your code to ensure that no problems will result from this minor yet common error.

When beginning to write your code, keep the following in mind:

- Code reuse
- Readability
- Ease of modification

You can use JavaScript tags in either the `<body>` or the `<head>` of a document. As I mentioned earlier, placing the `<script>` tag in the `<head>` rather than the `<body>` ensures that all statements will be evaluated (and executed, if necessary) before the user interacts with the document. The hazards of putting script statements in the `<body>` of the document are varied.

Depending on the specific tags and the order of the document, you can never know if the user will interact with the script in the correct manner or will react to the page before the script has fully loaded or executed. If either of these situations occurs, the effect that you want for your page might not be seen. (After all your effort, who wants that?)

The practice of defining your JavaScript functions and then calling them from the <body> will ensure that all the functions are evaluated before the user can begin interacting with the page. Listing 2.8 shows an example of this practice, and Listing 2.9 shows the alternative.

**LISTING 2.8    Calling from a Function**

```
<html>
<head>
  <title>Page with Pushbutton</title>
  <script type="text/javascript">
<!--
    function pushbutton(){
      alert("pushed");
    }
// -->
  </script>
</head>
<body>
  <form>
    <input type="SUBMIT" name="BUTTON1" value="PUSH" onclick="pushbutton()">
  </form>
</body>
</html>
```

**LISTING 2.9    Putting Script Directly in the `onclick` Event Handler**

```
<html>
<head>
  <title>Page with Pushbutton</title>
</head>
<body>
  <form>
    <input type="SUBMIT" name="BUTTON1" value="PUSH" onclick="alert('pushed')">
  </form>
</body>
</html>
```

Listing 2.9 shows that it's possible to put JavaScript statements directly into your HTML tags. I can relate the drawbacks of this practice to the code-writing guidelines I mentioned earlier. Modifying and reusing the code in tags is difficult. You must search for the tag and then cut and paste the code. Only then can it be reused or redefined in a function call.

You also limit readability and ease of modification both for yourself and for subsequent developers when you don't place your JavaScript statements in functions in the <head> section. Endlessly searching for code that could have been easily segregated is tedious and unnecessary.

Styles are as important in JavaScript as they are in any programming language. Keeping your styles consistent, your variables defined, and your formatting neat will save future development time.

Creating your JavaScript scripts function by function, piece by piece, will help you build stable interactive documents that have the functionality you want. Because JavaScript is interpreted and not compiled, the debugging process is not always completely straightforward. Many problems or bugs won't be apparent until the document is rigorously tested. I recommend that someone other than the developer test the page to ensure that all situations are encountered when testing the document and integrated JavaScript. (You never know what checking a check box out of order might do to your script.)

## Executing Scripts

As you've probably realized, JavaScript is as simple to load as HTML documents. You don't have to execute any code explicitly to run your scripts. Because you place your code in the HTML document or call it explicitly in the first script line, your script will run when the page loads. Remember that not all the code will necessarily execute immediately upon loading. Code that is enclosed in a function call is evaluated only when the page loads but doesn't execute until the function is explicitly called from a JavaScript event. Code that isn't enclosed in a function call runs after the page finishes loading but before the user has a chance to interact with the page.

## Summary

It is apparent that, although JavaScript is a scripting language separate from HTML, the two are very closely integrated when it comes to full-scale document design, development, and implementation. JavaScript can be written directly into HTML, expanding the current capabilities of your Web documents. It is also viewable and loadable right along with the HTML.

The enhancements that are continuously arising in HTML itself make it possible to add more functionality to your JavaScript code. By using these features, you can expand your documents to make them more interactive and user friendly.

# Assembling Your JavaScript Toolkit

Like any development language, JavaScript requires a development environment in which to work. Java sports Symantec's Visual Café as one example of an Integrated Development Environment (IDE), but JavaScript doesn't have any IDEs specifically available for it. Nonetheless, with the plethora of Web tools, you can create a toolkit that works for you. In this chapter, I examine the various tools that you can add to your toolkit for client-side JavaScript development. I'll close the chapter by looking at two products that you can use for developing server-side JavaScript applications.

# An Overview of Necessary Tools

To be productive as a developer, you need to assemble a group of tools that you are comfortable with. If you're developing applications in Delphi, Visual Basic, or VisualAge for Java, for example, your toolkit probably is relatively small, because these visual tools contain nearly everything you need out of the box. The same definitely can't be said of JavaScript. As a result, you need to work with the following principal tools to build a development environment:

- A JavaScript editor for writing JavaScript scripts

- An HTML editor for HTML page development

- A Web browser for testing your JavaScript scripts and applications

- A script debugger for helping find errors in your scripts

## JavaScript Editors

Choosing an editor is often a very personal choice for a software developer, much like choosing a bat is for a baseball player. Although no one can really recommend what's best for you, I'll offer some information to assist in your selection process by outlining three tool options for writing JavaScript code: text editors, HTML editors, and JavaScript-specific editors.

### Text Editors

Because JavaScript code is contained within HTML pages, all you really need in order to develop with JavaScript is a text editor. In Windows, I recommend TextPad, shown in Figure 3.1, or Notepad. In UNIX, you most likely will want to use emacs or vi. And for you Macintosh users, SimpleText and BBEdit, shown in Figure 3.2, are a couple of good choices.

The advantage of using an ordinary text editor is that you probably already have the software installed on your computer. However, the disadvantage is that it offers no features to facilitate learning the JavaScript language or to enhance your productivity (for example, code libraries or wizards).

**FIGURE 3.1**

*You can use TextPad as a JavaScript editor.*

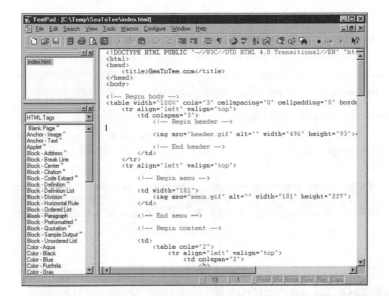

**FIGURE 3.2**

*BBEdit is an excellent editor for JavaScript development on the Macintosh.*

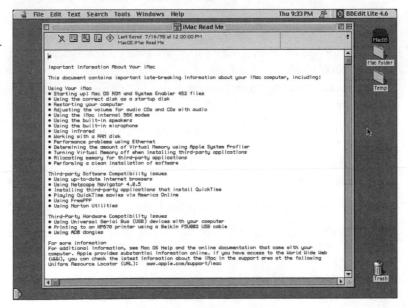

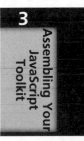

**3**

**Assembling Your JavaScript Toolkit**

As you consider the various options, look at what features are available in the editor before you decide. For example, you will find search-and-replace commands, especially those that perform regular expression pattern matching, critical once you start doing any serious JavaScript programming. You should also lean toward using one that color codes your scripts. This makes it easy to see what is code, HTML, and comments. These features alone make TextPad a much more attractive option than Notepad.

The more advanced text-based editors, TextPad and BBEdit, let you develop other code in their environments as well. This allows you to use the same tool to create your HTML code, JavaScript scripts, or even Java code. Additionally, third-party HTML editors such as Allaire HomeSite are providing support for JavaScript development.

A single environment eliminates the need to deal with multiple software packages, thereby reducing the number of applications you have to learn. Some of these editors also let you integrate with a Web browser for quick viewing or testing of your pages and scripts.

### Resource

You can find Allaire HomeSite at http://www.allaire.com.

## JavaScript Development Environments

In addition to text editors, there are a few editors specifically devoted to JavaScript script development. NetObjects ScriptBuilder, developed by NetObjects, was one of the first visual editors on the market for JavaScript developers. Netscape used to have a product called Visual JavaScript that allowed developers to build Web-based applications in its environment. Since the first release, its functionality has been rolled into their Application Builder product.

Some of the features included in these applications are as follows:

- Drag-and-drop text editing

- Drag-and-drop HTML tags

- Drag-and-drop JavaScript object methods and properties

- Syntax highlighting for JavaScript keywords and HTML tags

- Search-and-replace functionality

- Integration with multiple browsers for testing and debugging

> **Note**
>
> A trial version of NetObjects ScriptBuilder can be downloaded from the NetObjects Web site at `http://www.netobjects.com`.

These tools are not necessarily intended as replacements for an HTML text editor, but rather to work in concert with one.

# HTML Editors

Lest you forget the nature of the environment you're working in, a second tool you need to add to the toolkit is an HTML editor. The purpose of this tool is not so much to develop JavaScript scripts but to design the HTML pages to which you can later add your JavaScript code. The two types of HTML editors on the market are text and visual. Depending on your tastes and needs, you may use one or both.

## Text-Based Editors

As discussed earlier in this chapter, text-based HTML editors provide an environment that lets you work with HTML tags. A text-based HTML editor doesn't try to hide the messy details of HTML tags. Instead, it provides features supporting HTML development that make it more productive than a plain text editor.

## Visual HTML Editors

A second type of HTML editor is one that hides the hypertext formatting language from the page creator by providing a visual (or WYSIWYG—What You See Is What You Get) environment that generates HTML code behind the scenes. Therefore, page creation is performed in a point-and-click environment, as you would expect in this graphically based computer world.

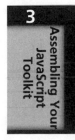

Netscape has a visual HTML editor component called Composer, which is built into its Communicator product. Composer lets you easily edit HTML documents within an integrated browser environment, as shown in Figure 3.3. Although Composer's visual environment lets you work with basic HTML page layout, it doesn't provide sufficient power to work visually with multiframe windows, style sheets, and so forth.

**FIGURE 3.3**

*Netscape Composer.*

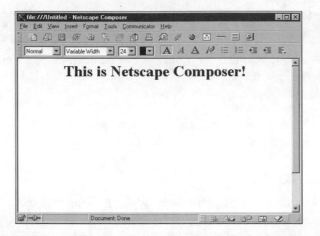

**Resource**

Check Netscape's home page at `http://home.netscape.com` for the latest build of Netscape Composer. Once Mozilla.org releases the first Open Source version of Communicator, you will be able to download Composer's successor from `http://www.mozilla.org`.

Microsoft FrontPage is a more sophisticated option. It includes one of the best visual HTML editors available. Not only does the FrontPage Editor support enhanced options (such as framesets and tables), but it also includes an expanded set of templates to speed up the process of developing a Web page.

FrontPage is more than just an editor, however. It lets you build and administer an entire Web site by working closely with Microsoft's Internet Information Server (IIS).

**Resource**

Check the Microsoft home page at `http://www.microsoft.com` for the latest information on FrontPage.

A current disadvantage of some visual HTML editors is their inability to let you go into a text-based mode and edit raw HTML. For the current release of Composer, you need an external editor to do that. Additionally, Composer hardly knows what to do with JavaScript code, so don't even think of using it as your JavaScript editing environment. Nonetheless, using an HTML editor will allow you to quickly develop the HTML around your scripts. Once you have the HTML created, you can use a text or JavaScript editor to add you scripts.

## Web Browsers

Another component you need is a Web browser that supports JavaScript. Chapter 1, "JavaScript and the World Wide Web," discussed the various Web browsers and their support for JavaScript, so I won't dive into that discussion here. However, because various versions of browsers provide different levels of JavaScript language support, you probably need to have many of these available during your testing phase.

The basic rule of thumb is to test your script using all the possible types of browsers that will access the page. For intranet applications, you might have only a single browser to test. However, for public Internet applications, you need to consider that many types of browsers might access your JavaScript-enabled site.

The best way to tell what browsers are hitting your site is to analyze your Web logs. All browsers send a user-agent string you can use to determine the browsers and operating systems of your users. You should find that they are the following:

- Real JavaScript browsers: Netscape Navigator 4.0+ and Microsoft Internet Explorer 4.0+

- Early JavaScript browsers: Netscape Navigator 2.0 and 3.0 and Internet Explorer 3.0

- Other JavaScript-enabled browsers: HotJava 3+, Opera 3+, NetPositive 2.1+

- Browsers that do not support JavaScript

Your JavaScript application doesn't necessarily have to support all browsers. For example, you might need to use a JavaScript feature that was added in the latest version of Netscape Navigator, so you require at least that version of the browser to view your pages. However, having previous versions available for testing can be invaluable to providing the best application environment possible.

## Script Debuggers

The last tool that you should have as part of your toolkit is a debugger. Currently, the two main debuggers are from Netscape and Microsoft. You will more than likely want to download both of these so that you can debug scripts in both Navigator and Internet Explorer browsers. Since Chapter 34, "Debugging," covers both of these applications, I will not talk about them here.

# The JavaScript Development Process

Once you have your toolkit elements, you need to assemble them into a workable development environment. Before you perform this process, it's helpful to understand how the JavaScript application development process is often structured. Figure 3.4 shows a typical scenario, in which basic HTML page creation is followed by the addition of JavaScript code to the HTML document. The page is then tested iteratively in the Web browser of choice.

**FIGURE 3.4**
*The JavaScript development process.*

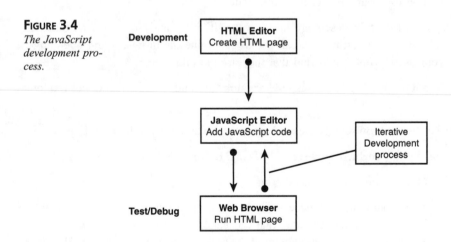

# Server-Side JavaScript Tools

JavaScript is featured as the scripting language for server-side Web development tools, such as Netscape's Server-Side JavaScript and Borland IntraBuilder. This section provides a brief overview of both of these tools.

## Netscape's Server-Side JavaScript

Server-Side JavaScript (SSJS) is Netscape's implementation of JavaScript on the server side. SSJS provides server-side language objects for file, mail, and database access. You can use Server-Side JavaScript to develop custom scripts that run on the Netscape server, eliminating the need for CGI in your applications. See Chapter 12, "Server-Side JavaScript," for more information on this implementation.

### Resource

Check the Netscape DevEdge home page at http://developer.netscape.com for the latest information on Server-Side JavaScript.

## Borland IntraBuilder

Borland's IntraBuilder is a Windows-based visual development environment designed to let you create, maintain, and administer Web database applications. If you've ever worked with a Windows visual development tool, you will feel at home with IntraBuilder.

### Resource

Check the Borland home page at http://www.borland.com for the latest technical and support information on IntraBuilder.

IntraBuilder's programming language is an extended version of JavaScript that supports true object orientation (including inheritance) and database-related objects. If you have used Borland's Visual dBASE, you will find that IntraBuilder has a similar look and feel.

# Summary

This chapter examined the basic building blocks needed by a JavaScript programmer: a JavaScript editor, an HTML editor, a Web browser, and script debuggers. I also introduced you to two server-side products that feature JavaScript as their native programming language.

# Writing Your First Script

**CHAPTER 4**

Over the past three chapters we have taken a look at JavaScript and how it fits into the Internet picture. I have given you insight to what you can do with the language and how it works with HTML. We have talked about browser support and server-side additions as well. I have approached the language from a coder's perspective by helping you understand the tools you will need to get started. Now we are going to tackle the task of writing your first scripts.

To do this, we are going to approach your first script the right way. By *the right way*, I mean that we are going to plan the script, implement it, and test it properly. While doing this, I will also remind you of some of the things you learned in the first three chapters.

# A Quick Reminder

First, remember that JavaScript is embedded into HTML documents by means of beginning and ending `<script>` tags. As the browser is loading the page, it starts interpreting the code by finding the beginning script tag, `<script>`, then reads everything that follows until the ending tag, `</script>`.

JavaScript interprets each line of code into instructions that it can follow. This is the same way you might follow directions to a party, for example. Just as you would read each instruction and act on it by turning or driving your car in the appropriate direction, JavaScript follows each of your instructions in order.

On your way to the party, you might need to stop at a red light until it turns green, or you might need to stop and pick up a friend. You can also emulate this with JavaScript if you want the computer to sit idle until something happens.

# Before You Start

Before you even start writing your code, you have to make some decisions. These decisions will help you understand what you have to do and how to write your code. The following sections will help you understand what you should be asking yourself.

## What Browsers Do You Want to Support?

The first question you need to ask yourself is what browsers you want or need to support. This is a huge question, because it will determine how much code you need to write.

As we said previously, JavaScript has changed drastically over the first several versions of the language. In fact, this language had a tendency to be all over the map until ECMAScript was standardized. Since ECMAScript defines only the core portion of the language, it still leaves a lot of gray area when client-side and server-side implementations are created. Because of this, you are going to find that you spend a substantial amount of coding time trying to write scripts that work in all browsers. Hence the question, "What browsers do you want to support?"

In deciding what browsers you want to support, there are a couple of factors that can help you. They are as follows:

- Do you have server-side functionality to determine the browser before your pages are sent out?

- Do browsers that you do not support need to fail gracefully?

## Help from the Server Side

If you can determine what browsers are requesting your page before it is sent, then you have a major advantage when creating client-side JavaScript programs and scripts. This allows you to avoid potential client-side errors by not sending code that is not supported.

True, it means that you may need several versions of your scripts, but the amount of download time for the browser and the chance of error will be reduced. You are no longer sending to determine what browser a user has, and excess lines that pertain only to one browser are not there. Having this functionality also allows you to handle known non-supporting browsers gracefully.

## Failing Gracefully

The second question you should ask is how gracefully you want to handle non-JavaScript browsers. This would include not only browsers that do not have JavaScript support but also those that have it turned off.

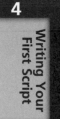

> **Caution**
>
> If you have ever taken a look at the preferences of your browser, you will notice that you can turn off JavaScript. See Figure 4.1 for Navigator 4.7's preference for turning off JavaScript. This is important to keep in mind, because you will need to be able to handle instances with JavaScript turned off gracefully. To do so, simply treat these instances as browsers that do not support JavaScript at all.

**FIGURE 4.1**

*Turning off
JavaScript in
Navigator 4.7.*

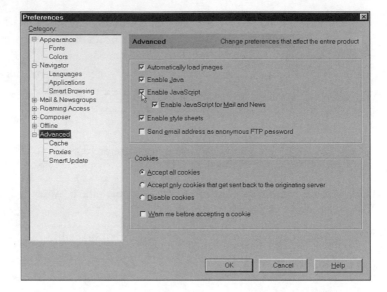

When asking yourself this question, you need to understand where you fit in the Internet space. Are you building a site that you want all people to access and get the full experience? Maybe you are developing an intranet for a company, and you know what browsers your users will have. You may even be building a site just to see what you can do with JavaScript.

What you are determining is the kinds of restrictions you are going to place on your users. Make this decision carefully and with the full understanding that leaving out some people may mean leaving out some potential traffic. If you have made the decision to lose users who do not have JavaScript enabled, then your task is a bit easier— simply do not provide secondary HTML for them to view your pages. Otherwise, you should try to provide them with as much functionality as you can.

## How Do You Want to Handle Non-JavaScript Browsers?

Up to this point, we have not talked about how to handle browsers that do not have JavaScript or have it turned off. If you have the ability, you can eliminate some of your worries by using the server-side functionality I spoke of earlier. However, this does not take care of those browsers that have JavaScript turned off. But there is hope: the `<noscript>` tag.

The `<noscript>` tag allows you to specify HTML that is to be displayed if JavaScript is turned off or not supported. This section of code usually goes directly under any `<script>`

sections you may have. Listing 4.1 shows how you can use this tag, and Figure 4.2 shows how it is rendered in Navigator 4.7 with JavaScript turned off.

**LISTING 4.1**   Using the `<noscript>` Tag

```html
<html>
<head>
  <meta http-equiv="Content-Script-Type" content="text/javascript">
  <title>My First JavaScript Script</title>
</head>
<body>
  <h1>What is returned?</h1>
  <script>
  <!--
    document.write('<p>JavaScript is turned on!</p>');
  //-->
  </script>
  <noscript>
    <p>JavaScript is turned off!</p>
  </noscript>
</body>
</html>
```

**FIGURE 4.2**
*Rendering the*
*`<noscript>` tag.*

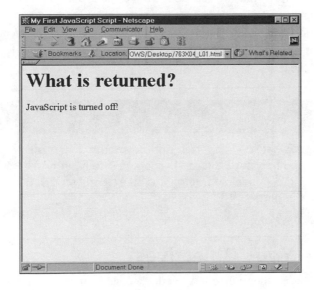

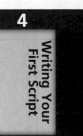

4

Writing Your
First Script

If you look at Listing 4.1 and Figure 4.2, you will notice that the `<noscript>` section tells the user that JavaScript is turned off. If it were turned on, this same page would interpret the JavaScript code and ignore the `<noscript>` section. This is a great tag to help handle non-supporting browsers gracefully.

> ### Warning
>
> Some of the older browsers, such as Navigator 2 and early versions of Internet Explorer, do not support the `<noscript>` tag. I have also seen problems with using this tag multiple times on a page when the browser supports JavaScript and has it turned off. Again, this seems to happen mostly in Navigator browsers.

## Inline or `src` It?

The final question you need to ask yourself before starting your code is how you want to put it on the page. Of course, this assumes that you have functions, variables, and other functionality that you want to place in the `<head>` of the document. The question becomes whether you want to put all of your code in external source (`.js`) files and include the files with the `src` attribute of the `<script>` tag or put the code in the document itself.

As I mentioned before, by placing your code in an external file, you will be able to edit one file to affect scripts on all of your pages. I like to put all of my functions in external source files. I even go so far as to split up my functions into separate files according to their functionality. For instance, I might have one file called `calculations.js` and another one called `formhandling.js`.

> ### Note
>
> The `src` attribute was not supported until JavaScript 1.1. This means that only Navigator 3+ and Internet Explorer 4+ support it fully. Internet Explorer 3.02 attempted to support this method of storing external scripts, but I have had limited success in getting it to work.

## What Are Your Objectives?

Defining objectives is among the most overlooked steps in starting a project. You would expect it to be the first step, but often it is not done thoroughly. I have seen many JavaScript programmers approach a script from what I call the *cool* angle rather than the *functional* angle.

JavaScript is definitely cool, and if the cool factor is your main focus, then I say go for it. However, if your main objective is a functional one, try to avoid excess coding that is nothing more than flashy. In the long run, other programmers and even you will find it hard to follow your code. You will also find it difficult to implement changes and fixes, because you will have to program around your *cool* code.

When defining your objectives, you fully determine what you want the end result of your program to be. For instance, you may want it to perform error checking on forms. With this goal in mind, you should work backward to determine what will accomplish this goal. Using the form example, you should ask yourself how many elements are going to be in the form. How many are radio buttons, text fields, selection options, and so on that you want to be able to process.

Once you have nailed down this second level of objectives, you can start figuring out how to code your scripts. You will want to write code that handles the radio buttons, text fields, and selection options. You may be able to create a function that will cover all the functionality you need and that works from a parameter that is passed in, such as `radio`. Remember that code reuse is a good thing and that you should apply any coding experience you have to reducing the number of lines of code your scripts need.

# Starting Your Script

By this time, you should be ready to start coding. You have decided what browsers you want to support, how you want to deal with non-supporting browsers, and where you want to store the scripts. This takes care of all of the technical aspects of writing JavaScript code.

## Defining Objectives

In your first script, we are going to create a simple pop-up dialog that asks the user for a password. If the password is incorrect, the user is redirected to an error page. If the password is valid, then the user is sent to the page he is requesting. Those whose browsers do not support JavaScript simply see a message saying they cannot access this page. Because this script is written in very basic JavaScript, it can be used in any supporting browser. We also will keep all of our scripts inline rather than in an external source file.

Here is a quick summary of what we have decided:

- Browser Support: Support all.

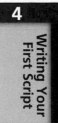

4

Writing Your
First Script

- Non-Supporting Browsers: Display a message saying they cannot access this portion of your site.

- Location of Script: Inline.

- Objective: Prompt the user for a password when the page is accessed. If the correct password is entered, the user is redirected to the secure page. If an incorrect password is entered, the user is redirected to an error page.

## Creating a Code Template

Now that our objectives are defined, the first thing I do when I start writing my code is to create a template. I usually include all the necessary <head> information and prepare the <body> portion. Listing 4.2 has a copy of the template I start with.

**LISTING 4.2   JavaScript Template File**

```
<html>
<head>
  <meta http-equiv="Content-Script-Type" content="text/javascript">
  <title>My First JavaScript Script</title>
  <script language="JavaScript">
  <!--

  // Your code will go here...


  //-->
  </script>
</head>
<body>

<!-- Content starts here -->

</body>
</html>
```

## Handling Non-Supporting Browsers

The first thing we want to get out of the way in this example is how we will handle non-supporting browsers. Since we are not performing an excessive amount of HTML for these users, it will be quick and easy to finish. Listing 4.3 shows what will be included in this section.

LISTING 4.3    Handling Non-Supporting Browsers

```
<body>
  <noscript>
    <b>
      Sorry, but your browser either does not support JavaScript or your
      have it turned off. For information on JavaScript supporting browsers
      or how to turn it back on, please see the website of your browser's
      creator.
    </b>
  </noscript>
</body>
```

As you can see, this was a very simple task, creating a message that will be displayed to the user. We included the text within bold tags (`<b>...</b>`) to ensure that it will show up well on the page.

# Writing Your Code

At this point the entire page is ready, except for writing the JavaScript code. By accomplishing all of the other tasks first, such as defining our objectives, creating a template, and handling non-supporting browsers, we have made sure that the page functions properly without any scripting on it. This is an important step; on many occasions I have thought that my script had a problem when in fact I had not properly closed the HTML, or I had misplaced some comments.

For this example, we will be working in the `<head>` portion of the page. The first thing we need to do is create a dialog for the user to enter the password. For this task, we will use the prompt method. This will give us a dialog like the one shown in Figure 4.3 to pass the entered information back to our script.

FIGURE 4.3
*The* prompt *dialog.*

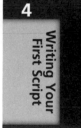

The key to using this dialog is that it returns what the user enters. Using this information, we can check to see if the proper password was entered and redirect the user's browser appropriately.

prompt, which is a method of the window object, takes two parameters and has the following syntax:

```
prompt("message","default");
```

When using this method, you should replace *message* with instructions for the user. This will be displayed above the field where the user will enter his data. The *default* parameter is used to specify a default for the user. In our first script, we do not want to have a default, so we will simply pass it an empty string.

In addition to the `prompt` method, we will also be using the `location` property of the `window` object. We will set this property to redirect the browser to the appropriate page according to the success of the user's entry. The last thing we need to note is that we will include all of this code in a function that is called after the entire page has loaded.

The code that accomplishes this task is relatively short and can be seen in Listing 4.4.

**LISTING 4.4**   JavaScript Needed to Prompt User for a Password

```
<script language="JavaScript">
<!--
  function passCheck(){
    if(prompt("Please enter your password","") == "letmein"){
      window.location = "/secure.html";
    }else{
      window.location = "/error.html";
    }
  }
//-->
</script>
```

Looking at Listing 4.4, you will see that we use the `language` attribute of the `<script>` tag. Our template had us specify the `Content-Script-Type` in a `<meta>` tag in the `<head>` portion of our document, so there is no need to set it in the `<script>` tag. Next, you see that we have defined a function called `passCheck()`.

Within this function, we use an `if..else` conditional statement to verify the password entered by the user. Don't worry too much right now about how this works—it is covered in detail in Chapter 7, "Control Structures and Looping." All you need to understand at this point is that it is checking to see if the user entered `letmein` as the password. The `==` evaluation operator, which will be covered in Chapter 6, "Operators," performs this task.

If the user enters the correct password, then he is redirected to the `/secure.html` page. If the user does not enter the correct password, his browser is redirected to the `/error.html` page.

## Calling the Function

The last step in getting our script to work is to call the function. For this, we will use the onLoad event handler to call the function after the page is loaded. This event handler is specified as an attribute to the <body> tag. It should look like the following:

```
<body onload="passCheck()">
```

# Your First Script

Your first script is now complete and needs only to be assembled into a single document. Listing 4.5 shows you the complete page as it should look in a text editor.

**LISTING 4.5** The Final Script

```html
<html>
<head>
  <meta http-equiv="Content-Script-Type" content="text/javascript">
  <title>My First JavaScript Script</title>
  <script language="JavaScript">
  <!--
    function passCheck(){
      if(prompt("Please enter your password","") == "letmein"){
        window.location = "/secure.html";
      }else{
        window.location = "/error.html";
      }
    }
  //-->
  </script>
</head>
<body onload="passCheck()">
  <noscript>
    <b>
      Sorry, but your browser either does not support JavaScript or your
      have it turned off. For information on JavaScript supporting browsers
      or how to turn it back on, please see the website of your browser's
      creator.
    </b>
  </noscript>
</body>
</html>
```

In this listing, you will see that we specified the default language type and our function in the <head> of the page and called it using an attribute of the <body> tag. Finally, we accommodate non-supporting browsers using the <noscript> tag in the <body> portion of the page. To see the result of running this script in a JavaScript-enabled browser, see Figure 4.4. Figure 4.5 shows what non-supporting browsers see.

**FIGURE 4.4**

*Running Listing 4.5 in a supported browser.*

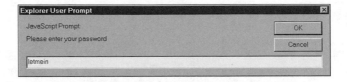

**FIGURE 4.5**

*Running Listing 4.5 in a non-supported browser.*

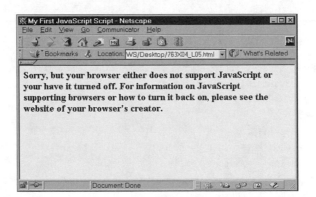

# Summary

In this chapter, you wrote your first script. Congratulations on making it this far! We could have done a simple "Hello World" script as your first, but I wanted to give you something a little more challenging and real-world. The "Hello World" script is nothing more than the use of the document.write() method, which you will learn more about later, in the <body> of your document. In fact, you should be able to do it now after completing your first script.

This chapter also concludes Part I of the book. In the next section you will learn more about the JavaScript language and how it works. We will dive into the syntax and semantics of the language, and you will learn about the operators and conditional statements I mentioned in this chapter.

# The Core JavaScript Language

# PART

# II

# Fundamentals of the JavaScript Language

## In This Chapter

**5**

**CHAPTER**

JavaScript is a high-level, object-based language designed to let Web authors and programmers easily create interactive Web documents. It offers the basic characteristics of an object-oriented language without the complicated features that accompany other languages such as Java and C++.

Also, JavaScript's relatively small vocabulary is easy to understand but gives way to a number of possibilities that were previously unavailable. In this chapter, I briefly explain how JavaScript got its start and how it relates to two well-known Web technologies. I'll then give you the information you need to create your own JavaScript scripts.

# A Very Brief Summary

While Sun was developing the much-lauded Java programming language, Netscape was busy developing a lightweight scripting language called LiveScript. This language was then redefined, renamed JavaScript, and jointly released by Sun and Netscape.

With JavaScript, you can provide almost limitless interactivity in your Web pages, because it lets you access events such as startups, document loads, exits, and user mouse clicks. You can also use JavaScript to control objects directly, such as the browser status bar, frames, and even the browser display window. JavaScript also provides interactivity between plug-in modules and Java applets.

# How JavaScript Relates to CGI, Plug-Ins, and Java

You might wonder what JavaScript has to offer that using a CGI (Common Gateway Interface) program, plug-in software, or Java doesn't. Semi-interactive Web pages were around long before JavaScript was born, thanks to CGI programs. Later came plug-in software and Java to give more interactivity to Web pages. I'll define these different technologies so that you can understand how JavaScript adds even more to your Web authoring toolbox.

## CGI

CGI is the standard for the way programs interface with a Web server. Using a programming language such as Perl, C/C++, Visual Basic, or AppleScript and complying with the CGI standard, you can create programs that pass information from the client to the Web server.

For example, developers have created many search utilities using CGI to help you locate your favorite sites on the Web or related information on the developers' sites. Typically, the user enters a word or phrase into an HTML text element and clicks a Search button. This submits the text to the server, where a CGI program is started by the Web server. The program takes the parameters passed and performs the functions included in the program. In the case of a search CGI, this will most likely search through a master database, finding only the sites that match the search criteria. Once the CGI program is finished with the search, the program creates a new HTML document that includes the results, which it then sends back to the user's Web browser.

In this example, you'll notice that all the hard work is done by the server. If you were limited to static Web pages that had to be written ahead of time, you would have to consider every search combination possible. Creating a Web document for each query would be impractical—a ridiculous way to emulate the type of searching function that users are accustomed to. This is one problem that CGI has solved to help the Web become more interactive.

### Resource

For all the information you need about CGI and links to existing CGI scripts, point your Web browser to `http://hoohoo.noea.uiuo.edu/ogi/overview.html`.

# Plug-Ins

Clicking a link tells the browser to request and download a file. If the file is a text, HTML, or graphic file, it is output to the display. If the browser doesn't recognize the file, it often asks you to save the file locally (on your hard disk) or select an application to handle the file. In addition to clicking through to these files, it is also possible to embed files of different formats within the body of your HTML.

Plug-ins, which Netscape first introduced in version 2.0 of its Navigator browser and Internet Explorer implemented in version 3.0, have increased the number of files that the browser recognizes. Plug-ins are program modules that you can use to handle files differently (such as to display them with extra controls) or to use files that were not originally designed to be understood. Such files might include audio, animation, Acrobat, and VRML files.

For example, if you click a link that points to an audio file and the browser does not natively support that format, it will look for a plug-in module to handle the file. If it finds one, the plug-in is loaded and begins playing the clip for you. The integration of the browser and audio player is practically seamless.

**Resource**

There are plenty of plug-ins to enhance your browsing experience. You can find a large list of them on Netscape's Netcenter site by pointing your Web browser to `http://home.netscape.com/download`.

## Java

Java is probably the technology most similar to JavaScript. However, there are substantial differences. For this reason, we will take a little closer look at Java than we did at CGI and plug-ins.

Unlike JavaScript, Java by nature does not have direct access to elements (that is, objects) within a Web page. There is not a client-side version that is specifically tailored to handling HTML and other objects that are retrieved by a browser. The structure and syntax of the Java language are closely correlated to the implementation of JavaScript. Reserved words, operators, and flow control statements are almost identical. Because Java is a compiled language, a more strict definition of the code tokens is required. As a result, in two main areas, Java diverges from JavaScript protocol: in variable type rules and in class encapsulation methodologies. Table 5.1 compares the attributes of JavaScript with those of Java.

**TABLE 5.1** Comparison of Attributes in the JavaScript and Java Languages

| *JavaScript* | *Java* |
| --- | --- |
| Scripting language | Programming language |
| Loose variable type checking | Strong variable type checking |
| Rudimentary access control | Tiered-access control definitions |
| No ability-derived types | Full object-oriented capabilities or inherited attributes |
| No array checking | Strict array access checks |
| Instance hierarchy | Object hierarchy |
| JavaScript objects | Java class |

In JavaScript, variables and functions are declared as either local or global in scope. Java enforces a flexible tiered-access convention for variables and methods (functions), whereby elements are visible according to their access modifier: private, protected, or public. The modifiers allow the programmer to hide object attributes and implementation details from the public interface of the object, giving more latitude in modifying the underlying code supporting a published interface while still maintaining backward compatibility.

Java instance variables are declared in a rigorous manner, and every variable specified must be assigned a primary or derived component type. In contrast, JavaScript code doesn't require a specification. Java has specialized, built-in data types that optimize the behavior and size of the variable.

Another distinction to note is that JavaScript currently has a more general classification schema (number or string) than Java (int, long, float, and char). Although JavaScript objects don't scale effectively into more complex object types, you can create Java classes that group the variables into object components.

> **Note**
>
> The next proposed release of JavaScript, which is currently dubbed 2.0, includes a stricter classification of elements. In JavaScript 2.0, such types as int, long, float, and char have been proposed.

You can consider JavaScript an object-oriented language because it supports an instance hierarchy. Objects are defined with specific variables and methods capable of being referenced using the dot convention but not extended through derivation of subclasses. Although the Java language syntax is similar to the JavaScript scripting language in relation to referencing and creating component objects, Java is a true programming language that bears a striking resemblance to C++.

Using Java code, object definitions can be reused to serve as the framework for a more complex architecture. Object classes are the building blocks of Java code. Unlike JavaScript, every Java function and variable must be defined inside the class structure. Furthermore, Java lets you aggregate the classes into packages of related objects or define abstract interface conventions for categories of objects.

Another difference is that Java source code is compiled into bytecode by the developer, creating binary components that can be used by other programmers. You can use the created components, class objects, to build derived classes that inherit the functionality of the base class and extend the attributes of the base class.

The capability to extend the base class is the basis for code reuse in large-scale application systems and improved programmer efficiency. Strong type checking is performed by the Java compiler, requiring the programmer to explicitly declare and cast instance variables as either built-in or derived types. JavaScript code allows the programmer to switch the type identifier of a variable transparently without regard to its original type definition.

There is a high level of integration between the two languages that allows the developer to embed JavaScript calls in Java code and access Java class methods in JavaScript. This capability enhances the value of JavaScript programmers who have knowledge of the Java framework. This technology, known as LiveConnect, will be discussed in Chapter 25, "Interacting with Other Technologies."

# Embedding Scripts in HTML Documents

What is unique about JavaScript is that you can use it to write programs that run on the server side (see Chapter 12, "Server-Side JavaScript") or on the client side within the browser. On the client side, you can implement JavaScript in one of two ways: either embedded in an HTML document between a set of `<script>` tags or inside an HTML tag to respond to an event. Each time an HTML page is downloaded, JavaScript is interpreted by the client's browser. Depending on the actions of the user and other events that occur while the HTML document is being viewed, portions of the embedded script or scripts are executed.

Suppose you have created an HTML document to collect data from people visiting a particular Web page. You could start out with a form that includes three text elements for name, company, and telephone number. At the bottom of the form, you could include a standard Submit button to send the visitor's information back to a database on your Web server. You could also require that each user complete every field and include the area code with the telephone number.

After the user clicks the Submit button, all the data in the form is passed to a server-side program for processing. If the program notices that the user left out some information, it can respond with a new HTML document, asking for the required data to be entered. The user can then submit the form again with all the required data in the correct format. Once the program is satisfied with what the visitor has typed, the program can continue by posting the data to the database.

Handling required entries like this can add up to substantial delays, which are now avoidable with JavaScript. You can perform data validation on the client side with JavaScript so that the Web server doesn't have to. Handling data validation is one example of how JavaScript can complement a server-side program by offering a quicker response to errors while freeing up more resources on the server. Chapter 14, "Handling Events," presents an in-depth look at data validation.

# Events

One of the key characteristics of JavaScript is its capability to catch a limited number of user actions, known to most programmers as *events*. Some HTML elements already react to events such as clicking the familiar link element that brings you to another HTML document.

As you move the mouse pointer over the text or graphic that makes up the link, the pointer changes from an arrow to a small pointing hand. Some browsers also respond by displaying the destination URL in the status bar. JavaScript calls this the MouseOver event and reacts whenever you move the mouse pointer over the element. If you click any part of the link, the browser responds by sending you to a different location on the Web or opening a new file. This action is cleverly called the Click event, which is triggered whenever you click the link. HTML catches these events, and the browser always reacts the same way.

With JavaScript, you can now create custom reactions to many events that can occur while the user views an HTML document. I will not go into a lot of detail here, but Chapter 14 shows you how to handle events in depth.

# Syntax Specifics

Like any programming language, JavaScript has a certain way of handling different items and elements. There are also specifics on keywords, reserved words, tokens, and more.

## Versions of JavaScript

As Netscape, Microsoft, and other leading companies have been improving the core ECMAScript standard and their individual implementations, JavaScript has seen new versions of the language, along with new versions of the various browsers. This book covers to JavaScript version 1.4 and mentions 1.5, which is currently in beta. For a full list of supported platforms, see Table 5.2.

**5**

**Fundamentals of the JavaScript Language**

**TABLE 5.2** JavaScript Support

| Version | Description |
|---------|-------------|
| JavaScript 1.0 | Supported in Netscape Navigator 2. |
| JavaScript 1.1 | Supported in Netscape Navigator 3, Internet Explorer 3, Opera 3, and Netscape Enterprise Server 2. |
| JavaScript 1.2 | Supported in Netscape Navigator 4 to 4.04 and Internet Explorer 4. |
| JavaScript 1.3 | Supported in Netscape Navigator 4.05 to 4.7 and Internet Explorer 5. |
| JavaScript 1.4 | Supported in some pre-alpha versions (before M12) of Mozilla, HotJava 3.0, Internet Explorer 5.5, and Netscape Enterprise Server 4.0. |
| JavaScript 1.5 | Planned support for Navigator 5 (Mozilla), the Open Source version of Netscape Navigator. |

See Tables 5.3, 5.4, and 5.5 to understand how these versions of JavaScript, JScript, and ECMAScript relate. The relationships of JavaScript, Jscript, and ECMAScript to each other are not necessarily the same. There are minor differences that make such comparisons incomplete.

**TABLE 5.3** JavaScript's Relationship to JScript

| JavaScript | JScript |
|------------|---------|
| 1.0 | n/a |
| 1.1 | 1.0 – 2.0 |
| 1.2 | 3.0 – 4.0 |
| 1.3 | 5.0 – 5.1 |
| 1.4 | 5.0 – 5.1 |
| 1.5 | 5.5 |

**TABLE 5.4** JavaScript's Relationship to ECMAScript

| JavaScript | ECMAScript |
|------------|------------|
| 1.0 | n/a |
| 1.1 | n/a—Foundation for standards submission |
| 1.2 | n/a—Contained most of ECMAScript 1.0 |
| 1.3 | 1.0 |
| 1.4 | 1.0 Revision 2 |
| 1.5 | 1.0 Revision 3 |

**TABLE 5.5**    JScript's Relationship to ECMAScript

| JScript | ECMAScript |
|---------|------------|
| 1.0 | n/a |
| 2.0 | n/a—Foundation for standards submission |
| 3.0—3.1 | 1.0 |
| 4.0 | 1.0 |
| 5.0 | 1.0 Revision 2 |
| 5.5 | 1.0 Revision 3 |

As a JavaScript developer, you must know the platform you are targeting so that you can develop for the correct version of JavaScript. Once this is decided, you can specify the version you want to use with the `language` attribute of the `<script>` tag.

**Note**

Remember that this tag has officially been deprecated in HTML 4.01 and XHTML 1.0. Currently, there is no standardized tag that allows you to specify the language version. However, I would recommend you continue to use the `language` attribute in conjunction with the `type` attribute until a definitive method is standardized.

For example, if your application must run on Netscape Navigator versions 2.0 and above and on Microsoft Internet Explorer 3.0, you would write scripts for JavaScript version 1.0. However, if your target platform is Navigator 5.0/Mozilla, and you would like to take advantage of its advanced features, you would use the following tag to specify version 1.5:

```
<script language="JavaScript1.5" type="text/javascript">
```

To specify version 1.4, use this:

```
<script language = "JavaScript1.4" type="text/javascript">
```

To specify version 1.3, use this:

```
<script language= "JavaScript1.3" type="text/javascript">
```

To specify version 1.2, use this:

```
<script language= "JavaScript1.2" type="text/javascript">
```

To specify version 1.1, use this:

```
<script language="JavaScript1.1" type="text/javascript">
```

**5**

**Fundamentals of the JavaScript Language**

To specify version 1.0, use this:

```
<script language="JavaScript" type="text/javascript">
```

> **Note**
>
> Do not try to use `"JavaScript1.0"` or `"JavaScript1"` as the language in order to specify version 1.0. These will not be recognized, and your script will be ignored.

> **Warning**
>
> Before jumping into the specifics of JavaScript, I would like to reiterate the importance of specifying the correct language in the `<script>` tag. A browser will ignore any scripts specifying a language version that it can't understand.

# Tokens

*Tokens* are the smallest individual words, phrases, or characters that JavaScript can understand. When JavaScript is interpreted, the browser parses the script into these tokens while ignoring comments and whitespace.

JavaScript tokens fall into four categories: identifiers, keywords, literals, and operators. As with all computer languages, you have many ways to arrange these tokens to instruct a computer to perform a specific function. The *syntax* of a language is the set of rules and restrictions for the way you can combine tokens.

## Identifiers

*Identifiers* are simply names that represent variables, methods, or objects. They consist of a combination of characters or a combination of characters and digits. Some names are already built into the JavaScript language and are therefore reserved.

Aside from these keywords, you can define your own creative and meaningful identifiers. Of course, there are a few rules to follow:

- You must begin all identifiers with either a letter or an underscore (_).
- You can then use letters, digits, or underscores for all subsequent characters.

- Letters include all uppercase characters, A through Z, and all lowercase characters, a through z.

- The sequence of characters that makes up an identifier should not include any spaces.

- Digits include the characters 0 through 9.

Table 5.6 shows some examples of valid and invalid identifiers.

**TABLE 5.6** Examples of User-Defined JavaScript Identifiers

| *Valid* | *Invalid* |
|---------|-----------|
| current_WebSite | current WebSite |
| numberOfHits | #ofIslands |
| n | 2bOrNotToBe |
| N | return |

Notice that `current WebSite` is invalid because it contains a space. JavaScript tries to interpret this as two identifiers instead of one. If a space is needed, it is standard practice to use an underscore in its place.

`#ofIslands` is invalid because the pound sign is not included in the set of characters that are valid for identifiers. `2bOrNotToBe` is not valid because it begins with a number. The `return` identifier is already used by JavaScript for another purpose. Attempting to use it as your own identifier would produce errors when you tried to run the script.

Also, both `n` and `N` are valid identifiers and are different from each other. JavaScript is case sensitive and therefore considers identifiers with different case to be unique, even though they might be spelled the same.

## Keywords and Reserved Words

*Keywords* are predefined identifiers that make up the core of a programming language. In JavaScript, they perform unique functions, such as declaring new variables and functions, making decisions based on the present state of the computer, or starting a repetitive loop inside your application.

Keywords are built into JavaScript and are always available for use by the programmer, but they must follow the correct syntax. The keyword `var` is the first that I describe in detail later in this chapter. As you progress through this book, I'll show you how you can use other keywords to create more dynamic programs.

*Reserved words* are identifiers that you may not use as names for JavaScript variables, functions, objects, or methods. These include keywords and identifiers that are set aside for possible future use. The following is a complete list of the reserved words for JavaScript:

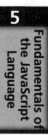

**5**

**Fundamentals of the JavaScript Language**

| | | | |
|---|---|---|---|
| Abstract | else | instanceof | switch |
| boolean | enum | int | synchronized |
| break | export | interface | this |
| byte | extends | long | throw |
| case | false | native | throws |
| catch | final | new | transient |
| char | finally | null | true |
| class | float | package | try |
| const | for | private | typeof |
| continue | function | protected | var |
| debugger | goto | public | void |
| default | if | return | volatile |
| delete | implements | short | while |
| do | import | static | with |
| double | in | super | |

## Literals

*Literals* are numbers or strings used to represent fixed values in JavaScript. They are values that don't change during the execution of your scripts. The following five sections describe the different types of literals.

### Integer

Integers can be expressed in decimal (base 10), octal (base 8), or hexadecimal (base 16) format. An integer literal in decimal format can include any sequence of digits that does not begin with 0 (zero). A zero in front of an integer literal designates octal form.

The integer itself can include a sequence of the digits 0 through 7. To designate hexadecimal, 0x (or 0X) is used before the integer. Hexadecimal integers can include digits 0 through 9 and the letters a through f or A through F. Here are some examples:

| | |
|---|---|
| Decimal | 33, 2139 |
| Octal | 071, 03664 |
| Hexadecimal | 0x7b8, 0X395 |

## Floating-Point

Floating-point literals represent decimal numbers with fractional parts. They can be expressed in either standard or scientific notation. With scientific notation, use either e or E to designate the exponent. Both the decimal number and the exponent can be either signed or unsigned (positive or negative), as shown in these examples:

```
3405.673
-1.958
8.3200e+11
8.3200e11
9.98E-12
```

## Boolean

JavaScript implements Boolean data types and therefore supports the two literals `true` and `false`, which represent the Boolean values 1 and 0, respectively. If you are new to programming, you will soon realize how often `true` and `false` values are needed. This is why JavaScript has built them into the language. The `true` and `false` keywords must appear in lowercase. As a result, the uppercase words `TRUE` and `FALSE` are left open to define as your own identifiers, but doing so is not recommended in order to avoid confusion.

## String

A string literal is zero or more characters enclosed in double quotes (`""`) or single quotes (`' '`). JavaScript gives you this option, but you must use the same type of quote to enclose each string. The following are examples of string literals enclosed in quotes:

```
"Allen's car"
'virtual "communities"'
"#12-6"
"Look, up in the sky!"
```

The use of either type of quotation mark is handy if you have a preference for one or the other. When you learn about JavaScript's built-in methods, be careful to note the guidelines that you must follow when using string literals as parameters. In some instances, in order to use the method properly, you might have to use both types of quotation marks when enclosing one string literal inside another. This is different from using escape codes, which is described in the next section.

## Special Characters

When writing scripts, you might sometimes need to tell the computer to use a special character or keystroke, such as a tab or a new line. To do this, use a backslash in front of one of the escape codes, as shown in the following list:

\b indicates a backspace.

\f indicates a form feed.

\n indicates a new line.

\r indicates a carriage return.

\t indicates a tab.

\\ indicates a backslash.

\' indicates a single quote.

\" indicates a double quote.

If you want to emulate a tab key to align two columns of data, you must use the tab character (\t). Listing 5.1 shows how to align text using tabs. The script itself can be harder to read after you add special characters but, as Figure 5.1 shows, the results look much better.

**LISTING 5.1**   Using Special Characters in JavaScript

```html
<html>
<head>
  <title>JavaScript Unleashed</title>
</head>
<body>
<!--
    Notice: Special characters do not take effect unless enclosed in a
    pre-formatted block
-->
  <pre>
    <script type="text/javascript">
    <!--
      document.writeln("\tPersonnel");
      document.writeln("Name\t\tAddress");
      document.writeln("Jeff\t\tjeff@company.com");
      document.writeln("Bill\t\tbill@company.com");
      document.writeln("Kim\t\tkim@company.com");
    // -->
    </script>
  </pre>
```

LISTING 5.1    continued

```
</body>
</html>
```

FIGURE **5.1**
*Aligning text using the tabs in JavaScript.*

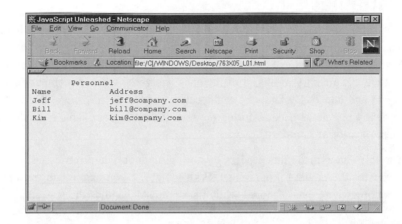

If you need to represent quotation marks within a string literal, precede them with a backslash:

```
document.write("\"Imagination is more important than knowledge.\"");
document.write(", Albert Einstein");
```

The preceding script would display the following line of text:

```
"Imagination is more important than knowledge.", Albert Einstein
```

# Operators

*Operators* are symbols or identifiers that represent a way in which a combination of expressions can be evaluated or manipulated. The most common operator you have used thus far is the assignment operator. In the example x = 10, both 10 by itself and the variable x are expressions. When JavaScript sees an assignment operator between two expressions, it acts according to the rules of the assignment operator. In this case, it takes the value from

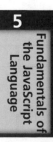

5

Fundamentals of the JavaScript Language

the expression on the right side and assigns it to the variable on the left side. Along with the common arithmetic operators, JavaScript supports over 30 others. I'll cover these more thoroughly in Chapter 6, "Operators."

# Variables

A *variable* is the name given to a location in a computer's memory where data is stored. The first computer programmers spent much of their time translating data such as the "Hello World" message into binary data. They would then find an empty area in the computer's memory to put all of the ones and zeros while remembering where the data began and ended. By knowing this location (address), they were able to find, update, or retrieve the data as needed during the rest of the program. This basically meant keeping track of a lot of numbers!

Variables have made this process of storing, updating, and retrieving information much easier for the modern programmer. With variables, you can assign meaningful names to locations where data is stored while the computer handles the rest.

## Naming

The name of a JavaScript variable is made up of one or more letters, digits, or underscores. It can't begin with a digit (0 through 9). Letters include all uppercase characters, A through Z, and all lowercase characters, a through z. JavaScript is case sensitive and therefore considers the following two examples to be different variable names:

```
internetAddress
internetaddress
```

The following are also valid variable names:

```
_lastName
n
number_2
```

When naming variables with a single word in JavaScript, it is common practice to use all lowercase letters. When using two or more words to name a variable, it is common to use lowercase letters for the first word and capitalize the first letter of all words thereafter. I make it a practice to use two or more words when naming variables to give others and myself a better idea of what the variable was created to do.

For example, suppose you need a variable to hold a Boolean value (`true` or `false`) that will let you know if a visitor to your Web page is finished typing his name into a text field. If you use a variable name such as `finish`, another programmer (or you, a couple of months down the road) could look at it and wonder, "Was this a flag that can be checked to find out if the visitor is done? Or was it a string stating what to write when the visitor was done, such as a thank-you message?"

The variable name `isDone` would be a better choice in this case. By using the word `is` as a prefix, you can indicate that this variable is posing a yes-or-no question, which indicates the variable will store a Boolean value. If the visitor is done entering his name, `isDone` is assigned the value `true`; otherwise, it's assigned the value `false`.

Although the length of a JavaScript variable is limited only by a computer's memory, it's a good idea to keep variables to a practical length. I recommend between 1 and 20 characters or two to three words. Try to prevent running over the end of a line while writing your scripts. Large variable names make this easy to do and can ruin the look and structure of your code.

Some traditional one-word and even single-character variables represent program or mathematical values. The most common are n for any number; x, y, and z for coordinates; and i for a placeholder in a recursive function or a counter in a loop. Again, these methods for using variables are simply traditional, and you may use them for whatever purpose you see fit.

There is a good chance, especially if you are in a professional environment, that at some point your code will need to be read by other people. Using consistent and meaningful naming conventions can be a big help to someone who is maintaining your scripts. Poorly thought out conventions cause big headaches and can significantly affect a company's bottom line.

## Declaring

To let JavaScript know you're going to use an identifier as a variable, you must first declare it. To declare variables in JavaScript, use the keyword var followed by the new variable name. This action reserves the name as a variable to be used as a storage area for whatever data you might want to hold in it. In the following examples, notice that you can also declare more than one variable at a time by using a comma between variable names:

```
var internetAddress;
```

```
var n;
```

```
var i, j, k;
```

```
var isMouseOverLink, helloMessage;
```

Once a variable is declared, it is then ready to be filled with its first value. This *initializing* is done with the assignment operator, =.

> **Note**
>
> The equals sign (=) is used to assign a value to a variable. You can read more about the assignment operator in Chapter 6.

You can initialize a variable at the same time you declare it or at any point thereafter in your script. Assigning a value when the variable is declared can help you remember what type of value you originally intended the variable to hold. The following shows the previous example, rewritten to include all initializations:

```
var internetAddress = "name@company.com";

var n = 0.00;

var i = 0, j = 0, k;

var isMouseOverLink = false;

var helloMessage = "Hello, thank you for coming!";

k = 0;
```

Notice that all variables have been initialized and declared at the same time except for k, which is initialized soon after. JavaScript reads from the top down, stepping through each line of code and performing the instructions in order. Until the program reaches the initializing step, the variable is said to be *undefined,* and you can't extract a value from it. Reading a value from a variable before it is initialized causes an error in your application when you execute it. JavaScript allows you to check if a variable has been assigned using the typeof operator. This is explained in Chapter 6.

JavaScript offers one other way of declaring a variable: by simply initializing it without using the var keyword. If you assign a value to a new variable before declaring it with var, JavaScript will automatically declare it for you.

> **Note**
>
> In older versions of JavaScript-enabled browsers, declaring variables without the var keyword will automatically declare the variable to be *global* in scope. Although this can be thought of as a shortcut, it's good programming practice to declare all variables specifically. Using the var keyword maintains the scope of the variable.

# Types

When storing a piece of data (more commonly known as a *value*), JavaScript automatically categorizes it as one of the five JavaScript data types. Table 5.7 shows the different types of data that JavaScript supports.

**TABLE 5.7** JavaScript Data Types

| Type | Examples |
| --- | --- |
| number | -19, 3.14159 |
| boolean | true, false |
| string | "Elementary, my dear Watson!", "" |
| function | unescape, write |
| object | window, document, null |

A variable of the number type holds either an integer or a real number. A boolean variable holds either true or false. string variables can hold any string literal that is assigned to it, including an empty string. Table 5.7 shows how to represent an empty string with two double quotes. functions are either user defined or built in. For example, the unescape function is built into JavaScript. You can learn how to create user-defined functions in Chapter 8, "Functions."

Functions that belong to objects, called *methods* in JavaScript, are also classified under the function data type. Core client-side JavaScript objects such as window or document are of the object data type, of course. object variables, or simply *objects*, can store other objects. A variable that holds the null value is said to be of the object type. This is because JavaScript classifies the value null as an object. Initializing a variable with null is a great way to prevent errors if you're not sure whether the variable will be used.

Typically, programming languages require that you define the type of data a new variable will represent. Throughout your program, any value assigned to that variable is expected to be of its defined data type. Furthermore, an error occurs when you attempt to assign a different data type to the variable. This doesn't happen with JavaScript, which is classified as a loosely typed language. You are not required to define data types, nor are you prevented from assigning different types of data to the same variable. JavaScript variables can accept a new type of data at any time, which in turn changes the type of variable it is. The following examples show valid uses of JavaScript variables:

```
var carLength;

carLength = 4 + 5;

document.writeln(carLength);
```

```
carLength = "9 feet";

document.writeln(carLength);
```

After you declare the variable, carLength is assigned the value of 4 + 5. JavaScript stores the number 9 as the number type. However, when you reassign carLength to "9 feet", JavaScript lets you store a new type of value, a string, in carLength. This eliminates the extra steps that are usually needed by other computer languages to let the computer know that you are switching data types.

## Scope

The *scope* of a variable refers to the area or areas within a program where a variable can be referenced. Suppose you embed one script in the head of an HTML document and another script (using another set of script tags) in the body of the same HTML document. JavaScript considers any variables declared within these two areas to be in the same scope. These variables are considered to be *global,* and they are accessible by any script in the current document. Later in this chapter, I'll more fully introduce functions, which are separate blocks of code. Variables declared within these blocks are considered *local* and are not always accessible by every script.

### Local

A variable declared inside a function is local in scope. Only that function has access to the value that the variable holds. Each time the function is called, the variable is created. Likewise, each time the function ends, the variable is destroyed. Another function declaring a variable with the same name is considered a different variable by JavaScript. Each addresses its own block of memory.

### Global

If you want more than one function to share a variable, declare the variable outside of any functions (but, of course, inside the <script> tags). With this method, any part of your application, including all functions, can share this variable.

> **Note**
>
> It is recommended that you declare global variables in the <head> of an HTML page to ensure that they are loaded before any other part of your application.

Listing 5.2 demonstrates how a global variable is declared and implemented. To show the difference between scopes, I included two functions in this program. You do not need to understand how functions work, but realize that they are like separate parts of a script, enclosed by curly braces ({}). If you are unfamiliar with functions, you can find this listing on the CD-ROM and load it into your browser. For more information on functions, refer to Chapter 8.

**LISTING 5.2** Global Versus Local Scope of a Variable

```html
<html>
<head>
  <title>JavaScript Unleashed</title>

  <script type="text/javascript">
  <!--
    // Global Variable
    var globalString = "A";

    // Functions
    function changeToB() {
      document.outputForm.beforeB.value = globalString;
      globalString = "B";
      document.outputForm.afterB.value = globalString;
    }

    function changeToC() {
      document.outputForm.beforeC.value = globalString;
      globalString = "C";
      document.outputForm.afterC.value = globalString;
    }

  // -->
  </script>
</head>
<body>

  <script type="text/javascript">
  <!--
    document.write("The initial value of globalString is \"" +
      globalString + "\".");
  // -->
  </script>
  <br>
```

LISTING 5.2   continued

```
  <form name="outputForm">
    <input name="changeButtonA" type="button" value="Change To B"
➥ onclick= "changeToB()">

    <input name="changeButtonB" type="button" value="Change To C"
➥ onclick="changeToC()">
    <p>
      Value of globalString
    <p>
    <input name="beforeB" type="TEXT" size="5,1">
    <p>
      Before clicking on "Change To B"
    <p>
    <input name="afterB" type="TEXT" size="5,1">
    <p>
      After clicking on "Change To B"
    <p>
    <input name="beforeC" type="TEXT" size="5,1">
    <p>
      Before clicking on "Change To C"
    <p>
    <input name="afterC" type="TEXT" size="5,1">
    <p>
      After clicking on "Change To C"
    <p>
  </form>
</body>
</html>
```

In this example, the initial value of globalString is displayed first. This shows that even though the variable was declared in the <head> block of the document, a script inside the <body> block of the document can use it. If you click the Change to B button, the function changeToB() first displays the initial value of globalString, changes it to B, and then displays the new value that globalString holds (see Figure 5.2).

To demonstrate that all functions in the document can use the same variable, I added a second button to call a different function. Clicking the Change to C button displays the current value of globalString, which is now B, and then changes globalString to C. Figure 5.2 shows the final output.

**FIGURE 5.2**

*The difference between local and global scopes.*

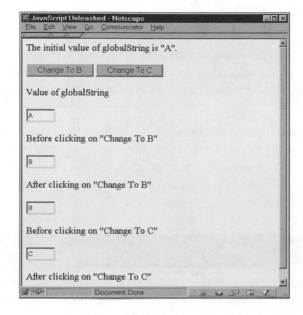

## Constants

A constant is a variable that holds the same value throughout a program's execution. JavaScript uses built-in constants to represent values used by common mathematical operations such as pi. They can be accessed through the math object. They are explained in Chapter 10, "Core Language Objects."

User-defined constants are variables that are defined by the programmer and whose values cannot change. Constants are usually represented by capitalized words and are defined at the beginning of a program.

JavaScript does not support constants in the traditional sense. Typically, a programming language that supports user-defined constants ensures that no other part of your application can change the value of a constant once it is defined. Attempting a change causes an error. JavaScript will not do this checking for you.

Even though there is no way to have JavaScript ensure that a variable is not altered, you can still use variables to hold values that are used repeatedly throughout a script. By replacing the multiple instances of a common value with a variable, you make it easier to update a script at a later time. All you have to do is change the initialization of the variable, and the entire script is updated.

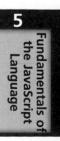

**5**

**Fundamentals of the JavaScript Language**

# Colors

JavaScript also supports the colors that are used in building HTML pages. To specify a color in your application, such as the color of a font, you can choose from the list of colors in Table 5.8. These values are string literals (not constants) that you can assign to specific object properties.

Listing 5.3 shows how you can use these values to set the color of strings that are written to the display. Notice that you can use either the name of the color or its hexadecimal equivalent. This method might look somewhat strange, but it simply sets the fontcolor property of the string literal that is written to the display. An invitation to the company picnic can be seen in Figure 5.3.

> **Note**
>
> You can't change the color of text once it has been displayed in the browser window. The document must be reloaded with a different font color specified.

**LISTING 5.3**    Using Colors in JavaScript

```html
<html>
<head>
  <title>JavaScript Unleashed</title>
</head>
<body>

  <h2>
    <script type="text/javascript">
    <!--
      document.writeln("Company Picnic!".fontcolor("crimson"));
    // -->
    </script>
  </h2>
  <h4>
    <script type="text/javascript">
    <!--
      document.writeln("July 19th at 1pm".fontcolor("blue"));
      document.writeln("<br>" + "Bring your family!".fontcolor("#008000"));
    // -->
    </script>
  </h4>
```

**LISTING 5.3** continued

```
</body>
</html>
```

**FIGURE 5.3**
*Changing the color of text in JavaScript.*

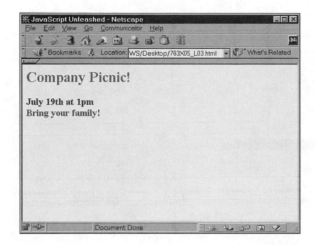

The hexadecimal string for each color is actually a combination of the RGB (red/green/blue) values that are used to make up each color. For example, the hexadecimal value for aqua is #00FFFF. This RGB value has 00 for the Red value, FF for the Green value, and FF for the Blue value. Two digits in hexadecimal allows for 256 degrees of each color. For the color aqua, the red is set to zero, which means that there is no red. The green and blue are each turned up all the way. Equal amounts of green and blue are combined to create the color aqua. With 256 combinations each for red, green, and blue, over 16 million colors are possible, but not all are supported by JavaScript. The full list of supported colors is shown in Table 5.8.

**TABLE 5.8** Color Values with Hexadecimal Equivalents

| Color | Red | Green | Blue | Color | Red | Green | Blue |
|---|---|---|---|---|---|---|---|
| aliceblue | F0 | F8 | FF | antiquewhite | FA | EB | D7 |
| aqua | 00 | FF | FF | aquamarine | 7F | FF | D4 |
| azure | F0 | FF | FF | beige | F5 | F5 | DC |
| bisque | FF | E4 | C4 | black | 00 | 00 | 00 |
| blanchedalmond | FF | EB | CD | blue | 00 | 00 | FF |
| blueviolet | 8A | 2B | E2 | brown | A5 | 2A | 2A |
| burlywood | DE | B8 | 87 | cadetblue | 5F | 9E | A0 |
| chartreuse | 7F | FF | 00 | chocolate | D2 | 69 | 1E |

**TABLE 5.8** continued

| Color | Red | Green | Blue | Color | Red | Green | Blue |
|-------|-----|-------|------|-------|-----|-------|------|
| coral | FF | 7F | 50 | cornflower-blue | 64 | 95 | ED |
| cornsilk | FF | F8 | DC | crimson | DC | 14 | 3C |
| cyan | 00 | FF | FF | darkblue | 00 | 00 | 8B |
| darkcyan | 00 | 8B | 8B | dark-goldenrod | B8 | 86 | 0B |
| darkgray | A9 | A9 | A9 | darkgreen | 00 | 64 | 00 |
| darkkhaki | BD | B7 | 6B | darkmagenta | 8B | 00 | 8B |
| darkolivegreen | 55 | 6B | 2F | darkorange | FF | 8C | 00 |
| darkorchid | 99 | 32 | CC | darkred | 8B | 00 | 00 |
| darksalmon | E9 | 96 | 7A | darkseagreen | 8F | BC | 8F |
| darkslateblue | 48 | 3D | 8B | darkslategray | 2F | 4F | 4F |
| darkturquoise | 00 | CE | D1 | darkviolet | 94 | 00 | D3 |
| deeppink | FF | 14 | 93 | deepskyblue | 00 | BF | FF |
| dimgray | 69 | 69 | 69 | dodgerblue | 1E | 90 | FF |
| firebrick | B2 | 22 | 22 | floralwhite | FF | FA | F0 |
| forestgreen | 22 | 8B | 22 | fuchsia | FF | 00 | FF |
| gainsboro | DC | DC | DC | ghostwhite | F8 | F8 | FF |
| gold | FF | D7 | 00 | goldenrod | DA | A5 | 20 |
| gray | 80 | 80 | 80 | green | 00 | 80 | 00 |
| greenyellow | AD | FF | 2F | honeydew | F0 | FF | F0 |
| hotpink | FF | 69 | B4 | indianred | CD | 5C | 5C |
| indigo | 4B | 00 | 82 | ivory | FF | FF | F0 |
| khaki | F0 | E6 | 8C | lavender | E6 | E6 | FA |
| lavenderblush | FF | F0 | F5 | lawngreen | 7C | FC | 00 |
| lemonchiffon | FF | FA | CD | lightblue | AD | D8 | E6 |
| lightcoral | F0 | 80 | 80 | lightcyan | E0 | FF | FF |
| lightgolden-rodyellow | FA | FA | D2 | lightgreen | 90 | EE | 90 |
| lightgray | D3 | D3 | D3 | lightpink | FF | B6 | C1 |
| lightsalmon | FF | A0 | 7A | lightseagreen | 20 | B2 | AA |
| lightskyblue | 87 | CE | FA | lightslate-gray | 77 | 88 | 99 |
| lightsteelblue | B0 | C4 | DE | lightyellow | FF | FF | E0 |
| lime | 00 | FF | 00 | limegreen | 32 | CD | 32 |
| linen | FA | F0 | E6 | magenta | FF | 00 | FF |
| maroon | 80 | 00 | 00 | medium-aquamarine | 66 | CD | AA |

**TABLE 5.8** continued

| Color | Red | Green | Blue | Color | Red | Green | Blue |
|-------|-----|-------|------|-------|-----|-------|------|
| mediumblue | 00 | 00 | CD | medium-orchid | BA | 55 | D3 |
| mediumpurple | 93 | 70 | DB | mediumsea-green | 3C | B3 | 71 |
| mediumslate-blue | 7B | 68 | EE | medium-springgreen | 00 | FA | 9A |
| medium-turquoise | 48 | D1 | CC | medium-violetred | C7 | 15 | 85 |
| midnightblue | 19 | 19 | 70 | mintcream | F5 | FF | FA |
| mistyrose | FF | E4 | E1 | moccasin | FF | E4 | B5 |
| navajowhite | FF | DE | AD | navy | 00 | 00 | 80 |
| oldlace | FD | F5 | E6 | olive | 80 | 80 | 00 |
| olivedrab | 6B | 8E | 23 | orange | FF | A5 | 00 |
| orangered | FF | 45 | 00 | orchid | DA | 70 | D6 |
| palegoldenrod | EE | E8 | AA | palegreen | 98 | FB | 98 |
| paleturquoise | AF | EE | EE | palevioletred | DB | 70 | 93 |
| papayawhip | FF | EF | D5 | peachpuff | FF | DA | B9 |
| peru | CD | 85 | 3F | pink | FF | C0 | CB |
| plum | DD | A0 | DD | powderblue | B0 | E0 | E6 |
| purple | 80 | 00 | 80 | red | FF | 00 | 00 |
| rosybrown | BC | 8F | 8F | royalblue | 41 | 69 | E1 |
| saddlebrown | 8B | 45 | 13 | salmon | FA | 80 | 72 |
| sandybrown | F4 | A4 | 60 | seagreen | 2E | 8B | 57 |
| seashell | FF | F5 | EE | sienna | A0 | 52 | 2D |
| silver | C0 | C0 | C0 | skyblue | 87 | CE | EB |
| slateblue | 6A | 5A | CD | slategray | 70 | 80 | 90 |
| snow | FF | FA | FA | springgreen | 00 | FF | 7F |
| steelblue | 46 | 82 | B4 | tan | D2 | B4 | 8C |
| teal | 00 | 80 | 80 | thistle | D8 | BF | D8 |
| tomato | FF | 63 | 47 | turquoise | 40 | E0 | D0 |
| violet | EE | 82 | EE | wheat | F5 | DE | B3 |
| white | FF | FF | FF | whitesmoke | F5 | F5 | F5 |
| yellow | FF | FF | 00 | yellowgreen | 9A | CD | 32 |

**5**

Fundamentals of
the JavaScript
Language

## Data Types

Although I have already discussed the basic data types that you can assign to variables, you should know that functions and objects are special types of data. They offer interesting ways to store and act upon the data that your scripts deal with. You will learn how to take advantage of these aspects of the language in Chapter 8.

## Expressions

An *expression* is a set of statements that, as a group, evaluates to a single value. This resulting value is then categorized by JavaScript as one of the following data types: `boolean`, `number`, `string`, `function`, or `object`.

An expression can be as simple as a number or variable by itself, or it can include many variables, keywords, and operators joined together. For example, the expression `x = 10` assigns the value `10` to the variable `x`. The expression as a whole evaluates to 10, so using the expression in a line of code such as `document.writeln(x = 10)` is valid.

JavaScript would rather see a string between the parentheses and simply display it, but in this case, it finds some work to do before moving on. It must first evaluate what is between the parentheses and then display the value. In this case, the number 10 is displayed.

Once the work is done to assign 10 to x, the following is also a valid expression: `x`. In this case, the only work that JavaScript needs to do is read the value from the computer's memory; no assignment needs to be performed. In addition to the assignment operator, there are many other operators you can use to form an expression (see Chapter 6).

## Comments

So far, I have used HTML comment tags for surrounding scripts, which ensures that old browsers don't display scripts that they can't execute. What if you want to place comments that JavaScript will ignore in your JavaScript code? The two solutions available to you are some of the same methods used in the C/C++ and Java languages. Here is the syntax:

```
// Here is a single line comment
```

The two forward slashes (`//`) hide text that follows until the end of the current line. For larger blocks of comments, you can use the multi-line syntax. To do this, use the following:

```
/* Use this method to contain multiple lines of

comments */
```

Whitespace is ignored in both of these types of comments. Because of this, either of the following is valid:

```
// Comments

/* Multiple lines

comments */
```

Listing 5.4 demonstrates the use of each type of comment. Two forward slashes do not hide code from older browsers. To avoid giving old browsers a headache, continue to use `<!--` and `-->` to surround all of your scripts. Anything that is commented in Listing 5.5 is not output to the display, as shown in Figure 5.4.

**FIGURE 5.4**
*Comments are
not displayed in
the browser.*

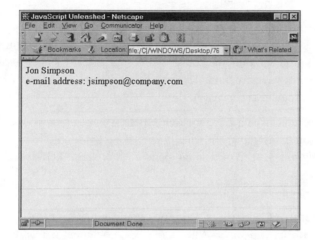

**LISTING 5.4**   Using JavaScript Comment Tags

```
<html>
<head>
  <title>JavaScript Unleashed</title>
</head>
<body>
  <script type="text/javascript">
  <!--
    // Variables
    var firstName = "Jon";
    var lastName = "Simpson";
    var internetAddress = "jsimpson@company.com";


    /*----------------------------------------
      Display the user's first and last name
```

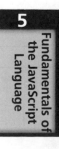

**5**

Fundamentals of
the JavaScript
Language

LISTING 5.4    continued

```
    along with their e-mail address.
- - - - - - - - - - - - - - - - - - - - - - - - - - - - - - - - - - - - - - */

    // Combine three strings
    document.writeln(firstName + " " + lastName + "<br>");
    document.writeln("e-mail address: " + internetAddress);
  // -->
  </script>
</body>
</html>
```

Being able to hide code from JavaScript gives you the ability to document your scripts. It is considered good programming practice to add design notes, friendly reminders, or warnings throughout your program. This can help you and others see what the different sections of your program are meant to do.

Another use of comments is debugging your scripts. You can hide your code to track down problems and then easily replace it when you're done by simply removing comment identifiers. Doing this instead of deleting parts of your script helps save time.

## Functions

In its simplest form, a function is a script that you can call by name at any time. This enhances JavaScript in two ways. When an HTML document is read by a JavaScript-enabled Web browser, the browser will find any embedded scripts and execute the instructions step-by-step. This is fine unless you would rather have part or all of your program wait before executing. Writing this part of your program in a function and assigning it a name is a great way to set up a script to be run at a later time.

When a specific event occurs, you can run this script by using the name that you gave to the function. Another advantage of functions is the ability to reuse scripts without typing in the same code repeatedly. Instead, you can just use the name given to the function to execute the code contained within.

Listing 5.5 shows how JavaScript executes a function. The first thing to notice is where the function is declared. Just as other variables need to be declared, so do functions. Be sure to enclose all function declarations within <script> tags.

> **Note**
>
> I recommend declaring your functions in the `<head>` block of the HTML document. Doing this ensures that the function is loaded by the browser before it is executed by the body.

To use the function, just place the name of it anywhere in your program. The main program is placed within the body and is surrounded by its own set of `<script>` tags. Take a look at Figure 5.5 to see how this is handled by the browser.

**LISTING 5.5**  Embedding a JavaScript Function

```html
<html>
<head>
  <title>JavaScript Unleashed</title>
  <script type="text/javascript">
  <!--
    function displayMessage() {
      document.write("JavaScript functions are easy to use!<br>");


    }
  // -->
  </script>
</head>
<body>
  <script type="text/javascript">
  <!--
    document.write("Calling a JavaScript function...<p>");
    displayMessage();
    document.write("</p>Done. ");
  // -->
  </script>
</body>
</html>
```

Starting with the main script, JavaScript executes the first line as always and then arrives at the `displayMessage()` function call. It looks up the function in memory and begins with the first line of `displayMessage()`. After writing JavaScript functions are easy to use!, a line break is displayed. The end of the function is reached, and program execution returns to where it left off in the main script.

**FIGURE 5.5**

*Calling a function in JavaScript.*

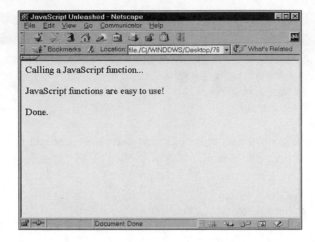

As you can see in Figure 5.5, each line of text is displayed in this sequence. If you have a lengthy program that displays this message many times, you can insert the function call in each place where you need it. If at a later time there is a need to update the message, you need only to change the message in one place. Change it within the function declaration, and your whole application is updated. You can learn more about functions and their advantages in Chapter 8.

# Summary

JavaScript is a great addition to the Web author's tool kit. It makes some things possible that CGI, plug-ins, and Java do not. It offers direct interaction with the user while an HTML document is being viewed.

Scripts are placed directly into HTML documents and surrounded by `<script>` tags. Use the correct types of comment to have either the browser or JavaScript itself ignore particular sections of your scripts.

Starting from the first line of code, the JavaScript interpreter reads the script line by line. Tokens are the smallest individual words, phrases, or characters that JavaScript can understand. Tokens can be literals, identifiers, or operators.

The different data types available include the `number`, `boolean`, `string`, `function`, and `object` types. Variables can store one data type at a time. To declare a variable, use the `var` keyword or simply initialize the variable. Try to use meaningful names for variables to make your scripts easier to read.

An expression is a set of statements that evaluates to a single value. The most common expressions assign values to variables. The assignment operator, =, is used to assign the value of its right operand to the variable that is its left operand. JavaScript supports all standard math operations, either through operators or by using the built-in `math` object.

Use comments to help document your scripts. This will make it easier for you or others to maintain.

Operators are symbols or identifiers that represent the way in which a combination of expressions is evaluated or manipulated. Operators are covered thoroughly in Chapter 6.

Functions are scripts that you can execute at any time before or after an HTML document is viewed by the user. With functions, you can set aside a script to be executed at any time and as often as you like. Using functions can also make your scripts easier to maintain. Chapter 8 explains functions in greater detail.

# Operators

## CHAPTER 6

The whole idea of writing a script is to input, evaluate, manipulate, or display data. Until now, you have concentrated on displaying data with JavaScript. To create more useful programs, you need to evaluate or even change the data that your scripts are dealing with. The tools for this job are called *operators*.

Operators are the symbols and identifiers that represent either the way that the data is changed or the way a combination of expressions is evaluated. The JavaScript language supports both binary and unary operators. Binary operators require there to be two operands in the expression, such as 9 + x, whereas unary operators need only one operand, for example x++.

Both of the examples used here are arithmetic operators, and their use will come naturally to those who understand basic math. Other types of JavaScript operators deal with strings and logical values. They aren't as familiar, but they're easy to learn and very handy when you're dealing with large amounts of text over the Internet. This chapter takes a close look at each type of JavaScript operator.

---

**Note**

Netscape offers a Console mode in which expressions are displayed as soon as you enter them. In versions before 4.05, this was displayed in the main browser window. From 4.05 on, this console was a separate pop-up window to allow for easy access and displaying of JavaScript errors.

This mode is an excellent way to check the value of an expression and an easy way to experiment. To enter this mode, simply type the following in the URL location field:

```
javascript:
```

You can now enter just about any line of JavaScript. This includes declaring variables, functions, and objects, along with evaluating expressions. An example of using this feature is seen in Figure 6.1. I entered 12 << 1 and pressed Enter twice.

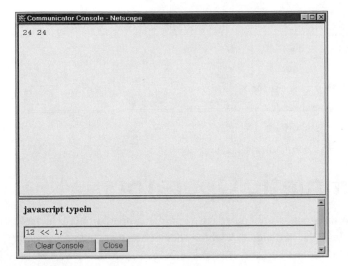

**Figure 6.1**
*Using Netscape's Console feature.*

# Assignment Operators

An operator you're already familiar with is the assignment operator. Its most basic function is assigning a value to a variable, thereby placing the value in memory.

For example, the expression x = 20 assigns the value 20 to the variable x. When JavaScript encounters the assignment operator (=), it first looks to the right for a value. It then looks to the left and ensures that there is a place to store the number. If it finds a variable, it assigns the value to it. In this case, x holds the value 20. It always works from right to left, so the expression 20 = x causes an error in JavaScript by trying to assign a new value to 20. This is not allowed, because 20 is not a variable; it is an integer whose value can't be changed.

JavaScript supports 11 other assignment operators that are actually combinations of the assignment operator and either an arithmetic or bitwise operator. These shorthand versions follow:

*The Combinations of Assignment and Arithmetic Operators*

x += y is short for x = x + y

x -= y is short for x = x - y

x *= y is short for x = x * y

x /= y is short for x = x / y

x %= y is short for x = x % y

x <<= y is short for x = x << y

x >>= y is short for x = x >> y

x >>>= y is short for x = x >>> y

x &= y is short for x = x & y

x ^= y is short for x = x ^ y

x |= y is short for x = x | y

# Arithmetic Operators

When working with numbers, you use arithmetic operators. The most basic operators of the group include the plus sign (+), which adds two values; the minus sign (-), which subtracts one value from another; the asterisk (*), which multiplies two values together; and the forward slash (/), which divides one value by another.

When JavaScript encounters one of these operators, it looks to the right and left sides of the operator to find the values to work on. In the example 7 + 9, JavaScript sees the plus operator and looks to either side of it to find 7 and 9. The plus operator then adds the two values together, resulting in the expression as a whole equating to 16. Using arithmetic operators with the assignment operator, you can assign the value of an expression to a variable:

```
x = 7 + 9
```

x will now equal 16 and can be used again, even to give itself a new value:

```
x = x + 1
```

Follow the last two examples in order. x is first assigned the value 16. Next, x is reassigned the present value of x (which, at that moment, is still 16) plus 1.

It is a very common operation to increment the value of a variable and then reassign that value to itself. It is used so often in computer programs that some languages incorporate special shorthand operators to increment and decrement the values that variables hold more easily. JavaScript is one such language. It uses ++ to increment and -- to decrement a value by 1. Note the following syntax:

++i is the same as i = i + 1

--i is the same as i = i - 1

You can use these operators as either prefixes or suffixes. That way, you can change the order in which a value is returned by the expression and when the new value is assigned. Listing 6.1 demonstrates how increment and decrement operators work.

**LISTING 6.1**    Examples of Increment and Decrement Operators

```
<html>
<head>
  <title>JavaScript Unleashed</title>
</head>
<body>

  <script type="text/javaScript">
  <!--
    var i = 0;
    var result = 0

    document.write("If i = 0, ");
    document.write("i returns the value of i");
    document.write(" after incrementing  : ");

    // Increment prefix
    result = ++i;

    document.write(result);

    // Reset variable
    i = 0;
    document.write("<br>i++ returns the value of i");
    document.write(" before incrementing : ");

    // Increment suffix
    result = i++;
    document.write(result);

    // Reset variable
    i = 0;
    document.write("<br>--i returns the value of i");
    document.write(" after decrementing  : ");

    // Decrement prefix
    result = --i;
    document.write(result)

    // Reset variable
    i = 0;
    document.write("<br>i-- returns the value of i");
    document.write(" before decrementing : ");
```

**LISTING 6.1**    continued

```
    // Decrement suffix
    result = i--;

    document.write(result);
    // -->
  </script>

</body>
</html>
```

The important thing to notice in Listing 6.1 is whether i is incremented before or after the expression is evaluated.

In the first example, result is set to the original value of i plus 1. In the second example, result is immediately set equal to the original value of i before i is incremented. The next two examples work the same way but demonstrate the decrement operator.

The results of these four examples are shown in Figure 6.2. Although these might seem like unnecessary ways to use the operator, they can come in handy when writing scripts that repeat a part of the program. This is shown in Chapter 7, "Control Structures and Looping."

**FIGURE 6.2**

*The increment and decrement operators shown in Listing 6.1.*

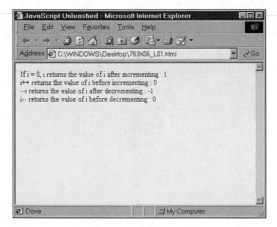

The unary negation operator (-) is used to change a value from positive to negative or vice versa. It is unary because it operates on only one operand. If, for example, you assign the value 5 to a variable x (x = 5) and then negate x and assign the value to y (y = -x), y will equal -5. The opposite is true when negating a negative number; the result will be positive. In both instances, the negation operator does not negate the value of x. The value of x remains equal to 5.

The modulus operator is symbolized by the percent sign (%). To find the modulus of two operands is to find the remainder after dividing the first operand by the second. In the example x = 10 % 3, x is assigned the number 1, because 10 divided by 3 is equal to 3 with 1 left over. With the modulus operator, you can easily determine that one number is the multiple of another if the modulus of the two numbers is equal to 0. This would be true for the expression x = 25 % 5. 25 divided by 5 is equal to 5 with no remainder, which leaves x equal to 0.

> **Caution**
>
> In some cases, Netscape Navigator returns an incorrect value when dealing with fractions. For example, 10/3 should return 3 1/3. If you use Netscape's Typein feature to evaluate 10/3, you will see that the result is 3.3333333333333335. The small inaccuracy at the sixteenth decimal place occurs due to the way in which fractions are stored in a computer's memory. Microsoft's Internet Explorer uses a workaround to this problem by displaying only 14 decimal places. Displaying the result of the same calculation shows 3.33333333333333.

# Comparison Operators

Comparison operators are used for just that—comparing. Expressions that use comparison operators are essentially asking a question about two values. The answer can be either `true` or `false`.

Two equal signs (==) make up the equal operator. When you use the equal operator in the middle of two operands, you're trying to determine whether the values of these two operands are equal. Listing 6.2 shows how to display the result when asking if two variables are equal.

**LISTING 6.2**  Using the Equal Operator

```
<html>
<head>
  <title>JavaScript Unleashed</title>
</head>
<body>
```

**LISTING 6.2** continued

```
<script type="text/javascript">
<!--
  // Declare variables
  var x = 5;
  var y = 5;
  var z = 10;
  // Output to display
  document.write("x = " + x + "<br>");
  document.write("y = " + y + "<br>");
  document.write("z = " + z + "<br>");
  document.write("Is x equal to y,(x == y)? ");
  document.write(x == y);
  document.write("<br>Is y equal to z,(y == z)? ");
  document.writeln(y == z);
// -->
</script>

</body>
</html>
```

Be sure to use the correct operator for the job. Again, the equal operator (==) tests to see if two values are equal, but the assignment operator (=) sets a variable equal to a value. If you happen to make a mistake and use the wrong one, the JavaScript interpreter is good about letting you know! Figure 6.3 shows the display after Listing 6.2 is executed.

**FIGURE 6.3**
*The equal operator from Listing 6.2.*

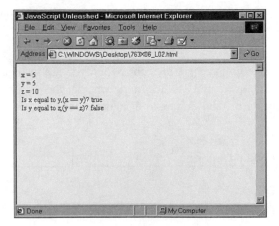

Table 6.1 is a list of all the comparison operators.

**6**

**TABLE 6.1**   Comparison Operators

| *Operator* | *Description* |
|---|---|
| == | The equal operator. Returns `true` if both of its operands are equal. |
| != | The not-equal operator. Returns `true` if its operands are not equal. |
| > | The greater-than operator. Returns `true` if its left operand is greater in value than its right operand. |
| >= | The greater-than-or-equal-to operator. Returns `true` if its left operand is greater than or equal to its right operand. |
| < | The less-than operator. Returns `true` if its left operand is less than the value of its right operand. |
| <= | The less-than-or-equal-to operator. Returns `true` if its left operand is less than or equal to its right operand. |

Comparison operators are normally used in JavaScript for making decisions. With them, you can ask, "What path in my script do I want to take?" Chapter 7 goes into detail on this topic.

## Comparison Operators in Navigator's Implementation of JavaScript 1.2

Until JavaScript 1.1, the language was very forgiving when comparing operands of different data types. For example, when comparing the number 7 with the string "7", JavaScript would first convert or *cast* the string operand to a number and then compare the two. JavaScript would then find them equal.

In JavaScript 1.2, it is up to the programmer to first cast the string as a number or cast the number as a string. If he doesn't, JavaScript will never find them equal. Listing 6.3 demonstrates a way to compare strings and numbers that returns the same results for all versions of JavaScript. Figure 6.4 shows how JavaScript 1.2 reacts to the three different scripts. Listing 6.3 can be fully executed only within a JavaScript 1.2–enabled browser, such as Netscape Navigator 4.0–4.04.

**LISTING 6.3**   Testing Different JavaScript Versions

```
<html>
<head>
  <title>JavaScript Unleashed</title>
</head>
<body>

  <script language="JavaScript">
  <!--
```

**LISTING 6.3** continued

```
    var x = "3";
    var y = 7;
    document.write('x = "3"');
    document.write("<br>");
    document.write("y = 7");
    document.write("<br><hr>");
    document.write("JavaScript 1.0 and 1.1<br>");
    document.write("x == 3 : ");
    document.write(x == 3);
    document.write("<br>");
    document.write('y == "7" : ');
    document.write(y == "7");
//-->
</script>
<script language="JavaScript1.2">
<!--
    document.write("<br><br>JavaScript version 1.2<br>");
    document.write("x == 3 : ");
    document.write(x == 3);
    document.write("<br>");
    document.write('y == "7" : ');
    document.write(y == "7");
//-->
</script>
<script language="JavaScript1.3">
<!--
    document.write("<br><br>JavaScript version 1.3 and higher<br>");
    document.write("x == 3 : ");
    document.write(x == 3);
    document.write("<br>");
    document.write('y == "7" : ');
    document.write(y == "7");
//-->
</script>
<script language="JavaScript">
<!--
    document.write("<br><br>Accomodate all versions.<br>");
    document.write("x - 0 == 3 : ");
    document.write(x - 0 == 3);
    document.write("<br>");
    document.write('"" + y == "7" : ');
    document.write("" + y == "7");
```

LISTING 6.3    continued

```
 //-->
 </script>
</body>
</html>
```

**FIGURE 6.4**

*The comparison strings and integers shown in Listing 6.3.*

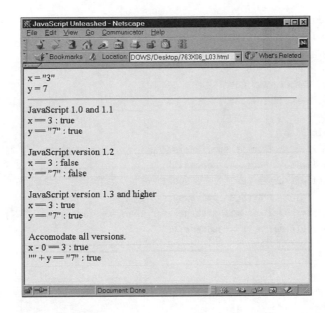

```
x = "3"
y = 7

JavaScript 1.0 and 1.1
x == 3 : true
y == "7" : true

JavaScript version 1.2
x == 3 : false
y == "7" : false

JavaScript version 1.3 and higher
x == 3 : true
y == "7" : true

Accomodate all versions.
x - 0 == 3 : true
"" + y == "7" : true
```

# String Operators

The set of string operators available in JavaScript includes all comparison operators and the concatenation operator (+). Using the concatenation operator, you can easily attach strings together to make a longer string, as shown in Listing 6.4.

LISTING 6.4    Concatenating Strings

```
<html>
<head>
  <title>JavaScript Unleashed</title>
</head>
<body>
  <script type="text/javascript">
  <!--
    // Declare variables
```

**LISTING 6.4** continued

```
    var a = "www";
    var b = "company";
    var c = "com";
    var sumOfParts;
    var address1;
    var address2;
    document.write("Part a is equal to \"" + a + "\".");
    document.write("<br>Part b is equal to \"" + b + "\".");
    document.write("<br>Part c is equal to \""+c+"\".\n");
    sumOfParts = a + "." + b + "." + c;
    address1 = "WWW.COMPANY.COM";
    address2 = "www.company.com";

    // Output to display
    document.write("<br><br>Is sumOfParts equal to " + address1 + "? ");
    document.write(sumOfParts == address1);
    document.write("<br>Is sumOfParts equal to " + address2 + "? ");
    document.write(sumOfParts == address2);
    document.write("<br>Is sumOfParts greater than " + address1 + "? ");
    document.write(sumOfParts > address1);
  //-->
  </script>

</body>
</html>
```

To begin, the script initializes three variables to hold three parts of an Internet Web address. Next, all three parts are added together, separated by the appropriate dots found in all Web addresses. To test if sumOfParts holds a specific Internet address, the script compares it to two possibilities.

Figure 6.5 shows that JavaScript is case sensitive when comparing strings and that it returns true only when comparing addresses with the same case. JavaScript goes from left to right, comparing the ASCII codes of each character in both strings. If all character codes match each other, the strings are equal. All uppercase letters have values less than their lowercase equivalents, which explains why the last comparison in Listing 6.3 returns true.

**FIGURE 6.5**

*The concatena-
tion of strings
shown in
Listing 6.4.*

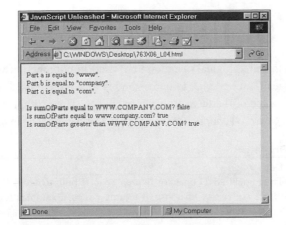

# Conditional Operators

JavaScript uses two operators, `?` and `:`, to form conditional expressions. The JavaScript conditional operators perform the same operation as an immediate `if` statement. Conditional expressions return one of two values, depending on the logical value of another expression.

For example, you can use the following conditional expression to alert the user if he is the millionth person to view the page:

```
var resultMsg = (numHits == 1000000) ? "Winner!" : "Loser!";
alert(resultMsg);
```

Provided that `numHits` is set equal to `1000000` elsewhere in the program, this expression returns the string `Winner!`; otherwise, it returns `Loser!`. The second line of the previous example displays the result to the user, using the built-in `alert()` function. If `numHits` is equal to one million, an alert dialog box pops up to let the visitor know. Otherwise, the expression returns `false`, and the failure message is displayed.

A conditional expression can be used to return any data type, such as `number` or `boolean`. The following expression returns either a string or a number, depending on whether `useString` is `true` or `false`:

```
var result = useString ? "seven" : 7;
document.write(result);
```

# Boolean Operators

Boolean operators (also called logical operators) are used in conjunction with expressions that return logical values. The best way to understand is to see them used with comparison operators. Table 6.2 is a list of the three Boolean operators. The examples are shown with either the syntax *expression1[operator]expression2* or *[operator]expression*.

**TABLE 6.2**   Boolean Operators

| Operator | Description |
|----------|-------------|
| && | The logical AND operator returns `true` if both *expression1* and *expression2* are `true`. Otherwise, it returns `false`. Examples follow: |
|    | `(1 > 0) && (2 > 1)` returns `true`. |
|    | `(1 > 0) && (2 < 1)` returns `false`. |
| \|\| | The logical OR operator returns `true` if either *expression1* or *expression2* is `true`. If neither *expression1* nor *expression2* is `true`, it returns `false`. Examples follow: |
|    | `(1 > 0) \|\| (2 < 1)` returns `true`. |
|    | `(1 < 0) \|\| (2 < 1)` returns `false`. |
| ! | The logical NOT operator is a unary operator that returns the opposite value of a Boolean *expression*. If *expression* is `true`, it returns `false`, and if *expression* is `false`, it returns `true`. This will not permanently change the value of *expression*, because it works the same way as the arithmetic negation operator. Examples follow: |
|    | `!(1 > 0)` returns `false`. |
|    | `!(1 < 0)` returns `true`. |

# The `typeof` Operator

The `typeof` operator returns the type of data that its operand currently holds. This is especially useful for determining if a variable has been defined. Note the following examples:

`typeof unescape` returns the string `"function"`.

`typeof undefinedVariable` returns the string `"undefined"`.

`typeof 33` returns the string `"number"`.

`typeof "A String"` returns the string `"string"`.

`typeof true` returns the string `"boolean"`.

`typeof null` returns the string `"object"`.

6

> **Caution**
>
> The `typeof` operator was added for Navigator 3.0 (JavaScript 1.1). It will work only with JavaScript 1.1 and higher browsers.

# Function Operators

Functions are covered in Chapter 8, "Functions." There are two operators you should be familiar with when dealing with functions. The first is the call operator, which is symbolized by a set of parentheses and always follows the function name. For example, a function named `displayName()` would be declared using the following syntax:

```
function displayName(){
    [statements]
}
```

The call operator is also used when calling the function from elsewhere in a script. It would look like this:

```
displayName()
```

The parentheses signify that a function is being used instead of any other user-defined identifier.

The second function operator is the comma. It's used to separate multiple arguments that a function can accept. Arguments are always enclosed by the call operator. The `displayName()` function modified to accept two arguments would look like the following:

```
function displayName(argument1,argument2){
    [statements]
}
```

# Data Structure Operators

*Data structure operators* is the term I use to classify two operators that are needed when dealing with data structures. Data structures are frameworks that are set up to store one or more basic pieces of data in an orderly fashion. In JavaScript, objects are used to group pieces of data to serve a more specific purpose.

An operator that you should be familiar with when dealing with objects is commonly referred to as the dot. Symbolized by a period, the dot is technically called the *structure-member operator*. It allows you to refer to a member (a variable, a function, or an object) belonging to the specified object. The syntax is as follows:

```
objectName.variableName
```

or

```
objectName.functionName()
```

or

```
objectName.anotherObject
```

This way of referring to a piece of data, usually called dot notation, returns the value of the rightmost variable, function, or object.

The member operator, also known as the *array subscript operator*, is used to access a piece of data from an array. Symbolized by a pair of square brackets, it allows you to refer to any one element of an array. Arrays are objects in JavaScript and are introduced in Chapter 10, "Core Language Objects." The following is the syntax for using the member operator:

```
arrayName[indexNumber]
```

The member operator encloses an integer, shown here as `indexNumber`. `indexNumber` specifies an index into `arrayName`, allowing access to any one member of the array.

# Bitwise Operators

At the lowest level, integers (along with all data) are stored in memory as bits. They are stored using the binary number system, which can represent any integer using the symbols `0` and `1`. Depending on placement, a bit set to `1` represents a value equal to 2 raised to $n$, where $n$ is the number of places from the right of the number.

For example, the integer 12 can be represented by the binary number 1100 and takes a minimum of 4 bits to store in memory. Starting from the right and moving to the left, 1100 can be calculated using the following expression:

```
0 x 2⁰ + 0 x 2¹ + 1 x 2² + 1 x 2³ = 12
```

A larger number such as 237 (11101101 in binary) requires 8 bits of memory to be stored. 11101101 can be calculated in the following way:

```
1 x 2⁰ + 0 x 2¹ + 1 x 2² + 1 x 2³ + 0 x 2⁴ + 1 x 2⁵ + 1 x 2⁶ + 1 x 2⁷ = 237
```

JavaScript sets aside 32 bits per integer when storing integers in memory. Once in memory, 237 conceptually looks like 00000000000000000000000011101101 but is typically written as 11101101, excluding the leading zeros, which are insignificant. You can enter an integer as a decimal, octal, or hexadecimal number, and JavaScript will store it in binary form.

To accommodate negative values, the leftmost bit or highest bit represents a negative value equal to $-(2^{31})$. Using the highest bit, you can start with $-(2^{31})$ and add positive values to it (represented by the remaining 31 bits) to generate any negative number greater than or equal to $-(2^{31})$. Note the following examples:

```
10000000000000000000000000000001 = -2147483648 + 1 = -2147483647
10000000000000000000000000000011 = -2147483648 + 3 = -2147483645
11111111111111111111111111111111 = -2147483648 + 2147483647 = -1
11111111111111111111111111111110 = -2147483648 + 2147483646 = -2
```

JavaScript gives you access to an integer's binary representative through bitwise operators. The simplest of bitwise operators is the unary *one's complement* operator, symbolized by the tilde (~). Its job is to "flip" every bit of its operand. This is classified as a negation operator because it negates each bit. If a bit is a 1, it will become a 0. If a bit is a 0, it will become a 1. Finding the one's complement of the number 6 can be visualized in the following ways:

```
x = ~6
x = ~00000000000000000000000000000110
x =   11111111111111111111111111111001
x = -7
```

## Bitwise Logical Operators

When you use bitwise logical operators, JavaScript pairs up each operand bit-by-bit. It then performs the operation on each pair of bits. For example, using the bitwise AND operator on the numbers 01111 and 11011 results in the number 01011. Their binary equivalents are aligned from right to left to form five pairs of bits. The pairs are then operated on separately, and a new number is generated. You can visualize this as shown in Table 6.3.

TABLE 6.3   The Use of Bitwise Logical Operators

| Equation | Result |
| --- | --- |
| 0 & 1 | 0 |
| 1 & 1 | 1 |
| 1 & 0 | 0 |
| 1 & 1 | 1 |
| 1 & 1 | 1 |
| & | The bitwise AND operator returns 1 if both operands are 1. Otherwise, it returns 0. For example, 15 & 27 returns 11 (01111 & 11011 returns 01011). |
| \| | The bitwise OR operator returns 1 if either operand is 1. Otherwise, it returns 0. For example, 15 \| 27 returns 31 (01111 \| 11011 returns 11111). |

**TABLE 6.3** continued

| Equation | Result |
|----------|--------|
| ^ | The bitwise exclusive OR operator returns 1 if one but not both operands are 1. Otherwise, it returns 0. For example, 15 ^ 27 returns 20 (01111 \| 11011 returns 10100). |

# Bitwise Shift Operators

All bitwise shift operators take two operands. The left operand is an integer whose bits are to be shifted. The right operand is the number of bits to shift the binary representation of the integer. Table 6.4 lists the bitwise shift operators.

**TABLE 6.4** Bitwise Shift Operators

| Operator | Description |
|----------|-------------|
| << | The left-shift operator returns the value of an integer if its bits were shifted a number of places to the left. All void rightmost bits are filled in with zeros. The following examples shift the number 15 to the left by 1 and then by 2. |
| | 15 << 1 returns 30 (1111 << 1 returns 11110) |
| | 15 << 2 returns 60 (1111 << 2 returns 111100) |
| | Note that shifting a positive integer to the left $n$ times is equivalent to multiplying the value by 2 $n$ times. In most cases, a computer can perform a left-shift faster than it can multiply by 2. For this reason, it is common to see the bitwise left-shift chosen over its higher-level counterpart when performing many multiplications. Any small increase in efficiency could result in a noticeable advantage. |
| | Using the left-shift on a negative integer could result in either a negative or positive integer, depending on the state of the highest bit after the left-shift has been performed. |
| >> | The sign-propagating right-shift operator returns the value of an integer if its bits were shifted a number of places to the right. All void bits are filled in with a copy of the leftmost bit (also called the *sign bit*). Copying the leftmost bit ensures that the integer will stay either positive or negative. This is also a more efficient way to divide a positive even integer by 2 $n$ times. In the case of a positive odd integer, a right-shift is the same as dividing by 2 $n$ times, but it throws away remainders. Note the following examples: |
| | 15 >> 1 returns 7 (1111 >> 1 returns 0111) |
| | -15 >> 1 returns -8 (11111111111111111111111111110001 >> 1 returns 11111111111111111111111111111000) |

TABLE **6.4** continued

| Operator | Description |
| --- | --- |
| >>> | The zero-fill right-shift operator returns the value of an integer if its bits were shifted a number of places to the right. All void high-order bits are filled in with zeros. When operating on positive integers, the zero-fill right-shift operator produces the same result as using the sign-propagating right-shift operator. This is due to the fact that the sign bit being copied is always zero for positive integers. As for negative integers, any zero-fill right-shift will change the highest bit from a 1 to a 0. The result will always be an integer that is greater than or equal to 0. Note the following examples: |

15 >>> 1 returns 7 (1111 >>> 1 returns 0111)

-15 >>> 1 returns 2147483640 (11111111111111111111111111110001 >> 1 returns 01111111111111111111111111111000)

## Why Mess with Bits?

Bitwise operators aren't needed in most scripts. It's possible that you may never have to deal with bits for your entire JavaScript career. However, there are special cases where dealing with data at its lowest level becomes practical or even necessary.

An example of when bitwise operators are needed is when converting a number from base 10 (decimal) to base 16 (hexadecimal). This takes a little extra effort, because JavaScript allows you to display only the decimal representation of a number stored in memory. There is no built-in way to display the number in an alternative base. Using bitwise operators, the solution to this obstacle is relatively easy. For instance, if you store the value 0xDC in a variable x, JavaScript converts it to binary. If you try to display x using the following lines of code, the number is displayed in decimal as 220:

```
var x = 0xDC;

// Will write "220" to the display
document.writeln(x);
```

JavaScript doesn't offer a method of displaying 220 as its hexadecimal equivalent, DC. This is a useful function if you are performing operations on HTML color values that are in hexadecimal. The easiest way to accomplish this is to use the binary value of the integer and translate it into hexadecimal. Hexadecimal values are easily represented in binary.

Four bits of memory can store 16 values. Because hexadecimal uses 16 digits, it takes 4 bits to store the value of each hexadecimal digit. In a 32-bit integer, the rightmost 4 bits of memory represent the rightmost digit of a hexadecimal integer. The next 4 bits store the next digit, and so on. To convert a 32-bit integer into hexadecimal, you can do this eight times, matching each 4-bit value to its hexadecimal equivalent.

To read in only 4 bits at a time, use the & operator with a control value. The control value should have a 1 in each bit location that you would like to copy from the integer being converted. Because you want the value of the first 4 bits, the control value should have a 1 in its first 4 bits. All other bits should be set to 0. The control value in this case must equal 1111 (15 or 0xF). This operation conceptually appears as the following:

Control: 00000000000000000000000000001111 &

Integer to convert: 00000000000000000000000011011100 =

Result: 00000000000000000000000000001100

The result is a copy of the first 4 bits of the integer you're converting. You can easily compare this to each of the 16 hexadecimal digits to find that it is equal to C. To find the next hexadecimal digit, copy the next 4 bits out of the integer. I have chosen to do this by shifting all the bits in the integer 4 bits to the right while using the same control. This will work as in the following:

Control: 00000000000000000000000000001111 &

Integer to convert: 00000000000000000000000000001101 =

Result: 00000000000000000000000000001101

Again, you can use the result to match up against the second digit, D. If the original integer was larger, you could continue this process up to six more times.

Listing 6.5 shows this algorithm in action. Using only the operators discussed up to this point, it can convert any 8-bit value into a string representing its hexadecimal equivalent. First I assign to the variable intValue the value to be converted. I then display the value to show that JavaScript will return only the decimal value of DC, which is 220. The program proceeds to translate the binary form of 220 into hexadecimal and displays the result. The output is shown in Figure 6.6.

**LISTING 6.5**  Converting Base 10 to Base 16 Using Bitwise Operators

```
<html>
<head>
  <title>JavaScript Unleashed</title>
</head>
<body>
  <script type="text/javascript">
  <!--
    // Declare variables
    var originalInt;

    // intValue can be any 8 bit value.
```

**LISTING 6.5**    continued

```
var intValue = 0xDC;
var controlValue = 0xF;
var fourBitValue;
var hexChar = "";
var hexString = "";

document.writeln("When displaying integers from memory,");
document.writeln("JavaScript always uses their decimal ");
document.writeln("equivalent: " + intValue);
originalInt = intValue;
fourBitValue =  controlValue & intValue;
hexChar = (fourBitValue == 0x0) ? "0" : hexChar;
hexChar = (fourBitValue == 0x1) ? "1" : hexChar;
hexChar = (fourBitValue == 0x2) ? "2" : hexChar;
hexChar = (fourBitValue == 0x3) ? "3" : hexChar;
hexChar = (fourBitValue == 0x4) ? "4" : hexChar;
hexChar = (fourBitValue == 0x5) ? "5" : hexChar;
hexChar = (fourBitValue == 0x6) ? "6" : hexChar;
hexChar = (fourBitValue == 0x7) ? "7" : hexChar;
hexChar = (fourBitValue == 0x8) ? "8" : hexChar;
hexChar = (fourBitValue == 0x9) ? "9" : hexChar;
hexChar = (fourBitValue == 0xA) ? "A" : hexChar;
hexChar = (fourBitValue == 0xB) ? "B" : hexChar;
hexChar = (fourBitValue == 0xC) ? "C" : hexChar;
hexChar = (fourBitValue == 0xD) ? "D" : hexChar;
hexChar = (fourBitValue == 0xE) ? "E" : hexChar;
hexChar = (fourBitValue == 0xF) ? "F" : hexChar;

// Build hexString placing digits from right to left
hexString = hexChar + hexString;

// Shift intValue four bits right
intValue = intValue >> 4;

// Extract the next four bit value
fourBitValue =  controlValue & intValue;

// Find the matching hex value and assign its string
// equivalent to hexChar.
hexChar = (fourBitValue == 0x0) ? "0" : hexChar;
hexChar = (fourBitValue == 0x1) ? "1" : hexChar;
hexChar = (fourBitValue == 0x2) ? "2" : hexChar;
```

**LISTING 6.5**    continued

```
    hexChar = (fourBitValue == 0x3) ? "3" : hexChar;
    hexChar = (fourBitValue == 0x4) ? "4" : hexChar;
    hexChar = (fourBitValue == 0x5) ? "5" : hexChar;
    hexChar = (fourBitValue == 0x6) ? "6" : hexChar;
    hexChar = (fourBitValue == 0x7) ? "7" : hexChar;
    hexChar = (fourBitValue == 0x8) ? "8" : hexChar;
    hexChar = (fourBitValue == 0x9) ? "9" : hexChar;
    hexChar = (fourBitValue == 0xA) ? "A" : hexChar;
    hexChar = (fourBitValue == 0xB) ? "B" : hexChar;
    hexChar = (fourBitValue == 0xC) ? "C" : hexChar;
    hexChar = (fourBitValue == 0xD) ? "D" : hexChar;
    hexChar = (fourBitValue == 0xE) ? "E" : hexChar;
    hexChar = (fourBitValue == 0xF) ? "F" : hexChar;
    hexString = hexChar + hexString;
    document.write("<br>" + originalInt + " displayed in");
    document.write(" hexadecimal :");
    document.writeln(hexString);
    // end hiding -->
  </script>
</body>
</html>
```

**FIGURE 6.6**

*Converting base 10 to base 16, as shown in Listing 6.5.*

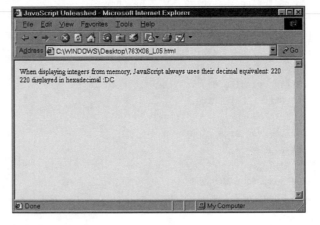

**Note**

The previous example uses multiple conditional expressions to find a match. More efficient ways to compare a range of numbers are possible using loops. Loops are discussed in Chapter 7.

Notice from the previous discussion how many zeros are left unused when storing a relatively small number. This is another area where bitwise operators can prove useful. Using bitwise operators, you can conserve memory by storing data in the unused portion of any variable.

For example, if your script uses a large group of positive integers less than or equal to 255, you could store four of them within one 32-bit word. Using a simple bitwise operation, you could then extract any number at will. With the amount of RAM most computers have today, it is usually not worth the extra coding effort. However, because JavaScript is designed to run on many platforms, you never know who will be running your script and who might run out of memory. Even so, you would have to be storing a lot of data in memory to begin worrying about this.

# Operator Precedence

When creating expressions that use more than one operator, you should be aware that JavaScript doesn't necessarily evaluate an expression from right to left or vice versa. Each part of an expression is evaluated in an order based on a predefined precedence for each operator. Note the following example:

```
x = a * b + c
```

a is multiplied by b; the result is added to c. The result of the addition is finally assigned to x. The multiplication operator has a higher precedence than the addition operator and therefore is evaluated first. If you need the addition to be evaluated first, you can enclose the expression in parentheses:

```
x = a * (b + c)
```

Parentheses are operators that boost the precedence of the expression that they enclose. When an expression has more than one operator of the same kind, JavaScript evaluates from left to right.

Table 6.5 shows operators in order of their precedence, from lowest to highest.

**TABLE 6.5** Operator Precedence

| Operator Name | Operator |
|---|---|
| Comma | , |
| Assignment | = += -= *= /= %= <<= >>= >>>= &= ^= \|= |
| Conditional | ?: |
| Logical OR | \|\| |
| Logical AND | && |
| Bitwise OR | \| |
| Bitwise XOR | ^ |
| Bitwise AND | & |
| Equality | == != |
| Comparison | < <= > >= |
| Bitwise shift | << >> >>> |
| Addition/subtraction | + - |
| Multiplication/division | * / % |
| Negation/increment | ! ~ - ++ -- |
| Call, data structure | () [] . |

One effect that operator precedence can have is determining the type of value that is returned by an expression. This becomes apparent when trying to concatenate strings and numbers, as shown in Listing 6.6.

**LISTING 6.6** Operator Precedence and Different Data Types

```
<html>
<head>
  <title>JavaScript Unleashed</title>
</head>
<body>
  <script type="text/javascript">
  <!--
    var carLength = 4 + 5;
    document.write(carLength);
    carLength = "<br>" + 4 + 5 + " feet";
    document.write(carLength);
    carLength = "<br>Length in feet: " + 4 + 5;
    document.write(carLength);
    carLength = "<br>Length in feet: " + (4 + 5);
    document.writeln(carLength);
  //-->
  </script>
```

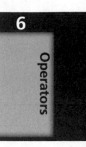

**LISTING 6.6** continued

```
</body>
</html>
```

When expressions have operators of the same precedence, JavaScript evaluates from left to right. The addition operator has the same precedence as the concatenate operator; therefore, JavaScript will evaluate all additions and concatenations from left to right throughout the statement.

Notice in Figure 6.7 that the first two examples work as you would expect. The third example shows what can happen when JavaScript works as designed. With the first + symbol, it converts the number 4 to a string and concatenates it to the end of `"Length in feet: "`. The result of this is the string `"Length in feet: 4"`. It then does the same with the number 5 to produce `"'Length in feet: 45"`. If, however, you want to display the sum of 4 and 5 instead, you can use parentheses to increase the precedence of 4 + 5. In this case, both operands are numbers, and JavaScript performs an addition rather than a string concatenation. Figure 6.7 shows this as the fourth example.

**FIGURE 6.7**
*Operator precedence and different data types, as shown in Listing 6.6.*

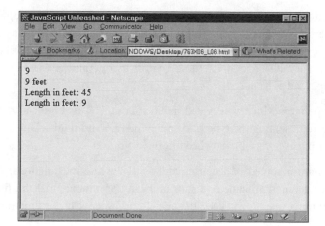

# Summary

Assignment operators assign values to variables. Along with the simple assignment operator, JavaScript supports 11 assignment operators that combine either arithmetic or bitwise operators with the simple assignment operator.

Arithmetic operators let you perform basic math operations in JavaScript. These include addition, subtraction, multiplication, division, and modulus. JavaScript also includes increment and decrement operators as shortcuts to two common math operations. More advanced math operations are also built into JavaScript, but they must be accessed through the `Math` object.

Comparison operators compare two values and return a value of `true` or `false`. You can check to see if one value is equal to another, greater or less than another, or any combination of these.

The conditional operators let you return one of two values that you can define to be of any data type. The value returned is decided by the value of a logical expression that you also define.

String operators include the concatenation operator and all comparison operators. The concatenation operator is used to append one string to another to form a new string. Comparison operators can be used with strings to compare their ASCII values. Starting with the leftmost character of each string and moving right, a single pair of characters is compared at a time. The returned value is either `true` or `false`.

Boolean operators are used with logical expressions to form another logical expression. The AND operator returns `true` if both of its operands are `true`. Otherwise, it returns `false`. The OR operator returns `true` if at least one of its operands is `true`. Otherwise, it returns `false`. The NOT operator returns `true` if its operand is `false`, and it will return `false` if its operand is `true`.

The `typeof` operator, which was added in JavaScript 1.1, is a built-in operator used to return a string representing the type of data that its operand holds. This is especially useful when determining if a variable has been defined yet.

Two operators are involved in declaring and using JavaScript functions. The call operator always follows a function name and surrounds any arguments that the function might accept. The comma operator is used to separate arguments if the function accepts more than one.

When you're dealing with arrays and other objects, two operators are needed. The dot is used to reference a member of an object. This is the standard dot notation. The member operator is used to index one element of an array object. It follows the array name and encloses an integer that refers to the location of the element being accessed.

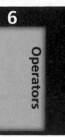

JavaScript allows access to the binary representation of any integer through its bitwise operators. The one's complement operator is used to flip each bit of an integer. Bitwise logical operators are included to compare two integers. The binary form of each operand is used to pair up the bits in each integer. The logical operation is then performed on each pair of bits to return the resulting integer. Bitwise shift operators shift the bits of an integer to the right or left *n* number of places. When shifting to the right, JavaScript allows you to specify either sign-propagating or zero-fill shifting.

When all operations in the expression are of the same precedence, JavaScript interprets from right to left when evaluating expressions. Otherwise, the operation with the highest precedence is performed first and then the next highest, and so on. The precedence of each operator is predefined by JavaScript.

# Control Structures and Looping

## In This Chapter

Designing a script to make decisions during runtime can be the most interesting part of JavaScript. When you have a script make a decision based on its present state, you're simply telling it to ask a question and then choose a path to take based on the answer.

For example, consider my morning commute to work. I can take a couple of different routes, and I choose one based on certain factors. I seldom cook, so the most important question I ask myself in the morning is whether I'm hungry. If I am, I choose the route that passes by the bagel shop. By the time I've finished picking up my breakfast, I'm usually running a little late. To make up for lost time, I drive directly to the highway, where I can quickly accelerate to just under the speed limit. On the other hand, if I'm not hungry, which is hardly ever the case, I choose to drive past the bagel shop and continue to work at a steady 10 miles per hour below the speed limit.

Using the same idea, you can design your JavaScript programs to perform specific operations based on one or more factors. For example, in Chapter 6, "Operators," you learned how to test whether a variable is equal to a particular value or even a range of values. Using control structures, you can now make your program take one or more different paths based on the result of such a test. This is the first topic I'll cover in this chapter.

As your programs become larger, one thing to watch for is the length of time it could take for the client to download them. One way to cut down on the amount of source code in a script is to use looping statements. Using a loop, you can make your scripts perform many similar operations with only a few lines of code. This can help you shrink the size of your scripts and avoid typing the same commands repeatedly. Also in this chapter, I'll demonstrate ways to make your scripts more efficient.

# Conditional Statements

In Chapter 6, I covered two conditional operators—? and :. These operators are used to create a two-step process. First, an expression is evaluated to be either true or false. Then, based on the result, one of two values is returned. If the statement is true, then the first value is returned. If the statement evaluated to false, then the second value is returned.

You can also have the script make a decision based on an expression using the if and else statements. However, the result is different. Instead of returning a value based on the result, the program takes one of two paths. With this capability, you can make JavaScript perform many different functions based on any information you have available.

## if

The if statement is one of the most popular statements you will use. Every programming language has it in one form or another, and its use cannot be avoided. You use the if statement in the following way:

```
if (condition) {
  [statements]
}
```

The *condition* can be any logical expression. If the result of *condition* is true, the *statements* are executed, and program execution continues. If *condition* returns false, JavaScript ignores the *statements* and continues.

In Listing 7.1, I emulate the type of influence an overbearing Marketing department might have on a company's Web site. The script begins by setting the value of visitorInterest to one of two values. I selected "Technical Support" for this example and commented out the alternative assignment.

Next, the script reaches the first if statement, which checks whether the value of visitorInterest is equal to the string "New Products". The resulting value of this expression is false, and the block of code immediately following the if statement is ignored. The script then reaches the second if statement and checks the value of visitorInterest against "Technical Support". The expression returns true, and the code that is enclosed in curly braces is executed.

Regardless of what value visitorInterest is equal to, the last statement always executes, and salesman Frank Zealous sends his pitch to the visitor. The entire display is shown in Figure 7.1. If you switch the value of visitorInterest, the output will change.

**LISTING 7.1** Using the if Statement to Make Decisions

```html
<html>
<head>
  <title>JavaScript Unleashed</title>
</head>
<body>
  <script type="text/javascript">
  <!--
    // Declare variables
    var visitorInterest;
    // visitorInterest = "New Products";
    visitorInterest = "Technical Support";

    document.writeln("Hello, my name is Frank Zealous!");
```

7

Control
Structures and
Looping

**LISTING 7.1**    continued

```
  // Evaluate value of vistorInterest
  if (visitorInterest == "New Products") {
    document.writeln("Thank you for inquiring about our products!");
  }
  if (visitorInterest == "Technical Support") {
    document.writeln("Technical support is now available.");
    document.write("But first, let me introduce you to our ");
    document.writeln("newest products!");
  }

  document.write("<br>Our newest products will satisfy all of your ");
  document.writeln("business needs!");
// -->
</script>
</body>
</html>
```

**FIGURE 7.1**

*Frank gives a customized sales pitch.*

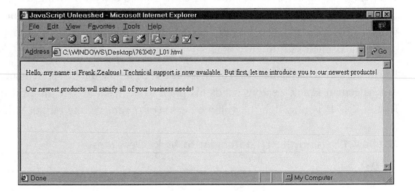

It's common practice to indent the set of statements enclosed in curly braces. This helps give your scripts a logical look and proves especially helpful when you nest `if` statements (that is, when you use an `if` statement within another `if` statement).

Listing 7.2 demonstrates how you can use logical variables by themselves to determine the path a script can take. The first `if` statement evaluates the variable `needsInfo`. `needsInfo` was set to `true`, so JavaScript enters the first `if` block and continues by displaying `"Our products are used all over the world"`. Next, the second, or nested, `if` block is reached, and `needsMoreInfo` is evaluated. Again, the value returned is `true`, and the statements within the second block are executed. The end of the nested `if` block is completed, and

JavaScript picks up where it left off with the first block. Notice how the indentation helps distinguish the separate blocks of code that may or may not be executed.

Figure 7.2 shows that JavaScript performed each line of code in sequence. By resetting the values of needsInfo and needsMoreInfo, you can create three different results. One important thing to realize is that if needsInfo is false, the second if block is never reached. In this case, it doesn't matter if needsMoreInfo is set to true or false, because it will never have a chance to be evaluated. Sorry, Frank, but if they don't need information, they certainly don't need *more* information.

**LISTING 7.2** Nested if Statements

```html
<html>
<head>
  <title>JavaScript Unleashed</title>
</head>
<body>
  <script type="text/javascript">
  <!--
    // Declare variables
    var needsInfo;
    var needsMoreInfo;

    // Set either of the following to false and the output notice the change.
    needsInfo = true;
    needsMoreInfo = true;

    document.writeln("I work for Best Products International!");
    if (needsInfo) {
      document.writeln("Our products are used all over the world.");
    if(needsMoreInfo){
      document.write("<br>I don't know how you have managed");
      document.writeln(" without them.");
    }
    document.writeln("<br>Ordering is easy using our on-line service.");
    }
  // -->
  </script>
</body>
</html>
```

FIGURE 7.2

*One of three possible outcomes.*

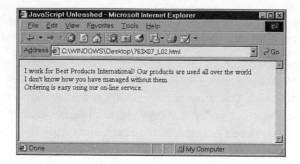

## if..else

Sometimes using the `if` statement alone is not enough. You can also reserve a set of statements to execute if the conditional expression returns `false`. You do this by adding an `else` block of statements immediately following the `if` block:

```
if(condition){
statements
}else{
statements
}
```

Additionally, if you don't want to go straight into a default block, you can combine the `else` portion with another `if` statement. Using this method, you are able to evaluate several different acceptable scenarios before performing the proper operation. The beauty of using this method is that you can finish it off with an `else` segment as well. The format for this type of statement is as follows:

```
if(condition){
statements
}else if (condition){
statements
}else{
statements
}
```

Nothing is worse than a nagging computer, but Listing 7.3 demonstrates how interactive a Web page can be with only a few lines of code. Again I have hard-coded the key value, `purchaseAmount`, which determines the outcome of the script. To truly interact with the users of your script, you need to be able to receive input from them. This way, `purchaseAmount` can be any value, depending on what the customer orders. You can do this using JavaScript and standard HTML input objects such as `checkbox` and `text` objects. Chapter 17, "Form Objects," covers this topic in more detail.

In this example, the user hasn't spent enough money to satisfy Frank. The `if` statement evaluates to `false`, and the `else` block is executed. Figure 7.3 shows how the user's purchase is questioned by a pushy salesman.

**LISTING 7.3**    The `else` Block Responds to a `false` Value

```html
<html>
<head>
  <title>JavaScript Unleashed</title>
</head>
<body>
  <script type="text/javascript">
  <!--
    // Declare variable
    var purchaseAmount;
    purchaseAmount = 10.00;

    if(purchaseAmount > 500.00){
      document.write("Thank you for your purchase!");
    }else{
      document.writeln("Thank you, but surely there is something ");
      document.writeln("else you would like to purchase.");
    }
  // -->
  </script>
</body>
</html>
```

**FIGURE 7.3**

*One of two possible outcomes.*

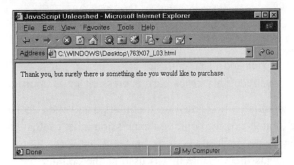

## try..catch

The `try..catch` statement is used to override the default environment handling of errors. Rather than go into a lot of detail in this section, check out Chapter 33, "Error Handling," for more information on `try..catch` and how to use it to handle errors.

# Looping Statements

Creating a loop inside a script can serve many purposes. One simple but very common use of a loop is counting. For example, writing a program that displays the numbers 0 through 9 is a quick and easy task. You could simply write 10 commands to display each number:

```
document.writeln("0");
document.writeln("1");
...
document.writeln("9");
```

This works for counting from 0 to 9, but what if you needed to count to 1,000? You can do this in the same manner, but the code takes much more time to write and download. The best way to count to 1,000 or any number is to use the same display statement with a variable in place of the string literal. By counting like this, the only thing you need is a way to increment the variable and repeat the display statement. JavaScript gives you the tools to handle this and other looping operations.

## for

You use the `for` statement to start a loop in a script. Before taking a closer look at the `for` statement in Listing 7.4, examine the following syntax:

```
for ([initializing_expr]; [condition_expr]; [loop_expr]) {
statements
}
```

The three expressions enclosed in parentheses are optional, but if you omit one, the semicolons are still required. This keeps each expression in its appropriate place.

You typically use the initializing expression to initialize and even declare a variable to use as a counter for the loop. Next, the condition expression must evaluate to `true` before each execution of the statements enclosed in curly braces. Finally, the loop expression typically increments or decrements the variable that is used as the counter for the loop.

Listing 7.4 demonstrates the use of a `for` statement to count from 0 to 99 while displaying each number. To fit the output on a standard page, I added a line break after each set of 10 numbers. The output is shown in Figure 7.4.

*Control Structures and Looping*

**CHAPTER 7**

157

7

Control
Structures and
Looping

**LISTING 7.4** A `for` Loop Used to Count from 0 to 99

```
<html>
<head>
  <title>JavaScript Unleashed</title>
<body>
  <script type="text/javascript">
  <!--
    // Write the header part to the page
    document.write("Numbers 0 through 99:");
    document.write('<hr size="0" width="50%" align="left">');

    for (var i = 0; i < 100; ++i) {

      // Put a break in between every 10th number
      if(i%10 == 0) {
        document.write('<br>');
      }

      // Write the number to the page
      document.write(i + ",");
    }

    // Finish up with the last number
    document.write("<br><br>After completing the loop, i equals : " + i);

  // -->
  </script>
</body>
</html>
```

In Listing 7.4, the order of execution is as follows: The initializing expression declares the variable `i` and sets it to `0`. The variable `i` is then tested to ensure that it's less than `100`. Where `i` is still equal to `0`, the condition expression returns `true`, and the program executes the statements between the curly braces. Once the program executes all the statements and reaches the ending curly brace, it evaluates the loop expression, `++i`. This increments `i` by 1, thus concluding the first full loop.

The process now begins again from the top. This time, JavaScript knows not to perform the initializing section of the `for` loop. Instead, the condition expression is evaluated again. Where `i` is still less than `100`, another loop is allowed to occur. This continues, and the set of statements inside the `for` block is repeated until `i` reaches `100`.

**FIGURE 7.4**

*The output after looping through the same code 100 times.*

At 99, the condition expression returns `true`, and the program executes the statements one last time. Once again, i is incremented and set to 100. When the condition expression is evaluated, it returns `false`, and the loop breaks. Program execution picks up immediately after the ending curly brace.

Because i was incremented to 100 before the loop was broken, 100 is the resulting value of i after the loop is finished. Notice also that the scope of i extends outside the `for` loop, obeying the rules of scope discussed in Chapter 5, "Fundamentals of the JavaScript Language."

> **Note**
>
> If the condition expression returns `false` on the first loop, the statements between the curly braces are never executed.

As with `if` statements, `for` loops can also be nested. Listing 7.5 shows how to step through each coordinate of a $10 \times 10$ grid. For each iteration of the first loop, there are 10 iterations of the nested loop. The result is that the nested loop is executed 100 times.

**LISTING 7.5** A Demonstration of a Nested Loop

```html
<html>
<head>
  <title>JavaScript Unleashed</title>
</head>
```

**LISTING 7.5**  continued

```
<body>
  <script type="text/javascript">
  <!--
    document.write("All x,y coordinates between (0,0) and (9,9):<br>")

    for (var x = 0; x < 10; ++x) {
      for (var y = 0; y < 10; ++y) {
        document.write("(" + x + "," + y + "),");
      }
    document.write('<br>');
    }

    document.write("<br>After completing the loop, x equals : " + x);
    document.write("<br>After completing the loop, y equals : " + y);
  // -->
  </script>
</body>
</html>
```

x is first assigned the value of 0. JavaScript reaches the nested loop and also assigns 0 to y. The nested loop displays the values of x and y and then increments y by 1. The nested loop continues until y is no longer less than 10. At this point, 10 sets of coordinates have been generated. The nested loop breaks, and control returns to the outer loop. x is incremented by 1, and again the nested loop starts.

JavaScript knows that the nested loop is starting from the beginning and that the initializing expression must be evaluated again. This resets y to 0, and the statements are run another 10 times. The entire process continues until x is no longer less than 10 and the outer loop finally breaks. This displays 100 sets of coordinates, as shown in Figure 7.5.

You aren't limited to a single nested loop, so you can increase the number of coordinates to three or even four. You can also use this same method to visit each element of a multidimensional array. Arrays are discussed in Chapter 10, "Core Language Objects."

## for..in

You need a basic understanding of JavaScript objects to use a for..in loop. After reading Chapter 9, "Client-Side Objects," you should be able to use the for..in construct with ease.

**FIGURE 7.5**

*One hundred sets of coordinates generated by two loops.*

With `for..in`, you can execute a set of statements for each property in an object. You can use the `for..in` loop with any JavaScript object, regardless of whether it has properties. One iteration is executed for each property, so if the object doesn't have any properties, no loops occur. The `for..in` loop also works with custom objects. A variable of a custom JavaScript object is considered a property and therefore executes a loop for each one. Here is the syntax:

```
for (property in object) {
statements
}
```

`property` is a string literal generated for you by JavaScript. For each loop, `property` is assigned the next property name contained in `object` until each one is used. Listing 7.6 uses this function to display each property name of the `Document` object, along with each of the property's values. The results are shown in Figure 7.6.

> **Caution**
>
> The `for..in` loop works only with JavaScript 1.1 and above. Note that it doesn't work properly in Microsoft Internet Explorer 3.0 (JScript 1.0).

**FIGURE 7.6**
*Each property
and its value for
the* Document
*object.*

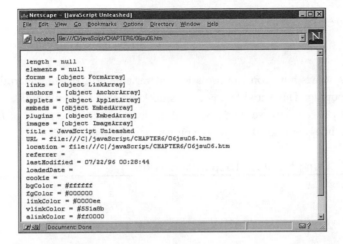

**LISTING 7.6**   Using a `for..in` Loop in JavaScript

```html
<html>
<head>
  <title>JavaScript Unleashed</title>
</head>
<body>
  <script language="JavaScript1.1" type="text/javascript">
  <!--
    // Declare variables
    var anObject = document;
    var propertyInfo = "";

    for (var propertyName in anObject) {
      propertyInfo = propertyName + " = " + anObject[propertyName];
      document.write(propertyInfo + "<br>");
    }
  // -->
  </script>
</body>
</html>
```

## while

The `while` statement acts much like a `for` loop but doesn't include the function of
initializing or incrementing variables in its declaration. You must declare variables
beforehand and increment or decrement the variables within the *statements* block. The
syntax follows:

```
while(condition_expr){
statements
}
```

Listing 7.7 shows how you can use a logical variable as a flag in determining whether to continue looping. This variable, status, is declared ahead of time and set to true. Once i is equal to 10, status is set to false, and the loop breaks. The result of Listing 7.7 is the sum of the integers from 0 to 10, as you can see in Figure 7.7.

**LISTING 7.7**  Using the while Loop in JavaScript

```
<html>
<head>
  <title>JavaScript Unleashed</title>
</head>
<body>
  <script type="text/javascript">
  <!--
    // Declare variables
    var i = 0;
    var result = 0;
    var status = true;

    document.write("0");
    while(status){
      result += ++i;
      document.write(" + " + i);
      if(i == 10){
        status = false;
      }
    }
    document.writeln(" = " + result);
    // -->
  </script>
</body>
</html>
```

## do..while

Starting with JavaScript 1.2, the language offers a do..while construct. This works exactly like the while statement, except that it doesn't check the conditional expression until after the first iteration. This guarantees that the script within the curly braces will be executed at least once.

**FIGURE 7.7**

*The result of Listing 7.7: Eleven iterations of a* while *loop.*

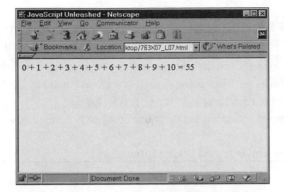

Listing 7.8 shows an example in which it's unknown what the exact value of userEntry might be (if it were actually entered by the user). A value of 0 is given to userEntry to demonstrate that the user might not enter a value that satisfies the conditional statement. The user's entry is still displayed.

**LISTING 7.8**   The do..while **Statement Ensures at Least One Iteration**

```
<html>
<head>
  <title>JavaScript Unleashed</title>
</head>
<body>
<script language="JavaScript1.2" type="text/javascript">
  <!--
    // Declare variables
    var userEntry = 0;
    var x = 1;

    do{
      document.writeln(x);
      x++;
    }while(x <= userEntry);
  // -->
  </script>
</body>
</html>
```

## break **and** continue

One thing to note when using a loop is that, by default, it doesn't stop repeating itself until the specified condition returns false. Sometimes, however, you might want to exit the loop before reaching the ending curly brace. This can be accomplished by adding either break or continue to the *statements* block of the loop.

break terminates the loop altogether, whereas continue skips the remaining statements for the current loop, evaluates the loop expression (if one exists), and begins the next loop. You can see the difference between these two statements in Listing 7.9. This script takes a very basic approach to finding the approximate square root of a number, n.

**LISTING 7.9**    Using the continue and break Statements

```html
<html>
<head>
  <title>JavaScript Unleashed</title>
</head>
<body>
  <script type="text/javascript">
  <!--
    // Declare variables
    var highestNum = 0;
    var n = 175;           // Sample value

    for(var i = 0; i < n; ++i){
      document.write(i + "<br>");
      if(n < 0){
        document.write("n cannot be negative.");
        break;
      }
      if (i * i <= n) {
        highestNum = i;
        continue;
      }
      document.write("<br>Finished!");
      break;
    }
    document.write("<br>The integer less than or equal to the Square Root");
    document.write(" of " + n + " = " + highestNum);
  // -->
  </script>
</body>
</html>
```

Starting with i set to 0, the for loop begins by displaying the value of i. Next, the script checks to ensure that n is not negative. If n is negative, the loop is broken, and program execution resumes after the ending curly brace. If n is positive, i is multiplied by itself, and the result is compared to n. If the result is less than n, i is stored as the highest number so far to be equal to or less than the square root of n.

The continue statement then skips the rest of the current loop and resumes from the top of the loop after incrementing i. As soon as i squared is greater than n, the script passes the continue statement and reaches the break statement, which stops the loop completely. The approximate square root of 175 is shown in Figure 7.8.

**FIGURE 7.8**
*The display after* break *is reached and the loop stops.*

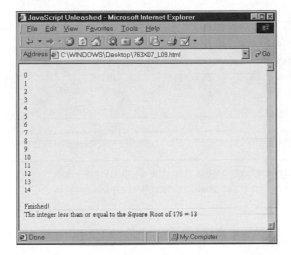

## label **Statements**

With the release of JavaScript 1.2, the language offers a way to be more specific when using the break or continue statement. The label statement can be placed before any control structure that can nest other statements. This allows you to break out of a conditional statement or loop to a specific location in your code. You can see its use in Listing 7.10.

**LISTING 7.10** Using the label Statement

```
<html>
<head>
  <title>JavaScript Unleashed</title>
</head>
<body>
  <script language="JavaScript1.2" type="text/javascript">
```

LISTING 7.10    continued

```
<!--
  // Declare variables
  var stopX = 3;
  var stopY = 8;

  document.write("All x,y pairs between (0,0) and (");
  document.write(stopX + "," + stopY + "):<br>");

loopX:
  for(var x = 0; x < 10; ++x){
    for(var y = 0; y < 10; ++y){
      document.write("("+x + "," + y +") ");
      if((x == stopX) && (y == stopY)){
        break loopX;
      }
    }
    document.write("<br>");
  }
  document.write("<br>After completing the loop, x equals : " + x);
  document.writeln("<br>After completing the loop, y equals : " + y);
  // -->
  </script>
</body>
</html>
```

In Listing 7.10, a for loop is "labeled" with the user-defined identifier loopX. This lets you break out of or continue in this for loop, regardless of how nested the program is at that time. loopX is added to the break statement to stop both for loops from continuing. Without the label, the break statement would have stopped only the loop generating values for y. Figure 7.9 displays the result when the x and y values reach 3 and 8, respectively.

**FIGURE 7.9**

*Using the* `label` *statement to break out of a nested* `for` *loop.*

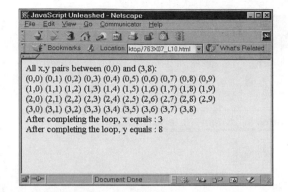

All x,y pairs between (0,0) and (3,8):
(0,0) (0,1) (0,2) (0,3) (0,4) (0,5) (0,6) (0,7) (0,8) (0,9)
(1,0) (1,1) (1,2) (1,3) (1,4) (1,5) (1,6) (1,7) (1,8) (1,9)
(2,0) (2,1) (2,2) (2,3) (2,4) (2,5) (2,6) (2,7) (2,8) (2,9)
(3,0) (3,1) (3,2) (3,3) (3,4) (3,5) (3,6) (3,7) (3,8)
After completing the loop, x equals : 3
After completing the loop, y equals : 8

**7**

Control
Structures and
Looping

# `with` Statements

The `with` statement is used to avoid repeatedly specifying the object reference when accessing properties or methods of that object. Any property or method in a `with` block that JavaScript doesn't recognize is associated with the object specified for that block. Here is the syntax:

```
with (object) {
statements
}
```

`object` specifies which object reference to use in the absence of one in the `statements` block. This is quite useful when you're using advanced math functions that are available only through the `Math` object. The `Math` object isn't covered until Chapter 10, so instead I'll demonstrate the `with` statement using the `Document` object, which you're more familiar with.

When using the `write()` or `writeln()` method associated with the `Document` object, I include the prefix `document.`, as in the following line:

```
document.writeln("Hello!")
```

When you display a large amount of data using this technique, it's not uncommon to use the same `document.writeln()` statement many times over. To cut down on the amount of code needed, enclose all statements that reference the `Document` object within a `with` block, as shown in Listing 7.11. This way, you can eliminate the `document` prefix when using a document's methods or properties.

Notice that `title` and `URL` are properties of the `Document` object and would normally be written as `document.title` and `document.URL`. Using the `with` statement, you need to reference the object only once to produce the same results as typing each line. Figure 7.10 shows the results.

> **Caution**
>
> Internet Explorer version 3.0 doesn't support the with statement.

**LISTING 7.11**  Using the with Statement in JavaScript

```html
<html>
<head>
  <title>JavaScript Unleashed</title>
</head>
<body>
  <script type="text/javascript">
  <!--
    with(document){
      write("Hello!");
      write("<br>The title of this document is, \"" + title + "\".");
      write("<br>The URL for this document is: " + URL);
      write("<br>Now you can avoid using the object's prefix each time!");
    }
  // -->
  </script>
</body>
</html>
```

**FIGURE 7.10**

*Displaying information using the* with *statement.*

> **Note**
>
> Depending on your browser, you may see an encoded format for the URL in this example.

# switch Statements

The switch statement is used to compare one value to many others. You might think that this task can be accomplished only by using many if statements, but the switch statement is your answer. It is more readable and allows you to specify a default set of statements to execute in case a match isn't found.

Listing 7.12 assumes that the variable request could change, depending on what the user has asked for. For this example, request is assigned "Names" as the value to compare to each case. The second case is equal to request, and it executes the statements that follow.

> **Note**
>
> The switch statement was not added until JavaScript 1.2.

**LISTING 7.12**  The switch Statement

```html
<html>
<head>
  <title>JavaScript Unleashed</title>
</head>
<body>
  <script language="JavaScript1.2" type="text/javascript">
  <!--
    // Declare variables
    var request = "Name";

    switch(request){
      case "Logo" :
        document.write('<img src="logo.gif" alt="Logo">');
        document.write("<br>");
        break;
      case "Name" :
```

LISTING 7.12    continued

```
        document.write("Software Inc.");
        document.write("<br>");
        break;
    case "Products" :
        document.write("MyEditor");
        document.write("<br>");
        break;
    default :
        document.write("www.mysite.com");
        break;
    }
//-->
</script>
</body>
</html>
```

The break statement is used to stop any further execution of the code remaining in the switch statement. If no break statements were used, the remaining code for each case would be executed, regardless of a match between request and that case. Figure 7.11 simply shows that request matched the value "Name" and displayed the company name.

FIGURE 7.11
*Using the* switch *statement.*

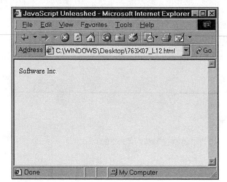

# Summary

To make decisions in JavaScript, use the conditional statements if and else. You can use if by itself to execute a section of code based on the condition of an expression. If the expression returns true, the code will be executed; otherwise, it will not.

Use the else statement immediately after the if block to have JavaScript execute code when the expression from the if block returns false. JavaScript lets you nest if and if..else statements within each other. Using this method, you can ask questions based on the answers to previous questions.

Use for loops to repeat a section of your script. In the declaration, you have the option of initializing a variable to be used inside the loop. You can also specify how to change the variable each time a loop is completed. Based on the conditional expression of the for loop, you can specify the reason for the loop to stop.

Use the for..in loop to perform a set of operations for each property of an object. JavaScript automatically assigns the name of the property to a variable that you specify. Using this variable, you can perform operations on that property.

Use the while loop to repeat a section of your script. You only need to specify a conditional expression that needs to return true before each loop is executed.

The break and continue statements are used to stop the execution of any loop. break stops the loop completely, and continue stops only the current iteration of the loop and skips to the beginning of the next iteration.

The with statement is used in conjunction with JavaScript objects. It allows you to reference an object once rather than each time you access a property or method of the object. Inside the with block, you can use the property and method names of an object without their object reference prefix.

And finally, we talked about the switch statement. This statement allows you to specify all possible values you would like to see in a given variable to perform the tasks you want. If the value passed is not a value you have specified, then it falls through to the default section.

# Functions

CHAPTER

8

Performing a function, or many functions, is the purpose of all JavaScript programs. In its simplest form, a script can read or take in data, perform operations on a set of data, or display and send out data. As you have seen in previous examples, you can use a combination of these basic tools or merely one of them to serve an overall purpose.

To entertain a casual browser, you might first inquire about his interests and then point him in the right direction. To welcome someone back to your Web page, you might let that person know what is new and exciting. If you have products to sell, JavaScript can easily quote a price for any combination of items that interests the user while storing this data for your Marketing department.

Accomplishing tasks such as these requires many lines of JavaScript code. Some sections of the script might need to execute as soon as a Web page is loaded into the browser. Other parts of the script might be most useful if they are delayed until an HTML form accepts data from the client. Sometimes, you might need parts of a script more than once or even an unlimited number of times, and intermittently repeating a section of code could become necessary.

These issues bring about the idea of splitting a script into smaller parts to serve a specific individual purpose. A specific purpose might be to signal a "direct hit" during a game developed with JavaScript. Validating data entered in an HTML form is another task you might want a script to run more than once while someone is viewing your Web page.

It makes a lot of sense to split a script logically into sections, each of which serves a single purpose. When the time comes, one particular section of a script can be called to execute. JavaScript gives you this capability through a structure known as a *function*.

# Understanding Functions

A JavaScript function is simply a script that is sectioned off as a separate piece of code and given a name. Using this name, another script can then call this script to execute at any time and as often as it needs to. Many programming languages, such as C/C++ and Java, also use functions, whereas others incorporate the same semantics but call them methods, procedures, or subroutines. They all do basically the same thing, but they have differences.

Functions are meant to serve the single purpose of helping split up the many tasks that one program is designed to do. You can think of this process as telling JavaScript to perform this list of related instructions and tell you when it's done.

Functions can be passed values, called *arguments*, when called. You can then use the arguments as *variables* within the statements block. Once data is assigned to a variable, you are able to process the data or use it in calculations and potentially return the result.

# Creating Functions

The following code fragment shows the syntax for declaring a function in JavaScript:

```
function functionName ([argument1] [...,argumentN]) {
    [statements]
}
```

The keyword `function` is used to specify a name, *functionName*, which serves as the identifier for the set of statements between the curly braces. Enclosed in parentheses and separated by commas are the argument names, which hold each value that a function receives.

Technically, arguments are variables that are assigned to literal values, other variables, or objects that are passed to the function by the calling statement. If you don't specify any arguments, you must still include an empty set of parentheses to complete the declaration.

The statements, which are the core of the function, are executed each time the function is called. For better readability, statements within the statement block are typically indented.

# Where to Declare Functions

Technically, you can declare a function anywhere inside of a `<script>` block. The only restriction is that you cannot declare one within another function or a control structure. However, keep in mind that just as different blocks of an HTML document are loaded ahead of others, so are any scripts that are embedded in these HTML blocks. For this reason, it is recommended that you declare functions in the `<head>` block of your HTML document. Declaring all your functions here ensures that the functions are available if another script needs to use them immediately.

Listing 8.1 shows a function named `defaultColors()` declared inside the `<head>` block of an HTML document. This function is then called once within the `<body>` block of the document.

**LISTING 8.1**   Declaring a Function in the `<head>` Block

```
<html>
<head>
  <title>JavaScript Unleashed</title>
  <script type="text/javascript">
  <!--
    function defaultColors() {
      document.writeln("Inside of defaultColors()");
      document.fgColor = "black";
      document.bgColor = "white";
```

8

Functions

**LISTING 8.1**   continued

```
    }
  // -->
  </script>
</head>
<body>
  <script type="text/javascript">
  <!--
    document.writeln("Functions are scripts just waiting to run!");
    defaultColors();
    document.writeln("All done.");
  // -->
  </script>
</body>
</html>
```

# Calling Functions

Listing 8.1 shows how the function `defaultColors()` is called from the second script block. This is an example of calling a function that takes no arguments. When the HTML document is loaded, the function is loaded into memory and "put on hold." The function is not executed until the main script block calls it with the following statement:

```
defaultColors()
```

At this point, program execution jumps immediately to the first line of the `defaultColors()` function. After executing all three lines of code, the program jumps back to where it left off and finishes what is left.

This result has the same effect as if you had inserted all the function's statements directly into that position in your code. Now that a name is assigned to this function, all you need to do to run the same statements is use its name again. You can view the results of this process in Figure 8.1. Reusing code like this is the ideal way to use functions.

> **Note**
>
> Unlike a string's `fontcolor` property, you can change a document's `fgcolor` and `bgcolor` properties without refreshing or reloading the page into the browser.

**FIGURE 8.1**
*Reusing code.*

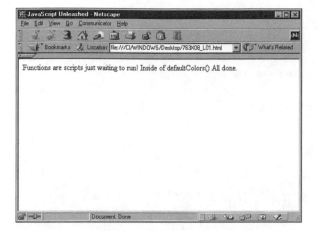

# Working with Arguments

Setting up functions to accept arguments can also be very useful. Doing so lets you reuse the function in several ways while serving the same general purpose. For example, you might want to create a function to be used many times throughout your program; however, one of the values inside the function might need to change each time the function is called.

One way to solve this problem without arguments is to use global variables that can be modified both outside and inside the function. This can get confusing if you happen to use the same variable names inside more than one function. The best thing to do is set up the function to accept an argument for each value you want it to receive. Listing 8.2 shows a function that takes advantage of using arguments.

**LISTING 8.2**    Using an Argument with a JavaScript Function

```
<html>
<head>
  <title>JavaScript Unleashed</title>
  <script type="text/javascript">
<!--
    function getBinary(anInteger) {
      var result = "";
      var shortResult = "";
      for(var i=1; i <= 32; i++) {
        if(anInteger & 1 == 1) {
        result = "1" + result;
        shortResult = result;
        } else {
```

8

Functions

LISTING 8.2    continued

```
            result =  "0" + result;
         }
         anInteger = anInteger >> 1;
      }
      return(shortResult);
   }
// -->
</script>
</head>
<body>
  <script type="text/javascript">
  <!--
    var binaryString = "";

    // Define an x variable
    x = 9;
    binaryString = getBinary(x);

    // Write results to the page
    document.write("The number " + x + " in binary form is : \n");
    document.writeln(binaryString);

    // Redefine x variable
    x = 255;
    binaryString = getBinary(x);

    // Write results to the page
    document.write("The number " + x + " in binary form is : \n");
    document.writeln(binaryString);
    document.writeln("The variable x is still equal to : " + x);
  // -->
  </script>

</body>
</html>
```

When the function is called with the statement `getBinary(x)`, the function receives a copy of the value that is stored in x. This process is called *passing by value*. The value is then assigned to `anInteger`, a variable local to the function. You can then use the variable throughout the statement block as a local variable. If `anInteger` changes value while inside the function, it doesn't affect the value of the variable x, which was passed as an argument, as shown in Figure 8.2.

Notice that you don't need to declare anInteger using the var keyword. JavaScript automatically declares a new variable every time the function is called.

**FIGURE 8.2**

*Passing by value doesn't affect the original variable.*

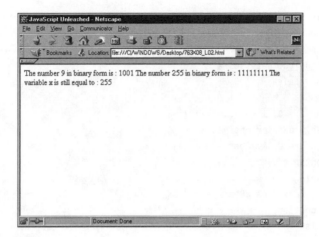

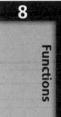

The last statement given in the getBinary() function is return(shortResult). Just as a function can receive a value, it can also return a value. The return statement returns a single value to the location in the program that first called the function. Returning a value from a function works in the same way as returning a value from an expression. The following statement assigns the value returned by getBinary() to the variable binaryString:

```
binaryString = getBinary(x)
```

In this case, the final value of shortResult is assigned to the binaryString variable.

You can use functions that return values anywhere you use a normal expression. Some functions return the result of a set of calculations, whereas others return a logical value just to let you know if everything went all right. This technique is demonstrated in Listing 8.3.

The function call isPhone(userInput) is used as the condition expression of an if statement. The function isPhone() is a function that returns a logical value. The value returned lets the caller know if a phone number was entered in the correct format. This is useful for validating data that the user has entered in an HTML form. Figure 8.3 shows that the phone number was entered correctly, and an appropriate message is displayed. You can find more information about validating data entry in Chapter 29, "Forms and Data Validation."

LISTING 8.3    Functions That Return Values Can Be Used in Expressions

```html
<html>
<head>
  <title>JavaScript Unleashed</title>
  <script type="text/javascript">
<!--
    function isPhone(aString) {
      var aChar = null;
      var status = true;
      if(aString.length != 13) {
        status = false;
      }else{
        for(var i = 0; i <= 12; i++) {
          aChar = aString.charAt(i);
          if ( i == 0 && aChar == "(" ){
            continue;
          }else{
            if( i == 4 && aChar == ")" ){
              continue;
            }else{
              if( i == 8 && aChar == "-" ){
                continue;
              }else{
                if( parseInt(aChar,10) >= 0 && parseInt(aChar,10) <= 9 ){
                  continue;
                }else {
                  status = false;
                  break;
                }
              }
            }
          }
        }
      }
      return(status);
    }
// -->
  </script>
</head>
<body>
  <script type="text/javascript">
<!--
    var userInput = "(800)555-1212";
```

**LISTING 8.3**   continued

```
  if(isPhone(userInput)) {
    document.writeln("Thank you for your phone number.");
    document.writeln("I will have a representative get you");
    document.writeln("more information.");
  }else{
    document.writeln("Please re-enter your phone number");
    document.writeln("using the format (###)###-####");
  }
  //-->
  </script>

</body>
</html>
```

**FIGURE 8.3**
*Using a function
as a conditional
expression.*

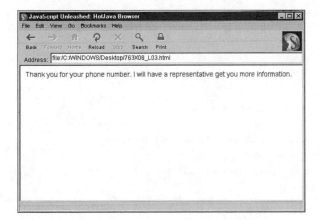

**8**

Functions

# Varying the Number of Arguments

A function is set up to accept a certain number of arguments. Although it's good programming practice to pass the same number of arguments as was declared, it's sometimes practical to allow a different number of arguments. This is common when calling a function that uses the same parameter each time but is set up to handle special cases.

In this case, you might want to use a default value inside the function if no arguments are passed. This lets you use the function without arguments or lets you specify a value other than the default. In Listing 8.4, I set up a function to display a very basic welcome message when the user arrives at a Web page.

**LISTING 8.4**  Accepting Either One or No Arguments

```html
<html>
<head>
  <title>JavaScript Unleashed</title>
  <script type="text/javascript">
  <!--
    // userName is optional
    function welcomeMessage(userName) {
      if (userName != null) {
        document.writeln("\"Hello again, " + userName + ".\"");
      }else{
        document.writeln("\"Welcome to our Web site!\"");
        document.write("\nIf a value is not passed to this ");
        document.writeln("function, displaying the");
        document.write("variable \"userName\" would show : ");
        document.writeln(userName);
      }
    }
  // -->
  </script>
</head>
<body>
  <script type="text/javascript">
  <!--
    document.writeln("First call to welcomeMessage(),\n");
    welcomeMessage("Mr. President");
    document.writeln("<HR>\nSecond call to welcomeMessage(),\n");
    welcomeMessage();
  // -->
  </script>
</body>
</html>
```

Depending on whether it knows the visitor's name, the program displays one of two messages. If userName is not equal to null, the variable was defined. This is possible only if a value, such as Mr. President, was passed to the function. If the function is equal to null, the program avoids using the variable in the welcome message altogether. Using it displays unwanted data, as shown in Figure 8.4. Depending on your Web browser, the unwanted data will be displayed as undefined or will be left blank.

**FIGURE 8.4**
*The result of passing either one of two arguments.*

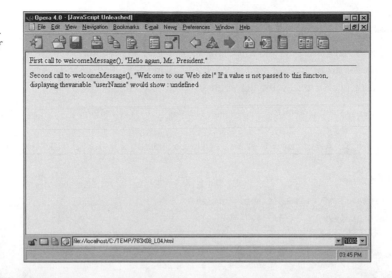

8

Functions

---

**Tip**

JavaScript now supports the `typeof` operator, which could be used to check if `userName` is undefined rather than `null`. This is the ideal way to check, but it is not supported by some of the older browsers.

---

**Resource**

For an up-to-date summary of new JavaScript features, check out Netscape's DevEdge site and look for links leading you to JavaScript documentation. You can access this site at `http://developer.netscape.com`.

---

Another possibility is for a function to be passed more arguments than were specified in the declaration. The extra values aren't lost; they're stored in an array named `arguments`, which is a property of every function. All arguments stored in the array can be extracted within the statements block. For example, to get the first argument passed to the `welcomeMessage` function, you can use the following statement:

```
firstArg = welcomeMessage.arguments[0]
```

JavaScript arrays are indexed starting at 0. To find the second item in the array, you would use 1, and so on. To find the total number of arguments that were passed, you can use the following statement to find the length of the array:

```
numArgs = welcomeMessage.arguments.length
```

Using these features, I modified the `welcomeMessage()` function to accept a variable number of arguments and included it in Listing 8.5. The `welcomeMessage()` function can therefore accept the following syntax:

```
welcomeMessage([userName] [,extraMessage1] [,extraMessage2]...)
```

**LISTING 8.5**  A Function Can Be Set Up to Accept a Variable Number of Arguments

```html
<html>
<head>
  <title>JavaScript Unleashed</title>
  <script type="text/javascript">
  <!--
    // Use this syntax for welcomeMessage function:
    // welcomeMessage([userName] [,extraMessage1] [,extraMessage2]...)
    function welcomeMessage(userName) {
      if (userName != null) {
        document.writeln("\"Hello again, " + userName + ".\"");
      }else{
        document.writeln("\"Welcome to our Web site!\"");
      }
      numArgs = welcomeMessage.arguments.length;
      // If more arguments than the userName were sent,
      // display each one.
      if(numArgs > 1) {
        for(var i = 1; i < numArgs; i++) {
          document.writeln("\""+welcomeMessage.arguments[i]+"\"");
        }
      }
    }
  // -->
  </script>
</head>
<body>
  <script type="text/javascript">
  <!--
    var userName = "David", extraMsg = "It has been a long time!";
    var userName2 = null;
    var extraMsg1 = "Would you like to become a member?";
    var extraMsg2 = "You can enroll online!";
    welcomeMessage(userName, extraMsg);
    document.writeln("<hr>");
```

**LISTING 8.5**    continued

```
    welcomeMessage(userName2, extraMsg1, extraMsg2);
  // -->
  </script>
</body>
</html>
```

Notice that Listing 8.5 can still handle the situation in which the userName is unknown but extra messages need to be displayed. The variable userName2 is assigned null to fill the first element in the arguments array, so that a message isn't displayed as the user's name. Figure 8.5 shows the resulting output.

**FIGURE 8.5**
*Accepting multiple arguments to display many messages.*

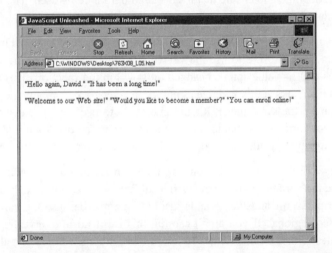

8

Functions

---

**Tip**

When you're developing with a group of people, it's important to document the intricacies of your scripts so that others can understand the full potential of what you have written. Without descriptive comments, reading through an application takes much more time to understand.

# Using Global and Local Variables

In Chapter 5, "Fundamentals of the JavaScript Language," I described the difference between local and global variables. I demonstrated how a global variable can be modified from anywhere in a document, whereas a local variable can be modified only within the function in which it is declared. You can choose which type of variable to use by following these guidelines:

- If the value of a variable is meant to be used and possibly modified by any part of a program, both inside and outside functions, the variable should be declared outside any function. This has the effect of making it global and modifiable by any part of the program. The best place to declare a global variable is in the <head> block of your HTML document to ensure that it's declared before being used. The variable need not be declared again inside any function.

- If the variable is needed only within a particular function, it should be declared inside that function. Be sure to use the keyword var when declaring the variable. This ensures that its value can be changed only within the function. This also ensures that JavaScript looks at this variable as unique and separate from any global variables that might have the same name. It's not necessary to use the var keyword to declare argument variables. Variables that are specified in the declaration of the function are automatically considered local, as if they were declared with the var keyword.

- If you want to use a variable only in the main script and not within any functions, declare the variable somewhere outside all functions. Unfortunately, nothing prevents the script from using the variable inside functions, because the variable is still considered global. If you aren't careful, this can lead to overwriting values held by variables with the same name. To avoid this problem completely, always follow the preceding guideline.

- If you want the value of a variable to be modifiable by one function, but you need to use the variable in another function, pass the variable as an argument to that function. This has the effect of making a copy of the variable and assigning its value to the argument variable set up to receive it. As the function works and modifies its own copy of the variable, it will not affect the original. Argument variables are automatically declared as local to that function. Even if the argument variable has the same name as the variable being passed, making changes to it doesn't affect the variable that was passed. The one exception to this is objects. When an object is passed as an argument, it's passed by reference, as opposed to being passed by value. Instead of making a copy of the object, the function uses the original object. Changes made to an object's properties within the function have an effect on the original object.

To see examples of passing variables by value, look at Listing 8.6. I made it a point to demonstrate how JavaScript considers some variables with the same name to be different. This is shown when the variable `numberB` is passed to the function `doublePassedVar()`. JavaScript automatically creates a local variable also named `numberB`. Even though this local variable has the same name as the global variable, modifications to it don't affect the global variable. Figure 8.6 shows the results.

**LISTING 8.6**   The Effects of Local and Global Variables

```html
<html>
<head>
  <title>JavaScript Unleashed</title>
  <script type="text/javascript">
  <!--
    // Global variable modified in any function
    var numberA;

    // Global variable only modified in main script
    var numberB;

    function doubleGlobalVar(){
      // This will change the value of the global variable.
      numberA *= 2;
    }

    function tripleLocalVar() {
      // This uses the same name as the global variable, but is considered
      // different by JavaScript.
      var numberA = 1;
      numberA *= 3;
}

    function doublePassedVar(numberB) {
      // I purposely gave the argument variable the same name as the
      // variable being passed. This shows that JavaScript considers them
      // to be different.
      numberB *= 2;
    }
  //-->
  </script>
</head>
<body>
  <script type="text/javascript">
```

**LISTING 8.6**    continued

```
<!--
  numberA = 1;
  document.writeln("Initial value of numberA: " + numberA);
  doubleGlobalVar();
  tripleLocalVar();
  document.writeln("Final value of numberA: " + numberA);
  numberB = 1;
  document.writeln("Initial value of numberB: " + numberB);
  doublePassedVar(numberB);
  document.writeln("Final value of numberB: " + numberB);
// -->
</script>
</body>
</html>
```

**FIGURE 8.6**

*The resulting values of the* numberA *and* numberB *variables.*

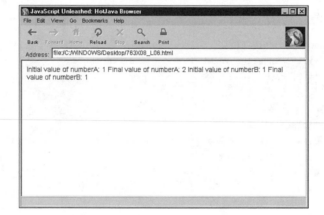

# Passing Objects by Reference

A formal introduction to creating custom JavaScript objects is given in Chapter 11, "Creating Custom JavaScript Objects," but when dealing with functions, it's important to know what happens when you use an object as one of the arguments for a function call.

When a simple data type such as a string, number, or Boolean is passed to a function, it's passed by value. This means that a copy of the variable instead of the original is used by the function. Any changes made to the copy don't affect the original.

On the other hand, when an object is passed to a function, it's passed by reference. This allows the function to alter the original version of the object. Knowing this, you have the ability to wrap simple data types inside an object if you would rather pass the variable by reference. Listing 8.7 demonstrates how to do this.

**LISTING 8.7**   Passing by Reference Versus Passing by Value

```html
<html>
<head>
  <title>JavaScript Unleashed</title>
  <script type="text/javascript">
<!--
    // wrap and integer inside an object
    function intObject() {
      this.i;
      return this;
    }

    function start() {
      // declare two ways to store an integer
      var I;
      var myIntObject = new intObject();

      // assign initial values
      i = 0;
      myIntObject.i = 0;

      // display current values
      document.write("<br>Before<br>");
      document.write("i = " + i);
      document.write("<br>");
      document.write("myIntObject = " + myIntObject.i);
      document.write("<br>");

      // pass variables
      modify(i, myIntObject);

      // display current values
      document.write("<br>After<br>");
      document.write("i = " + i);
      document.write("<br>");
      document.write("myIntObject = " + myIntObject.i);
      document.write("<br>");
```

8

Functions

---

**LISTING 8.7**    continued

```
    }

    function modify(n, obj) {
      n++;
      obj.i++;
    }
  //-->
  </script>
</head>
<body>
  <script type="text/javascript">
  <!--
    start();
  //-->
  </script>
</body>
</html>
```

---

The function `intObject()` is actually used to wrap the variable i inside an object. An instance of the object is created with the line

```
var myIntObject = new intObject()
```

`myIntObject` can now be used to access the variable i with the code

```
myIntObject.i
```

This also allows you to pass the number by reference if you pass the entire object to the function. The `modify()` function is used to show the difference between modifying a simple data type and modifying an object. In Figure 8.7, you can see that the original value of i was not affected, while the original value of `myIntObject.i` was.

**FIGURE 8.7**
*Passing a custom JavaScript object by reference.*

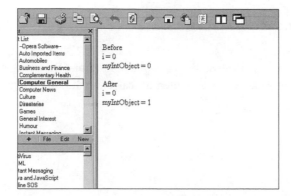

# More Information on Functions

So far in this chapter, we have covered a lot of ground on functions. Without them, JavaScript would be nothing more than a simple scripting language that could be used only for very simple scripts. In addition to what you have learned so far, functions can be reused, and they can be recursive.

## Reusing Functions

A function is great for separating an application into its logical parts, but its best benefit is in promoting the reuse of code.

Unlike sections of code enclosed in loops to be repeated many times in succession, a function can be reused at any given time simply by calling its name. Creating functions that serve one purpose but that are useful in many situations takes practice and a little foresight.

For example, in Listing 8.4, the `welcomeMessage()` function serves one purpose on more than one occasion throughout the execution of the program. By allowing a more flexible argument list in Listing 8.5, the `welcomeMessage()` function became useful in more situations. It still serves the same purpose, but it's a better candidate for reuse in its more flexible form.

Also keep in mind that you can store your functions in external JavaScript source files. This allows you to include these files using the `src` attribute of the `<script>` tag. Following this approach, it becomes an easy job for a Webmaster to change a function across his entire site, because he has to edit it in only one location.

## Recursive Functions

A JavaScript function can be *recursive,* which means that it can call itself. Solving factorial equations is a common way to demonstrate how recursion works. Since JavaScript doesn't

offer a factorial operator, I have included an example of how to solve factorials using a recursive function.

To find the factorial of any positive integer n, you simply find the product of all integers 1 through n. To find the factorial of 6, written 6!, calculate the following:

$$6! = 6 \times 5 \times 4 \times 3 \times 2 \times 1$$
$$= 720$$

To calculate 7!, you would use the following:

$$7! = 7 \times 6 \times 5 \times 4 \times 3 \times 2 \times 1$$

Comparing these two calculations, you can produce a general formula to use in your function. Notice that 7! is equal to $7 \times 6!$. For any positive integer n greater than 0, n! = n $\times$ (n - 1)!. The first iteration would process this:

$$7! = 7 \times (7 - 1)!$$
$$= 7 \times 6!$$

From here, you have to stop and calculate 6! before continuing with the rest of the calculation. This occurs six more times before you can back out of each one and find the final solution. Instead of doing that, you can use a recursive function such as the following:

```
function getFactorial(n) {
  var result;
  if(n > 0){
    result = n * getFactorial(n - 1);
  }else if(n==0){
    result = 1;
  }else{
    result = null;
  }
  return(result)
}
```

The function first checks to see if n is greater than 0, which is the case the majority of the time. If this is true, the function multiplies n by the result returned from calling the function again with a different argument—in this case, n-1. This continues to put many getFactorial functions on hold until n is equal to 0. At this point, the most nested occurrence of the function finishes and returns the first value. JavaScript then backs out and finishes each nested function until it reaches the original call to getFactorial, and then it returns the final result.

Developing useful functions can be one of the most rewarding and interesting aspects of programming. After you see a function in action, it's common to go back and modify it to make it more flexible. If you do this, be sure that the function still serves one purpose and doesn't do more than you expect.

# Summary

Becoming experienced in writing functions prepares you for the next exciting step in JavaScript programming—creating custom objects. This is covered in Chapter 11. For now, there is much to be learned about the objects that are already built into HTML and JavaScript. JavaScript also includes functions that are built into the language and can be used at any time. These are covered in Chapter 10, "Core Language Objects."

JavaScript functions serve several purposes. They let you put code on hold so that it doesn't execute immediately when the document is loaded. Used with arguments, they let you duplicate code easily and use the same code to perform the same operations on different sets of data. Here is a quick list of what functions can do and reminders on how each is accomplished.

- A function is a set of JavaScript code that is grouped and given a name. To declare a function, use the `function` statement, followed by the name you want to give it, a set of parentheses, and the script you want the function to include. Function names must adhere to the rules applied to all variables.

- Functions can be declared anywhere inside an HTML document, as long as the declaration is surrounded by `<script>` tags. It is suggested that functions be declared in the `<head>` of the document.

- To call a function, use its name followed by a set of parentheses. The parentheses enclose any arguments that the function can accept.

- JavaScript arguments are passed by value. Functions can accept a variable number of arguments, regardless of how the function was declared. Each function has an array named `arguments` associated with it. This array can be used to extract an argument that might have been passed to the function.

- JavaScript functions can return values. Functions that return values can be used as expressions or in other expressions.

- Argument variables don't need to be declared. They are automatically declared as local variables each time the function is called. To declare a global variable within a function, don't use the `var` keyword. Instead, just initialize the variable.

8

Functions

- Functions that serve one purpose but are flexible enough to deal with different pieces of data are the most reusable functions.

- In JavaScript, functions can call themselves. Functions that do so are called *recursive functions*.

# Client-Side Objects

So far in this book, you have looked at the basic language elements of JavaScript. But you can't stop there. Undoubtedly, the heart and soul of client-side JavaScript is its object model. With that in mind, this chapter takes a top-level view of JavaScript's object model and presents all objects currently defined in the language.

However, before diving into JavaScript objects, you should first take a brief high-level look at some of the basic concepts of object-oriented programming (OOP). JavaScript isn't object oriented (OO) in the same way that Java or C++ is, but it is object based. Therefore, understanding OO terminology is fundamental to a good understanding of how to maximize your use of JavaScript objects.

After the OOP primer, this chapter continues by looking exactly at what the JavaScript object model is and, just as importantly, what it is not. Finally, I conclude by providing a brief description of all the objects in the model.

# Understanding Objects

If you're new to object-oriented concepts, you might find that developers who are comfortable with OOP seem to be speaking a different language. After all, terms such as *OOP*, *method*, and *property* may be confusing if you're used to programming functions or macros. However, once you take a moment to understand OO, you will find it to be very intuitive. In this section, I'll look at some of the basic OO concepts, including objects, properties, and methods.

## Objects

Programs are developed for executing a particular business case. For example, an order management system handles customer orders. The business tasks of an application—in addition to the end user's requirements—form the "problem world" or "problem space" of a software system. This area also includes technical components such as a graphical user interface (GUI).

In constructing OO software applications, objects are the central logical building blocks. Objects in program code are often representations of real-world objects found in the problem space. Additionally, you can build technical helper objects for solving special computer science problems.

An object can be any of the following:

- A tangible or visible thing in the problem space—for example, an order or a customer. If you are developing software for a car dealer business, probable objects are the cars to be sold, car models, employees, customers, and so on.

- An abstract concept in the mind of the developer or something that can be comprehended intellectually. For example, if you are building an application for chemists, you might need chemical structures for objects such as molecules, atoms, chemical models, and the like. Date and time might be considered intellectual objects, too, because they are certainly not tangible. The Math object in JavaScript is another good example of a purely logical concept. The Math object provides advanced mathematical functions (arithmetic and trigonometric) for processing numbers in JavaScript.

- A visible GUI object. JavaScript has many different GUI objects such as windows, frames, buttons, and input fields.

Historically, the object-oriented model stems from the concept of data structures. Think of a data structure as a more complex data type. A data structure is very similar to the idea of an object. It is a model of an abstract concept in computer science for solving primitive technical programming tasks. A data structure is a container of corresponding data variables, together with the operations defined for it.

Many examples cited as objects in computer science books are essentially data structures, such as records, arrays, complex numbers, or stacks. A stack is a storage container of data values and works basically like a stack of paper. A stack can store only a single data item at a time, which is always put on top of the other data items. Moreover, you can remove a data item only from the top position of the stack.

Other popular data structures are strings and dates, which are also implemented in JavaScript as core objects. A string is a collection of single characters. A string is considered a single entity, even though some string functions extract substrings out of strings. A Date object contains the data values resembling dates and time.

An object includes the data values needed to describe its nature (its properties) and the functions it can perform (its methods). You can consider an object an entity with a defined boundary, as shown in Figure 9.1. The kernel of an object is built by its data values. The data items of an object describe the object's special characteristics and its identity. In object-oriented jargon, object data items are called *properties* (or *attributes*).

Generally, an object supports several functions. The functions of an object visible to the outside form the behavior of an object. In object-oriented terms, an object function is often called a *method*. A method is a chunk of source code performing one single task that is an important feature of the object. A method is a function of the object that can be called. In other words, the methods of an object represent its behavior, which is its outwardly visible and testable activity.

9

Client-Side
Objects

FIGURE 9.1

*A graphical view
of an object.*

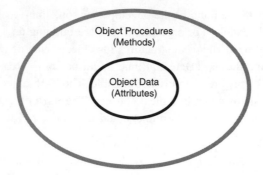

Figure 9.1 shows the popular donut view of an object. The methods of an object are drawn in the outer circle because they are visible to other objects. This means these functions could be called and executed on the object. The attributes are in the inner circle.

One example of an object is my car. My car is represented as the object myCar in the object-oriented world. It is a red Renault 19 built in 1992, so its data attributes include the following:

| | |
|---|---|
| make | Renault |
| model | 19 |
| age | 1992 |
| color | red |

My car can park or drive. Those are the important functions it provides. Figure 9.2 shows a graphical image of my car as an object in the donut-view perspective.

FIGURE 9.2

*A graphical view
of my car as an
object.*

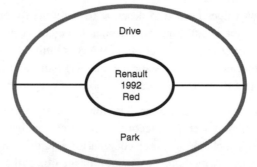

In addition to specific characteristics and identifying values, an object's attribute can also represent the state of the object or a role that an object could play at a given time. State and role are special time-dependent object characteristics. A *state* is a kind of data item that changes over time and generally shows a current value for the object. Add to the list another attribute of `myCar`, `position`, which always contains the current geographic position of my car. The attribute `position` is a typical example of a state attribute.

An employee might be a team leader or department head at any given time in his professional career. An employee object can contain an attribute for professional status that stores the different roles (such as team leader or department head) an employee could fulfill.

Let's look at an example that uses factorials. Figure 9.3 shows a simple graphical user interface for computing factorials. The source code for constructing the HTML for this form is shown in Listing 9.1, which contains the body of an HTML document. Do note that the source code for the calculation functionality is not included in this listing, just the HTML.

**FIGURE 9.3**
*A graphical user interface for computing n!*

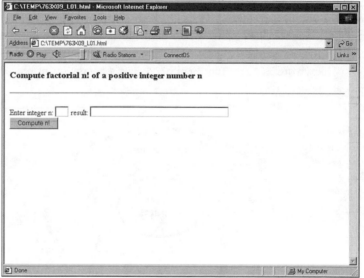

**9**

Client-Side Objects

**LISTING 9.1**   Computing *n*!

```
<body>
  <h3>
    Compute factorial n! of a positive integer number n
  </h3>
  <hr>
  <form>
    Enter integer n:
```

**LISTING 9.1    continued**

```
    <input type="text" name="fn" size="2">
    result:
    <input type="text" name="fresult" size="40">
    <br>
    <input type="button" name="compute" value="Compute n!"
      onClick="xcompute(this.form)">
  </form>
</body>
```

In JavaScript, an object's attributes are referred to as the object's *properties*. For example, the pushbutton `compute` in the example is a GUI object in JavaScript. A pushbutton has the JavaScript properties `name` and `value`. In the HTML document example (see Listing 9.1), the properties are specified by the attributes `name` and `value`.

The user can click a GUI button, so the object `compute` supports the function `click`. The function `click` presents a way to trigger the object `compute` through the programmed script instead of through a user action. All the functions of an object build its behavior. In object-oriented terms, an object's function is often called a method. In JavaScript, however, the respective keyword is `function`. Figure 9.4 shows a JavaScript object drawn in the graphical donut view.

**FIGURE 9.4**

*A graphical view of a JavaScript object.*

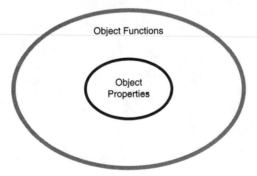

The built-in object string is a special object type. You can simply create the string `myString` with the `var` statement. The `var` statement creates new variables in JavaScript, as shown here:

```
var myString = "This is my text. It resembles a string object";
```

`MyString` has the property `length`, which all strings possess. The attribute `length` contains the length of the string `myString`—in this case, the number 45. Strings feature several different methods (see Chapter 10, "Core Language Objects," for details), including `blink()`, which results in a blinking string. This statement has the same effect as the following HTML tag:

```
<blink>This is my text. It resembles a string object</blink>
```

The following statement makes the text "This is my text. It resembles a string object" blink onscreen:

```
myString.blink();
```

An object's properties can contain simple variable types such as characters, integers, and so on, as well as other objects. Figure 9.5 illustrates this idea.

For example, the object `myCar` can be defined through attributes such as `make`, `model`, `year`, and `owner`, where `owner` is a person object defined through attributes such as `name`, `age`, and `address`. The inclusion of objects in the data attributes of the containing object is often called *aggregation* or a *whole-part* relationship. The expression "whole-part" signifies a typical example for containment, where a machine consists of several smaller parts, as in a car with an engine, four wheels, and so on.

**FIGURE 9.5**
*A graphical view of object containment.*

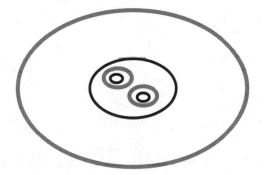

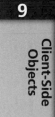

JavaScript has many different objects, such as `String`, `Date`, `Button`, and `Math`. You can use all those objects. In fact, you can have several different objects of one type.

For example, your HTML form can have various pushbuttons. Every button possesses the same properties and methods; that is, every button has a value and supports a `click` method. A button is only a kind of construction plan for creating new existing buttons in a form. Such a construction specification is called a *class* in object-oriented terms. The different built-in objects in JavaScript actually form a set of classes that you can reuse. Such a set of classes is called a *class library*. Because JavaScript doesn't really deal with classes in the way object-oriented languages do, the built-in objects in JavaScript as a whole are often called the *JavaScript object library*.

> **Tip**
>
> To save development time and programming effort, use as many of the JavaScript objects as suitable. Study the JavaScript object library carefully. Don't invent your own object types if it isn't necessary. Reusing already existing software components is a beneficial strategy when you're programming the object-oriented way.

## Encapsulation

The data attributes and functions of an object form one inseparable entity, as shown in Figure 9.6, which is the same representation you saw in Figure 9.1. The information about the inner workings of an object should be hidden.

**FIGURE 9.6**

*A graphical view of an object as one encapsulated entity.*

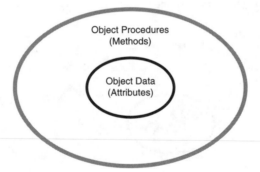

An object presents itself to the world through its published public methods, which form the interface. Take another look at the object `myCar`.

The published methods of the object `myCar` are `park` and `drive`, which are the functions the object `myCar` supports. They are called *public* because the methods are accessible from the outside. They can be invoked by other objects to perform their tasks. The interface of an object is the set of public methods it offers.

The opposite of a public method is a *private* method. Private methods are helper functions for an object. They are used only inside the object itself. Private methods can't be called from the outside. JavaScript has no private methods, so all functions declared in an object are public.

Even the attributes of an object should not be manipulated outside the object. In software engineering, this principle is called *information hiding*. Return to the object `myCar` and extend the list of attributes (`make`, `model`, `age`, and `color`) with additional ones such as `engine` and `wheels`. I'm not particularly interested in the type of engine or what kind of wheels `myCar` has. The only thing that is important to me is that my car works all right and can be driven. If I have a mechanic change the type of car engine, it should not change the working condition of `myCar`. Moreover, the type of new engine doesn't interest me. I only want to drive around with `myCar`.

The abstraction of an object should precede the decisions of its implementation. The source code specifying the inner part of an object should be changeable without interfering with the abstract view. For a better and simpler software design, no part of a complex application should depend on the internal details of any object declared in it.

You can gain a couple of important benefits through encapsulation and information hiding:

- Consider an object a small software component. You could easily use it in many situations and places in a program. Reusing software components is highly supported through encapsulation. Possible reuse is one of the great advantages of object orientation. Rightly used, it could save a lot of time and money in developing software projects.

- Hiding the object's implementation details gives the programmer the opportunity to modify the data representation later without changing the object's representation to the outside world. The same applies to changes inside methods. The object's interface stays the same. The source code of collaborating objects remains the same. This means maintenance efforts are greatly reduced, and the architecture of the software system is far more stable than in conventional applications.

# Messages

If you want an object to do something for you, you send a message to it. A message invokes an object's function. Figure 9.7 illustrates message passing between objects.

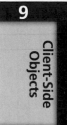

**FIGURE 9.7**
*A graphical view of object messaging.*

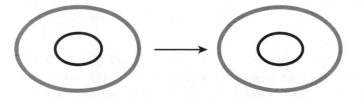

For example, if you need the current time in your application, you create a new object `currTime` of type `Date` and set it to the current date and time:

```
var currTime = new Date();
```

The statement var simply creates a new variable in JavaScript. New objects are created with the new method of the object type. The new method creates a new object of type Date. This new object automatically contains the current date and time. Because of the assignment (=) in the previous statement, the variable currTime contains an object of type Date set with the current date and time.

You might want to extract the current time in hours and minutes:

```
var hours;
var minutes;

hours = currTime.getHours();
minutes = currTime.getMinutes();
```

What you do is send the message getHours to your object currTime to extract the number of hours. Then you use the message getMinutes to get the number of minutes. In JavaScript, messages are essentially function calls. You know from the documentation of the core JavaScript objects that an object of type Date understands the messages getHours and getMinutes. This means the object type Date includes an implementation of the functions getHours() and getMinutes().

When creating custom objects, you define object methods as well. Inside one method, you might need other objects to accomplish a certain task. For example, in a car dealer application, you have an object currSale, resembling a car sale, with a method getSaleData(), extracting data about the sale. Inside the function getSaleData(), you address an object of type Car and another of type Customer. Both objects are sent messages to get the necessary information. If you take this concept further, you'll see that an object-oriented application consists of a world of objects communicating through messages.

## Classes

Objects are concrete, existing software entities in a program. For example, okButton, myWindow, and currTime are all objects. An object is a concrete entity that exists in time and space; a class represents only an abstraction of several similar objects, as shown in Figure 9.8.

Objects with the same properties and behavior form a class or object type. A class features a construction plan for the objects contained in it. This means a class defines the number, name, and structure of data attributes and methods. Additionally, a class provides the behavior (implementation) of the functions. New objects are created due to the primarily defined construction plan. Every object is a member of a certain class; the object is said to be an *instance* of this class. An object property is also called an *instance variable* of a class or an object.

**FIGURE 9.8**
*A graphical view of a class.*

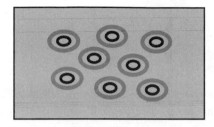

For example, your car, my car, and your neighbor's car are all cars, although they have different makes, ages, and colors. Every car has a make, model name, model year, and color. Moreover, every car can drive or sit in a parking space. The features and possible functions are the same. The class car describes the data characteristics and methods for all cars.

JavaScript is not a class-based, object-oriented language, because there is no class statement. However, JavaScript includes a similar concept: an object type. First, client-side object types include the different GUI objects or core objects such as Date, String, and Math. New objects are created with the new method of the object type. This is true for all objects. The following statement creates the object currTime as a new instance of the object type Date:

```
var currTime = new Date();
```

In JavaScript, you can define your own object type. For example, if your system should display time values, you might want to implement a new object type Clock. A Clock object should know the hours and minutes it is set to, so the properties of the Clock object are hours and minutes. The methods a Clock object should implement are displayTime() and setTime(). The following segment shows the definition of the object type Clock:

```
function Clock(hours, minutes){
  this.hours = hours;
  this.minutes = minutes;
  this.setTime = setTime;
  this.displayTime = displayTime;
}

function setTime(hours, minutes){
  this.hours = hours;
  this.minutes = minutes;
}
```

**9**

**Client-Side Objects**

```
function displayTime(){
  var line = this.hours + ":" + this.minutes;
  document.write ("<hr><p>Time of clock:   " + line);
}
```

JavaScript is an instance-based language, because there is no class construct. *Instance-based* is an object-oriented term that means that the programming language has objects but no classes.

JavaScript is not very well structured in this context. It has no classes, but it does have a concept like an object type. Moreover, new objects aren't constructed through existing objects; instead, they are created with the new statement. Netscape calls JavaScript an instance-based programming language.

I want to point out that the function statement in JavaScript serves many purposes. Creating a new object type means defining a function with the name of the object type as the function name. The result is a source code that always looks a little confusing to the reader. The properties of the new object type are declared as parameters of the defining function. This means there is only one constructor for a new class. As the name already points out, a constructor is a method of a class that creates a new object from the class template. A constructor initializes the new object with the given data values in the parameter part of the constructor method. The following code shows a template for declaring a new object type in JavaScript:

```
function ObjectType(instVar1, instVar2, ...){
  this.property1 = instVar1;
  this.property2 = instVar2;
  ...
  this.method1 = function1;
  this.method2 = function2;
  ...
}


function1 (param1, param2, ...){
  here goes the implementation
}


function2 (param1, param2, ...){
  here goes the implementation
}
```

The special object this addresses the current object in the object type declaration. The properties and methods of the new object are defined with assignments to this. The initial properties for the new object are given as parameters of the creating function; in the template, they are named `instVar1` and `instVar2`. In the object type definition, only the method names (`method1` and `method2`) are present. The implementation for the methods as JavaScript functions (`function1` and `function2`) is given later.

Declarations of new object types are best placed in the <head> section of the HTML document so that they are read at the beginning of the document-loading process. This ensures that the class declarations are known when the rest of the program is interpreted. You usually put the action tasks in the <body> segment of the HTML document.

To give you a better understanding of classes, Listing 9.2 shows a short description of the `Clock` class in a simple but complete HTML document.

**LISTING 9.2**   Creating a `Clock` Object and Displaying the Results on the Page

```
<html>
<head>
  <title>JavaScript Unleashed</title>
  <script type="text/javascript">
  <!--
    function Clock (hours, minutes){
      this.hours = hours;
      this.minutes = minutes;
      this.setTime = setTime;
      this.displayTime = displayTime;
    }

    function setTime (hours, minutes){
      this.hours = hours;
      this.minutes = minutes;
    }

    function displayTime (){
      var line = this.hours + ":" + this.minutes;
      document.write ("<hr>Time of clock:  " + line);
    }
  //-->
  </script>
</head>
<body>
  <script type="text/javascript">
  <!--
    var currTime = new Date();
    var myClock = new Clock(currTime.getHours (), currTime.getMinutes ());
    myClock.displayTime ();
```

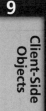

**9**

**Client-Side Objects**

**LISTING 9.2**  continued

```
//-->
</script>
</body>
</html>
```

With the following statement, the new Clock object myClock is created and initialized with the current system time in the <body> section of the document:

```
var myClock = new Clock(currTime.getHours(), currTime.getMinutes());
```

> **Note**
>
> Because JavaScript is an instance-based language, you can extend any existing object with new properties and methods at runtime. This adds a new feature to only one particular object and doesn't affect the other objects of the same object type.

# JavaScript Objects

As discussed at the start of this chapter, JavaScript is not an object-oriented language but an object-based language. It follows the notions of objects, properties, methods, and encapsulation. It is loosely typed, because variables aren't declared in conjunction with an object type. For example, you declare the variable currTime with the following statement:

```
var currTime;
```

You provide no variable type (such as int or char) or other object type. You could put any variable or object type in the variable currTime.

Interpretation is always done through dynamic binding at runtime. Dynamic binding means that the types of all the variables and expressions are not known until the program is executed.

JavaScript doesn't implement the class concept and is, instead, largely instance based. Still more significant is the lack of inheritance. Therefore, JavaScript falls into the category of object-based programming languages.

# Dot Notation

In JavaScript, you access the properties and methods of an object through dot notation. This notation, which is demonstrated in the following syntax example, provides a hierarchy-style method of accessing these properties and implementing the methods.

```
objectName.propertyName
objectName.methodName(arguments)
```

The current object is addressed through the special variable `this`. In the method declaration of an object type (class), you address the object itself with the variable `this`. The object itself, meaning the current object, is the object for which you are declaring the method.

In an object type defining complex numbers, you write a method for adding two complex numbers as follows:

```
// add x + z  giving rz

function add(z){
  var a;
  var b;
  var rz;

  a = this.real + z.getReal(z);
  b = this.img  + z.getImg(z);
  rz = new Complex(a,b);
  return rz;
}
```

The numbers x and y are then summed with the following statement:

```
x.add(y);
```

In the method `add`, the term `this.real` addresses the `real` property of the current object—in this case, `x.real`. Similarly, `this.img` addresses the `img` property—that is, `x.img`, which is the `img` part of x.

# Exploring the JavaScript Object Model

JavaScript objects are truly objects, in the sense that they have properties and methods and can respond to events. However, as you have learned in this chapter, JavaScript doesn't have the same true OOP capabilities of inheritance. When you look at the JavaScript object model, it is critical that you look at it in that context. Rather than a class hierarchy that is inheritance based, the JavaScript object model is a containership hierarchy, as shown in Figure 9.9. If you are experienced in object-oriented programming languages such as Java, C++, or Delphi, this might be the biggest adjustment you need to make in your thinking when developing with JavaScript.

**FIGURE 9.9**

*The JavaScript built-in object model hierarchy.*

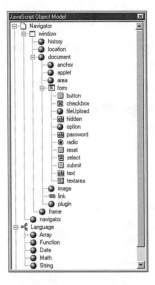

*Containership* is the principle of one object containing another object. If you look again at Figure 9.9, you can see that the relationship between the Form object and the Radio object is not one of ancestor and descendant (or class and subclass), but one of container and contained. Stated differently, there is no bloodline between these objects, because one did not descend from the other. As a result, an object cannot inherit properties and methods from another object, nor can you subclass an object in the hierarchy.

# Containership in JavaScript

Containership is an important term to understand as you develop JavaScript scripts and applications—not only in terms of how one object relates to another, but in practical terms of how you reference an object. Recall from the discussion of dot notation earlier in this chapter that when you reference an object's properties or methods, you use a dot to denote ownership. For example, in the following command, the write method is said to be owned by the Document object:

```
document.write("<h1>A cow jumping over the moon.</h1>");
```

However, you can extend this to include not only properties and methods of an object but also objects contained by that object. If you wanted to return the name of a `Button` object to a variable, you would use the following command:

```
buttonName = document.formMain.okButton.name;
```

`document` is the default name of the `Document` object, and `formMain` is the name of the `Form` object, which contains the `okButton` button.

An important fact to understand when you work with objects is knowing when you need to reference a container object and when you don't. For example, the `Window` object is essentially the highest-level object you work with in your code on the client side. Most of the references you make are to objects within its containership. You could also write the previous `document.write` example like this:

```
window.document.write("<h1>A cow jumping over the moon.</h1>");
```

Although you can ignore the `window` reference in most cases, it is necessary when you deal with multiple windows or frames. For instance, Listing 9.3 creates a `Window` object in the `showStats()` function and then closes it in the `closeWindow()` function.

**LISTING 9.3**   Creating a New Window and Writing Information to It

```
<html>
<head>
  <title>JavaScript Unleashed</title>
  <script type="text/javascript">
  <!--
    var windowObject

    function showStats() {
      windowObject = window.open("", "ViewStats", "toolbar=0,width=300,
          height=50,resizable=1");
      windowObject.document.write("<h2>We outperformed all goals this month.
          Congratulations!</h2>");
    }

    function closeWindow(){
      windowObject.close();
    }
  // -->
  </script>
</head>
<body OnUnload="closeWindow()">
  <h1>
```

**LISTING 9.3**    continued

```
     Click the following button to view the monthly stats.
   </h1>
   <form>
     <input type="button" value="Show Stats" onclick="showStats()">
   </form>
</body>
</html>
```

The `Window` object is the only one that provides any leniency in object references. For example, if you want to reference a form within an HTML page, you must add its parent object (`Document`) for JavaScript to understand which object you are referencing. If you want to reference the first form within the `Document` object and retrieve the number of elements in it, you use the following command:

```
var num = document.forms[0].length;
```

Even if the form had a `name` attribute, you still need to add the parent reference:

```
var num = document.queryForm.length;
```

# Properties

Properties in JavaScript resemble the data attributes of an object. The properties of an object explain the characteristics and identity of the given object. In addition to specific characteristics and identifying values, an object's attributes can also represent the state of the object or a role that an object could play at a given time.

When modeling projects, you could define the object type `Project` as follows:

```
function Project(members, leader, currentMilestone, time){
   this.members = members;
   this.leader = leader;
   this.currentMilestone = currentMilestone;
   this.time =  time;
}
```

You would then create the particular software project `myProject` as follows:

```
var myProject = new Project(memberGroup, "Claudia", "starting", currTime);
```

The object `myProject` consists of a group of persons described in the object `memberGroup`. The project leader is `"Claudia"` and the current milestone is `"starting"` because the project just recently began. The variables `memberGroup` and `currTime` contain other objects that are not described here.

In addition to dot notation, you have other ways to access the properties of an object. The following example shows array notation:

```
objectName["propertyName"]
```

The next line demonstrates indexing through ordinal numbers:

```
objectName[integerIndex]
```

This technique returns the attribute of number `integerIndex`.

Outside an object itself, you might not want to access an object's attributes directly, because it damages the principle of encapsulation. (See the section "Encapsulation," earlier in this chapter.)

# Methods

A method denotes a service the class offers to other objects. Generally, methods belong to one of the following four categories:

- Modifier: A method that changes the state of an object. This method changes the value of one or more data attributes of the object. A popular modifier method is a `set` function that sets the value of one particular object attribute.

- Selector: A method that accesses the data attributes of an object but makes no changes. An important selector is a `get` function that returns (gets) the value of one particular object attribute.

- Iterator: A method that accesses all the parts of an object, such as all the data attributes, in some defined order. As the name denotes, an iterator method iterates over the data attributes of an object.

- Constructor: A constructor is a method of an object type that creates a new object from the class template. A constructor initializes the new object with the given data values in the parameter part of the constructor method.

In JavaScript, object methods are normal JavaScript functions. You access them through dot notation:

```
objectName.functionName(arguments)
```

Generally, an HTML file includes a `<body>` section that creates the special `Document` object in JavaScript. The `Document` object supports the method `write()`. With this method, you can dynamically extend the text layout of your HTML page through JavaScript. The following statement prints the string `This is sample text`:

```
document.write("This is sample text");
```

9

Client-Side
Objects

When constructing new object types in JavaScript, you use a source code template such as the one presented here:

```
function ObjectType(instVar1, instVar2, ...){
  this.property1 = instVar1;
  this.property2 = instVar2;
  ...
  this.method1 = function1;
  this.method2 = function2;
  ...
}

function1(param1, param2, ...){
  here goes the implementation
}

function2(param1, param2, ...){
  here goes the implementation
}
```

The implementation for the object methods is given later in a function declaration following the rules for regular JavaScript functions. The arguments of a function can be strings, numbers, or complete objects. The following segment shows an example of defining a class representing complex numbers:

```
// define complex numbers

function Complex(real, img){
  this.real = real;
  this.img = img;
  this.getReal = getReal;
  this.getImg = getImg;
  this.add = add;
  this.subtract = subtract;
  this.multiply = multiply;
  this.divide = divide;
}

// get real part
function getReal(){
  return this.real;
}

// get img part
```

```
function getImg(){
  return this.img;
}

// add x + z  giving rz
function add(z){
  var a;
  var b;
  var rz;

  a = this.real + z.getReal (z);
  b = this.img  + z.getImg  (z);
  rz = new Complex (a,b);
  return rz;
}

// methods subtract, multiply and divide not yet implemented
```

The object method `add` takes one argument of type `Complex`. You can add two complex numbers x and y as follows:

```
var x = new Complex(a,b);
var y = new Complex(c,d);

var z = x.add(y);
```

Inside a function declaration, you can refer to the properties of the current object with the special object `this`, as shown here:

```
a = this.real + z.getReal (z);
```

## Events

Often, JavaScript statements create or manipulate graphical user interface elements such as forms or windows. Figure 9.10 shows a simple graphical user interface.

Listing 9.4 serves only for generating a form shown in Figure 9.10. Other parts are not fully programmed yet and generally produce `Not yet implemented` messages.

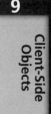

9

Client-Side
Objects

**FIGURE 9.10**

*A graphical user interface.*

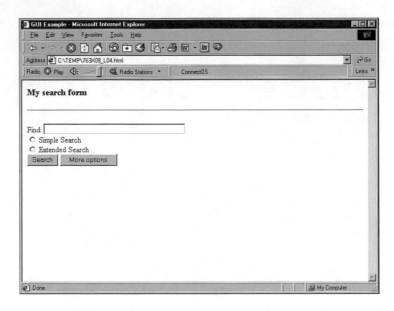

**LISTING 9.4    A Simple GUI**

```html
<html>
<head>
  <title>GUI Example</title>
  <script type="text/javascript">
  <!--

    // search function not yet implemented
    // here: create display of result list
    function fsearch(aForm){
      alert ("Sorry, search function not yet implemented");
    }

    // display of options not yet implemented
    function foptions(aForm){
      alert ("Sorry, no options available");
    }
    //-->
  </script>
</head>
<body>
  <h3>
    My search form
  </h3>
  <hr>
```

**LISTING 9.4**    continued

```
<form>
  Find:
  <input type="text" name="tfield" size="40">
  <br>
  <input type="radio" name="search">
  Simple Search
  <br>
  <input type="radio" name="search">
  Extended Search
  <br>
  <input type="button" name="bsearch" value="Search"
    onclick="fsearch(this.form)">
  <input type="button" name="boptions" value="More options"
    onclick="foptions(this.form)">
</form>
</body>
</html>
```

In the context of a graphical user interface, an event is a result of a user action. It takes place when the user does something. For example, when the user clicks a button on the user interface, a `click` event occurs. Other GUI events include clicking a check box, selecting a string in a list box, double-clicking an item, and opening or closing a window.

The best way to control GUIs is through event-driven programming. Events can be *captured*, or handled by event handlers in JavaScript. See Chapter 14, "Handling Events," for more information.

Generally, events are not considered object-oriented features, although some object-oriented programming languages also support events. Most GUI elements, such as windows, buttons, text fields, and check boxes, react to certain events. These elements exist in JavaScript as built-in object types. For example, you can create a button in JavaScript to trigger the `onClick` event when a button is clicked:

```
<form>
  <input type="button" value="press me" onClick="myfunc()">
</form>
```

In this example, the function `myfunc` is executed when the user clicks the Press Me button. Some built-in objects feature methods that emulate an event. For example, the object type `checkbox` defines a `click()` method that emulates the check box being clicked. The same applies to the object type `Button`. The event-emulation method doesn't trigger an event

9

**Client-Side Objects**

declared elsewhere for the object. If you need an action on the event, you have to handle the event explicitly.

Because event handlers are allowed only for HTML tags, newly created object types have no event handlers. See Chapter 14 on events and event handlers in JavaScript for a more detailed description of this subject.

# Object Breakdown

When you begin to look closely at the overall JavaScript object hierarchy, you can see that most objects are either client-side objects, server-side objects, or core objects. This section of the book takes a look at client-side objects and introduces you to each of the properties and methods within them. Chapter 10 and Chapter 12, "Server-Side JavaScript," will cover the other types of objects that JavaScript contains.

> **Note**
>
> In addition to these three types of objects, Microsoft has also created some extensions to the language for its Windows Script Host. These extensions allow users to access files, move folders, and open applications, in much the same manner as batch files—just more powerfully. Microsoft Extensions are not covered in this book, but they can be found in the book *Pure JavaScript*, also by Sams.

The client-side functionality built into JavaScript centers on what you can do with HTML pages. The first set of objects generally has a correlation to the browser and HTML tags within it. Figure 9.11 shows HTML source code for a Web page and highlights the JavaScript objects in it.

As you can see, most JavaScript objects are object representations of HTML tags. Table 9.1 lists the client-side objects and the corresponding HTML tags.

**FIGURE 9.11**
*Many JavaScript objects match HTML tags.*

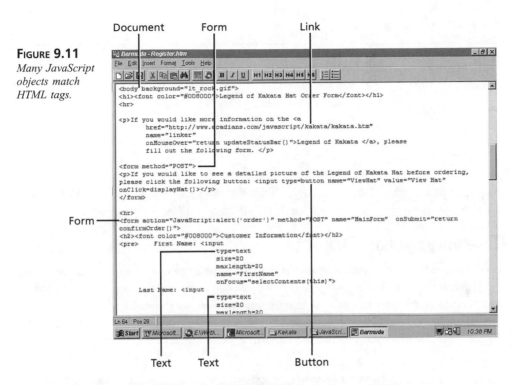

TABLE 9.1   Client-Side JavaScript Objects and HTML Tags That Create Instances of Them

| JavaScript Object | Corresponding HTML Tag |
| --- | --- |
| Button | `<input type="button">` |
| Checkbox | `<input type="checkbox">` |
| Hidden | `<input type="hidden">` |
| Fileupload | `<input type="file">` |
| Password | `<input type="password">` |
| Radio | `<input type="radio">` |
| Reset | `<input type="reset">` |
| Select | `<select>` |
| Frame | `<frame>` |
| Document | `<body>` |
| Layer | `<layer>` or `<ilayer>` |
| Link | `<a href="">` |
| Image | `<img>` |
| Area | `<map>` |
| Anchor | `<a name="">` |
| Applet | `<applet>` |

**9**

**Client-Side Objects**

**TABLE 9.1** continued

| JavaScript Object | Corresponding HTML Tag |
|---|---|
| Plugin | `<embed>` |
| Form | `<form>` |
| Submit | `<input type="submit">` |
| Text | `<input type="text">` |
| Textarea | `<textarea>` |
| Option | `<option>` |

As you explore each of these objects, you'll look at the various ways they are presented to users and developers: user interface view, HTML tag, and JavaScript object code.

## The `navigator` Object

Boldly named by the inventors of JavaScript (Netscape), the `navigator` object represents the browser software in use. Using this object, you can retrieve information about the name and version of the browser, as well as other information, as shown in Figure 9.12. Both Netscape Navigator and Microsoft Internet Explorer support the `navigator` object. The object itself has two child objects: the `Plugin` object and the `Mimetype` object.

**FIGURE 9.12**
*Using the* navigator *object to return information about the browser.*

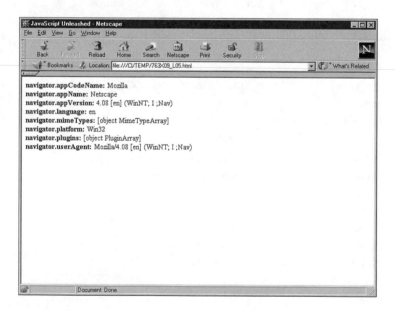

The code I used to retrieve this information is seen in Listing 9.5. Table 9.2 lists the methods and properties of the `navigator` object.

**LISTING 9.5**   Accessing the Properties of the navigator Object

```
<html>
<head>
  <title>JavaScript Unleashed</title>
</head>
<body>
  <script language="JavaScript">
  <!--

    document.write("navigator.appCodeName: ".bold() + navigator.appCodeName
      ➥ + "<br>");
    document.write("navigator.appName: ".bold() + navigator.appName
      ➥ + "<br>");
    document.write("navigator.appVersion: ".bold() + navigator.appVersion
      ➥ + "<br>");
    document.write("navigator.language: ".bold() + navigator.language
      ➥ + "<br>");
    document.write("navigator.mimeTypes: ".bold() + navigator.mimeTypes
      ➥ + "<br>");
    document.write("navigator.platform: ".bold() + navigator.platform
      ➥ + "<br>");
    document.write("navigator.plugins: ".bold() + navigator.plugins
      ➥ + "<br>");
    document.write("navigator.userAgent: ".bold() + navigator.userAgent
      ➥ + "<br>");document.close();

  //--->
  </script>

</body>
</html>
```

**TABLE 9.2**   The Methods and Properties of the navigator Object

| Type | Item | Description |
|------|------|-------------|
| Method | javaEnabled() | Function that tests to see if Java is supported in the browser. This method was added in JavaScript 1.1. |
| | plugins.refresh() | Checks for any newly installed plug-ins. This method was added in JavaScript 1.2. |
| | preference() | Allows reading and setting of various user preferences in the browser. This method was added in JavaScript 1.2. |

9

Client-Side
Objects

TABLE 9.2  continued

| Type | Item | Description |
|---|---|---|
| | `taintEnabled()` | Tests to see if data-tainting is enabled. This method was added in JavaScript 1.1. |
| Property | `appCodeName` | Represents the code name of the browser. |
| | `appName` | Refers to the official browser name. |
| | `appVersion` | Refers to the version information of the browser. |
| | `language` | Refers to the language of the browser. This property was added in JavaScript 1.2. |
| | `mimeTypes` | Refers to an array of `Mimetype` objects that contains all the MIME types that the browser supports. This property was added in JavaScript 1.1. |
| | `platform` | A string representing the platform on which the browser is running. This property was added in JavaScript 1.2. |
| | `plugins` | Refers to an array of `Plugin` objects that contains all the plug-ins installed on the browser. This property was added in JavaScript 1.1. |
| | `userAgent` | A string that represents the user-agent header. |

## The `Mimetype` Object

The multipurpose Internet mail extensions (MIME) object, which is a subobject of the navigator object, was added in JavaScript 1.1. It allows you to access information about the MIME types your plug-ins support. Like the `Plugin` object, it is not supported by Internet Explorer. The properties of the `Mimetype` object are contained in Table 9.3.

TABLE 9.3  Properties of the `Mimetype` Object

| Property | Description |
|---|---|
| `description` | Contains the description of `Mimetype`. |
| `enabledPlugin` | Contains the plug-in for a specific `Mimetype`. |
| `suffixes` | Contains the file extension for `Mimetype`. |
| `type` | Contains the string representation of `Mimetype`. |

## The `Plugin` Object

The `Plugin` object, which was added in JavaScript 1.1 and is not supported by Internet Explorer, is created by having plug-ins installed for the browser. This object contains an array of elements and MIME types handled by each plug-in. It has only properties, as shown in Table 9.4; however, there is a `plugins.refresh()` method of the `navigator` object that allows you to rebuild the plug-in array. Figure 9.13 shows how you can use this object with the `document.write()` method to display information on installed plug-ins.

**TABLE 9.4** Properties of the `Plugin` Object

| Property | Description |
| --- | --- |
| description | Refers to a description of the plug-in. |
| filename | Refers to the filename of a plug-in program. |
| length | Refers to the number of MIME types contained in the array. |
| name | Refers to the plug-in's name. |

**FIGURE 9.13**
*Displaying the installed plug-ins using the* Plugin *object.*

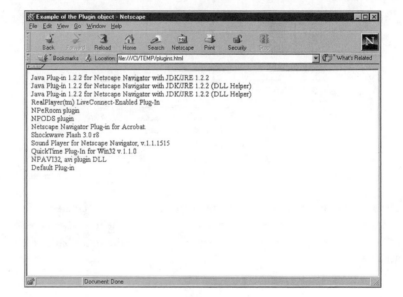

## The `Window` Object

A Web browser—whether it's Netscape Navigator, Microsoft Internet Explorer, or whatever—is presented to the user in a window. Everything a user does with the browser is performed within that window. Moreover, every screen element is also contained inside that window.

The `Window` object provides a direct corollary to this metaphor (see Figure 9.14). It is considered the highest of all objects in the client-side JavaScript object hierarchy and contains all other client-side objects (except for the `navigator` object itself). Just as you

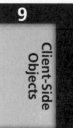

can have multiple windows open in your browser, you can work with multiple `Window` objects at once in your code.

**FIGURE 9.14**

*A* Window *object contains all other elements—both visually and in code.*

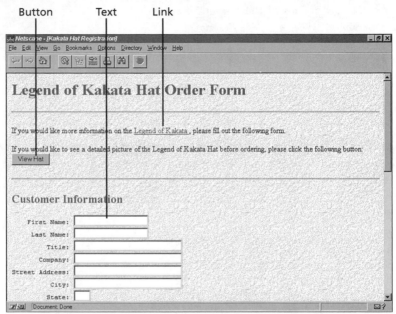

The `Window` object has no HTML tag equivalent, but it is created when a new browser window is opened. Within JavaScript code, you work with a `Window` object as shown in the following example. Suppose you want to add text to the status bar of the window. The code follows:

```
window.status = 'Welcome to my home page.';
```

Like the other objects, the `Window` object has several different properties and methods. Because it is the top-level object, some of these can be called or referenced without having `window.` in front of them. The `alert()` method is an example of this. Table 9.5 lists all the methods and properties of the `Window` object.

**TABLE 9.5**  Properties and Methods of the `Window` Object

| Type | Item | Description |
|------|------|-------------|
| Method | atob() | Decodes a string that has been encoded using base 64 encoding. This method was added in JavaScript 1.2. |
| | alert() | Displays an alert dialog box with the text string passed. |

**TABLE 9.5**    continued

| Type | Item | Description |
|------|------|-------------|
| | back() | Loads the previous page in place of the window instance. This method was added in JavaScript 1.2. |
| | blur() | Removes the focus from a window. |
| | btob() | Encodes a string with base 64 encoding. This method was added in JavaScript 1.2. |
| | captureEvents() | Sets the window to capture all events of a specified type. This method was added in JavaScript 1.2. |
| | clearInterval() | Clears the interval set with the setInterval() method. This method was added in JavaScript 1.2. |
| | clearTimeout() | Clears the timeout set with the setTimeout() method. |
| | close() | Closes the instance of the window. This method was added in JavaScript 1.1. |
| | confirm() | Displays a confirmation dialog box. |
| | crypto.random() | Generates a random string of data whose length is specified by the number of bytes passed. This method was added in JavaScript 1.2. |
| | crypto.signText() | Returns a string of encoded data that represents a signed object. This method was added in JavaScript 1.2. |
| | disableExternalCapture() | Disables external event capturing. This method was added in JavaScript 1.2. |
| | enableExternalCapture() | Enables external event capturing for the pages loaded from other servers. This method was added in JavaScript 1.2. |
| | find() | Displays a Find dialog box in which the user can enter text to search the current page. This method was added in JavaScript 1.2. |
| | focus() | Assigns the focus to the specified window instance. This method was added in JavaScript 1.1. |
| | forward() | Loads the next page in place of the window instance. This method was added in JavaScript 1.2. |
| | handleEvent() | Invokes the handler for the event passed. This method was added in JavaScript 1.2. |

**9**

**Client-Side Objects**

**TABLE 9.5** continued

| Type | Item | Description |
| --- | --- | --- |
| | home() | Loads the user's specified home page in place of the window instance. This method was added in JavaScript 1.2. |
| | moveBy() | Moves the window by the specified amount. This method was added in JavaScript 1.2. |
| | moveTo() | Moves the window to the specified location. This method was added in JavaScript 1.2. |
| | open() | Opens a new instance of a window. |
| | print() | Invokes the Print dialog box so the user can print the current window. This method was added in JavaScript 1.2. |
| | prompt() | Displays a prompt dialog box. |
| | releaseEvents() | Releases the captured events of a specified type. This method was added in JavaScript 1.2. |
| | resizeBy() | Resizes the window by the specified amount. This method was added in JavaScript 1.2. |
| | resizeTo() | Resizes the window to the specified size. This method was added in JavaScript 1.2. |
| | routeEvent() | Passes the events of a specified type to be handled natively. This method was added in JavaScript 1.2. |
| | scroll() | Scrolls the document in the window to a specified location. This method was added in JavaScript 1.1. |
| | scrollBy() | Scrolls the document in the window by a specified amount. This method was added in JavaScript 1.2. |
| | scrollTo() | Scrolls the document's width and height to a specified location in the window. This method was added in JavaScript 1.2. |
| | setHotKeys() | Allows you to toggle on or off the window hotkeys when no menus are present. This method was added in JavaScript 1.2. |
| | setInterval() | Invokes a function or evaluates an expression every time the number of milliseconds has passed. This method was added in JavaScript 1.2. |
| | setResizable() | Allows you to specify whether a user can resize a window. This method was added in JavaScript 1.2. |
| | setTimeout() | Invokes a function or evaluates an expression when the number of milliseconds has passed. |

TABLE **9.5** continued

| Type | Item | Description |
|------|------|-------------|
| | setZOptions() | Allows you to specify the z-order stacking of a window. This method was added in JavaScript 1.2. |
| | stop() | Stops the current window from loading another item within it. This method was added in JavaScript 1.2. |
| Property | closed | Specifies if the window instance has been closed. |
| | crypto | Allows access to Navigator's encryption features. This property was added in JavaScript 1.2. |
| | defaultStatus | Specifies the default message in the window's status bar. |
| | document | References all the information about the document within this window. See the Document object for more information. |
| | frames | References all the information about the frames within this window. See the Frame object for more information. |
| | history | References the URLs the user has visited. This property was added in JavaScript 1.1. |
| | innerHeight | Contains the height in pixels of the display area of the current window. This property was added in JavaScript 1.2. |
| | innerWidth | Contains the width in pixels of the display area of the current window. This property was added in JavaScript 1.2. |
| | length | Represents the number of frames in the current window. |
| | location | Contains the current URL loaded into the window. |
| | locationbar | Refers to the browser's location bar. This property was added in JavaScript 1.2. |
| | locationbar.visible | Contains Boolean value that tells you if the location bar on the user's browser is visible. This property was added in JavaScript 1.2. |
| | menubar | Refers to the browser's menu bar. This property was added in JavaScript 1.2. |
| | menubar.visible | Contains Boolean value that tells you if the menu bar on the user's browser is visible. This property was added in JavaScript 1.2. |
| | name | Contains the name of the window. |

**9**

**Client-Side Objects**

**TABLE 9.5** continued

| Type | Item | Description |
|---|---|---|
| | offscreenBuffering | Contains a Boolean value that allows you to determine if any window updates are performed in an off screen buffer. This property was added in JavaScript 1.2. |
| | opener | Contains the name of the window from which a second window was opened. |
| | outerHeight | Contains the height in pixels of the outer area of the current window. This property was added in JavaScript 1.2. |
| | outerWidth | Contains the width in pixels of the outer area of the current window. This property was added in JavaScript 1.2. |
| | pageXOffset | Contains the x-coordinate of the current window. This property was added in JavaScript 1.2. |
| | pageYOffset | Contains the y-coordinate of the current window. This property was added in JavaScript 1.2. |
| | parent | Refers to the uppermost window that is displaying the current frame. |
| | personalbar | Reference to the browser's personal bar. This property was added in JavaScript 1.2. |
| | personalbar.visible | Contains Boolean value that tells you if the personal bar on the user's browser is visible . This property was added in JavaScript 1.2. |
| | screenX | Refers to the browser's x-coordinate at the left edge of the window. This property was added in JavaScript 1.2. |
| | screenY | Refers to the browser's y-coordinate at the top edge of the window. This property was added in JavaScript 1.2. |
| | scrollbars | Refers to the browser's scrollbars. This property was added in JavaScript 1.2. |
| | scrollbars.visible | Contains Boolean value that tells you if the scrollbars on the user's browser are visible. This property was added in JavaScript 1.2. |
| | self | Refers to the current window. |
| | status | Refers to the message in the window's status bar. |
| | statusbar | Refers to the browser's status bar. This property was added in JavaScript 1.2. |

**TABLE 9.5**  continued

| Type | Item | Description |
|------|------|-------------|
| | `statusbar.visible` | Contains Boolean value that tells you if the status bar on the user's browser is visible. This property was added in JavaScript 1.2. |
| | `toolbar` | Refers to the browser's toolbar. This property was added in JavaScript 1.2. |
| | `toolbar.visible` | Contains Boolean value that tells you if the toolbar on the user's browser is visible. This property was added in JavaScript 1.2. |
| | `top` | Refers to the uppermost window that is displaying the current frame. |
| | `window` | Refers to the current window. |

# Top-Level Objects

The `Window` object, the top-level client-side object, contains four child objects. These objects lay the foundation for all of the other objects that you will work with on a daily basis when programming in JavaScript. It is important to know these objects and how they function together. They are as follows:

- `Document`
- `Frame`
- `History`
- `Location`

## The `Document` Object

Although the `Window` object is the top-level object in the hierarchy, the `Document` object is arguably the most important. The `Document` object, shown in Figure 9.15, is responsible for all the actual content displayed on a given page. You can work with the `Document` object to display dynamic HTML pages. Also contained within the document are all the typical user interface (UI) elements of a Web application. Table 9.6 contains the methods and properties of the `Document` object.

9

Client-Side
Objects

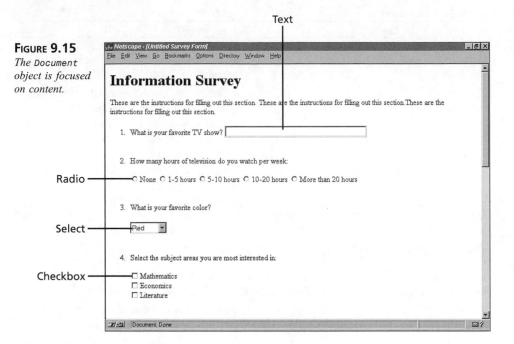

**FIGURE 9.15**
*The Document object is focused on content.*

**TABLE 9.6   Methods and Properties of the Document Object**

| Type | Item | Description |
|------|------|-------------|
| Methods | captureEvents() | Captures events to be handled by the document. This method was added in JavaScript 1.2. |
| | close() | Closes output stream to the document. |
| | contextual() | Allows you to selectively apply a style to an HTML element that appears in a specific context. This method was added in JavaScript 1.2. |
| | getSelection() | Returns the selected text. This method was added in JavaScript 1.2. |
| | handleEvent() | Invokes the handler for the specified event. This method was added in JavaScript 1.2. |
| | open() | Opens output stream to document. |
| | releaseEvents() | Releases events captured by the document. This method was added in JavaScript 1.2. |
| | routeEvent() | Routes captured events to other objects. This method was added in JavaScript 1.2. |
| | write() | Appends text to the document. |
| | writeln() | Appends text and a newline character to the document. |

**TABLE 9.6** continued

| *Type* | *Item* | *Description* |
| --- | --- | --- |
| Property | alinkColor | Color of an activated link. |
| | all | Array of all HTML tags in the document. This method was added in JScript 3.0. |
| | anchors | Array of Anchor objects. This property was added in JavaScript 1.2. |
| | applets | Array of Applet objects. This property was added in JavaScript 1.1. |
| | bgcolor | Background color of the document. |
| | classes | Style sheet classes array. This property was added in JavaScript 1.2. |
| | cookie | Cookie associated with the document. |
| | domain | Domain of the document. This property was added in JavaScript 1.1. |
| | embeds | Array of embedded objects. This property was added in JavaScript 1.1. |
| | fgcolor | Color of text in the document. |
| | forms | Array of Form objects. |
| | formName | Specifies Form instance, which is accessed by using the value of the name attribute in the `<form>` tag. This property was added in JavaScript 1.1. |
| | height | Specifies height in pixels of the document. This property was added in JavaScript 1.2. |
| | ids | Style sheet IDs array. This property was added in JavaScript 1.2. |
| | images | Array of Image objects. This property was added in JavaScript 1.2. |
| | lastModified | Date when the document was last modified. |
| | layers | Array of Layer objects. This property was added in JavaScript 1.2. |
| | linkColor | Color of links. |
| | links | Array of Link objects. |
| | plugins | Array of embedded objects. This property was added in JavaScript 1.1. |
| | referrer | URL of the document to which the current document was linked. |
| | tags | Style sheet tag array. This property was added in JavaScript 1.2. |
| | title | Title of the document. |

**9**

Client-Side
Objects

**TABLE 9.6** continued

| Type | Item | Description |
| --- | --- | --- |
| | URL | URL of the current document. This property was added in JavaScript 1.1. |
| | vlinkColor | Color of visited links. |
| | width | Specifies width in pixels of the document. This property was added in JavaScript 1.2. |

> **Note**
>
> Many of the properties above have subproperties and submethods. You should refer to Netscape's (http://developer.netscape.com) or Microsoft's (http://msdn.microsoft.com) documentation for more information on these.

A common use of the Document object is to generate HTML pages through JavaScript. You can do this using the document.write() or document.writeln() method. For example, the following code displays the HTML text specified as the method parameter:

```
<html>
<body>
  <script type="text/javascript">
  <!--
    document.write("<h1>Text created by JavaScript</h1>");
  //-->
  </script>
</body>
</html>
```

## The Frame Object

As you will learn in this book, frames are especially important objects to use to enhance the presentation of your Web application. The Frame object represents a frame within a frameset. In a multiframe presentation, your Window object is the page that contains the <frameset> definition, whereas the other pages are considered frames in that context. Table 9.7 contains the methods and properties of the Frame object.

**TABLE 9.7** Methods and Properties of the `Frame` Object

| Type | Item | Description |
|------|------|-------------|
| Method | `blur()` | Removes focus from the frame. This method was added in JavaScript 1.1. |
| | `clearInterval()` | Cancels a repeated execution. This method was added in JavaScript 1.2. |
| | `clearTimeout()` | Cancels any delayed execution. |
| | `focus()` | Applies focus to a frame. This method was added in JavaScript 1.1. |
| | `print()` | Invokes the Print dialog box. This method was added in JavaScript 1.2. |
| | `setInterval()` | Sets function schedule for repeated execution. This method was added in JavaScript 1.2. |
| | `setTimeout()` | Sets function schedule for delayed execution. |
| Property | `document` | Current document loaded within a frame. |
| | `frames` | Array containing references to child frames. |
| | `length` | Length of the frames array. |
| | `name` | name attribute of the `<frame>` tag. |
| | `parent` | Main window or frame from which child frames are created. |
| | `self` | Refers to the current frame. |
| | `top` | Browser window that executes script. |
| | `window` | Refers to current window or frame. |

## The `History` Object

A long-time feature in browser software is the capability to track where you have surfed within a given session. This feature has come to be known as a *history list*, and the `History` object is the JavaScript equivalent to this list. You can work with it as a user might, moving forward or backward in a list to navigate where a user has been.

Suppose you want to go back two pages in your history list when the user clicks a button. The event handler for that button could call a function that looks like the following. All of the methods and properties of this object are shown in Table 9.8.

```
<script type="text/javascript">
<!--
  function goBackTwoPages() {
    window.history.go(-2);
  }
//-->
</script>
```

**9**

**Client-Side Objects**

**TABLE 9.8**    Methods and Properties of the History Object

| Type | Item | Description |
|------|------|-------------|
| Method | back() | Loads the last URL in the history list. |
| | forward() | Loads the next URL in the history list, assuming you have gone back at some point. |
| | go() | Loads a URL from the history list by using the offset passed. |
| Property | current | Refers to the current URL in the history list. This property was added in JavaScript 1.1. |
| | length | Returns the number of entries in the history list. |
| | next | Refers to the next URL in the history list. This property was added in JavaScript 1.1. |
| | previous | Refers to the previous URL in the history list. This property was added in JavaScript 1.1. |

# The Location Object

The Web is all about content presentation. Every Window object is designed to display content to the user, but that content must come from somewhere. The origin of the page is thus contained in the Location object. This object is used to store all URL information for a given window. Although users see URL information in the location box onscreen, as shown in Figure 9.16, you can work with that same information with the Location object.

If you want to retrieve the protocol portion of the current URL and evaluate it, you use the following:

```
<script type="text/javascript">
<!--
  function evalProtocol(){
    curProtocol = window.location.protocol;
    if (curProtocol == "http:"){
      alert("The document comes from the Web.");
    }else{
      if (curProtocol == "file:"){
        alert("This document comes from your hard drive.");
      }else{
        alert("This document comes from somewhere else.");
      }
    }
  }
//-->
</script>
```

Location

**FIGURE 9.16**
*Users work with the location box, and you can work with the* Location *object.*

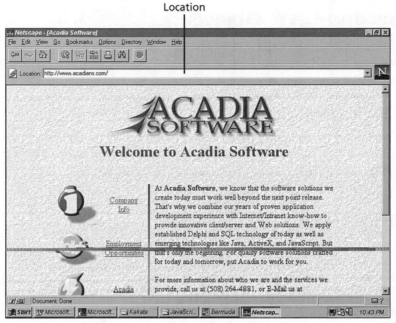

The methods and properties of this object can be seen in Table 9.9.

**TABLE 9.9   Methods and Properties of the** Location **Object**

| Type | Item | Description |
|------|------|-------------|
| Method | reload() | Reloads the current URL in the browser window. This method was added in JavaScript 1.1. |
|  | replace() | Loads the new page passed in the current browser. This method was added in JavaScript 1.1. |
| Property | hash | Represents an anchor name in the URL that begins with the # character. |
|  | host | Represents the hostname and port number of the URL. |
|  | hostname | Represents the hostname part of the URL. |
|  | href | Represents the complete URL. |
|  | pathname | Represents the PATH_INFO part of the URL. |
|  | port | Represents the port part of the URL. |
|  | protocol | Represents the protocol part of the URL. |
|  | search | The search part of the URL, including the ?. |

**9**

**Client-Side Objects**

# Second-Level Objects

Just as there are subobjects of the Window object, we have second level objects of the Document object. In this section of the chapter we will look at these objects and how they are used.

## The Anchor Object

The Anchor object is text or an image in the HTML page that can be the target of a hypertext link. In practical terms, you use this object very little with JavaScript, making it perhaps the least important of all client-side objects. See Table 9.10 for a list of the properties of this object.

**TABLE 9.10**   Properties of the Anchor Object

| Property | Description |
| --- | --- |
| name | A name that provides access to the anchor from a link. |
| text | The text that appears between the <a> and </a> tags. |
| x | The x-coordinate of the anchor. |
| y | The y-coordinate of the anchor. |

## The Area Object

The Area object, which was also added in JavaScript 1.1, lets you define an area of an image as an imagemap. An <area>'s href attribute is loaded in a target window when a specified location is clicked by the user. Table 9.11 shows the properties and methods of this object.

**TABLE 9.11**   Methods and Properties of the Area Object

| Type | Item | Description |
| --- | --- | --- |
| Method | handleEvent() | Calls the event handler associated with this event. This method was added in JavaScript 1.2. |
| Property | hash | The portion of the URL that is the anchor, including the # symbol. |
| | host | The hostname (IP address) and port specified in the URL. |
| | hostname | The hostname specified within the URL. |
| | href | The entire URL. |
| | pathname | The path of the file specified in the URL, beginning with the / symbol. |
| | port | The port specified in the URL. |
| | protocol | The protocol specified in the URL, including the ending colon (:). |

**TABLE 9.11** continued

| Type | Item | Description |
|------|------|-------------|
| | search | The search part of the URL, including the beginning question mark (?). |
| | target | The name of the target window in which the URL should be displayed. |
| | text | The text that appears between the <area> and </area> tags. |
| | x | The x-coordinate of the area. |
| | y | The y-coordinate of the area. |

## The `Applet` Object

The `Applet` object, which was added in JavaScript 1.1, represents the JavaScript equivalent of the <applet> HTML tag. In a generic sense, these JavaScript objects have no methods associated with them, but that is really irrelevant, because you can use JavaScript to access the specific methods of a given Java applet. Because of this, the properties of the `Applet` object are all public fields of a Java applet, and the methods are all public methods.

## The `Form` Object

Forget for a moment such add-ins as Java applets or ActiveX controls that can interact with the user. If you think only in terms of the HTML world, the only way to interact with the user is through a form and its elements (see Figure 9.17). Forms give life to static pages by providing an interface users can interact with through controls. You can place only a button, text, or other UI object within the confines of a form. The `Form` object is your means of interacting with this HTML element in your scripts. Table 9.12 contains the methods and properties of the `Form` object.

**TABLE 9.12** Methods and Properties of the `Form` Object

| Type | Item | Description |
|------|------|-------------|
| Method | handleEvent() | Calls the event handler associated with this event. This method was added in JavaScript 1.2. |
| | reset() | Resets form elements to their default values. This method was added in JavaScript 1.1. |
| | submit() | Triggers a submit event to tell the browser to send the data to the server program specified in the action attribute of the <form> tag. |
| Property | action | Contains the action attribute of a <form> instance. |
| | elements | Array contain all the elements within <form>. |
| | encoding | Contains the enctype attribute of a <form> instance. |

9

Client-Side
Objects

**TABLE 9.12**   continued

| Type | Item | Description |
|------|------|-------------|
| | length | Number of elements contained in the form. |
| | method | Contains the method attribute of a `<form>` instance. |
| | name | Contains the name attribute of a `<form>` instance. |
| | target | Contains the target attribute of a `<form>` instance. |

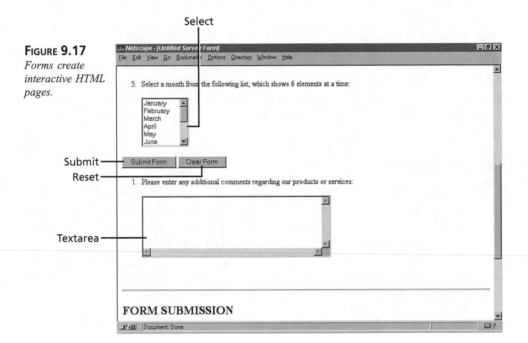

**FIGURE 9.17**
*Forms create interactive HTML pages.*

## The `Image` Object

An `Image` object is an encapsulation of an HTML image. Perhaps the most effective use of this object type is to cache images you want to display. You can construct an `Image` object in your code and download the image data from the server before it is needed for display by the browser. When the image is requested, you can pull the image from cache rather than from the server. Table 9.13 contains the methods and properties of the `Image` object.

**TABLE 9.13**   Methods and Properties of the Image Object

| Type | Item | Description |
|------|------|-------------|
| Method | handleEvent() | This method invokes the handler for the specified event. This method was added in JavaScript 1.2. |
| Property | border | Width of border around the image. |
| | complete | Tells you if the image has finished loading. |
| | height | Height of the image. |
| | hspace | Padding on left and right of the image. |
| | lowsrc | Alternate image for low-resolution displays. |
| | name | Name of the image. |
| | src | URL of the image. |
| | vspace | Padding on top and bottom of the image. |
| | width | Width of the image. |

# The Layer Object

The Layer object, which was added in JavaScript 1.2 and is supported only by Navigator browsers, allows JavaScript to access *layers* within the document. Refer to Part III of this book, "Scripting the Document Object Model," for more information on layers and how they work inside a browser. Additionally, you can check out Chapter 23, "Layers," for more information on using this object. See Table 9.14 for a list of methods and properties of the Layer object.

**TABLE 9.14**   Methods and Properties of the Layer Object

| Type | Item | Description |
|------|------|-------------|
| Method | captureEvents() | Specifies the event types to capture. |
| | handleEvent() | Invokes handler for specified event. |
| | load() | Loads a new URL. |
| | moveAbove() | Moves the layer above another layer. |
| | moveBelow() | Moves the layer below another layer. |
| | moveBy() | Moves the layer to a specified position. |
| | moveTo() | Moves the top-left corner of the window to the specified screen coordinates. |
| | moveToAbsolute() | Changes the layer position to the specified pixel coordinates within the page. |
| | releaseEvents() | Sets the layer to release captured events of the specified type. |
| | resizeBy() | Resizes the layer by the specified height and width values. |
| | resizeTo() | Resizes the layer to have the specified height and width values. |

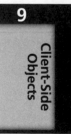

TABLE 9.14   continued

| Type | Item | Description |
|------|------|-------------|
| | routeEvent() | Passes a captured event along the normal event hierarchy. |
| Property | above | Specifies the layer above. |
| | background | Refers to the background image of the layer. |
| | below | Specifies the layer below. |
| | bgColor | Refers to the background color of the layer. |
| | clip.bottom | Refers to the bottom of the layer's clipping area. |
| | clip.height | Refers to the height of the layer's clipping area. |
| | clip.left | Refers to the left of the layer's clipping area. |
| | clip.right | Refers to the right of the layer's clipping area. |
| | clip.top | Refers to the top of the layer's clipping area. |
| | clip.width | Refers to the width of the layer's clipping area. |
| | document | Refers to the Document object that contains the layer. |
| | left | Refers to the x-coordinate of the layer. |
| | name | Refers to the name of the layer. |
| | pageX | Refers to the x-coordinate relative to the document. |
| | pageY | Refers to the y-coordinate relative to the document. |
| | parentLayer | Refers to the containing layer. |
| | siblingAbove | Refers to the layer above in the zIndex. |
| | siblingBelow | Refers to the layer below in the zIndex. |
| | src | Refers to the source URL for the layer. |
| | top | Refers to the y-coordinate of the layer. |
| | visibility | Refers to the visibility state of the layer. |
| | window | Refers to the Window or Frame object that contains the layer. |
| | x | Refers to the x-coordinate of the layer. |
| | y | Refers to the y-coordinate of the layer. |
| | zIndex | Refers to the relative z-order of this layer with respect to its siblings. |

## The Link Object

Lest you forget, the whole reason the Web was developed back in 1989 was the simple hypertext link of an HTML page. Perhaps overlooked in the latest Web application craze, the link remains the very heart of Web technology. The Link object lets you work with links in JavaScript code. Because a link simply references another HTML page or other destination, it's very similar to the Location object (which contains the same information for the current HTML page). The methods and properties of this object are shown in Table 9.15.

**TABLE 9.15** Methods and Properties of the Link Object

| Type | Item | Description |
|------|------|-------------|
| Method | handleEvent() | Invokes the handler for the specified event. This method was added in JavaScript 1.2. |
| Property | hash | Represents an anchor name in the URL for the link, which begins with the # character. |
| | host | Represents the host portion of the URL associated with a link. |
| | hostname | Represents the hostname portion of the URL associated with a link. |
| | href | Represents the complete URL associated with a link. |
| | pathname | Represents the pathname portion of the link URL. |
| | port | Represents the port portion of the URL link. |
| | protocol | Specifies the protocol portion of the URL link. |
| | search | Represents the query portion of the URL link. |
| | target | Represents the name of the Window object in which the link is displayed. |
| | text | The text used to create the link. This property was added in JavaScript 1.2. |
| | x | Refers to the x-coordinate of the link. |
| | y | Refers to the y-coordinate of the link. |

## The Plugin Object

Much like the Applet object, the Plugin object is a way to access all of the plug-ins currently installed in the browser. Do note that this object, which was added in JavaScript 1.1, is not supported by Internet Explorer. Table 9.16 contains the properties of this object.

**TABLE 9.16** Properties of the Plugin Object

| Property | Description |
|----------|-------------|
| description | Contains the description of the plug-in. |
| filename | Contains the filename of a plug-in program. |
| length | Contains the number of MIME types supported by the plug-in. |
| name | Contains the name of the plug-in. |

# Third-Level Objects

The next level of objects contained in client-side JavaScript is what I call the third-level objects. All of these objects are subobjects of the Form object. In much the same manner that you nest HTML elements inside the beginning and ending <form> tags, these objects are nested inside the Form object.

## The Button Object

Unless you jumped into Web development from a character-based environment, you're undoubtedly familiar with pushbuttons. JavaScript has three "button" objects: Button, Submit, and Reset. Each of these has an object representation of the HTML tag.

The Button object is a generic button to which you need to add code in order for it to be useful, while the other two have specific purposes. However, it is possible to use a Button object to serve the same role as the Submit object (by calling Form.submit()) or the Reset object (by calling Form.reset()). Table 9.17 contains the methods and properties of the Button object.

---

**Tip**

The width of the button is determined by the length of the text within the value parameter. To enlarge a button's width, add spaces around the text as follows:

```
<INPUT type=button value="  OK  " onClick="doThis()">
```

---

**TABLE 9.17**   Methods and Properties of the Button Object

| Type | Item | Description |
| --- | --- | --- |
| Method | blur() | Removes focus from the button. This method was added in JavaScript 1.1. |
| | click() | Invokes a click event for that button. |
| | focus() | Applies focus to a button. This method was added in JavaScript 1.1. |
| | handleEvent() | Passes an event to the appropriate event handler associated with a button. This method was added in JavaScript 1.2. |
| Property | form | Returns the Form object of which the button is a member. |
| | name | Returns the string that is specified in the name attribute of the HTML <input> tag. |

**TABLE 9.17** continued

| Type | Item | Description |
|---|---|---|
| | type | Returns the string that is specified in the type attribute of the HTML <input> tag. This string is always button for the Button object. This property was added in JavaScript 1.1. |
| | value | Returns the string that appears in the graphical representation of a button. |

## The Checkbox Object

Another industry-wide standard user interface (UI) control is the check box. This element allows the user to specify a yes/no or true/false value by clicking a check box. Table 9.18 contains the properties and methods of the Checkbox object.

**TABLE 9.18** Methods and Properties of the Checkbox Object

| Type | Item | Description |
|---|---|---|
| Method | blur() | Removes focus from the check box. This method was added in JavaScript 1.1. |
| | click() | Calls the check box's onClick event handler. This method was added in JavaScript 1.1. |
| | focus() | Applies focus to this check box. |
| | handleEvent() | Passes an event to the appropriate event handler associated with the check box. This method was added in JavaScript 1.2. |
| Property | checked | Returns a Boolean value that determines if the check box is checked. |
| | defaultChecked | Returns a Boolean value that holds the initial state of the check box. This value is set with the checked attribute. |
| | form | Returns the Form object of the check box. |
| | name | Returns a string that is specified in the name attribute of the HTML <input> tag. |
| | type | Returns a string that is specified in the type attribute of the HTML <input> tag. This string is always checkbox for the Checkbox object. This property was added in JavaScript 1.1. |
| | value | Returns a value returned when the form is submitted. |

9

Client-Side
Objects

## The `FileUpload` Object

The `FileUpload` object, which was added in JavaScript 1.1, is the equivalent to the HTML file upload element. You can't do much with this object in JavaScript, however, other than reference its properties. The `FileUpload` object has no real methods to act on. Table 9.19 contains the properties of the `FileUpload` object.

**TABLE 9.19**   Methods and Properties of the `FileUpload` Object

| *Type* | *Item* | *Description* |
|---|---|---|
| Method | `blur()` | Removes focus from the FileUpload box. |
| | `focus()` | Sets focus on the FileUpload box. |
| | `handleEvent()` | Invokes the default handler for the specified event. This method was added in JavaScript 1.2. |
| | `select()` | Selects input area for the FileUpload box. |
| Property | `name` | Contains the value of the name attribute for the FileUpload box. |
| | `form` | Reference the Form object containing the FileUpload box. |
| | `type` | Contains the value of the type attribute for the FileUpload box. |
| | `value` | String specifying the pathname of the selected file. |

## The `Hidden` Object

Another field object, the `Hidden` object, is like a text object with a `visible` property set to `false`. It's used to store values to pass to a server process. The `Hidden` object comes from the pre-JavaScript days of HTML, when there were no such things as variables, arrays, or objects to store values. Although you might still want to employ them for transferring data among pages of a multiple-page data entry application, much of the data storage value of `Hidden` objects is no longer needed with JavaScript. Table 9.20 contains the properties of the `Hidden` object.

**TABLE 9.20**   Properties of the `Hidden` Object

| *Property* | *Description* |
|---|---|
| `form` | Specifies the form containing the Hidden object. |
| `name` | Contains the name of the Hidden object. |
| `type` | Contains the value of the type attribute of the Hidden object. This property was added in JavaScript 1.1. |
| `value` | Contains the value of the value attribute of the Hidden object. |

## The `Password` Object

If JavaScript supported inheritance, the `Password` object would be a subclass of the `Text` object. The only difference between the two is that all the characters entered into the `Password` object are displayed as asterisks so as not to reveal their value. Table 9.21 contains the methods and properties of the `Password` object.

**TABLE 9.21** Methods and Properties of the `Password` Object

| Type | Item | Description |
|------|------|-------------|
| Method | `blur()` | Removes focus from the password box. |
| | `focus()` | Sets focus to the password box. |
| | `handleEvent()` | Invokes the default handler for the specified event. This method was added in JavaScript 1.2. |
| | `select()` | Selects the text entered in the password box. |
| Property | `defaultValue` | Refers to the `value` attribute of the HTML password box. |
| | `form` | Refers to the form that contains the password box. |
| | `name` | Refers to the `name` attribute of the HTML password box. |
| | `type` | Refers to the `type` attribute of the HTML password box. This property was added in JavaScript 1.1. |
| | `value` | Refers to the current contents of the password box. |

## The `Radio` Object

Radio buttons are mutually exclusive controls, such that if one radio button is selected, all other buttons in the set become unselected. The `Radio` object provides this element in an HTML form. You define a set of radio buttons by giving them the same `name` property. Table 9.22 contains the properties and methods of the `Radio` object.

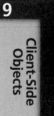

> **Note**
>
> Radio buttons are grouped based on a common `name` property.

9

Client-Side
Objects

TABLE 9.22  Methods and Properties of the Radio Object

| Type | Item | Description |
|------|------|-------------|
| Method | blur() | Removes focus from the Radio object. |
| | click() | Simulates a mouse click on the button. |
| | focus() | Sets the focus to a button. |
| | handleEvent() | Invokes the default handler for the specified event. This method was added in JavaScript 1.2. |
| Property | checked | Specifies whether a button is checked or unchecked. |
| | defaultChecked | Refers to the checked attribute of the HTML <input> tag. |
| | form | Refers to the Form object that contains the Radio object. |
| | name | Refers to the name attribute of the HTML <input> tag. |
| | type | Refers to the type attribute of the HTML <input> tag. |
| | value | Refers to the value attribute of the HTML <input> tag. |

## The Reset Object

The second kind of button-related object is the Reset object, which was added in JavaScript 1.2. When pressed, this object fires an event that resets all the values in a form to their original values. Table 9.23 is a list of the objects and properties of this object.

TABLE 9.23  Methods and Properties of the Reset Object

| Type | Item | Description |
|------|------|-------------|
| Method | blur() | Removes focus from the button. |
| | click() | Simulates a mouse click on the button. |
| | focus() | Sets the focus to the button. |
| | handleEvent() | Passes an event to the appropriate event handler associated with a button. This method was added in JavaScript 1.2. |
| Property | form | Returns the Form object of which the button is a member. |
| | name | Contains the name attribute for the button. |
| | type | Contains the type attribute for the button. |
| | value | Contains the value attribute for the button. |

# The `Submit` Object

The final button-related object is the `Submit` object. This object, when pressed, fires an event that submits all the values in a form to the program specified in the `action` attribute of the `<form>` tag. Table 9.24 is a list of the methods and properties of this object.

**TABLE 9.24**   Methods and Properties of the `Submit` Object

| Type | Item | Description |
|------|------|-------------|
| Method | blur() | Removes focus from the Submit button. This method was added in JavaScript 1.1. |
| | click() | Simulates a mouse click on the Submit button. |
| | focus() | Gives the focus to the Submit button. This method was added in JavaScript 1.1. |
| | handleEvent() | Invokes the handler for the event specified; was added in JavaScript 1.2. |
| Property | form | Returns the entire form the Submit button is in. |
| | name | Returns the name of the Submit button specified by the `name` attribute. |
| | type | Returns the type of this Submit button, specified by the `type` attribute. This property always returns submit. This property was added in JavaScript 1.1. |
| | value | Returns the value of this Submit button, specified by the `value` attribute. |

# The `Select` Object

Another common control in windowed environments is a drop-down list or selection list box, both of which let the user select from a predefined list of values. The difference is that the user can select only one value from a drop-down list, whereas he can select multiple choices from a selection list. The `Select` object encapsulates the behavior of both of these UI elements. In other words, it can appear as a drop-down list (default) or a selection list (if its `multiple` property is set to `true`). Table 9.25 contains the properties and methods of the `Select` object.

**TABLE 9.25**   Methods and Properties of the `Select` Object

| Type | Item | Description |
|------|------|-------------|
| Method | blur() | Removes the focus from the select box. |
| | focus() | Gives the focus to the select box. |
| | handleEvent() | Invokes the handler for the event specified; was added in JavaScript 1.2. |
| Property | form | Returns the entire form the select box is in. |

**TABLE 9.25** continued

| Type | Item | Description |
|------|------|-------------|
| | length | Returns the number of options in the select box. |
| | name | Returns the name of this select box, specified by the name attribute. |
| | options | Returns an array containing each of the items in the select box. These items are created using the \<option\> HTML tag. There are also length and selectedIndex subproperties of this property. |
| | selectedIndex | Returns an integer specifying the indexed location of the selected option in the select box. |
| | type | Returns the type of this select box specified by the type attribute. For \<select\> instances that contain the multiple attribute, this property returns select-multiple. Instances without this attribute return select-one. This property was added in JavaScript 1.1. |

## The Text Object

A principal element for any data entry application is a field in which the user can input data. The Text object serves as this data-capturing device as the representation of the text input HTML tag. Table 9.26 contains the properties and methods of the Text object.

**TABLE 9.26** Methods and Properties of the Text Object

| Type | Item | Description |
|------|------|-------------|
| Method | blur() | Removes the focus from the text box. |
| | focus() | Gives the focus to the text box. |
| | handleEvent() | Invokes the default handler for the specified event. This method was added in JavaScript 1.2. |
| | select() | Selects the text in the text box. |
| Property | defaultValue | Returns the value of this text box, specified by the value attribute. Note that this property is not supported by Opera browsers. |
| | form | Returns the entire form the text box is in. |
| | name | Returns the name of this text box, specified by the name attribute. |
| | type | Returns the type of this text box, specified by the type attribute. This is always text; it was added in JavaScript 1.1. |
| | value | Returns the value that is actually displayed in the text box. |

## The `Textarea` Object

Related to the `Text` object is the `Textarea` object, which allows you to enter multiple lines of text, as opposed to a single line. If you've worked with other programming environments, it might be helpful to think of the `Textarea` object as a memo field. Table 9.27 contains the properties and methods of the `Textarea` object.

**TABLE 9.27**  Methods and Properties of the `Textarea` Object

| *Type* | *Item* | *Description* |
| --- | --- | --- |
| Method | `blur()` | Removes the focus from the text area. |
| | `focus()` | Gives the focus to the text area. |
| | `handleEvent()` | Invokes the default handler for the specified event. This method was added in JavaScript 1.2. |
| | `select()` | Selects the text in the text area. |
| Property | `defaultValue` | Returns the value of this text area defined between the beginning and ending `<textarea>` tags. This property is not supported by Opera browsers. |
| | `form` | Returns the entire form the text area is in. |
| | `name` | Returns the name of this text area, specified by the name attribute. |
| | `type` | Returns the type of this text area. This is always `textarea`; it was added in JavaScript 1.1. |
| | `value` | Returns the value that is actually displayed in the text area. |

# Fourth-Level Objects

As of JavaScript 1.4, there is only one fourth-level object, and it is a subobject of the `Select` object. Keep an eye on this section in future editions though, because advancements in ECMAScript and the Document Object Module (DOM) seem to be growing in this area.

## The `Option` Object

The `Option` object is used to reference the various `<option>` elements that occur within the beginning and ending `<select>` tags. Table 9.28 contains the properties of the `Option` object.

**9**

**Client-Side Objects**

TABLE 9.28 Properties of the Option Object

| Property | Description |
| --- | --- |
| defaultSelected | Refers to the option that is selected by default from the select box. This property was added in JavaScript 1.1. |
| index | Refers to the zero-based indexed location of an element in the Select.options array. |
| selected | Refers to the selected value of the select box. This property was added in JavaScript 1.2. |
| text | Refers to the text for the option. |
| value | Refers to the value that is returned when the option is selected. |

# Summary

JavaScript's client-side language objects serve as the fundamental tools by which you can construct scripts. This chapter took a high-level view of the JavaScript object hierarchy and each of the JavaScript objects.

Much of the object model consists of HTML elements that are "objectified," allowing you to work with HTML tags in an object-oriented manner. If you come from an HTML background, begin to think of these elements not just as tags, but as objects. Chapter 10 covers the core language objects, Chapter 11, "Creating Custom JavaScript Objects," talks about creating your own objects, and Chapter 12 will introduce you to server-side JavaScript and the objects that are contained in that environment.

# Core Language Objects

CHAPTER

10

You could be justified in calling the client-side objects the heart of JavaScript, but an important part of developing sophisticated JavaScript applications comes in working with its core language objects. It is these core objects that are consistent across the various implementations, whether it be Microsoft, Netscape, Sun, Be, or Opera Software, as well as across the various platforms, such as client-side or server-side. These are also the objects that are standardized by the ECMAScript 1.0 specification.

In this chapter, we'll look at the `String`, `RegExp`, `Array`, `Date`, `Math`, `Boolean`, `Number`, and `Function` objects. This chapter also explores the differences that exist in working with these objects in the various JavaScript versions. Some things have changed in the implementations, and ECMAScript has brought on some additions as well.

> **Note**
>
> Even though we will go over all of the core objects and mention the properties and methods of each, this book will not cover the complete syntax of each object, property, and method. For this information, we recommend you go to `http://developer.netscape.com` to find information on Netscape's implementation, and `http://msdn.microsoft.com/scripting` for Microsoft's. Additionally, you can check out `http://www.mozilla.org/js` for future implementation in the soon-to-be-released Open Source version of Navigator (*aka* 5.0).

# The `Global` Object

Those of you who have programmed in JavaScript before might ask what in the world the `Global` object is. This is most likely because you have never heard of it. Before I go into the properties and methods of this object, I wanted to give you some background on it.

The `Global` object seemed to first show its head right around the time when ECMAScript 1.0 was nearing approval as a standard. All of a sudden I noticed that Microsoft grouped some "top-level" properties and methods under a `Global` object. Netscape also mentioned this object in some of its documentation. This became the birth of the `Global` object: top-level properties and methods that had no parent object.

There are several methods and properties that fall under this object. These are listed in Table 10.1. As you will see, they are commonly used in many JavaScript scripts and, if you have programmed in JavaScript before, you more than likely have used them.

**TABLE 10.1**   Methods and Properties of the `Global` Object

| Type | Item | Description |
|---|---|---|
| Method | escape() | Returns a `String` object in which all non-alphanumeric characters are converted to their numeric equivalents. |
| | eval() | Accepts a string of JavaScript statements and evaluates it as source code. |
| | isFinite() | Determines if a variable has finite bounds. This method was added in JavaScript 1.3. |
| | isNaN() | Determines whether or not a variable is a valid number. This method was added in JavaScript 1.1. |
| | parseFloat() | Converts a string to a number of type `float`. |
| | parseInt() | Converts a string to an integer. |
| | unescape() | Takes a hexadecimal value and returns the ISO-Latin-1 ASCII equivalent. |
| Property | Infinity | Keyword that represents positive infinity. This property was added in JavaScript 1.3. |
| | NaN | Represents an object not equal to any number. This property was added in JavaScript 1.3. |

# The `String` Object

Strings are a fundamental part of any programming language. A string, which is a set of alphanumeric characters, can be either a *literal* string, such as `"Push the envelope"`, or a variable representing a string, such as `thePhrase`. You learned about strings as data types in Chapter 5, "Fundamentals of the JavaScript Language," but a string in the JavaScript language is also an object, complete with its own suite of methods and properties.

As JavaScript has matured, strings have gained more power. The first version of JavaScript did not treat strings as true objects, but starting with JavaScript 1.1 it does. For example, if you were creating a string and checking its length in JavaScript 1.0, you would use the following code:

```
<script type="text/javascript">
<!--
  var str = "My name is Richard";
  alert(str.length);
//-->
</script>
```

However, starting with JavaScript 1.1, you could use the `new` operator, just like another object, to create an instance of the `String` object. If you try this using a browser that doesn't support the `String` object definition, you get an error complaining that a `String` is not defined. The following shows how this works in JavaScript 1.1+ browsers:

```
<script type="text/javascript" language="JavaScript1.1">
<!--
  var str = new String("My name is Richard");
  alert(str.length);
//-->
</script>
```

You might be wondering at this point what the purpose is of explicitly declaring a `String` object. The major benefit is that `String` objects can be accessed from other frames in a manner that is easier and more reliable than it was in JavaScript 1.0. For example, if you wanted to access a variable called `custName` from the parent window, you would use the following:

```
var customer = new String();
customer = parent.custName;
```

In JavaScript 1.0, you had to add an empty string to the end of the expression to use it successfully:

```
var customer = parent.custName + "";
```

In addition to some of the simplicity, this is simply good programming practice. ECMAScript is a standard now, and both JavaScript and JScript are implementations of this standard. As a programmer, you want to be sure that your code uses the proper syntax and semantics so that it will work across implementations as flawlessly as possible. To allow you to handle strings, JavaScript has the properties and methods shown in Table 10.2. Because of the amount of work you will do with strings, you should become familiar with them and how they work.

**TABLE 10.2** Methods and Properties of the `String` Object

| Type | Item | Description |
|------|------|-------------|
| Method | `anchor()` | Creates an instance of the `<a>` tag with the name attribute set to the string passed to the method. |
| | `big()` | Converts the string into an instance of the `<big>` tag. |
| | `blink()` | Converts the string into an instance of the `<blink>` tag. |
| | `bold()` | Converts the string into an instance of the `<bold>` tag. |
| | `charAt()` | Returns the character at the index passed to the method. |
| | `charCodeAt()` | Returns the ISO-Latin-1 number of the character at the index passed to the method. |

**TABLE 10.2** continued

| Type | Item | Description |
|---|---|---|
| | concat() | Concatenates the two strings passed to return a new string. This method was added in JavaScript 1.2. |
| | fixed() | Converts the string into an instance of the `<tt>` fixed pitch font tag. |
| | fontcolor() | Sets the `color` attribute of an instance of the `<font>` tag. |
| | fontsize() | Sets the `size` attribute of an instance of the `<font>` tag. |
| | fromCharCode() | Returns the string value of the ISO-Latin-1 number passed to the method. |
| | indexOf() | Returns the index of the first occurrence of the string passed to the method within an instance of a `String` object. |
| | italics() | Converts the string into an instance of the `<i>` tag. |
| | lastIndexOf() | Returns the index of the last occurrence of the string passed to the method within an instance of a `String` object. |
| | link() | Converts the string into an instance of the `<a>` tag and sets the `href` attribute with the URL that is passed to the method. |
| | match() | Returns an array containing the matches found based on the regular expression passed to the method. This method was added in JavaScript 1.2. |
| | replace() | Performs a search and replace, using the regular expression and replace string passed to the method, on the instance of a `String` that calls it. This method was added in JavaScript 1.2. |
| | search() | Returns the index location of the match found in the string passed to the method. A $-1$ is returned if the string is not found. This method was added in JavaScript 1.2. |
| | slice() | Returns the string between the beginning and ending indexes passed to the method. If a negative number is passed, the index is referenced from the end of the string passed. This method was added in JavaScript 1.2. |
| | small() | Converts the string into an instance of the `<small>` tag. |
| | split() | Returns the string split into segments defined by the string and instance limit passed to the method. This method was added in JavaScript 1.1. |

**10**

**Core Language Objects**

TABLE **10.2**    continued

| Type | Item | Description |
|---|---|---|
| | strike() | Converts the string into an instance of the `<strike>` tag. |
| | sub() | Converts the string into an instance of the `<sub>` tag. |
| | substr() | Returns the string beginning with the indexed location and number of characters to return. If a negative number is passed, the index is referenced from the end of the string passed. This method was added in JavaScript 1.2. |
| | substring() | Returns the string between the beginning and ending indexes passed to the method. |
| | sup() | Converts the string into an instance of the `<sup>` tag. |
| | toLowerCase() | Converts all the characters in the string to lowercase. |
| | toSource() | Returns the string representation of the `String` passed. This method was added in JavaScript 1.3. |
| | toString() | Returnsthe characters passed as type `String`. This method was added in JavaScript 1.3. |
| | toUpperCase() | Converts all the characters in the string to uppercase. |
| Property | length | Returns the length of the string. |
| | prototype | Provides the capability for a programmer to add properties to instances of the `String` object. This property was added in JavaScript 1.1. |

Because strings are one of the primary types of data you must work with, it is critical to have ways to extract data from strings and obtain information about them. For instance, you can use the `length` property to determine the size of a string. This example, for instance, returns 16:

```
var myString = new String("This is the day.");
var len = myString.length;
```

You can also search for text within strings by using `indexOf()`and `lastIndexOf()` methods. Use these when you want to search for a particular character or substring within a string and return the position (or index) of the occurrence within the string. Whereas `indexOf()` starts at the left of the string and moves right, `lastIndexOf()` performs the same operation but starts at the left. Both methods start at the 0 position for the first character encountered, and both return a value of -1 if the search text isn't found. For example, the following code returns a value of 3:

```
var myString = new String("Time and time again");
var results = myString.indexOf("e");
```

On the other hand, the following code returns a value of 12 in the result variable:

```
var myString = new String("Time and time again");
var result = myString.lastIndexOf("e");
```

Both methods have an optional second parameter that allows you to specify where in the string you want to start the search. For example, the script shown in Listing 10.1 searches through the variable graf and counts the number of occurrences of the letter *e*.

**LISTING 10.1**  Using the indexOf() Method to Find All Occurrences of the Letter *e* in a Sentence

```
<script type="text/javascript" language="JavaScript1.1">
<!--
  // Declare variables
  var pos = 0;
  var num = -1;
  var i = -1;
    var graf = "While nearly everyone agrees on the principle of reuse,"
              + "the priority we give it varies wildly.";

  // Search the string and counts the number of e's
  while (pos != -1) {
    pos = graf.indexOf("e", i + 1);
    num += 1;
    i = pos;
  }

  // Write the response to the page
  document.write(graf)
  document.write("<hr size='1'>")
  document.write("There were " + num + " e's in that paragraph.");  document.close();
//-->
</script>
```

Figure 10.1 shows the result of the script.

If you want more than just to find the index of a specific character, you can retrieve a portion of a string variable or literal by using the substring() method. It has two parameters—the start position and the end position of the substring you want to return. Just like indexOf() and lastIndexOf(), this method is also zero based, such that the first position of the string begins at 0. For example, the following code returns New:

```
var myString = new String("New England");
var results = myString.substring(0,3);
```

**FIGURE 10.1**
*The result of the*
`indexOf()`
*example.*

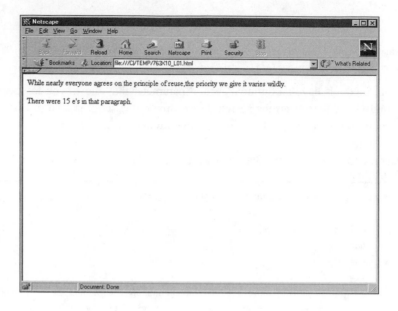

If you want to retrieve a single character, you can use `charAt()`. The `charAt()` method returns the character at the position you specify as a parameter. For example, the following code returns a value of v:

```
var myString = new String("Denver Broncos");
var results = myString.charAt(3);
```

If you specify a position that is out of the string's range, a value of -1 is returned:

```
var myString = new String("007");
var results = myString.charAt(20102);
```

The true power of these string-handling routines is demonstrated when you combine them to solve a problem. Consider a common routine that you might want in JavaScript: a routine to replace specified text within a string with something else. To do this, develop a generic string-replace function that uses the `length` property, `indexOf()`, and `substring()`. Additionally, I will demonstrate both the procedural and the object-oriented approaches to solving this problem.

---

**Note**

Because we are about to build a function that performs search and replace on a string, it is worth mentioning that JavaScript 1.2 includes a new object called `RegExp` that allows you to perform regular expression string functions. With this object, it is easier to perform searches and replaces because there are included methods for this functionality. The RegExp object will be touched on in this chapter and discussed in detail in Chapter 31, "Pattern Matching Using Regular Expressions."

# An Example of String Manipulation

Using a traditional approach, you could develop a stringReplace() function that has three parameters:

- originalString: The original string upon which you want to perform the replacement.

- findText: The string that you want to replace.

- replaceText: The string that you want to insert into the originalString.

The function then uses that information to perform the replacement process. You can see that Listing 10.2 uses the indexOf() method to look for the findText parameter, and the substring() method pulls out the strings that are before and after findText. The function then concatenates preString, replaceText, and postString and assigns the result to the originalString variable.

This happens for each occurrence of findText throughout the string. When findText is no longer found, the originalString value is returned to the user.

**LISTING 10.2**   Creating a Function That Will Search and Replace in Strings

```
<html>
<head>
  <title>JavaScript Unleashed</title>
  <script language="JavaScript1.1" type="text/javascript">
<!--
    function stringReplace(originalString, findText, replaceText) {
      var pos = 0;
      var len = findText.length;
      pos = originalString.indexOf(findText);
      while (pos != -1) {
        preString = originalString.substring(0, pos);
        postString = originalString.substring(pos + len,
            originalString.length);
        originalString = preString + replaceText + postString;
        pos = originalString.indexOf(findText);
      }
      return originalString;
```

**10**

Core Language
Objects

LISTING 10.2   continued

```
    }
  //-->
  </script>
</head>
<body>
  <script language="JavaScript1.1" type="text/javascript">
  <!--
    // Declare variables
    var origString = new String("Allen");
    var findString = new String("All");
    var replaceString = new String("Ell");
    var resultString = stringReplace(origString, findString, replaceString)

    // Write results to the page
    document.write("The original string was: " + origString + "<br>");
    document.write("We searched for: " + findString + "<br>");
    document.write("We replaced it with: " + replaceString + "<hr size='1'>");
    document.write("The result was:   " + resultString);
  //-->
  </script>
</body>
</html>
```

Another way to code this same function is to take advantage of JavaScript 1.1's object prototype capabilities and add a replace() method to the String object type. You can restructure the stringReplace() code to work within the object framework, the result of which is shown in Listing 10.3.

LISTING 10.3   Adding a replace() Method to the String Object

```
<html>
<head>
  <title>JavaScript Unleashed</title>
  <script language="JavaScript1.1" type="text/javascript">
  <!--

    // Define a new method for the String object
    String.prototype.replace = stringReplace;

    function stringReplace(findText, replaceText) {
```

LISTING **10.3**    continued

```
      // Had to add this variable to inherit calling object
      var originalString = new String(this);

      var pos = 0;
      var len = findText.length;
      pos = originalString.indexOf(findText);
      while (pos != -1) {
        preString = originalString.substring(0, pos);
        postString = originalString.substring(pos + len,
            originalString.length);
        originalString = preString + replaceText + postString;
        pos = originalString.indexOf(findText);
      }
      return originalString;
    }
  //-->
  </script>
</head>
<body>
  <script language="JavaScript1.1" type="text/javascript">
  <!--
    // Declare variables
    var origString = new String("Allen");
    var findString = new String("All");
    var replaceString = new String("Ell");

    // Notice the difference here
    var resultString = origString.replace(findString, replaceString)

    // Write results to the page
    document.write("The original string was: " + origString + "<br>");
    document.write("We searched for: " + findString + "<br>");
    document.write("We replaced it with: " + replaceString + "<hr size='1'>");
    document.write("The result was: " + resultString);
  //-->
  </script>
</body>
</html>
```

**10**

Core Language
Objects

As you can see, you can put the `replace()` method into action by creating a `String` object, assigning a value to it, and then calling the newly created method to replace all occurrences of a particular string.

## Formatting Strings

JavaScript has several methods you can use to format strings. Most of these methods are simply equivalents of HTML formatting tags. Using the formatting methods gives you an object-oriented way of dealing with HTML formatting tags, and it's also easier than continuously concatenating HTML tags to strings. In other words, if you have a string literal `"This is the day"` and you want to add bold formatting to it, you can do so by one of two means. You could add HTML formatting tags:

```
"<b>" + "This is the day" + "</b>"
```

Or you could use the `String` object `bold()` method to add the formatting:

```
var myString = new String("This is the day");
var result = myString.bold();
```

When you use this string, the following HTML text is returned:

```
<b>This is the day</b>
```

> **Note**
>
> Keep in mind the context in which you can use the formatting methods. You can't use them outside a JavaScript script as a substitute for HTML formatting tags.

To demonstrate how the basic formatting methods are used in JavaScript, let's create a sample JavaScript page that lets you format a user-defined string based on the options set using an HTML form.

In the code behind the form, we will create a single JavaScript method called `showWindow()` that is called when the Show button is clicked. The method assigns the value of the form's text field to a string variable called `txt`.

Each of the formatting options shown as check boxes is either `true` or `false`. There will also be code that checks to see if each of the boxes is checked. If so, it calls the appropriate formatting method for the `txt` variable.

None of these formatting options are mutually exclusive—although some might cancel out each other. As a result, you will be able to use as many of the methods at the same time as you want. JavaScript simply processes each of the methods, adding the appropriate HTML tags in sequential order.

When we try to specify a font color and size, these settings aren't simply logical settings, so they require a parameter to be set. The select boxes on the form are used to specify these settings.

Finally, the `txt` variable is used in a `document.write()` method on a new window that is created. This will write the full string to the new window with all the formatting tags around the text.

Figure 10.2 shows the window with all the options, and Figure 10.3 shows the result window based on the settings selected.

**FIGURE 10.2**

*The initial page that allows you to select the format-ting options.*

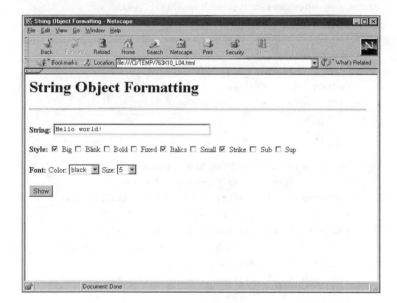

Listing 10.4 shows the entire source code for this example.

**FIGURE 10.3**

*The result of the string-formatting options.*

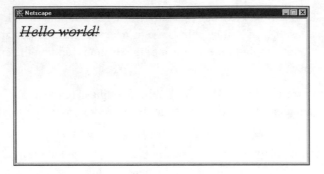

---

**LISTING 10.4    Source Code for Our String-Formatting Script**

```html
<html>
<head>
  <title>String Object Formatting</title>
  <script language="JavaScript1.1" type="text/javascript">
  <!--

    function showWindow() {

      // Declare your variables
      var txt = document.form1.stringField.value;
      var clr = "";
      var sze = "";

      // Check to see what options are selected
      if (document.form1.bigBox.checked) txt = txt.big();
      if (document.form1.blinkBox.checked) txt = txt.blink();
      if (document.form1.boldBox.checked) txt = txt.bold();
      if (document.form1.fixedBox.checked) txt = txt.fixed();
      if (document.form1.italicsBox.checked) txt = txt.italics();
      if (document.form1.smallBox.checked) txt = txt.small();
      if (document.form1.strikeBox.checked) txt = txt.strike();
      if (document.form1.subBox.checked) txt = txt.sub();
      if (document.form1.supBox.checked) txt = txt.sup();

      // Special checking for select box
      clr = document.form1.colorList.options[document.form1
➥.colorList.options.selectedIndex].text;
      txt = txt.fontcolor(clr);
      sze = document.form1.sizeList.options[document.form1
➥.sizeList.options.selectedIndex].text;
      txt = txt.fontsize(sze);
```

LISTING **10.4**   continued

```
      // Open a new window to write the results to
      objWindow = window.open("", "","width=600,height=300");
      objWindow.document.write(txt);
      objWindow.document.close();
  }
  //-->
  </script>
</head>
<body>
  <h1>
    String Object Formatting
  </h1>
  <hr>
  <form method="POST" name="form1">
    <p>
      <strong>
        String:
      </strong>
      <input type=text size=40 maxlength=256 name="stringField">
    </p>
    <p>
      <strong>
        Style:
      </strong>
      <input type=checkbox name="bigBox" value="ON">
      Big
      <input type=checkbox name="blinkBox" value="ON">
      Blink
      <input type=checkbox name="boldBox" value="ON">
      Bold
      <input type=checkbox name="fixedBox" value="ON">
      Fixed
      <input type=checkbox name="italicsBox" value="ON">
      Italics
      <input type=checkbox name="smallBox" value="ON">
      Small
      <input type=checkbox name="strikeBox" value="ON">
      Strike
      <input type=checkbox name="subBox" value="ON">
      Sub
      <input type=checkbox name="supBox" value="ON">
```

**10**

Core Language
Objects

**LISTING 10.4**    continued

```
      Sup
    </p>
    <p>
      <strong>
        Font:
      </strong>
      Color:
      <select name="colorList" size=1>
        <option selected>black</option>
        <option>green</option>
        <option>red</option>
      </select>
      Size:
      <select name="sizeList" size=1>
        <option selected>1</option>
        <option>2</option>
        <option>3</option>
        <option>4</option>
        <option>5</option>
        <option>6</option>
        <option>7</option>
      </select>
    </p>
    <input type="button" name="Show" value="Show" onClick="showWindow()">
  </form>
</body>
</html>
```

> **Tip**
>
> The `toUpperCase()` and `toLowerCase()` methods work just as you would expect. They are useful when you need to compare text without concerning yourself with the case of the text. For example, if you want to compare user-entered text with a string literal, it is helpful to use all uppercase or all lowercase when making the evaluation.

You can also use the `String` object's `anchor()` and `link()` methods to create `Anchor` and `Link` objects. These methods make it much easier to work with anchors and links in your code, avoiding painful string concatenations of HTML tags. To illustrate, we can use an idea similar to the previous formatting example to work with hypertext formatting.

A similar showWindow() method (triggered by the Show button's onClick event handler) processes the user-entered options and calls either the link() or anchor() method of the txt variable.

Figure 10.4 shows an HTML form you can use to specify the elements of a hypertext link: text, anchor/link designation, and URL/anchor to associate with the underlined text. Figure 10.5 shows the resulting window with a new hypertext link created.

**FIGURE 10.4**
String *object hypertext formatting.*

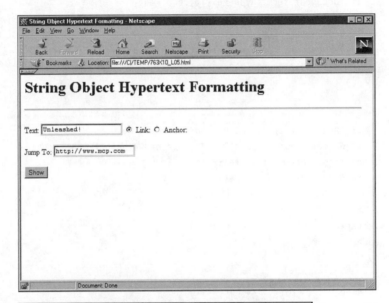

**FIGURE 10.5**
A Link *object created using the* link() *method.*

Listing 10.5 shows the entire source code for our example.

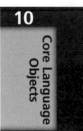

**LISTING 10.5**  Source Code for a Sample Page That Formats a `String` Object with the `<a>` Tag

```html
<html>
<head>
  <title>String Object Hypertext Formatting</title>
  <script language="JavaScript1.1" type="text/javascript">
  <!--
    function showWindow(){
      var txt = document.form1.stringField.value

      if (document.form1.hypertext[0].checked){
        txt = txt.link(document.form1.jumptoField.value);
      }else{
        if (document.form1.hypertext[1].checked){
          txt = txt.anchor(document.form1.jumptoField.value);
        }
      }

      // Create and open a window to write the results
      objWindow = window.open("", "","width=600,height=300");
      objWindow.document.write(txt);
      objWindow.document.close();
    }
  //-->
  </script>
</head>
<body>
  <h1>
    String Object Hypertext Formatting
  </h1>
  <hr>
  <form method="POST" name="form1">
    <p>
      Text:
      <input type=text size=20 maxlength=256 name="stringField">
      <input type=radio name="hypertext" value="Link" checked>
      Link:
      <input type=radio name="hypertext" value="Anchor">
      Anchor:
    </p>
    <p>
      Jump To:
      <input type=text size=20 maxlength=256 name="jumptoField">
```

**LISTING 10.5** continued

```
      </p>
      <input type="button" name="Show" value="Show" onClick="showWindow()">
  </form>
</body>
</html>
```

# Working with Special Characters

When working with strings in any language, you will discover certain characters that are difficult to use. JavaScript lets you work with these special-case characters by using a backslash character (\) followed by the character or its code. Table 10.3 lists the JavaScript inline symbols.

**TABLE 10.3** Inline Symbols

| Symbol | Description |
|--------|-------------|
| \t | Tab |
| \n | Newline |
| \r | Carriage return |
| \f | Form feed |
| \\ | Backslash |
| \b | Backspace |
| \" | Double quote |
| \' | Single quote |

For example, if you want to use a backslash in a string literal, use the following method:

```
var myString = new String("Your file is located in C:\\WINDOWS\\TEMP");
```

When displayed with the document.write() method, it looks like this:

```
Your file is located in C:\WINDOWS\TEMP
```

**Tip**

Use the \r inline symbol to add a carriage return to an alert() message box message.

10

Core Language Objects

Because these inline symbols can be confusing to use, you might find it helpful to assign variables to them. In fact, if you use them often, you can pull these defined "constants" from a JavaScript code library and use them over and over. Listing 10.6 shows these inline characters treated as constants and shows how to use them in a `document.write()` method.

**LISTING 10.6**   Defining Special Characters as Variables for Later Use

```
<script type="text/javascript">
<!--
  // Inline Character Constants
  var TAB = "\t";
  var CR = "\r";
  var LF = "\n";
  var CRLF = "\r\n";
  var FF = "\f";
  var DQUOTE = '\"';
  var SQUOTE = "\'";
  var BACKSLASH = "\\";
  var BACKSPACE = "\b";

  document.write("Column1" + TAB + "Column2" + TAB + "Column3")
//-->
</script>
```

In addition to these inline symbols, you also have other ways of working with non-alphanumeric values in JavaScript. If you need to convert a non-alphanumeric value to an ASCII-encoded value, you can use the built-in `escape()` method. One example is the following code:

```
escape("Jim's Favorite ASCII character is the tilde(~)");
```

This code returns the following value:

```
Jim%27s%20Favorite%20ASCII%20character%20is%20the%20tilde%28%7E%29
```

If you need to convert an ASCII-encoded string—perhaps a string retrieved from a server—you can use the `unescape()` method. The following code is a good illustration:

```
unescape("email%20me%20at%20someone@anywhere.com%21");
```

This code returns the following string value:

```
email me at someone@anywhere.com!
```

# Converting Strings and Numbers

JavaScript provides two built-in methods that you can use to convert strings to numbers: `parseInt()` and `parseFloat()`. Both functions take strings as their parameters and attempt to convert the string data into a numeric value. `parseInt()` tries to convert the string to an integer value, and `parseFloat()` attempts to convert into a floating point value. For example, the following code returns `123`:

```
var myString = new String ("123.88888");
document.write(parseInt(myString));
```

The following code returns `1234.0012121`:

```
var myString = new String("1234.0012121");
document.write(parseFloat(myString));
```

Both of these routines start the conversion from the left side of the string and convert until they come to something other than a numeric digit (0 to 9), a decimal (.), or a plus or minus sign (+/-). If the routine encounters a nonnumeric character, the rest of the string is ignored. For example, the following code returns `1234.01`:

```
var myString = new String("1234.01 is the total price");
document.write(parseFloat(myString));
```

However, the following code returns `NaN` (Not a Number) because the dollar sign is a nonnumeric value:

```
var myString = new String("$1234.01 is the total price");
document.write(parseFloat(myString));
```

These conversion functions are very useful when you're working with text objects. Because the `value` property of a `Text` object returns a string, you must convert this data any time you want to treat text entered by the user as a numeric value.

You can also convert numeric values to strings, but in JavaScript versions prior to 1.3, there were no built-in methods to do so. Instead, you could perform this task based on how JavaScript processes the addition (+) operator. If JavaScript encounters a string while it adds elements of an expression, the whole expression is treated as a string from that point on. For example, `35 + 100` returns a numeric value of `135`. However, `35 + "100"` returns a string value of `"35100"`.

**10**

**Core Language Objects**

---

> **Note**
>
> If you're working with a `Number` object and JavaScript 1.3+, you can use its `toString()` method to convert it to a string value.

Interestingly, because JavaScript processes the addition operator from left to right, you could actually add two numeric digits together before the expression is converted into a string. For example, 10+20+ "40" returns a string value of "3040" because the 10 + 20 pair is added before its result is added to the string value. In contrast, "40" + 10 + 20 returns a string value of "401020" because the string is on the left of the numeric values.

In most programming languages, you must convert a numeric value before you can use it in the context of a string value. As you can see, the only thing you need to do is either use it in a string expression with other string values or add an empty string to it. For example, the expression 1300 + "" returns a string value of "1300". Rather than add an empty string each time you want to perform this conversion, you could use a simple conversion function to do this for you:

```
function numToString(number) {
  number += "";
  return number;
}
```

Listing 10.7 shows a sample script that demonstrates this function. The first alert message box displays Number as the data type for the number variable. After the numToString() function is performed, the second alert box displays String as the number's data type.

**LISTING 10.7** Converting a Number to a String

```
<script type="text/javascript">
<!--
  function numToString(number) {
    number += "";
    return number;
  }

  var number = 100;
  alert(typeof number);
  number = numToString(number);
  alert(typeof number);
//-->
</script>
```

# The RegExp Object

As you saw in the previous section, it is possible to create functions that perform string evaluation and searching. With the release of JavaScript 1.2, the language now has a core RegExp object that allows you to perform regular expression functions on your strings.

Because Chapter 31 goes into detail on this topic, we will not cover it here. However, Table 10.4 does have a short description of the various properties and methods of the RegExp object.

**TABLE 10.4**  Methods and Properties of the RegExp Object

| Type | Item | Description |
|------|------|-------------|
| Method | compile() | Compiles the regular expression for faster execution. |
| | exec() | Executes the search for a match in a specified string. |
| | test() | Tests for a string match. |
| Property | RegExp,$* | Represents multiline. |
| | RegExp.$& | Represents lastmatch. |
| | RegExp.$_ | Represents input. |
| | RegExp.$` | Represents leftContext |
| | RegExp.$' | Represents rightContext. |
| | RegExp.$+ | Represents lastParen. |
| | RegExp.$1,$2,...$9 | Represents a substring of matches. |
| | global | Specifies whether to check the expressions against all possible matches. |
| | ignoreCase | Specifies whether case is ignored during a string search. |
| | input | The string that is matched. |
| | lastIndex | Specifies the index at which to start matching the next string. |
| | lastMatch | The last matched characters. |
| | lastParen | The last parenthesized substring match. |
| | leftContext | The substring preceding the most recent match. |
| | multiline | Specifies whether to search on multiple lines. |
| | rightContext | The substring following the most recent match. |
| | source | The string pattern. |

# The Array Object

An array is a programming construct fundamental to nearly all modern languages. JavaScript is no different, providing the capability to construct and work with arrays. An *array* is simply a container holding a set of data elements. Each of the elements in an array is a separate value, but they exist as part of the array and cannot be accessed except by going through the array. Table 10.5 shows all the methods and properties of the Array object.

TABLE 10.5  Methods and Properties of the Array Object

| Type | Item | Description |
|------|------|-------------|
| Method | concat() | Concatenates the elements passed into an existing array. This method was added in JavaScript 1.2. |
| | join() | Concatenates all elements of an array into one string. |
| | pop() | Deletes the last element of an array. |
| | push() | Adds elements to the end of an array. |
| | reverse() | Reverses the order of the elements in the array. This method was added in JavaScript 1.2. |
| | shift() | Deletes elements from the front of an array. This method was added in JavaScript 1.2. |
| | slice() | Returns a subsection of the array. This method was added in JavaScript 1.2. |
| | sort() | Sorts elements in array. |
| | splice() | Inserts and removes elements from an array. This method was added in JavaScript 1.2. |
| | toSource() | Converts elements to a string with square brackets. This method was added in JavaScript 1.3. |
| | toString() | Converts the elements in an array to a string. |
| | unshift() | Adds elements to the front of an array. This method was added in JavaScript 1.2. |
| | valueOf() | Returns an array of elements separated by commas. |
| Property | index | For an array created by a regular expression match, this property returns the indexed location of the match. This was added in JavaScript 1.2. |
| | input | For an array created by a regular expression match, this property returns the original string. This was added in JavaScript 1.2. |
| | length | The number of elements in the array. |
| | prototype | Provides the capability for a programmer to add properties to instances of the Array object. This property was added in JavaScript 1.1. |

**Note**

Although strongly typed languages require that all array values be of the same type, JavaScript does not. Consequently, your array can contain mixed data types, just as an object can have properties of varying types.

> **Warning**
>
> In JavaScript 1.0, an array is not a native object—the `Array` object was not added until JavaScript 1.1. For JavaScript 1.0 you have to create a function, as follows, to define an array. Note that it does not have all the functionality of the native `Array` object.
>
> ```
> function createArray(size) {
>   this.length = size;
>   for (var i = 1; i <= size; i++) {
>     this[i] = null ;
>   }
>   return this;
> }
> ```

To define or access a particular element, you need to add brackets and an index value to the array variable. For example, you can define an array called `coffee` as follows:

```
coffee[0] = "Ethiopian Sidamo"
coffee[1] = "Kenyan"
coffee[2] = "Cafe Verona"
coffee[3] = "Sumatra"
coffee[4] = "Costa Rica"
coffee[5] = "Columbian"
coffee[6] = "Bristan"
```

If you wanted to use any of these elements within a script, you could access them using the array variable along with an index value representing the location of the element within the array. Therefore, if you wanted to write the following line

```
My favorite coffee is Ethiopian Sidamo
```

You would code the following:

```
document.write("My favorite coffee is " + coffee[0])
```

If arrays are new to you, you might find it helpful to think of an array as JavaScript's equivalent of a numbered list. It's really no more complicated than that. For example, suppose you have a list of 10 items:

1. JavaScript
2. Java
3. Delphi
4. C++

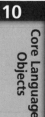

**10**

Core Language Objects

5. Visual Basic

6. Oracle Power Objects

7. SmallTalk

8. PowerBuilder

9. Paradox

10. Access

If you wanted to assemble this group of items in a JavaScript array, it would look like this. Do notice, however, that arrays are zero based—the first element in the array has an index of 0:

```
devTools[0] = "JavaScript"
devTools[1] = "Java"
devTools[2] = "Delphi"
devTools[3] = "C++"
devTools[4] = "Visual Basic"
devTools[5] = "Oracle Power Objects"
devTools[6] = "SmallTalk"
devTools[7] = "PowerBuilder"
devTools[8] = "Paradox"
devTools[9] = "Access"
```

You can create instances of an `Array` object using the `new` operator, and the statements following fill the array with data elements. For example, if you wanted to create the `coffee` array defined earlier, you would define it as follows:

```
var coffee = new Array();
coffee[0] = "Ethiopian Sidamo";
coffee[1] = "Kenyan";
coffee[2] = "Cafe Verona";
coffee[3] = "Sumatra";
coffee[4] = "Costa Rica";
coffee[5] = "Columbian";
coffee[6] = "Bristan";
```

> **Tip**
>
> An alternative way to define an `Array` object is to specify the data elements as parameters of the `new` call. For example, the following line is the functional equivalent of the previous example:
>
> ```
> var coffee = new Array("Ethiopian Sidamo", "Kenyan", "Cafe Verona",
> ➡"Sumatra", "Costa Rica", "Columbian", "Bristan");
> ```

Notice that you didn't specify a size of the array, as is common in many programming languages. JavaScript doesn't require that you specify the size of the array, which allows you to incrementally expand the array as you add each new data element. However, if you want to, you can specify the size of the array initially as a parameter in the new expression:

```
var coffee = new Array(7);
```

Alternatively, you could also resize an array simply by defining a data element at the $n$ position. If $n$ is the highest number defined in the array, the new array size is expanded to $n$ + 1. Note the following example:

```
var javaDrinks = new Array();
javaDrinks[0] = "Regular coffee";
javaDrinks[1] = "Decaf coffee";
javaDrinks[2] = "Cafe Mocha";
javaDrinks[3] = "Cafe au Lait";
javaDrinks[199] = "Cafe Latte";
```

The size of the `javaDrinks` array is 200, even though only five data elements are defined. Each undefined element returns a null value if you access it.

You can retrieve the size of the array using the `Array` object's `length` property. For example, if you wanted to iterate through each element in an `Array` object, you could use the script shown in Listing 10.8.

**LISTING 10.8**    Displaying the Contents of an Array

```
<script language="JavaScript1.1" type="text/javascript">
<!--
  var coffee = new Array();
  coffee[0] = "Ethiopian Sidamo";
  coffee[1] = "Kenyan";
  coffee[2] = "Cafe Verona";
  coffee[3] = "Sumatra";
  coffee[4] = "Costa Rica";
  coffee[5] = "Columbian";
  coffee[6] = "Bristan";

  document.write("Coffees of the World:<p>");
  for (var i = 0; i < coffee.length; i++) {
    document.write(i + 1 + ". " + coffee[i] + "<br>");
  }
  document.write('</p>');
//-->
</script>
```

**10**

**Core Language Objects**

Figure 10.6 shows the result.

**FIGURE 10.6**
*Using JavaScript to display a coffee list.*

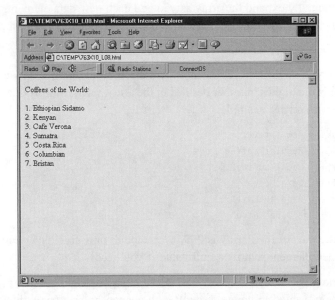

> **Caution**
>
> The `Array` object's `length` property is read only. As a result, you can't resize an array by assigning a value to the `length` property.

# The `Date` Object

The `Date` object is the means by which you work with date and time values in JavaScript. You should understand three significant facts regarding this object before using it:

- Following the UNIX convention, JavaScript considers January 1, 1970, to be the baseline date. Consequently, you can't work with dates prior to that.

- When you create a `Date` object, the time reflected within the object is based on the client machine. You are thus dependent on the client computer to have a working and accurate clock. Keep this dependency in mind as you consider time-sensitive code in your JavaScript scripts.

- JavaScript keeps track of date/time values in the form of milliseconds since the baseline date (1/1/70).

Encapsulated within the Date object is an impressive array of methods to get and set date values and convert them into various forms. Table 10.6 shows all the methods and properties of the Date object.

> **Note**
>
> Like almost everything else in JavaScript, relative date values are also zero based. This is perhaps counterintuitive, because days of the week are 0 to 6 rather than 1 to 7, and months of the year are 0 to 11 rather than 1 to 12. As you process these values in your code, you need to account for these zero-based values.
>
> However, note that the date within the month is an exception (1 to 31), because this is an absolute value.

**TABLE 10.6** Methods and Properties of the Date Object

| Type | Item | Description |
|---|---|---|
| Method | getDate() | Returns the date within month (1 to 31). |
| | getDay() | Returns the day within the week (0 to 6). |
| | getFullYear() | Returns the year in local time with four digits. This method was added in JavaScript 1.2. |
| | getHours() | Returns the hour within the day (0 to 23). |
| | getMilliseconds() | Returns the milliseconds. This method was added in JavaScript 1.2. |
| | getMinutes() | Returns the minutes within the hour (0 to 59). |
| | getMonth() | Returns the month within the year (0 to 11). |
| | getSeconds() | Returns seconds within the minute (0 to 59). |
| | getTime() | Returns the number of milliseconds since 1/1/70 00:00:00. |
| | getTimeZoneOffset() | Returns minutes offset from GMT/UTC. |
| | getUTCDate() | Returns the day of the month. This method was added in JavaScript 1.2. |
| | getUTCDay() | Returns the day of the week converted to universal time. This method was added in JavaScript 1.2. |

**10**

Core Language Objects

**TABLE 10.6** continued

| Type | Item | Description |
|------|------|-------------|
| | getUTCFullYear() | Returns a four-digit representation of the year converted to universal time. This method was added in JavaScript 1.2. |
| | getUTCHours() | Returns the hour converted to universal time. This method was added in JavaScript 1.2. |
| | getUTCMilliseconds() | Returns the milliseconds converted to universal time. This method was added in JavaScript 1.2. |
| | getUTCMinutes() | Returns the minutes converted to universal time. This method was added in JavaScript 1.2. |
| | getUTCMonth() | Returns the month converted to universal time. This method was added in JavaScript 1.2. |
| | getUTCSeconds() | Returns the seconds converted to universal time. This method was added in JavaScript 1.2. |
| | getYear() | Returns number of years since 1900. |
| | parse() | Converts the passed-in string date to milliseconds. |
| | setDate() | Sets the date within the month (1 to 31). |
| | setFullYear() | Sets the year as a four-digit number. This method was added in JavaScript 1.2. |
| | setHours() | Sets hour within day (0 to 23). |
| | setMilliseconds() | Sets the milliseconds. This method was added in JavaScript 1.2. |
| | setMinutes() | Sets the minutes within the hour (0 to 59). |
| | setMonth() | Sets the month within the year (0 to 11). |
| | setSeconds() | Sets the seconds within the minute (0 to 59). |
| | setTime() | Sets the number of milliseconds since 1/1/70 00:00:00. |
| | setUTCdate() | Sets the day of the month in universal time. This method was added in JavaScript 1.2. |
| | setUTCFullYear() | Sets the year as a four-digit number in universal time. This method was added in JavaScript 1.2. |
| | setUTCHours() | Sets the hour in universal time. This method was added in JavaScript 1.2. |
| | setUTCMilliseconds() | Sets the milliseconds in universal time. This method was added in JavaScript 1.2. |
| | setUTCMinutes() | Sets the minutes in universal time. This method was added in JavaScript 1.2. |
| | setUTCMonth() | Sets the month in universal time. This method was added in JavaScript 1.2. |
| | setUTCSeconds() | Sets the seconds in universal time. This method was added in JavaScript 1.2. |

**TABLE 10.6** continued

| Type | Item | Description |
|------|------|-------------|
| | setYear() | Sets the number of years since 1900. |
| | toGMTString() | Returns the date string in universal format. |
| | toLocalString() | Returns the date string in the local system's format. |
| | toSource() | Returns the source of the Date object. This method was added in JavaScript 1.3. |
| | toString() | Returns the date and time as a string in local time. |
| | toUTCString() | Returns the data and time as a string in universal time (UTC). This method was added in JavaScript 1.2. |
| | UTC() | Convertscomma-delimited values to milliseconds of UTC date. |
| | valueOf() | Returns the equivalence of the Date object in milliseconds. This method was added in JavaScript 1.1. |
| Property | prototype | Property that allows you to add methods and properties to the Date object. This property was added in JavaScript 1.1. |

Creating a Date object is similar to creating a String or Array object. You can create as many of these objects as you want in your scripts. Using the new operator, you can define a Date object as follows:

```
var dateVariable = new Date([parameters]);
```

The various sets of parameters that can be passed in creating these object instances are shown in Table 10.7.

**TABLE 10.7** Parameters That Can Be Passed to Create an Instance of the Date Object

| Parameter | Description | Example |
|-----------|-------------|---------|
| Nothing | Creates an object with the current date and time. | var today = new Date() |
| "month dd, yyyy hh:mm:ss" | Creates an object with the specified date and time in the string. (All omitted time values are automatically set to zero.) | var someDate = new Date ("September 22, 2000") |
| yy, mm, dd | Creates an object with the specified date of the set of integer values (zero-based). | var someDate = new Date(00,1,0) |

**10**

Core Language
Objects

**TABLE 10.7** continued

| Parameter | Description | Example |
|---|---|---|
| yy, mm, dd, hh, mm, ss | Creates an object with the specified date and time of the set of integer values (zero-based). (All omitted time values are automatically set to zero.) | var someDate = new Date(00,7,12,7,10,29) |

Once the object is created, you can use one of several methods to either get or set date values. For example, to return the date of the current month, you would code the following:

```
var today = new Date();
result = today.getDate();
```

To change the month defined for the Date object appt, you can use the following:

```
var appt = new Date(1996,06,12);
result = appt.setMonth(7);
```

I discussed earlier how zero-based date values can make it difficult to work with getting dates. You can get around this annoyance by extending the Date object methods by prototyping more user-friendly get methods. If you recall, JavaScript 1.1 lets you extend the capabilities of built-in objects by letting you prototype new methods or properties. All objects of this type will inherit this new prototype. Add these new methods to the Date object:

- getActualMonth() returns the actual numeric value for the month.

- getCalendarMonth() returns the name of the month.

- getActualDay() returns the actual numeric value of the day of week.

- getCalendarDay() returns the name of the day of week.

Listing 10.9 shows the method definitions for each of these prototype methods. This listing would make a great example of storing commonly used functions in an external JavaScript library or source file that you can load using the src attribute of the <script> tag.

**LISTING 10.9** Extending the Date Object to Include Some New Methods

```
<script type="text/javascript" language="JavaScript1.1">
<!--
  Date.prototype.getActualMonth = getActualMonth;
  Date.prototype.getActualDay = getActualDay;
  Date.prototype.getCalendarDay = getCalendarDay;
  Date.prototype.getCalendarMonth = getCalendarMonth;
```

LISTING **10.9**    continued

```
function getActualMonth() {
  var n = this.getMonth();
  n += 1;
  return n;
}

function getActualDay() {
  var n = this.getDay();
  n += 1;
  return n;
}

function getCalendarDay() {
  var n = this.getDay();
  var dow = new Array(7);
  dow[0] = "Sunday";
  dow[1] = "Monday";
  dow[2] = "Tuesday";
  dow[3] = "Wednesday";
  dow[4] = "Thursday";
  dow[5] = "Friday";
  dow[6] = "Saturday";
  return dow[n];
}

function getCalendarMonth() {
  var n = this.getMonth();
  var moy = new Array(12);
  moy[0] = "January";
  moy[1] = "February";
  moy[2] = "March";
  moy[3] = "April";
  moy[4] = "May";
  moy[5] = "June";
  moy[6] = "July";
  moy[7] = "August";
  moy[8] = "September";
  moy[9] = "October";
  moy[10] = "November";
  moy[11] = "December";
  return moy[n];
}
```

**10**

Core Language
Objects

**LISTING 10.9**    continued

```
// Test the new methods you created
var today = new Date();

document.write("<b>I hereby declare that on "
  + today.getCalendarDay() + ", the " + today.getDate()
  + "th day of " + today.getCalendarMonth() + " in the year "
  + today.getFullYear() + " A.D. at the " + today.getHours()
  + "th hour of the day, absolutely nothing is happening.</b>");
//-->
</script>
```

After the methods are declared, the script creates a Date object and then generates an HTML document using a combination of the prototype methods. Figure 10.7 shows the result.

**FIGURE 10.7**
*Using the enhanced* Get *methods.*

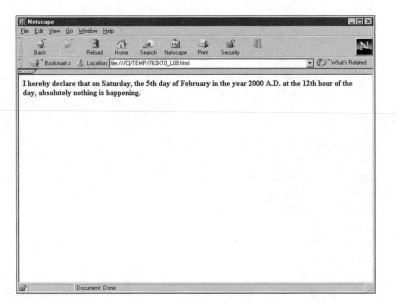

Given that JavaScript is an application for the World Wide Web, it is only fitting that it include some methods to deal with time zones. getTimezoneOffset() returns the number of minutes difference between the client computer and GMT (Greenwich Mean Time). For example, as I write this, I am in the U.S. Eastern time zone. If I want to return the number of time zone offset hours, I could use the following code:

```
var today = new Date();
offset = today.getTimezoneOffset() / 60;
if (offset == 5) {
    alert("You are in the Eastern Timezone");
}
```

Figure 10.8 shows the result when I run the script.

**FIGURE 10.8**
*Using* getTime-
zoneOffset() *to
determine the
time zone.*

You can also perform calculations between date values, determining such things as the number of days until the end of the next century. When you perform calculations with dates, it's important to keep the dates in their "native" millisecond format during the calculation and then extract the relevant data later.

# The Math Object

For mathematical calculations, JavaScript encapsulates a host of mathematical constants and procedures into a single entity—the Math object. This object is quite different from the other core objects. First, you can perform basic arithmetic calculations (addition, subtraction, multiplication, and division) outside a Math object, so unless you regularly require advanced math functions, you might rarely use it.

Second, although you can create instances of String, Array, and Date objects using new, you work with a core instance of the Math object. This quality of the object parallels the navigator object, for example, which is not created on-the-fly. Consequently, the Math object is commonly referred to as a *static* object.

The Math object's properties are really nothing more than a list of common mathematical constants. Table 10.8 shows a list of these properties as well as all the methods of the object. Note the case of the constants. Although nearly all JavaScript properties are lowercase or mixed case, these properties are all uppercase.

**TABLE 10.8**  Methods and Properties of the Math Object

| Type | Item | Description |
|------|------|-------------|
| Method | abs() | Absolute value of the value passed. |
| | acos() | Arc cosine, in radians, of the value passed. |
| | asin() | Arc sine, in radians, of the value passed. |

**TABLE 10.8** continued

| Type | Item | Description |
|------|------|-------------|
| | atan() | Arc tangent, in radians, of the value passed. |
| | atan2() | Arc tangent (in radians) of the quotient of the value passed. |
| | ceil() | Next integer greater than or equal to the value passed. |
| | cos() | Cosine of the value passed. |
| | exp() | Euler's constant to the power of the value passed. |
| | floor() | Next integer less than or equal to the value passed. |
| | log() | Natural logarithm, base e, of the value passed. |
| | max() | The highest number of the two values passed. |
| | min() | The lowest number of the two values passed. |
| | pow() | Power of the first number to the second number passed. |
| | random() | A random number between 0 and 1. This method was added in JavaScript 1.1. |
| | round() | The value passed, rounded to the nearest whole number. |
| | sin() | Sine, in radians, of the value passed. |
| | sqrt() | Square root of the value passed. |
| | tan() | Tangent, in radians, of the value passed. |
| | toSource() | A copy of an object. This method was added in JavaScript 1.3. |
| | toString() | A string representation of an object. |
| Property | E | Euler's constant (2.718281828459045). |
| | LN2 | Natural log of 2 (0.6931471805599453). |
| | LN10 | Natural log of 10 (2.302585092994046). |
| | LOG2E | Log base −2 of E (1.4426950408889633). |
| | LOG10E | Log base −10 of E (0.4342944819032518). |
| | PI | Pi (3.141592653589793). |
| | SQRT1_2 | Square root of 0.5 (0.7071067811865476). |
| | SQRT2 | Square root of 2 (1.4142135623730951). |

# The Boolean Object

Boolean values are an important part of any programming language. The Boolean object, which was added in JavaScript 1.1, is used to convert a non-Boolean value into a Boolean value. You can then use this object as if it were a normal Boolean value (true or false).

You can create a Boolean object using the now familiar new operator with the following syntax:

```
var booleanObjectName = new Boolean(initialValue);
```

The initialValue parameter specifies the initial setting of the object. If initialValue is false, 0, null, or an empty string (""), or if it is omitted altogether, a value of false is implied. All other values will set the object to true. Table 10.9 shows a list of all the methods and properties of the Boolean object.

**TABLE 10.9**   Methods and Properties of the Boolean Object

| Type | Item | Description |
| --- | --- | --- |
| Method | toString() | This method returns a string representation of the primitive Boolean value stored in the object. If the object contains true, the string "true" is returned. Similarly, if the object contains false, the string "false" is returned. |
| Property | prototype | This property allows you to add methods and properties to the Boolean object. |

# The Number Object

The Number object, which is supported in JavaScript 1.1 and higher, does for number values what the String object does for string values. However, in practice, it is typically used much less. You will find this object useful when you need to access certain constant values, such as the largest and smallest representable numbers, positive and negative infinity, and the Not a Number (NaN) value. JavaScript represents these values as Number object properties. Table 10.10 shows a list of these properties and the methods of the Number object.

**TABLE 10.10**   Methods and Properties of the Number Object

| Type | Item | Description |
| --- | --- | --- |
| Method | toSource() | Returns a string representation of the Number object. This method was added in JavaScript 1.3. |
|  | toString() | Returns a string representing the specified Number object. |
|  | valueOf() | Returns the primitive value of a Number object as a number data type. |
| Property | MAX_VALUE | Largest representable number (1.7976931348623157e+308). |
|  | MIN_VALUE | Smallest representable number (5e-324). |
|  | NaN | Special Not-a-Number value. |

**10**

Core Language Objects

**TABLE 10.10** continued

| Type | Item | Description |
|------|------|-------------|
| | NEGATIVE_INFINITY | Special negative infinite value (-Infinity); returned on overflow. |
| | POSITIVE_INFINITY | Special infinite value; returned on overflow. |
| | prototype | Allows you to add properties and methods to the Number object. |

Like many of the other core objects, Number instances are instantiated in your script using the new operator, with the following syntax:

```
var numberObjectName = new Number(initialValue);
```

You can create Number objects when you need to add properties to them. For example, the code in Listing 10.10 demonstrates a scenario in which Number objects would be very useful. This avoids the necessity of making several string-to-number conversions.

**LISTING 10.10**  Creating Number Objects Rather than Performing String-to-Number Conversions

```
<html>
<head>
  <script language="JavaScript1.1" type="text/javascript">
<!--
  // Add description property to Number objects
  Number.prototype.description = null;

  // Speed Limit Numbers
  slHighway = new Number(65);
  slCity = new Number(35);
  slSchoolZone = new Number(25);

  // Add Descriptions
  slHighway.description = "Interstate Highway Speed Limit";
  slCity.description = "City Speed Limit";
  slSchoolZone.description = "School Zone Speed Limit";

  // Subtract num2 from num1 and display the value of the difference
  // between the two along with the original number descriptions.
  function tellDifference(num1, num2) {
    diff = num1 - num2;
    document.write("The speed difference between " + num1.description +
              " and " + num2.description + " is " + diff);
```

**LISTING 10.10**    continued

```
    }


  //-->
  </script>
</head>
<body>
  <script language="JavaScript1.1" type="text/javascript">
  <!--
    // Call function
    tellDifference(slHighway,  slCity);
  //-->
  </script>
</body>
</html>
```

This script will generate the text seen in Figure 10.9.

**FIGURE 10.9**
*Using the* Number
*object.*

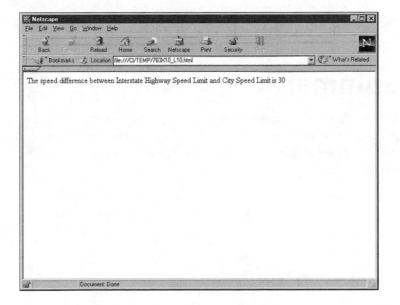

# The `Function` Object

The last core object is the `Function` object, which was added in JavaScript 1.1. This object lets you define a string at runtime and compile it as a function. Here is the syntax for declaring a `Function` object:

```
functionObjectName = new Function ([arg1, arg2, ... argn], functionBody);
```

Keep in mind that a `Function` object and a standard JavaScript `function` are similar but also different. The object name of a `Function` object is considered a *variable* representing the current value of the function defined with `new Function()`, whereas a name of a standard JavaScript function is not a variable, just the name of a function.

> **Note**
>
> `Function` objects are evaluated each time they are used. Not surprisingly, they are slower in execution than normal JavaScript functions.

You can use a Function object as an event handler, as shown in the following code:

```
window.onload = new Function("document.bgColor = 'aqua'" );
```

# Summary

You can think of the core language objects as the nuts and bolts of JavaScript, because much of the hard programming work is performed within the constructs of these objects. Also remember that it is these core objects that are standardized in the ECMAScript specification.

In this chapter, you learned how to use these core language objects and the differences that exist when working with different versions of browser software. In the next chapter, you will apply what you learned in this chapter about arrays as you examine how to create custom objects.

# Creating Custom JavaScript Objects

This chapter's discussion is a natural follow-up to the previous chapters. Chapter 9, "Client-Side Objects," covered many basics of object-oriented programming, and Chapter 10, "Core Language Objects," discussed the entire spectrum of built-in objects within the JavaScript language. But if you stop there, you limit a great deal of the power that JavaScript has: letting you create your own custom objects. In this chapter, I discuss how to create custom objects in JavaScript, the major capabilities of JavaScript, and its limitations.

# Creating an Object

Custom objects in JavaScript have a close association with arrays. Arrays are a means of structuring data into a container. Yet, as powerful as arrays are, they fail to meet the needs of everything you would like to do as a JavaScript developer. Although they store data, they cannot store behavior.

As discussed in Chapter 9, an object contains both data, known as *properties*, and behavior, known as *methods*. Therefore, although an array is essentially the same thing as an object with properties, it doesn't store information on how the array can respond to methods. Our mission, then, is to create an entity that can encapsulate data elements and responses to methods.

To create a JavaScript object, you need to create a *constructor*. A constructor is a special JavaScript function that defines what the object will look like and how it will act. The constructor doesn't actually create the object; instead, it provides a template for what an instantiated object will look like. (Creating an instance of an object is called *instantiating* an object.) The following is the basic structure of an instantiated object:

```
function object(parameter1, parameter2,...) {
    this.property1 = parameter1
    this.property2 = parameter2
    this.property3 = parameter3
    this.property4 = parameter4
    this.method1 = function1
    this.method2 = function2
}
```

As you can see, the actual structure of the constructor is relatively straightforward. First, you name the method itself. The name of the function will serve as the name of your object type. Therefore, it's critical for clarity's sake to give your constructor method a descriptive name. If you're creating an object to represent an invoice, call it `invoice`. I've seen some people name their constructors in a verb format, such as `createInvoice`. This practice can lead to confusing and hard-to-read code, because a property of the object would look like this:

*Creating Custom JavaScript Objects*

**CHAPTER 11**

293

11

Creating
Custom
JavaScript
Objects

```
myDate = createInvoice.date;
```

Even worse, if you had `create()` as a method of the object, your code would look like this:

```
createInvoice.create();
```

A much clearer method of presentation is to use a noun-based approach, which would make the preceding two lines much more readable:

```
myDate = invoice.date;
```

and

```
invoice.create();
```

Second, add parameters to the function for all the properties of the object. With this approach, when you instantiate the object, you pass the property values to the function as parameters.

Third, assign the value of the incoming parameters to the properties of the object. The `this` keyword comes in handy here; it's used to represent the object as you define the properties.

Fourth, define the methods that the object type will have. Whereas properties are assigned values by parameters of the constructor itself, methods are created as functions outside of the constructor and are assigned to the method definition of the object.

To illustrate, suppose I want to create a custom object in which I can store information on my favorite books. In particular, I want to track a book's title, author, ISBN, subject, and a personal rating. The constructor can be defined as follows:

```
function book(title, author, ISBN, subject, rating) {
  this.title = title;
  this.author = author;
  this.ISBN = ISBN;
  this.subject = subject;
  this.rating = rating;
}
```

Also, I want to add a method called `show()`, which displays the information on the instantiated object to the user. Therefore, I need to create a function, separate from the constructor itself, to do this:

```
function show() {
  objWindow = window.open("", "", "width=600,height=300");
  objWindow.document.write("<html><body >");
  objWindow.document.write("<h1>Object Description</h1>");
  objWindow.document.write("<p>");
  objWindow.document.write("Book Title: " + this.title + "<br>");
```

```
objWindow.document.write("Author: " + this.author + "<br>");
objWindow.document.write("ISBN: " + this.ISBN + "<br>");
objWindow.document.write("Subject: " + this.subject + "<br>");
objWindow.document.write("Allen's Rating: " + this.rating + "<br>");
objWindow.document.write("</body ></html>");
objWindow.document.close();
}
```

Even though this code is outside of the constructor, you can consider it a part of the object declaration. Therefore, you can use the `this` keyword and have it refer to the object instance that is being called.

I can then add a new entry to my constructor for the method:

```
function book(title, author, ISBN, subject, rating) {
  this.title = title;
  this.author = author;
  this.ISBN = ISBN;
  this.subject = subject;
  this.rating = rating;
  this.show = show; // New method to display
}
```

Notice two details about the `show()` method declaration. First, although the object method name is the same as the associated external function, it doesn't have to be. You can name each object method anything you like. For readability, some developers prefer to use identical names, and others prefix the external function with the object name, such as `book_show()`. Second, the external function doesn't include parentheses in the constructor, only the function name itself.

In older versions of Netscape Navigator, you needed to place a method definition above the object constructor, because all references were executed in a top-down format. This is no longer the case in Navigator 3+. The placement of the `show()` method relative to the constructor method isn't important from JavaScript's point of view.

I find it helpful to take advantage of this new capability and make the code easier to read by placing any method definitions immediately under the object constructor. I also use comments to keep the set of functions together and treated as a unit. Listing 11.1 shows the complete object declaration for the `Book` object.

**LISTING 11.1**  The `Book` Object Definition

```
<script type="text/javascript">
<!--
  function book(title, author, ISBN, subject, rating) {
```

*Creating Custom JavaScript Objects*

**CHAPTER 11**

295

11

Creating
Custom
JavaScript
Objects

**LISTING 11.1**   continued

```
    this.title = title;
    this.author = author;
    this.ISBN = ISBN;
    this.subject = subject;
    this.rating = rating;
    this.show = show;
  }
  function show() {
    objWindow = window.open("", "", "width=600,height=300");
    objWindow.document.write("<html><body >");
    objWindow.document.write("<h1>Object Description</h1>");
    objWindow.document.write("<p>");
    objWindow.document.write("Book Title: " + this.title + "<br>");
    objWindow.document.write("Author: " + this.author + "<br>");
    objWindow.document.write("ISBN: " + this.ISBN + "<br>");
    objWindow.document.write("Subject: " + this.subject + "<br>");
    objWindow.document.write("Allen's Rating: " + this.rating + "<br>");
    objWindow.document.write("</body ></html>");
    objWindow.document. close();
  }
//-->
</script>
```

# Instantiating Objects

To use the object I have declared in the book() constructor method, I need to create an instance of it in my JavaScript code. The new operator is used for this purpose. It has the following syntax:

```
objectInstance = new objectType(parameter1, parameter2, parameter3,...)
```

Using the new operator, I create a Book object using the following code:

```
dbBook = new book("Cost of Discipleship", "Dietrich Bonhoeffer",
➥"1-57521-118-1", "Grace", 5)
```

I can now refer to this object anywhere in my code using the dbBook variable. The instance will exist in memory as long as the page is loaded in my browser. After the user moves to a new page or closes the browser, the instance of the object disappears. This is important to understand when you start assigning values to object properties. If you want persistent objects, you will need to pass them to the server for processing.

> **Note**
>
> Persistence is a buzzword of the object community. In a nutshell, it means the capability to create an object instance and save the state of the object, so that the next time the object is accessed, it is retrieved in its saved state.
>
> You can't store objects persistently using client-side JavaScript.

To demonstrate what has been developed so far, Listing 11.2 has all the code necessary to create an instance of the Book object and call its show() method. Figure 11.1 shows the result of loading this page in a browser.

**LISTING 11.2**  Using the Book Object Constructor

```
<html>
<head>
  <title>Using the book object</title>
  <script type="text/javascript">
<!--
  function book(title, author, ISBN, subject, rating) {
    this.title = title;
    this.author = author;
    this.ISBN = ISBN;
    this.subject = subject;
    this.rating = rating;
    this.show = show;
  }

  function show() {
    objWindow = window.open("", "", "width=600,height=300");
    objWindow.document.write("<html><body >");
    objWindow.document.write("<h1>Object Description</h1>");
    objWindow.document.write("<p>");
    objWindow.document.write("Book Title: " + this.title + "<br>");
    objWindow.document.write("Author: " + this.author + "<br>");
    objWindow.document.write("ISBN: " + this.ISBN + "<br>");
    objWindow.document.write("Subject: " + this.subject + "<br>");
    objWindow.document.write("Allen's Rating: " + this.rating + "<br>");
    objWindow.document.write("</body ></html>");
    objWindow.document.close();
  }
//-->
```

*Creating Custom JavaScript Objects*

**CHAPTER 11**

297

11

Creating
Custom
JavaScript
Objects

**LISTING 11.2** continued

```
  </script>
</head>
<body>
  <script type="text/javascript">
  <!--
    // Book object defined here
    dbBook = new book("Cost of Discipleship", "Dietrich Bonhoeffer",
➡    "1-57521-118-1",  "Grace", 5);
    dbBook.show();
  //-->
  </script>
</body>
</html>
```

**FIGURE 11.1**
Book *object
information is
displayed in a
new window.*

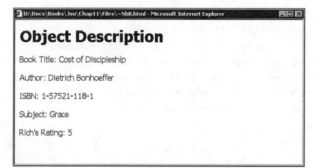

**D:\Docs\Books\Jsu\Chap11\Files\~SbB.html - Microsoft Internet Explorer**

# Object Description

Book Title: Cost of Discipleship

Author: Dietrich Bonhoeffer

ISBN: 1-57521-118-1

Subject: Grace

Rich's Rating: 5

# Working with Object Instances

After an object instance is created, you can work with it by assigning values to it or by performing one of its methods. You can also connect objects to user interface elements.

For example, suppose you want to create a form that will let you change the rating for books, as well as display the book information form for each of the Book objects you have instantiated. You can define the Book object as shown earlier and create five instances using the following code:

```
dbBook = new book("Cost of Discipleship", "Dietrich Bonhoeffer", "1-57521-118-1",
➡   "Grace", 5);
fkBook = new book("The Once and Future King", "T.H. White", "1-57521-112-1",
➡   "Camelot", 5);
olBook = new book("On Liberty", "John Stuart Mill", "1-53221-118-1",
```

```
➡  "Political Philosophy", 4);
iaBook = new book("Icarus Agenda", "Robert Ludlum", "1-53221-118-1",
➡  "Politcal Thriller", 2);
cnBook = new book("Chronicles of Narnia", "C.S. Lewis", "1-53231-128-1",
➡  "Children's Fiction", 5);
```

For the form itself, use a Select object with an <option> element defined for each of the books, as well as one for the rating (a range of 1 to 5). Add two buttons—one for the rating assignment and another for displaying the book information form. The form code looks like the following (and is shown in Figure 11.2):

```html
<body>
  <h1>Book Objects</h1>
  <form name="form1">
    <p>
      Select a book:
    </p>
    <p>
      <select name="bookList" size=1>
        <option value="dbBook">Cost of Discipleship</option>
        <option value="fkBook">The Once and Future King</option>
        <option value="olBook">On Liberty</option>
        <option value="iaBook">Icarus Agenda</option>
        <option value="cnBook">Chronicles of Narnia</option>
      </select>
    </p>
    <p>
      Assign a rating:
    </p>
    <p>
      <select name="rating" size=1>
        <option>1</option>
        <option>2</option>
        <option>3</option>
        <option>4</option>
        <option>5</option>
      </select>
    </p>
    <p>
      Click to assign:
    </p>
    <p>
      <input type="button" name="Assign" value="Assign" onClick="assignRating()">
    </p>
```

```
   <p>
     Click to show:
   </p>
   <p>
     <input type="button" name="Show" value="Show" onClick="showBook()">
   </p>
 </form>
</body>
```

**FIGURE 11.2**
*The* Book *object
form.*

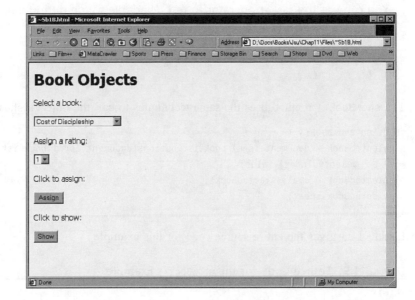

The heart of this example will be in the event handlers for the Assign and Show buttons. The `assignRating()` method assigns the value of the selected rating to the selected book:

```
function assignRating() {
  selectedBook = document.form1.bookList.options[document.form1.bookList.
      selectedIndex].value;
  selectedBook = eval(selectedBook);
  selectedBook.rating = document.form1.rating.options[document.form1.
      rating.selectedIndex].text;
}
```

Looking at this more closely, you can see that the method retrieves the value of the selected `bookList` option and assigns it to the `selectedBook` variable. To get this value, I use the `bookList` object's `options` property, along with its `selectedIndex` property. I now have the name of the Book object contained in the `selectedBook` variable, but JavaScript looks at this as a string value, not as a reference to an object instance. Therefore, the eval() method is used to convert the variable to an object reference.

The last line of the method uses the selectedBook variable to assign its rating property the value of the currently selected option in the ratingSelect object.

> **Note**
>
> You can use the typeof operator to test a variable's type during a method's execution. For example, you could display an alert message box showing the selectedBook variable's type using the following code:
>
> ```
> alert(typeof selectedBook);
> ```

The showBook() method uses the same techniques to call the object's show() method:

```
function showBook() {
  selectedBook = document.form1.bookList.options[document.form1.bookList.
      selectedIndex].value;
  selectedBook = eval(selectedBook);
  selectedBook.show();
}
```

Listing 11.3 gives the entire source code for this example.

**LISTING 11.3**   Source Code for the showBook() Example

```
<html>
<head>
  <title>Using the book object</title>
  <script type="text/javascript">
  <!--

  function book(title, author, ISBN, subject,  rating) {
    this.title = title;
    this.author = author;
    this.ISBN = ISBN;
    this.subject = subject;
    this.rating = rating;
    this.show = show;
  }

  function show() {
```

**11**

**LISTING 11.3** continued

```
    objWindow = window.open("", "", "width=600,height=300");
    objWindow.document.write("<html><body >");
    objWindow.document.write("<h1>Object Description</h1>");
    objWindow.document.write("<p>");
    objWindow.document.write("Book Title: " + this.title + "<br>");
    objWindow.document.write("Author: " + this.author + "<br>");
    objWindow.document.write("ISBN: " + this.ISBN + "<br>");
    objWindow.document.write("Subject: " + this.subject + "<br>");
    objWindow.document.write("Allen's Rating: " + this.rating + "<br>");
    objWindow.document.write("</body ></html>");
    objWindow.document.close();
  }


  function assignRating() {
    selectedBook = document.form1.bookList.options[document.form1.bookList.
➥      selectedIndex].value;
    selectedBook = eval(selectedBook);
    selectedBook.rating = document.form1.rating.options[document.form1.
➥      rating.selectedIndex].text;
  }


  function showBook() {
    selectedBook = document.form1.bookList.options[document.form1.bookList.
➥      selectedIndex].value;
    selectedBook = eval(selectedBook);
    selectedBook.show();
  }
  // Execute on loading
  dbBook = new book("Cost of Discipleship", "Dietrich Bonhoeffer",
➥    "1-57521-118-1", "Grace", 5);
  fkBook = new book("The Once and Future King", "T.H. White",
➥    "1-57521-112-1", "Camelot", 5);
  olBook = new book("On Liberty", "John Stuart Mill",
➥    "1-53221-118-1", "Political Philosophy", 4);
  iaBook = new book("Icarus Agenda", "Robert Ludlum",
➥    "1-53221-118-1", "Political Thriller", 3);
  cnBook = new book("Chronicles of Narnia", "C.S. Lewis",
➥    "1-53231-128-1", "Children's Fiction", 5);


  //-->
  </script>
</head>
```

**LISTING 11.3**   continued

```html
<body>
  <h1>Book Objects</h1>
  <form name="form1">
    <p>
      Select a book:
    </p>
    <p>
      <select name="bookList" size=1>
        <option value="dbBook">Cost of Discipleship</option>
        <option value="fkBook">The Once and Future King</option>
        <option value="olBook">On Liberty</option>
        <option value="iaBook">Icarus Agenda</option>
        <option value="cnBook">Chronicles of Narnia</option>
      </select>
    </p>
    <p>
      Assign a rating:
    </p>
    <p>
      <select name="rating" size=1>
        <option>1</option>
        <option>2</option>
        <option>3</option>
        <option>4</option>
        <option>5</option>
      </select>
    </p>
    <p>
      Click to assign:
    </p>
    <p>
      <input type="button" name="Assign" value="Assign" onClick="assignRating()">
    </p>
    <p>
      Click to show:
    </p>
    <p>
      <input type="button" name="Show" value="Show" onClick="showBook()">
    </p>
  </form>
```

**LISTING 11.3**    continued

```
</body>

</html>
```

# Creating Complex Objects

The objects covered so far have been *simple objects,* those with a single level of properties and methods. Another quick but more complex example of creating your own objects is the following buttonSet object. This object gives you a way to add buttons to an array of buttons on-the-fly, place a buttonSet in any Document object, space buttons, and conditionally display individual buttons. The constructor for the buttonSet object is shown in Listing 11.4.

**LISTING 11.4**   The buttonSet Object Constructor

```
<script type="text/javascript">
<!--
function buttonSet(name) {
  this.name = name;
  this.length = 0;
  this.addBtn = addBtn;
  this.print = print;

  // Point at which to add additional members to this object. If this
  // must be changed, reflect it in this.print()
  this.index = 4;      return this;
}

// print() method for buttonSet object
function print(dObj) {
  var spaceInt;
  for(var i = 5; this.index >= i; i++) {
    if(eval(this[i].condition)) {
      dObj.writeln('<a href="'+this[i].url+'"><img src="' +
        this[i].file+'" alt="'+this[i].alt +
        '" width="44" height="46" border=0></a>');

      // Add space if specified.
      spaceInt = 0 + this[i].spacer;
      if(navigator.appName == "Microsoft Internet Explorer") {
        spaceInt = spaceInt + 3 ;
```

**LISTING 11.4**    continued

```
      }
      if(spaceInt != 0) {
        dObj.write('<img src="images/space.gif" width=' + spaceInt +
➥        'height=46 border=0>');
      }
    }
  }
}
//-->
</script>
```

JavaScript also supports *complex objects,* with which an object's property can itself be an object. Complex objects let you structure your code in a more logical manner rather than being forced to dump all data into a single-level object.

Suppose you would like to track information on employees, their current projects, and their related clients. Obviously a client address really shouldn't be part of an employee object definition, so JavaScript's complex objects let you structure the data around three separate but related entities: employee, project, and client.

In the `employee` constructor, define the basic properties (name, phone, and email address) and a method called `showSummaryInfo()`. However, for project information, define a `project` property in the `employee` object. You would define this in much the same way you would a normal property, except that the `project` parameter is actually a reference to another object rather than a string value:

```
function employee(FirstName, LastName, HomePhone, Ext, EmailAddress, project) {
  this.FirstName = FirstName;
  this.LastName = LastName;
  this.HomePhone = HomePhone;
  this.Ext = Ext;
  this.EmailAddress = EmailAddress;
  this.Project = project;
  this.showSummaryInfo = summaryInfo;
}
```

Define the `project` object in asimilar manner, using the `client` object as a property:

```
function project(ProjectName, client, DevTool) {
  this.ProjectName = ProjectName;
  this.Client = client;
  this.DevTool = DevTool;
}
```

*Creating Custom JavaScript Objects*

**CHAPTER 11**    305

**11**

Creating
Custom
JavaScript
Objects

```
function client(ClientName, Address, City, State, Zip) {
  this.ClientName = ClientName;
  this.Address = Address;
  this.City = City;
  this.State = State;
  this.Zip = Zip;
}
```

To show how these nested objects can be referenced, define the `showSummaryInfo()` method of the `employee` object. This method opens a new window to display an employee summary information sheet—essentially a listing of all the properties for the `employee` object and the objects contained within it.

```
function summaryInfo() {
  objWindow = window.open("", "", "width=600,height=400");
    objWindow.document.write("<html><body>");
  objWindow.document.write("<h1>Employee Summary Information Sheet</h1>");

  objWindow.document.write("<h2>" + this.FirstName + " " + this.LastName
➡      + "</h2>");
  objWindow.document.write("<p><em><Sstrong>Contact Information</strong>
➡         </em></p>");
  objWindow.document.write("<p>Home Phone: " + this.HomePhone + "</p>");
  objWindow.document.write("<p>Ext.: " + this.Ext + "</p>");
  objWindow.document.write("<p>Email: " + this.EmailAddress + "</p>");


  objWindow.document.write("<p><em><strong>Project Information</strong>
➡         </em></p>");
  objWindow.document.write("<p>Current Project: " + this.project.ProjectName
➡          + "</p>");
  objWindow.document.write("<p>Client: " + this.Project.Client.ClientName
➡          + "</p>");
  objWindow.document.write("<p>Client: " + this.Project.Client.Address
➡          + "</p>");
  objWindow.document.write("<p>Client: " + this.Project.Client.City + ", " +
➡ this.Project.Client.State + " " + this.Project.Client.Zip + "</p>");
  objWindow.document.write("<p>Developmnt Tool Used: " + this.Project.DevTool
➡          + "</p>");
    objWindow.document.write("</body></html>");
  objWindow.document.close();
}
```

Child objects are referenced using familiar dot notation, so that the client's address is referenced with `this.Project.Client.Address`. The dot notation makes it easy to follow the code, since it specifies the path to the actual method or property being used. You can follow the parent object (before the first dot) down through the child objects, until you hit the final method or property.

Now that the constructors are defined for each of these object types, you can instantiate sample `employee`, `project`, and `client` objects:

```
CoastTech = new client("Coastal Techonology", "100 Beacon Hill", "Boston",
➡          "MA", "01220");
Coastal = new project("Coastal01", CoastTech, "JavaScript");
Allen = new employee("Allen", "Wyke", "617/555-1212", "100",
➡          "allen@anywhere.com", "Coastal");
```

The `project` parameter in the employee definition and the `client` parameter in the project definition are not strings; they are the names of the newly created objects. Also, notice the order in which these objects are created. Because the `Allen` object uses the `Coastal` project object as a parameter, `Coastal` must be instantiated first, or you will get an error. The same principle applies to creating the `CoastTech` instance of the `client` object before creating the `Coastal` project.

After the object instances are created, call `Allen.showSummaryInfo()` to display the window shown in Figure 11.3.

**FIGURE 11.3**
*The Employee Summary Information Sheet.*

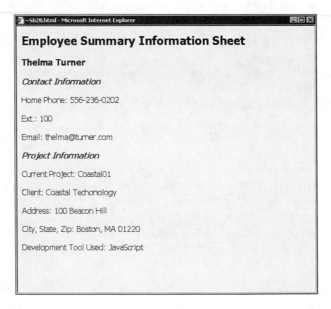

Listing 11.5 provides the entire source code for this example.

**LISTING 11.5**  Complete Example of Using the `employee`, `client`, and `project` Objects

```
<html>
<head>
  <title>Using the book object</title>
  <script type="text/javascript">
  <!--


  function employee(FirstName, LastName, HomePhone, Ext, EmailAddress, project) {
    this.FirstName = FirstName;
    this.LastName = LastName;
    this.HomePhone = HomePhone;
    this.Ext = Ext;
    this.EmailAddress = EmailAddress;
    this.Project = project;
    this.showSummaryInfo = summaryInfo;
  }

  function summaryInfo() {
    objWindow = window.open("", "", "width=600,height=400");
    objWindow.document.write("<html><body>");
    objWindow.document.write("<h1>Employee Summary Information Sheet</h1>");
    objWindow.document.write("<h2>" + this.FirstName + " " + this.LastName
        + "</h2>");
    objWindow.document.write("<p><em><Sstrong>Contact Information</strong>
        </em></p>");
    objWindow.document.write("<p>Home Phone: " + this.HomePhone + "</p>");
    objWindow.document.write("<p>Ext.: " + this.Ext + "</p>");
    objWindow.document.write("<p>Email: " + this.EmailAddress + "</p>");
    objWindow.document.write("<p><em><strong>Project Information</strong>
        </em></p>");
    objWindow.document.write("<p>Current Project: " + this.project.ProjectName
        + "</p>");
    objWindow.document.write("<p>Client: " + this.Project.Client.ClientName
        + "</p>");
    objWindow.document.write("<p>Client: " + this.Project.Client.Address
        + "</p>");
    objWindow.document.write("<p>Client: " + this.Project.Client.City + ", " +
        this.Project.Client.State + " " + this.Project.Client.Zip + "</p>");
    objWindow.document.write("<p>Development Tool Used: " + this.Project.DevTool
```

**LISTING 11.5    continued**

```
➡      + "</p>");
objWindow.document.write("</body></html>");
    objWindow.document.close();
}

  function project(ProjectName, client, DevTool) {
    this.ProjectName = ProjectName;
    this.Client = client;
    this.DevTool = DevTool;
  }

  function client(ClientName, Address, City, State, Zip) {
    this.ClientName = ClientName;
    this.Address = Address;
    this.City = City;
    this.State = State;
    this.Zip = Zip;
  }

  //-->
  </script>
</head>
<body>
  <script type="text/javascript">
  <!--
  CoastTech = new client("Coastal Techonology", "100 Beacon Hill", "Boston",
➡    "MA", "01220");
  Coastal = new project("Coastal01", CoastTech, "JavaScript");
  Allen = new employee("Allen", "Wyke", "617/555-1212", "100",
➡    "allen@anywhere.com", "Coastal");
  Allen.showSummaryInfo();
  //-->
  </script>
</body>
</html>
```

# Creating Objects Dynamically

The capability to create objects in code gives the JavaScript developer power and flexibility, but all the examples I've shown so far have dealt with objects being created as the window loads using the new operator. You might be wondering what capability you

*Creating Custom JavaScript Objects*

CHAPTER 11

309

11

Creating
Custom
JavaScript
Objects

have to dynamically create objects at runtime. After all, with other object-oriented programming environments, you can create object instances on-the-fly.

JavaScript allows you to create object instances on-the-fly, but with certain definite limitations. Initially, my plan was to create a generic instantiator function that created an object instance each time it was called. If this were successful, you could avoid using new statements that have already been defined and create objects based on input from the user. The idea was that the method would look like this:

```
function addEmployee(ObjectName,FirstName, LastName) {
  ObjectName = new employee(FirstName, LastName);
}
```

Ideally, this method would instantiate an object and give the object's name based on the ObjectName parameter. Unfortunately, no matter what was tried, JavaScript wouldn't allow the name of the object instance to be a variable. Instead, it used ObjectName as the name of the object. In contrast, the following is valid as long as Frank has already been defined as the object reference:

```
function addFrank(FirstName, LastName) {
  Frank = new employee(FirstName, LastName);
}
```

Although you can't dynamically name an object being instantiated, you can create an object as an element of a container array. You could, therefore, have an employeeList array that stores each employee object that is created. Therefore, if you modify the addEmployee() method, you could use the following:

```
function addEmployeeObject(FirstName, LastName, HomePhone, Ext, EmailAddress) {
  empList[i] = new employee(FirstName, LastName, HomePhone, Ext, EmailAddress);
}
```

Using this method, you can actually create object instances based on user input and dynamically create the object by calling the addEmployeeObject() method. For example, the form shown in Figure 11.4 allows a user to enter basic employee information. When the user clicks the Add button, a new object instance is created. Listing 11.6 shows the source code for this sample form.

**FIGURE 11.4**
*Dynamic object creation.*

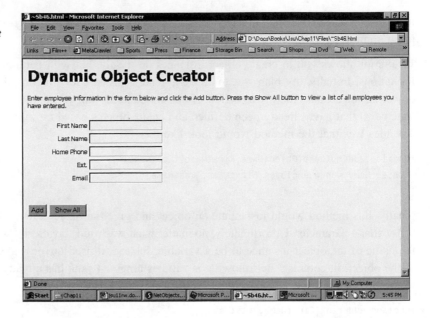

**LISTING 11.6**  Creating Objects Dynamically

```html
<html>
<head>
  <title>Intranet Employee Database</title>
  <script type="text/javascript">
<!--

    // Global variables
    var i = 0;

    // Create Array objects
    var empList = new Array();

    // Employee object constructor
    function employee(FirstName, LastName, HomePhone, Ext,  EmailAddress) {
      this.FirstName = FirstName;
      this.LastName = LastName;
      this.HomePhone = HomePhone;
      this.Ext = Ext;
      this.EmailAddress = EmailAddress;
      this.show = show;
    }


    function show() {
```

*Creating Custom JavaScript Objects*

**CHAPTER 11**    311

11

Creating
Custom
JavaScript
Objects

**LISTING 11.6**    continued

```
     alert(this.FirstName + "/n" +
➥       this.LastName + "/n" +
➥       this.HomePhone + "/n" +
➥
       this.Ext + "/n" +
➥       this.EmailAddress);
     }

   function addEmployeeObject(FirstName, LastName, HomePhone, Ext,
➥     EmailAddress) {
     empList[i] = new employee(FirstName, LastName, HomePhone, Ext,
➥     EmailAddress);
     }

   function insertRecord() {
     FirstName = document.form1.FirstName.value;
     LastName = document.form1.LastName.value;
     HomePhone = document.form1.HomePhone.value;
     Ext = document.form1.Ext.value;
     EmailAddress = document.form1.EmailAddress.value;
     i++;
     addEmployeeObject(FirstName, LastName, HomePhone, Ext, EmailAddress);
     }

   function showAll() {
     objWindow = window.open("", "", "width=600,height=300");
     objWindow.document.write("<html><body>");
     objWindow.document.write("<h1>Object Description</h1>");
     objWindow.document.write("<p>");
     for (var q=1; q<empList.length; q++) {
       objWindow.document.write("<strong>" + empList[q].FirstName
➥         + " " + empList[q].LastName + "</strong></p>");
       objWindow.document.write("<p>" + empList[q].HomePhone + "</p>");
       objWindow.document.write("<p>" + empList[q].Ext + "</p>");
       objWindow.document.write("<p>" + empList[q].EmailAddress + "</p>");

     objWindow.document.write("</body></html>");
     }
     objWindow.document.close()
   }
//-->
</script>
```

**LISTING 11.6   continued**

```
</head>
<body>
  <h1>Dyanamic Object Creator</h1>
  <p>Enter employee information in the form below and click the Add button.
  Press the Show All button to view a list of all employees you have
  entered.</p>
  <form name="form1">
    <pre>
      First Name:
      <input type=text size=20 maxlength=256 name="FirstName">
    </pre>
    <pre>
      Last Name:
      <input type=text size=20 maxlength=256 name="LastName">
    </pre>
    <pre>
      Home Phone:
      <input type=text size=20 maxlength=256 name="HomePhone">
    </pre>
    <pre>
      Ext.:
      <input type=text size=20 maxlength=256 name="Ext">
    </pre>
    <pre>
      Email Address:
      <input type=text size=20 maxlength=256 name="EmailAddress">

    </pre>
    <pre>
      <input type="button" name="Add" value="Add" onClick="insertRecord()">
      <input type="button" name="ShowAll" value="Show All"
        onClick="showAll()">

    </pre>
  </form>
</body>
</html>
```

The Show All button lets you see all the objects that have been created during that session. Figure 11.5 shows a list of employee objects that have been instantiated.

*Creating Custom JavaScript Objects*

**CHAPTER 11**

313

11

Creating
Custom
JavaScript
Objects

**Note**

Array objects were not supported in Netscape Navigator until 3.0. Keep this in mind when you are creating scripts for version 2.0, which does not support them.

**FIGURE 11.5**

*A list of objects created dynamically.*

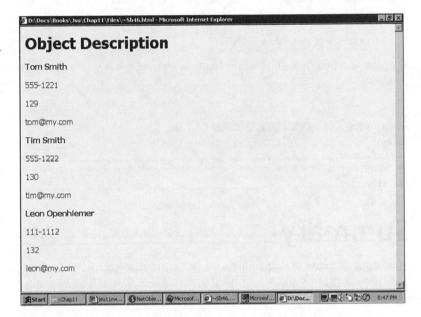

# Extending Instantiated Objects

Just as JavaScript is aloosely typed language in terms of data types, it's also flexible in terms of object definitions. You can extend the definition of any object instance by declaring the new property and assigning it a value. Using the Book object example from earlier in this chapter, suppose you wanted to add a Series property to the cnBook object after it has been defined. As you recall, it is defined as follows:

```
cnBook = new book("Chronicles of Narnia", "C.S. Lewis",
    "1-53231-128-1", "Children's Fiction", 5);
```

Later in the script, add a Series property to it using the following code:

```
cnBook.Series = "True";
```

This technique applies to that object instance only, not to the object type. However, browsers that support at least JavaScript 1.1 let you extend objects you already created using an object prototype. Its syntax is as follows:

```
objectType.prototype.propertyName;
```

An object prototype lets you add a property or method to each instance of an object type. Therefore, if you wanted to add a new `recommended` property to each `Book` object and it had the value of `true`, you could use the following line:

```
book.prototype.recommended = True;
```

You can test this by calling `alert(cnBook.recommended)`. The result is shown in Figure 11.6.

**FIGURE 11.6**

*Showing the value of a property using* `alert()`.

## Summary

JavaScript supports the capability to create custom objects in your client-side scripts. This adds a great deal of power and flexibility to JavaScript and allows you to structure your code in an object-based manner.

In this chapter, you learned all about the various aspects of creating and instantiating object types. You also learned about how to extend the power of normal objects by creating complex objects, which can also be referred to as "objects within objects." You can use complex objects to encapsulate data that spans multiple levels, much in the same way a relational database does with one-to-many table relationships. Finally, you learned how to extend objects that have already been instantiated by using the prototype operator.

As you proceed through the rest of this book, you will find many instances where custom objects are used.

# Server-Side JavaScript

Although JavaScript plays a key role on the client side, it can also be used to create server-based applications using Netscape's Server-Side JavaScript (SSJS). SSJS, like its client-side counterpart, is a set of objects, functions, and methods that extends the ECMAScript standard. It is used as a server-based scripting language in place of CGIs and other technologies to build Web-based applications.

### Note

Server-Side JavaScript was originally called LiveWire. Starting with Netscape Enterprise Server 3, LiveWire was integrated into the server and was therefore no longer considered a separate product. LiveWire now refers to its database connectivity functionality.

### Note

SSJS works only on Netscape servers, so you can't use it with other Web servers at this time. Microsoft does support JScript in its Active Server Pages (ASP), but those server-side language extensions are different than the SSJS extensions. Additionally, JavaServer Pages (JSP) is also a different technology.

Before we dive into SSJS, it is important to understand how to build client/server applications. SSJS and the Application Manager, which is used to manage these applications, represent the server in a client/server model. The client is the browser or application to which information is being sent. A firm grasp on these client/server theories will accelerate your learning, so we will take a quick look at them here.

# Using Client/Server Architecture

The client and server are separate entities, completely independent of each other until the client needs information from the server. The client/server concept has evolved beyond the server being a host for HTML pages; the server side of a Web application could be a true server, supporting application processing and database storage—not just the static document storage facility it has been in the past.

# Web-Based Client/Server

Web-based client/server development is slightly different from traditional client/server development. Traditionally, the server is a form of a database server used to store and process data requests from the client. In a Web-based client/server, the server might not necessarily be a database; it is just the Web server that is used for processing, administering, and performing calculations on HTML documents. The capability still exists to split processing between client and server, but the processing is usually centralized on the server.

## Two-Tier Application Structure

When developing such an application, you will partition it into two distinct pieces. This is the two-tier structure for client/server architecture. One piece is the user interface (UI), or frontend, where the user can interact with the application. The second is the server, the backend, where most of the processing capabilities reside. Because of client-side JavaScript, processing can be split between the client and the server according to the application's requirements.

In a traditional environment, it is reasonable to put more processing on the clients, because you usually have some control over the configuration and setup of those machines. You, the developer, can partition the application as you see fit, moving more or less processing to the client side, depending on its capabilities, server processing load, and network traffic flow.

The server is the processing engine for the application. It usually stores and manages large amounts of data and performs the processor-intensive, large-scale calculations and system processing.

The capability to segregate the two parts of a system, making them largely independent of each other, has contributed to significant advances in the development of large-scale database systems. The capability to split these two pieces gives the developer more flexibility in application design.

## *N*-Tier Application Structure

The *n*-tier methodology is used to overcome some of the limitations associated with the two-tier methodology. *N*-tier architecture involves splitting user interface, processing, and data storage into distinct levels, spreading the workload even further. The frontend remains responsible for the user interface and minor processing, and the backend is still responsible for data storage, but processing and calculations (or *business rules* as they are often referred to) have been moved to a middle layer. This allows changes to be made to the business rules without affecting the user interface or the database.

**12**

Server-Side
JavaScript

You have far less control over the frontend computer (both Web browser and desktop workstation) in the Web environment than you do in the normal application environment. It is more difficult to judge how well processes run on the client side. This makes it more reasonable to run processes on the backend, because you have control over that environment and can predict the outcome.

On the other hand, normal client/server applications face some problems that a Web-based client/server doesn't. In a normal client/server database application, if the client-side module is modified, you might need to redistribute the entire application. With a Web-based client/server, because the client is a Web page, the new frontend is just redistributed the next time the page is loaded.

The browser client initiates the transaction by sending a request to the server to perform some operation, database request, calculation, processing request, or Server-Side JavaScript function call. The client then waits for a response from the server before continuing. Server-side processing allows code to remain on one centralized server for easier modification and also gives you the benefit of faster processing, because the processing occurs on the server.

## Questions to Avoid Pitfalls

JavaScript presents you with client/server architecture questions as well. JavaScript processing can be distributed between the client and the server, depending on your preferences. Processing speed on the client is completely dependent on the client's environment, memory, speed, and other internal factors; processing on the server is dependent on the amount of traffic on the Internet as well as traffic and processing on the server. Dividing processing among multiple entities is a good idea, keeping intense processing on the more known quantity—the server.

> **Note**
>
> Thinking about architecture design early in the development phase of a Web application helps you build a more stable application that gives you the most processing power available.

# Client/Server Communication

Communication between client and server in a Web-based environment is an important component to consider—one that presents a new hurdle to overcome. Unlike client/server environments on a normal network, the Web environment doesn't provide a constant connection to the server; instead, communication is through HTTP protocols using TCP/IP.

## Client to Server

The first substantial exchange of information between client (browser) and server is the client request. Because of the nature of HTTP, it is necessary for browser clients to send requests to servers for all the information they want. Servers do not have a way of initiating an HTTP document transfer/connection.

The format for the HTTP request to the server can be a basic HTML page request or it can be a request that contains content information or data that needs to be processed or posted to the server. Additionally, a piece of information included in the request message, called the body, contains data (content) to be used by the server, either from functions or data-entry fields on the HTML document.

The HTTP request contains three basic groups of information:

- Request line: Method (`GET`, `HEAD`, `POST`), URL, and HTTP version

- Name/value pairs for fields such as `accept`, `referer`, `if-modified`, `user-agent`, `content-type`, and `content-length`

- Content: Information (data) being sent to the server for processing

## Server to Client

Once a client has sent a request to a server for information, that server will in turn send a message back to the client containing information that the client has requested. HTTP responses take a similar format to HTTP requests, but they include the returned HTML document (response) at the end.

The HTTP response contains three basic groups of information:

- Response line

- Response headers

- Response data

The response line from the server has the syntax of HTTP version, status code (a three-digit return code), and the response line of the text (not used by the browser, but it can be used for document interpretation). This might look like the following:

```
HTTP/1.1 200 OK
Server: Netscape-Enterprise/3.5.1G
Date: Wed, 19 Apr 2000 17:13:33 GMT
Content-type: text/html
Connection: close
```

The response line gives the browser some initial information about what it can expect to follow in the rest of the response. The HTTP version tells it how to begin interpreting the document response, and the status code tells it what to expect as far as the return. For example, a response status code of 200 is "OK."

> **Note**
>
> There is a variety of response codes (such as 200, 302, and 404) that relate to the state and content of the document being returned.

The response data, or body, is the final part of the HTTP response and is in the format defined by the content-type passed. The significance of this data depends on the status code that is returned in the response header. The response data is usually in the form of an HTML document to be displayed in the client browser.

## Session Management

One of the benefits of the Web and its design is also one of its biggest obstacles in applications that require client interaction with the server itself. Because a server operates in a stateless environment, it can run faster, but it has to rely on the client to remind it who the client is when a client makes a request. The evolution of HTML from static pages to interactive applications has made a formerly stateless environment look for ways to maintain state.

Because the client is not continuously connected to the Web server, there is the problem of knowing how to tell a Web server who the client is when the client reconnects to send a request back to the server. If Web applications remained continuously connected to the server, Web development would be as uncomplicated as generic client/server applications—but they aren't.

There are several techniques for session management, including the use of client cookies, URL encoding, and IP addresses on the server. The first two techniques can involve complete client-side state maintenance or help from the server. IP addresses require the server to maintain the information, while the client can help.

# Cookies

Cookies provide a Web server with a mechanism, through identification, to save client information that can be used in future connections to the server. Cookies are a client-based state maintenance methodology. The server saves the information that it needs about the client on the client itself, and the client sends the information back with every HTTP request.

Cookies are stored in a text file on the client drive. The server, as a means of keeping track of the client's state, has the capability to set the information in a cookie as long as the browser allows it. Different browsers handle cookies different ways. Some (such as Navigator) have only one cookie file where all servers write cookie information to the same file, tagging sections in the cookie with the specific URL names as they are saved and updated. Others (such as Internet Explorer) store cookie information in multiple files located in a cookie directory.

> **Warning**
>
> The size of the cookie file is limited, so only a certain amount of information can be stored on any given client. This limits the amount of information that each server can store and the number of Web servers that can store information on a specific client computer.

With cookies, the possibility always exists that the user could delete the cookie file by mistake (after all, it's only a text file). Then every server would lose whatever state information it had been maintaining, and the client would need to start from scratch in establishing itself with the server.

Because cookie information is stored on the client side, it is not affected by server issues. It also allows the client to resend a request successfully, even if problems are encountered on the server side. Another benefit of cookies is that, because the server isn't required to store any information about the client, the server can forget about the client after the initial request for information, and no storage of information is required on the server.

Cookies increase the amount of Internet traffic, because the server is sending and receiving extra information with every client URL request. Cookie information is transferred in the name/value pair methodology, using the cookie protocol for transferring cookie information with requests.

## URL Encoding

The client URL encoding methodology for maintaining state information between client and server involves sending `name/value` pairs or unique key fields of information as part of the URL string at client HTTP request time. This method of storing state information has the same benefits for the server as cookies, in that no information needs to be stored on the server.

> **Note**
>
> Using this process to maintain client state requires that the URL be built dynamically each time a request is made, which can cause a significant increase in the size of the URL.

Using client-side URL encoding allows more flexibility when the need for state maintenance exists. Unlike cookies, client URL encoding isn't browser specific. Because you don't know which type of browser is accessing your server, this is a more reliable method of maintaining state.

## IP Address on the Server

A third method of maintaining state is to store IP addresses and state information on the server. The server must have database access or shared memory in which to store the information. The state information of a client is stored based on the IP address of the client, and this information is held and usable only by this particular server.

Because of these drawbacks, this type of state maintenance is useful only if the following criteria apply:

- Clients are known to have fixed IP addresses.

- Only one server supports the application.

The practice of dynamically allocating IP addresses for machines that in turn run a Web browser makes this type of state maintenance impossible to implement. Multiple Web servers can't be supported using this methodology, either.

# Developing Server-Side JavaScript Applications

Now that we have gone over the specifics of the server-side JavaScript language, let's look at the process of developing an application in this environment using SSJS. Figure 12.1 details the process.

**FIGURE 12.1**

*The Server-Side JavaScript development process.*

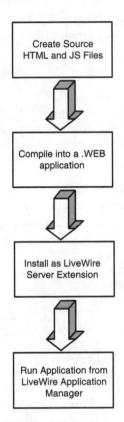

Create Source HTML and JS Files

Compile into a .WEB application

Install as LiveWire Server Extension

Run Application from LiveWire Application Manager

## Creating Source Files

The first step in building a Server-Side JavaScript application is to create your source files, which can be one of two types:

- Source HTML documents: These documents can be either static pages or JavaScript-enabled pages. They have an .htm or .html extension.

- JavaScript library files: These files, which have a .js extension, serve as library files containing JavaScript functions. You don't need to use HTML tags in these files.

These files are needed because, unlike client-side JavaScript, SSJS has to be compiled into bytecode before it can be loaded in the Web server. This is an advantage and a disadvantage of using JavaScript on the server side. The advantage is that it should be faster because it has been precompiled. However, it is a disadvantage because it means most things built with SSJS have to be Web-based applications and not everyday pages, which is something most developers need as well.

## HTML Documents

In many cases, you will want to embed JavaScript code in your HTML documents, just as you do with client-side JavaScript. However, the way you embed server JavaScript in your HTML file can change the result. To embed JavaScript into your documents, you can use one of two options.

First, you can use the <server> and </server> tags to surround server JavaScript code. In many ways, the use of these tags is very similar to the <script> and </script> tags you use in client-side JavaScript. Suppose you want to generate a line that displays the person's ID, which he would have passed to you in a form earlier. You could use the <server> tag to do the following:

```
<server>
  if (client.custid == null) {
    write("You have no customer ID");
  }else{
    write("Your customer ID is " + client.custid);
  }
</server>
```

The second option does not require you to use the <server> tag, because it is within another HTML tag (that is, between the < and > of another tag). If you need to add a JavaScript expression inside another HTML tag, you can surround the code with backquotes (\Q). You will find that backquotes are useful when working with Link, Anchor, and Form objects. For example, if you want to generate HTML with a link created on-the-fly based on the client's Web address, again entered previously, you could use the following:

```
<A HREF=\'client.WebAddress\'>Your Home Page</A>
```

When you embed server JavaScript into your source HTML documents, the user sees only the result of the code, not the code itself. Server-Side JavaScript thus contrasts with client-side JavaScript, which the user can see simply by viewing the source file in any Web browser.

Listing 12.1 is a source HTML file with embedded JavaScript. When the application runs, however, the HTML source shown in Listing 12.2 is what the client can see if the source code is viewed in the browser. (Figure 12.2 shows the actual presentation of the HTML.) In case you're wondering about the meaning of the JavaScript expressions, I'll talk about the Client object a little later in this chapter. At this point, think of these expressions as properties of an object that has already been created and defined elsewhere.

**LISTING 12.1**   An Embedded Server Script

```html
<html>
<head>
  <title>Feedback</title>
</head>
<body>
  <h1>
    "Superiffic" Feedback Confirmation
  </h1>
  <p>
    Dear <server>client.firstName</server>,
  </p>
  <p>
    Thank you for submitting feedback about our product. If you have asked
    us to contact you, we will be using the following information:
  </p>
  <blockquote>
    <p>
      <strong>
        E-mail: <server>client.email</server>
      </strong><br>
      <strong>Telephone: <server>client.phone</server>
      </strong><br>
      <strong>FAX: <server>client.fax</server>
      </strong>
    </p>
  </blockquote>
  <p>
```

**LISTING 12.1    continued**

```
    If any of this information is incorrect, please go back to the feedback
    form and change it. We thank you for taking the time to help us be a
    "superiffic" company.
  </p>
  <p>
    Sincerely,
  </p>
  <p>
    Rupert Mydryl
    <br>
    Manager, Customer Services
  </p>
</body>
</html>
```

**LISTING 12.2    The Resulting Document Given to the Client**

```
<html>
<head>
 <title>Feedback</title>
</head>
<body>
  <h1>
    "Superiffic" Feedback Confirmation
  </h1>
  <p>
    Dear Charles:
  </p>
  <p>
    Thank you for submitting feedback about our product. If you have asked
    us to contact you, we will be using the following information:
  </p>
  <blockquote>
    <p>
      <strong>
        E-mail: chappy@smiles.com
      </strong><br>
      <strong>
        Telephone: 808-555-1212
      </strong><br>
      <strong>
        FAX: 808-555-5050
```

**LISTING 12.2**    continued

```
        </strong>
    </p>
</blockquote>
<p>
    If any of this information is incorrect, please go back to the feedback
    form and change it. We thank you for taking the time to help us be a
    "superiffic" company.
</p>
<p>
    Sincerely,
</p>
<p>
    Rupert Mydryl
    <br>
    Manager, Customer Services
</p>
</body>
</html>>
```

**FIGURE 12.2**
*The HTML document in the browser.*

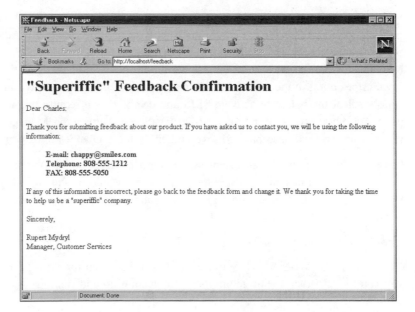

## JavaScript Library Files

Any serious development environment needs somewhere to place generic functions that can be called from a variety of sources. As on the client side, the server-side version of JavaScript allows you to place JavaScript code in external text files, denoted with a `.js` extension.

Inside this JavaScript library file, there should be functions, not HTML. You can then reference these functions inside your HTML files. When your SSJS application is compiled, the compiler resolves all the calls to external functions by looking at the `.js` files that you have included in the application.

# Preparing Your Application

Unlike client-side JavaScript, the server-side implementation requires that you compile your source files into a `.web` application file. For this reason, most implementations of SSJS are Web-based applications. Over the next few sections we will talk about how you build these applications and run them on your Netscape Enterprise Server (NES), which includes the releases under the iPlanet product line.

## Enabling Server-Side JavaScript

Before users can access your application, you need to enable server-side JavaScript on your instance of Enterprise Server. To do this, simply access the Enterprise Administration Server and select the server instance on which you want to enable SSJS. Once the Server Manager for that instance comes up, select the Programs tab and click the Server Side JavaScript option in the menu. All you need to do on this page, shown in Figure 12.3, is simply select the button to activate SSJS and decide if you require the administrator password when accessing the Server-Side JavaScript Application Manager (which is a good idea). You will also have to save and apply these changes once completed.

Once you have restarted that instance of Enterprise Server as the Administration Server requires, you will be able to access the Application Manager, shown in Figure 12.4, from the following URL. You should replace *www.yourinstance.com* with the name of your server:

`http://www.yourinstance.com/appmgr`

Now that the Server-Side JavaScript environment has been turned on and is ready to go, you can move forward with getting your application up and running.

**FIGURE 12.3**
*Enabling Server-Side JavaScript in Netscape Enterprise Server 4.*

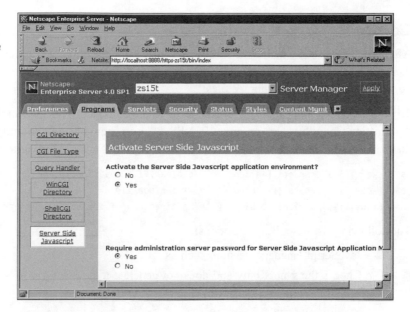

**FIGURE 12.4**
*The Server-Side JavaScript Application Manager.*

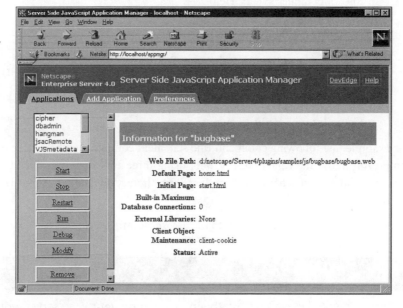

# Compiling Your Applications

After you've finished creating the source files for your application, you're ready to compile them. The compiler that comes with NES creates a bytecode .web file from the HTML documents and JavaScript library files.

To compile these applications, you need to go to the command line and run the JavaScript Application Compiler (jsac) program. In NES 4.0, you should be able to find this binary in the bin\https\bin subdirectory of the installation. Here is a list of the variations of syntax:

```
jsac [-cdv] [-l charSet] [-a langVer] -o binaryFile [-i] inputFile1 [-i] inputFile2...
jsac [-cdv] [-a langVer] -o binaryFile -f includeFile
jsac [-cdv] [-a langVer] -o binaryFile -p directory -f includeFile -r errorFile
```

The following list describes the options:

-a JavaScript language version, such as "1.2."

-c Checks the syntax only and does not generate a binaryFile.

-d Enables debug output.

-f includeFile Filename to include.

-h Shows compiler syntax Help.

-i Input filename.

-l Character set name (iso-8859-1 or x-sjis, for example).

-o Creates a .web file using the specified name.

-p Path is set to current path when processing files.

-r Redirects error output to the specified errorFile.

-v Compiles with verbose output.

For example, the following command-line statement compiles (with verbose output) a SSJS application into a file called policy.web, using three HTML source files (index.htm, toc.htm, and polpage.htm) and two JavaScript library files (jsroutine.js and jsdates.js):

```
lwcomp -v -o policy.web index.htm toc.htm polpage.htm jsroutines.js jsdates.js
```

> **Tip**
>
> Once Server-Side JavaScript has been enabled on your Web server, you can remotely compile applications by accessing the jsacRemote program that comes with the Application Manager. Simply enter the URL to your instance of Enterprise Server, and use /jsacRemote as the path to access this application.

# Installing Applications

To install applications on the server using the Server-Side JavaScript Application Manager, click the Add Application tab to begin the installation process. After you click this tab, the right frame of the window displays an HTML form for you to fill out, as shown in Figure 12.5.

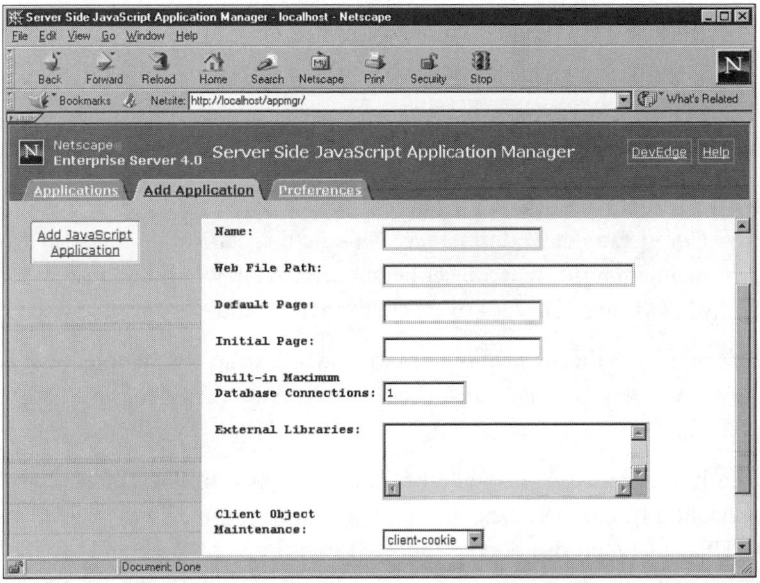

**FIGURE 12.5**
*Adding an application.*

Fill out the form based on the following information.

- **Name:** Enter the name of the application. This name is used to access the application after it is installed. For example, if you name an application `fireball` on a server with a URL of www.junebug.com, you could access it with the following request:

  `http://www.junebug.com/fireball`

### Caution

Be sure you don't give an application the same name as an existing directory on the Web server. If you do, a client will be unable to access that directory on the server.

- **Web File Path:** Enter the full path and filename of the `.web` application file.

- **Default Page:** Optionally, enter an HTML filename to serve as the default page of an application. The default page is served when a client who has already accessed the application doesn't specify a file in the request.

- **Initial Page:** Optionally, enter an HTML filename to serve as the opening page when the application is accessed by a client.

- **Built-in Maximum Database Connections:** If you're accessing a database and running from an NT server, enter the maximum number of concurrent connections your database server permits.

- **External Libraries:** If your application uses external libraries (for example, dynamic link libraries), enter the full path in the space provided.

- **Client Object Maintenance:** This field specifies the mode in which you're maintaining `Client` object persistence. Available options are `client-cookie`, `client-url`, `server-ip`, `server-cookie`, and `server-url`.

After you enter the application information, click the OK button at the bottom of the page. The Application Manager then checks your input values for any errors, and installs the application on the server.

Once it is installed, you should be able to go back to the Applications tab and see your application listed. Start the application by clicking Run. Then you can access it by entering the URL to Enterprise Server, followed by a forward slash and the name of your application. The following shows an example of how to call the myApp application.

```
http://www.mysite.com/myApp
```

> **Note**
>
> When you modify the source of an application and recompile, you must restart the application using the Application Manager before changes take effect.

## Troubleshooting

Now that everything is running, you can access your application to make sure it is functioning properly. If all is working perfectly, you are finished and ready to allow your users access to the application. If there are problems, then you need to start debugging the application to find out what the problem is.

## General Debugging

If you work with both client-side and server-side JavaScript, you might get spoiled when you start working with the server-side debugger; you will probably soon wish you could use the debugger for client-side JavaScript as well. There is a debugger within the Application Manager that can be accessed by selecting the application from the list and clicking Debug. This results in the opening of a new browser window with a trace frame (or window) displayed beside it, as shown in Figure 12.6. The trace window shows the current objects and their properties. You can also use the built-in debug() function, which operates just like the write() function, to bring the result of a JavaScript expression to the trace window.

**FIGURE 12.6**
*The Server-Side JavaScript Application Manager debugger.*

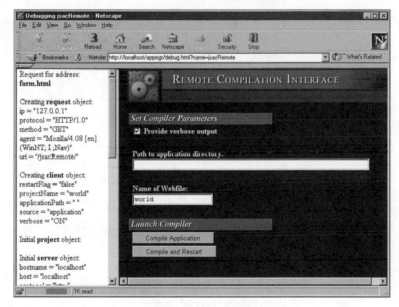

## Database Problems

Most of the methods you use to interact with a database return a status code. A status code is an integer in the range 0 to 27. A code of 0 indicates that the command finished successfully, whereas the other values, shown in Table 12.1, indicate specific errors from the server.

TABLE **12.1**  Database Status Codes

| Status Code | Description |
| --- | --- |
| 0 | No error. |
| 1 | Out of memory. |
| 2 | Object not initialized. |
| 3 | Type conversion error. |
| 4 | Database not registered. |
| 5 | Error reported by server. |
| 6 | Message from server. |
| 7 | Error from vendor library. |
| 8 | Lost connection. |
| 9 | End of fetch. |
| 10 | Invalid use of object. |
| 11 | Column does not exist. |
| 12 | Invalid positioning within object (bounds error). |
| 13 | Unsupported feature. |
| 14 | Null reference parameter. |
| 15 | Database object not found. |
| 16 | Required information is missing. |
| 17 | Object cannot support multiple readers. |
| 18 | Object cannot support deletions. |
| 19 | Object cannot support insertions. |
| 20 | Object cannot support updates. |
| 21 | Object cannot support updates. |
| 22 | Object cannot support indices. |
| 23 | Object cannot be dropped. |
| 24 | Incorrect connection supplied. |
| 25 | Object cannot support privileges. |
| 26 | Object cannot support cursors. |
| 27 | Unable to open. |

The database object includes four error-handling methods that return error codes and messages from the database server. The values of what is returned depend greatly on the backend database server. Tables 12.2 through 12.5 list the return values for each of the SQL databases natively supported by SSJS.

**TABLE 12.2** Informix Vendor Library Errors (Status Code 7)

| Method | What It Returns |
|---|---|
| majorErrorMessage() | Vendor Library Error:*errorMsg* (*errorMsg* is text from Informix). |
| minorErrorMessage() | ISAM Error:*errorMsg* (*errorMsg* is text of the ISAM error code from Informix or an empty string (" ") if no ISAM error occurred). |
| majorErrorCode() | Informix error code. |
| minorErrorCode() | ISAM error code (or zero if there is no ISAM error). |

**TABLE 12.3** Oracle Server Errors (Status Code 5)

| Method | What It Returns |
|---|---|
| majorErrorMessage() | Server Error:*errorMsg* (where *errorMsg* is translation of Oracle return code). |
| minorErrorMessage() | Oracle server name. |
| majorErrorCode() | Return code as reported by Oracle Call-level Interface (OCI). |
| minorErrorCode() | Operating system error code as reported by OCI. |

**TABLE 12.4** Sybase Vendor Library Errors (Status Code 7)

| Method | What It Returns |
|---|---|
| majorErrorMessage() | Vendor Library Error:*errorMsg* (where *errorMsg* is error text from DB-Library). |
| minorErrorMessage() | Operating system error text (as specified by DB-Library). |
| majorErrorCode() | DB-Library error number. |
| minorErrorCode() | Severity level (as specified by DB-Library). |

**TABLE 12.5** Sybase Server Errors (Status Code 5)

| Method | What It Returns |
|---|---|
| majorErrorMessage() | Server Error:*errorMsg* (where *errorMsg* is text from SQL server). If severity and message number are both zero, just the message text is returned. |
| minorErrorMessage() | SQL server name. |
| majorErrorCode() | SQL server message number. |
| minorErrorCode() | Severity level (as specified by SQL server). |

**12**

**Server-Side JavaScript**

# Understanding Core Server-Side Objects

Now that we have an understanding of how the client/server model works in the Internet space and how server-side JavaScript operates, it is time to discuss the objects (shown in Figure 12.7) you have at your disposal for building your applications. The central purpose of these server objects is to manage persistent data. Within the Web's stateless environment, these objects can store various types of data persistently across multiple requests per client, across multiple clients, and even across multiple SSJS applications.

**FIGURE 12.7**
*Basic Server-Side JavaScript object framework.*

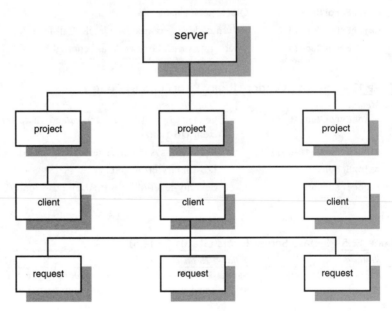

## The Server Object

The Server object is used to manage global data about the server itself. This object is always present on an SSJS server and is created when the server is started. It is destroyed only when the server shuts down. It has several built-in properties and methods, as shown in Table 12.6.

**TABLE 12.6**  Built-In Methods and Properties of the `Server` Object

| Type | Item | Description |
|------|------|-------------|
| Method | `lock()` | Locks your code while you perform data manipulation that should have only a single thread connected to it. |
| | `unlock()` | Unlocks the previously locked code. |
| Property | `host` | String specifying the server name, subdomain, and domain of the Web server. |
| | `hostname` | Full name of the server (including port); the same as concatenating the `host` and `port` properties. |
| | `jsVersion` | Contains the JavaScript server version and platform. |
| | `port` | Server port number used by the server. |
| | `protocol` | Internet protocol in use, which is the information in the URL up to the first colon. |

Read through the next section on the `Project` object to better understand the `lock()` and `unlock()` methods. They operate in the same manner.

## The `Project` Object

The `Project` object is designed to maintain application-wide information across clients and maintain persistence until the application is closed on the server. This object does not contain any properties, but it does have two methods, which are described in Table 12.7.

**TABLE 12.7**  Built-In Methods of the `Project` Object

| Method | Description |
|--------|-------------|
| `lock()` | Locks your code while you perform data manipulation that should have only a single thread connected to it. |
| `unlock()` | Unlocks the previously locked code. |

With the multiuser nature of a Web, hundreds or thousands of users could access an SSJS application concurrently. As a result, it is not unusual for multiple persons to be either reading or writing to a `Project` object at the same time. SSJS automatically enforces implicit locking for the length of time it takes to read or set a property value.

> **Note**
>
> Beginning with version 4.01 of the Netscape Enterprise Server, there is no implicit locking for the `Project` and `Server` objects as there was in previous releases.

12

Server-Side
JavaScript

You might sometimes need to lock a property explicitly. The best example of this is if you want to base the value of an incrementing number, such as an invoice number, on the existing value of a property. To do so, you need to read the old value, add a value to it, and then reassign the new value to the property.

Implicit locking doesn't work in this context; however, you can use the `Project` object's `lock()` method to perform this process. The `lock()` method places an explicit lock on the object itself until an `unlock()` method is called. For example, to assign a new invoice number based on the existing one, you could use the following code:

```
project.lock();
project.invoiceNum += 1;
project.unlock();
```

If another client tries to access the `Project` object during this process, it is forced to wait until the process is finished.

> **Note**
>
> SSJS ensures that a deadlock, where two objects have a lock on the database, can't occur within a `Project` instance by automatically releasing any locks after each client request.

## The `Client` Object

As you will see, `Request` objects exist for a specific moment in time. However, because a client's interaction with a server application often spans more than a single request, the `Client` object is used to provide state throughout a series of stateless requests. A new `Client` object is instantiated each time a new client accesses the application. Like the `Project` object, the `Client` object has no properties, but it does have two methods. Table 12.8 lists these two methods and a short description of each.

**TABLE 12.8**   Built-In Methods of the `Client` Object

| Method | Description |
|---|---|
| `destroy()` | This method explicitly destroys the object and all properties maintained by the object. |
| `expiration()` | This method allows you to change the default 10-minute expiration of `Client` objects to another time period. |

The `Client` object is designed to self-destruct after a specific length of time. The reason behind this is that you want to maintain state across client requests, but you have no way to determine which request is a client's last request. Because you obviously don't want to leave unused `Client` objects in memory any longer than necessary, you need to determine when they should expire automatically. The default time period is 10 minutes, but you can change this value by using the object's `expiration()` method.

For example, to extend the expiration period to 20 minutes, you would use the following code:

```
client.expiration(1200);
```

If you change the default time period, the `expiration()` method must be defined in each page of the application. Any page that doesn't have this method uses the default expiration setting.

## The `Request` Object

A `Request` object is instantiated for each new request received by the server. This newly created `Request` object contains data from the current request of the client. The `Request` object has several built-in properties, which are listed in Table 12.9.

TABLE **12.9**   Built-In Properties of the `Request` Object

| Property | Description |
|----------|-------------|
| agent | Client software information (such as name and version). |
| auth_type | Authorization type; corresponds to the CGI environment variable AUTH_TYPE. |
| auth_user | The name of the local HTTP user of the browser, if HTTP access authorization has been activated. Corresponds to the CGI environment variable REMOTE_USER. |
| formKey | Represents any form key that is sent by the browser. |
| imageX | Horizontal location of the mouse pointer over an imagemap. |
| imageY | Vertical location of the mouse pointer over an imagemap. |
| ip | IP address of the client. |
| method | HTTP method (typically GET or POST). |
| protocol | HTTP protocol level of the client. |
| query | Contains information submitted after the ? on the URL. Corresponds to the CGI environment variable QUERY_STRING. |

As mentioned in Table 12.9, the `Request` object also has corresponding properties for each input element of a submitted HTML form—`formKey`. Suppose, for example, that a user submitted the form shown in Listing 12.3.

**LISTING 12.3**   Registration Form Example

```html
<html>
<head>
  <title>Online Registration</title>
</head>
<body>
<h1>Registration</h1>
<hr>
  <form action="/ssjs/objects" method="POST">
    <p>
      Please provide the following contact information:
    </p>
    <em>Name</em>
    <input type="text" size="35" maxlength="256" name="FullName"><br>
    <em>Title</em>
    <input type="text" size="35" maxlength="256" name="Title"><br>
    <em>Organization</em>
    <input type="text" size="35" maxlength="256" name="Organization"><br>
    <em>E-mail</em>
    <input type="text" size="25" maxlength="256" name="Email"><br>
    <p>
      <input type="submit" value="Submit">
      <input type="reset" value="Reset">
    </p>
</form>
</body>
</html>
```

When a `Request` object is created based on this form's submission, the following properties are associated with it:

```
request.FullName
request.Title
request.Organization
request.Email
```

The one form element that is a special case occurs when a `Select` object is set to accept multiple values (that is, the `multiple` parameter is set in the `<select>` definition). You can use the built-in `getOptionValue()` and `getOptionValueCount()` functions to iterate through multiple values of a `Select` object. The `getOptionValue()` function is defined as

```
getOptionValue(name, index);
```

The *name* parameter is the Select object name, and the *index* parameter is the index of the options array. For example, look at the list of options in the Select object defined in Listing 12.4 and shown in Figure 12.8. When the form is submitted to the server, Listing 12.5 is requested. Using a familiar-looking for loop, you can iterate through each element that was selected. Figure 12.9 shows the resulting HTML form that the write() function creates dynamically.

**LISTING 12.4** A Form to Pick Songs

```html
<html>
<head>
  <title>Song-Picker</title>
</head>
<body>
  <h2>Pick Your Favorite Songs From the List:</h2>
  <form action="topsongs.htm" method="post" name="songSelect">
    <select name="songs" size="10" multiple>
      <option>1979 (Smashing Pumpkins)</option>
      <option>Breakfast at Tiffany's (Deep Blue Something)</option>
      <option>Don't Cry (Seal)</option>
      <option>Flood (Jars of Clay)</option>
    </select>
    <input type="submit" value="Submit">
  </form>
</body>
</html>
```

**FIGURE 12.8**
*A multiselection list before it is submitted.*

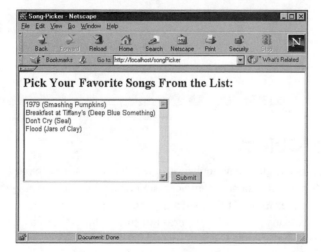

LISTING 12.5   Server-Side Code to Process Song Submission

```
<html>
<head>
  <title>Results Page</title>
</head>
<body>
<server>
  write("<h2>The songs selected included:</h2>");
  write("<ul>");
  var size = getOptionValueCount("songs");
  for (var i = 0; i < size; i++) {
    write("<li>" + getOptionValue("songs", i) + "</li>\n");
  }
  write("</ul>");
</server>
</body>
</html>
```

FIGURE **12.9**

*A document generated on-the-fly.*

## The Lock **Object**

The Lock object is used to create locks for other objects. As mentioned before, these locks prevent any other object instance from accessing data when only a single thread is desired. A counter is a great example of this, such as when you might want to count the number of clients or requests being made over a period of time. This object has three methods and a single property, which are defined in Table 12.10.

**TABLE 12.10**    Built-In Methods and Property of the Lock Object

| Type | Item | Description |
|------|------|-------------|
| Method | isValid() | Verifies that the construction of the Lock object was successful. |
| | lock() | Locks your code while you perform data manipulation that should have exclusive access. |
| | unlock() | Unlocks the previously locked code. |
| Property | prototype | Allows you to add methods and properties to the Lock object. |

# The File Object

Up to this point, we have looked only at some of the "automatic" objects. By automatic I mean those that are created within the SSJS environment simply by starting the server, getting requests, maintaining projects, or performing locks. The first object we are going to look at outside of the automatic ones is the File object.

The File object lets you read and write data to a file on the server's file system, which is very helpful. The commands for reading and writing to files are largely standard across programming languages, so if you have had any experience with other languages, you should feel right at home. This object has only one property but several methods. Table 12.11 contains a list of these and a short description.

**TABLE 12.11**    File Object Property and Methods

| Type | Item | Description |
|------|------|-------------|
| Method | byteToString() | Converts a number that represents a byte into a string. |
| | clearError() | Clears the file error status. |
| | close() | Closes a file. |
| | eof() | Determines whether the file pointer is at the end of the file. |
| | error() | Returns the current error status. |
| | exists() | Determines whether the specified file exists. |
| | flush() | Writes the content of the internal buffer to a file. |
| | getLength() | Gets the length of the file. |
| | getPosition() | Gets the current position in the file. |
| | open() | Opens the file for access. |
| | read() | Reads data from the file into a string. |
| | readByte() | Reads the number of bytes you specify and returns its value. |
| | readln() | Reads the current line of the file into a string. |

12

Server-Side JavaScript

**TABLE 12.11** continued

| Type | Item | Description |
|------|------|-------------|
| | setPosition() | Sets the current position in the file. |
| | stringToByte() | Converts the first number of a string into a number to represent a byte. |
| | write() | Writes data to a file. |
| | writeByte() | Writes a byte of data to a file. |
| | writeln() | Writes data to a file and appends a carriage return. |
| Property | prototype | Allows you to add methods and properties to the File object. |

New instances of a `File` object are created using the new operator. An example of this is as follows:

```
var fileObject = new File("path");
```

Because the `File` object deals with the server's file system, the `path` parameter is a full path to the file, not a URL. After the object has been instantiated, you need to open it to prepare it for either reading or writing. You will use the `open()` method for this task. This method takes a `mode` parameter that can be one of the options outlined in Table 12.12.

**TABLE 12.12** `open()` Method Parameters for the `File` Object

| Mode | Description |
|------|-------------|
| a[b] | Opens an existing file for appending new text. If the file does not exist, one is created. |
| a+[b] | Opens an existing file for reading and writing. If the file does not exist, `false` is returned. The position of the pointer is the end of the file. |
| r[b] | Opens an existing file for reading. If the file does not exist, a `false` value is returned. |
| r+[b] | Opens an existing file for reading and writing. If the file does not exist, `false` is returned. The position of the pointer is the start of the file. |
| w[b] | Opens a new file for writing. If the file exists, it is overwritten. |
| w+[b] | Opens a new file for reading and writing. If the file exists, it is overwritten. |

You may notice that there is an optional b parameter that can be used to open these files in binary mode for Windows operating systems only. When you have finished working with an open file, issue a `close()` method to close access to it.

> **Tip**
>
> Although the `File` object doesn't have `lock()` and `unlock()` methods, you can still take advantage of the locking capabilities of the `Project` and `Server` objects to prevent multiple users from accessing the file simultaneously.

Listing 12.6 demonstrates the process of working with files. You can use this source HTML file to record a log of persons who submit the attached form. Each time a form is submitted, the server script opens the `contlog.txt` file and writes each field entry into the comma-delimited file.

**LISTING 12.6**   Working with Files Using the `File` Object

```html
<html>
<head>
  <title>Online Registration</title>
</head>
<body>
  <server>
  if (request.FullName != null) {
    cLog = new File("d:/netscape/suitespot/server4/logs/contlog.txt");
    project.lock();
    if (cLog.open("a") == true) {
      cLog.write(request.FullName + ",");
      cLog.write(request.Title + ",");
      cLog.write(request.Organization + ",");
      cLog.write(request.Email + ",");
      cLog.close();
    }
    project.unlock();
  }
  </server>
<h1>Registration</h1>
<hr>
  <form action="/ssjs/objects" method="POST">
    <p>
      Please provide the following contact information:
    </p>
    <em>Name</em>
    <input type=text size=35 maxlength=256 name="FullName"><br>
    <em>Title</em>
    <input type=text size=35 maxlength=256 name="Title"><br>
```

LISTING 12.6    continued

```
      <em>Organization</em>
      <input type=text size=35 maxlength=256 name="Organization"><br>
      <em>E-mail</em>
      <input type=text size=25 maxlength=256 name="Email"><br>
      <p>
        <input type=submit value="Submit">
        <input type=reset value="Reset">
      </p>
    </form>
  </body>
</html>
```

# The `SendMail` Object

The `SendMail` object is another useful object, because it allows you to send messages through your existing mail server. As you might guess, with this object you can easily create a page in your application that allows your users to send mail. `SendMail` has several methods and properties, all of which are shown in Table 12.13.

**TABLE 12.13**    `SendMail` Object Methods and Properties

| Type | Item | Description |
| --- | --- | --- |
| Method | `errorCode()` | Returns an integer representing an error code encountered when sending email. |
| | `errorMessage()` | Returns a string related to any error message that may be encountered when sending email. |
| | `send()` | Sends the email. |
| Property | `Bcc` | A comma-delimited list of recipients you want to blind carbon copy. |
| | `Body` | The body text of the message. |
| | `Cc` | A comma-delimited list of recipients you want to carbon copy. |
| | `Errorsto` | The username to which to send errors concerning the message. The default value is the `From` property. |
| | `From` | The username of the message sender, which is required. |
| | `Organization` | Organization name or other company information of the sender. |
| | `prototype` | Allows you to create new properties and methods for the `SendMail` object. |

**TABLE 12.13** continued

| Type | Item | Description |
|---|---|---|
| | Replyto | A username to use instead of the From property as the address to which replies to the message should be sent. |
| | Smtpserver | The SMTP hostname or IP address. |
| | Subject | The subject of the message. |
| | To | A comma-delimited list of message recipients, which is required. |

Like the File object, you can create a SendMail object using the new operator, in the following format:

```
var myMessage = new SendMail();
```

# Database-Specific Objects

One of the best things you are going to find about Server-Side JavaScript is its ability to interact with databases. As mentioned early in the chapter, SSJS used to be called LiveWire. Now, LiveWire refers to database access functionality within the SSJS environment. Over the next several sections, we are going to look at the core objects that make up this powerful access.

## The Database Object

The Database object encapsulates all functionality related to interacting with a relational database. This object contains only one property, so most of its utility stems from its methods. Take a look at Table 12.14 for a complete list and short description of these. If you have worked with databases using other programming languages, you can see that JavaScript has almost everything you would expect for interacting with relational databases.

**TABLE 12.14** Database Object Methods and Property

| Type | Item | Description |
|---|---|---|
| Method | beginTransaction() | Starts a SQL transaction. |
| | commitTransaction() | Commits the current SQL transaction. |
| | connect() | Connects the application to the specified database. |
| | connected() | Returns true if the application is connected to a database. |
| | cursor() | Creates a Cursor object for the specified SQL SELECT statement. |
| | disconnect() | Closes the database connection. |

**TABLE 12.14** continued

| Type | Item | Description |
|------|------|-------------|
| | execute() | Executes the specified SQL statement. Used for SQL statements that do not return a cursor. |
| | majorErrorCode() | Major error code returned by the database server or ODBC. |
| | majorErrorMessage() | Major error message returned by the database server or ODBC. |
| | minorErrorCode() | Secondary error code returned by the vendor library. |
| | minorErrorMessage() | Secondary message returned by the vendor library. |
| | rollbackTransaction() | Rolls back the current SQL transaction. |
| | SQLTable() | Generates an HTML table to display the results of the SELECT query. |
| | storedProc() | Creates a Stproc object and runs the specified stored procedure. |
| | storedProcArgs() | Creates a prototype for DB2, ODBC, or Sybase stored procedures. |
| | toString() | Returns a string representing the specified object. |
| Property | prototype | Allows you to add methods or properties to your instances of Database objects. |

## The DbPool Object

The DbPool object, which was added in Netscape Enterprise Server 3, is much like the Database object, except that it represents an entire pool of connections to a database. Once you have created a pool, you can pull connections from that pool as needed. Table 12.15 has a list of the methods and the one property this object has.

**TABLE 12.15** DbPool Object Methods and Property

| Type | Item | Description |
|------|------|-------------|
| Method | connect() | Connects a pool in the application to the specified database. |
| | connected() | Returns true if the pool is connected to a database. |
| | connection() | Grabs an available connection from the pool. |
| | DbPool() | Creates the pool of connections to the database. |
| | disconnect() | Closes all database connections in the pool. |
| | majorErrorCode() | Major error code returned by the database server or ODBC. |

**TABLE 12.15** continued

| Type | Item | Description |
|------|------|-------------|
| | majorErrorMessage() | Major error message returned by the database server or ODBC. |
| | minorErrorCode() | Secondary error code returned by the vendor library. |
| | minorErrorMessage() | Secondary message returned by the vendor library. |
| | storedProcArgs() | Creates a prototype for DB2, ODBC, or Sybase stored procedures. |
| | toString() | Returns a string representing the specified object. |
| Property | prototype | Allows you to add methods or properties to your instances of DbPool objects. |

## The Connection Object

The Connection object, which was added in Netscape Enterprise Server 3, represents a given connection when pulled from a pool of connections to a database. This object is created by calling the DbPool.connection() method. Table 12.16 has a list of the methods and the one property *this* object has.

**TABLE 12.16** Connection Object Methods and Property

| Type | Item | Description |
|------|------|-------------|
| Method | beginTransaction() | Starts a SQL transaction. |
| | commitTransaction() | Commits the current SQL transaction. |
| | connected() | Returns true if the application is connected to a database. |
| | cursor() | Creates a Cursor object for the specified SQL SELECT statement. |
| | execute() | Executes the specified SQL statement. Used for SQL statements that do not return a cursor. |
| | majorErrorCode() | Major error code returned by the database server or ODBC. |
| | majorErrorMessage() | Major error message returned by the database server or ODBC. |
| | minorErrorCode() | Secondary error code returned by the vendor library. |
| | minorErrorMessage() | Secondary message returned by the vendor library. |
| | release() | Releases the connection, returning it to the pool. |
| | rollbackTransaction() | Rolls back the current SQL transaction. |

**12**

Server-Side
JavaScript

**TABLE 12.16** continued

| Type | Item | Description |
|---|---|---|
| | SQLTable() | Generates an HTML table to display the results of the SELECT query. |
| | storedProc() | Creates a Stproc object and runs the specified stored procedure. |
| | toString() | Returns a string representing the specified object. |
| Property | prototype | Allows you to add methods or properties to your instances of Connection objects. |

## The Cursor Object

The Cursor object is created by calling the Connection.cursor() or database.cursor() method. Because a query on the database is said to return a cursor, this object contains a reference to the rows that are returned by the query. Table 12.17 has a list of the methods and the one property this object has.

**TABLE 12.17** Cursor Object Methods and Properties

| Type | Item | Description |
|---|---|---|
| Method | close() | Closes the cursor and frees any memory it took up. |
| | columnName() | Takes in an indexed column location and returns the name of the column in that location. |
| | columns() | Returns the number of columns in the cursor. |
| | deleteRow() | Deletes the current row of the table passed to the method. |
| | insertRow() | Inserts a new row into the table passed to the method. |
| | next() | Moves the instance of the Cursor object from the current row to the next. |
| | updateRow() | Updates the current row of the table passed in. |
| Property | columnName | Represents the column names that are returned by the cursor. |
| | prototype | Allows you to add methods or properties to your instances of Cursor objects. |

## The Resultset Object

The Resultset object is created by calling the Stproc.resultSet() method. This object stores the results of running a stored procedure. For procedures run on DB2, Oracle, Sybase, and ODBC databases, one Resultset object is returned for each SELECT statement executed in the procedure. For Informix, only one object is returned. Table 12.18 has a list of the methods and the one property for this object.

**TABLE 12.18** Resultset Object Methods and Property

| Type | Item | Description |
|---|---|---|
| Method | close() | Closes the result set along with freeing any memory it had taken up. |
| | columnName() | Takes in an indexed column location and returns the name of the column in that location. |
| | columns() | Returns the number of columns in the result set. |
| | next() | This moves the current row in the instance of the Resultset object to the next. |
| property | prototype | Allows you to add methods or properties to your instances of Resultset objects. |

## The Stproc Object

The Stproc object is created by calling the Connection.storedProc() or database.storedProc() method, and it executes a stored procedure on the accessed database. Be sure that you call the close() method of this object when you have finished running your procedure. Table 12.19 has a list of this object's methods and one property.

**TABLE 12.19** Stproc Object Methods and Property

| Type | Item | Description |
|---|---|---|
| Method | close() | Closes the stored procedure instance along with freeing any memory it had taken up. |
| | outParamCount() | Returns the number of output parameters form the procedure. |
| | outParameters() | Returns the value of the output parameter passed to the method. |
| | resultSet() | Creates a new Resultset object. |
| | returnValue() | Returns the return value of the stored procedure. |
| Property | prototype | Allows you to add methods or properties to your instances of Stproc objects. |

## The BLOB Object

The last core object that we are going to look at provides support for working with Binary Large Objects (BLOBs) in your database. This object has no properties, but it does have two methods. These are described in Table 12.20.

**TABLE 12.20** BLOB Object Methods

| Method | Description |
| --- | --- |
| blobImage() | Retrieves and displays a BLOB data instance in the database. |
| blobLink() | Retrieves and displays an HTML link that references a BLOB data instance in the database. |

# Summary

Much thought needs to go into the architecture of the application before you can begin to build it for successful Internet use. Knowing your predicted audience and being able to anticipate access to your server helps when defining the methodologies and techniques that you choose to use to implement a client/server application. Adding JavaScript and database functionality brings on a whole new level of concerns and issues that must be accounted for.

Server-side versus client-side processing needs to be taken into account when deciding test speed and functionality of the JavaScript application. The two-tier and *n*-tier methodologies need to be evaluated for advantages and disadvantages on your particular application and its complexity and maintainability.

In this chapter, you learned that JavaScript is not just for the client side anymore. Using Netscape's Server-Side JavaScript, you can employ the scripting language to produce Web-based applications.

# Scripting the Document Object Model

## IN THIS PART

# Fundamentals of the Document Object Model (DOM)

This chapter is something of a primer about the Document Object Model (DOM) and its purpose, its characteristics, its entities, and some of the important methods and properties that surround it. Of course, we will look at only the fundamentals here, such as navigating documents and other entities and how they can be visualized as DOM trees. We will look at some of the important DOM methods that operate on the trees directly, though these are explained more thoroughly in Chapter 19, "Other DOM Objects," where we will look at the DOM more from a JavaScript perspective.

# Understanding the Document Object Model

Key advancements of the Web always remedy long-standing problems. For instance, Java provided a way of developing platform-independent Web applications by using applets. Although not quite as momentous as this, the Document Object Model solves another fairly old problem of making JavaScript scripts and Java programs portable in the context of Web browsers. It achieves this by using standard application programming interfaces (APIs) that are defined in Object Management Group (OMG) Interface Definition Language (IDL), and they may therefore be used by any IDL-compliant language. You can think of the collective DOM API as a way of standardizing objects across browsers when delivering HTML and XML documents. Of course the Web browser has to be DOM compliant, and the move toward this is occurring at a rapid pace.

There's really not a lot to DOM actually. It merely defines a logical and standardized document structure. This lets you build, edit, and browse elements and content in HTML or XML documents. The DOM structure is nothing more than an object hierarchy that is comparable to that of JavaScript or any other object-based language. The difference is that DOM has a useful API that is language neutral and defines a standard set of interfaces. That's not to say that all DOM applications will be based on the same objects; they might define their own interfaces and objects. This might be the case if you renovate an application so that it can become DOM compliant, for example.

## Resource

You can obtain the W3C Document Object Model (DOM) Level 2 Specification from http://www.w3.org/TR/1999/CR-DOM-Level-2-19991210. The earlier Level 1 specification can also be obtained from this site. The information contained in the specification is not pitched directly at JavaScript or other ECMA-complaint scripting languages. Appendix E of the specification shows the appropriate

ECMAScript language binding. There is a growing number of DOM tutorials on the Web, and numerous articles and papers accompany them.

## From DHTML to DOM

The transition of Web pages to an object model has many phases, but few are as significant as DHTML, which is itself rather insignificant when compared to DOM. This is because DOM is a standardized object model that Web developers have been wanting for some time. As an example, if a Web developer has to update or renovate a Web page with the DHTML object model, a considerable amount of information would be required, possibly in the form of a programmer's guide. This is because of the myriad of HTML tags, properties, methods, and events. DHTML is really nothing more than a means of allowing you to change objects that are accessed and manipulated using their id and name attributes. It does not introduce the standardization or simplification of DOM, which encapsulates the whole document as an object model, representing it as a hierarchy, or tree. The tree's nodes represent HTML tags and text segments they may hold. The entire HTML document is in that tree, showing all objects and their relationships as children, parents, and siblings. Unlike with DHTML, you can navigate the DOM document tree and make changes easily. To change text entries, for example, simply use the nodeValue property to change the value of the tree node. You can create, delete, and move nodes in the DOM document tree. (The methods that permit you to do this are described later, in Table 13.2.)

## Navigating a Table

To understand tree structures, take a look at the DOM tree structure for a simple table in Figure 13.1. This illustrates the properties childNodes, firstChild, lastChild, nextSibling, and previousSibling. These may be used to understand the structure and to navigate to any part of it.

Taking the table DOM tree shown as a reference, we have <TABLE> at the root. It follows that we can move to any point in the tree by specifying the appropriate node. Navigating downward through the tree, we can arrive at its various parts using the expressions shown in Table 13.1.

**13**

**Fundamentals of the Document Object Model (DOM)**

**FIGURE 13.1**
*A simple DOM tree structure of a table.*

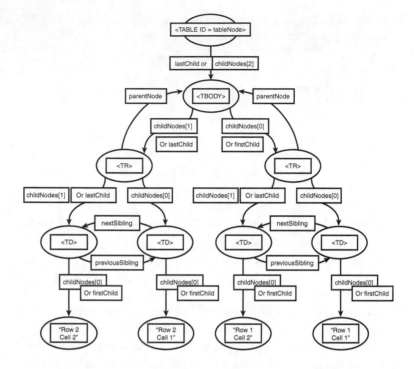

**TABLE 13.1**    Navigating Expressions

| Navigate to | Expression |
| --- | --- |
| Second row of the table | `tableNode.firstChild.childNodes[1]` |
| First cell of the second row | `tableNode.firstChild.childNodes[1].childNodes[0]` |
| The content of the second cell in the first row | `tableNode.firstChild.firstChild.childNodes[1].firstChild` |
| The root from the second row | `Tr2Node.parentNode.parentNode`<br>or<br>`Tr2Node.previousSibling.parentNode.parentNode`<br>or<br>`Tr2Node.previousSibling.previousSibling.parentNode.`<br>`parentNode` |

**TABLE 13.1** continued

| Navigate to | Expression |
|---|---|
| Each of the cells, and then back to the root | `tableNode.firstChild.firstChild.firstChild.firstChild.` `parentNode.parentNode.parentNode.parentNode` `tableNode.firstChild.firstChild.childNodes[1].firstChild.` `parentNode.parentNode.parentNode.parentNode` `tableNode.firstChild.childNodes[1].firstChild.firstChild.` `parentNode.parentNode.parentNode.parentNode` `tableNode.firstChild.childNodes[1].childNodes[1].` `firstChild.parentNode.parentNode.parentNode.parentNode` |
| Each of the cells | `tableNode.firstChild.firstChild.firstChild.firstChild` `tableNode.firstChild.firstChild.childNodes[1].firstChild` `tableNode.firstChild.childNodes[1].firstChild.firstChild` `tableNode.firstChild.childNodes[1].childNodes[1].firstChild` |

# Manipulating Documents

Let's take a look at some of the basic DOM methods that let you perform some everyday tasks. In its API, DOM has methods that are defined to create, delete, insert, move, swap, and replace nodes or objects. These are described briefly in Table 13.2, together with their arguments, descriptions, and returned values or *out* parameters. It's pretty obvious stuff actually; the `removeNode()` method deletes a subtree rooted at the specified node when `deep` is `true`. When `deep` is `false`, only the specified node is removed, and its children objects revert back to the current grandfather. Another method that depends on a Boolean parameter is `cloneNode()`. When this Boolean is `true`, a subtree is cloned, and when it is `false` only a node is cloned.

**TABLE 13.2** Useful DOM Methods for Manipulating Documents

| `<TBODY>` DOM Method Syntax | Argument or Parameter | Description |
|---|---|---|
| `AppendChild fatherObj.` `appendChild(childObj)` | Object | Append a child (`childObj`) to a father object (`fatherObj`). |
| `ApplyElement childObj.` `applyElement(fatherObj)` | Object | Apply an element object to another object (`fatherObj`). |
| `ClearAttributes clearedObj.` `clearAttributes()` | NA | Remove all attributes and values from the object (`clearedObj`) |
| `CloneNode newObj =` `existingObj. cloneNode(deep)` | Boolean | Clone an existing object to create a new one (`newObj`). |
| `CreateElement newObj =` `document. createElement` `("Tag")` | HTML Tag | Create a new tag node (`newObj`). |

**TABLE 13.2**   continued

| <TBODY> *DOM Method Syntax* | *Argument or Parameter* | *Description* |
| --- | --- | --- |
| CreateTextNode newObj = document. createTextNode (string) | String | Create a new text node (newObj). |
| HasChildNodes hasChildrenFlag = testedObj. hasChildNodes() | NA | Determine whether an object has children. |
| InsertBefore parentObj. insertBefore(childObj, brotherObj) | Object | Insert an object (childObj) as a child of (parentObj). |
| MergeAttributes targetObj. mergeAttributes (sourceObj) | Object | Merge all attributes from (sourceObj) to (targetObj). |
| RemoveNode deletedObj. removeNode(deep) | NA | Remove an object's subtree when deep is true and just the node when deep is false. |
| ReplaceNode oldObj. replaceNode(newObj) | Object | Replace a node (oldObj) with a new one (newObj). |
| SwapNode firstObj. swapNode(secondObj) | Object | Swap one node for another. |

# The Object Model and Attributes

The DOM document structure may actually include multiple trees, which are object hierarchies showing all their relating links. But DOM compliance does not require the implementation of documents as trees, and neither does it require specific relationships between objects. However, every document might have a document type node, a root element node that serves as the root of the document's tree, and comments or processing instructions. The tree representation, or *structure model*, has information items that are accessed using the tree-walking methods. DOM also adheres to *structural isomorphism*, in which different DOM-compliant implementations, used to create representations of the same document, result in the same structure model. The nodes that we have discussed exhibit various attributes, and many of these are listed in Table 13.3.

**TABLE 13.3**   Useful DOM Attributes

| *Attribute* | *Read/Write* | *Description* |
| --- | --- | --- |
| Attributes of type NamedNodeMap | Read-only | A NamedNodeMap holding the attributes of a node. |
| childNodes of type NodeList | Read-only | A NodeList that holds all children of a node. |

**TABLE 13.3** continued

| Attribute | Read/Write | Description |
|---|---|---|
| firstChild of type Node | Read-only | The first child of a node; if the node does not exist, then a null is returned. |
| lastChild of type Node | Read-only | The last child of a node; if the node does not exist, then a null is returned. |
| localName of type DOMString | Read-only | Returns the local part of the qualified name of this node. When used with nodes created with the DOM Level 1 method, including createElement, it returns a null value. |
| namespaceURI of type DOMString | Read-only | Holds the namespaceURI value given when created. It is always null for node types other than ElementNode and AttributeNode. It is null for nodes created with the DOM Level 1 method, including createElement from the Document interface. |
| nextSibling of type Node | Read-only | The next consecutive node; when there is no such node, a null is returned. |
| nodeName of type DOMString | Read-only | A node's name. |
| nodeType of type unsigned short | Read-only | Code holding the defined object type. |
| ownerDocument of type Document | Read-only | The document object that owns the node; this document object is used to create new nodes. |
| parentNode of type Node | Read-only | The parent of the node. Provided it is not an Attr, Document, DocumentFragment, Entity, or Notation. ParentNode is null when a node is newly created and has yet to become part of the tree, or when it is removed from the tree. |
| Prefix of type DOMString | | The namespace prefix of the node; null is returned if none is specified. Setting this attribute changes the nodeName attribute, which holds the qualified name tagName and name attributes of the Element and Attr interfaces. |
| previousSibling of type Node | Read-only | The next preceding node; when no such node exists, null is returned. |

13

Fundamentals of
the Document
Object Model
(DOM)

> **Note**
>
> Changing an attribute's prefix, which has a default value, does not create a new attribute with this default value and the original prefix, because `namespaceURI` and `localName` are not changed.

# Navigating Documents

Having looked at how to navigate a simple table, it is natural to move on to do the same with a document. Listing 13.1 shows a DOM structure that contains a document title, a text entry, and four paragraphs:

**LISTING 13.1**   A Simple Document

```
<HTML>
<HEAD>
<TITLE> DOM document tree </TITLE>
</HEAD>
<BODY ID="bodyNode"><P ID = "Node1">A first paragraph</P>
The main document
<P ID = "Node2">   </P>
<P ID = "Node3"></P>
<P ID = "Node4"></P>
</BODY>
</HTML>
```

The `<BODY>` tag is at the tree's top level and has five children, including four `<P>` tags and a single text entry. A document's DOM tree has nodes for tags and textual entries. You may navigate the tree from nodes that have `ID` attributes. Using the DOM properties, you can navigate to any point in the document, as shown in Table 13.4.

**TABLE 13.4**   Navigating a Document

| Navigate to | Expression |
|---|---|
| The first child | `bodyNode.firstChild` or `bodyNode.childNodes[0]` |
| The second child | `bodyNode.childNodes[1]` |
| The fourth or last child | `bodyNode.childNodes[4]` or `bodyNode.lastChild` |
| Root's second child (the text node) from Node 1 | `Node1.nextSibling` |
| Root's third child from Node 1 | `Node1.nextSibling.nextSibling` |
| Root's last child | `Node1.nextSibling.nextSibling. nextSibling` |

**TABLE 13.4** continued

| Navigate to | Expression |
| --- | --- |
| Children of the fourth child | Node1.nextSibling.nextSibling. nextSibling. childNodes[0] |
| The second <P> from the third <P> | Node3.previousSibling.previous Sibling. previousSibling.childNodes[0] |
| The grandchild of the <BODY> tag. | bodyNode.firstChild.firstChild |
| <BODY> root tag from a <P> tag | Node1.parentNode |
| The grandchild of the <BODY> and back to the <BODY> | bodyNode.firstChild.firstChild. parentNode. parentNode |

# Summary

This chapter has explained DOM's fundamentals and its basic object model when applied to standard entities on simple Web pages. We have looked at navigating and how you may move between nodes that define the documents themselves. We have also looked at properties and how they can be changed and used to gather information that is on the tree model. We have looked at the terminology that surrounds DOM, such as nodes that have names such as firstChild, lastChild, nextSibling, and previousSibling. With this basic information now covered, we can expand on the application of DOM in JavaScript context. I have left this particular chore to Chapter 19, when we will take a more detailed look at DOM.

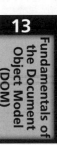

**13**

Fundamentals of
the Document
Object Model
(DOM)

# Handling Events

**CHAPTER**

**14**

If you have done much programming over the past several years, chances are you've worked with an event-driven programming language. Procedural programs of the past dictated which task a user could perform at any given time. However, the graphical, windowed environments of today have a completely different paradigm and require applications to respond to events initiated by users rather than the other way around.

Given JavaScript's object-based nature (discussed in Chapter 9, "Client-Side Objects," in the section, "JavaScript Objects"), it should come as no surprise that JavaScript is primarily an event-driven language. This chapter discusses JavaScript events and how you can respond to them and thus create interactive scripts for your site.

# Understanding Events and Event Handlers

Much of the code you write in JavaScript will respond to an event performed by either the user or the browser software. This event-driven environment lets you focus only on the events that affect your application; what the browser performs between events is its burden, not yours. In addition, you don't need to concern yourself with all the events performed by the user—only those to which you care to respond.

Each JavaScript event has a corresponding *event handler* that is charged with the responsibility of automatically responding to the event when it occurs. When you work with an event, you never add code to it or modify the event itself; rather, you manage the event handler to which that event corresponds.

# JavaScript Event Handlers

If you've created HTML pages, you know that each element on a form has a tag and attributes associated with it. For example, you would define text input in the following way:

```
<input type=text size=30 maxlength=30 name="LastName">
```

JavaScript implements event handlers by embedding them as attributes of HTML tags. For example, suppose you want to perform a method you created each time the value of the Text object changes. To do so, assign the method (called, for example, checkField()) to the Text object's onChange event handler:

```
<input type=text size=30 maxlength=256 name="LastName" onChange="checkField( this )">
```

Within the quotes, you can either write in-place JavaScript code or call a separate function. Although the previous example calls the checkField() function, the following code is also valid:

```
<input type=text size=30 maxlength=256 name="LastName"
    onChange= "if ( confirm( 'Are you certain you wish to change this value?'))
              { alert('Changed' )}">
```

> **Tip**
>
> If you use in-place code, you can place multiple lines within the event handler assignment by using a semicolon to separate each JavaScript command. However, use multiple lines of code with caution. It's much easier to work with code separated as a function than work within the event handler itself. For example, if the code is located in a central location, it becomes much easier to make changes to it over the life of your Web site.

As you proceed through this chapter, you will examine the most common events supported by both Microsoft Internet Explorer and Netscape Navigator. We will pay particular attention to the events for which you will most often want to trap. In doing so, you will take a typical HTML form (shown in Figure 14.1) and add life to it by adding code to its event handlers. The form you will use initially is a sample order form for a fictitious company.

## Clicking an Object (onClick)

One of the most common uses of JavaScript is to enhance HTML forms to provide a greater degree of interactivity. If that is true, perhaps the single most common event many developers will work with is the click event. The click event is triggered when the user clicks a clickable object.

As is standard for most computer environments, the click event is triggered only after the default mouse button is pressed and released. A user holding the mouse button down without releasing it on the object will not cause the object's click event to be triggered.

When a click event occurs, the onClick event handler for the object that is clicked executes one or more JavaScript commands or calls a custom function. For example, note the View Hat button in Figure 14.1. Suppose you would like to add code that displays a second browser window showing an image of the hat when the button is clicked.

In the HTML source, the Button object is defined as follows:

```
<input type=button name="ViewHat" value="View Hat" onClick="displayHat()">
```

**14**

**Handling Events**

**FIGURE 14.1**

*A sample HTML form.*

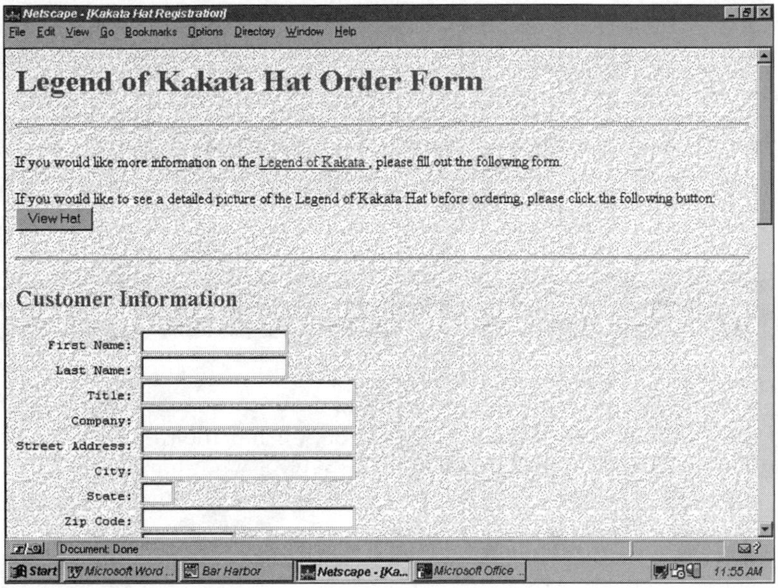

In the <head> section of the HTML file, you can then write the displayHat() method that will be called when the button's onClick event handler is triggered:

```
<head>
<script language="JavaScript">
<!--


    //onClick event handler
    function displayHat() {
       hatWindow = window.open("http://www.myhat.com", "View MyHat",
          "toolbar=0,width=200,height=400,resizable=0");
    }
</script>
</head>
```

When the user clicks the button, the event handler uses the open() method for the Window object to display a window showing the hat image, as shown in Figure 14.2.

The onClick event handler isn't just for buttons; you can use it to respond to clicks of check boxes, radio buttons, and Link objects. Because of the nature of these controls, a customized click event for them is much less common. Check boxes and radio buttons are often used for data entry and evaluated at a later point rather than when a control is clicked. Also, the Link object is used primarily as a reference to the location specified in its href property, so adding code is often not necessary unless you want to modify its default behavior.

**FIGURE 14.2**

*The second window is displayed using the open() method.*

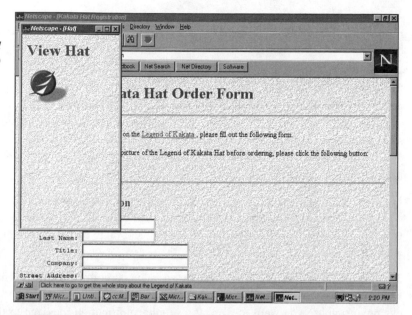

> **Note**
>
> For check boxes, links, radio buttons, and reset and submit buttons, you can return a false value from the onClick event handler to cancel the triggered action. For example, if you wanted to confirm whether or not to check a check box, you could add the following code to its onClick event handler:
>
> ```
> <input type="checkbox" name="checkbox1" value="DeluxeRoom"
> onClick="return confirm('Deluxe rooms are very expensive.
> ➥Are you sure?')">Deluxe Room
> ```

Because the appearance of a Web page is important, you might want to use images rather than buttons to respond to click events. Although an image can't actually respond to any event, you can imitate a click event through the smart use of a link object. I'll demonstrate this by using an image, rather than the View Hat button, to execute the displayHat() method from the previous example. To do so, you can define the Link object as follows:

```
<a href="JavaScript:displayHat()">
  <img src="minihat.gif" align=bottom border=0 width=89 height=75>
</a>
```

Rather than add code to the link's onClick event handler, I used JavaScript: as the protocol for the href property. Using JavaScript:*JavaScriptExpression* as the href property tells the browser to execute a JavaScript expression rather than navigate to a defined link.

## Submitting a Form (`onSubmit`)

As discussed in Chapter 1, "JavaScript and the World Wide Web," one of the advantages of using JavaScript in HTML forms is that you can perform data validation on the client side rather than pass this task onto an overloaded server. You can perform validation on a field-by-field basis or on a form-wide basis. Depending on the context, you might want to use one or both methods.

For form-wide data validation as well as for other tasks, the submit event is your primary concern. This event occurs just before the submission of an HTML form. Adding code to the onSubmit event handler of a form object enables you to check the submission and either allow it to proceed or block it and notify the user.

The submit event will occur unless a false value is returned from the onSubmit event handler. Any other value (true or otherwise) will cause the submission to occur. For example, suppose you want to display a simple confirmation message to the user of the Kakata Hat order form before processing the submission. The form is defined in the HTML source as follows:

```
<form action="process.cgi" method="POST" onSubmit="return confirmOrder()">
```

The confirmOrder() method referenced in the form's onSubmit event handler is declared in the <head> section of the file:

```
//onSubmit event handler
function confirmOrder() {
   return confirm('Are you certain you wish to order the Kakata hat?');
}
```

When triggered, the confirmOrder() method displays a Confirm dialog box with buttons labeled OK and Cancel. If the user clicks OK, the dialog box is closed, and a true value is returned to the onSubmit event handler. If the user clicks Cancel, false is returned. The return statement in the onSubmit event handler examines the incoming value and determines whether the form should continue to process. The return in the event-handler assignment is essential for the code to work correctly. Assigning onSubmit= "confirmOrder()" to the event handler causes the form to process regardless of the returned value from the dialog box.

The onSubmit event handler is similar to an onClick event handler of a Submit object. Both of these are events you can use to trap a form before it's processed. As shown in

Figure 14.3, the Submit object's onClick event handler is triggered first, followed by the form's onSubmit.

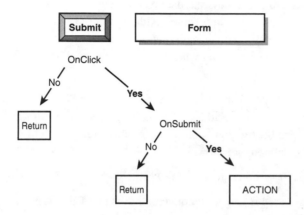

FIGURE **14.3**
*Event sequencing on a form submission.*

The onSubmit event handler is an ideal location to place form-level data validation before it is sent to a server or other process.

## Resetting a Form (onReset)

You might have to trigger an event when a form is submitted, as well as when it is reset. The onResetevent handler triggers JavaScript code when a reset event occurs. Just as with onSubmit, onReset is an event handler of a Form object.

To illustrate, look again at the Kakata hat order form used in the last section. After you add a new event handler to the Form object's definition, the code would look like this:

```
<form action="process.cgi" method="POST" onSubmit="return confirmOrder()"
➥onReset="return confirmReset()">
```

The confirmReset() method referenced in the form's onReset event handler is declared in the <HEAD> section of the file:

```
//onReset event handler
function confirmReset() {
    return confirm('Are you certain you wish to clear the order form?');
}
```

**Note**

The onReset event handler is supported in JavaScript 1.1 and higher.

14

Handling Events

## Modifying Data (onChange)

As mentioned with the submit event, when your JavaScript applications deal with data, you'll typically want to preprocess the data entered by the user to avoid validation problems when the data is sent to a server. Although submit is designed for form-wide verification, the change event is typically the most important event for field-level validation. The change event occurs when the value of a field object changes and the field itself loses focus.

You use the onChange event handler to execute JavaScript code or call a function to handle the event. Suppose you want to add a basic validity-checking routine to the Kakata Hat data-entry form. Specifically, you want to ensure that the State field is always uppercase. The Text object is defined as follows:

```
<input type=text size=3 maxlength=2 name="State" onChange="convertToUppercase(this)">
```

The convertToUppercase() method converts the value of the State field to uppercase using the string method toUpperCase():

```
function convertToUppercase(fieldObject) {
  fieldObject.value = fieldObject.value.toUpperCase()
}
```

## Receiving Focus (onFocus)

The focus event is triggered when a field object receives focus—when the user either tabs into the object or clicks it with the mouse or when you call an object's focus() method. Only one object can receive focus at a given time.

> **Note**
>
> JavaScript 1.1 and higher expands the scope of onFocus to include it as an event handler for Window, Frame, and Frameset objects. For each of these objects, the onFocus event handler specifies the action that should execute when the window receives focus.
>
> The onFocus event handler should be placed in the <BODY> tag of the Window, Frame, or Frameset object.

You can add an onFocus event handler to these objects to trigger an action. For example, enhance the standard behavior of the Text objects on the form. When you move onto a Text object, an insertion point appears by default. However, a standard in many environments (such as Windows) is that if the field already has a value, the contents are selected when the object receives focus. To code this behavior (see Listing 14.1), you need to add an onFocus event handler for each of the Text objects, as well as the Textarea object:

**LISTING 14.1**  Using the onFocus Event with Form Fields

```
<pre>    First Name: <input
                    type=text
                    size=20
                    maxlength=20
                    name="FirstName"
                    onFocus="selectContents(this)">
       Last Name: <input
                    type=text
                    size=20
                    maxlength=20
                    name="LastName"
                    onFocus="selectContents(this)">
           Title: <input
                    type=text
                    size=30
                    maxlength=256
                    name="Title"
                    onFocus="selectContents(this)">
         Company: <input
                    type=text
                    size=30
                    maxlength=256
                    name="Company"
                    onFocus="selectContents(this)">
  Street Address: <input
                    type=text
                    size=30
                    maxlength=256
                    name="StreetAddr"
                    onFocus="selectContents(this)">
            City: <input
                    type=text
                    size=30
                    maxlength=256
                    name="City"
                    onFocus="selectContents(this)">
```

**14**

**Handling Events**

**LISTING 14.1** continued

```
    State: <input
                     type=text
                     size=3
                     maxlength=2
                     name="State"
                     onFocus="selectContents(this)"
                     onChange="convertToUppercase(this)">
 Zip Code: <input

                     type=text
                     size=30
                     maxlength=10
                     name="ZipCode"
                     onFocus="selectContents(this)">
Telephone: <input

                     type=text
                     size=12
                     maxlength=12
                     name="Phone"
                     onFocus="selectContents(this)">
      FAX: <input

                     type=text
                     size=12
                     maxlength=12
                     name="FAX"
                     onFocus="selectContents(this)">
   E-mail: <input

                     type=text
                     size=30
                     maxlength=256
                     name="Email"
                     onFocus="selectContents(this)">
      URL: <input

                      type=text
                      size=30
                      maxlength=256
                      name="URL"
                      onFocus="selectContents(this)"></pre>

<textarea name="worthyBox" rows=3 cols=49 onFocus="selectContents(this)">
</textarea>
```

Although you could write separate event handlers for each of these fields, it would be unwise to do so unless the processes were completely different. Instead, the selectContents() method takes advantage of the this keyword to reference the object making the call. The following function is then used as a global function for all the objects:

```
function selectContents(fieldObject) {
    fieldObject.select();
}
```

When any of the Text or Textarea objects calls the selectContents() method, the method uses the fieldObject parameter as a reference to the calling object. The select() method then selects the input area of the specified object.

## Losing Focus (onBlur)

The blur event (the inverse of the focus event) is triggered when an object loses focus.

> **Note**
>
> As with the onFocus event handler, JavaScript 1.1 and higher expand the scope of onBlur to include it as an event handler for Window, Frame, and Frameset objects. For each of these objects, the onBlur event handler specifies the action that should execute when the window loses focus.
>
> The onBlur event handler should be placed in the <body> tag of the Window, Frame, or Frameset object.

For example, suppose that on the data-entry form you want to ensure that the EmailText object is not left blank by the user. You could add this check to the onBlur event handler of the object. Because this affects a single field of the form, you can just add the JavaScript code to the Text object definition:

```
<input type=text size=30  maxlength=256  name="Email"
    onFocus="selectContents(this)" onBlur="if (this.value == ''){
        alert('You must enter something.');this.focus();}">
```

If the user tries to tab out of the object without entering text, an alert dialog box notifies the user not to leave the field blank. The next command returns focus to the EmailText object. If that command hadn't been used, the cursor would have moved on to the next tab stop.

As you have probably noticed, onChange and onBlur are similar. When should you use one over the other? onChange is best for checking or analyzing the content of an object and has the advantage of not being called if the user doesn't change the value. On the other hand, for required fields, you might want to use onBlur.

The sequencing of the onChange, onBlur, and onFocus event handlers is important to understand before you use them. As Figure 14.4 illustrates, onFocus occurs when you enter the field. As you leave, onChange is called, followed by the onBlur event handler, and finally by the onFocus handler of the next input object. Keep in mind that the code you might add—for example, to the onChange event handler—could have an impact on an onBlur event handler of the same object. As a general rule, you should use these three events conservatively.

**FIGURE 14.4**
*Event sequencing from one* Text *object to another* Text *object.*

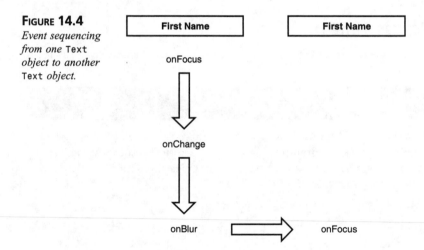

## Selecting Text (onSelect)

The next JavaScript event is the select event, which occurs when the user selects text from a Text or Textarea object. The object's onSelect event handler either executes JavaScript code or calls a predefined function.

Regardless of whether it works, the select event's scope is rather limited for most purposes, and most developers will have little occasion to use it.

# Moving the Mouse Over Objects (`onMouseOver` and `onMouseOut`)

If you are an experienced Web user, you have come to expect that the act of moving your mouse over link text will display the link's target destination (typically a URL address). However, no matter how much a power user might want to see the URL address, beginning users usually want something less esoteric. This is particularly the case in intranet environments where the destination URL is probably not that meaningful. Trapping the `mouseOver` and `mouseOut` events lets you change the default text in the status bar.

> **Note**
>
> The `onMouseOver` and `onMouseOut` event handlers are also supported by the `Area` object in JavaScript 1.1 and higher.

The `mouseOver` event takes place when the user moves the mouse cursor over a `Link` or `Area` object. As you might expect, `onMouseOut` behaves in much the same way, except that it occurs each time a mouse pointer leaves an area or link. These objects' `onMouseOver` and `onMouseOut` event handlers can then change the default behavior of the browser. If you want to set the window's `status` and `defaultStatus` properties, you need to return a value of `true` to the event handler.

For example, suppose you want to display the following text in the status bar when a `mouseOver` event occurs for the Kakata Hat link:

`Click here to get the whole story about the Legend of Kakata.`

To do this, add the `onMouseOver` event handler to the `Link` tag:

```
<a href="http://www. kakata.com" name="linker" onMouseOver="return updateStatusBar()"
   >Legend of Kakata
</a>
```

The `updateStatusBar()` method is defined as follows:

```
// onMouseOver event handler
function updateStatusBar() {
   window.status = 'Click here to get the whole story about the
      Legend of Kakata';
   return true
}
```

Each of the examples discussed in this chapter is contained in the `Register.htm` file. Listing 14.2 lists the complete source code for the examples.

**LISTING 14.2**   Source Code for `Register.htm`

```
<html>
<head>
<title>Kakata Hat Registration</title>

<script language="JavaScript">
<!--

    var noticeWindow

    //onClick event handler
    function displayHat() {
       hatWindow = window.open("http:/../kakata/viewhat.htm",
       "ViewHat" ,"toolbar=0,width=200,height=400,resizable=0");
    }

    //onSubmit event handler
    function confirmOrder() {
      return confirm('Are you certain you wish to order the Kakata hat?');
    }

    //onChange event handler
    function convertToUppercase(fieldObject) {
        fieldObject.value = fieldObject.value.toUpperCase();
    }

    // onFocus event handler
    function selectContents(fieldObject) {
        fieldObject.select();
    }

    // onMouseOver event handler
    function updateStatusBar() {
      window.status = 'Click here to get the whole story
        ➥about the Legend of Kakata';
      return true
    }

    // onMouseOut event handler
```

LISTING 14.2    continued

```
      function updateStatusBarOut() {
        window.status = '';
        return true
      }

      // onSelect event handler
      function accessText() {
        alert('Success');
      }

// -->
</script>
</head>
<body background="lt_rock.gif">
<h1><font color="#008000">Legend of Kakata Hat Order Form</font></h1>
<hr>

<p>If you would like more information on the <a
      href="http://www.acadians.com/javascript/kakata/kakata.htm"
      name="linker"
      onMouseOver="return updateStatusBar()"
      onMouseOut="return updateStatusBarOut()">Legend of Kakata </a>, please
      fill out the following form. </p>
<form method="POST">
<p>If you would like to see a detailed picture of the Legend of Kakata
Hat before ordering, please click the following button: <input
type=button name="ViewHat" value="View Hat" onClick=displayHat()></p>
</form>

<hr>
<form
      action="JavaScript:alert('order')"
      method="POST"
      name="MainForm"
      onSubmit="return confirmOrder()">
<h2><font color="#008000">Customer Information</font></h2>
<pre>    First Name: <input
                          type=text
                          size=20
                          maxlength=20
                          name="FirstName"
                          onFocus="selectContents(this)">
```

**LISTING 14.2**    continued

```
    Last Name: <input
                    type=text
                    size=20
                    maxlength=20
                    name="LastName"
                    onFocus="selectContents(this)">
        Title: <input
                    type=text
                    size=30
                    maxlength=30
                    name="Title"
                    onFocus="selectContents(this)">
      Company: <input
                    type=text
                    size=30
                    maxlength=30
                    name="Company"
                    onFocus="selectContents(this)">
Street Address: <input
                    type=text
                    size=30
                    maxlength=30
                    name="StreetAddr"
                    onFocus="selectContents(this)">
         City: <input
                    type=text
                    size=30
                    maxlength=30
                    name="City"
                    onFocus="selectContents(this)">
        State: <input
                    type=text
                    size=3
                    maxlength=2
                    name="State"
                    onFocus="selectContents(this)"
                    onChange="convertToUppercase(this)">
     Zip Code: <input
                    type=text
                    size=30
                    maxlength=10
                    name="ZipCode"
```

**LISTING 14.2**    continued

```
                        onFocus="selectContents(this)">
        Telephone: <input

                        type=text
                        size=12
                        maxlength=12
                        name="Phone"
                        onFocus="selectContents(this)">
            FAX: <input

                        type=text
                        size=12
                        maxlength=12
                        name="FAX"
                        onFocus="selectContents(this)">
        Email: <input
size=30

                        maxlength=50
                        name="Email"
                        onFocus="selectContents(this)">
            URL: <input

                          type=text
                          size=30
                          maxlength=100
                          name="URL"
                          onFocus="selectContents(this)"></pre>
<hr>

<p><strong>Are you &quot;Kakata worthy&quot;? Please use the space below to
enter a thorough reason for your order.</strong></p>
<blockquote>
<p><textarea
        name="worthyBox"
        rows=3
        cols=49
        onFocus="selectContents(this)">
</textarea></blockquote></p>

<h2><font color="#008000">Form Submission</font></h2>
<p><em>Please click the Order button to order your free Legend of Kakata hat.
You will receive email confirmation of your order in 24 hours.</em></p>
<p><input
        type=submit
        value="Order"
```

**LISTING 14.2**  continued

```
    onClick="confirmOrder('Submit object')">
<input
    type=reset
    value="Clear Form"
    onClick="alert('Clearing!')"></p>
<p> </p>
<p>
</form>

<a
    href="JavaScript:displayHat()">
    <img src="ball.gif" align=bottom border=0 width=16 height=16>
</a>

</body>
</html>
```

> **Tip**
>
> If you're trapping for multiple mouseOver and mouseOut events in an Area object, onMouseOut will be triggered when you leave an area, followed by onMouseOver when you enter the next area.

# Loading a Document (onLoad)

The initial opening of a window or frameset can be an important time to perform a JavaScript process. The load event lets you harness this by adding an onLoad event handler to a single-frame window's <body> tag or a multiframe window's <frameset> tag. The load event is executed when the browser finishes loading a window or all frames within a frameset. The Window object is the only object that can handle this event.

To illustrate, suppose you want to ensure that all intranet users in your company are using the correct version of Netscape Navigator. You could evaluate the browser being used in the onLoad event handler and then notify the user if his software version is incorrect. In the <body> tag for the document, you would add the onLoad event handler:

```
<body onLoad="checkBrowser()">
```

Next, the checkBrowser() method is defined in the document's <head> tag as follows:

```
//onLoad event handler
function checkBrowser() {
if ((navigator.appName == 'Netscape') &&
  (navigator.appVersion == '4.0 (Win95; I)')) {
noticeWindow = window.open("", "NoticeWindow",
        "toolbar=0,width=300,height=100,resizable=0");
    noticeWindow.document.write("<head><title>Upgrade Notice</title></head>");
    noticeWindow.document.write("<center><big><b>Your Web Browser needs
      to be updated. Please see your supervisor before noon.
      </b></big></center>")}
}
```

When the document is loaded, the JavaScript method is executed. Figure 14.5 shows the Upgrade Notice window displayed for versions that don't pass the test.

**FIGURE 14.5**
*The Upgrade Notice window is opened by the* onLoad *event handler.*

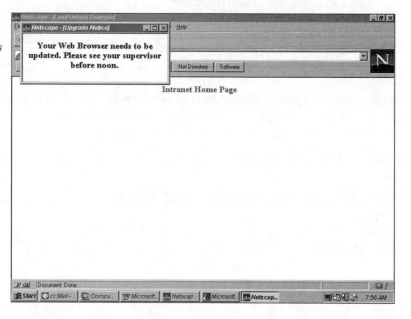

## Note

The Image object also has an onLoad event handler. This event is triggered when an image is displayed by the browser. Note that this event does not occur during the loading of an image to a client, but during the display of that image.

# Exiting a Document (`onUnload`)

The unload event, which is the counterpart to the load event, is triggered just before the user exits a document. As with onLoad, you can add an onUnload event handler to a single-frame window's `<body>` tag or a multiframe window's `<frameset>` tag. If you have a frameset and multiple onUnload event handlers, the `<frameset>` event handler always happens last.

One example of how you can use the onUnload event handler is cleaning up the browser environment before continuing to the next page. For instance, suppose you want to close the View Hat window when leaving the Kakata order page. You can add onUnload to the `<body>` tag as follows:

```
<body onLoad="checkBrowser()" onUnload="clean()">
```

Next, you can define the clean() method:

```
// onUnload event handler
function clean() {
    noticeWindow.close();
}
```

noticeWindow is a global variable declared in the `<HEAD>` tag of the document and refers to the Upgrade Notice window displayed in the onLoad event handler. If open, the Upgrade Notice window is closed when the user exits the current page.

Listing 14.3 provides the complete source code for the onLoad and onUnload examples.

**LISTING 14.3** The Source Code for `LoadUnload.htm`

```
<html>
<head>
<title>Load/Unload Example</title>

<script language="JavaScript">
<!--

    var noticeWindow

//onLoad event handler
function checkBrowser() {
if ((navigator.appName == 'Netscape') &&
    (navigator.appVersion == '4.0 (Win95; I)')) {
noticeWindow = window.open("", "NoticeWindow",
        "toolbar=0,width=300,height=100,resizable=0");
    noticeWindow.document.write("<HEAD><TITLE>Upgrade Notice</TITLE></HEAD>");
```

**LISTING 14.3** continued

```
    noticeWindow.document.write("<CENTER><BIG><B>Your Web Browser needs to be updated.
Please see your supervisor before noon.
    </B></BIG></CENTER>")}
}

// onUnload event handler
  function clean() {
    if ( noticeWindow != null ) { noticeWindow.close() };
  }
// -->
</script>
</head>
<body onLoad="checkBrowser()" onUnload="clean()">
<font color="#008000">
<center><big><b>Intranet Home Page</b></big></center>
</body>
</html>
```

# Handling Errors (onError)

The window and image objects have an onError event handler that lets you trap for errors occurring during the loading of a document or image. The error that will be trapped will be either a JavaScript syntax error or a runtime error, not a browser error (such as an unresponsive server message). See Chapter 33, "Error Handling," for full coverage of trapping errors with onError.

> **Note**
>
> The onError event handler is supported in JavaScript 1.1 and higher.

# Aborting an Image Load (onAbort)

Depending on its size, loading an HTML image can be a time-intensive process. As a result, users may become impatient and stop the image load before it is complete. For example, a user may abort the loading process by clicking a link to another page or the browser's Stop button.

**14**

**Handling Events**

> **Note**
>
> The Image object and the onAbort event handler are supported in JavaScript 1.1 and higher.

However, having the user work with a partially downloaded HTML file may not be what you would like to occur and will likely have some ramifications on any image-specific code in your script. The onAbort event handler lets you react to this aborting of an image load and trigger a JavaScript function as a response. For example, suppose you wanted to alert your user that the entire HTML document hasn't been downloaded. You would add the following event handler to your <img> tag:

```
<img name="mapworld" SRC="global.gif" onAbort="alert('You have not downloaded the
entire document.')">
```

# Changing Event Handlers

In JavaScript 1.1 and higher, you can change an event handler defined in the HTML tag definition. For example, in the following listing, the optionA() function is assigned by the <input> definition to be the event handler for the button1 object. However, the second script defined evaluates the choice variable. If choice isn't equal to "A", the code changes the event handler assignment to the optionB() function, as shown in Listing 14.4.

**LISTING 14.4**  An Example of Changing Event Handlers

```
<script language="JavaScript">        var choice = "A"
    function optionA() {
       ...
    }

    function optionB() {
       ...
    }
    ...
</script>
<body>

<form name="form1">
<input type="button" name="button1"
   onClick="optionA()">
</form>
```

**LISTING 14.4**    continued

```
<script language="JavaScript">

    if (choice != "A") {
        document.form1.button1.onclick=optionB
    }

</script>
</body>
```

Notice that event handlers are function references and therefore do not have parentheses added to them when defined in code. If the code had been defined as follows, the optionB() function would have been triggered, not assigned as an event handler:

```
document.form1.button1.onclick=optionB()
```

# Triggering Events in Code

So far, this chapter has discussed responding to events generated by either the user (such as a click event) or the system (such as an onUnload event). In most cases, you will design your code to respond to these events as they occur. However, as a JavaScript developer, you don't have to rely on external forces to cause an event to happen. In fact, you can trigger some of these events to occur within your code.

For example, you can simulate a click event for a Button object by calling its click() method. Although this is valid for a Button object, a Link object—which has an onClick event handler—doesn't have a click() method.

# Timer Events

Many event-driven programming environments use a timer event, which is an event triggered every time a given time interval elapses. Although JavaScript offers no event called timer, you can use the Window object's setInterval method to serve the same function.

**Note**

The setInterval method is supported in JavaScript 1.2 and higher.

**14**

Handling Events

The setInterval method repeatedly calls a function or evaluates an expression each time a time interval (in milliseconds) has expired. This method continues to execute until the window is destroyed or the clearInterval method is called.

For example, in Listing 14.5, the setInterval method is executed when the document opens and begins to call the dailyTask() function every 10,000 milliseconds. The dailyTask() function evaluates the time each time it is called, and when it is 8:30 a.m., the code within the if statement is called, alerting the user and then clearing the interval. Once the clearInterval method is called, setInterval halts execution.

**LISTING 14.5**  Source Code for Timer12.htm

```
<head>
<script language="JavaScript">
<!--
    function dailyTask() {
      var tdy = new Date();
      if ((tdy.getHours() == 8) && (tdy.getMinutes() == 30)) {
          alert('Good morning sunshine!')
          clearInterval(timerID)
        }
      }

//-->


timerID = setInterval('dailyTask()', 10000)

</script>
</head>
```

If you're using JavaScript 1.1 or earlier, you can perform a similar process, albeit in a much less straightforward way, using the setTimeout() and clearTimeout() methods.

You usually use the setTimeout()method to evaluate an expression after a specific amount of time. This evaluation is a one-time process that is not repeated an infinite number of times. However, because you can make recursive function calls in JavaScript, you can use recursion to create a *de facto* timer event.

Suppose that each morning at 8:30 a.m. you want to perform the task just shown. You could have a timer evaluate the time of day; when that time is reached, the process is spawned. The dailyTask() method is defined as follows:

```
function dailyTask() {
  var tdy = new Date();
```

```
    if ((tdy.getHours() == 8) && (tdy.getMinutes() == 30)) {
       performProcess()}
    timerID = setTimeout("dailyTask()",10000)
}
```

The method creates a date object to get the current time using getHours() and getMinutes(). If these evaluate to 8:30 a.m., the performProcess() method is called. The next line—the heart of the timer process—uses the setTimeout() method to call the dailyTask() method recursively every 10,000 milliseconds.

> **Caution**
>
> This example demonstrates a "kludge" method of using a timer, but you would probably want to be careful implementing such a solution in the real world. Implementing a continuous looping process like that in a browser could lead to resource constraints over time.

To trigger this timer initially when the document is loaded, you can add an onLoad event handler to the <body> tag of the HTML document:

```
<body onLoad="dailyTask()">
```

Listing 14.6 provides the entire source code listing for this example.

**LISTING 14.6**   Source Code for Timer11.htm

```
<head>
<script language="JavaScript">
<!--
    function performProcess() {
        alert('Good morning sunshine!
');
    }

    function dailyTask() {
        var tdy = new Date();
        if ((tdy.getHours() == 8) && (tdy.getMinutes() == 30)) {
           performProcess()}
           timerID = setTimeout("dailyTask()",10000)
        }
//-->
</script>
```

**14**

Handling Events

---

LISTING **14.6**   continued
_____

```
</head>

<body onLoad="dailyTask()">
</body>
```
_____

# Summary

Given JavaScript's event-driven nature, a solid understanding of its built-in events is key to maximizing its power. This chapter discussed events and their associated event handlers. I focused on the events that are most useful to you, as well as specific examples of how you can use them. Having this foundation in place will assist you over the next few chapters as you look in depth at JavaScript's built-in events.

# Window Object

**CHAPTER 15**

The Navigator objects are the highest-level objects in the JavaScript object hierarchy. These objects don't deal with the nuts and bolts of HTML; instead, they deal primarily with browser issues, such as opening a new browser window, traversing the History list, or obtaining the hostname from the current URL. This chapter concerns itself with the Window object, which, as we have said, is at the pinnacle of the object hierarchy, and we'll then descend to some of the other objects, though these are explained in greater detail elsewhere. These include the Frame object, which is discussed in Chapter 18, "Frame Objects." Other objects include the Location and History objects and the application-level Navigator object.

# The Window Object

The top-level Window object is the parent of all other child objects, and is present on every page, and of course a multiplicity of them are possible in a single JavaScript application. The basic methods that surround the operation of the Window object have obvious functionalities and include those described in Table 15.1:

**TABLE 15.1**  Basic Window Object Methods

| Method | Description |
| --- | --- |
| Open and Close | Open and close browser windows; you can specify the size of the window, its content, and whether it has a button bar, location field, and other *chrome* attributes. |
| Alert | Show an alert dialog with an appropriate message. |
| Confirm | Show a confirm dialog with OK and Cancel buttons. |
| Prompt | Show a prompt dialog with a text entry field. |
| Blur and Focus | Remove or add focus to a window. |
| ScrollTo | Scroll a window to specified point. |
| SetInterval | A specified period between a functional call and the evaluation of an expression. |
| SetTimeout | A single specified period prior to a functional call or the evaluation of an expression. |

As discussed in Chapter 9, "Client-Side Objects," in the section "JavaScript Objects," the Window object is the top-level object in the JavaScript object hierarchy. Unlike other objects that may or may not be present, the Window object is always there, whether it's in a single or multiframe display. However, the Window object is unusual in that you can often simply ignore it, for two reasons.

First, if you're working in a single-frame environment, you can ignore explicit referencing of the Window object. JavaScript infers the reference to the current window. For example, the following two statements are equivalent and produce the same result:

```
myTitle = window.document.title
myTitle = document.title
```

Second, because of the structure of the JavaScript language, some system-level methods, such as displaying message boxes or setting a timer, are assigned to the Window object. However, you don't need to reference the window itself when calling these methods; the reference to the window is implicit.

Working with Window objects is important when programming in JavaScript because of the way people use browser windows. Although most people browsing the Web typically use only one instance of the browser, having two or more windows open is sometimes beneficial. You can compare pages from different sites, enter information into a form using data from a different Web page, and conduct research from a list on one page and look at the references with another browser instance.

The term *browser window* is often shortened to just *window*, although you should be careful not to confuse separate copies of the browser with frames, which are also referred to as windows (subwindows of the browser window). The browser window is also called the *top window*, because frames are subwindows of the browser. Browsers that support JavaScript let you programmatically open and close browser windows and navigate through these windows. A site with separate windows can provide several simultaneous views of the site's content, increase access to the information and features, and offer new ways to fully interact with the site.

> ### Note
>
> JavaScript 1.2 added several new Window methods: atob, back, btoa, captureEvents, clearInterval, crypto.random, crypto.signText, disableExternalCapture, enableExternalCapture, find, forward, handleEvent, home, moveBy, moveTo, releaseEvents, resizeBy, resizeTo, routeEvent, scrollBy, scrollTo, setHotKeys, setInterval, setResizable, and setZOptions.
>
> At the same time it added new properties: crypto, innerHeight, innerWidth, locationbar, menubar, offscreenBuffering, outerHeight, outerWidth, pageXOffset, pageYOffset, personalbar, screenX, screenY, scrollbars, statusbar, and toolbar properties;
>
> JavaScript 1.2 requires Navigator 4.0-4.05, while JavaScript 1.3 requires Navigator 4.06-4.5.

**15**

Window Object

In many cases, frames might be better for simultaneous viewing, as discussed in Chapter 18. However, multiple browser windows can be individually resized and positioned by the user. Users can also minimize and maximize the window, move the window to the foreground or background as needed, and typically keep all the tools and other features (menu bar, location field, status bar, bookmarks, and so on) with each instance of the browser.

> **Tip**
>
> Many users might find it distracting and annoying to unexpectedly open new browser windows, especially if they have to keep closing them. Let the visitor know that an action will cause a window to open—for example, a short note next to a link. In the following, `Spike` is a link that opens a new window:
>
> `See a picture of my dog Spike. (new window)`

# Opening and Closing Windows

> **Note**
>
> A user can always open a new window by selecting File, New Browser (or a similar option). However, any window opened by a user in this way can't be referenced by JavaScript in other windows.

You can use JavaScript to open and close browser windows. As a developer, you can create a new window with a particular document loaded into it, based upon specific conditions. You can also specify, for example, the size of the new window and the options that are available in the window, and you can assign names for referencing it. Although the act of opening a window is similar to creating a new `Window` object, you don't use the `new` constructor. Instead, you use the following syntax:

```
windowVar = window.open(URL, windowName, [, windowFeatures])
```

The parameters for the `open()` method are

- *URL*: The URL of the target window. This parameter is optional. If the URL is an empty string (`""`), the browser opens a blank window, allowing you to use the `write()` method to create dynamic HTML.

- *windowName*: The name of the `Window` object. *Name* is also optional; however, to target the window with a link or a form, you need a name. You can provide a name at a later time by assigning the `window.name` property.

- *windowFeatures*: A list of display attributes for the browser window.

If successful, the `open()` method returns a handle to a `Window` object. If `open()` fails, it returns a null value.

> **Note**
>
> The two names that can refer to a window aren't the same functionally. Consider the following code:
>
> ```
> myWindow=window.open("","newWindow");
> ```
>
> `myWindow` is a variable of the object that opened `newWindow`. `newWindow` is the new window's name. The new window's properties can be referenced through the variable `myWindow`. Links and forms can be targeted to the new window with its name `newWindow`.

# Referencing Windows

When working with single and multiple frames in your JavaScript applications, you probably need to use other ways to reference windows. JavaScript provides four references to windows, and each is implemented as a property of the `Window` object. There is more information about referencing windows and frames in Chapter 18.

> **Note**
>
> Separate browser windows don't have a hierarchy structure; however, the window containing the code that opens another window is often referred to as the *parent window*. The new window is often referred to as the *child window*. Any new window can assign a variable in other windows so that other windows can reference it and its properties. To reference a property in the new window, use `windowName.property`.

Consider the following code:

```
newWindow = window.open();
newWindow.location.href = "http://www.mcp.com/";
```

Although this segment isn't the most efficient way to write the code, it demonstrates referencing a child window's property. The new window is opened and named (in this case, newWindow). Then, the new window's location.href is referenced and assigned.

# The Current Window

Chapter 9 discussed using windows to reference the current window. However, what wasn't covered is that the Window object contains a property called window that can be used as a self-referencing tool. In addition, the self property of the Window object is another means of referring to the current or active window. For example, the following two code lines are functionally the same:

```
window.defaultStatus = "Welcome to the Goat Farm Home Page"
self.defaultStatus = "Welcome to the Goat Farm Home Page"
```

Because both window and self are synonyms of the current window, you might find it curious that both are included in the JavaScript language. As shown in the previous example, the rationale is flexibility; you can use window or self as you want.

However, as useful as window and self can be, it can easily become confusing to think about the logic behind it all. After all, an object's property that is used as an equivalent term for the object itself is rather unusual. Consequently, you might find it helpful to think of window or self as reserved words for the Window object rather than its properties.

Because window and self are properties of the Window object, you can't use both window and self in the same context. For example, the following code doesn't work:

```
window.self.document.write("<h1>Test.</h1>")
```

Finally, in multiframe environments, window and self always refer to the window in which the JavaScript code is executed.

> **Note**
>
> In some object-oriented or object-based languages, self might refer to the active object, no matter what type it is. In JavaScript, self refers only to the active Window or Frame object—nothing else.

# Specifying Window Content

The URL parameter specifies what content appears in the new window. If you specify a value, the browser attempts to locate and display the specified document:

```
newWindow = window.open("http://www.acadians.com", "AcadiaPage", LO:WRONG)
```

Alternatively, you can display a blank page by specifying an empty string ("") as the URL parameter. Use this technique if you want to create an HTML page dynamically using JavaScript:

```
newWindow = window.open("", "DynamicPage", "")
newWindow.document.write("<H1>Document created using JavaScript.</H1>")
newWindow.document.close()
```

See Chapter 16, "Document Object," for complete details on using the Document object's write() method to create dynamic HTML.

# Specifying Window Attributes

The windowFeatures parameter is important as you display windows, because it lets you customize the look of the window you're opening. The windowFeatures parameter is optional; not using it gives you a window with attributes identical to the current one. Table 15.2 lists the attributes that you can specify.

**TABLE 15.2**   The open() Method's Window Display Attributes

| Attribute | Description |
| --- | --- |
| width | Width of the Navigator client area in pixels. See innerWidth, which was introduced in JavaScript 1.2. |
| height | Height of the Navigator client area in pixels, but see innerHeight, which was introduced in JavaScript 1.2. |
| dependent | When yes, creates a child window of the current window, and when using Windows the child window does not appear on the task bar. Child windows close in unison with their parent windows. Introduced in JavaScript 1.2. |
| toolbar | Shows/hides the browser toolbar. |
| menubar | Shows/hides the browser menu bar. |
| scrollbars | Shows/hides the browser horizontal and vertical scrollbars. |
| innerWidth | Specifies the width of a window's content area. Windows smaller than $100 \times 100$ pixels require signed script. Introduced in JavaScript 1.2, supersedes width, which can also be used for backward compatibility. |
| innerHeight | Specifies the height of a window's content area. Windows that are smaller than $100 \times 100$ pixels require signed script. Introduced in JavaScript 1.2, supersedes height, which can also be used for backward compatibility. |
| resizable | Allows/disallows resizing of the browser window. |

**15**

**Window Object**

TABLE **15.2**  continued

| Attribute | Description |
|-----------|-------------|
| screenX | Specifies the distance from the left side of the screen to a new window. A window may be placed offscreen using this feature in signed scripts. Introduced in JavaScript 1.2. |
| screenY | Specifies the distance from the top of the screen to a new window. A window may be placed offscreen using this feature in signed scripts. Introduced in JavaScript 1.2. |
| status | Shows/hidesthe browser status bar. |
| location | Shows/hides the URL location box. |
| directories | When yes, shows a secondary toolbar (Netscape) with familiar buttons such as What's New and What's Cool. |
| copyhistory | Copies the current window's Go history for a new window. |
| outerWidth | Width of the Navigator window in pixels (JavaScript 1.2). |
| outerHeight | Height of the Navigator window in pixels (JavaScript 1.2). |
| left | Distance in pixels from the left side of the screen (JavaScript 1.2). |
| top | Distance in pixels from the top of the screen (JavaScript 1.2). |
| alwaysLowered | Creates a browser window that floats below other windows, regardless of whether or not it is active (introduced in JavaScript 1.2). A secure feature requiring signed scripts. |
| alwaysRaised | When yes, creates a browser window that floats on top of other windows, regardless of whether or not it is active. Introduced in JavaScript 1.2 and a secure feature requiring signed scripts. |
| z-lock | Creates a new browser window that doesn't rise above other windows when given focus (JavaScript 1.2). |

**Note**

The alwaysRaised and z-lock attributes added in JavaScript 1.2 work only on Windows and Macintosh platforms.

The width and height attributes specify the dimensions of the window in pixels and are backward compatible with JavaScript 1.0 and 1.1, though you might prefer their replacement keywords, including innerWidth and innerHeight. The remaining attributes are set by using Boolean values: true values are 1, yes, or the attribute alone; false values are 0, no, or leaving the attribute out altogether. For example, if you want to display the new window with only a toolbar and menu bar, use the following syntax:

```
newWindow = window.open(LO:WRONG, "myWindow", "toolbar=1,menubar=1")
```

The following syntaxes are also valid:

```
newWindow = window.open("", "myWindow", "toolbar=yes,menubar=yes")
newWindow = window.open("", "myWindow", "toolbar,menubar")
```

As you see, you can simply leave out attributes that aren't specified. They are assumed to have `false` values.

---

**Note**

The `outerWidth`, `outerHeight`, `left`, and `top` attributes added in JavaScript 1.2 let you provide absolute positioning of browser windows on your desktop. `innerWidth` and `innerHeight` provide control over the exact size of browser windows, though if you are using JavaScript 1.0 or 1.1, you will have to use the `width` and `height` keywords instead.

---

**Tip**

A bug in certain versions of the Netscape Navigator browser prevents the display of a document with the `window.open()` method. The workaround for this bug is to repeat the window-opening statement:

```
myWindow = window.open("new.html","newWindow");
myWindow = window.open("new.html","newWindow");
```

Repeating the statement forces the display of `newWindow` and its document in all versions of the Netscape Navigator browser.

---

**Note**

In addition to the `Windowopen()` method, you can also provide a link attribute of `TARGET="_blank"` or even a target attribute value of any name (window or frame) not currently in use to open a new window. The link `<A HREF="foo.html" TARGET="bar">foo</A>` opens a browser window, names the window bar, and loads the document `foo.html` in it, as long as one of the current windows or frames in use isn't named `bar` (window and frame names are case sensitive).

Additionally, the link `TARGET="_blank"` creates an unnamed window, which makes it difficult to update the window. With a target of `_blank`, a link (whether the same link or a different one) simply adds another new window instead of updating the one previously opened.

**15**

**Window Object**

# Closing Windows

To close a window, you can use the `Window` object's `close()` method. If you're closing the current window, your method call is simply `window.close()`. Unlike other `Window` object methods such as `alert()` or `setTimer()`, the `close()` method must always accompany an object reference. If you use `close()` by itself, you could close the current document rather than the window, depending on the context of the method call. The reason is that the `Document` object has a `close()` method, too. Table 15.3 illustrates some typical code scenarios in which we see the `close()` method applied.

**TABLE 15.3**  The `close()` Method and Open Windows

| Close()/Opener | Description |
| --- | --- |
| `window.opener.close()` | Close the window that opened the current window. |
| `document.write("<br>opener property is " + window.opener.name)` | Determine the name of its opener as follows. |
| `top.opener.close()` | Close the main browser window. |
| `window.opener.document.bgColor='bisque'` | Change the background color of the window that the opener property specifies. |
| `window.opener=null` | Change the value of the opener property to null, preventing closure of the opener window. |

> **Note**
>
> Later versions of Netscape prevent `window.close()` from closing a window that wasn't created by JavaScript. This security measure prevents pranksters from inserting the code in poorly written guest books and the like. This measure shouldn't affect any legitimate use of the `window.close()` method.

A function or event handler with `window.close()` closes the window containing it:

```
<FORM>
<INPUT TYPE="BUTTON" VALUE="Close Window" onClick="top.close()">
</FORM>
```

> **Note**
>
> For an event handler such as `onClick`, you must specify a window name such as `window`, `parent`, `top`, `self` or an assigned variable name such as `myWindow`, as in

> window.close() or myWindow.close(). Simply using close() in an event handler implies document.close().

You can close a window by reference in the same window that opened it, through the variable assigned to the new window:

```
myWindow = window.open("new.html","newWindow");
.....
<FORM>
<INPUT TYPE="BUTTON" VALUE="Close Window" onClick="myWindow.close()">
</FORM>
```

## Note

newWindow.close(); won't work. You can use the name newWindow in the preceding example to identify the window (the window.name property) and target the window in links and forms. However, you can't use newWindow to reference the new window and its properties.

## Tip

A good use of the window.close() method is to provide a button or link for users to close a new window when they're finished with it. (Some users, especially new ones, might not know how to close the window or might mistakenly exit the browser instead of closing the window.) You can use a conditional statement to provide a close button or link if the document is loaded in a window named explicitly (a new window):

```
<SCRIPT LANUAGE="JavaScript">
<!--
//newWindow is the name given the new window
if(top.name == "newWindow"){
➥   document.write('<A HREF="javascript:top.close()>close</A>"' +
                " this window to return to previous window.");
    }    //  For clarity the angle brackets
         //  are not encoded, unescape("%3C"), unescape("%3E").
//However in actual code they would be encoded to
//prevent misinterpretation as comment tags by older browsers.
// -->
</SCRIPT>
```

The form in Figure 15.1 demonstrates the various aspects of opening and closing windows. By filling out the form, you can specify how you want the new window to look.

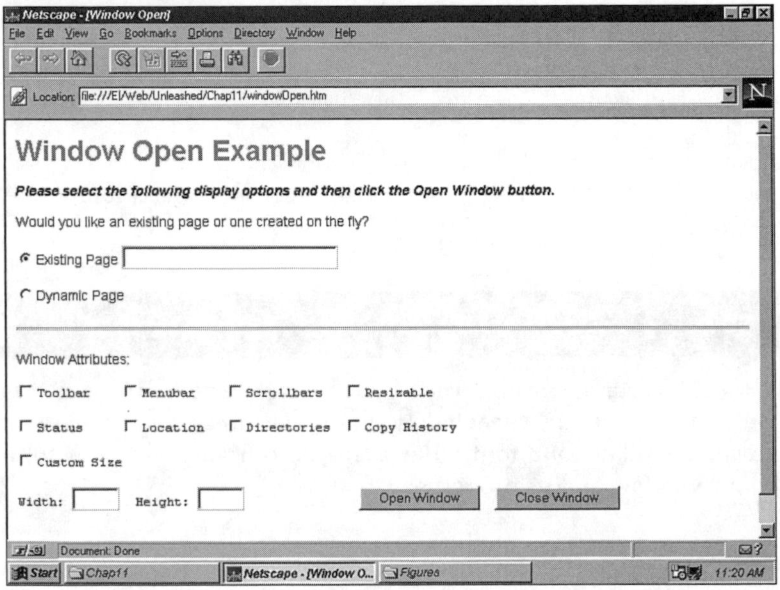

**FIGURE 15.1**

*A window open sample form.*

In the first section, you can specify the URL parameter—to use an existing URL or create a page on-the-fly. The second section lets you specify each of the window attributes available. By default, all are unchecked. You can check all the ones you want to display. By checking the Custom Size box, you can specify the dimensions of the new window.

By clicking the Open Window button, you can see the new window that is created, as shown in Figure 15.2.

Listing 15.1 provides the source code for this example.

**LISTING 15.1**   OpenWindow.htm

```
<html>
<head>
<title>Window Open</title>
<SCRIPT LANGUAGE="JavaScript">
<!--
    var newWindow

    // Open Window based on user defined attributes
```

**LISTING 15.1**     continued

```
function openWindow() {

    // Build the windowFeatures parameter list
    var winAtts = ""
    if (document.winOptions.toolbarOption.checked) {
        winAtts += "toolbar=1," }
    if (document.winOptions.menubarOption.checked) {
        winAtts += "menubar=1," }
    if (document.winOptions.scrollbarsOption.checked) {
        winAtts += "scrollbars=1," }
    if (document.winOptions.resizableOption.checked) {
        winAtts += "resizable=1," }
    if (document.winOptions.statusOption.checked) {
        winAtts += "status=1," }
    if (document.winOptions.locationOption. checked) {
        winAtts += "location=1," }
    if (document.winOptions.directoriesOption.checked) {
        winAtts += "directories=1," }
    if (document.winOptions.copyHistoryOption.checked) {
        winAtts += "copyhistory=1," }
    if (document.winOptions.customSizeOption.checked) {
        winAtts += "height=" + document.winOptions.heightBox.value + ","
        winAtts += "width=" + document.winOptions.widthBox.value + ","
    }
    winAtts = winAtts.substring(0, winAtts.length-2)

    // Determine URL and show window
    if (document.winOptions.pageType[1].checked) {
        var urlVar = ""
        urlVar = document.winOptions.urlBox.value
        newWindow = window.open(urlVar,"newWindow",winAtts) }
    else {
        newWindow = window.open("","newWindow",winAtts)
        newWindow.document.write("<H1>Window Open Test</H1><p>")
    }
}


// Close Window
function closeWindow() {
    newWindow.close()
}
// -->
```

15

Window Object

**LISTING 15.1**  continued

```
</SCRIPT>
</head>

<body background="../lt_rock.gif">
<h1><font color="#008040">Window Open Example</font></h1>
<p><i><b>Please select the following display options and then click
the Open Window button. </i></B></p>
<form name="winOptions" method="POST">
<p>Would you like an existing page or one created on the fly?</p>
<input
    type=radio
    checked
    name="pageType"
    value="existing">Existing Page
    <input
        type=text
        size=30
        maxlength=256
        name="urlBox"></p>
    <input
        type=radio
        name="pageType"
        value="dynamic">Dynamic Page</p>
<hr>
<p>Window Attributes:</p>
<pre><input
    type=checkbox
    name="toolbarOption"
    value="ON"
    >Toolbar     <input
    type=checkbox
    name="menubarOption"
    value="ON">Menubar      <input
    type=checkbox
    name="scrollbarsOption"
    value="ON">Scrollbars    <input
    type=checkbox
    name="resizableOption"
    value="ON">Resizable</pre>
 <pre><input
    type=checkbox
    name="statusOption"
```

**LISTING 15.1** continued

```
    value="ON">Status       <input
    type=checkbox
    name="locationOption"
    value="ON">Location     <input
    type=checkbox name="directoriesOption"
    value="ON">Directories   <input
    type=checkbox name="copyHistoryOption"
    value="ON">Copy History</pre>
<pre><input
    type=checkbox
    name="customSizeOption"
    value="ON">Custom Size</pre>
<pre>Width: <input
    type=text
    size=5
    maxlength=5
    name="widthBox">  Height: <input
    type=text
    size=5
    maxlength=5
    name="heightBox">              <input
    type="button"
    name="OpenButton"
    value="Open Window"
    onClick="openWindow()">  <input
    type="button"
    name="CloseButton"
    value="Close Window"
    onClick="closeWindow()"></pre>
</form>
<p> </p>
</body>
</html>
```

**15**

**Window Object**

**FIGURE 15.2**
*The new window is displayed.*

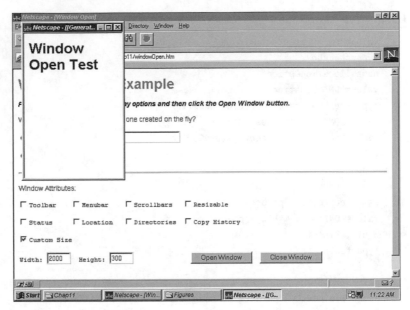

# Navigating Between Windows

It's possible to have a number of windows open during a session; however, only one window can be active, or have focus, at a time. Having focus means that the window can directly receive and respond to user input. Also, the window with the focus is typically the top window on the display, the one in the foreground overlapping the other windows. (In UNIX and X Window, the window with focus can be in the background.)

The user can navigate between the windows by using the mouse. Often, clicking the window gives the window focus. With some varieties of UNIX, moving the mouse cursor on a window is enough to give it focus; conversely, moving the cursor off the window blurs (removes focus or deactivates) the window.

Relying on user action isn't the only way, nor at times the best way, to give focus to a window and blur others. JavaScript and HTML provide several methods to focus and blur windows automatically through code. This automatic focusing and blurring allow navigation through the windows with little or no user action. Instead of providing a message to tell the user to click a window, the code can focus the window automatically for the user. The intent isn't to remove user control of the session but to assist the user—as cruise control in an automobile does.

Although many sites don't need multiple windows, sites that do might benefit by controlling these windows programmatically. JavaScript provides a good means of controlling windows through the opening and closing techniques previously described and through techniques to apply and remove window focus. All these techniques for controlling windows combine to provide a programmatic window navigation system.

In JavaScript, merely specifying an object of the window or its document or even changing a property in the window doesn't give the window focus. You can give focus to a window in two ways:

- Indirectly, by giving focus to an object in the window

- Directly, by giving focus to the window itself

## Indirect Focus

A window opened with a variable `myWindow`, containing a document with a form named `myForm` and an input element named `myInput`, can receive focus through the window that opened it with the following code:

```
myWindow.document.myForm.myInput.focus();
```

The input element, `myInput`, gains focus and, as a result, `myWindow`, which contains `myInput`, also gets focus.

A new window can give focus to the window that opened it through its `opener` property:

```
window.opener.focus();
```

> **Note**
>
> The `opener` property is supported in JavaScript 1.1 and higher.

To provide focus from a new window to the window that opened it in early versions of JavaScript-capable browsers, the new window needs a variable to reference the opening window:

```
myWindow = window.open("new.html","newWindow");
myWindow.oldWindow = top;
```

The new window can reference the old window and indirectly give it focus:

```
oldWindow. document.myForm.myInput.focus();
```

**15**

**Window Object**

# Direct Focus

A window receives focus directly if you use the `window.focus()` method. If the window can reference another window through a variable such as `myWindow`, it can give focus to the other window:

```
myWindow.focus();
```

A new window can give focus to the window that opened it through its `opener` property:

```
window.opener.focus();
```

A call to a function in a window can provide focus to the window if the function containsd `window.focus()`:

```
function focusDemo(){
    top.focus;
    ... rest of function
}
```

> **Note**
>
> The `window.focus()` and `window.blur()` methods, like the `opener` property, are supported only in JavaScript 1.1 and higher. To support the early versions of the browser, you have to use the indirect focusing technique.

# Removing Focus

To blur (remove focus from) a window, just give focus to another window. Because only one window at a time can have focus, giving focus to a window directly or indirectly blurs the other windows.

Through the `window.blur()` method, a window can lose focus directly without another window gaining the focus. You can use any of the means that you employ with `window.focus()` for `window.blur()` as well.

> **Note**
>
> According to Netscape documentation, you're supposed to give focus to a window by targeting a link at the window:
>
> ```
> <A HREF="some.html" TARGET="myWindow">My Window</A>
> ```

Clicking the link should load the document `some.html` in the window `myWindow` and give focus to `myWindow`. If `myWindow` doesn't exist, a new window is opened with `some.html` loaded in it, and the new window has the focus.

This technique doesn't always work in every version of the browser. If the window is already open, it might not gain focus.

# Displaying Message Boxes

Dialog boxes are typically an important part of an application environment. If you've used Windows much, you know that dialog boxes are a given in this and other graphical user interfaces. JavaScript can display standard dialog boxes to either notify a user or receive information before proceeding. However, because of the nonmodal nature of the Web, I recommend that you not use dialog boxes. You can usually communicate with the user in some other way.

### Tip

Modal dialog boxes are common in Windows applications. If you come from a Windows 4GL background, be sure to adjust your thinking about their use.

The JavaScript language itself not so subtly enforces this notion by adding a prefix to the messages you display. For alert messages, "JavaScript Alert" appears before the message you specify. For confirm dialog boxes, it's "JavaScript Confirm"; in prompt dialog boxes, you see "JavaScript Prompt." One reason for this is that the user can better determine the source of the dialog box that is displayed.

### Note

Other than providing the message itself, you can't customize the look of JavaScript message boxes. The title and icons are always the same.

## Simple Notification

You use the `Window` object's `alert()` method to display information to the user. The alert dialog box displays a message to the user with a single OK button to close the box. It is modal, so the user must close the dialog box before continuing in the browser (even in multiframe documents). No value is returned when the dialog box closes. Its syntax is as follows:

```
[window.]alert(message)
```

You can display information about the current window in an alert message with the code shown in Listing 15.2.

**LISTING 15.2**   DisplayWindowInfo.htm

```html
<HTML>
<HEAD NAME = "WindowPane">
<SCRIPT LANGUAGE = "JavaScript">

    function displayWindowInfo() {
        var winInfo = ""
        winInfo = "Number of frames: " + window.length + "\r"
        winInfo += "Window object name: " + window.window + "\r"
        winInfo += "Window parent name: " + window.parent + "\r"
        winInfo += "URL: " + window.location + "\r"
        alert(winInfo)
    }

</SCRIPT>
</HEAD>

<BODY>
<FORM>
<INPUT
    Type="button"
    Value="Display Window Information"
    OnClick="displayWindowInfo()"
</INPUT>
</FORM>
</BODY>
```

Figure 15.3 shows the alert dialog box that is displayed when the user clicks the button.

The message parameter of the alert() method is typically a string, although it isn't required to be. Because JavaScript isn't a strongly typed language, you can display other data type information without converting the data to a string. You can even use an object as a parameter, as shown in Listing 15.3. Figure 15.4 shows the result.

**FIGURE 15.3**

*An alert
dialog box.*

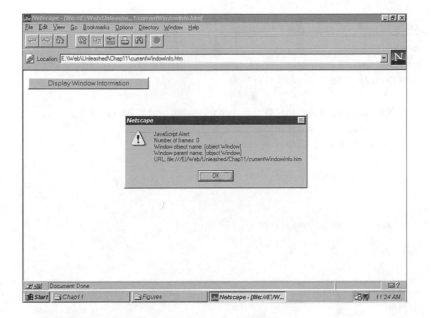

**FIGURE 15.4**

*An object defini-
tion, displayed in
an alert
dialog box.*

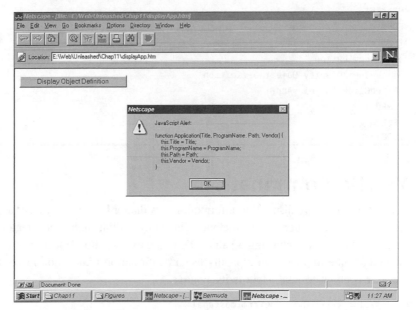

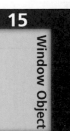

**15**

**Window Object**

**LISTING 15.3**    DisplayWindowObjectInfo.htm

```
<HTML>
<HEAD>
<SCRIPT LANGUAGE = "JavaScript">

    function Application(Title, ProgramName, Path, Vendor) {
        this.Title = Title
        this.ProgramName = ProgramName
        this.Path = Path
        this.Vendor = Vendor
    }

    function displayApp() {
        alert(Application)
    }

</SCRIPT>
</HEAD>
<BODY>
<H1></H1>
<FORM>
<INPUT
    Type="button"
    Value="Display Object Definition"
    OnClick="displayApp()"
</INPUT>
</FORM>
</BODY>
```

# Yes/No Confirmation

In addition to simply displaying information in a dialog box, you can ask a question using the Window object's confirm() method. The confirmation dialog box features OK and Cancel buttons, each returning a value. OK returns true, and Cancel returns false. As the method's name implies, you typically use a confirmation dialog box to confirm an action the user is about to take. Here is its syntax:

```
returnValue = [window.]confirm(message)
```

A common use of the confirmation dialog box is to ask the user to confirm a form submission or send an email message. Listing 15.4 shows how you can use confirm() to return a value to the form's onSubmit event handler. If the user clicks OK, the form is emailed to the specified address. If the Cancel button is clicked, the submit event is canceled.

**LISTING 15.4**    JavaScriptChronicles.htm

```
<html>
<head>
<title>Untitled Normal Page</title>
<SCRIPT LANGUAGE="JavaScript">

    function confirmAction() {

      return confirm("Do you really want this subscription?")
    }

</SCRIPT>
</head>

<body>
<h2><em>JavaScript Chronicles -- Free Subscription Form</em></h2>
<form
    action="mailto:subscribe@jschronicles.com"
    method="POST"
    name="SubscribeForm"
    onSubmit="return confirmAction()">
<ol>
<li>What other magazines do you currently subscribe to?
<pre><input type=checkbox name="C1-SKU01" value="SKU01">PC Week
<input type=checkbox name="C1-SKU04" value="SKU04">DBMS
<input type=checkbox name="C1-SKU07" value="SKU07">Wired
<input type=checkbox name="C1-SKU10" value="SKU10">Yahoo
<input type=checkbox name="C1-SKU02" value="SKU02">InfoWorld
<input type=checkbox name="C1-SKU05" value="SKU05">Databased Advisor
<input type=checkbox name="C1-SKU08" value="SKU08">Web Publisher
<input type=checkbox name="C1-SKU11" value="SKU11">Internet Advisor
<input type=checkbox name="C1-SKU03" value="SKU03">PC Magazine
<input type=checkbox name="C1-SKU06" value="SKU06">Delphi Informant
<input type=checkbox name="C1-SKU09" value="C1-SKU09">Web Informant
<input type=checkbox name="C1-SKU12" value="SKU12">JavaWorld
</pre>

</li>
<li>Please enter the reason you would like to subscribe to
```

LISTING **15.4**    continued

```
<em>JavaScript Chronicles:</em><br>
<br>
<textarea
    name="Comments"
    rows=6
    cols=46>
    </textarea></li>
</ol>
<p>
<input
    type=submit
    name="Submit"
    value="Submit">

</form>
</body>
</html>
```

Figure 15.5 shows the confirmation message box that is displayed when the user clicks the Submit button.

**FIGURE 15.5**
*The confirmation dialog box returns the user's response.*

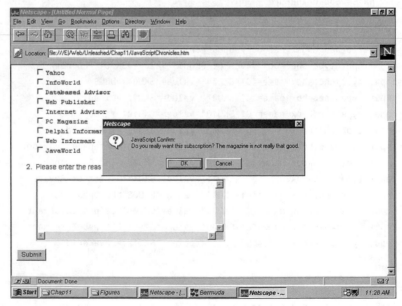

# User Input

A third message box that you can use for obtaining user input is invoked with the `prompt()` method of the `Window` object. Use the prompt dialog box when you want to obtain a value from a user. This dialog box features a message, an edit box for user input, and OK and Cancel buttons. The `prompt()` method has the following syntax:

```
returnValue = [window.]prompt(message, defaultReply)
```

As you can see, in addition to specifying the message of the dialog box, you need to specify a *defaultReply* parameter. This value becomes the default text inserted in the edit box of the message box. You must specify this parameter, even if it has no default value.

### Note

Always be sure to use a default reply when displaying a prompt dialog box. If you don't add this parameter, JavaScript places Undefined in the edit box, which can be confusing for users. If you have no default value, use an empty string ("") for the parameter.

If the user clicks OK, the `prompt()` method returns the string value entered by the user. If nothing is entered in the edit box, an empty string ("") is returned. However, if the user clicks Cancel, a null value is returned.

### Caution

Don't assume that the user will always click OK in the prompt dialog box. Every time you use the `prompt()` method, you should first ensure that a non-null value is returned before proceeding to evaluate it. Otherwise, if the user clicks Cancel, you will be working with a string value of "null" rather than what the user actually entered.

Listing 15.5 shows one example of how you can use the prompt message box. The user is asked to enter text in the box, as shown in Figure 15.6. This text is then used in a new window, as shown in Figure 15.7.

**LISTING 15.5**   UserText.htm

```
<HTML>
<HEAD>
<SCRIPT LANGUAGE = "JavaScript">

    function showBox() {
            userText = prompt("Enter the text for your " +
              "personalized browser window.","My own browser text")
        if (userText != null) {
            userWindow = window.open("", "userTextWindow", "toolbar=0")
            userWindow.document.write("<h1>" + userText + "</h1>") }
    }

</SCRIPT>

<BODY>
<FORM>
<INPUT
    Type="button"
    Value="Create Your Own HTML Page"
    OnClick="showBox()"
</INPUT>
</FORM>
</BODY>
```

The return value is always a string. If you want to treat it as another value, you must convert it first. For example, if you want to calculate a total price based on a user-defined interest rate, you could get that value using the prompt() method, as shown in Figure 15.8. Next, you could convert the value into a float using parseFloat()before calculating. Listing 15.6 shows the code.

**FIGURE 15.6**
*The prompt message box.*

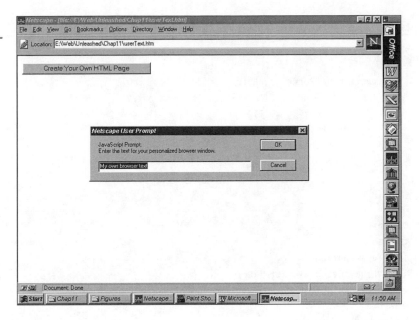

**FIGURE 15.7**
*The new window displays content provided by the user.*

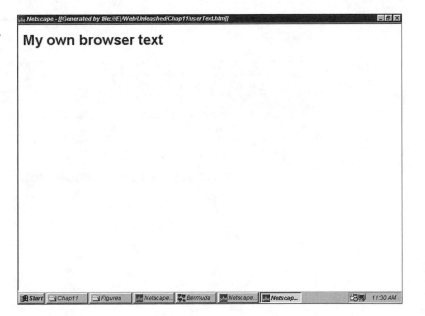

**LISTING 15.6**   Calc.htm

```
<HTML>
<HEAD>
```

**LISTING 15.6    continued**

```
<SCRIPT LANGUAGE = "JavaScript">

    function getPercentageRate() {
      percent = prompt("What is the current rate?", "8.5")
      if (percent != null) {
        totalPrice = parseFloat(percent) * 20000
        alert(totalPrice) }
     }

</SCRIPT>
<BODY>
<FORM>
<INPUT
    Type="button"
    Value="Calculate Total Price"
    OnClick="getPercentageRate()"
</INPUT>
</FORM>
</BODY>
```

**FIGURE 15.8**

*Retrieving input from the user.*

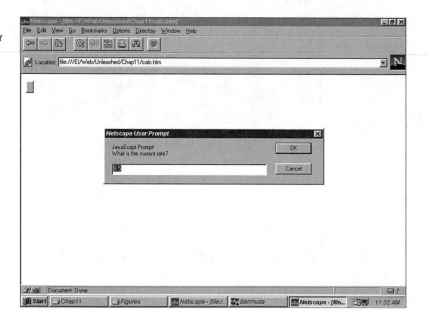

# Working with Status Bar Messages

The status bar of a browser can be an important means of communicating with the user. You can use two properties of the Window object—defaultStatus and status—to control the text that is displayed.

Generally, there are two ways to use the status bar. First, you can display a default message on the status bar. The user sees this message without performing any action. You can display a default message using the defaultStatus property. The defaultStatus property can be set at any time—either upon loading the window or while the window is already open.

Second, you can display a temporary message that overrides the default text. In practice, this message usually appears when a user performs an event, such as moving a mouse over a jump. You can set this message using the status property.

Figure 15.9 demonstrates the use of the defaultStatus and status properties.

**FIGURE 15.9**
*Setting the*
defaultStatus
*and* status
*properties.*

The code behind this page shows three actions that you code to change the status bar message. First, the following code sets a default message when the window opens:

```
window.defaultStatus = "Welcome to the large URL page."
```

Second, when the user passes over the Go link, its `onMouseOver` event handler calls the following function:

```
function changeStatus() {
    window.status = "Click me to go to the Acadia Software home page."
}
```

Third, to change the text of the default status message, the user can select a different message from the `Select` object. When the Change button's `onClick` event handler is triggered, it executes the following function:

```
function changeDefaultStatus() {
    window.defaultStatus = window.document.statusForm.messageList.
    options[window.document.statusForm.messageList.selectedIndex].
    text
}
```

Listing 15.7 provides the complete source code for this example.

**LISTING 15.7**   `Status.htm`

```
<html>
<head>
<title>Status Bar</title>
<SCRIPT LANGUAGE="JavaScript">
<!--
    window.defaultStatus = "Welcome to the large URL page."

    function changeStatus() {
        window.status = "Click me to go to the Acadia Software" +
         " home page."
    }

    function changeDefaultStatus() {
        window.defaultStatus = window.document.statusForm.messageList.
         options[window.document.statusForm.messageList.
         selectedIndex].text
    }
//-->
</SCRIPT>
</head>

<body>
<p> </p>
<p> </p>
```

**LISTING 15.7** continued

```
<p align=center>
<font color="#008040">
<font size=7>
<strong>http://www.acadians.com</strong></font></font></p>
<p align=oenter>
<a href="http://www.acadians.com" onMouseOver="changeStatus()
     ;return true">Go...</a></p>


<form name="statusForm" method="POST">
<p><br>
<br>
<br>
<br>
</p>
<p align=center>
<font size=1>To change the default status bar message, select
a message from the list below and click the Change button. </font></p>
<p align=center><select
     name="messageList"
     size=1>
     <option selected>Welcome to the large URL page.</option>
     <option>En route to Acadia Software</option>
     <option>This page intentionally left (nearly) blank.</option>
     <option>An exciting example of changing status bar text.</option>
     </select>
<input
     type=button
     name="Change"
     value="Change"
     onClick="changeDefaultStatus()"></p>
</form>
</body>
</html>
```

# Summary

This chapter dived into the top level of the JavaScript object hierarchy. The objects I discussed have much less to do with HTML tags than with various aspects of a browser window. As the top-level object in the hierarchy, the Window object is charged with many responsibilities—in both single and multiframe windows. The Frame, Location, and

History objects are all properties of the Window object and provide a means to work with their respective browser counterparts. This chapter also discussed how to use JavaScript to reference objects and properties in other frames and browser windows.

# Document Object

Chapter 9, "Client-Side Objects," began the look at JavaScript objects by examining each object tier, starting with the first. In that chapter, we took a brief look at the Document, Link, Anchor, and Image objects, but we did not go into detail on how they work or how to use them. Because these objects represent such substantial functionality from a Web developer's point of view, they warrant their own chapter.

This chapter continues the initial discussion by looking at these objects—often referred to as the *document* objects. This set of objects includes the core client-side Document object and three of its "child" objects: Link, Anchor, and Image.

# The Document Object

The Window object is the highest-level object for client-side JavaScript objects. In this role, it serves as a container, but it doesn't actually have any content associated with it. It leaves the content of a Web document up to the Document object. The Document object serves as the JavaScript equivalent of an HTML document and is used as the method of access to its child objects.

In this role, the Document object is a container for all HTML-related objects that are associated with the <head> and <body> tags. The Document object gets the value of its title property from the <title> tag (located within the <head> section) and several color-related properties from the <body> section, which is shown here:

```
<body
    [background="backgroundImage"]
    [bgcolor="backgroundColor"]
    [text="foregroundColor"]
    [link="unfollowedLinkColor"]
    [alink="activatedLinkColor"]
    [vlink="followedLinkColor"]
    [onload="methodName"]
    [onunload="methodName"]>
</body>
```

> **Note**
>
> Although onLoad and onUnload events can be captured with the onload and onunload event handlers in the <body> tag, they are events of the Window object, not the Document object.

The Document object is critical as you work with JavaScript and HTML, because all the action happens on a Web page within a document. Because of this, you need to refer to the Documentobject when you access an object within it. For example, if you want to access a Form object named invoiceForm, you must preface your reference with document:

```
document.invoiceForm.submit();
```

If you don't, JavaScript can't locate the object within the page.

# Creating HTML Documents Programmatically

As you will see throughout this book, you can use JavaScript to react to events generated on static Web pages. You can also use it to generate HTML pages on-the-fly. In fact, you can use each of the methods of the Document object to alter documents programmatically:

- open(["*mimeType*"]) prepares a stream for write() and writeln() statements. Its parameter can be one of several MIME types (text/html is the default):

  text/html

  text/plain

  image/gif

  image/jpeg

  image/x-bitmap

  plugIn (any Netscape plug-in MIME type)

- write(*JavaScriptExpression*) writes a JavaScript expression to a document.

- writeln(*JavaScriptExpression*) also writes a JavaScript expression to a document but appends a newline character to the end of the expression.

- close() closes the stream that was opened by the open() method.

Whereas open() and close() prepare or close a generated document, the write() and writeln() methods give the document content. You can use any valid JavaScript expression as their parameter, including a string literal, a variable, and an integer value. For example, each of the following is a valid use of write():

```
var loc = "Ashford, Kent"
document.write("The castle is located in " + loc)
document.write("I stayed in the Robert Courtneys room.")
document.write("I would like " + 70 + "copies of that report.")
```

Keep in mind that you are writing HTML, not straight text. You can use HTML tags just as if you were writing the document in an HTML editor, as in the following example:

```
document.write('<h3>Return to the <a
➥href="http://www.mcp.com">MCP</a> home
➥page.</h3><p>');
```

Figure 16.1 shows the result.

**FIGURE 16.1**

*A link generated
using JavaScript.*

The one key limitation you need to keep in mind when using `write()` or `writeln()` is that you can't change the contents of the current document without completely reloading the window. The following sections describe the three valid contexts in which you can create HTML documents on-the-fly.

## Creating in the Current Window

You can create a new document in the current window when the document loads. You typically place this code within a `<script>` tag either in the `<head>` section or by itself if it stands alone. For example, if you want to evaluate the browser and change the text based on its type, you can use the script shown in Listing 16.1.

**LISTING 16.1**  Writing Different Text to a Page Based on the Browser

```
<script type="text/javascript">
<!--
  var browser = navigator.appName;
  document.open();

  if(browser == "Netscape"){
    document.write("<h2>Welcome <a href='http://home.netscape.com'>
```

**LISTING 16.1** continued

```
➥       Navigator</a> user.</h2>");
    }else if(browser == "Microsoft Internet Explorer"){
      document.write("<h2>Welcome <a href='http://www.microsoft.com'>

➥       Internet Explorer</a> user.</h2>");
    }else{
      document.write("<h2>Welcome. But what browser are you using?</h2>")
    }
    document.write("We are glad you came to our Web site. Do you know how");
    document.write(" we knew your browser type?");
    document.close();
//-->
</script>
```

Figure 16.2 shows the result in Navigator 4, and Figure 16.3 shows the result in Internet Explorer 5.

**FIGURE 16.2**

*A customized
Navigator page.*

**FIGURE 16.3**
*A customized Internet Explorer page.*

## Creating in a Frame

You can also generate a new document in another frame of a multiframe window. The techniques are similar to those used in the preceding example, but you must reference the correct document using dot notation. For example, to reference the first frame of a frameset, you could use the following code:

```
parent.frames[0].document.write("test");
```

Listing 16.8, which you'll see later in this chapter, has an example of setting a frame document programmatically.

## Creating in a Separate Window

The third technique for creating documents on-the-fly is opening a new window and writing to its document. If you want to enumerate a list of installed Navigator plug-ins for the browser in a separate window, use the code shown in Listing 16.2.

**LISTING 16.2**    Displaying a List of Navigator Plug-Ins

```
<html>
<head>
  <script type="text/javascript">
<!--
    function showWindow(){
      var len = navigator.plugins.length;
      newWin = window.open("", "", "height=400,width=500");
      newWin.document.write("<h2>Plug-In Info:</h2>");
```

**LISTING 16.2**    continued

```
    for(var i = 0; i < len; i++){
      newWin.document.write("<li>" + navigator.plugins[i].description +
➥       "</li>");
    }

    newWin.document.close()
  }
//-->
</script>
</head>
<body>
  <form>
    <input type="button" value="Show Plug-In Information"
➥      onclick="showWindow()">
  </form>
</body>
</html>
```

Figure 16.4 shows the result of the script in a Navigator browser.

**FIGURE 16.4**

*Generating a new
document in a
separate window.*

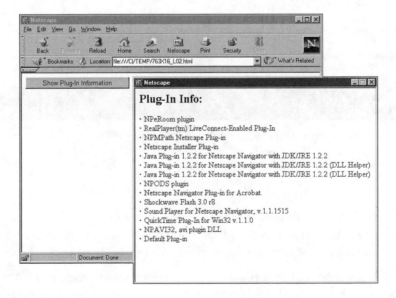

# Changing Document Colors

Color settings for documents are by default set in the user's browser configuration, but HTML gives you the capability to change these color settings, and with JavaScript you can do it programmatically. The Document object has five properties that reflect the colors of various attributes within the document—alinkColor, bgColor, fgColor, linkColor, and vlinkColor. These are described in Table 16.1.

**TABLE 16.1** Document Color-Related Properties

| Property | HTML <body> Attribute | Description |
|----------|----------------------|-------------|
| alinkColor | alink | The color of an activated link (after mouse down and before mouse up). |
| bgColor | bgcolor | The background color of the document. |
| fgColor | text | The foreground color (text) of the document. |
| linkColor | link | The color of unvisited links. |
| vlinkColor | vlink | The color of visited links. |

These properties are expressed either as string literals or as hexadecimal RGB triplet values. For example, if you want to assign a background color of chartreuse to a document, use the string literal chartreuse:

```
document.bgColor="chartreuse";
```

You could also use the equivalent hexadecimal RGB triplet value:

```
document.bgColor="7fff00";
```

> **Note**
>
> You can find the JavaScript color values table in Table 5.8 in Chapter 5, "Fundamentals of the JavaScript Language." It lists the color values as both string literals and hexadecimal RGB triplets.

A hexadecimal RGB triplet is a combination of three hexadecimal values representing red, green, and blue. When combined, the values form a hexadecimal RGB triplet. The number should take one of two case-sensitive forms: rrggbb or #rrggbb.

When applying color changes to a Document attribute, you must follow the same principles as when changing text. You can make the changes only when the page is set, such as in a document.write() statement—not on a page that has already been "painted" in the browser window.

To see how to set these color settings, look at the example shown in Figure 16.5. The bottom frame has a selection list with all the colors and a group of radio buttons associated with the Document attribute color options. You can select a color and the property you want to use and then click the Apply button. JavaScript code reloads the top frame based on your setting.

**FIGURE 16.5**
*Changing the color of a frame on-the-fly.*

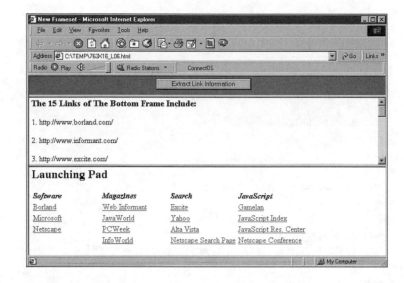

Listing 16.3 provides the HTML source of the frameset document. Listing 16.4 shows the code for the main body of text. Listing 16.5 lists the code from the lower frameset that performs this process. When the user clicks the Apply button, the refreshMain() method assigns a value to the newColor variable based on the currently selected option in the selection list. Next, using dot notation, the document of the upper frame is referenced (parent.main.document) and reloaded based on write() and a color property assignment.

**LISTING 16.3** The Source for the Frameset of the Document

```
<html>
<head>
  <title>Color Example</title>
</head>
<frameset rows="75%,25%">
  <frame src="763X16_L04.html" name="main" marginwidth="1"
➡    marginheight="1">
  <frame src="763X16_L05.html" name="colorDef" marginwidth="1"
➡    marginheight="1">
```

**LISTING 16.3** continued

```
</frameset>
</html>
```

**LISTING 16.4** Code for the Main Body of the Sample Text

```
<html>
<head>
  <title>Main Body</title>
</head>
<body>
  <h2>
    <em>
      JavaScript Unleashed
    </em>
  </h2>
  <p>
    Here is some sample text
  </p>
  <p>
    Here is a sample link:
    <a href="http://home.netscape.com">Netscape</a>
  </p>
  </body>
</html>
```

**LISTING 16.5** Code for the Actual JavaScript Code and Color Selectors

```
<html>
<head>
  <title>Color Definition</title>
  <SCRIPT LANGUAGE="JavaScript">
  <!--
    var graf = '<body>';
    graf += '<h2><em>JavaScript Unleashed</em></h2>';
    graf += '<p>Here is some sample text</p>';
    graf += '<p>Here is a sample link: <a href="http://home.netscape.com">
        Netscape</a></p>';
    graf += '</body>'

    function refreshMain() {
      var newColor = document.form1.colorList.options[document.form1.
```

**LISTING 16.5** continued

```
➥          colorList.selectedIndex].text
        var selProp = null

        with(parent.main.document){
          open();
          write(graf);
          if(document.form1.type[0].checked){
            bgColor = newColor
          }else{
            if(document.form1.type[1].checked){
              fgColor = newColor;
            }else{
              if(document.form1.type[2].checked){
                alinkColor = newColor;
              }else{
                if(document.form1.type[3].checked){
                  linkColor = newColor;
                }else if (document.form1.type[4].checked){
                  vlinkColor = newColor;
                }
              }
            }
          }
        }
        close()
      }
  //-->
  </script>
</head>

<body bgcolor="tomato">
  <form name="form1">
    <p>
      Select Color:
      <select name="colorList" size="1">
        <option>black</option>
        <option>blue</option>
        <option>brown</option>
        <option>cyan</option>
        <option>gold</option>
        <option>gray</option>
        <option>green</option>
```

**LISTING 16.5** continued

```
            <option>indigo</option>
            <option>lavender</option>
            <option>lime</option>
            <option>maroon</option>
            <option>navy</option>
            <option>olive</option>
            <option>orange</option>
            <option>pink</option>
            <option>purple</option>
            <option>red</option>
            <option>royalblue</option>
            <option>silver</option>
            <option>slategray</option>
            <option>tan</option>
            <option>teal</option>
            <option>turquoise</option>
            <option>violet</option>
            <option>white</option>
            <option>yellow</option>
        </select>
        <br>
        <input type="radio" name="type" value="bgColor" checked>Background
➥           </input>
        <input type="radio" name="type" value="fgColor">Foreground</input>
        <input type="radio" name="type" value="alinkColor">Activated Link
➥           </input>
        <input type="radio" name="type" value="linkColor">Unvisted Link
➥           </input>
        <input type="radio" name="type" value="vlinkColor">Visited Link
➥           </input>
        <br>
        <input type="button" name="Apply" value="Apply"
➥           onclick="refreshMain()">
    </p>
  </form>
</body>
</html>
```

Although this is a limited example, you can build on this base to develop much more flexible scripts to change colors on-the-fly.

> **Tip**
>
> For a comprehensive example of using colors in your documents, see the hIdaho Color Center at `http://www.hidaho.com/colorcenter/`.

# The `Link` Object

Perhaps love makes the world go 'round, but links are what make the World Wide Web go 'round. HTML links are the core elements of any Web document, allowing you to jump to another Web page with the click of a mouse. The location of the document is immaterial; it could be on the same Web server or thousands of miles away. All that matters is that the URL is valid. The JavaScript equivalent of the hypertext link is the `Link` object, which is defined in HTML syntax as

```
<a href=locationOrURL
    [name="objectName"]
    [target="windowName"]
    [onclick="methodName"]
    [onmouseover="methodName"]>
 linkText
</a>
```

> **Tip**
>
> For more information on `link` events, see Chapter 14, "Handling Events."

The `Link` object has several properties that are the same as the parameters for the `Location` object. These include `hash`, `host`, `hostname`, `href`, `pathname`, `port`, `protocol`, and `search`. See Chapter 9 for more information on these properties.

## Referencing `Link` Objects

`Link` objects do not have a `name` property, so you can't refer to a specific `Link` object by itself. The only way you can refer to a `Link` object in your JavaScript code is by using the `document.links` array. The `document.links` array is a collection of all the links within the current document. The order of the array is based on the order in which the links are located within the source file. I'll present an example that demonstrates how you can use the `document.links` array to deal with individual `Link` objects.

Suppose you want to extract the URLs from each link on a page and list them on another page. Using a triple-frame frameset, you can set the bottom frame to be the "free" window that is used for browsing, the top frame to contain a button to set off the process, and the middle frame to list the URLs. Figure 16.5 shows the triple-frame frameset in an Internet Explorer window after this process is performed.

Listing 16.6 displays the frameset source code, Listing 16.7 shows the code for the bottom frame, which contains all the lines, and Listing 16.8 lists the JavaScript source code for the top frame, which contains the processing power for this example. Clicking the Extract Link Information button triggers the getLinkInfo() method. This method references the links array of the bottom frame (named bFrame) and sets the len variable equal to its length. While writing to the middle frame, the method loops through each element in the links array and retrieves the href property value.

**LISTING 16.6**   Source Code for the Frameset

```html
<html>
<head>
  <title>New Frameset</title>
</head>
<frameset rows="80,*,185">
  <frame src="763X16_L08.html" name="tFrame" marginwidth="2"
     marginheight="4">
  <frame src="about:blank" name="mFrame" marginwidth="5"
     marginheight="2">
  <frame src="763X16_L07.html" name="bFrame" marginwidth="5"
     marginheight="2">
</frameset>
</html>
```

**LISTING 16.7**   Source Code for the Bottom Frame

```html
<html>
<head>
  <title>Links</title>
</head>
<body>
<h2>Launching Pad</h2>
  <table width="80%">
    <tr>
      <td width="25%">
        <em>
          <strong>
```

**LISTING 16.7**    continued

```
        Software
      </strong>
    </em>
  </td>
  <td width="25%">
    <em>
      <strong>
        Magazines
      </strong>
    </em>
  </td>
  <td width="25%">
    <em>
      <strong>
        Search
      </strong>
    </em>
  </td>
  <td width="25%">
    <em>
      <strong>
        JavaScript
      </strong>
    </em>
  </td>
</tr>
<tr>
  <td width="25%">
    <a href="http://www.borland.com">Borland</a>
  </td>
  <td width="25%">
    <a href="http://www.informant.com">Web Informant</a>
  </td>
  <td width="25%">
    <a href="http://www.excite.com">Excite</a>
  </td>
  <td width="25%">
    <a href="http://www.gamelan.com">Gamelan</a>
  </td>
</tr>
<tr>
  <td width="25%">
```

**LISTING 16.7**   continued

```
            <a href="http://www.microsoft.com">Microsoft</a>
          </td>
          <td width="25%">
            <a href="http://www.javaworld.com">JavaWorld</a>
          </td>
          <td width="25%">
            <a href="http://www.yahoo.com">Yahoo</a>
          </td>
          <td width="25%">
            <a href="http://www.c2.org/~andreww/javascript">JavaScript Index</a>
          </td>
        </tr>
        <tr>
          <td width="25%">
            <a href="http://home.netscape.com">Netscape</a>
          </td>
          <td width="25%">
            <a href="http://www.pcweek.com">PCWeek</a>
          </td>
          <td width="25%">
            <a href="http://www.altavitsa.digital.com">Alta Vista</a>
          </td>
          <td width="25%">
            <a href="http://www.intercom.net/user/mecha/java/index.html">
➥           JavaScript Res. Center</a>
          </td>
        </tr>
        <tr>
          <td width="25%">
             
          </td>
          <td width="25%">
            <a href="http://www.infoworld.com">InfoWorld</a>
          </td>
          <td width="25%">
            <a href="http://home.netscape.com/escapes/search/search4.html">
➥           Netscape Search Page</a>
          </td>
          <td width="25%">
            <a href="http://home.netscape.com/misc/developer/conference
➥           /proceedings">Netscape Conference</a>
          </td>
```

**LISTING 16.7**    continued

```
    </tr>
  </table>
</body>
</html>
```

**LISTING 16.8**    Source Code for the Top Frame

```
<html>
<head>
  <base target="middle">
  <script type="text/javascript">
  <!--
    function getLinkInfo() {
      var len = parent.tFrame.document.links.length;

      with(parent.mFrame.document){
        open();
        write("<h3>The " + len + " Links of The Top Frame Include:
          </h3><p>");

        for(var i = 0; i < len; i++){
          write((i + 1) + ". " + parent.tFrame.document.links[i].href
            + "<p>");
        }
        close()
      }
    }
  //-->
  </script>
</head>
<body bgcolor="red">
  <form>
    <div align="center">
      <input type="button" name="Extract" value="Extract Link Information"
        onclick="getLinkInfo()">
    </div>
  </form>
</body>
</html>
```

# Executing JavaScript Code Within Links

Using `javascript:` as the protocol element of the link's `href`, you can perform a
JavaScript expression in place of a typical link action, such as jumping to a new Web page
or sending a mail message. However, the code you execute must be self contained. You
can't reference another object outside of its context, such as another window.

You could use a link to evaluate the type of browser in use, such as in the following code:

```
<a href="javascript:if(navigator.appName != 'Netscape')
➥{ alert('You should not have clicked this link!') } else
➥{ alert('Thanks for clicking.')} ">All Netscape users, click me</a>
```

As a second example, I set up a table of contents for the first edition of this book in an
HTML document and added a link to each of the part names. For the `href` attribute of these
links, I placed a description of each part in an alert message box. Listing 16.9 shows the
HTML code for this example, and Figure 16.5 shows the result of clicking the Part III link.

**LISTING 16.9**    Table of Contents with `document.alert()` Links

```
<html>
<head>
  <title>JavaScript Unleashed Table of Contents</title>
</head>
<body>
  <a href="javascript:alert('In this first section, you will get a complete
➥      introduction to JavaScript. Chapter 1 takes a unique look at JavaScript,
➥      focusing on how and where it fits into the Web application development
➥      framework. You will also see how it relates to other Web technologies
➥      both on the client- and server-side. Next, in Chapter 2, you will learn
➥      about the relationship between JavaScript and Hypertext Markup Language
➥      (HTML) and how the browser interprets your code at runtime. Chapter 3
➥      looks at the software tools you need to develop in JavaScript.')">
    <h3>Part I: Getting Started with JavaScript</h3>
  </a>
  <h4>
    1) JavaScript and the World Wide Web <br>
    2) How JavaScript and HTML Work Together <br>
    3) Assembling Your JavaScript Toolkit
  </h4>
  <a href="javascript:alert('The second part presents a thorough look at the
➥      JavaScript language. In Chapters 4-7, you will learn about language
➥      basics, control structures, operators, and functions.')">
    <h3>Part II: The JavaScript Language</h3>
```

**Listing 16.9**    continued

```
  </a>
  <h4>
    4) Fundamentals of the JavaScript Language<br>
    5) Control Structures and Looping <br>
    6) Operators<br>
    7) Functions
  </h4>
  <a href="javascript:alert('Part three dives into the heart of JavaScript--
➥    objects. After an introduction to object-oriented concepts in Chapter 8,
➥    Chapter 9 looks at how you can handle user and system events. Chapter 10
➥    then looks at the built-in JavaScript hierarchy and introduces you to
➥    each of the Navigator and Built-in language objects. Chapters 11-14
➥    continue where the previous chapter left off by exploring in-depth
➥    each of the built-in JavaScript objects. Chapter 15 rounds out the
➥    discussion on objects, focusing on how you can create your own. It
➥    includes many innovative ideas related to custom object development
➥    within JavaScript.')">
   <h3>Part III: JavaScript Objects</h3>
  </a>
  <h4>
    8) Fundamentals of Object-Orientation <br>
    9) Handling Events <br>
    10) JavaScript Built-In Object Model <br>
    11) Navigator Objects <br>
    12) Document Objects <br>
    13) Form Objects <br>
    14) Built-in Language Objects <br>
    15) Creating Custom JavaScript Objects
  <h4>
  <a href="javascript:alert('The next section builds upon everything you
➥    learned up to that point to look at specific areas of interest to the
➥    JavaScript developer. Chapter 16 explores how you can enhance HTML forms
➥    with JavaScript, such as providing client-side data validation. Both
➥    Chapters 17-18 really focus on frames and how you can use JavaScript
➥    in multi-frame windows. I have found frame management to be perhaps
➥    the most common use of JavaScript on the Web. Chapter 19 looks at yet
➥    another key topic, cookies and other techniques for handling and
➥    maintaining state in the stateless environment of the Web.')">
    <h3>Part IV: JavaScript Programming</h3>
  </a>
  <h4>
    16) Enhancing Forms with JavaScript <br>
```

**LISTING 16.9**    continued

```
  17) Working with Frames and Windows<br>
  18) Scripting Outlines and Table of Contents <br>
  19) Cookies &amp; State Maintenance
</h4>
<a href="javascript:alert('While Parts I-IV focused on client-side
➥   JavaScript, this section focuses on its server-side counterpart. Within
➥   Netscape LiveWire and other products such as Borland IntraBuilder, you
➥   can use JavaScript as a server-side scripting language. In doing so,
➥   you are freed from writing CGI scripts and dealing with such languages
➥   as PERL. Chapter 20 looks at server-side JavaScript, focusing on
➥   LiveWire and IntraBuilder. Chapter 21 takes look at the issue of how to
➥   architect client/server applications on the Web. Covered are many of the
➥   issues you will encounter as you plan such an application.')">
    <h3>Part V: JavaScript on the Server</h3>
  </a>
  <h4>
  20) Server-Based JavaScript <br>
  21) Partitioning Client and Server Applications
</h4>
<a href="javascript:alert('Part VI explores five advanced subjects, many
➥   of which are emerging as key topics as JavaScript matures. Chapter 22
➥   dives into Error Handling and Debugging JavaScript applications. Chapters
➥   23-24 cover the hot topic of integrating JavaScript with Netscape
➥   Plug-Ins and ActiveX controls. Chapter 25 looks at integrating
➥   JavaScript with VRML and multimedia data. Chapter 26 closes the section
➥   by looking at a more conceptual topic--JavaScript security. The chapter
➥   not only looks at the key issues surrounding this subject, but provides
➥   some helpful advice as you consider using JavaScript for your Web
➥   site.')">
    <h3>Part VI: Advanced JavaScript</h3>
  </a>
  <h4>
  22) Error Handling and Debugging in JavaScript <br>
  23) Working with Netscape Plug-ins <br>
  24) ActiveX Scripting with JavaScript <br>
  25) VRML and Multimedia <br>
  26) JavaScript and Web Security
</h4>
<a href="javascript:alert('JavaScript is an important tool to glue HTML
➥   and Java applets. In this section, we will look at Java from a
➥   JavaScript perspective in Chapter 27 and see how similar or different
➥   the language is for JavaScripters. Chapter 28 provides a good
```

**LISTING 16.9**    continued

➥    introduction on how to build a Java applet, while Chapter 29 is
➥    where the rubber meets the road when it focuses on integrating Java
➥    and JavaScript.')">
    &lt;h3&gt;Part VII: Java and JavaScript&lt;/h3&gt;
  &lt;/a&gt;
  &lt;h4&gt;
    27) Java from a JavaScripter Perspective &lt;br&gt;
    28) Building Java Applets&lt;br&gt;
    29) Integrating JavaScript with Java
  &lt;/h4&gt;
  &lt;a href="javascript:alert('Many corporations will use the Web as a way to
➥    get at their data. As a result, how JavaScript can access data will be
➥    an increasingly important topic as the technology matures. In this
➥    section, we will look at how you can work with data both on the
➥    client-side and server-side. Chapter 30 introduces the notion of
➥    maintaining lookup tables on the client side to lessen the need to
➥    access the server. Chapter 31 then gets into how you can use JavaScript
➥    to access server-side data. LiveWire and IntraBuilder will again be used
➥    in this context.')">
    &lt;h3&gt;Part VIII: JavaScript Database Applications&lt;/h3&gt;
  &lt;/a&gt;
  &lt;h4&gt;
    30) Using Client-Side Tables in JavaScript &lt;br&gt;
    31) Working with Server-Side Database Objects
  &lt;/h
  &lt;a href="javascript:alert('The final section provides some extra
➥    information that will assist you as you read the book. Appendixes A-B
➥    provide basic references on the JavaScript and HTML respectively.
➥    Appendix C looks at how VBScript and JavaScript compare. Appendix D
➥    lists JavaScript resources that are available online.')">
    &lt;h3&gt;Part IX: Appendixes&lt;/h3&gt;
  &lt;/a&gt;
  &lt;h4&gt;
    A) JavaScript Language Summary &lt;br&gt;
    B) Fundamentals of HTML &lt;br&gt;
    C) Comparing JavaScript with Microsoft&#146;s VBScript &lt;br&gt;
    D) JavaScript Resources on the Internet
  &lt;h4&gt;
&lt;/body&gt;
&lt;/html&gt;

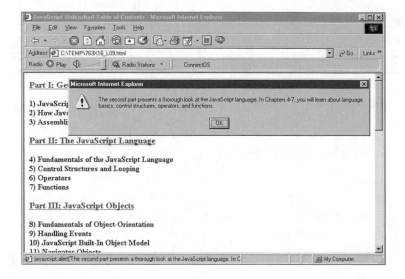

**FIGURE 16.6**
*Clicking a link displays a message box.*

# The Anchor Object

You most often use a Link object to jump to another Web page or another location within the current document. Within the current document, the link locates a specific place in the text, called an *anchor*. This is defined in HTML syntax as

```
<a [href=locationOrURL]
   name="objectName"
   [target="windowName"]>
  anchorText
</a>
```

You could say that the Anchor object is "JavaScript-challenged," because you can do little in JavaScript with anchors. By itself, an Anchor object has no properties, methods, or events. The only way you can really use one in JavaScript is through an anchors array of the Document object. You can use the document.anchors array to determine the number of anchors in a document and iterate through them as desired.

# The Image Object

**Note**

The Image object is supported in JavaScript 1.1 and later. It is not supported in JavaScript 1.0 or JScript 1.0.

If you've spent much time on the Web, you probably realize how important graphics are to the Web. You can hardly go to a page without seeing several graphics scattered throughout. New in Navigator 3, the Image object represents an HTML image, which is defined in the following format:

```
<img
    [name="objectName"]
    src="Location"
    [lowsrc="Location"]
    [height="Pixels"|"Value"%]
    [width="Pixels"|¦"Value"%]
    [hspace="Pixels"]
    [wspace="Pixels"]
    [border="Pixels"]
    [align="left"|"right"| "top"|
        "absmiddle"|"absbottom"|
        "texttop"|"middle"|"baseline"|
        "bottom"]
    [ismap]
    [usemap="Location#MapName"]
    [onabort="methodName"]
    [onerror="methodName"]
    [onload="methodName"]>
```

### Tip

For more information on Image object events, see Chapter 14.

For example, to display an image called dot.gif in HTML, you would use the following syntax:

```
<img src="dot.gif" height="200" width="200">
```

You can create an instance of an Image object using the new operator, as shown here:

```
companyLogo = new Image();
companyLogo.src = "logo.gif";
```

You can set the dimensions of the graphic as a parameter to the Image() constructor. For example, if you want to display the logo in a $200 \times 300$-pixel format, use the following:

```
companyLogo = new Image(200,300);
companyLogo.src = "logo.gif";
```

By assigning a value to the src property, you can change the image that is displayed. However, if you do this, the new URL or graphic loads in the image area.

Because you still define an image using the <img> tag, an Image object you create serves a rather limited purpose. You can use it to retrieve an image before it's actually needed for display purposes. Because this image is now in memory, it would be much quicker to display it when a document is reloaded. The most common example is an animation-like series of images that are retrieved using the Image object and then displayed later while they are in memory.

> **Tip**
>
> See Chapter 20, "Rollovers," and Chapter 21, "Visual Effects," for more information on how you can use Image objects.

# Summary

The document objects discussed in this chapter are the JavaScript equivalent of some of the most basic HTML elements around. These objects include the HTML Document, Link, Anchor, and Image. Although you can use JavaScript to enhance or retrieve information from these objects, much of the JavaScript interaction usually comes from working with forms. Therefore, the next chapter looks closely at Form objects.

# Form **Objects**

One of the key milestones in the evolution of the Web was the emergence of HTML forms from the world of static pages. With forms, the Web could actually be more than a one-directional mode of communication. Forms provided a means by which any user on any machine could transfer data to a server for processing.

With JavaScript, HTML forms grow even more powerful. Not only can you preprocess form data before it's sent to the user, but you can also use forms in an application that is contained completely on the client side. This chapter discusses the `Form` object and the numerous objects it can contain, including `Text` objects, `Button` objects, `Radio` objects, and `Select` objects. The aim of this chapter is simply to provide all the information you need to implement forms quickly and at the same time bring your attention to some really useful tips.

You can also *pattern mine* using this chapter, which is fun and saves lots of time when developing sites. With pattern mining, you simply look at the listings and their general structures and then reshape their code to suit your own needs. At the same time, you don't actually copy the code directly. More and more developers are working this way, and this chapter attempts to provide lots of patterns that you can use.

> **Note**
>
> The `Form` objects discussed in this chapter can exist only within a form—not outside one.

# The `Form` Object

One of the principal uses of JavaScript is to provide a means to interact with the user on the client side. Most of the time, this interaction with the user happens through an HTML form. As a result, the JavaScript `Form` object is an important object within the JavaScript object model. You don't do that much with a `Form` object in and of itself. Rather, the `Form` object provides a container with which you can retrieve data from the user.

In HTML, the `Form` object is defined as

```
<FORM
    [NAME="formName"]
    [ACTION="serverURL"]
    [ENCTYPE="encodingType"]
    [METHOD=GET ¦ POST]
    [TARGET="windowName"]
```

```
    [onSubmit="methodName"]>
</FORM>
```

To define a form, follow standard HTML conventions:

```
<FORM NAME="form1" ACTION="http://www.acadians.com/js/script.jfm" METHOD=GET>

  <!-- Enter form objects here -->

</FORM>
```

---

**Note**

For more information on using forms in JavaScript, see Chapter 29, "Forms and Data Validation."

---

## Submitting Forms to the Server

Before JavaScript came along, the only real purpose of an HTML form was to send the data elements gathered on the client side to the server. Because the client side itself wasn't powerful enough to process the data intelligently, it was up to the server to then react to the information it received. JavaScript lets you add a great deal of frontend processing to your HTML forms, but that doesn't eliminate the need to submit a form to a server for more industrial-strength purposes.

You can submit a form using one of two processes. You can call the Form object's submit() method, or you can click a Submit button, which automatically submits the form with which it is associated.

---

**Note**

See Chapter 14, "Handling Events," for more information on performing validity checks using JavaScript before submitting a form.

---

Many of the Form object properties deal with additional information that is sent to the server from the form. These properties include the following:

- action (same as the ACTION= parameter): The action property specifies the server URL to which the form is sent.

```
form1.action = "http://www.acadians.com/js/surv.cgi"
```

This is usually a CGI program, a LiveWire application, or an IntraBuilder JFM file.

- enctype (same as the ENCTYPE= parameter): The enctype property specifies the MIME encoding of the form. The default is application/x-www-form-urlencoded, as shown here.

```
if (form1.enctype == "application/x-www-form-urlencoded") {
    alert("Encoding type is normal.") }
```

- method (same as the METHOD= parameter): The method property defines how the form is sent to the server. The value of GET is used most often, but you can use POST as well. This parameter is based on the server-side process, so as you design the HTML form, you need to check the server program's requirements. The following code shows an example of using the method parameter.

```
var methodType
methodType = form1.method
alert("The method type for this form is: " + methodType)
```

- target (same as the TARGET= parameter): The target property specifies the destination window that the server should send information back to. If the target property isn't specified, the server displays results in the window that submitted the form. If you're using a frameset, the target property can be a frame specified by the NAME parameter of the <FRAME> tag. You can also use one of the following reserved window names: _top, _parent, _self, and _blank. Keep in mind that you are in HTML for this specification, not JavaScript. You can't use a JavaScript Window object name, such as parent.resultsWindow. The following code shows an example.

```
if (document.form1.newWindowCheckBox.checked) {
    document.form1.target = "resultsForm" }
else {
    document.form1.target = "_self" }
```

The HTML form shown in Listing 17.1 uses a combination of HTML tags and JavaScript code to submit a form. Note that if the user checks the Rush Order check box, the Form's action property changes to a new value during the Form's onSubmit event. Setting the action property programmatically overrides the default value.

**LISTING 17.1**  formSubmit.htm

```
<html>
<head>
```

**LISTING 17.1**   continued

```
<title>For More Information</title>
<SCRIPT LANGUAGE="JavaScript">

    function checkType() {
        if (document.form1.rush.checked) {
            document.form1.action = "http://www.acadians.com/js/rush.cgi" }
    }
</SCRIPT>
</head>

<body>
<h1>Order Form</h1>
<hr>
<form name="form1" action="http://www.acadians.com/js/order.cgi"
method="POST" onSubmit="checkType()">
<p>Please provide the following contact information:</p>
<blockquote>
<pre><em>     First name </em><input type=text size=25 maxlength=256
name="Contact_FirstName">
<em>      Last name </em><input type=text size=25 maxlength=256
name="Contact_LastName">
<em>          Title </em><input type=text size=35 maxlength=256
name="Contact_Title">
<em>    Organization </em><input type=text size=35 maxlength=256
name="Contact_Organization">
<em>     Work Phone </em><input type=text size=25 maxlength=25
name="Contact_WorkPhone">
<em>            FAX </em><input type=text size=25 maxlength=25
name="Contact_FAX">
<em>         E-mail </em><input type=text size=25 maxlength=256
name="Contact_Email">
<em>            URL </em><input type=text size=25 maxlength=25
name="Contact_URL">
</pre>
</blockquote>
<p>Please provide the following ordering information:</p>
<blockquote>
<pre><strong>QTY     DESCRIPTION
</strong><input type=text size=6 maxlength=6
name="Ordering_OrderQty0">
<input type=text size=45 maxlength=256 name="Ordering_OrderDesc0">
<input type=text size=6 maxlength=6 name="Ordering_OrderQty1">
```

**LISTING 17.1** continued

```
<input type=text size=45 maxlength=256 name="Ordering_OrderDesc1">
<input type=text size=6 maxlength=6 name="Ordering_OrderQty2">
<input type=text size=45 maxlength=256 name="Ordering_OrderDesc2">
<input type=text size=6 maxlength=6 name="Ordering_OrderQty3">
<input type=text size=45 maxlength=256 name="Ordering_OrderDesc3">
<input type=text size=6 maxlength=6 name="Ordering_OrderQty4">
<input type=text size=45 maxlength=256 name="Ordering_OrderDesc4">

<em>                </em><strong>BILLING</strong>
<em>Purchase order # </em><input type=text size=25 maxlength=256
name="Ordering_PONumber">
<em>    Account name </em><input type=text size=25 maxlength=256
name="Ordering_POAccount">

<em>                </em><strong>SHIPPING</strong>
<em>   Street address </em><input type=text size=35 maxlength=256
name="Ordering_StreetAddress">
<em> Address (cont.) </em><input type=text size=35 maxlength=256
name="Ordering_Address2">
<em>            City </em><input type=text size=35 maxlength=256
name="Ordering_City">
<em>   State/Province </em><input type=text size=35 maxlength=256
name="Ordering_State">
<em> Zip/Postal code </em><input type=text size=12 maxlength=12
name="Ordering_ZipCode">
<em>         Country </em><input type=text size=25 maxlength=256
name="Ordering_Country">
</pre>
<pre><input type=checkbox name="rush" value="ON">Rush Order!</pre>
</blockquote>
<p><input type=submit value="Submit Form"> <input type=reset
value="Reset Form"> </p>
</form>
</body>
</html>
```

**Note**

For more information on the onSubmit event handler, see Chapter 14.

# Checking Elements on a Form

The `Form` acts as a container object for all objects on a form. Because these types of objects, such as `Text` or `Button` objects, are for user interaction, you can refer to them as *user interface objects* or *UI objects*. The `Form` object has an `elements` property that you can use to either refer to an element on a form or check all elements on a form to perform a particular task. The order of the array is based purely on the order in which the elements of the HTML form are defined in the source file. The first element listed is `element[0]`, the second is `element[1]`, and so on.

You can refer to each `Form` element either by name or by its index in the `elements` array. For example, if the `Text` object named `LastName` is the first element defined on the form, it can be accessed with the following code:

```
custLastName = form1.elements[0].value
```

You could also use this:

```
custLastName = form1.LastName.value
```

You can also use the `elements` property to do something with each object within the form. For example, suppose you want to make sure that each field on your form isn't blank. Using the `elements` property, you can use a `for` loop to iterate through each array element and check the values. This code is shown in Listing 17.2.

**17**

**Form Objects**

> **Note**
>
> You will notice that the following form validation procedures do not check that the year is a numeric entry. For information on useful validation techniques, refer to Chapter 29, in the section "Frequently Used Validation Code."

**LISTING 17.2**   formElements.htm

```
<html>
<head>
<title>Online Registration</title>
<SCRIPT LANGUAGE="JavaScript">
<!--
    function checkFields() {
        var num = document.form1.elements.length
        var validFlag = true
        for (var i=0; i<num; i++) {
```

**LISTING 17.2**    continued

```
            if ((document.form1.elements[i].value == null ¦¦
                document.form1.elements[i].value == "") &&
                (typeof document.form1.elements[i] != 'submit' ¦¦
                typeof document.form1.elements[i] != 'reset'))
    {

                validFlag = false
                alert("The " + document.form1.elements[i].name +
                    " field is blank. Please enter a value.")
                break }
        }
        return validFlag

    }
// -->
</SCRIPT>
</head>

<body>
<form name="form1" method="POST" onSubmit="return checkFields()">
<h2>Online Registration</h2>
<p>Username:<br>
<input type=text size=25 maxlength=256 name="Username"><br>
Category of Interest:<br>
<input type=text size=25 maxlength=256 name="Category"><br>
Starting Year:<strong><br>
</strong><input type=text size=25 maxlength=256 name="StartYear"><br>
Email address:<strong><br>
</strong><input type=text size=25 maxlength=256 name="EmailAddress"></p>
<h2><input type=submit value="Register"> <input type=reset value="Clear"></h2>
</form>
<p> </h5>
</body>
</html>
```

Notice that the checkFields() method uses the elements.length property to determine
the number of iterations in the for loop. Next, because the elements array includes all
objects in the form, including the two Button objects, the typeof operator is used to
qualify the element before checking its value. Figure 17.1 shows the alert message box that
appears if a field is blank.

**FIGURE 17.1**
*Checking the values of fields on a form.*

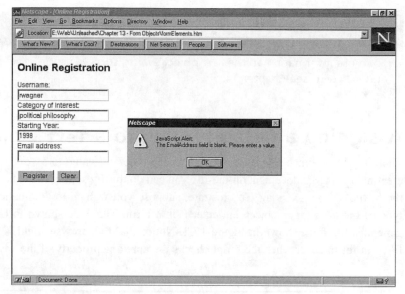

# The Text Object

For most tasks, the Text object is the element you use most often to gather data entered by the user. The Text object is used for capturing single-line, free-flow information. For information that spans multiple lines, use the Textarea object, discussed in the section "The Textarea Object." As with other Form objects, the Text object is the "objectified" version of an HTML tag, and it has the following syntax:

```
<INPUT
    TYPE="text"
    [NAME="objectName"]
    [VALUE="value"]
    [SIZE=size]
    [MAXLENGTH=size]
    [onBlur="methodName"]
    [onChange="methodName"]
    [onFocus="methodName"]
    [onSelect="methodName"]>
```

For example, to define a Text object for a last name, you could use the following:

```
<INPUT TYPE="text" NAME=LastName SIZE=20 MAXLENGTH=25>
```

> **Note**
>
> For more information on the Text object events, such as onBlur, onChange, onFocus, and onSelect, see Chapter 14.

## Assigning a Default Value to a Text Object

There might be times when you want to assign a default value to a Text object. If you're creating an HTML document on-the-fly, you can do this by setting the VALUE= parameter of the <INPUTtype=text> tag. To illustrate, suppose you wanted to automatically check the type of the Navigator object and enter it in a form. The code shown in Listing 17.3 generates the form shown in Figure 17.2. Notice that the Browser field is automatically filled in for the user when the script checks the appName property of the Navigator object.

**LISTING 17.3**   textDefaultValueWrite.htm

```
<SCRIPT LANGUAGE="JavaScript">
var browserVar = navigator.appName
document.write('<body>')
document.write('<form name="form1" method="POST">')
document.write('<h2>Online Registration</h2>')
document.write('<p>Username:<br>')
document.write('<input type=text size=25 maxlength=256 name="Username"><br>')
document.write('Browser used:<br>')
document.write('<input type=text size=25 maxlength=256
➥        name="Browser" value="' + browserVar + '"><br>')
document.write('Email address:<strong> <br>')
document.write('</strong><input type=text size=25 maxlength=256')
document.write('name="EmailAddress"></p>')
document.write('<h2><input type=submit value="Register">  ')
document.write('<input type=reset value="Clear"></h2>')
document.write('</form>')
document.write('</body>')
document.write('</html>')
// -->
</SCRIPT>
```

A second way to assign a default value to a Text object already generated is to set its value property. For example, you could create the same form using the code shown in Listing 17.4. In this example, the window's onLoad event handler assigns a value to the Browser field.

**FIGURE 17.2**

*The default value is set for the user.*

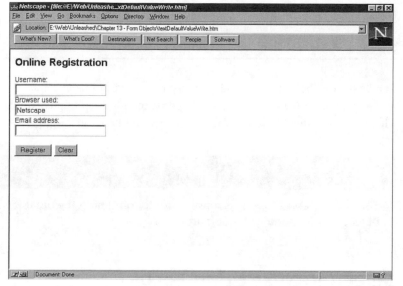

**LISTING 17.4**   `textDefaultValue.htm`

```html
<html>
<head>
<title>Online Registration</title>
<SCRIPT LANGUAGE="JavaScript">
<!--
    function findBrowser() {
        document.form1.Browser.value = navigator.appName
    }
// -->
</SCRIPT>
</head>

<body onLoad="findBrowser()" >
<form name="form1" method="POST">
<h2>Online Registration</h2>
<p>Username:<br>
<input type=text size=25 maxlength=256 name="Username"><br>
Browser used:<br>
<input type=text size=25 maxlength=256 name="Browser"><br>
Email address:<strong> <br>
</strong><input type=text size=25 maxlength=256 name="EmailAddress"></p>
<h2><input type=submit value="Register"> <input type=reset value="Clear"></h2>
</form>
```

---

**LISTING 17.4**    continued

```
</body>
</html>
```

---

Paradoxically, the `defaultValue` property isn't used in this example. Although you can assign a value to the `defaultValue` property, the form isn't updated when you do so. Therefore, you should use the `value` property, as shown in Listing 17.4.

> **Tip**
>
> The `defaultValue` property is most useful for obtaining the default value of a `Text` object, not for setting the default value.

## Selecting Text Upon Focus

By default, when you enter a `Text` object, the cursor is an insertion point. If the field currently has text you want to type over, you have to select the text, delete it, and retype a value. You can change this behavior by using the `select()` method of the `Text` object. Listing 17.5 shows an HTML form with four `Text` objects, each of which call `this.select()` when the `onFocus` event is triggered. As a result, when the user enters each of these fields, any existing text is highlighted automatically. Figure 17.3 shows the result.

---

**LISTING 17.5**    textSelect.htm

```
<html>
<head>
<title>Online Registration</title>
</head>

<body>
<form name="form1" method="POST">
<h2>Online Registration</h2>
<p>Username:<br>
<input type=text size=25 maxlength=256 name="Username"
onFocus="this.select()"><br>
Browser used:<br>
<input type=text size=25 maxlength=256 name="Browser"
onFocus="this.select()"><br>
Email address:<strong> <br>
</strong><input type=text size=25 maxlength=256 name="EmailAddress"
```

**LISTING 17.5**    continued

```
onFocus="this.select()"></p>
<h2><input type=submit value="Register"> <input type=reset value="Clear"></h2>
</form>
</body>
</html>
```

**FIGURE 17.3**

*Highlighting text automatically.*

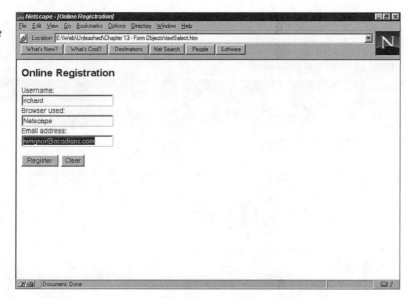

## Capturing Data Using the Textarea Object

All the other Form objects that you work with are designed for capturing data of limited size (less than 256 characters). The Textarea object provides a means for capturing information that doesn't lend itself to simple text fields, radio buttons, or selection lists. You can use the Textarea object to enter free-form data that spans several lines. You're limited to displaying ASCII text, but such basic formatting as paragraphs is allowed. The Textarea object is defined using the standard HTML syntax:

```
<TEXTAREA
    NAME="objectName"
    ROWS="numRows"
    COLS="numCols"
    [WRAP="off|virtual|physical"]
    [onBlur="methodName"]
```

17

Form Objects

```
    [onChange="methodName"]
    [onFocus="methodName"]
    [onSelect="methodName"]>
  displayText
</TEXTAREA>
```

For example, to define a `Textarea` for submitting online comments, you could define the object as follows:

```
<textarea name="Comments" rows=12 cols=78></textarea>
```

Figure 17.4 shows the result in a form.

**FIGURE 17.4**
*The* Textarea *object.*

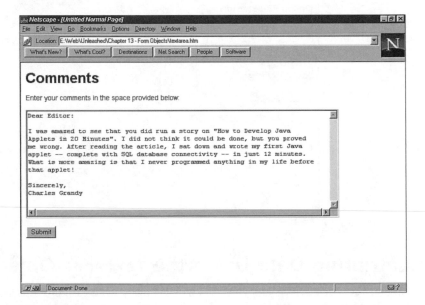

> **Note**
>
> For more information on `Textarea` events, such as `onBlur`, `onChange`, `onFocus`, and `onSelect`, see Chapter 14.

## Wrapping Text in a `Textarea` Object

By default, text doesn't wrap in a `Textarea` object. The user must manually enter a new line using the Enter key. However, working with such an element can be frustrating for the user, so you can set text wrapping options with the WRAP= parameter of the <TEXTAREA> HTML tag. Besides off, the default setting, you have two additional options:

- virtual: If the WRAP= parameter is set to virtual, the lines wrap onscreen at the end of the Textarea object, but a new line is defined only when you actually enter a carriage return.

- physical: If the WRAP= parameter is set to physical, the lines wrap onscreen, but a carriage return is automatically placed at the end of each onscreen line when it is sent to the server.

# The Button Objects: Submit, Reset, and Button

Because graphical operating environments have become dominant over the past decade, the pushbutton is perhaps the most ubiquitous of all user interface components. HTML has three types of buttons you can use in your forms: Button, Submit, and Reset. As you can see, two are specialized forms of the more generic Button object. Using conventional HTML syntax, a button is defined as

```
<INPUT
    TYPE="button|submit|reset"
    [NAME="objectName"]
    [VALUE="labelText"]
    [onClick="methodName"]>
```

The three button types have different purposes:

- The Submit button submits the form in which it is contained to the server, based on the parameters of the form. No JavaScript code is needed to perform this action, because its behavior is built into the object itself.

- The Reset button clears the values in the fields of the current form, restoring any default values that might have been set. As with the Submit button, no JavaScript code is used for this.

- The Button object is a generic object with no predefined behavior built into it. In order for this object to do anything, you need to add an onClick event handler to the button.

If you're new to HTML, you might be wondering about the reasons for the Submit and Reset buttons, because you could use a Button object to perform these same tasks. These originated before the days of JavaScript, when you couldn't use a generic button because you had no way to make it do anything. Additionally, although not all browsers support JavaScript (and thus the Button object), all modern browsers do support the Reset and Submit buttons. For compatibility reasons, it's usually best to use the Submit and Reset buttons unless JavaScript support is a requirement for accessing your page. In that case, it wouldn't matter.

> **Note**
>
> For more information on the onClick event for the Button type objects, see Chapter 14.

Listing 17.6 shows an example of how you can use all three buttons. As you would expect, the Submit and Reset buttons are used to submit or clear the form, although their VALUE= parameters were changed to reflect a more user-friendly verbiage. The Button object is used to display a Help window that tells users how to fill out the registration form.

Additionally, in the Help window that is generated by the showHelp() method, a Button object is defined using the document's write() method. Let me point out two things about this button. First, to center the button on the page, I used the <DIV ALIGN=> tag. Second, to add a little "beef" to the width of the button, I added a few blank spaces before and after the OK in the VALUE= parameter. Figure 17.5 shows the form that is generated by the HTML.

**LISTING 17.6**   buttons.htm

```
<html>
<head>
<title>Online Registration</title>

<SCRIPT LANGUAGE="JavaScript">

    function showHelp() {

        helpWin = window.open("", "Help", "height=200,width=400")
        helpWin.document.write("<body><h2>Help on Registration</h2>")
        helpWin.document.write("1. Please enter your product
        information into the fields.<p>")
        helpWin.document.write("2. Press the Register button
        to submit your form.<p>")
        helpWin.document.write("3. Press the Clear button to
        clear the form and start again.<p>")
        helpWin.document.write("<p>")
```

**17**

Form Objects

**LISTING 17.6**  continued

```
        helpWin.document.write("<form><DIV ALIGN='CENTER'>")
        helpWin.document.write("<input type=button value='
        OK  'onClick='window.close()'>")
        helpWin.document.write("</DIV></form></body>")


    }


</SCRIPT>

</head>

<body>
<h1>Online Registration</h1>
<form method="POST">
<p>Please provide the following product information:</p>
<blockquote>
<pre><em>    Product name </em><input type=text size=25 maxlength=256
name="ProductName">
<em>          Model </em><input type=text size=25 maxlength=256
name="Product_Model">
<em>  Version number </em><input type=text size=25 maxlength=256
name="Product_VersionNumber">
<em>Operating system </em><input type=text size=25 maxlength=256
name="Product_OperatingSystem">
<em>   Serial number </em><input type=text size=25 maxlength=256
name="Product_SerialNumber">
</pre>
</blockquote>
<p><input type=submit value="Register"> <input type=reset value="Clear">
<input type=button value="Help" onClick="showHelp()"></p>
</form>
</body>
```

---

> **Note**
>
> For better performance using JavaScript 1.4, you need not specify a function name if you use argument arrays. Using JavaScript 1.4, the argument array is no longer a property of Function objects, but is a variable. Think of a function that concatenates strings, like that shown, which only has an argument that represents the characters that separate concatenated items.

```
function ConcatenateUnleashed(separator) {
   result="" // initialize list
   for (var i=1; i<arguments.length; i++) {
      result += arguments[i] + separator
   }
   return result
}
```

The function simply creates lists that correspond with the arguments that it is passed:

```
// returns "Ford; GM; Chrysler;"
ConcatenateUnleashed("; ","Ford","GM","Chrysler")
```

**FIGURE 17.5**

*The* Button *(OK),* Reset *(Clear), and* Submit *(Register) buttons are used in this application.*

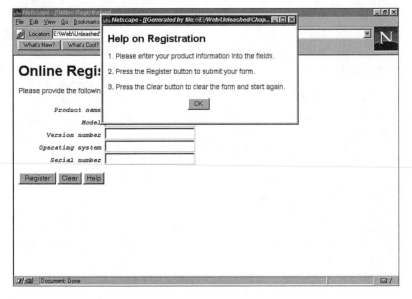

# The Checkbox Object

The Checkbox object is the Form object that is best equipped to denote logical (true or false) data. It acts as a toggle switch that can be turned on or off either by the user or by your JavaScript code. To define a Checkbox, use the following HTML syntax:

```
<INPUT
   TYPE="checkbox"
   [NAME="objectName"]
```

```
[VALUE="value"]
[CHECKED]
[onClick="methodName"]>
[displayText]
```

For example, the following Checkbox lets users specify their foreign-language proficiencies:

```
<input type=checkbox name="language">I speak multiple languages.
```

Following user interface conventions, a Checkbox shouldn't usually cause a "processing action" to be performed (as do Button objects). As a result, you probably won't use its onClick event handler extensively. However, the exceptions to this rule include changing the state of other objects on the form.

> **Note**
>
> For more information on the onClick event for the Checkbox object, see Chapter 14.

## Determining Whether a Checkbox Object Is Checked

Perhaps the most important property of the Checkbox object is its checked property. You can evaluate this property to determine whether the user has checked a check box. You shouldn't use the value property to test a Checkbox object, as clarified in the following.

> **Caution**
>
> The value property can be misleading at first. Unlike some environments, the value property is static and doesn't change in response to the Checkbox's change of state. Therefore, don't check the value property to determine whether a check box is checked.

To illustrate, I'll build on an example I used in the discussion of Text objects earlier in this chapter. As you'll recall, one of the examples automatically highlighted the contents of a Text object by calling the Text object's select() method. Suppose you want to give users the option of having the text selected or not. You can use a check box to achieve this result. Listing 17.7 shows this code, and Figure 17.6 shows the resulting form.

**17**

Form Objects

FIGURE 17.6
*Using a
check box.*

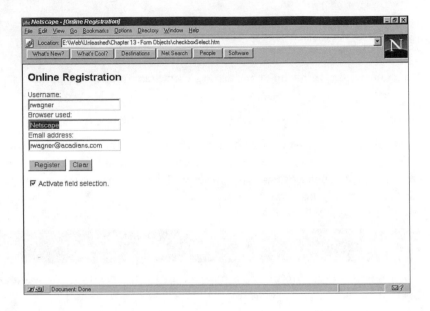

**FIGURE 17.6**
*Using a
check box.*

**LISTING 17.7**   checkboxSelect.htm

```
<html>
<head>
<title>Online Registration</title>
<SCRIPT LANGUAGE="JavaScript">

    function selectText(currentObject) {
        if (document.form1.selectBox.checked) {
            currentObject.select()
        }
    }

</SCRIPT>
</head>

<body>
<form name="form1" method="POST">
<h2>Online Registration</h2>
<p>Username:<br>
<input type=text size=25 maxlength=256 name="Username"
onFocus="selectText(this)"><br>
Browser used:<br>
```

LISTING 17.7    continued

```
<input type=text size=25 maxlength=256 name="Browser"
onFocus="selectText(this)"><br>
Email address:<strong> <br>
</strong><input type=text size=25 maxlength=256 name="EmailAddress"
onFocus="selectText(this)"></p>
<h2><input type=submit value="Register"> <input type=reset value="Clear"></h2>
<p><input type=checkbox name="selectBox">Activate field selection.
</form>
</body>
</html>
```

**Note**

The example shown in Listing 17.7 is useful in demonstrating how to evaluate the checked property during a process. However, it should be noted that this code doesn't necessarily work as you would expect. Once the check box is checked, text is highlighted from that point on, regardless of whether you uncheck the check box. This is because once a `select()` method is called for a `Text` object, the highlighted state remains in effect until the page is reloaded.

Interestingly, if you reload the page using Netscape Navigator's Reload toolbar command, it works fine thereafter without erasing the contents of the form. If you try to use Netscape Navigator 3.0's `reload()` method, your existing values are cleared.

# The `Radio` Object

You use the `Radio` object to let a user select a single option from a group of options. If one option within a set is selected, no others can be selected at the same time. The act of clicking a radio button deselects any other radio button that was selected.

The `Radio` object is different from the other `Form` objects you have worked with. Whereas other `Form` objects have a one-to-one correspondence with an HTML tag, a `Radio` object has a one-to-many relationship with a set of `<INPUT type="radio">` elements within the HTML source code. Each element of a `Radio` object is defined like this:

```
<INPUT
   TYPE="radio"
   [NAME="groupName"]
```

```
[VALUE="value"]
[CHECKED]
[onClick="methodName"]>
[displayText]
```

You don't group each of these elements as you do with the items in a Select object (discussed later in this chapter). The way they are grouped is based on the NAME= parameter of the radio buttons. Each element in a Radio object must use the same value in that parameter. For example, the following set of radio buttons is treated as a single Radio object called weekdays:

```
<INPUT TYPE="radio" NAME="weekdays" VALUE="Monday">Monday
<INPUT TYPE="radio" NAME="weekdays" VALUE="Tuesday">Tuesday
<INPUT TYPE="radio" NAME="weekdays" VALUE="Wednesday">Wednesday
<INPUT TYPE="radio" NAME="weekdays" VALUE="Thursday">Thursday
<INPUT TYPE="radio" NAME="weekdays" VALUE="Friday">Friday
<INPUT TYPE="radio" NAME="weekdays" VALUE="Saturday">Saturday
<INPUT TYPE="radio" NAME="weekdays" VALUE="Sunday">Sunday
```

**Note**

For more information on the onClick event for the Radio object, see Chapter 14.

## Determining the Value of the Selected Radio Button

One of the most common programming needs you will have when using a Radio object is retrieving the value of the currently selected radio button. To do so, you must determine which of the radio buttons is selected and then return its value. Rather than custom coding each time you need this routine, you could more easily use a generic function I call getRadioValue(), which returns the value of the Radio object used as the method's parameter.

Look at the code shown in Listing 17.8. The SongsRadio object lists a set of three songs. The Show Selected Button object displays the currently selected object by calling the getRadioValue() method using the Songs object as the function's parameter. The getRadioValue() method performs a for loop to analyze which of the radio buttons is checked (selected). It uses the length property of the Radio object to determine the number of iterations. When the for loop encounters the checked value, it assigns the variable the value of the radio button, breaks the loop, and then returns the value to the Button event handler.

**LISTING 17.8**   radio.htm

```
<html>
<head>
<script language = "JavaScript">
    function getRadioValue(radioObject) {
        var value = null
        for (var i=0; i<radioObject.length; i++) {
            if (radioObject[i].checked) {
                value = radioObject[i].value
                break }
        }
        return value
    }
</script>
</head>
<body>
<form name="form1">
<p><input type=radio name="songs" value="Liquid">Liquid</p>
<p><input type=radio name="songs" value="Flood">Flood</p>
<p><input type=radio name="songs" value="World's Apart">World's Apart</p>
<input type=button value="Show Selected"
onClick="alert(getRadioValue(this.form.songs))">
</form>
</body>
</html>
```

Figure 17.7 shows the result of clicking the Show Selected button.

**Note**

Listings 17.12 and 17.17, which you'll see later in this chapter, show how to check a radio button automatically.

FIGURE **17.7**
*Determining the
value of the*
Radio *object.*

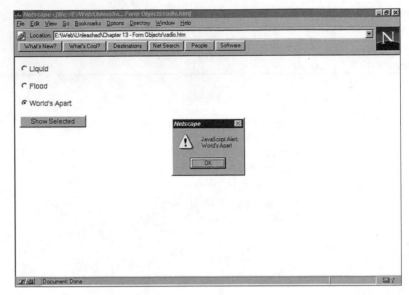

# The Select Object

The Select object is one of the most useful and flexible of all the Form objects. You can use it in instances where you might otherwise use a Radio object. The Select object can take up less real estate than a Radio object, which needs space for each of its radio buttons. Here is the basic HTML syntax for a Select object:

```
<SELECT
    [NAME="objectName"]
    [SIZE="numberVisible"]
    [MULTIPLE]
    [onBlur="methodName"]
    [onChange="methodName"]
    [onFocus="methodName"]>
    <OPTION VALUE="optionValue" [SELECTED]>displayText</OPTION>
    [<OPTION VALUE="optionValue">displayText</OPTION>]
</SELECT>
```

The Select object is flexible and can take three different forms: a selection list, a scrolling list, and a multiselection scrolling list.

> **Note**
>
> For more information on Select object events, see Chapter 14.

## Creating a Selection List

A selection list is a drop-down list of options in which the user can select a single item from the list. A selection list usually displays a single value at a time, as shown in Figure 17.8, but it expands to show a list when the user clicks its arrow, as shown in Figure 17.9. Unlike combo boxes in the Windows world, you can't enter a value in the box; you can only select from an existing array of values.

**FIGURE 17.8**

*A selection list in its normal state.*

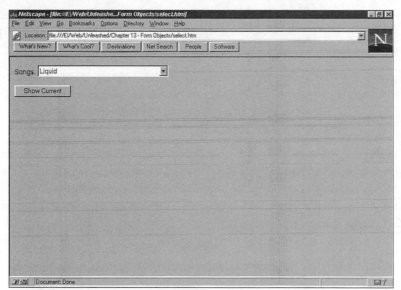

The selection list shown in Figures 17.8 and 17.9 can be defined like this:

```
<select NAME="songs" SIZE=1>
<option VALUE="Liquid">Liquid</option>
<option VALUE="World's Apart">World's Apart</option>
<option VALUE="Ironic">Ironic</option>
<option VALUE="1979">1979</option>
<option VALUE="Wonderwall">Wonderwall</option>
<option VALUE="Standing Outside a Broken Phone Booth">
Standing Outside a Broken Phone Booth</option>
```

FIGURE **17.9**

*A selection list in
an expanded
state.*

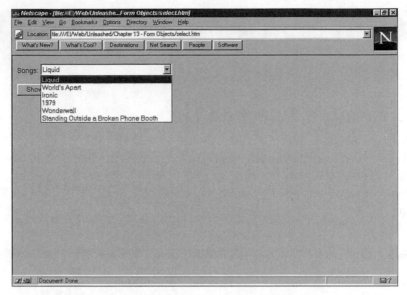

The key to defining a selection list is to give the SIZE= parameter a value of 1 (or leave it out entirely). This ensures that the list shows only a single line at a time.

## Creating a Scrolling List

The second form a Select object can take is a scrolling list—commonly known in many operating environments as a *list box*. Rather than retract all the items in a drop-down list, a scrolling list displays a designated number of items at one time in a list format. The scrolling list includes scrollbars so that the user can scroll up or down to see more than what fits in the space provided.

To define a scrolling list, the only change you make to the HTML <select> definition is in the SIZE= parameter. Making this value greater than 1 transforms the Select object into a scrolling list. For example, when you change the SIZE= parameter of the previously defined Songs object from 1 to 5, the list takes on a new look, as shown in Figure 17.10. As with the selection list, a scrolling list lets you select a single value from the list.

## Creating a Multiselection List

The final form a Select object can take is a multiselection list. It looks the same as a normal scrolling list but has different behavior. You can select one or more items from this type of Select object. The task of selecting multiple items depends on the operating environment. In most cases, you can either drag the mouse across multiple contiguous items or hold the Shift or Ctrl key while you click an item.

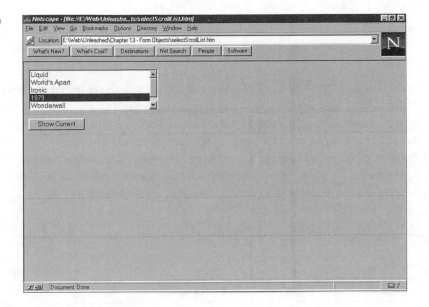

**FIGURE 17.10**

*A scrolling list.*

To define a multiselection list, you simply add the MULTIPLE parameter to the Select object definition:

```
<select NAME="songs" SIZE=5 MULTIPLE>
<option VALUE="Liquid">Liquid</option>
<option VALUE="World's Apart">World's Apart</option>
<option VALUE="Ironic">Ironic</option>
<option VALUE="1979">1979</option>
<option VALUE="Wonderwall">Wonderwall</option>
<option VALUE="Standing Outside a Broken Phone Booth">
Standing Outside a Broken Phone Booth</option>
```

## Determining the Value or Text of the Selected Option

In a selection or scrolling list, you can determine the value of the selected option by using a combination of the options and selectedIndex properties of the Select object. For example, if I wanted to determine the song that was selected in our Songs object example, I could use the following:

```
favorite = document.form1.songs.options[document.form1.songs.selectedIndex].
   value
```

The options property is an array containing each option defined within a Select object. Using this property, you can access the properties of each option. You can use the selectedIndex property to return the index of the selected option. When options and selectedIndex are used in combination, you can return the value of the currently selected option.

With JavaScript's dot notation requirements, trying to retrieve the currently selected value can involve long code lines. You can avoid this by making a generic getSelectValue() method to use instead. Listing 17.9 shows how to define this method. As you can see, the Select object is passed as the getSelectValue() method's parameter when the user clicks the Show Current button. The selectObject variable is treated as an object type variable and retrieves the value of the currently selected option. This value is passed back to the Button object's event handler and displayed in an alert message box.

**LISTING 17.9**   select.htm

```
<html>
<head>
<script language = "JavaScript">

    function getSelectValue(selectObject) {
        return selectObject.options[selectObject.selectedIndex].value
    }

</script>
</head>
<body>
<form name="form1">
Songs: <select NAME="songs" SIZE=1>
<option VALUE="Liquid">Liquid</option>
<option VALUE="World's Apart">World's Apart</option>
<option VALUE="Ironic">Ironic</option>
<option VALUE="1979">1979</option>
<option VALUE="Wonderwall">Wonderwall</option>
<option VALUE="Standing Outside a Broken Phone Booth">
Standing Outside a Broken Phone Booth</option>
</SELECT><p>
<input type=button value="Show Current"
onClick="alert(getSelectValue(this.form.songs))">
</form>
</body>
</html>
```

One important difference between the Select and Radio objects is that the Select object has a text property in addition to the value property. If the value you want to define is the same as what is being displayed to the user—as in Listing 17.9—you can return the `text` value of the currently selected object rather than the `value` property. If the `Select` object were defined like this

```
<select NAME="songs" SIZE=1>
<option>Liquid</option>
<option>World's Apart</option>
<option>Ironic</option>
<option>1979</option>
<option>Wonderwall</option>
<option>Standing Outside a Broken Phone Booth</option>
```

you could use the `text` property rather than the `value` property to return the song name:

```
function getSelectValue(selectObject) {
    return selectObject.options[selectObject.selectedIndex].text
}
```

# Determining the Values of Multiselection Lists

In lists where a single option is selected at any given time, the `selectedIndex` property efficiently returns information you need from the currently selected option. If you have a multiselection scrolling list, however, `selectedIndex` returns only the first option that is selected, not all of them. When you use multiselection lists, you must use the `selected` property of the options array to determine the status of each option in the list. Listing 17.10 shows an example of this in its `showSelection()` method. In this function, a `for` loop iterates through each option in the `Select` object and tests to see if the `selected` property is `true`. If it is, the value of the element's `text` property is added to the list variable. The result is then presented in a second window, as shown in Figure 17.11.

**LISTING 17.10**  selectMultiple.htm

```
<html>
<head>
<script language = "JavaScript">

    function showSelection(objectName) {
        var list = ""
        for (var i=0; i<objectName.length; i++) {
            if (objectName.options[i].selected) {
                list += objectName.options[i].text + "<p>"
            }
        }
        selWindow = window.open("", "Selections", "height=200,width=400")
```

**LISTING 17.10** continued

```
        selWindow.document.write("<h2>You picked the following songs:
➥    </h2><p><p>")
        selWindow.document.write(list)
    }

</script>
</head>
<body>
<form name="form1">
Pick Your Favorite Songs From the List:<p>
<select NAME="songs" SIZE=5 MULTIPLE>
<option>Fortress Around Your Heart</option>
<option>Breakfast at Tiffany's</option>
<option>Flood</option>
<option>The Chess Game</option>
<option>Liquid</option>
<option>World's Apart</option>
<option>Ironic</option>
<option>1979</option>
<option>Wonderwall</option>
<option>Standing Outside a Broken Phone Booth</option>
</SELECT><p>
<input type=button value="Show Selection"
onClick="showSelection(this.form.songs)">
</form>
</body>
</html>
```

# Selecting an Option Using JavaScript

You can select an option programmatically by setting the selected property of a Select object's options array. Suppose you have a Favorite Band field and a list of songs. If the value of the Favorite Band field is Oasis, you want to locate a song written by that group in the Songs field. Listing 17.11 shows this example.

**FIGURE 17.11**

*Displaying multiple selections.*

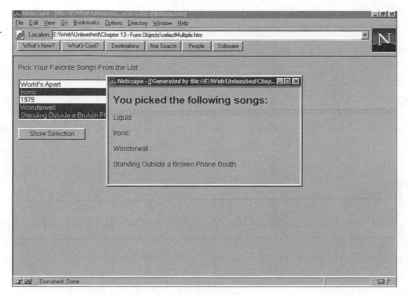

**LISTING 17.11** selectSelected.htm

```
<html>
<head>
<script language = "JavaScript">

    function quickSelect() {
        var bnd = document.form1.band.value
        bnd = bnd.toUpperCase()
        if (bnd == "OASIS") {
            document.form1.songs[4].selected = "1"
        }
    }

</script>
</head>
<body>
<form name="form1">
Favorite Band: <input type=text name="band" size=20 onBlur="quickSelect()"><p>
Songs: <select NAME="songs" SIZE=1>
<option VALUE="Liquid">Liquid</option>
<option VALUE="World's Apart">World's Apart</option>
<option VALUE="Ironic">Ironic</option>
<option VALUE="1979">1979</option>
<option VALUE="Wonderwall">Wonderwall</option>
```

LISTING 17.11    continued

```
<option VALUE="Standing Outside a Broken Phone Booth">
Standing Outside a Broken Phone Booth</option>
</SELECT><p>
<input type=button value="Show Current" onClick="quickSelect()">
</form>
</body>
</html>
```

# The `Password` Object

As you can tell from its name, the `Password` object has but a single purpose: to capture a password value from a user. A `Password` object is similar to a `Text` object but displays any character the user types in the field as an asterisk (*). It can be defined in HTML syntax like this:

```
<INPUT
    TYPE="password"
    [NAME="objectName"]
    [VALUE="defaultPassword"]
    [SIZE=integer]>
```

The following line shows an example:

```
<INPUT TYPE="password" NAME="passwordField" SIZE=15>
```

JavaScript has little control over the `Password` object. For example, you can't retrieve the value of the text entered by the user to evaluate it; you can only retrieve default text that has been defined using the VALUE= parameter of the <INPUT type=password> tag. Part of the reason JavaScript can't access this is that JavaScript code is currently embedded into the HTML document so that the user can access it. As JavaScript matures, it might get more control over this `Form` object.

# The `Hidden` Object

As one might infer from its name, the `Hidden` object is invisible to the user. The `Hidden` object is a hidden text field that you can use to store values that you don't want to present to the user with a normal text field. You can then pass this information to the server for processing. You can define a `Hidden` object in HTML using the following syntax:

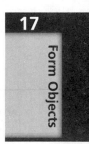

```
<INPUT
   TYPE="hidden"
   NAME="objectName"
   [VALUE="value"]>
```

The following line shows an example:

```
<INPUT TYPE="hidden" NAME="hiddenField1">
```

In a pure HTML world, hidden fields played an important role in holding specific bits of information on the user side that the server could use later. With the advent of JavaScript, the Hidden object makes less sense to use in combination with JavaScript. The reason is that a JavaScript global variable serves the same purpose as the Hidden object, and it's much easier to manipulate.

The following two examples demonstrate this. Figure 17.12 shows a set of radio buttons the user can click. However, you want to add code to the Undo Last button so that the user can undo the last selection he made. You can't use a Reset button for this, because that will either clear the radio buttons or return the default value. Instead, you need to add JavaScript code to perform this task. The code shown in Listings 17.12 and 17.13 is charged with performing this task. Listing 17.12 uses a set of hidden fields to carry this out, whereas Listing 17.13 uses global variables. Keep in mind that neither of these methods is incorrect; both are valid techniques.

**FIGURE 17.12**

*Storing the last value using a* Hidden *object.*

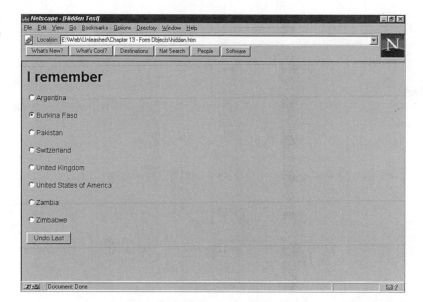

17

Form Objects

**LISTING 17.12**   hidden.htm

```
<html>
<head>
<title>Hidden Test</title>
<script language="JavaScript">

    function postData(value) {
        document.form1.holder2.value = document.form1.holder.value
        document.form1.holder.value = value

    }


    function resetValue() {
        var len = document.form1.ctyList.length
        for (var i=0; i<len; i++) {
            if (document.form1.ctyList[i].value ==
               document.form1.holder2.value) {
                 document.form1.ctyList[i].checked = "1"
                 break }
        }
    }

</script>
</head>


<body>
<h1>I remember</h1>
<form name="form1" method="POST">
<p><input type=radio name="ctyList" value="Argentina"
onClick="postData(this.value)">Argentina</p>
<p><input type=radio name="ctyList" value="Burkina Faso"
onClick="postData(this.value)">Burkina Faso</p>
<p><input type=radio name="ctyList" value="Pakistan"
onClick="postData(this.value)">Pakistan</p>
<p><input type=radio name="ctyList" value="Switzerland"
onClick="postData(this.value)">Switzerland</p>
<p><input type=radio name="ctyList" value="United Kingdom"
onClick="postData(this.value)">United Kingdom</p>
<p><input type=radio name="ctyList" value="United States of America"
onClick="postData(this.value)">United States of America</p>
<p><input type=radio name="ctyList" value="Zambia"
onClick="postData(this.value)">Zambia</p>
<p><input type=radio name="ctyList" value="Zimbabwe"
onClick="postData(this.value)">Zimbabwe</p>
```

**LISTING 17.12**    continued

```
<p><input type=button name="UndoLast" value="Undo Last"
onClick="resetValue()"></p>
<INPUT TYPE="hidden" NAME="holder" value="">
<INPUT TYPE="hidden" NAME="holder2" value="">
</form>
</body>
</html>
```

In this first example, each time the user clicks a radio button, the postData() method places the current radio button value in the Hidden object called holder and the current holder value into the holder2 object. This value is then retrieved when the user clicks the Undo Last button and the appropriate radio button is selected.

**LISTING 17.13**    hiddenVars.htm

```
<html>
<head>
<title>Hidden Var Test</title>
<script language="JavaScript">

    var holder = ""
    var holder2 = ""

    function postData(value) {
        holder2 = holder
        holder = value
    }

    function resetValue() {
        var len = document.form1.ctyList.length
        for (var i=0; i<len; i++) {
            if (document.form1.ctyList[i].value == holder2) {
                document.form1.ctyList[i].checked = "1"
                break }
        }
    }

</script>
</head>

<body>
<h1>I remember</h1>
```

LISTING 17.13    continued

```
<form name="form1" method="POST">
<p><input type=radio name="ctyList" value="Argentina"
onClick="postData(this.value)">Argentina</p>
<p><input type=radio name="ctyList" value="Burkina Faso"
onClick="postData(this.value)">Burkina Faso</p>
<p><input type=radio name="ctyList" value="Pakistan"
onClick="postData(this.value)">Pakistan</p>
<p><input type=radio name="ctyList" value="Switzerland"
onClick="postData(this.value)">Switzerland</p>
<p><input type=radio name="ctyList" value="United Kingdom"
onClick="postData(this.value)">United Kingdom</p>
<p><input type=radio name="ctyList" value="United States of America"
onClick="postData(this.value)">United States of America</p>
<p><input type=radio name="ctyList" value="Zambia"
onClick="postData(this.value)">Zambia</p>
<p><input type=radio name="ctyList" value="Zimbabwe"
onClick="postData(this.value)">Zimbabwe</p>
<p><input type=button name="UndoLast" value="Undo Last"
onClick="resetValue()"></p>
</form>
</body>
</html>
```

In this second example, the holder and holder2 variables are defined globally at the start of the script. This script uses these variables in place of the Hidden object references of the first example.

# Summary

Forms play an important role in JavaScript. Not only can you qualify and sharpen data before it's sent to the server for processing, but you can also use HTML forms to create client-side applications using JavaScript. In this chapter, you learned about the Form object and the various objects that can exist only inside its borders. You also learned how to submit forms to the server and how to work with and check the values of input controls before data is sent on.

# Frame **Objects**

**CHAPTER 18**

This chapter discusses the Frame object and its myriad of applications when building Web sites. I will begin by looking at the creation of single and multiframe windows and discuss the methods, properties, and events that surround them. I will then move on to popular objects that include the History and Navigator objects. The former is of course a well-known repository for recording user interaction and paths, and the latter permits the gathering of information from the current browser. This is obviously a fairly long chapter, because it has to negotiate many essential topics that relate to frames and windows.

# The Frame Object

Frames were introduced in Netscape Navigator 2.0. A *frame* is a subwindow of a full window; its specifications are determined by the designer. Frames quickly became popular because they allow the user to display multiple documents simultaneously in the same window.

Each frame can contain a separate document (HTML, text, image, and so on), each one individually addressable and scrollable. As with windows, you can name and reference frames. You can load documents in a frame without affecting the documents in the other frames.

Frames provide a means to view and interact with a site that isn't accessible otherwise. It allows you to have a permanently displayed index or navigation bar that provides quick and effective location of content in the site. You can simultaneously display the input and output of forms and view multiple documents simultaneously. You can select different image files from a menu for viewing. A new window can open to provide an expanded view of a document and close when it's no longer needed. You can give slide show presentations. The uses and implementations of a framed site are limited only by the Web site author's imagination.

For example, a window might hold a number of scrollable frames that point to URLs, and URLs can point at the frame as well. Frame objects are created using<FRAME> tags within <FRAMESET> tags, and they are essentiallyWindow objects, from which they inherit methods and properties. For more information about these methods, properties, and general behaviors, refer to Chapter 15, "Window Object."

> **Caution**
>
> Some visitors find frames and new windows distracting. Also, sometimes too much of the display area is lost due to frames, especially with small monitors. The author of a framed site should make sure that using frames provides a benefit to the visitor; he also should make an alternative frameless version of the site available.

JavaScript greatly enhances a frame site and adds to the interaction of the site. You can open and close new windows programmatically. You can update and synchronize frames through the script without relying on a server-side program. Imagemaps and links can be dynamic, changing with different configurations and uses of the site. Documents in different frames and windows can interact and pass information to each other.

> **Resource**
>
> You can find online resources for JavaScript and frames at the Netscape site at `http://home.netscape.com/`.

A real benefit of frames is the capability to provide a permanent navigation menu for the site. Instead of hopping from one page to another to navigate, a user can select a page from the menu and see it appear in another frame (a main display frame). A table of contents might be displayed in one frame and documents displayed in another. You might place a button bar frame along one edge of the window, with which the user can click the buttons to load different portions of the site in the display frame.

> **Tip**
>
> Using frames does have some drawbacks. The major drawback is that the area to display each document is reduced. Users with small monitors, laptop computers, or palmtop computers might have difficulty viewing some of the documents in frames. It's considered a good idea to provide frame and no-frame versions of a site and give frame-capable users the option of viewing either version (which is fairly easy to accomplish with JavaScript).

**18**

**Frame Objects**

The `Frame` object is essentially the same element as a `Window` object, and you can deal with it in a similar manner. If you're working with a single window, the `Window` object is the top-level object. If you're working within a frameset, the top-level window is considered the parent window, whereas its child windows are considered `Frame` objects.

## Creating Frames

Frames are created with `<FRAMESET>` tags and specified with `<FRAME>` tags.

```
<HTML>
<HEAD>
<TITLE>Creating frames</TITLE>
</HEAD>
<FRAMESET COLS="60%,*,5%">
      <FRAME SRC="doc1.html" NAME="frame1">
      <FRAME SRC="doc2.html" NAME="frame2">
      <FRAME SRC="doc3.html" NAME="frame3">
</FRAMESET>

</HTML>
```

By adding a few lines of code, I can easily set up a window with three frames, like those I have just created:

```
<HTML>
<HEAD>
<TITLE>Window frames: Window One</TITLE>
</HEAD>
<FRAMESET ROWS="45%,45%" COLS="60%,60%"
   onLoad="alert('Windows have frames')">
      <FRAME SRC="doc1.html" NAME="frame1">
      <FRAME SRC="doc2.html" NAME="frame2">
<FRAME SRC="doc3.html" NAME="frame3">
      <FRAME SRC="doc4.html" NAME="frame4">
</FRAMESET>

</HTML>
```

### Tip

Indenting the `<FRAME>` tags isn't necessary but is frequently done to provide the Web author a better view of the tags and the frame hierarchy within the code. Some HTML editors indent automatically, and they may also color certain code segments for improved readability.

## <FRAMESET> Tags

The <FRAMESET> tag has an attribute that describes how to divide the window into frames. This attribute is either COLS or ROWS (for *columns* or *rows*), but not both. The author can specify the number of rows or columns in the window and the size of each. Each row or column can be specified as an absolute size in pixels, a relative size in percentage of the window, or as the remainder of the window after others are set. The following line creates two frames as columns, one with 60% of the window and the other with the remainder of the window's width (specified by *, in this case 40%):

```
<FRAMESET COLS="60%,*">
```

The next code line creates the two frames as before, but without the percent sign. The width of the first frame is an absolute value of 60 pixels:

```
<FRAMESET COLS="60,*">
```

The second frame still has the remainder of the window's width.

The following line creates four frames as columns; three of the frames take 30% of the screen's width each, and the fourth takes the remainder:

```
<FRAMESET COLS="30%,30%,30%,*">
```

You could replace the * with 10% in this case. You aren't required to use *. However, if you specify all the frames with percentages, they must add up to 100% of the window's width.

The next code line creates two frames as rows, the first with 70% of the window's height and the second with 30%:

```
<FRAMESET ROWS="70%,30%">
```

The frame sizes can be a mix of absolute, relative, and remainder, but if the total size of all the frames doesn't equal the window size, the results are unpredictable. Specifying frame sizes with just * might seem obvious; however, you can use * for each frame. The following line creates three equal frames, each with one third of the window's height:

```
<FRAMESET ROWS="*,*,*">
```

## <FRAME> Tags

The <FRAME> tag attributes specify the document to be loaded in the frames, the name of the frame, frame margins, scrollbars, and the resizing option. All the following attributes of the <FRAME> tag are optional:

- The SRC attribute is the URL (relative or absolute) of the document to be loaded in the frame. The document can be from the same server as the frameset file or from another server. If you don't use the SRC attribute, the frame contains blank space. This blank space might be what you want, especially if you use JavaScript to write content to the frame.

- The NAME attribute, if specified, provides a means to reference the frame from other frames and with JavaScript. JavaScript can also reference the frame through the frames array, which is covered in the section "Referencing Frames," later in this chapter. The value for the NAME attribute must begin with an alphanumeric character.

- You set the margins with two attributes, MARGINWIDTH and MARGINHEIGHT:

    - MARGINWIDTH controls the side margins of the frame. Its value, in pixels, can be as low as 1. The maximum value is limited only by the size of the frame. (You can't set the margin in such a way as to leave no room to display the document.)

    - The MARGINHEIGHT attribute is the same as MARGINWIDTH, except that it controls the top and bottom margins.

    - Both MARGINWIDTH and MARGINHEIGHT, if not specified, default to a value determined by the browser.

- The SCROLLING attribute controls whether the frame has scrollbars. The values for SCROLLING are YES, NO, and AUTO. YES causes scrollbars always to be present in the frame. NO prevents scrollbars from being displayed. AUTO displays scrollbars only if the document is larger than the frame; otherwise, scrollbars are suppressed. The default value for SCROLLING is AUTO.

- NORESIZE prevents the user from resizing the frame. There is no value specified for this attribute. By default, all frames are resizable unless you specify this attribute. Frames that border a frame with the NORESIZE attribute can't be resized along the common border.

### Tip

If possible, it's best to let the user resize the frame by not specifying this attribute.

Use the following code segment to name a frame frame1, load the document doc1.html, set the side margins to 5 pixels, set the upper and lower margins to 10 pixels, always display scrollbars, and prevent the user from resizing the frame:

```
<FRAME SRC="doc1.html" NAME="frame1" MARGINWIDTH=5
MARGINHEIGHT=10 SCROLLING=YES NORESIZE>
```

Netscape and Microsoft are introducing more advanced features for their latest browsers. Visit the Web sites of these companies to find detailed information (`http://home.netscape.com/` and `http://www.microsoft.com/`, respectively).

Event handling is an additional consideration when using frames, debugging JavaScript code, or modifying it for target browsers. JavaScript events that are common to both Microsoft Explorer and Netscape Navigator are shown in Table 18.1.

**TABLE 18.1** JavaScript Events and Frames

| Object | Event | Description |
|---|---|---|
| Window or Frame<br>`<BODY><FRAMESET><FRAME>` | `dragdrop` | A user has dropped an object on the window. |
| | `error` | An error is thrown when a window is loaded. |
| | `focus` | A window gets current focus. |
| | `load` | A window is loaded. |
| | `Move` | A window has been moved. |
| | `Resize` | A window has been resized. |
| | `unload` | A user has exited a window. |

## Tag Placement

You usually place the `<FRAMESET>` and `<FRAME>` tags in the body of the document. However, in several versions of Netscape Navigator, enclosing them in `<BODY>` and `</BODY>` tags prevents the browser from reading the `<FRAMESET>` tags. Because the `<BODY>` tags are optional, place the `<FRAMESET>` tags after the `<HEAD>` section of the document and omit the `<BODY>` tags, as shown here:

```
<HTML>
<HEAD>
<TITLE>Frame Demo</TITLE>
</HEAD>
<FRAMESET COLS="60%,*">
     <FRAME SRC="doc1.html" NAME="frame1">
     <FRAME SRC="doc2.html" NAME="frame2">
</FRAMESET>
</HTML>
```

This code sets up the frames and loads the appropriate documents. Actually, you can make the file smaller, because the `<HTML>`, `<HEAD>`, and `<BODY>` tags are optional; the file can contain only the `<TITLE>`, `<FRAMESET>`, and `<FRAME>` tags, as shown in the next segment. (The `<TITLE>` opening and closing tags are the only tags required by HTML specification to be in every HTML document.)

18

Frame Objects

```
<TITLE>Frame Demo</TITLE>
<FRAMESET COLS="60%,*">
     <FRAME SRC="doc1.html" NAME="frame1">
     <FRAME SRC="doc2.html" NAME="frame2">
</FRAMESET>
```

## The `<NOFRAMES>` Tag

Many authors also include a set of `<NOFRAMES>` tags to display a message for browsers that don't use frames:

```
<NOFRAMES>
code and text content to display to nonframe-capable browsers
</NOFRAMES>
```

The content can contain HTML tags as well as text. A frames-capable browser ignores the content between the `<NOFRAMES>` and `</NOFRAMES>` tags, whereas a frames-incapable browser ignores the `<FRAMESET>`, `<FRAME>`, and `<NOFRAMES>` tags and displays the content between the `<NOFRAMES>` and `</NOFRAMES>` tags. You place the `<NOFRAMES>` tags within `<FRAMESET>` tags:

```
<TITLE>Frame Demo</TITLE>
<FRAMESET COLS="60%,*">
     <FRAME SRC="doc1.html" NAME="frame1">
     <FRAME SRC="doc2.html" NAME="frame2">
<NOFRAMES>
code and text content to display to nonframe-capable browsers
</NOFRAMES>
</FRAMESET>
```

> **Tip**
>
> A number of authors actually duplicate the main document of the site in the `<NOFRAMES>` tags for a non-frame version. However, it isn't usually necessary to use this technique, because you can create a framed version of the site with JavaScript from the same pages that are displayed to frames-incapable users.

It's interesting to note that you can include the `<BODY>` tags in the `<NOFRAMES>` tags, using the attributes of background, bgcolor, text, and so on for the no-frames version of the document. The frames-incapable browser ignores the `<FRAMESET>` tags and initiates the body section at the first appropriate content (that is, a `<BODY>` tag) in the `<NOFRAMES>` tag. The frames-capable browser initiates the body section at the first `<FRAMESET>` tag and ignores the contents of the <NOFRAMES> tag. Of course, the frames-capable browser loads the documents specified by the <FRAME> tags, and the <BODY> tags of these documents are properly recognized by the browser.

## Nested Frames

You can create nested frames in which a frame is divided into more frames. Of the two different ways to create nested frames, both appear the same. However, there's a big difference in the frame hierarchy and the way nested frames are referenced.

The following code creates frames with multiple framesets in a single window. Figure 18.1 shows the frames, and Figure 18.2 shows the structure (hierarchy).

```
<FRAMESET COLS="30%,*">
    <FRAME SRC="doc1.html" NAME="frame1">
    <FRAMESET ROWS="*,20%">
        <FRAME SRC="doc2.html" NAME="frame2">
        <FRAME SRC="doc3.html" NAME="frame3">
    </FRAMESET>
</FRAMESET>
```

**FIGURE 18.1**

*Creating frames with multiple framesets in a single window.*

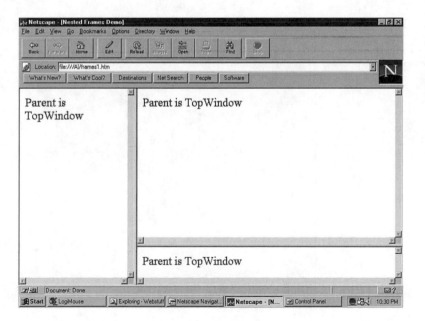

**FIGURE 18.2**

*The frame hierarchy of multiple framesets in a single window.*

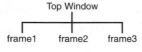

The following code creates frames with multiple framesets in two windows. (A frame is considered a window.) Figure 18.3 shows these frames, and Figure 18.4 shows the hierarchy.

```
<FRAMESET COLS="30%,*">
    <FRAME SRC="doc1.html" NAME="frame1">
    <FRAME SRC="frame2.html" NAME="frame2">
</FRAMESET>
```

The file `frame2.html` contains the following additional frameset information:

```
<FRAMESET ROWS="*,20%">
        <FRAME SRC="doc2.html" NAME="frame3">
        <FRAME SRC="doc3.html" NAME="frame4">
</FRAMESET>
```

**FIGURE 18.3**

*Creating frames with multiple framesets in two windows.*

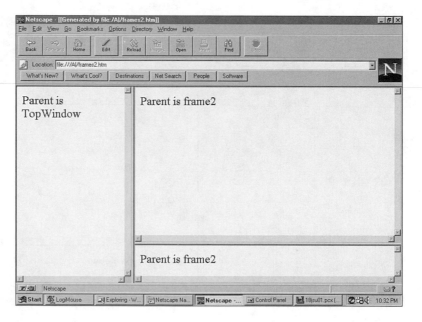

**FIGURE 18.4**
*The frame hierarchy of multiple framesets in two windows.*

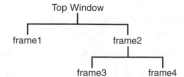

The two code snippets produce frames that appear exactly the same, as shown in Figures 18.1 and 18.3. However, the structures, as shown in Figures 18.2 and 18.4, are completely different. In the code for Figure 18.2, all three frames have the same parent, the top window. In the code for Figure 18.4, only frame1 and frame2 have the top window as parent; the parent frame3 and frame4's is frame2. This can make a big difference in how the frames are referenced, as discussed in the following sections.

# Adding JavaScript Code to Frames

The frameset files and most of the files of the documents that appear in frames are HTML files. As a result, you can use JavaScript in them, as you do in other HTML files. The only difference is that JavaScript can reference properties of other documents in frames and use certain features to reference those properties.

You can refer to the top window and its frames by their relationships to each other. A window can be referenced with the Window properties top, parent, window, and self. The top property refers to the main window (the browser window); parent refers to the window containing the frameset for a particular frame. For frames with a frameset in the top window, parent and top are the same. The properties self and window refer to the particular frame or window.

Consider the following code:

```
<FRAMESET COLS="10%,*">
    <FRAME SRC="doc1.html" NAME="frame1">
    <FRAMESET COLS="50%,*">
        <FRAME SRC="frame2.html" NAME="frame2">
        <FRAME SRC="doc3.html" NAME="frame3">
</FRAMESET>
```

The file frame2.html contains the following additional frameset information:

```
<FRAMESET ROWS="*,20%">
        <FRAME SRC="doc4.html" NAME="frame4">
        <FRAME SRC="doc5.html" NAME="frame5">
 </FRAMESET>
```

The parent of frame1, frame2, and frame3 is top because the frameset for each of these frames is in the top window. The parent for frame4 and frame5 is frame2 because the

18

Frame Objects

frameset for these two frames is in the window `frame2`. To reference the top frame from the document in `frame4`, you use the `top` property; to reference `frame2`, you use the `parent` property; and finally, to reference its own frame, you use `self` or `window`.

You can refer to functions, variables, and other properties with the relational `Window` properties:

```
<HTML>
<HEAD>
<TITLE>Frame Demo</TITLE>
<SCRIPT LANGUAGE="JavaScript">
<!--
a1 = 2;
function addA1(){
    a2 = a1 + 1;
   return a2;
 }
// -->
</SCRIPT>
</HEAD>
<BODY>
<FRAMESET COLS="10%,*">
     <FRAME SRC="doc1.html" NAME="frame1">
     <FRAMESET COLS="50%,*">
             <FRAME SRC="frame2.html" NAME="frame2">
             <FRAME SRC="doc3.html" NAME="frame3">
</FRAMESET>
.....
```

The file `frame2.html` contains additional frameset information:

```
<HTML>
<HEAD>
<TITLE>Frame Demo</TITLE>
<SCRIPT LANGUAGE="JavaScript">
<!--
b1 = 2;
function addB1(){
    b2 = b1 + 1;
   return b2;
 }
// -->
</SCRIPT>
</HEAD>
```

```
<BODY>
 <FRAMESET ROWS="*,20%">
             <FRAME SRC="doc4.html" NAME="frame4">
             <FRAME SRC="doc5.html" NAME="frame5">
 </FRAMESET>
```

To access variable a1 and function addA1() from frame1, frame2, or frame3, you could use either top.a1 or parent.a1 and either top.addA1() or parent.addA1(). However, from frame4 or frame5, you can use only top.a1 and top.addA1, because parent refers to frame2. You can access variable b1 and function addB1() from frame4 and frame5 with parent.b1 and parent.addB1().

I hope you aren't thoroughly confused. I'll discuss more ways to refer to various frames and windows in the section "Referencing Frames," later in this chapter.

You must exercise several precautions when dealing with framed documents and JavaScript. Your script can produce errors if a referenced frame doesn't contain the correct document or doesn't even exist.

Trying to access top.a1 from any of the documents in the previous example when the document isn't in frames causes an error. However, JavaScript offers the means to prevent such errors, as discussed in the next section.

## Synchronizing Frames

As I mentioned, not having the right documents or the right frames loaded can cause errors and other problems. A session can stop dead in its tracks if it can't find one variable. Furthermore, the problem might be that the documents haven't finished loading. Synchronizing the frames ensures that the frames and documents have finished loading before they are needed or that alternative actions are taken.

## Verifying Frames

A common problem occurs when a page contains JavaScript that can be viewed either in or out of frames. The window.length property is quite useful for letting JavaScript determine whether a document is being viewed in frames. The length property is equal to the number of frames a window contains. You can set a conditional statement that performs an action if frames are being used:

```
if( top.length != 0 ){
     document.write("Frames are being used");
   }
```

You usually use top or parent instead of window, because window implies the frame containing the code, which doesn't contain frames unless the document is a frameset file. If

**18**

Frame Objects

a window or frame does have frames, its length is greater than zero. However, writing > for "greater than" could be misinterpreted as the end of an HTML comment by older browsers, so using != (not equal to) is preferable.

The short-circuit feature of the if statement is useful for preventing an error when a document that isn't in frames attempts to access a variable in another frame or frameset. If the top frameset contains a a1 variable that is used in a conditional statement by a framed document, an error is produced if the document is viewed as a standalone (no-frame) document. However, if the length property is checked first in the conditional and found to be false, the statement ends, which prevents an error from attempting to access a nonexistent variable.

The first part of the following statement, parent.length != 0, is false when frames aren't used, so further evaluation is stopped and the error doesn't occur:

```
if( (parent.length != 0) && (top.a1 == x ) )
```

## Verifying Documents Loaded

Various techniques have been developed to synchronize the frames—some rather simple, others rather complex. One of the easiest techniques is to use JavaScript to verify that a particular document is present in a certain frame before proceeding with the rest of the code. The framesarray lets you specify a frame as an element of the array. (Refer to the section "Referencing Windows and Frames," later in this chapter, for information on the frames array.) Consider the following code line:

```
if( (parent.length == 3)&&(parent.frames[1].title == "My Page") )
```

The if statement verifies that the correct frame structure is present (in this case, three frames) and that the document in the second frame (which, in this case, is to be referenced) is the correct one. If the frame structure is incorrect, the conditional evaluation stops, and no further action is taken or an alternative action is taken. If the frame structure is correct but the wrong document is present, the script initiates either no action or an alternative action. Initiating no further action simply maintains the session at its current position, allowing the user to proceed with other actions or retry a failed action. (Perhaps the page wasn't finished loading and another attempt will be successful.) Alternative actions could include providing an alert to the user, loading the correct page and proceeding, or proceeding with the action but skipping the steps that require the missing document.

The previous example checked a simple frame structure (three frames). You can check more complex structures using the frames array of various windows in a multipart if statement. The multipart if statement has to verify the structure from the top down; otherwise, referencing a missing frame causes an error. Note the following line of code:

```
if(top.length==3)&&(top.frames[1].length==2)&&(top.frames[1].frames[1]==3)...
```

If a portion of the frame structure isn't present, the `if` statement stops at that point, and the script can perform an alternative action by using an `else` statement or perform no action at all.

In verifying that the correct document is present, the code can check other properties besides the title, such as the frame's `location.href`. You can assign a common variable in each document a unique name or number and then check that document identity variable instead of the document title or other property.

## Registering Documents

Simply verifying that the required document is present can get complicated with larger sites and doesn't necessarily verify that the document is loaded. Another technique involves having the documents indicate when they are loaded and unloaded. Using the `onLoad()` and `onUnload()` events, documents record their presence in a `topWindow` variable or a cookie. The following code shows that you don't have to use the title to identify the document; you could use another property or a identity variable:

```
<BODY onLoad="top.funRecord(document.title)"
    onUnload="top.funRemove(document.title)">
```

The following example shows a simple document registration scheme. The first code segment contains the top frameset file:

```
<SCRIPT LANGUAGE="JavaScript">
<!--
var a4 = "";    // variable for document registration string

function funRecord{ // add the document to the registration string on load
    a4 += a;
}

function funRemove{        // remove document registration on unload
    a4 = a4.substring( 0,a4.indexOf ) +
            a4.substring(a4.indexOf+a.length,a4.length);
}

function funCheck{    // check whether document is registered or not
  if( a4.indexOf != -1)  return true;
  else  return false;
 }
// -->
</SCRIPT>
```

The next code segment shows the document file:

```
<HTML>
<TITLE>The Harley FXSTC</TITLE>
<SCRIPT LANGUAGE="JavaScript">
<!--
function funRegister{
  // check that top frameset is present to register document, else ignore
  if( ( top.length != 0 )&&(top.document.title == "Main Frameset") )
     if( a =="R") top.funRecord(document.title);
     else top.funRemove(document.title);
 }
function funCheck{   // check whether document is registered or not
  if( ( top.length != 0 )&&(top.document.title == "Main Frameset") )
     return top.funCheck;
 else return false;
}
// -->
</SCRIPT>
<BODY onLoad="top.funRecord(document.title)"
    onUnload="top.funRemove(document.title)">
```

The following code checks whether the document is registered:

```
if( funCheck("The Softtail Series") )
        top.frames[2].fxnames();   // document registered, proceed with action
else                     // document not registered, take alternative action
      top.location.href = "http://www.foo.com/fx.html";
```

## Using Extensive Registration Schemes

More complex schemes not only register the document but also register the document's
position in the frame structure hierarchy. If a document position changes due to different
possible loading scenarios or a site update, the code dependent on referencing the
document can locate the document through the document's registration information.
Instead of using a single variable or a cookie to hold registration information, some
schemes employ an array of variables with each element (variable) containing identity and
position information for a registered document. These schemes are complex to set up;
however, they do provide great benefit in very large sites where a small change in the
structure could throw off the code references in many of the documents.

The hIdaho frameset (`http://hidaho.com/frameset/`) is a registration scheme that is
effective for large, complex frame structures. It registers functions and locations of
functions within the frame structure. It determines the location by passing its frame name

(self.name) to its parent, which attaches its own name and passes the information to its parent. The process continues upward, parent by parent, until the top window is reached. Also included are functions to unregister a particular function (all functions must have a unique name) and unregister a frame name (all the functions that were located in that frame) on a document's unload.

Also included in the hIdaho frameset is a function to check whether a specified function is registered (it returns `false` if the specified function isn't registered) and a function, `Exec()`, that calls other functions and passes parameters to the other functions. Because all function names must be unique, the author can call a particular function without knowing its location and pass parameters to it through `Exec(function,parameter1,parameter2,...)`.

## Updating Frames

A significant benefit of frames is the capability to update or change the document in a frame while other frames remain unchanged. Whether a frame gets updated from user input in another frame or gets updated programmatically, you can provide the means to direct the changes to the appropriate frame through several techniques. These techniques can employ HTML (with certain Netscape extensions), JavaScript, or a combination of both.

## Links

Perhaps the simplest updating technique is using a link to update its own frame (by loading a new document). To direct the new document into another frame, the anchor tag has a `target` attribute for which you can specify either the value of a frame name or a relational name. The relational words (called *magic target names* by Netscape) correspond to the relational window properties discussed previously. The relational names used for targeting links all begin with an underscore and are always lowercase. These names are `_top`, `_parent`, and `_self`, which correspond to the window properties `top`, `parent`, and `self`. There is no `_window`, however.

The following code represents frames in which a link in one frame must update another frame:

```
<FRAMESET COLS="10%,*">
    <FRAME SRC="doc1.html" NAME="frame1">
    <FRAMESET COLS="50%,*">
            <FRAME SRC="frame2.html" NAME="frame2">
            <FRAME SRC="doc3.html" NAME="frame3">
</FRAMESET>
```

The file `frame2.html` contains the following additional frameset information:

```
<FRAMESET ROWS="*,20%">
                <FRAME SRC="doc4.html" NAME="frame4">
                <FRAME SRC="doc5.html" NAME="frame5">
 </FRAMESET>
```

To load a new document in `frame2` from a link in `doc4.html` (in `frame4`), write the link as follows:

```
<A HREF="new.html" TARGET="_parent">
```

Use the following line to load the document in the top window and clear all the frames:

```
<A HREF="new.html" TARGET="_top">
```

## Dynamic Links

Because links are objects in JavaScript and `href` and `target` are properties of links, you can create a dynamic link by reassigning the values of `href` and `target`:

```
<A HREF="#" TARGET="_top" onClick='this.href="new.html";this.target="_self";'>
```

For JavaScript-enabled browsers, the document `new.html` loads in the current frame; otherwise, the current document loads in the top window. (A fragment specifier, #, without a URL and an anchor name, or fragment identifier, refers to the current document.) This reassignment of the link's `href` and `target` properties can be more dynamic if you combine the assignment statements with conditional and other statements. For example, load a frameset file in the parent if frames are being used; otherwise, load the main document of the frameset:

```
<A HREF="main.html" TARGET="_top"
   onClick='if( top.length != 0 ){this.href="frameset1.html";
                              this.target="_parent";}'>
```

Watch those quotes; the event handler must be enclosed in a set of quotes (either double or single).

You don't need to reassign both the `href` and `target` properties for every dynamic link. The previous example could have had the target attribute set to _parent.

For the no-frames user, _parent and _top are equivalent. If the user doesn't have a frames-capable browser, the `target` attribute is ignored. The example could be written this way:

```
<A HREF="main.html" TARGET="_parent"
   onClick='if( parent.length != 0 ){this.href="frameset1.html";}'>
```

The link tag can get pretty long and cumbersome as you add more statements to the event handler. To simplify the link, you can use function calls:

```
<A HREF="main.html" TARGET="_top" onClick='this.href=theHref();
                             this.target=theTarget();'>
```

theHref() is a user-defined function that determines the conditions and returns the appropriate value for the href property. Likewise, theTarget() returns the appropriate value for the target property. These functions must return a value regardless of whether the evaluated condition is true or false; only the non-JavaScript-enabled browser uses the default values set by the HREF and TARGET attributes. For our frame-to-noframe examples, consider the following code:

```
function theHref(){
    if( top.length != 0 )
      a = "frameset1.html";
    else
      a = "main.html";
    return a;
}
```

theTarget() would be similarly constructed. You could also use the functions for other links on the page by passing the appropriate URLs and target names in the function calls. You could use one or two generic functions for a number of links.

You will often find that dynamic links aren't necessary. Typically, a page is loaded into the current frame or the links appear on a navigational menu that isn't seen by no-frames users and can always be targeted to a particular frame. However, for the few circumstances when they're necessary, dynamic links can be quite effective. Also, the frames/no-frames condition isn't the only case where dynamic links might be necessary; you can set up these links for any circumstance you can imagine.

## The `location.href` Property

Another way to update a frame that doesn't necessarily require a link is by using the href property of the Location object. You can also use the href property in conjunction with a form button event handler or a function. Don't confuse the Location object with the location property of the document. document.location is a read-only property, but you can write to window.location.href. The following statements are equivalent and update the current frame with the home page of http://www.mcp.com/:

```
location.href = "http://www.mcp.com/";
self.location.href = "http://www.mcp.com/";
window.location.href = "http://www.mcp.com/";
```

18

Frame Objects

The following statements update the parent and top frames, respectively:

```
parent.location = "http://www.mcp.com/";
top.location = "http://www.mcp.com/";
```

Instead of using relational `Window` properties, you can use a frame name:

```
parent.frame3.location.href = "http://www.mcp.com/";
```

In addition to writing the `href` property, you can also write the `pathname` property of the `Location` object, which lets you specify the path or filename from the server root. (Of course, the host name, as well as the protocol and port, remains unchanged from the current location.) Use the following code to load the document `http://www.abc.com/foo/doc2.html` in `frame1`, which currently has `http://www.abc.com/index.htm`:

```
frame1.location.pathname="/foo/doc2.html";
```

However, if the current document is `http://www.def.org/home.html` or `ftp://ftp.abc.com/pub/abc.txt`, you must use the `href` property.

## The `write()` Method

A third way to update a frame is using the `write()` or `writeln()` method. JavaScript can dynamically generate a document in a frame:

```
<HTML>
<HEAD>
<TITLE>Updating Demo Frameset</TITLE>
</HEAD>
<FRAMESET COLS="40%,*">
    <FRAME SRC="doc1.html" NAME="frame1">
    <FRAME SRC="doc2.html" NAME="frame2">
</FRAMESET>
</HTML>


file doc1.html
```

The file `doc2.html` can be any file, even empty. However, you should place at least a space or carriage return in the file so that you don't cause a `Document contains no data` error.

Dynamically uploading a frame can be interactive with the user through links or forms:

```
<HTML>
<HEAD>
<TITLE>Updating Demo frame1</TITLE>
<SCRIPT LANGUAGE="JavaScript">
```

```
<!--
function docWrite(){
    top.frame2.document.clear();
    top.frame2.document.write("<HTML><HEAD>" +
        "<TITLE>Updating Demo frame2</TITLE>");
    top.frame2.document.write(" </HEAD><BODY BGCOLOR=\"" +
                    document.form1.bginput.value + "\">");
    top.frame2.document.write("<H1>Updated Page</H1>");
    top.frame2.document.write("Update by " + document.form1.input1.value);
    top.frame2.document.write("</BODY></HTML>");
    top.frame2.document.close();
  }
// -->
</SCRIPT>

</HEAD>
<BODY>
<FORM NAME="form1">
<INPUT TYPE="TEXT" NAME="input1">
<P>
Select a Background Color<BR>
<INPUT TYPE="RADIO" NAME="radio1" VALUE="white" CHECKED
    onClick='document.form1.bginput.value="white"'>White<BR>
<INPUT TYPE="RADIO" NAME="radio1" VALUE="red"
    onClick='document.form1.bginput.value="red"'>Red<BR>
<INPUT TYPE="RADIO" NAME="radio1" VALUE="blue"
    onClick='document.form1.bginput.value="blue"'>Blue<BR>
<INPUT TYPE="RADIO" NAME="radio1" VALUE="green"
    onClick='document.form1.bginput.value="green"'>Green<BR>
<P>
<INPUT TYPE="HIDDEN" NAME="bginput" VALUE="white">
<P>
<INPUT TYPE="BUTTON" VALUE="Update frame2" onClick="docWrite()">
</FORM>
</BODY>
</HTML>
```

18

Frame Objects

The JavaScript code used to update a frame can be very sophisticated. You can use conditional statements, calculations, or any script imaginable to create a document to update the frame. Games, slide shows, highlighted maps, and database query results are some examples of what you can use to update the frame.

## Caching Files

Image files to be included in an updated frame can be cached ahead of time to prevent the download from delaying the update. You use the Image object to cache an image until it's needed. However, this object isn't available in early versions of JavaScript-capable browsers. Another technique is to use a document in a hidden frame to download the image:

```
<HTML>
<HEAD>
<TITLE>Hidden Frame to Cache Images</TITLE>
</HEAD>
<FRAMESET COLS="100%,*">
    <FRAME SRC="doc1.html" NAME="frame1">
    <FRAME SRC="cache.html" NAME="frame2">
</FRAMESET>
</HTML>
```

The following is an undisplayed document just for downloading images so that the image files are stored in the cache:

```
<HTML>
<HEAD>
<TITLE>Updating Demo frame1</TITLE>
<SCRIPT LANGUAGE="JavaScript">
<!--
var a1 = 0;
// -->
</SCRIPT>
</HEAD>
<BODY onLoad="a1 = 1;">
<IMG SRC="image1.gif" WIDTH=100 HEIGHT=200>
<IMG SRC="image2.jgp" WIDTH=300 HEIGHT=120>
<IMG SRC="image3.gif" WIDTH=200 HEIGHT=200>
</BODY>
</HTML>
```

### Tip

You should size the image tags to prevent problems when the script executes in certain browser versions.

Although good practice usually dictates that you use the `alt` attribute with image tags, the attribute isn't necessary here because the document isn't displayed in any browser—let alone a nongraphical browser.

Variable `a1` is a flag that is set when the images are downloaded. You aren't required to use this flag, but it's useful to prevent the execution of a frame update script until the images are downloaded:

```
if(top.frame2.a1 !=1 ){
   alert("Please wait, images are still downloading");
  }
else{
   ...continue with rest of script
```

## Scripting Imagemap Frames

Netscape Navigator 2.0 began implementing client-side imagemaps (although Netscape wasn't the first browser to do so) along with frames and JavaScript. Client-side imagemaps (CSIM) offer enormous benefits over the server-side imagemaps used previously. With CSIM, you can include the map file in the document with the image or reference it as a separate file. No longer do you have to send a request to the server for processing and redirecting the appropriate URL. Users can see in the status bar the URLs associated with the map. Furthermore, you can use CSIMs in conjunction with the older server-side imagemaps for downward compatibility with older browsers.

### Imagemap Properties

Imagemaps have several objects and properties. The area tags in the map are JavaScript objects. The `href` and `target` attributes are properties of the `Area` object that can change programmatically with JavaScript. The `Area` object has event handlers such as `onClick`, `onMouseOver`, and `onMouseOut`. In fact, the `Area` object has all the same properties and events as the `Link` object. The area tag also has a `nohref` attribute that prevents the loading of the document URL assigned to the `href` attribute.

> **Note**
>
> The imagemap objects and properties aren't available in early versions of JavaScript-capable browsers. The `Area` object and its properties were introduced in JavaScript 1.1. Furthermore, in JavaScript 1.1, the `onClick` event handler and the `nohref` attribute aren't functional for all platforms.

**18**

**Frame Objects**

# Referencing Area Objects

You can reference the Area objects with the links array. The links array consists of all the Link and Area objects in the document. The elements are numbered from zero to one less than the total number of link and area tags. The following code is an example of a document with a link and a CSIM.

```
<HTML>
<HEAD>
<TITLE>CSIM DEMO</TITLE>
</HEAD>
<BODY>
<A HREF="doc1.html" target="frameA">The Softtails</A>
<MAP NAME="map1">
<A NAME="areaA" COORDS="20,20,80,80" HREF="doc2.html" TARGET="frameA">
<A NAME="areaB" COORDS="100,20,180,80" HREF="doc3.html" TARGET="frameA">
<A NAME="areaC" COORDS="20,100,80,180" HREF="doc4.html" TARGET="frameA">
<A NAME="areaD" COORDS="100,100,180,180" HREF="doc5.html" TARGET="frameA">
</MAP>
<IMG SRC="map1.gif" WIDTH=200 HEIGHT=200 ALT="Menu" USEMAP="#map1">
<!-- Code for alternative server-side map and a text menu for
non-graphical browsers omitted for clarity in the above example -->.
</BODY>
</HTML>
```

In the preceding example, the link is referenced by document.links[0] because it's the first link or area tag in the document. Area areaA is referenced by document.links[1] because it's the second link or area tag. areaB is document.links[2], areaC is document.links[3], and areaD is document.links[4].

The href and target properties of the Area objects, as with the Link objects, can be referenced and assigned new values through the links array. The following line changes the value of areaB's href property so that when its area of the imagemap is clicked, the document doc6.html loads instead of doc3.html:

```
document.link[2].href="doc6.html"
```

Likewise, you can change the target property:

```
document.link[2].target="frameB"
```

The target attribute and property must be specified as a frame name or one of the special relational frame words (_top, _parent, _self, or _blank) and not with a JavaScript property (top, parent, and so on).

You can open and name new windows by assigning to the target a name that isn't already in use. A new window opened in this manner has the name specified as the value of the `target` attribute.

## Calling Functions

The area tags don't always have to reference a document. You can make function calls by using a protocol of `javascript:` followed by the function name:

```
<A NAME="areaA" COORDS="20,20,80,80" HREF="javascript:fun1()">
```

The script calls the user-defined function `fun1()` instead of a document. You can also use JavaScript methods and statements. This technique is particularly suited for a framed version of a site in which the imagemap server is a navigation button bar. The function can perform various statements to determine whether frames are used and certain flags are set or perform a calculation or evaluation. The function can then take the appropriate action, such as loading a certain document, or take no action at all.

The following code segments contain a rather simple slide show script with a button bar imagemap that allows the user to cycle forward and backward through slides. The imagemap also contains buttons to return to the menu so the user can select another slide show or return to the home page. Each slide show has a sequence name that forms the first part of the filenames of the slides in the sequence. The second part of the filename is a sequential number unique to each slide in the sequence. Each of the slide files has three variables: the sequence name, the sequential number of the slide, and the total number of slides in the sequence. The script reads these three variables to load the next slide file based upon which portion of the imagemap was clicked.

The following segment is the frameset file:

```
<HTML>
<HEAD>
<TITLE>Slide Show Main Frameset</TITLE>
</HEAD>
<FRAMESET ROWS="*,55">
    <FRAME SRC="slide1.html" NAME="frameA">
    <FRAME SRC="button.html" NAME="frameB">
</HTML>
```

The next segment is the `slide1` file:

```
<HTML>
<HEAD>
<TITLE>Slide Show - First Slide</TITLE>
<SCRIPT LANGUAGE="JavaScript">
```

**18**

Frame Objects

```
<!--
var a1 = "slide";     //first portion of slide file names
var a2 = 1;              // sequential number of the slide
var a3 = 3;              // total number of slides
// -->
</SCRIPT>
</HEAD>
<BODY>
<IMG SRC="slide1.gif" WIDTH=300 HEIGHT=200
     ALT="The 1992 FXSTC, Softtail Custom">
</BODY>
</HTML>
```

The following segment contains the button bar file:

```
<HTML>
<HEAD>
<TITLE>Slide Show Demo Image Map</TITLE>
<SCRIPT LANGUAGE="JavaScript">
function fun1{
  a1 = top.frames[0].a1; // root file name for series of slides
  a2 = top.frames[0].a2; // sequential slide number
  a3 = top.frames[0].a3; // number of slides
  if( a == "f" )
    if(a2 == a3)
      a2 = 0;
  if( a == "r" )
    if(a2 == 1)
      a2 = a3 - 1;
    else
      a2 = a2 - 2;
  a2 = a2 + 1;
  a1 += a2;
  a1 += ".html";
  top.frames[0].location.href = a1;
 }
</SCRIPT>
</HEAD>
<BODY BGCOLOR="000000">
<MAP NAME="map1">
  <AREA COORDS="1,1,75,50" HREF='javascript:fun1("f")'
   onMouseOver='window.status="Cycle forward through slide show";
   return true'>
  <AREA COORDS="76,1,150,50" HREF="menu.html" TARGET="frameA"
```

```
   onMouseOver='window.status="Return to Menu to Select Another Slide Show";
   return true'>
 <AREA COORDS="151,1,225,50" HREF="home.html" TARGET="_top"
   onMouseOver='window.status="Quit Slide Show and Return to Home Page";
   return true'>
 <AREA COORDS="226,1,300,50" HREF='javascript:fun1("r")'
   onMouseOver='window.status="Cycle backward through slide show";
   return true'>
</MAP>
<IMG SRC="buttons.gif" WIDTH=300 HEIGHT=50 USEMAP="#map1">
</BODY>
</HTML>
```

# Working with Frame URLs

There are no real differences between framed and unframed documents regarding URLs. Within the entire window, however, you can use different sites and base HREFs. One frame might contain a document from a certain directory on a server, another frame might have a document from another directory, and a third frame could have a document from a different server. Regardless of which frame is targeted, a relative URL in a link is referenced from the document containing the link. You can use the <BASE> tag <BASE HREF="http:// www.foo.com/some.html"> in a document to set all links relative to the base HREF, if needed. You can override the base HREF by specifying an absolute URL in the link.

As with the HREF attribute of the <BASE> tag, you can also specify a base target. <BASE TARGET="frameA"> directs all links in the document to the specified frame. You can also override the base target with the TARGET attribute in the link. For example, <A HREF="some.html" TARGET="_self"> overrides the base target and loads the document into its own frame.

## Note

You must place the <BASE> tag <BASEHREF="some.html"TARGET="someframe"> in the <HEAD> section of the document. No content or closing tag is associated with the <BASE> tag. The <BASE> tag with both the HREF and TARGET attributes is shown in the following example:

```
<HTML>
<HEAD>
<TITLE>Base Demo</TITLE>
```

```
<BASE HREF="http://www.foo.com/home.html" TARGET="frameA">
</HEAD>
<BODY>
...
```

You can find additional information on using URLs in frames throughout this chapter, especially in the next section and the section "Updating Frames."

# Referencing Frames

When working with single and multiple frames in your JavaScript applications, you probably need to use other ways to reference windows. JavaScript provides four references to windows. Each is implemented as properties of the Window object.

> **Note**
>
> Separate browser windows don't have a hierarchy structure; however, the window containing the code that opens another window is often referred to as the parent window. The new window is often referred to as the child window. Any new window can assign a variable in other windows so that other windows can reference it and its properties. To reference a property in the new window, you simply use windowName.property.
>
> Consider the following code:
> ```
> newWindow = window.open();
> newWindow.location.href = "http://www.mcp.com/";
> ```
>
> Although this segment doesn't exhibit the most efficient way to write the code, it demonstrates referencing a child window's property. The new window is opened and named (in this case, newWindow). Then, the new window's location.href is referenced and assigned.

## Referencing the Current Window

Chapter 9, "Client-Side Objects," discusses using window to reference the current window. However, what wasn't said at the time is that the Window object also contains a property called window that can be used as a self-referencing tool. In addition, the self property of the Window object is another means of referring to the current or active window. For example, the following two code lines are functionally the same:

```
window.defaultStatus = "Welcome to the Goat Farm Home Page"
self.defaultStatus = "Welcome to the Goat Farm Home Page"
```

Because `window` and `self` are both synonyms of the current window, you might find it curious that both are included in the JavaScript language. As shown in the previous example, the rationale is flexibility; you can use `window` or `self` as you want.

However, as useful as `window` and `self` can be, it can easily become confusing to think about the logic behind it all. After all, an object's property that is used as an equivalent term for the object itself is rather unusual. Consequently, you might find it helpful to think of `window` or `self` as "reserved words" for the `Window` object rather than its properties.

Because `window` and `self` are properties of the `Window` object, you can't use both `window` and `self` in the same context. For example, the following code doesn't work as desired:

```
window.self.document.write("<h1>Test.</h1>")
```

Finally, in multiframe environments, `window` and `self` always refer to the window in which the JavaScript code is executed.

> **Note**
>
> In some object-oriented or object-based languages, `self` might refer to the active object, no matter what type it is. In JavaScript, `self` refers only to the active `Window` or `Frame` object—nothing else.

## Parent to Child

A child frame is referenced by the parent in one of two ways. First, you can use a frame's name, which is defined by the `NAME` parameter of the `<FRAME>` tag. For example, in the following code, the `myFrameFlicka` variable references the name of the `frameA` frame:

```
<HTML>
<HEAD>
<TITLE>Parent to Child Demo</TITLE>
<SCRIPT LANGUAGE="JavaScript">
function childCall(){
   var myFrameFlicka = self.frameA.name
}
</SCRIPT>
</HEAD>
<FRAMESET COLS="50%,*">
    <FRAME SRC="doc1.html" NAME="frameA">
```

```
            <FRAME SRC="doc2.html" NAME="frameB">
</FRAMESET>
</HTML>
```

You can also reference child frames using the frameset's frames array. Every frame in the window, or parent frame, is an element of the array. The frames array elements are referenced by frames[i], where i is the number corresponding to the order in which the frame is created in the parent window. The frames are numbered from zero to one less than the total number of frames. The following frameset contains four frames:

```
<FRAMESET ROWS="25%,25%,25%,25%">
    <FRAME SRC="doc1.html" NAME="frameA">
    <FRAME SRC="doc2.html" NAME="frameB">
    <FRAME SRC="doc3.html" NAME="frameC">
    <FRAME SRC="doc4.html" NAME="frameD">
</FRAMESET>
```

The window's frames array has four elements:

> frames[0] for frame frameA
>
> frames[1] for frame frameB
>
> frames[2] for frame frameC
>
> frames[3] for frame frameD

Note the plural, frames, when referring to an element in the frames array.

## Child to Parent

As you've learned in this chapter, frames are the same as Window objects within a frameset. Within this multiframe setting, you need to distinguish between the various frames displayed in the browser. The parent property of a Window object helps you do that by referencing its parent—the window containing the <FRAMESET> definition. For example, if you want to retrieve some information about the current window's parent, you use the example in Listing 18.1.

**LISTING 18.1**   childWindow.htm

```
<html>
<head>
<title>Child Window</title>
<SCRIPT LANGUAGE="JavaScript">
<!--
    function getParentInfo() {
        myParentTitle = parent.document.title
```

**LISTING 18.1**    continued

```
        alert("My daddy's name is " + myParentTitle)
    }
// -->
</SCRIPT>
<form>
<input
    type="button"
    value="Get Info"
    onClick="getParentInfo()">
</form>
</body>
</html>
```

Not only can you retrieve property values, but you can also access the parent's methods. For example, Listing 18.2 shows the HTML source for a parent window in a frameset with a showInfo() method defined with no means of implementation in it. Listing 18.3 shows how the child window accesses this method. When the user clicks the childButton Button object, its onClick event handler calls runDadMethod() using the this keyword as its parameter. The runDadMethod() in turn calls the parent object's showInfo() method, passing the current object's name as the parameter. Figure 18.5 shows the result.

**LISTING 18.2**    parentWindow.htm

```
<html>
<head>
<title>Parent Window Title</title>
<SCRIPT LANGUAGE="JavaScript">

    function showInfo(objectName) {
        alert(objectName)
    }

</SCRIPT>
</head>
<Frameset Cols="35%,65%">
<Frame Name = "FRAME1" SRC="childWindow.htm">
<Frame Name = "FRAME2" >
</Frameset>
</html>
```

> **Tip**
>
> To define a blank frame, simply leave off the SRC attribute in the <FRAME> definition.

**LISTING 18.3**   anotherChildWindow.htm

```
<html>
<head>
<title>Child Window</title>
</head>
<SCRIPT LANGUAGE="JavaScript">
<!--
    function runDadMethod(curObject) {
        parent.showInfo(curObject.name)
    }

// -->
</SCRIPT>
<form>
<input
    type="button"
    name="childButton"
    value="Run Dad's Method"
    onClick="runDadMethod(this)">
</form>
</body>
</html>
```

The parent is often the topmost window within a multiframe window environment, but not necessarily. You can have nested levels of framesets, as you will see in the following discussion on the top property. Therefore, the parent property refers to the current window's immediate parent. If you want to access the parent's parent (the "grandparent" window), you could use the following:

```
myGranddadTitle = parent.parent.document.title
```

In more complex frame structures, all the frames can still be referenced by their positions in the structure, as shown in Figure 18.6 and Table 18.2.

**FIGURE 18.5**
*Calling a method of a parent.*

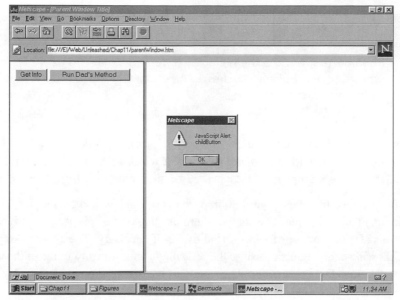

**FIGURE 18.6**
*The hierarchy of a complex nested frame site.*

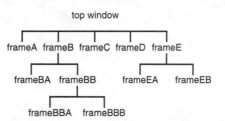

**TABLE 18.2**   Referencing Other Frames from `frameBBB`

| Frame | Reference |
|-------|-----------|
| frameA | top.frameA or top.frames[0] |
| frameBA | top.frames[1].frameBA or top.frames[1].frames[0] |
| frameBB | parent, top.frames[1].frameBB, or top.frames[1].frames[1] |
| frameEA | top.frames[4].frameEA or top.frames[4].frames[0] |

Use the following line to reference the title of the document in `frameEA` and assign it to a variable a1:

```
a1 = top.frames[4].frames[0].document.title;
```

Other properties are referenced similarly.

> **Note**
>
> It's important to note the hierarchy differences that can exist between two similar-looking frame structures, as mentioned in the section "Creating Frames," earlier in this chapter.

JavaScript 1.1 and higher supply the `opener` property, which is used to reference the window (the parent) that opened the current window. From the new (child) window, you can reference a property of the opener (parent) window with the `top.opener.property`.

To reference the opener window from the new window in JavaScript 1.0, you can use an assignment technique. The samples here use the `Window` property `top`; however, you can use `self`, `parent`, or `window` instead of `top` if necessary. The `top` property is used in the following code segment because the code might appear in any frame of the windows. Using `top` ensures that the appropriate property of the top window is identified. `self`, `parent`, or `window` could be any frame in the top window.

```
newWindow = window.open("doc1.html");
newWindow.oldWindow = top;
```

Use the following syntax to reference a property in the opener window from the new window:

```
top.oldWindow.property
```

## Using Child to Child References

The `parent` property is important not only for accessing a child window's parent window, but also for referencing another object in one of its "sibling" windows. As shown in Figure 18.7, any communication between child frames must go through their parent.

Frames on the same level with different parents must be referenced by the absolute position in the frame structure:

```
<FRAMESET COLS="50%,*">
    <FRAME SRC="doc1.html" NAME="frameA">
    <FRAME SRC="doc2.html" NAME="frameB">
</FRAMESET>
```

The following segment contains `doc1.html`:

```
<FRAMESET ROWS="50%,*">
    <FRAME SRC="doc3.html" NAME="frameAA">
    <FRAME SRC="doc4.html" NAME="frameAB">
</FRAMESET>
```

**FIGURE 18.7**
*Using the* parent *property to reference siblings.*

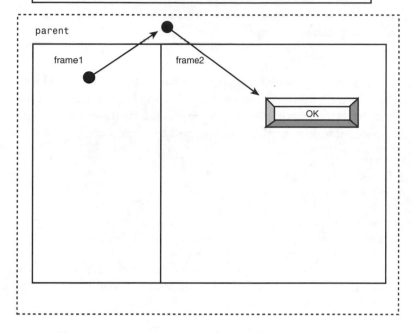

In this example, frame1 wants to reference the value of the OK button in frame2. Using the parent property, it could do that with the following code:

```
buttonLabel = parent.frame2.document.form[0].okButton.value
```

The next segment contains doc2.html:

```
<FRAMESET ROWS="50%,*">
    <FRAME SRC="doc5.html" NAME="frameBA">
    <FRAME SRC="doc6.html" NAME="frameBB">
</FRAMESET>
```

frameAB is referenced by frameBB as in the following:

```
top.frames[0].frameAB
```

You can also use the following line:

```
top.frames[0].frames[0]
```

There is no intermediate level between top and parent, such as grandparent, to reference frames. It's probably a good thing that parent is the only term borrowed from genealogy; imagine referring to a frame as third.cousin.twice.removed.

**18**

Frame Objects

If browser windows are always assigned a name when opened, it's no problem for one of the new (child) windows to reference another child window through the opener (parent window). The name of the window is simply referenced as described in the previous sections. If a window is assigned a variable name of myWindow when it is opened, another child window can reference it like this:

```
top.opener.myWindow
```

You can synchronize the window with the same techniques employed for frames. However, because there is no one top browser window or window hierarchy, one window, such as the opener for the other windows, has to serve as the synchronization point. The following code segment is an example of a script used to synchronize windows:

```
<HTML>
<TITLE>The Harley FXSTC</TITLE>
<SCRIPT LANGUAGE="JavaScript">
<!--
function funRegister{
   // check that page is in its own window and that the opener
   //window contains the correct document
  if( (top.name=="newWindow1") && (top.opener.document.title=="Main Frameset") )
     if( a =="R") top.opener.funRecord(document.title);
     else top.opener.funRemove(document.title);
  }
function funCheck{    // check whether document is registered or not
  if( (top.name=="newWindow1") && (top.opener.document.title=="Main Frameset") )
     return top.opener.funCheck;
  else return false;
}
// -->
</SCRIPT>
<BODY onLoad="top.funRecord(document.title)"
    onUnload="top.funRemove(document.title)">
...
```

The following code checks whether the document is registered:

```
if( funCheck("The Softtail Series")
   newWindow2.frames[2].fxnames(); // document registered, proceed with action
else                     // document not registered, take alternative action
     top.location.href ="http://www.foo.com/fx.html";
...
```

As with frames, you can use more complex schemes to register the location information for the document. Those schemes employ the same scripts as those for frames but would extend one level to incorporate separate browser windows.

## The Top Window

Similar in function to the `parent` property, the `Window` object's `top` property allows you to reference the topmost window within a frameset or set of framesets. If you're working with a single frameset, the `top` and `parent` properties refer to the same window. However, if you have nested levels of framesets, `top` refers to the highest level window, whereas `parent` may or may not refer to that same window.

> **Tip**
>
> The top and parent windows can be excellent locations for storing global methods.

This difference is best illustrated through an example. Suppose you have two framesets. The first frameset divides the window horizontally using `80%` , `20%` (as shown in Figure 18.8). Divided into four quadrants, the second frameset (shown in Figure 18.9) is intended for the lower 20% of the top-level frameset.

For each child frame, suppose you want to get the titles of its top and parent windows. To do so, you can define a common function called `getName()` that returns this information to the calling window. Just as child windows can access a method in a parent window, all frames in a multiframeset window can access methods in the top window. Therefore, the top window serves as a good repository for functions you want to be globally available to all windows. The `getName()` method is defined as follows:

```
function getName(callingObject, relation, parentName) {
 callingObject.document.write("My " + relation + "'s name is " +
  parentName +".")
}
```

The `callingObject` parameter represents the window that is calling the function. Using dot notation, you can then assign the `document.write` command to be performed within the window in question. The `relation` and `parentName` parameters are strings provided by the calling window but aren't manipulated in this function.

This `getName()` method is called by the child frames upon loading. You can do this by putting the following code in each of the child frames:

**18**

Frame Objects

FIGURE **18.8**
*A top-level
frameset.*

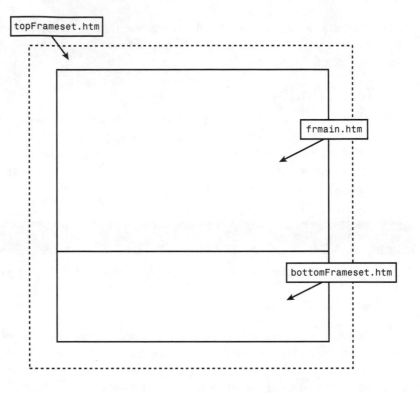

FIGURE **18.9**
*A lower-level
frameset.*

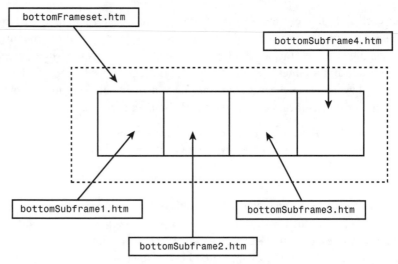

```
<SCRIPT LANGUAGE="JavaScript">
    top.getName(self, "parent", parent.document.title)
    document.write("<p>")
```

```
        top.getName(self, "top", top.document.title)
</SCRIPT>
```

The script uses top to access the getName() method, self to identify itself as the calling window, and parent and top to retrieve the titles for both windows. Figure 18.10 shows the result when the frameset is loaded.

Listings 18.4, 18.5, and 18.6 provide the source code for the top-level frameset (topFrameset.htm), lower-level frameset (bottomFrameset.htm), and one of the bottom child frames (bottomSubframe1.htm).

**LISTING 18.4**   topFrameset.htm

```
<HTML>
<HEAD>
<TITLE>Top-Level Frameset</TITLE>
<SCRIPT LANGUAGE="JavaScript">

    function getName(callingObject, relation, parentName) {
     callingObject.document.write("My " + relation +
       "'s name is " + parentName +".")
    }

</SCRIPT>
</HEAD>
<FRAMESET ROWS="80%,20%">
  <FRAME SRC="frmain.htm"
         NAME="main"
         MARGINWIDTH="1"
         MARGINHEIGHT="1">
  <FRAME SRC="bottomFrameset.htm"
         NAME="footnotes"
         MARGINWIDTH="1"
         MARGINHEIGHT="1">
  <NOFRAMES>
Warning text should go here for browsers with no frame support.
<BODY>
</BODY>
</NOFRAMES>
</FRAMESET>
</HTML>
```

**FIGURE 18.10**

*The* top *and*
parent *proper-
ties.*

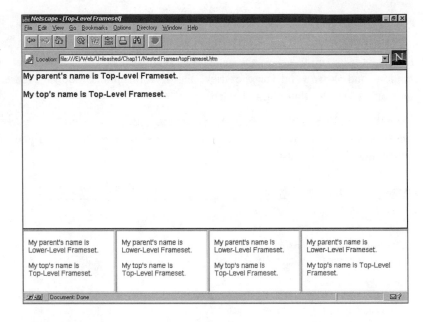

**LISTING 18.5**  bottomFrameset.htm

```
<HTML>
<HEAD>
<TITLE>Lower-Level Frameset</TITLE>
</HEAD>
<FRAMESET COLS="24%,24%,24%,28%">
  <FRAME SRC="bottomSubframe1.htm">
  <FRAME SRC="bottomSubframe2.htm">
  <FRAME SRC="bottomSubframe3.htm">
  <FRAME SRC="bottomSubframe4.htm">
</FRAMESET>
</HTML>
```

**LISTING 18.6**  bottomSubframe1.htm

```
<HTML>
<HEAD>
<TITLE>Footnotes Frame in Bottom Frameset</TITLE>
<SCRIPT LANGUAGE="JavaScript">
     top.getName(self, "parent", parent.document.title)
     document.write("<p>")
     top.getName(self, "top", top.document.title)
</SCRIPT>
</HEAD>
```

**Listing 18.6** continued

```
<BODY>
</BODY>
</HTML>
```

> **Note**
>
> A possible concern about referencing documents in other frames and windows is a security restriction that prevents JavaScript from accessing the properties of documents from a different server. Starting with Netscape Navigator 2.02, this restriction was implemented to keep people from accessing information on the user's history, passwords in HTML forms, directory structure, and other confidential items.
>
> Netscape Navigator 3.0 incorporates a security measure called *data tainting*, which permits people to access a different server's documents without the possible security risk. With data tainting, JavaScript code can access and use properties of documents from different servers. The data obtained is marked (tainted) so that it can't be sent to a different server (a security and privacy concern) without user confirmation.
>
> You can find more information on data tainting in Chapter 35, "JavaScript and Web Security."

# The Location Object

The `Location` object encapsulates the URL of the current page. Its purpose is twofold, allowing you to do the following:

- Set the `Location` object to move to a new URL.

- Extract specific elements of the URL and work with them. Without the `Location` object, you would be forced to perform string manipulations on a URL string to get at the information you needed.

The basic structure of a URL is as follows:

```
protocol//hostname: port pathname search hash
```

A typical URL could look something like the following:

```
http://www.acadians.com/javascript/search/Hats?qt=RFC+1738+&col=XL
```

The Location object has the properties shown in Table 18.3, each of which is an element in the URL.

**TABLE 18.3**   Location **Object Properties**

| Attribute | Description |
|-----------|-------------|
| HREF | Complete URL |
| PROTOCOL | Initial element of a URL (before and including colon) |
| HOSTNAME | Host and domain name or IP address |
| HOST | *Hostname:port* element of a URL |
| PORT | Communications port of the server |
| PATHNAME | Path element of a URL |
| SEARCH | Query definition portion of a URL (begins with ?) |
| HASH | Anchor name of a URL (begins with #) |

**Note**

It's important to distinguish the Location object from the Document object's location property. Although you can set the Location object, the Document object's location property is read-only.

## Opening a New URL

Instead of using a specific method to go to a new URL in a window, you can open a new URL by setting the value of the Location object. Interestingly, you can do this by either assigning a URL to the object itself or assigning a URL to the Location object's href property. For example, the following two lines perform the same action:

```
window.location = "http://www.acadians.com/"
window.location.href = "http://www.acadians.com/"
```

For example, to simulate a browser's location edit box using JavaScript, you could use the code in Listing 18.7.

**LISTING 18.7**   moveTo.htm

```
<HTML>
<HEAD>
<SCRIPT LANGUAGE = "JavaScript">
```

**LISTING 18.7**   continued

```
    function moveon() {
        var urlAddress = ""
        urlAddress = document.forms[0].Edit1.value
        window.location = urlAddress
    }

</SCRIPT>
</HEAD>
<BODY>
<FORM>
<INPUT type="text" name="Edit1">
<INPUT type="button" value="move" onClick="moveon()">
</FORM>
</BODY>
</HTML>
```

In multiframe windows, you can specify the value of the Location object in other frames by referring to the appropriate window name. For example, Figure 18.11 displays a multiframe window in which you can change the URL based on the entry of the form in the footnote frame. Listing 18.8 shows the source code for the footnote frame.

**18**

Frame Objects

**FIGURE 18.11**
*Using the*
Location *object*
*to change*
*another frame's*
*URL.*

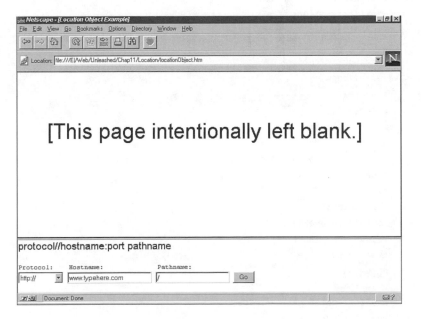

**LISTING 18.8**  frfootno.htm

```
<html>
<head>
<title>Footnotes Frame in Location Object Example</title>
<SCRIPT LANGUAGE="JavaScript">
<!--
    function gotoPage() {
      parent.frames[0].location.href = window.document.loc.ProtocolField.
       options[window.document.loc.ProtocolField.selectedIndex].text
       + document.loc.HostnameField.value + document.loc.PathnameField.value
    }
//-->
</SCRIPT>
</head>


<body>
<p><font size=5>protocol//hostname:port pathname</font></p>
<form name="loc" method="POST">
<pre>Protocol:    Hostname:              Pathname:
<select name="ProtocolField" size=1>
<option>http://</option>
<option>file://</option>
<option>javascript:</option>
<option>ftp:</option>
<option>mailto:</option>
<option>gopher:</option>
<option>about:</option>
</select> <input
    type=text
    size=23
    maxlength=256
    name="HostnameField"
    value="www.typehere.com"> <input
    type=text
    size=20
    maxlength=100
    name="PathnameField"
    value="/"> <input
    type=button
    name="Go"
    value="Go"
    onClick="gotoPage()"></pre>
</form>
```

**LISTING 18.8**   continued

```
</body>
</html>
```

## Working with the `protocol` Property

The `protocol` property of the `Location` object lets you specify the type of URL with which you're working. Table 18.4 lists the most common protocols used.

**TABLE 18.4**   Location **Object Protocols**

| URL Type | Protocol |
|---|---|
| Web | http: |
| File | file: |
| FTP | ftp: |
| MailTo | mailto: |
| Usenet | news: |
| Gopher | gopher: |
| JavaScript | javascript: |
| Navigator | about: |

# The `History` Object

If you've done much Web surfing, you're probably very familiar with a browser's History list. Just as the History list lets a user traverse where she has been, JavaScript's `History` object lets you as a JavaScript developer maneuver through previously visited Web pages. The `History` object has no events and only the properties and methods that are shown in Tables 18.5 and 18.6.

**TABLE 18.5**   History **Object Properties**

| Property | Description |
|---|---|
| current | The URL of the current document. |
| length | The History list's length. |
| next | The History list's next URL. |
| previous | The History list's previous URL. |

**TABLE 18.6**   History **Object Methods**

| Method | Description |
|---|---|
| Back() | Loads the History list's previous document. |
| Forward() | Loads the History list's next document. |
| Go() | Goes to a specific document. |

| Method | Description |
|--------|-------------|
| Go(*n*) | If *n*>0, loads the document that is *n* entries ahead in the History list. |
| Go(*string*) | Loads the History list document whose URL contains the specified string. |

TABLE **18.6**   continued

## Determining the Size of the List

You can use the length property of the History object to determine the number of entries in the list. For example, suppose you want to track the number of History list entries in the right frame of a multiframe window. The left frame contains the following code:

```
<HTML>
<HEAD>
<SCRIPT LANGUAGE = "JavaScript">

    function moveon() {
        var urlAddress = ""
        urlAddress = document.forms[0].Edit1.value
        parent.frames[1].location = urlAddress
        document.forms[0].Edit2.value = parent.frames[1].history.length
    }

</SCRIPT>
</HEAD>

<BODY>
<FORM>
<INPUT type="text" name="Edit1">
<INPUT type="button" value="move" onClick="moveon()">
<INPUT type="text" name="Edit2">
</FORM>
</BODY>
</HTML>
```

The user can use the Edit1 text object to enter a destination URL. As the user clicks the Move button to move to the URL, the Edit2 text object is updated to provide the length of the History list for the right frame.

## Navigating the History List

Just knowing the length of the History list is rarely useful, but it can become useful if you want to navigate a list using the History object methods back(), forward(), and go().

## Moving Back a Page

The back() method is the functional equivalent of clicking the Back (left-arrow) button on the browser's toolbar. For example, the following code moves a window to its previous position:

```
window.history.back()
```

## Moving Forward a Page

As you would expect, the forward() method is the same as clicking the right-arrow button on the browser's toolbar. It is used as follows:

```
window.history.forward()
```

## Going to a Specific Page Based on a Number

The go() method jumps to a specific place in the History list. Its syntax follows:

```
[window.]history.go(delta | "location")
```

The *delta* parameter is a positive or negative integer that can specify the number of places to jump. For example, the following line moves to the next document in the History list (the equivalent of using the forward() method):

```
window.history.go(1)
```

Table 18.7 lists the possible *delta* values.

TABLE **18.7**   delta Values

| Method | Description |
| --- | --- |
| *delta* < 0 | Moves backward *delta* number of entries |
| *delta* > 0 | Moves forward *delta* number of entries |
| *delta* = 0 | Reloads the current document |

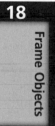

## Going to a Specific Page Based on a String

Alternatively, you can use the location parameter to specify a specific URL in the list. Note that this doesn't have to be an exact URL—only a substring. The following example moves to the URL in the History list that contains www.acadians.com/filenew:

```
window.history.go("www.acadians.com/filenew")
```

You can add the back(), forward(), and go() to the earlier example to provide a more fully functional multiframe navigating system. Figure 18.12 shows the frameset. Listing 18.9 provides the HTML source for the parent frameset page, and Listing 18.10 provides the HTML source for the History list. The right pane contains no JavaScript code related to this example.

**FIGURE 18.12**
*The History frame example.*

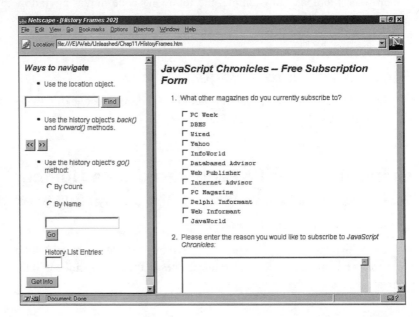

**LISTING 18.9**   HistoryFrames.htm

```
<html>
<head>
<title>History Object Example</title>
</head>
<Frameset Cols="35%,65%">
<Frame Name = "FRAME1" SRC="History.htm">
<Frame Name = "FRAME2" SRC="JavaScriptChronicles.htm">
</Frameset>

</html>
```

**LISTING 18.10**   History.htm

```
<html>
<head>
<title>History Page</title>
</head>
<body bgcolor="#FFFFFF">
```

**LISTING 18.10**    continued

```
<SCRIPT LANGUAGE="JavaScript">
<!--
    function goPrev() {
        parent.frames[1].history.back()
    }

    function goNext() {
        parent.frames[1].history.forward()
    }

    function moveOn() {
        var urlAddress = ""
        urlAddress = document.forms[0].LocationBox.value
        if (urlAddress != "") {
            parent.frames[1].location = urlAddress
            document.forms[0].ListLen.value = parent.frames[1].history.length }
        else {
            alert("Please enter a URL before clicking the Go button.")
        }
    }

    function jump() {
        if (document.forms[0].goParam[1].checked) {
            var goVal = 0
            goVal = parseInt(document.forms[0].GoBox.value) }
        else {
            var goVal = ""
            goVal = document.forms[0].GoBox.value
        }
        parent.frames[1].history.go(goVal)
    }
// -->
</SCRIPT>

<form method="POST">
<h3><em>Ways to navigate</em></h3>
<ul>
<li>Use the location object.</li>
</ul>
<p><input
    type=text
    size=20
```

**18**

Frame Objects

**LISTING 18.10**  continued

```
        maxlength=50
        name="LocationBox"> <input
        type="button"
        value="Find"
        onClick="moveOn()"> </p>
<ul>
<li>Use the history object's <em>back()</em> and<em> forward() </em>methods.
</li>
</ul>
<p align=center><input
        type="button"
        value="&lt;&lt;"
        onClick="goPrev()"> <input
        type="button"
        value="&gt;&gt;"
        onClick="goNext()"></p>
<ul>
<li>Use the history object's <em>go()</em> method:</li>
</ul>
<blockquote>
<p><input type=radio name="goParam" value="ByCount">By Count</p>
<p><input type=radio name="goParam" value="ByName">By Name</p>
<p><input
        type=text
        size=20
        maxlength=30
        name="GoBox"> <input
        type="button"
        value="Go"
        onClick="jump()"> </p>
<p>History List Entries: <input
        type=text
        size=3
        maxlength=4
        name="ListLen"> </p>
</blockquote>
</form>
</body>
</html>
```

# The `Navigator` Object

The `Navigator` object is the one object that just doesn't seem to fit into the JavaScript built-in object hierarchy. On first glance, it would seem to be the top level of the pyramid, because the browser software—the element the `Navigator` object represents—contains information about the browser that is running a script. However, the `Navigator` object has no real connection to any other object in the hierarchy; it really stands alone, providing only a way to obtain information about the current Web browser.

> **Note**
>
> Keep in mind that you can't use the `Navigator` object to obtain information from browsers that don't support JavaScript. If the browser doesn't support JavaScript, it doesn't process the request for information. You obviously couldn't use a JavaScript routine to determine whether the browser supports JavaScript.

The `Navigator` object has four properties, as shown in Table 18.8.

**TABLE 18.8**    Properties of the `Navigator` Object

| Property | Description |
|---|---|
| `appName` | Name of the browser. |
| `appVersion` | Version of the browser. |
| `appCodeName` | Code name for the browser. |
| `userAgent` | User-agent header for the browser. |
| `appCodeName` | Browser's code name; supported by Navigator 2 and Internet Explorer 3. |
| `AppMinorVersion` | Browser's minor version number; supported by Internet Explorer 4. |
| `AppName` | Browser's name; supported by Navigator 2 and Explorer 3. |
| `AppVersion` | Version of the browser; supported by Navigator 2 and Explorer 3. |
| `BrowserLanguage` | Language configuration of the browser; supported by Explorer 4. |
| `ConnectionSpeed` | Connection speed of the browser; supported by Explorer 4. |
| `CookieEnabled` | Whether the browser is cookie enabled; supported by Explorer 4. |
| `CpuClass` | Processor class on the browser's platform; supported by Explorer 4. |
| `OnLine` | Indicates whether the browser is on-line, and is supported by Explorer 4. |
| `Language` | Language configuration of the browser; supported by Explorer 4. |
| `MimeTypes` | MIME types supported by the browser; compliant with Navigator 3 and Explorer 4. |
| `Platform` | OS upon which the browser is operating; supported by Navigator 4 and Explorer 4. |

**TABLE 18.8** continued

| Property | Description |
| --- | --- |
| Plugins | Array of plug-ins currently installed; supported by Navigator 3 and Explorer 4. |
| SystemLanguage | OS's default language; supported by Explorer 4. |
| UserAgent | User agent header sent from the browser to the server; supported by Explorer 3 and Navigator 2. |
| UserLanguage | User's language; supported by Explorer 4. |
| UserProfile | Access to the user profile information; supported by Explorer 4. |

Both Netscape Navigator and Microsoft Internet Explorer support the Navigator object. Listing 18.11 provides an example of displaying browser information in a dialog box when the user clicks the Show Browser Info button. Figures 18.13 and 18.14 show the alert message boxes that appear when the script is run in Netscape and Internet Explorer, respectively.

**LISTING 18.11**    navigatorInfo.htm

```
<HTML>
<HEAD>
<SCRIPT LANGUAGE = "JavaScript">

    function displayBrowserInfo() {

        var browserStr = ""
        browserStr += "Browser: " + navigator.appName + "\r"
        browserStr += "Version:" + navigator.appVersion + "\r"
        browserStr += "Codename: " + navigator.appCodeName + "\r"
        browserStr += "User agent: " + navigator.userAgent + "\r"
        alert(browserStr)
    }

</SCRIPT>

<BODY>
<H1></H1>
<FORM>
<INPUT
    Type="button"
    Value="Show Browser Information"
    OnClick="displayBrowserInfo()"
</INPUT>
</FORM>
```

**LISTING 18.11** continued

```
</BODY>
</HTML>
```

**FIGURE 18.13**
*Netscape
Navigator
browser
information.*

**FIGURE 18.14**
*Microsoft Internet
Explorer browser
information.*

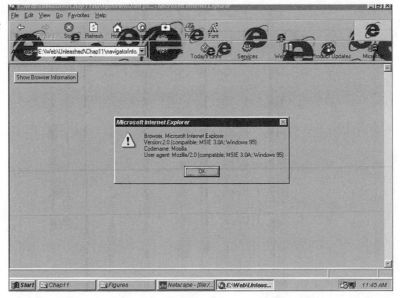

**18**

**Frame Objects**

# Summary

This chapter dived into single and multiframe windows. The `Frame`, `Location`, and `History` objects provide a means to work with their respective browser counterparts. The `Navigator` object, much different in purpose from the other JavaScript objects, lets you retrieve information about the current browser being used.

This chapter also discussed how to use JavaScript to reference objects and properties in other frames and browser windows. I outlined basic window creation and frame setup and covered references to properties in different frames and windows. I also explained updating frames and synchronizing frames and windows, providing a few examples of windows and frames interacting with each other through JavaScript.

Although using JavaScript in a framed site might be a little more complex than using it in a no-frames site, the benefits are often worth the small amount of added complexity. I only touched upon a few examples of JavaScript with frames and windows. The possible uses and implementations of a framed site are limited only by the Web site author's imagination and the depth of his perseverance.

# Other DOM Objects

In Chapter 13, "Fundamentals of the Document Object Model (DOM)," we looked at the fundamentals of the Document Object Model (DOM), and we saw that it standardizes the object model of documents using intuitive tree representations. In this chapter, we will look at the application of the common DOM methods using some JavaScript listings. We also will discuss the various DOM nodes and elements and how these may be manipulated in a practical way, as well as some important issues that surround browsers.

# DOM Browsers

DOM uses document parts to represent a logical hierarchy, using the pages' tags, their numbers, their sequences, their properties, and their attributes. But the recently changing DOM of Netscape Navigator and Internet Explorer is linked to the work of W3C (World Wide Web Consortium). The attributes of image and anchor tags could be read and written using Netscape Navigator 3, and their information could be queried to determine what plug-ins it had, which MIME types it supported, and other items. Navigator 4.0 introduced layer tags for trees and improved methods for determining the width and height of containers and windows. Historically this level of DOM was held in JavaScript, and Java applets and plug-ins could manipulate the DOM using LiveConnect, which is the JavaScript scripting engine. Internet Explorer 4.0 integrated the DOM in the browser itself, instead of in a scripting language. This eliminates differences between different scripting languages, which may include the position of tags, for example. Instead, the information is standardized and consistent across different browsers, and interaction with the DOM can be the same using JavaScript, VBScript, ActiveX controls, Java applets, or any other language component that is compatible with the DOM API, written in OMG IDL. So it follows that the navigation processes we looked at in Chapter 13 are relevant. Nodes have been described as the atomic units of DOM trees and, as we saw in Chapter 13, it is these that permit programs to interact with document contents. They are described in Table 19.1.

**TABLE 19.1    XML and HTML Document Nodes**

| Node | Description |
| --- | --- |
| Attribute | A tag's property where, for instance, the `img` element may have the `src` attribute. |
| CDATA section | Text content that excludes markup characters. The `createCDATASection` method makes a node with a value that is a specified string. |
| Comment | Comments about the page that may describe the code and other facets of the page or Web site as a whole. |
| Document type | Every document has a `DocumentType` object or a `doctype` attribute that may be `null`. The `DocumentType` interface is able to list such defined entities. |

**TABLE 19.1** continued

| Node | Description |
| --- | --- |
| Document | An object representation of the entire document. The Document interface represents the entire HTML or XML document and holds the factory methods to create Document objects that include elements, text nodes, comments, and processing instructions. Resulting Node objects have an ownerDocument attribute. |
| Element | Aside from text, most Element nodes are the most common objects that authors navigate when traversing documents such as the following XML example: |

<elementUnleashed id="Unleashed demo">

</elementUnleashed>

Obviously the DOM tree has as its top node the Document node containing an Element node for elementUnleashed that has two child Element nodes, subelement1 and subelement2, while subelement1 has no child nodes.

| Entity reference | An ampersand (&) prefix indicates that an entity is inserted in a document using a reference. With DOM Level 2 version 1.0, it is not possible to edit Entity nodes; rather, every related EntityReference in the structure model has to be replaced with a clone of the entity's contents, and then these may be altered. Descendants of an Entity node are read only, and an Entity node does not have a parent. |

*Attributes*

systemId of type DOMString (read-only)—This holds the specified system identifier, or null if unspecified.

notationName of type DOMString (read-only) —This holds the name of the notation for unparsed entities, or null for those that are parsed.

publicId of type DOMString (read-only)—This holds the specified public identifier, or null if unspecified.

| Node | A reference to an element, attribute, or string of text. |
| Processing instruction | An instruction for an XML parser; the DOM keeps this processing information in XML documents. |

*Attributes*

Target of type DOMString (read-only)—This is the target of the processing instruction or the first token following the processing instruction.

Data of type DOMString—The content of the processing instruction, which is between the first non-whitespace character after the target and the character immediately preceding the ?>.

| Text | An object that holds text. |

## Note

The World Wide Web Consortium (W3C) DOM is supported by Netscape Navigator 5 and Microsoft Internet Explorer 5. Navigator 4 writes new HTML to a Layer object. To change a text element with a given ID and the value newtext, the form is

```
var lyr = document.layers[id].document
        lyr.open()
        lyr.write(newtext)
        lyr.close()
```

Internet Explorer 4.0 works in a different way and exposes the HTML document elements using the keyword ALL. To change a text element with a given ID and the value newtext, the form is

```
document.all[id].innerHTML = newtext
```

Explorer 5 continues to have its ALL keyword for backward compatibility. Equally Navigator 5.0 also clings to the Layers model for objects for backward compatibility.

## Tip

To produce version 4 cross-browser DHTML, you must create a fork that can detect the browser and make the appropriate adjustments:

```
ns4 = (document.layers)? true:false
    ie4 = (document.all)? true:false
    function simpleLayerWrite(id,newtext) {
      if (ns4) {
      var lyr = document.layers[id].document
      lyr.open()
      lyr.write(text)
      lyr.close()
      }
      else if (ie4) document.all[id].innerHTML = newtext
}
```

> **Note**
>
> From here on we look mainly at the DOM of the IE5 implementation (and the Gecko browser engine). This note, however, will obviously have a short lifespan, and it may be that Netscape Navigator and Explorer have a compatible DOM when you read it.

# DOM Document Manipulation and DOM Methods

We now know that the DOM defines useful and practical methods for manipulating the object or node structure of a document. It gives us common methods to do simple things like cloning, copying, inserting, and swapping nodes. These methods allow us to build easily changed documents that anyone can modify and understand, provided they know DOM. The methods also provide shortcuts to making the documents themselves, and at the same time they harness a key aspect of object-based documents, which is reusability; rather than make new nodes and objects repeatedly, you can simply clone them. This timely debate now brings us to the nuts and bolts of these methods and their practical application when making and manipulating documents, as described in the following sections.

## Using the `cloneNode` Method

The operation of the `cloneNode` method is dictated by its in parameter, the Boolean argument, and when this is `true`, the entire subtree rooted at the node is cloned. Alternatively, using the `false` parameter, namely `cloneMode()`, causes the browser to clone only the specified node and ignores its children and parent. The `cloneNode` method is demonstrated in Listing 19.1, which uses the `false` parameter to clone, as we have said, only the node. The script does not do a great deal, other than to create an array of nodes including a table, and this is achieved in HTML. The JavaScript script holds the `cloneNode` method, specifying which node to clone, and it invokes an Alert dialog that indicates the status of the cloned node. In this instance, the Alert message shows that the `cloneNode` method returned the cloned object. Accompanying this information is an indication that the cloned object has no children and no parent(s), proving that we have cloned only the node. By replacing the `cloneNode`'s parameter `false` with `true` causes the entire subtree to be cloned, including its children and parent(s).

**LISTING 19.1** The `cloneNode` Method

```
<HTML>
<HEAD>
<TITLE> DOM cloneNode example </TITLE>
</HEAD>
<BODY ID="bodyNode">
    <TABLE ID="tableNode">
      <TBODY>
        <TR ID="tr1Node"><TD BGCOLOR="yellow">Row 1, Cell 1</TD>
➥ <TD BGCOLOR="orange">Row 1, Cell 2</TD></TR>
        <TR ID="tr2Node"><TD BGCOLOR="red">Row 2, Cell 1</TD>
➥ <TD BGCOLOR="magenta">Row 2, Cell 2</TD></TR>
        <TR ID="tr3Node"><TD BGCOLOR="lightgreen">Row 3, Cell 1</TD>
➥ <TD BGCOLOR="beige">Row 3, Cell 2</TD></TR>
        <TR ID="tr4Node"><TD BGCOLOR="blue">Row 4, Cell 1</TD>
➥ <TD BGCOLOR="lightblue">Row 4, Cell 2</TD></TR>
        <TR ID="tr5Node"><TD BGCOLOR="orange">Row 5, Cell 1</TD>
➥ <TD BGCOLOR="purple">Row 5, Cell 2</TD></TR>
      </TBODY>
    </TABLE>
<SCRIPT LANGUAGE="JavaScript">
<!--
tr30bj = tr1Node.cloneNode(false);
alert(
        "tr30bj.firstChild = " + tr30bj.firstChild + "\n" +
        "tr30bj.nodeName = " + tr30bj.nodeName
      );
 // -->
</SCRIPT>
</BODY>
</HTML>
```

# Using the `insertBefore` Method with DOM

The `insertBefore` method is a means of building object structures by inserting objects before the occurrence of other specified objects. You use two parameters that are objects:

```
tbodyObj.insertBefore(tr2obj, tr3obj)
```

Building a table is possible using the `insertBefore` method, as well as other DOM methods. For example, we can create a node, clone it, and then use `insertBefore` to create a table. Listing 19.2 illustrates the construction of a table using these methods. `tbodyObj` has three children: `tr1Obj`, `tr2Obj`, and `tr3Obj`, which are created using the following expressions:

```
tr1Obj = document.createElement("TR");
tr1td1Obj = document.createElement("TD");
tr1td2Obj = tr1td1Obj.cloneNode(false);
tr2td1Obj = tr1td1Obj.cloneNode(false);
```

Using the `insertBefore` method the objects are assembled as follows:

```
tbodyObj.insertBefore(tr3Obj);
tbodyObj.insertBefore(tr2Obj, tr3Obj);
tbodyObj.insertBefore(tr1Obj, tr2Obj);
tr1Obj.insertBefore(tr1td2Obj);
tr1Obj.insertBefore(tr1td1Obj, tr1td2Obj);
tr2Obj.insertBefore(tr2td2Obj);
tr2Obj.insertBefore(tr2td1Obj, tr2td2Obj);
```

As can be seen from the code fragment, the last child (`tr3Obj`) is inserted first, the second child is inserted in front of it, and the first child (`tr1Obj`) is inserted in front of the second (`tr2Obj`).

**LISTING 19.2**   Creating a Table Using `insertBefore`

```
<HTML>
<HEAD>
<TITLE> Building tables using DOM </TITLE>
</HEAD>
<BODY ID="bodyNode">
<SCRIPT LANGUAGE="JavaScript">
<!--
row1column1Obj = document.createTextNode("Row 1, column 1  ");
tableObj = document.createElement("TABLE");
tbodyObj = document.createElement("TBODY");
tr1Obj = document.createElement("TR");
tr1td1Obj = document.createElement("TD");
tr1td2Obj = tr1td1Obj.cloneNode(false);
tr2td1Obj = tr1td1Obj.cloneNode(false);
tr2td2Obj = tr1td1Obj.cloneNode(false);
tr3td1Obj = tr1td1Obj.cloneNode(false);
tr3td2Obj = tr1td1Obj.cloneNode(false);
tr2Obj = tr1Obj.cloneNode(false);
tr3Obj = tr1Obj.cloneNode(false);
row1column2Obj = row1column1Obj.cloneNode(false);
row2column1Obj = row1column1Obj.cloneNode(false);
```

**19**

**Other DOM Objects**

LISTING **19.2**   continued

```
row2column2Obj = row1column1Obj.cloneNode(false);
row3column1Obj = row1column1Obj.cloneNode(false);
row3column2Obj = row1column1Obj.cloneNode(false);
row1column2Obj.nodeValue = "Row 1, column 2   ";
row2column1Obj.nodeValue = "Row 2, column 1   ";
row2column2Obj.nodeValue = "Row 2, column 2   ";
row3column1Obj.nodeValue = "Row 3, column 1   ";
row3column2Obj.nodeValue = "Row 3, column 2   ";
returnValue = tableObj.insertBefore(tbodyObj);
tbodyObj.insertBefore(tr3Obj);
tbodyObj.insertBefore(tr2Obj, tr3Obj);
tbodyObj.insertBefore(tr1Obj, tr2Obj);
tr1Obj.insertBefore(tr1td2Obj);
tr1Obj.insertBefore(tr1td1Obj, tr1td2Obj);
tr2Obj.insertBefore(tr2td2Obj);
tr2Obj.insertBefore(tr2td1Obj, tr2td2Obj);
tr3Obj.insertBefore(tr3td2Obj);
tr3Obj.insertBefore(tr3td1Obj, tr3td2Obj);
tr1td2Obj.insertBefore(row1column2Obj);
tr1td1Obj.insertBefore(row1column1Obj);
tr2td2Obj.insertBefore(row2column2Obj);
tr2td1Obj.insertBefore(row2column1Obj);
tr3td2Obj.insertBefore(row3column2Obj);
tr3td1Obj.insertBefore(row3column1Obj);
bodyNode.insertBefore(tableObj);
// -->
</SCRIPT>
</BODY>
</HTML>
```

# Using the swapNode Method

The swapNode method swaps specified subtrees that are rooted at the specified elements. The swapNode method returns the whole subtree and may be applied as shown in Listing 19.3.

LISTING **19.3**   Swapping Paragraphs

```
<SCRIPT LANGUAGE="JavaScript">
<!--
var msg = "";
function printChildObjects()  {
```

LISTING **19.3**    continued

```
    childCount = bodyNode.childNodes.length;
    msg += "bodyNode.childNodes.length = " + bodyNode.childNodes.length + "\n" ;
    for(var i = 0; i < childCount; i++)  {
    msg += "bodyNode.childNodes[i].nodeName = " + bodyNode.childNodes[i].nodeName +
➥"\n";
    }
}
printChildObjects();
msg += "Swap Paragraph 2 with paragraph1\n";
var b = p2Node;
var swappingNode = p3Node.swapNode(b);
msg += "swappingNode.nodeName = " + swappingNode.nodeName + "\n";
msg += "swappingNode.childNodes.length = " + swappingNode.childNodes.length + "\n";
msg += "p2Node.nodeName = " + p2Node.nodeName + "\n";
printChildObjects();
alert(msg);
// -->
</SCRIPT>
```

The `printChildObjects` function prints the `bodyNode`'s children together with the `nodeName` property.

## Using the `removeNode` Method

`removeNode(false)` deletes specified nodes and assigns their children to the previous parent of the deleted node. The form is this:

```
erasedNode = p3Node.removeNode(false);
```

Listing 19.4 illustrates the `removeNode` method and again includes the `printChildObjects` function.

**19**

Other DOM Objects

LISTING **19.4**   Removing Nodes

```
<SCRIPT LANGUAGE="JavaScript">
<!--
var msg = "";
function printChildObjects()  {
    childCount = bodyNode.childNodes.length;
    msg += "bodyNode.childNodes.length = " + bodyNode.childNodes.length + "\n" ;
    for(var i = 0; i < childCount; i++)  {
    msg += "bodyNode.childNodes[i].nodeName = " + bodyNode.childNodes[i].nodeName +
➥"\n";
```

**LISTING 19.4**    continued

```
    }
}
printChildObjects();
msg += "Erase paragraph 3\n";
var deletedNode = p3Node.removeNode(false);
msg += "deletedNode.nodeName = " + deletedNode.nodeName + "\n";
msg += "deletedNode.childNodes.length = " + deletedNode.childNodes.length + "\n";
printChildObjects();
alert(msg);
// -->
</SCRIPT>
```

> **Tip**
>
> DOM objects refer to the entire Web page contents, including its graphics, which may be in GIF format. The first graphic in a document may be altered by changing its src (or source) property. In the DOM form like that below, this simply exchanges the first image for the GIF image file called New_Title.
>
> ```
> window.document.images[0].src='New -Title.gif';
> ```
>
> GIF images and other graphics files may be edited using Paint Shop Pro from Jasc Software. It is shareware and may be downloaded from the Web at various sites, including the Jasc site. It is filled with useful editing tools and effects that are excellent for producing Web graphics.

# Summary

This chapter has taken the debate about DOM in this book a step further, in that it is used to build as well as change document entities. It follows then that by knowing the structure and characteristics of DOM, it may be applied literally anywhere, and by using virtually any software entity, including the scripts that we have used here. But beyond these, you can do the same with ActiveX controls and with Java applets. There is a new landscape of standardized target platforms or client browsers that are for the first time speaking the same language, which is defined by DOM.

# Dynamic HTML Programming Techniques

# PART

# IV

## In This Part

# Rollovers

A rollover is a common method of spicing up a site's pages with JavaScript. In fact, it was one of the first globally used JavaScript functions that is still used. Others, such as scrolling status bar messages and text fields, have gone by the wayside.

Using rollovers is a fairly easy task and does not involve a lot of code. However, you should note that there are different kinds of rollovers. You will have to determine whether you want to use image rollovers or layer rollovers.

# Knowing Your Events

When creating rollover effects on your site, you will need to fully understand the various rollover-related events that can be used in JavaScript. Although these events are discussed fully in Chapter 14, "Handling Events," we will take another quick look at those related to rollovers in this chapter.

## onMouseOver

The onMouseOver event can be used by Links and Document objects to indicate when the mouse cursor has been moved over an element. Internet Explorer allows the capturing of this event in almost all elements on a page—not just the Links and Document objects. We will use the onMouseOver event, in conjunction with the <a> tag, to trigger most of the "over" events in our examples. A sample is as follows:

```
<a href="http://www.mcp.com" onmouseover="alert('You rolled over!')">Here</a>
```

## onMouseOut

The onMouseOut event is very similar to the onMouseOver event and can be used by Links and Document objects. This event indicates when the mouse cursor has been moved off of a particular element. Internet Explorer also allows the capturing of this event in most elements on a page—not just the Links and Document objects. A sample follows:

```
<a href="http://www.mcp.com" onmouseout="alert('You rolled off!')">Here</a>
```

## onMouseDown

The onMouseDown event is used by Links and Document objects to indicate when a mouse button has been pressed down on an element. We will use the onMouseDown event, in conjunction with the <a> tag, to trigger most of the "down" events in our examples. A sample is as follows:

```
<a href="http://www.mcp.com" onmousedown="alert('You pressed!')">Here</a>
```

### onMouseUp

The onMouseUp event is used by Links and Document objects to indicate when a mouse button has been released after being pressed down on an element. We will use this event, in conjunction with the <a> tag, to trigger most of the "up" events in our examples. A sample follows:

```
<a href="http://www.mcp.com" onmouseup="alert('You released!')">Here</a>
```

# Types of Rollovers

As a Web developer, you need to decide not only what kind of rollover your application needs, but also how you want to implement it. Many of these rollovers can simulate the others, so your choice will most likely reflect what your users' browsers support or what you know how to do.

## Image Rollovers

There are several methods of implementing image rollovers, but the easiest is to create two arrays that contain the images you want to use, then reference their indexed location within the document, using the document.images array. To accomplish this, we will store all of the images in an array of Image objects. For our example, shown in Figure 20.1, we will have two images on a single page. When the user rolls over an image, the image is replaced with the "rollover" version of the image. The array of images can be created with the following code:

```
// Create arrays to hold images
var overImg = new Array();
overImg[0] = new Image(24,24);
overImg[1] = new Image(24,24);

var defaultImg = new Array();
defaultImg[0] = new Image(24,24);
defaultImg[1] = new Image(24,24);

// Preload images in the array
overImg[0].src = "back-over.gif";
overImg[1].src = "forward-over.gif";

defaultImg[0].src = "back.gif";
defaultImg[1].src = "forward.gif";
```

**20**

Rollovers

FIGURE 20.1
*Our rollover
page.*

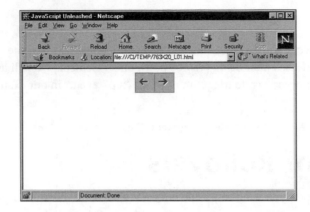

The next thing we need is a function to do the actual swapping of the images. The function that we are going to use will take two parameters: One is the indexed location of the image that needs to be swapped, and the second is the type of swap ("over" or "out") that is occurring. Once these parameters are passed in, a `switch` statement will be used to determine which array to pull the replacement image from. Once this has been determined, the actual assignment, or replacement, of the image is accomplished through the use of the `src` property of the `Image` object. The following function is used:

```
function rollImage(img,type){
  switch(type){
    case "over":
      document.images[img].src = overImg[img].src;
      break;
    case "out":
      document.images[img].src = defaultImg[img].src;
      break;
  }
}
```

The last task we need to accomplish in our example is the capturing of the `onMouseOver` and `onMouseOut` events. As indicated before, this is accomplished through the use of the `<a>` tag. Listing 20.1 shows the complete source code for the capturing of these events, and Figure 20.2 shows the replaced image with the mouse over one of the buttons.

LISTING 20.1   Complete Source Code for Our Image Rollover

```
<html>
<head>
  <title>JavaScript Unleashed</title>
  <script type="text/javascript" language="JavaScript1.2">
```

**LISTING 20.1**    continued

```
<!--

  // Create arrays to hold images
  var overImg = new Array();
  overImg[0] = new Image(24,24);
  overImg[1] = new Image(24,24);

  var defaultImg = new Array();
  defaultImg[0] = new Image(24,24);
  defaultImg[1] = new Image(24,24);

  // Preload images in the array
  overImg[0].src = "back-over.gif";
  overImg[1].src = "forward-over.gif";

  defaultImg[0].src = "back.gif";
  defaultImg[1].src = "forward.gif";

  // Change the state of image depending on the event that fired.
  function rollImage(img,type){
    switch(type){
      case "over":
        document.images[img].src = overImg[img].src;
        break;
      case "out":
        document.images[img].src = defaultImg[img].src;
        break;
    }
  }
  //-->
  </script>
</head>
<body bgcolor="#ffffff">
  <table border="1" cellpadding="5" cellspacing="0" align="center"
     bgcolor="#c0c0c0">
    <tr>
      <td align="center">
        <a href="javascript:void(0)"
            onmouseout="rollImage('0','out')"
            onmouseover="rollImage('0','over')">
          <img border="0" src="back.gif" width="24" height="24" alt="Back">
        </a>
```

**20**

**Rollovers**

**LISTING 20.1**    continued

```
      </td>
      <td align="center">
        <a href="javascript:void(0)"
             onmouseout="rollImage('1','out')"
             onmouseover="rollImage('1','over')">
          <img border="0" src="forward.gif" width="24" height="24"
            alt="Forward"></a>
      </td>
    </tr>
  </table>
</body>
</html>
```

**FIGURE 20.2**

*Rolling over one of our images.*

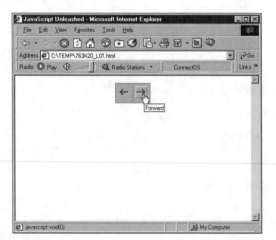

---

**Note**

Chapter 24, "DHTML Menus and Toolbars," contains a more in-depth example and description of using image rollovers. Please read through it for a better understanding of how this works and how you can use it.

# Layer Rollovers

The next method we are going to talk about is layer rollovers. These are generated by hiding and exposing layers within a document. This is covered in Chapter 23, "Layers," but we will do a quick introduction on accessing the `visibility` property of cascading style sheets (CSS) in JavaScript.

The first thing we are going to do is create the HTML that makes up our example. In this example we are going to have a simple link and an initially hidden layer. As you would imagine, our HTML is very simple.

```
<div name="layer1" id="layer1">
  Hello World!
</div>
<a href="javascript:void(0)"
  onmouseout="changeState('layer1','hidden')"
  onmouseover="changeState('layer1','visible')">
  Rollover to show and hide the layer.
</a>
```

Again, do not worry about the layer concept at this point—we will cover it in detail in Chapter 23. Just focus on the JavaScript we are using to process the rollovers.

As with image rollovers, we will be using the `<a>` tag to capture the `onMouseOver` and `onMouseOut` events. In the `<a>` tag, you see three JavaScript interactions. The first is located in the `href` attribute. This call (`javascript:`) tells the browser that nothing should happen (`void(0)`) if the user clicks the link. The second and third instances call a `changeState()` function and pass it two variables. As you can see, one is `name` (for Navigator browsers) and `id` (for Internet Explorer browsers) of the layer instance, and the second is an indicator of whether to hide or show the layer.

> **Tip**
>
> It is possible to use this same syntax, commonly referred to as a "JavaScript URL," to call functions or even execute other JavaScript code—all contained within the `href` attribute.

The next step is to set up the style sheet for the layer so that it is hidden. To make it easier to see and position properly, I have also included several other CSS properties and values. Chapter 22, "Cascading Style Sheets," and Chapter 23 will go over the use of these

**20**

**Rollovers**

properties; for now, focus only on the use of the visibility property. As you can see, it is set to hidden.

```
<!--
  #layer1{
    background-color: red;
    height: 100;
    left: 10;
    position: absolute;
    top: 50;
    width: 100;
    visibility: hidden;
  }
-->
</style>
```

The next section of code is here only because the implementation of accessing layers in Navigator and Internet Explorer browsers is different. Because of this, we have to determine which one is accessing the page and set variables that will allow us to use a single function to process the rollovers. We will not cover the details of this right now, because it is covered in Chapter 23. The code we are going to use, however, is as follows:

```
// Create global variables for browser type
var isIE = new Boolean(false);
var isNav = new Boolean(false);
var layer = new String();
var style = new String();


 // Determine if the browser is Internet Explorer, Navigator,
// or other. Also, set the layer variable depending on the
// type of access it needs.
function checkBrowser(){
  if(navigator.userAgent.indexOf("MSIE") != -1){
    isIE = true;
    layer = ".all";
    style = ".style";
  }else if(navigator.userAgent.indexOf("Nav") != -1){
    isNav = true;
    layer = ".layers";
    style = "";
  }
}
```

The final function in our example shows and hides the layer. As you saw in the HTML, it takes two parameters: the layer's name and the state to which you want to switch the layer. Because of the processing we did beforehand, this function contains only one line of code:

```
function changeState(layerRef, state){
  eval("document" + layer + "['" + layerRef + "']" + style
➡      + ".visibility = '" + state + "'");
}
```

As you can see in this function, we use the top-level `eval()` method. This method will take a `String` object and execute it as if it were JavaScript code. In our example, it turns

```
"document" + layer + "['" + layerRef + "']" + style
➡  + ".visibility = '" + state + "'");
```

into

```
document.layers['layer1'].visibility = "hidden";
```

when hidden on Navigator browsers, and

```
document.all['layer1'].style.visibility = "hidden";
```

when hidden on Internet Explorer browsers. You are now seeing the differences in accessing layers in these two browsers.

Now that we have completed the construction of our code, let's see it in action. Listing 20.2 contains the complete source code for our example. Figure 20.3 shows the page loaded in the browser. Figure 20.4 shows the result of rolling over the link and exposing the layer.

**LISTING 20.2** Our Layer Rollover Example

```
<html>
<head>
  <title>JavaScript Unleashed</title>
  <style type="text/css">
  <!--
    #layer1{
      background-color: red;
      height: 100;
      left: 10;
      position: absolute;
      top: 50;
      width: 100;
      visibility: hidden;
    }
  -->
```

LISTING 20.2    continued

```
</style>
<script type="text/javascript" language="JavaScript1.2">
<!--
  // Create global variables for browser type
  var isIE = new Boolean(false);
  var isNav = new Boolean(false);
  var unSupported = new Boolean(false);
  var layer = new String();
  var style = new String();

  // Determine if the browser is Internet Explorer, Navigator,
  // or other. Also, set the layer variable depending on the
  // type of access it needs.
  function checkBrowser(){
    if(navigator.userAgent.indexOf("MSIE") != -1){
      isIE = true;
      layer = ".all";
      style = ".style";
    }else if(navigator.userAgent.indexOf("Nav") != -1){
      isNav = true;
      layer = ".layers";
      style = "";
    }else{
      unSupported = true;
    }
  }


  // Take the state passed in, and change it.
  function changeState(layerRef, state){
    eval("document" + layer + "['" + layerRef + "']"
      + style + ".visibility = '" + state + "'");
  }
//-->
</script>
</head>
<body onload="checkBrowser()">
  <div name="layer1" id="layer1">
    Hello World!
  </div>
  <a href="javascript:void(0)"
    onmouseout="changeState('layer1','hidden')"
    onmouseover="changeState('layer1','visible')">
```

**LISTING 20.2**   continued

```
    Rollover to show and hide the layer.
  </a>
</body>
</html>
```

**FIGURE 20.3**
*The example without rolling over the link.*

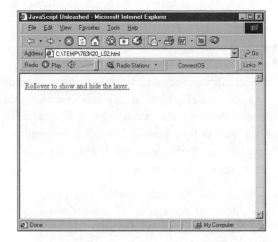

**FIGURE 20.4**
*The layer while rolling over the link.*

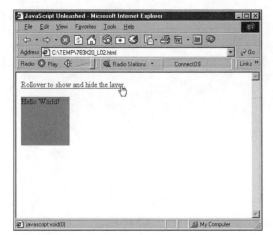

**20**

**Rollovers**

> **Note**
>
> Both Navigator and Internet Explorer have *implementations* of CSS, so do not be surprised when you see slightly different results in running some of these scripts. When loading Listing 20.2, for example, Navigator 4 will color only the background of the text, not the entire layer.

# Summary

Even though this was a short chapter, we have covered some very important JavaScript applications. Implementing rollover effects on your site is one of the easiest and safest applications of JavaScript you can perform. But do not limit yourself to what you have learned here. The *effect* of rollovers lays the foundation for many other tasks that you can accomplish with JavaScript. It familiarizes you with events and accessing elements on a page and introduces you to user interface design.

The rest of this part of the book will take you through some additional visual effects, CSS, and layers. You will also see how to build a DHTML toolbar and menu and how to interact with other components on your page using JavaScript.

# Visual Effects

CHAPTER

21

Web technologies such as JavaScript and Java are important because of the practical purposes they serve in the realm of Web application development. At the same time, some of the primary reasons JavaScript and Java are so popular are the "cool" things you can do with them on your Web site. Think back: As Java was gaining popularity, how many meaningless Java marquees and other applets did you see spread across the Web? And, in the JavaScript realm, as the language has matured, you can do many more exciting things with JavaScript.

# Scrolling Marquees

A scrolling marquee is a popular effect for Web site developers. Its purpose is to relay the latest news or tidbit to visitors of your Web site. The marquee, or "ticker tape," was first popularized with Java applets.

You can create a scrolling marquee in JavaScript as well, although the visual appearance is typically less stunning than a Java applet. This is because you're forced to use a Text object as the container for the scrolling text, and none of the HTML form objects are going to dazzle you with their appearance. Nonetheless, JavaScript marquees don't require a separate applet and can be created quickly and easily, so you may find them very useful in a variety of situations.

To create a JavaScript marquee, you need to do three things:

1. Create an HTML form with an embedded Text object.
2. Write a function that scrolls text within the Text object.
3. Associate this function as an event handler of the window's onLoad event, to set the wheels in motion.

To begin, create a Form object with a Text object within it. As you do so, it's helpful to name these objects appropriately. Because they are created specifically for the marquee and irrelevant to other forms on the page, I often label the form "marqueeForm" and the text "marqueeText", or something to that effect. Next, enter the marquee message as the value attribute of the <input> tag. Here is the <form> definition code:

```
<CENTER>
  <form name="marqueeForm">
  <input name="marqueeText" size="50" value=""THIS JUST IN...JavaScript
    is selected as official scripting language of the 2000 Summer Olympics">
  </form>
</center>
```

Once we have the marquee container defined, we can get to the heart of the matter. We first want to define two global constants to use in the marquee: the rate (in milliseconds) at which to scroll and the number of characters to scroll at a time. Also, we will create a String object called marqueeMessage:

```
var SCROLL_RATE = 100;
var SCROLL_CHARS = 1;
var marqueeMessage = new String();
```

The next task is to create a function called JSMarquee(), which gives your ordinary Text object the look of a marquee. Because a marquee requires continuous updating, you will need to make JSMarquee() recursive by calling setTimeout() at the start of the function. See Chapter 14, "Handling Events," for more information on the setTimeout() method, as well as the "Billboards" section of this chapter. The global variable SCROLL_RATE is used as the method parameter to determine how often to call the function.

The heart of the JSMarquee() function is first to get the value of the Text object and assign it to the marqueeMessage string. You can then simulate word wrapping by chopping off a chunk of the message at the front and placing it on the end of the string. The String object's substring() method is used to do this, as shown here:

```
function JSMarquee(){
  setTimeout('JSMarquee()', SCROLL_RATE);
  marqueeMessage = document.marqueeForm.marqueeText.value;
  document.marqueeForm.marqueeText.value =
      marqueeMessage.substring( SCROLL_CHARS ) +
      marqueeMessage.substring( 0, SCROLL_CHARS );
}
```

Figure 21.1 shows the scrolling effect of the marquee as it runs continuously while you are on the page.

The complete source code for the marquee example is shown in Listing 21.1.

**Note**

The code shown in Listing 21.1 adds a little extra JavaScript code to the example so you can define the text of the message to be a global variable. If you change the scrolling text message often, you may find it easier to maintain.

**FIGURE 21.1**
*The start of the scrolling marquee.*

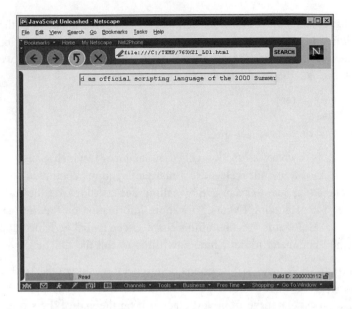

**LISTING 21.1**   A Marquee Using JavaScript

```html
<html>
<head>
  <title>JavaScript Unleashed</title>
  <script type="text/javascript">
  <!--
    // Declare variables
    var SCROLL_RATE = 100;
    var SCROLL_CHARS = 1;
    var MESSAGE = "THIS JUST IN...JavaScript is selected as " +
        "official scripting language of the 2000 Summer Olympics..."
    var marqueeMessage = new String();

    function JSMarquee(){
      setTimeout( 'JSMarquee()', SCROLL_RATE );
      marqueeMessage = document.marqueeForm.marqueeText.value;
      document.marqueeForm.marqueeText.value = [
        marqueeMessage.substring( SCROLL_CHARS ) +
        marqueeMessage.substring( 0, SCROLL_CHARS );
    }
  //-->
  </script>
</head>
<body onload="JSMarquee()">
```

**LISTING 21.1**    continued

```
<center>
  <form name="marqueeForm">
    <input name="marqueeText" size="50">
    <script type="text/javascript">
    <!--
      document.marqueeForm.marqueeText.value = MESSAGE;
    //-->
    </script>
  </form>
</center>
</body>
</html>
```

# Billboards

Billboards are another common component found on Web pages. They are eye-catching teasers, often used for advertising. Invariably, their mission is to be interesting enough to be noticed and tantalizing enough to get a user to click them. Using JavaScript `Image` objects, you can create professional-caliber billboards without the need for animated GIFs or Java applets.

> **Note**
>
> Before creating the script itself, you need to get two sets of GIF files with the same dimensions. First, you need to have two or three images that will be used as the main billboard images. Second, to create a transition effect, you need a series of transitional images that, when drawn sequentially, look like an animation. You will typically want five to seven transition images for the effect to be smooth.
>
> Always be mindful, however, of the total size of the GIF files required. Someone downloading your page at 28.8 may not appreciate it if you use 15 transition images to create the ultimate smoothing effect.

Once your billboard GIF files are ready, you need to follow these steps to create a JavaScript billboard:

1. Create an image placeholder on your Web page.

2. Define an array to hold your primary images and one to hold your transitional images.

3. Develop a routine to manage image presentation.

4. Associate this function as an event handler of the window's `onLoad` event.

To begin, create an `Image` object on your Web page that will serve as the placeholder for all the action. Because a billboard typically takes you somewhere once it's clicked, you'll probably want to put the `<img>` tag inside a link:

```
<a href = "http://www.mcp.com"
   onmouseover="window.status='http://www.mcp.com'; return true;"
   onmouseout="window.status = ''; return true;">
 <img name="billboard" height="49" width="333" src="./visjs.gif">
</a>
```

> **Note**
>
> Note the `onMouseOver` and `onMouseOut` event handlers that are defined in the `Link` object. Although they aren't needed if you're hardcoding the URL, they become useful if each of the primary images in your billboard has a different URL destination. You would then create a URL array and have the `mouseOver` text dependent on the active image.

Within the `<head>`, you need to add a `<script>` tag and define a series of variables and objects. You have two global constants for the amount of time (in milliseconds) to display the primary images and an additional constant for the amount of time to display the transitional images. Two additional variables are defined for use later:

```
// Global constants
var DISPLAY_TIME = 3500;
var TRANSITION_TIME = 50;

// Global variables
var primaryIdx = 0;
var transIdx = 0;
```

Two arrays should now be defined to hold the information about the primary and transitional image sets. For each array element, the image `src` property is declared:

```
// First array contains primary images
JSBillboardArray = new Array( 3 );
```

```
JSBillboardArray[0] = new Image( 49, 333 );
JSBillboardArray[0].src = "./visjs.gif";
JSBillboardArray[1] = new Image( 49, 333 );
JSBillboardArray[1].src = "./url.gif";
JSBillboardArray[2] = new Image( 49, 333 );
JSBillboardArray[2].src = "./bltwith.gif";

// Second array contains transitionary images
transArray = new Array( 6 );
transArray[0] = new Image( 49, 333 );
transArray[0].src = "./bw7.gif";
transArray[1] = new Image( 49, 333 );
transArray[1].src = "./bw6.gif";
transArray[2] = new Image( 49, 333 );
transArray[2].src = "./bw5.gif";
transArray[3] = new Image( 49, 333 );
transArray[3].src = "./bw4.gif";
transArray[4] = new Image( 49, 333 );
transArray[4].src = "./bw3.gif";
transArray[5] = new Image( 49, 333 );
transArray[5].src = "./bw2.gif";
```

The main function used to run the billboard is called `runJSBillboard()`. First it determines the rate of change for each billboard cycle, and then it uses that value in a recursive `setTimeout()` method call. The `runJSBillboard()` function then calls a second function called `repaint()`:

```
function runJSBillboard() {
  changeRate = DISPLAY_TIME + ( transArray.length * TRANSITION_TIME );
  setTimeout( "runJSBillboard()", changeRate );
  repaint();

}
```

The `repaint()` function is the nuts and bolts of a JavaScript billboard. It determines which image to display in this cycle. First up are the transitional images, and `repaint()` begins by checking their state and determining if they have completed cycling. If so, the `if` section of code is processed, displaying the current primary image. If not, the `else` section of code is executed:

```
function repaint() {
  if ( transIdx > transArray.length - 1 ) {
    primaryIdx++;
    transIdx = 0;
```

```
    if ( primaryIdx > JSBillboardArray.length - 1 ) primaryIdx = 0;

      document.billboard.src = JSBillboardArray[primaryIdx].src;
      return;
    }else{


      document.billboard.src = transArray[transIdx].src;
      setTimeout( "repaint()", TRANSITION_TIME );
    }
  transIdx++;
}
```

The repaint() function deserves a closer look. The if section is designed to display a primary image—specifically, the one that is current in the JSBillboardArray. When it does so, it resets the transIdx variable to 0 so that the transitional cycle will begin the next time through repaint(). After checking to see if primaryIdx should be reset as well, it returns control to the calling function runJSBillboard().

Because runJSBillboard() is recursive, the repaint() function is immediately processed again. Because the if clause was processed last time, you can be assured that the else clause will kick in this time around. This section of code displays the current transitional image from the transArray array. It then calls setTimeout() to recursively call repaint(). For each transitional cycle, the else clause is triggered until the last transitional image is displayed. The next time repaint() is called (by itself), the if clause resets everything when it executes.

> **Note**
>
> Recursion can be a difficult programming concept to understand. But, as this example shows, you can use it for some powerful coding techniques.

Figures 21.2, 21.3, and 21.4 show snapshots of the billboard cycling process.

Listing 21.2 provides the full source code for the billboard example.

**FIGURE 21.2**
*The initial primary image.*

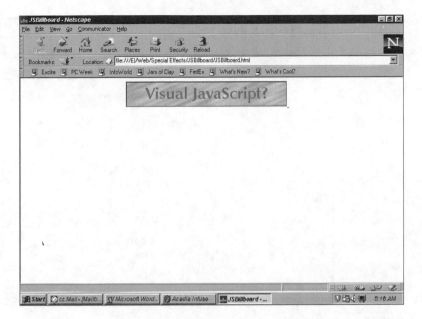

**FIGURE 21.3**
*One of the five transitional images.*

**FIGURE 21.4**
*The second primary image.*

**LISTING 21.2**   Building a Billboard with JavaScript

```
<html>
<head>
  <title>JavaScript Unleashed</title>
  <script type="text/javascript" language="JavaScript1.1">
  <!--

    // Global constants
    var BB_URL = 'http://www.mcp.com';
    var DISPLAY_TIME = 3500;
    var TRANSITION_TIME = 50;

    // Global variables
    var primaryIdx = 0;
    var transIdx = 0;

    // First array contains primary images
    JSBillboardArray = new Array( 3 );
    JSBillboardArray[0] = new Image( 49, 333 );
    JSBillboardArray[0].src = "./visjs.gif";
    JSBillboardArray[1] = new Image( 49, 333 );
    JSBillboardArray[1].src = "./url.gif";
    JSBillboardArray[2] = new Image( 49, 333 );
    JSBillboardArray[2].src = "./bltwith.gif";
```

**LISTING 21.2**    continued

```
// Second array contains transitional images
transArray = new Array();
transArray[0] = new Image( 49, 333 );
transArray[0].src = "./bw7.gif";
transArray[1] = new Image( 49, 333 );
transArray[1].src = "./bw6.gif";
transArray[2] = new Image( 49, 333 );
transArray[2].src = "./bw5.gif";
transArray[3] = new Image( 49, 333 );
transArray[3].src = "./bw4.gif";
transArray[4] = new Image( 49, 333 );
transArray[4].src = "./bw3.gif";
transArray[5] = new Image( 49, 333 );
transArray[5].src = "./bw2.gif";

function runJSBillboard() {
  changeRate = DISPLAY_TIME + (transArray.length * TRANSITION_TIME);
  setTimeout("runJSBillboard()", changeRate);
  repaint();
}

function repaint() {
  if (transIdx > transArray.length - 1){
    primaryIdx++;  // Increment primary image index
    transIdx = 0;  // Reset transitional image index
    if (primaryIdx > JSBillboardArray.length - 1){
          primaryIdx = 0;  // Reset primary index
    }
    document.billboard.src = JSBillboardArray[primaryIdx].src;
    return; // Return to runJSBillboard()
  }else{

    // Display transitional image
    document.billboard.src = transArray[transIdx].src;

    // Run repaint() recursively through cycle
    setTimeout( "repaint()", TRANSITION_TIME );
  }

  transIdx++; // Increment transitionary index
}
```

---

**LISTING 21.2**   continued

```
//-->
  </script>
</head>
<body onload="runJSBillboard()">
  <center>
    <a href="http://www.mcp.com" onmouseover="window.status=BB_URL;
➥    return true;" onmouseout="window.status=''; return true;">
      <img name="billboard" height="49" width="333" src="./visjs.gif">
    </a>
  </center>
</body>
</html>
```

---

# Color Fading

So far in this chapter, we have looked at how you can use JavaScript to simulate a control that is typically implemented using Java, such as a billboard or a marquee. However, ignore the hype you read in the press: Java can't do everything. A case in point is the next technique—fading the color of an HTML page. Because JavaScript has a capability to control an HTML document that Java doesn't, it works best for techniques such as this.

Color fading is performed by gradually changing the value of the Document object's bgColor property. This property is either a hexadecimal RGB triplet or a string literal representing an RGB triplet, such as "aqua" or "red". Although string literals are easy to work with when setting the bgColor property on a one-time basis, you need to use a hexadecimal RGB triplet value in the format rrggbb.

Using JavaScript, you can create a function called JSFade() to perform the color fading and then simply make a call to that function when the document loads. The JSFade() function has seven parameters:

- Initial RGB values for red, green, and blue

- Ending RGB values for red, green, and blue

- The number of milliseconds to perform the fading process

Next, a for loop is used to step through the fading process. It's dependent on the delay parameter to determine the actual number of times the for loop is processed. Two variables are defined: finishPercent tells the percentage of the process left until the process is finished, and startPercent tells the percentage of the process that has completed. The heart of the color fade process is in the next statement, which assigns a value to the `document.bgColor` property based on adding the quotient of the starting red value times the `startPercent` variable and the quotient of the finishing red value times the `finishPercent` variable. This process is repeated for the green and blue sets as well.

```
function JSFade(startRed, startGreen, startBlue, finishRed,
➡ finishGreen, finishBlue, delay){
  for(var i = 1; i <= delay - 1; i++){
    var finishPercent = i/delay;
    var startPercent = 1 - finishPercent;
    document.bgColor = Math.floor(startRed * startPercent + finishRed *
➡     finishPercent) * 256 * 256 + Math.floor(startGreen  * startPercent
➡ + finishGreen * finishPercent) * 256 + Math.floor(startBlue *
➡ startPercent + finishBlue * finishPercent );
  }
}
```

You can then call this function in your script. For example, to fade from off-white to teal green, you would use the following:

```
JSFade(255, 255, 240, 0, 128, 128, 170);
```

To fade from blue to red, you would use this:

```
JSFade(0, 0, 198, 196, 2, 40, 170);
```

Finally, to fade from black to white, you would use this:

```
JSFade(0, 0, 0, 255, 255, 255, 170);
```

Listing 21.3 provides the source code for this color fade example.

**LISTING 21.3**   Using JavaScript to Change the Background Color of Your Document

```
<html>
<head>
  <title>JavaScrip Unleashed</title>
  <script type="text/javascript">
  <!--
    function JSFade(startRed, startGreen, startBlue, finishRed, finishGreen,
➡       finishBlue, delay){
      for(var i = 1; i <= delay - 1; i++){
        var finishPercent = i/delay;
        var startPercent = 1 - finishPercent;
        document.bgColor = Math.floor(startRed * startPercent + finishRed *
➡         finishPercent) * 256 * 256 + Math.floor(startGreen *
➡         startPercent + finishGreen * finishPercent) * 256 +
➡         Math.floor(startBlue * startPercent + finishBlue *
```

LISTING 21.3    continued

```
➥          finishPercent );          }
    }
  //-->
  </script>
</head>
<body>
  <script type="text/javascript">
  <!--
    JSFade( 255,255,240,0,128,128,170 );
  //-->
  </script>
</body>
</html>
```

# Animated Pushbuttons

The look-and-feel of the Web has come a long way over the past three years. Originally a text-based technology medium, the Web today sports graphics, multimedia, and sophisticated page layouts. However, one aspect of the old "ugly" look is form objects, such as text input boxes and pushbuttons. After all, you can't even specify the font for those controls yet.

It isn't surprising, therefore, that many Web developers are looking to JavaScript to provide alternatives to one of the most common UI (user interface) controls today: buttons. Although no graphical button objects are available yet, with the Image object, JavaScript does a remarkably good job of simulating the behavior of a pushbutton.

> **Note**
>
> As with the billboard example from earlier in this chapter, you need to first assemble the appropriate GIF files to use on your Web page.

In this example, I'll show you how to use JavaScript to simulate the look-and-feel of the Windows 98/2000—style buttons, first popularized with Microsoft Internet Explorer 3. A button of this style looks flat until you place the mouse cursor on top of it, at which point it takes on a three-dimensional appearance. With that in mind, you will add Previous and Next buttons to the page to simulate the Prev and Next buttons of any browser.

To create animated pushbuttons like these, you need to do the following:

1. Create image placeholders on your Web page for each of the buttons.
2. Define Image objects and associate a GIF or JPG file with these language constructs.
3. Create a routine to display images on demand.
4. Add handlers for onMouseOver and onMouseOut events.
5. Add handler code for the Link object's click event.

To use Image objects to serve as button replacements, you can define the <img> tags. However, because Image objects don't respond to events, you need to encapsulate each of the images in a Link object. This is shown in the following code:

```
<a href="">
  <img src="./prev_off.gif" border="0" width="52" height="42" name="prev">
</a

<a href="">
  <img src="./next_off.gif" border="0" width="52" height="42" name="next">
</a>
```

Within a <script> tag in the <head> section of the HTML document, you need to define Image objects for each of the four images to be used: two representing the flat button look and two representing the 3D look. At this time, you also associate the Image object with an external source:

```
var prevBtnOff = new Image( 42, 52 );
prevBtnOff.src = "./prev_off.gif";

var prevBtnOn =  new Image( 42, 52 );
prevBtnOn.src = "./prev_on.gif";

var nextBtnOff = new Image( 42, 52 );
nextBtnOff.src = "./next_off.gif";

var nextBtnOn =  new Image( 42, 52 );
nextBtnOn.src = "./next_on.gif";
```

So far we have defined placeholder <img> tags for both the Previous and Next buttons and instantiated the associated Image objects for both their "off" and "on" states. Next, we can add a function called highlightButton() that changes the state of an image being displayed on demand.

The highlightButton() function has two parameters: One is the name of the <img> image placeholder, and one is the name of the Image object to be displayed. You can use the built-in document.images array to reference the <img> image placeholder:

```
function highlightButton(placeholder, imageObject){
  document.images[placeholder].src = eval(imageObject + ".src")
}
```

We now need to return to the <img> tag definitions to add the appropriate event handler code to them. For both animated buttons, when a mouse cursor passes over, we want the button to reflect an on, 3D-like state; otherwise, we want it to appear flat. You can add onMouseOver and onMouseOut event handlers to do just that. Therefore, when an onMouseOver event is triggered, the highlightButton() function is called for that button. Then, when the onMouseOut event is called, the highlightButton() function is called again for the off state image to appear:

```
<a href="javascript:history.back()"
  onmouseover="highlightButton('Prev','prevBtnOn');window.status='Previous';
     return true;"
  onmouseout="highlightButton('Prev','prevBtnOff');window.status='';
     return true;">
 <img src="./prev_off.gif" border="0" width="52" height="42" name="Prev">
</a>
<a href="javascript:history.forward()"
  onmouseover="highlightButton('Next','nextBtnOn');window.status='Next';
     return true;"
  onmouseout="highlightButton('Next','nextBtnOff');window.status='';
     return true;">
 <img src="./next_off.gif" border="0" width="52" height="42" name="Next">
</a>
```

The final step is to add code to respond to the clicking of an animated button. Because the Image object can't respond to a click event, you need to use the javascript: protocol in the <a> Link object's href property. As shown in the preceding code, the History object's back() and forward() methods are employed to provide the desired capabilities.

As a last cleanup, you need to add some code to the onMouseOver and onMouseOut event handers to customize the message in the browser's status bar. If you don't do this, the javascript: protocol is shown.

Figures 21.5 and 21.6 show the code in action.

Listing 21.4 provides the complete source code.

**FIGURE 21.5**
*The buttons in their normal flat state.*

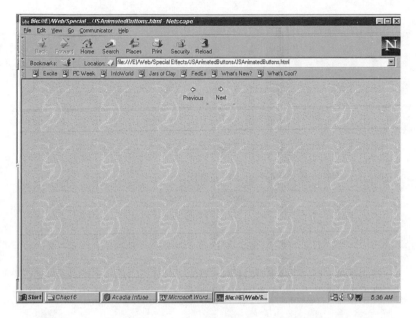

**FIGURE 21.6**
*The Previous button changes to the 3D state when the mouse cursor is over it.*

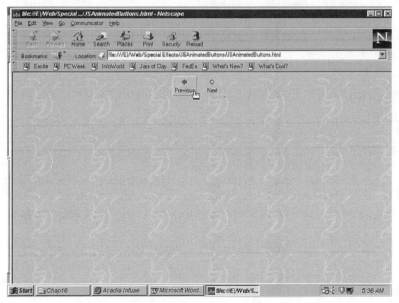

**LISTING 21.4**  Animating Buttons with JavaScript

```
<html>
<head>
```

LISTING 21.4    continued

```html
<title>JavaScript Unleashed</title>
<script type="text/javascript" language="JavaScript1.1">
<!--

  // Define image objects
  var prevBtnOff = new Image(42, 52);
  prevBtnOff.src = "./prev_off.gif";


  var prevBtnOn =  new Image(42, 52);
  prevBtnOn.src = "./prev_on.gif";


  var nextBtnOff = new Image(42, 52);
  nextBtnOff.src = "./next_off.gif";


  var nextBtnOn =  new Image(42, 52);
  nextBtnOn.src = "./next_on.gif";


  // Changes image being displayed.
  function highlightButton(placeholder, imageObject) {
    document.images[placeholder].src = eval(imageObject + ".src")
  }

//-->
  </script>
</head>
<body background="./aiback.gif">
  <center>
    <a href="javascript:history.back()"
      onmouseover="highlightButton('Prev','prevBtnOn');window.status='Previous';
        return true;"
      onmouseout="highlightButton('Prev','prevBtnOff');window.status='';
        return true;">
    <img src="./prev_off.gif" border="0" width="52" height="42" name="Prev">
    </a>
    <a href="javascript:history.forward()"
      onmouseover="highlightButton('Next','nextBtnOn');window.status='Next';
        return true;"
      onmouseout="highlightButton('Next','nextBtnOff');window.status='';
        return true;">
    <img src="./next_off.gif" border="0" width="52" height="42" name="Next">
    </a>
```

**LISTING 21.4**    continued

```
  </center>
</body>
</html>
```

# Summary

Let's be honest: Many Web sites are boring to look at and have little visual appeal. HTML by itself can do nothing more than place a flat image on a page and display it. Many people are using Java applets to add life to HTML but, as JavaScript matures, it's becoming an increasingly popular option as well.

JavaScript has added several capabilities, especially in the 1.1 and 1.2 versions, that let you enhance the appearance of your Web site. In this chapter, you looked at four of the most popular examples of using JavaScript to create special effects: marquees, billboards, animated buttons, and fading backgrounds.

# Cascading Style Sheets

**22**

**CHAPTER**

The introduction of cascading style sheets (CSS) into HTML has given developers a more powerful way to express style, enhance presentation, and define more consistent styles in HTML documents. Before CSS, one of the major disadvantages of publishing information to the Web was the fact that it was nearly impossible to have the control the traditional desktop publishing world had. You had to use all kinds of workarounds to have items placed in the right locations or for fonts to be of the right type and size. Often, you were forced to use HTML tables or rely on browser bugs to position your elements the way you wanted.

This all ended when CSS became a formalized recommendation from the World Wide Web Consortium (W3C). CSS enabled developers to specify the exact fonts and sizes they wanted their text to be, as well as the exact location (CSS positioning, or CSS-P) of elements.

In this chapter, I am going to introduce you to CSS and touch on some Navigator-only arrays that allow you to work with styles. This chapter is not meant to be a complete coverage of CSS, but rather a primer, so that you are familiar with CSS when we go over Dynamic HTML (DHTML) in Chapter 24, "DHTML Menus and Toolbars." We will also touch on CSS in terms of positioning in Chapter 23, "Layers."

> **Note**
>
> Complete coverage of CSS and its variations is beyond the scope of this book because only a subset pertains to JavaScript. If you would like more information on CSS, please visit the W3C Web site at http://www.w3.org.

# Basic Style Sheet Concepts

A style sheet consists of one or more style definitions (font sizes, font styles, text alignment, font and background colors, margins, padding, line height, and so on) for HTML elements that can be either linked or embedded in HTML documents. This functionality was created to give developers and Web designers the ability to have consistent styles and positioning throughout the document.

Over the next few pages, you are going to take an introductory look at this technology and how it applies to JavaScript. Additionally, you will get into some of the details of using CSS because it is an integral piece of technology in the implementation of DHTML.

# Standards

To successfully implement any kind of technology on a wide scale, there must be some kind of standard or formalized method of implementation. Like many of the standards being used by Internet developers today, CSS was created and is maintained by the World Wide Web Consortium (W3C). You will take a quick look at the various releases of the CSS Recommendation (*aka* standard), so that you have a better understanding of the history and direction of this technology.

## CSS Level 1

In December 1996, the first version of cascading style sheets (CSS1) was made an official Recommendation by the W3C. This was the first attempt to create a standardized method of applying styles to Web documents. It was obviously a giant step for developers and companies, because they were being given the flexibility and formatting they needed for their documents.

However, this Recommendation, which was last updated in January 1999, did not contain everything that was needed by developers—primarily the capability to position elements on a page and functions that would be needed for future uses, such as handheld and wireless devices.

## CSS-P

In August 1997, the W3C issued the Positioning with Cascading Style Sheet (CSS-P) Recommendation. This Recommendation contained a subset of properties that allowed developers to explicitly specify the location of their elements on a page. This, combined with CSS, gave developers the majority of the control, down to the pixel, that they needed to create stylish pages. It was also the combination of CSS1 and CSS-P that was first implemented in browsers, such as Navigator 4, Internet Explorer 4, and Opera 3.5.

## Level 2 Enhancements

The second version of the CSS Recommendation, CSS Level 2 or CSS2 for short, did several things. First and foremost, it combined the CSS1 and CSS-P Recommendations into a single Recommendation. It also implemented the concept of media types to best accommodate the need for styling print material or data delivered to Internet appliances or devices. CSS2 even added a property that specified the type of cursor that the application should use as the pointing device.

## Proposal for Level 3

The CSS group of the W3C is currently working on CSS Level 3 (CSS3). This latest edition, which has not been released yet, is attempting to provide not only support for scaleable vector graphics and international layout, but many other user interface enhancements as well. It will be this version that will take CSS to a more globally supported Recommendation, in much the same manner that HTML 4 did for HTML.

# Inheritance

It's important to remember the concept of inheritance when defining styles. The term *inheritance* is used to describe the concept by which a child has the same properties as the parent. For the definitions used here, *parent* and *child* refer to HTML elements that are grouped or contained within other elements. Style sheets give you the ability to set global styles for your documents and allow those styles to be passed to other elements within the document, thus saving you the time of defining styles for each element.

For example, the <body> element can have many children within it, including <h1> and <p>, whereas the <p> element will have fewer children (<em> is an example). For the majority of styles, the style of a parent is inherited by the child if the child has the same properties. You can safely assume that a <p> within the <body> will reflect the font size of the <body>, unless the <p> specifically overrides it. Styles are inherited inside containers for which they are defined. This functionality gives the document a more consistent look and feel.

Font sizes, text placement, and margins are excellent examples of how style sheets can help give a Web site consistency. When you define these styles generically in the parent elements, the styles will be inherited in the children of the document. Each document can have the same look and feel, while still giving the developer the option of manipulating and overriding the styles during runtime if desired.

> **Note**
>
> For the most part, styles that aren't inherited will be obvious. If the child doesn't have the same property as the parent, the child can't inherit the style.

# Margins and Padding

Not only can text properties be defined with CSS, padding, borders, and margins for block-level elements can also be defined. Block-level elements are elements such as <h1> and

<p>, which always start on a new line. These properties allow you to specify everything from the margins and padding around elements to borders.

## Comments

As in all coding, comments are important in your code. Writing comments in CSS is similar to defining comments in other well-known programming languages, except that it only officially supports what is commonly known as multi-line comments. For example

```
/* comment type 1 */
```

is an acceptable comment format in CSS.

# Using Styles in Your Document

There are several different methods of using styles in your documents. They can be placed inline, using the `style` attribute defined within a `<style>` section, or linked in, using the `<link>` tag. In addition to the methods of placing styles in your documents, there are also several ways to apply them. Styles can be applied globally, by assigning a class with the `class` attribute, or even on an individual basis with the `id` attribute.

## Defining Styles

As mentioned, styles are defined in one of three ways. By "defining a style," I mean that there are three locations where you can place a style. When creating a document that is using style sheets, you should use these methods to define your styles. There is not an exact rule on how you should do this; just try to implement it in a way that makes the most sense to you and those editing your documents.

### `<style>`

The first location for defining styles is within the `<style>` tag. This tag takes a single attribute (`type`) that tells the browser what kind of style is being defined. The value of this attribute for CSS is `text/css`. Between the beginning and ending tag are style definitions. Listing 22.1 gives an example of using this method of defining styles. In this example, you will see four different styles that are being applied to the text in the body of the document. Figure 22.1 shows the result of loading this example in a browser. Don't worry about the different types at this moment. We will cover them shortly.

**FIGURE 22.1**
*Header text over-ridden with class for Internet Explorer brow-sers.*

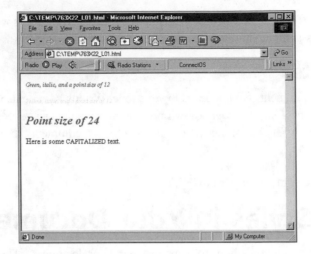

**LISTING 22.1**  Defining Styles in the `<style>` Tag

```html
<html>
<head>
  <style type="text/css">
  <!--
    h1{
      color: green;
      font-style: italic;
      font-size: 12pt;
    }

    h1.special{
      font-size: 24pt;
    }

    .newheader{
      color: yellow;
    }

    #caps{
      font-variant: small-caps;
    }
  -->
  </style>
</head>
<body>
  <h1>Green, italic, and a point size of 12</h1>
```

**LISTING 22.1**    continued

```
  <h1 class="newheader">Yellow, italic, and a point size of 12</h1>
  <h1 class="special">Point size of 24</h1>
  <p>
    Here is some <span id="caps">capitalized</span> text.
  </p>
</body>
</html>
```

## `<link>`

If you prefer to store all or a set of your styles in single location so that changes are applied globally across your site, you can use the `<link>` element. This element is used to link external style sheets to a document. The attributes of the `<link>` element, `type` and `href`, are used to define the type of link and the URL where the external style sheet can be located.

External cascading style sheets are built similarly to the CSS defined within the document. The style sheet is stored as a URL containing the style definitions, but the `<style>` and `</style>` HTML elements are not needed. This element should be contained in the `<head>` section of your document. The following example shows how you might include the style sheet named `chapters.css` in a given document:

```
<head>
  <link rel="stylesheet" type="text/css" href="http://www.mcp.com/stylesheets/
chapters.css">
</head>
```

## The `style` Attribute

The final method to define styles and include them in your documents is through the use of the `style` attribute of any HTML text element. `style` defines a new style to be used for that particular element instance only. This allows each element to have its own style, independent of any style defined in the current style sheet. The lowest-level selector involves defining a style for a particular instance of an element. This allows for very specific style definitions for each element. Styles are not often defined in this manner because of the difficulty of editing the style in the future. However, defining styles in this manner becomes extremely useful when the need to override a style occurs for only one particular instance of an element in the document.

For example, the code line

```
<h3 style="font-size: 36pt;">Hello</h3>
```

will make this particular <h3> a point size of 36.

# Applying Styles

After you have styles defined, you can apply them by using the id or class attributes or at a global level. Of course, the last method of defining styles discussed, using the style attribute, could also be a method of applying a style. It is actually a one-step method of defining and applying a style.

## Applying Styles Globally

To apply a style globally across all instances of an element, you have to specify the element and the corresponding style changes in your definition. For example, if I wanted to change all instances of the <p> tag to be displayed in italic 16-point font, I would put the following in the <head> portion of my document. When I use this method, these styles will be applied every time I use the <p> tag in this document.

```
<style type="text/css">
<!--
  p{
    font-style: italic;
    font-size: 16pt;
  }
-->
</style>
```

## The id Attribute

The second method of applying a style is with the the id attribute. When you use this method, you will define your styles in the <head> of your document and prepend the style name with a #. Listing 22.2 shows an example of creating a "heading" style that I then use on a <p> tag. Notice that only the <p> tag with the id="heading" value is affected. See Figure 22.2 for the result of loading this page in a browser.

**LISTING 22.2**   Using the id Attribute

```
<html>
<head>
  <style type="text/css">
  <!--
    #heading{
```

**Listing 22.2** continued

```
      font-style: italic;
      font-size: 24pt;
    }
  -->
  </style>
</head>
<body>
  <p id="heading">
    Welcome to my page!
  </p>
  <p>
    Here is some text.
  </p>
</body>
</html>
```

**Figure 22.2**
*Specifying styles with the* id *attribute.*

## The `class` Attribute

Styles that are defined by `class` are explicitly called with the HTML elements at each use. Style classes, as shown in Listing 22.3, are a way to group together style properties that you are going to use in several locations in your document. Defining styles to the document in classes rather than generically gives you more control over the use of the styles and allows for more flexibility on an element-by-element basis. This method can also make CSS more complicated because the HTML document has now become more complex, with much interwoven CSS class usage.

Defining classes of styles can be especially useful when styles need to apply to more than one type of HTML. It would be extremely tedious to define a style for multiple elements, each of which set the color to yellow. You can use classes to define one `yellowClass` and then use that class with any element that has the color property. Defining classes is the most effective method for making use of the flexibility of style sheets. Listing 22.3 shows an example of defining two classes of styles and applying them to different instances of the `<p>` tag.

**LISTING 22.3**  Using the `class` Attribute to Select a Style

```html
<html>
<head>
  <style type="text/css">
  <!--
    .heading{
      font-style: italic;
      font-size: 24pt;
    }

    .content{
      font-size: 12pt;
    }
  -->
  </style>
</head>
<body>
  <p class="heading">
    Welcome to my page!
  </p>
  <p class="content">
    Here is some text.
  </p>
</body>
</html>
```

## `<span>` Tags

The final method of applying a style is through the use of the `<span>` and `</span>` tags. These tags are used to mark a specific piece of text to which a style will be applied. This element is used when a section of text within an element (not the entire element) needs to have a style applied. This allows you to apply a style to content that has already had a style applied. Listing 22.4 shows an example of how you can override default styles using this tag.

**LISTING 22.4**   Using the `<span>` Tag

```html
<html>
<head>
  <style type="text/css">
  <!--
    p{
      font-style: italic;
      font-size: 24pt;
    }

    #smaller{
      font-size: 12pt;
    }
  -->
  </style>
</head>
<body>
  <p>
    Here is some text that has global styles applied, but
    <span id="smaller">here is some smaller text</span> in
    the middle of this paragraph.
  </p>
</body>
</html>
```

## Mixing Selectors

The implementation of multiple style sheets brings up the possibility of multiple style definitions for HTML elements. Any style definitions in a style sheet will always take precedence over any styles that have been previously defined for the document. The use of multiple style sheets can be beneficial when generic styles apply to the entire document and certain styles need to be overwritten for only a portion of the document. This is helpful when a corporate style is defined for the beginning of a document and the developer would like different styles to take precedence.

Listing 22.5 mixes selectors of different types, to achieve the effect shown in Figure 22.3. This includes applying attributes of different selector types (one `class` and one `id` attribute) and using the `<span>` tag inside of another tag with a class defined.

FIGURE **22.3**
*Mixed and matched selectors.*

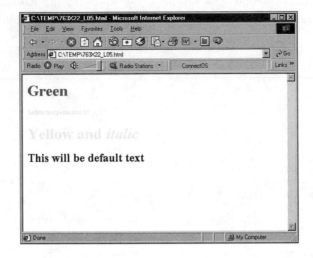

LISTING 22.5    Combining Styles in a Single Style Definition

```html
<html>
<head>
  <style type="text/css">
  <!--
    h1{
      color: green;
    }

    #ital{
      font-style: italic;
    }

    .newheader{
      color: yellow;
    }

    #myid{
      font-size: 12pt;
    }
  -->
  </style>
</head>
<body>
  <h1>Green</h1>
```

**LISTING 22.5**    continued

```
 <h1 class="newheader" id="myid">Yellow and point size 12</h1>
 <h1 class="newheader">Yellow and <span id="ital">italic</span></h1>
 <h2>This will be default text<h2>
</body>
</html>
```

## Determining Style Precedence

To find the value or precedence of a style for an element (and property), you must adhere to the following rules:

1. Locate all references to the element by any selector.

2. Sort the references by explicit weight.

3. Sort by origin of style sheet. Default values are overridden by user style sheets, which are overridden by author style sheets.

4. Sort by specificity. Give one point for each of the following three options, and then sum the points to get specificity:

   - The number of `id` attributes
   - The number of `class` attributes
   - The number of tag names referenced

5. Sort by the order specified. For two rules with identical weights, the latter rule will take precedence.

Using these five rules, you can accurately determine and account for the style that will be applied for an element when you're developing documents using CSS.

# JavaScript Style Objects

In JavaScript 1.2, Netscape added three new JavaScript objects—`tag`, `class`, and `id`—for use with style sheets. These objects are used to define the types of styles that can be applied to style definitions. These style definitions can be in external style sheets that are linked to the HTML document, or they can be defined in the document itself, within the `<style>` and `</style>` elements.

> **Note**
>
> Currently, only Navigator 4+ supports the method of accessing styles through these objects. While other browsers may or may not provide a method to do so, take special care if you use these tags to assign styles.

## document.tags

The `document.tags` array is a reference to HTML tags and, in truth, is a sub-object of the `Document` object. Following the definition is the element to which it applies. After the element definition is the style property that is being defined (which does not necessarily have the same name as defined in CSS). The full syntax of a definition specifying that all `<p>` tags should have a font size of 20 is as follows:

```
document.tags.p.fontSize = "20pt";
```

## document.classes

`document.classes` is also an array and a sub-object of the `Document` object. This array contains access to tags with the `class` attribute specified. A style class can apply to one particular element

```
document.classes.fontclass.blockquote.fontSize = "20pt";
```

or it can be defined to be accessible to all elements

```
document.classes. fontclass.all.fontSize = "20pt";
```

Following the object in the dot notation is the name of the `class` and then the element for which the class is defined. Classes defined as `all` can be applied to all elements, as shown in the second example.

## document.ids

The `document.ids` object is similar to `document.classes`, except that any element that references that `id` will be rendered with the style defined.

```
document.id.myid.fontSize = "20pt";
```

The `document.ids` object tag is followed by the name of the `id` and, unlike the `document.classes` and `document.tags` objects, it doesn't take the element name (or `all`) as part of the definition. `document.ids` objects can be used with any element to which they apply.

# Properties

Table 22.1 shows the properties available through the JavaScript style objects that you can use to define styles on your pages.

**TABLE 22.1**  JavaScript Style Objects Properties

| Property Name | What It Applies To | Possible Values | Value Definitions |
| --- | --- | --- | --- |
| | | *Font Properties* | |
| fontSize | All elements | Absolute sizes | x-small, small, medium, large, x-large, point size |
| | | Relative sizes | smaller, larger |
| | | Percentage | 150% bigger |
| fontStyle | All elements | | normal, italic, oblique, small-caps |
| | | *Text Properties* | |
| lineHeight | Block-level elements | Number | Units to increase height by |
| | | Length | Absolute value of line height |
| | | Percentage | Percentage of parent |
| verticalAlign | All elements | | baseline, sub, sup, top, text-top middle, bottom, text-bottom |
| textDecoration | All elements | | none, underline, overline, line-through, blink |
| textTransform | All elements | | capitalize, uppercase, lowercase, none |
| textAlign | Block-level elements | | left, right, center, justify |
| textIndent | Block-level elements | Length | Numerical units to indent |
| | | Percentage | Percentage of parent |
| | | *Block-Level Properties* | |
| paddings() | All elements | Number | Number of units of padding |
| | | Percentage | Percentage of parent |
| borderWidths() | All elements | Number | Number of units for width of border |
| margins() | All elements | Length | Margins in number of units |
| | | Percentage | Percentage of parent |
| | | Auto | Document autosizes margins |

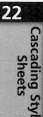

**22**

**Cascading Style Sheets**

**TABLE 22.1** continued

| Property Name | What It Applies To | Possible Values | Value Definitions |
|---|---|---|---|
| *Block-Level Properties* | | | |
| borderStyle | All elements | | none, solid, 3D |
| width | Block-level elements | Length | Width in units |
| | | Percentage | Percentage of parent |
| | | Auto | Document autosizes width |
| length | Block-level elements | Length | Length in units |
| | | Auto | Document autosizes length |
| align | All elements | | left, right, none |
| *Color Properties* | | | |
| color | All elements | Color | color names, RGB colors |
| backgroundImage | All elements | | URL |
| backgroundColor | All elements | Color | color names, RGB colors |
| *Classification Properties* | | | |
| display | All elements | | block, inline, list-item, none |
| listStyleType | Elements with display property | | disc, circle, square, decimal, lower and upper-roman, lower and upper-alpha, none |
| whiteSpace | Block-level elements | Normal and pre | |

# Summary

Cascading style sheets offer Web developers greater control over the style of documents they create. Developers can define default styles both internally and externally to the document, and these styles can be applied against a wide range of elements. A wide range of style properties are currently available that allow developers control over how their content looks.

# CHAPTER 23

# Layers

Until recently, one of the fundamental limitations of Web pages has been the inability to position text or images on a page precisely. Additionally, there was no way to overlap HTML elements on a page. One of the most innovative aspects of the newer browsers is the support for layers. Layers let you define overlays of transparent or solid content in an HTML document, which can be positioned precisely where you want it. Layers can be implemented using several different techniques, and for those of you who are knee-deep in the Web publishing world, you know this is often a cause of confusion.

In the non-Navigator 4 world, a layer was created using an HTML tag and applying several cascading style sheet (CSS) properties to position, show, and control the stacking of the tag. Simply by the nature of what the `<div>` tag represents (a division of data), it was the most logical choice for creating layers, and it is what was commonly used. Now, let's introduce Navigator 4, which was released with Netscape's Communicator suite of Internet tools in 1997.

Navigator 4 included two new tags: `<layer>` and `<ilayer>` (the "i" stands for *inflow*). These tags took a different path from the standardized use of `<div>` tags, which Navigator does support, to create layers in an HTML document. Unlike the `<div>` tag, the `<layer>` and `<ilayer>` tags did have attributes that essentially allow you to "style" them. To create a layer with absolute positioning (that is, to locate the layer at specific coordinates), use the `<layer>` tag. To create a layer with relative positioning (to appear exactly where you put the tag in the HTML page), use the `<ilayer>` tag.

The only real benefit that I saw in these two tags from Netscape, other than their capability to be styled within their attributes (which is a very minor benefit), was their capability to pull in external HTML files for their content. This was accomplished using the `src` attribute of the tag. However, to combat that argument, there is an `<iframe>` tag (the "i" is for *inline*) that is part of the HTML 4 Recommendation, which can be styled with CSS, that has the same functionality. Unfortunately, Navigator 4 did not support his tag. Hence the fork in the implementation of layers.

> **Note**
>
> At this point your head is probably beginning to hurt, and you are wondering why anyone would even mess with layers. Well, help is on the way. As mentioned, the real problem lies in the fact that Navigator 4 broke from the standards. However, there is hope. Navigator 5, the Open Source browser from Mozilla.org, supports CSS and HTML 4, which includes the styles you need for positioning, and the tags such as `<iframe>`, which you want for pulling in external files.

That is all the specifics of these implementations we are going to talk about for now. They will be covered in more detail later in the chapter, so we are going to move on to assessing the use and benefits of layers from a higher level. In this chapter we are going to look at not only some universal practices, but also at using the `<div>` and `<iframe>` method and the `<layer>` and `<ilayer>` method for deploying layers.

# Universal Practices

Despite the fork in the implementation of layers we spoke of earlier, things are definitely moving toward a more universal implementation. In this section of the chapter, we will look at some of the universal practices and theories that apply no matter what method you use to deploy layers on your pages.

## Using Style Sheets for Layering

As we mentioned in the introduction of this chapter, the proper and standardized way of implementing layers is to control them through the use of style sheets. This would include everything from the positioning and styling of the data included in the layer to the stacked location and visibility of the layer. The properties of CSS that we are going to focus on are in the following bulleted list.

- position
- left, right, top, and bottom
- height and width
- z-index
- visibility

**23**

Layers

> **Note**
>
> Please note that we will not go into all the properties of CSS in this chapter. Please refer to Chapter 22, "Cascading Style Sheets," for more information on style sheets.

### position

The `position` property is used to tell the browser how and where to place elements that have this property applied. There are four different values of this property, all of which are listed and described in Table 23.1.

TABLE 23.1   Values of the position Property

| Value | Description |
|-------|-------------|
| absolute | This value tells the browser that you will be specifying the absolute coordinates of the element. When you use this value, you also use the top and left properties. If these are not specified, the browser assumes the x and y coordinates are 0 (the top-left corner of the browser window). |
| fixed | This value is the same as absolute, except that it does not move when the window is scrolled. |
| relative | This value lets you offset the element based on the previous element. |
| static | This is the default value that is used in rendering HTML in today's browsers. |

To help you understand how this property works, look at Listing 23.1. In this listing, I placed three <p> tags within the body of the document. Each of these has been named and has a style ID. In the <head> of the document, I have given each of the IDs a different background-color (for ease of seeing the difference), left, and top value. You will also notice that I have set the position property to absolute. Figure 23.1 shows what this looks like in an Internet Explorer browser.

**Note**

I purposely did not use the <div> tag in this example to demonstrate that these types of styles can be applied to any element.

**FIGURE 23.1**

*Specifying the absolute positioning of HTML elements.*

**LISTING 23.1**  Specifying the Absolute Positioning of HTML Elements with CSS Properties

```html
<html>
<head>
  <title>JavaScript Unleashed</title>
  <style type="text/css">
  <!--
  #first{
  background-color: green;
  left: 0;
  position: absolute;
  top: 0;
  }

  #second{
  background-color: red;
  left: 30;
  position: absolute;
  top: 30;
  }

  #third{
  background-color: blue;
  left: 60;
  position: absolute;
  top: 60;
  }
  -->
  </style>
</head>
<body>
  <p name="layer1" id="first">
    Layer 1
  </p>
  <p name="layer2" id="second">
    Layer 2
  </p>
  <p name="layer3" id="third">
    Layer 3
  </p>
</body>
</html>
```

**23**

**Layers**

## left, right, top, and bottom

As you saw in the previous example, there are certain CSS properties that allow you to specify the exact location of an element. When using these properties, which take numerical values for coordinates, you will not use all of them at once. For instance, an element cannot have the `right` property set at the same time a `left` property is set. The same is true for `top` and `bottom`. If you try to do this, most browsers default to the property that is last in your style definition to be applied.

For example, look at Listing 23.2. I have expanded on the previous listing and added a fourth layer and style definition. I have used the various combinations of the `right`, `left`, `top`, and `bottom` properties to place squares in each of the four corners of the browser window, as shown in Figure 23.2.

**LISTING 23.2**   Using the `right`, `left`, `top`, and `bottom` Properties

```html
<html>
<head>
 <title>JavaScript Unleashed</title>
 <style type="text/css">
 <!--
 #first{
 background-color: green;
 left: 0;
 position: absolute;
 top: 0;
 }

 #second{
 background-color: red;
 position: absolute;
 right: 0;
 top: 0;
 }

 #third{
 background-color: blue;
 bottom: 0;
 position: absolute;
 right: 0;
 }

 #fourth{
 background-color: yellow;
```

**LISTING 23.2**  continued

```
  bottom: 0;
  left: 0;
  position: absolute;
  }

  -->
  </style>
</head>
<body>
  <p name="layer1" id="first">
    Layer 1
  </p>
  <p name="layer2" id="second">
    Layer 2
  </p>
  <p name="layer3" id="third">
    Layer 3
  </p>
  <p name="layer4" id="fourth">
    Layer 4
  </p>
</body>
</html>
```

**FIGURE 23.2**
*Specifying the right, left, top, and bottom positions of HTML elements.*

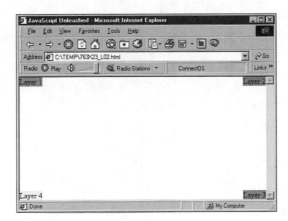

## height **and** width

The next two properties allow you to specify the height and width of your layers. Understandably, these properties are called `height` and `width`. Like the properties that allow you to specify the location of layers, these two properties take numerical values for how tall and wide a layer should be. In Listing 23.3, I have worked even more on our example by giving our four layers specified `height` and `width` values. You can see the result in Figure 23.3.

LISTING 23.3    Using `height` and `width` to Specify the Size of Your Layers

```
<html>
<head>
  <title>JavaScript Unleashed</title>
  <style type="text/css">
<!--
#first{
background-color: green;
height:20;
left: 0;
position: absolute;
top: 0;
width: 40;
}

#second{
background-color: red;
height:10;
position: absolute;
right: 0;
top: 0;
width: 30;
}

#third{
background-color: blue;
bottom: 0;
height:100;
position: absolute;
right: 0;
width: 50;
}
```

**LISTING 23.3** continued

```
#fourth{
background-color: yellow;
bottom: 0;
height:100;
left: 0;
position: absolute;
width: 200;
}

-->
</style>
</head>
<body>
  <p name="layer1" id="first">
    Layer 1
  </p>
  <p name="layer2" id="second">
    Layer 2
  </p>
  <p name="layer3" id="third">
    Layer 3
  </p>
  <p name="layer4" id="fourth">
    Layer 4
  </p>
</body>
</html>
```

**FIGURE 23.3**
*Specifying how tall and wide layers are.*

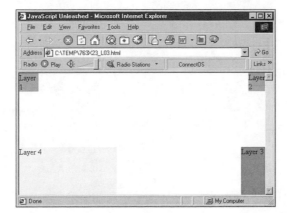

## z-index

Now it is time to get into the good stuff in terms of layers. Up to this point, we have only been defining how the layer looks—its style characteristics. Now we are going to start stacking those layers so that we can get the effect of overlapping layers. To do this, we will use the z-index property.

The z-index property contains a numerical value that specifies the location of the layer relative to the browser window, which is zero (0). Setting z-index to a value of 1 would mean that you place the layer above the browser window. This is how they appear on a page. However, if you have overlapping layers and one of them has a z-index of 1, it will overlap the other. Remember that the browser window is 0, which is below 1.

Before we jump into an example, look at Listing 23.4. It has four layers that overlap. This is not because they have z-index values set, but because of the order in which they appear in the document. The first layer is at the bottom, then the second, third, and fourth. Figure 23.4 shows what this looks like.

**LISTING 23.4**  Layers That Have Overlapping Coordinates

```html
<html>
<head>
  <title>JavaScript Unleashed</title>
  <style type="text/css">
<!--
#first{
background-color: green;
height: 100;
left: 0;
position: absolute;
top: 0;
width: 100;
}

#second{
background-color: red;
height: 100;
left: 20;
position: absolute;
top: 20;
width: 100;
}
```

**LISTING 23.4**    continued

```
#third{
background-color: blue;
height: 100;
left: 40;
position: absolute;
top: 40;
width: 100;
}

#fourth{
background-color: yellow;
height: 100;
left: 60;
position: absolute;
top: 60;
width: 100;
}

-->
</style>
</head>
<body>
  <p name="layer1" id="first">
    Layer 1
  </p>
  <p name="layer2" id="second">
    Layer 2
  </p>
  <p name="layer3" id="third">
    Layer 3
  </p>
  <p name="layer4" id="fourth">
    Layer 4
  </p>
</body>
</html>
```

**23**

**Layers**

**FIGURE 23.4**
*Layers overlapping due to their order in the document.*

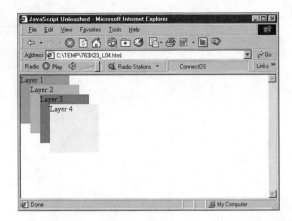

As you can see, the order of the layers plays an important role in how they are displayed. Are they really stacked on top of each other? No—they just appear to be. However, we can order them by specifying the z-index property. Of course, if we place them in the same order, they will look exactly the same, so this property is most often used to change the order, rather than to specify them in the default order when building your pages.

Let's now take a look at Listing 23.5. As you can see in this listing, I have given both the first and third layer a z-index value. Because I want the first layer to be on top, I have given it a value of 2 and the third layer a value of 1. Look at Figure 23.5 to see the result of loading this listing in a browser.

**LISTING 23.5**  Changing the z-index of the Layers

```
<html>
<head>
  <title>JavaScript Unleashed</title>
  <style type="text/css">
<!--
#first{
background-color: green;
height: 100;
left: 0;
position: absolute;
top: 0;
width: 100;
z-index: 2;
}

#second{
background-color: red;
```

LISTING 23.5    continued

```
  height: 100;
  left: 20;
  position: absolute;
  top: 20;
  width: 100;
  }

  #third{
  background-color: blue;
  height: 100;
  left: 40;
  position: absolute;
  top: 40;
  width: 100;
  z-index: 1;
  }

  #fourth{
  background-color: yellow;
  height: 100;
  left: 60;
  position: absolute;
  top: 60;
  width: 100;
  }

  -->
  </style>
</head>
<body>
  <p name="layer1" id="first">
    Layer 1
  </p>
  <p name="layer2" id="second">
    Layer 2
  </p>
  <p name="layer3" id="third">
    Layer 3
  </p>
  <p name="layer4" id="fourth">
    Layer 4
  </p>
```

**LISTING 23.5**    continued

```
</body>
</html>
```

**FIGURE 23.5**
*Changing the overlap of the previous example.*

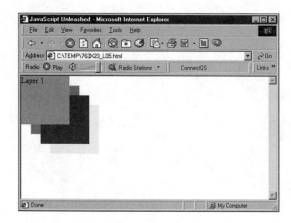

## visibility

The final property that we are going to look at is the `visibility` property. This property has four possible values, which are listed and defined in Table 23.2. As you might guess, this property is responsible for hiding and exposing layers.

**TABLE 23.2**    Values of the `visibility` Property

| Value | Description |
| --- | --- |
| collapse | This is the same as `hidden` (below), except when used on tables. |
| hidden | This hides the element. |
| inherit | This is the browser's default value; takes the same value as its parent. |
| visible | This makes the element visible. |

To demonstrate this property, I am going to take the code from the previous example and add two lines to it. Remember the two layers that we gave a `z-index` value to? This brought them to the front of the page. In their style definition, I am going to set their `visibility` to `hidden`. Listing 23.6 shows the code that I used, and Figure 23.6 shows that these two layers are no longer seen.

**LISTING 23.6**    Using the `visibility` Property to Hide Elements

```
<html>
<head>
```

**LISTING 23.6**   continued

```
<title>JavaScript Unleashed</title>
<style type="text/css">
<!--
#first{
background-color: green;
height: 100;
left: 0;
position: absolute;
top: 0;
width: 100;
z-index: 2;
visibility: hidden;
}

#second{
background-color: red;
height: 100;
left: 20;
position: absolute;
top: 20;
width: 100;
}

#third{
background-color: blue;
height: 100;
left: 40;
position: absolute;
top: 40;
width: 100;
z-index: 1;
visibility: hidden;
}

#fourth{
background-color: yellow;
height: 100;
left: 60;
position: absolute;
top: 60;
width: 100;
}
```

**LISTING 23.6**    continued

```
    -->
    </style>
</head>
<body>
  <p name="layer1" id="first">
    Layer 1
  </p>
  <p name="layer2" id="second">
    Layer 2
  </p>
  <p name="layer3" id="third">
    Layer 3
  </p>
  <p name="layer4" id="fourth">
    Layer 4
  </p>
</body>
</html>
```

**FIGURE 23.6**
*Hiding layers.*

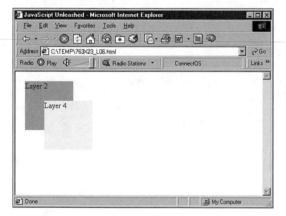

## Managing Overlying Layers

Using the CSS properties that we have talked about allows you to perform some interesting visual effects. For example, suppose you wanted to display some chart report data on a Web page. Your goal is to display one chart at a time and to give the user the option of viewing one of the other charts. Perhaps if you were working in a Windows environment, you could imagine the use of a tabbed window for this purpose, with each chart being shown on a separate tab. Layers make it possible to have a similar effect on a Web page.

In creating these layers, however, it is important to remember that you need to manage them effectively. Reproducing tabs, lists, or other menu style items you see in everyday applications is not easy. You have to remember the previous state of an element or an entire set of elements, so that when one changes, they all do. For instance, if you click outside a cascading menu, you want the menu to go away—which means you also have to capture clicks. We will not discuss these items here; they are covered in more detail in Chapter 24, "DHTML Menus and Toolbars."

## Creating Animation Effects

Another intriguing aspect of layers is the way you can use them to create animations. Because JavaScript lets you position layers dynamically, you can create recursive routines in which layers can appear to slide or jump across the document. It is this combination of HTML and JavaScript that allows you to create Dynamic HTML (DHTML).

Using layers, JavaScript, and style sheets, you can create (with HTML), design (with CSS), and manipulate (with JavaScript) elements on a page. With advancements such as better support of the Document Object Model (DOM) and XML (eXtensible Markup Language) in browsers around the corner, the possibilities are endless.

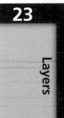

## `<div>` and `<iframe>`

Now that we have covered the basics of creating layers, it is time to get into the specifics. Even though the Netscape method of using `<layer>` and `<ilayer>` for implementing layers has been deprecated, we will still cover it later in this chapter. For now, we will look at the more universal method of implementing them, using the `<div>` and `<iframe>` tags.

# Defining Data Blocks

One of the first steps in creating layers is to define the block of data that you consider to be a layer. If you think of a regular application such as a browser, the window might be considered the first layer. When you click on a menu, however, the menu itself is displayed above the window—this would be a second layer on top of the first layer. If you click on a submenu that cascades out, then this is another layer (it might or might not be of the same level as the first).

The current method of defining these blocks of data is through the use of the <div> tag. This tag creates a defined block-level structure in a document. In terms of rendering, it is similar to the <p> tag, except that <p> is supposed to not only dictate the start of a new paragraph but also define the data within it as part of a paragraph. The <div> tag, on the other hand, defines the data more than it tells the browser how to render it.

Before we get into moving layers, or <div> blocks, in this method, we are going to take a look at the attributes of this tag and what they mean. These are all contained in Table 23.3.

**TABLE 23.3**  Attributes of the <div> Tag

| Value | Description |
|---|---|
| align | Used to align the data contained inside the <div> tag  and can take values of left, right, center, and justify. Deprecated in favor of using CSS to align elements. |
| class | A comma-separated list of style classes that make the tag an instance of those classes. |
| dir | Specifies the text direction of any text contained in the tag. Value ltr means *left to right* and rtl means *right to left*. |
| id | Often used by style sheets to define the type of style that should be applied to the data in the tag. |
| lang | Identifies the human language code of the data within the tag. |
| name | Used to give the instance of the block a name. Can be used by JavaScript to manipulate the layers. |
| style | Allows you to specify a style definition within the tag, rather than in a style sheet. |
| title | Allows you to provide a more informative title for the tag than the <title> tag, which applies to the whole document. |

# Defining a Data Block

Using the <div> tag is easy. All you have to do is place it around the elements you want to define as a block of data. Listing 23.7 shows how this is done. As you see, there are two <div> blocks in this example. Within the first one are two horizontal rules (<hr> tags), and the text DIV 1. In the second block, I have included a level 3 heading (<h3> tag) and a paragraph (<p> tag). I have also included some text before and after each <div> block so that you can see where they start and end. Figure 23.7 shows what this looks like in an Opera browser.

**LISTING 23.7**   Using the <div> Tag

```
<html>
<head>
  <title>JavaScript Unleashed</title>
</head>
<body>
  Before the first block.
  <div name="layer1">
    <hr>
    DIV 1
    <hr>
  </div>
  After the first block.
  <br>
  Before the second block.
  <div name="layer2">
    <h3>
      DIV 2
    </h3>
    <p>
      I am inside the second DIV block.
    </p>
  </div>
  After the second block.
</body>
</html>
```

## Positioning Your <div> Blocks

The next thing is to apply positioning to these blocks of data. To do this, we assign the id property of the tags and define style properties for each. We are going to define the location, size, and background colors first, so that they are readily apparent. These are all items we looked at earlier in the chapter. Listing 23.8 shows the code to do this, and Figure 23.8 shows what it looks like. As you see in the figure, I have set the positioning so that the second block appears to the left of the first one, and the first one also overlaps some of the text.

**FIGURE 23.7**
*Defining blocks
of data in your
documents.*

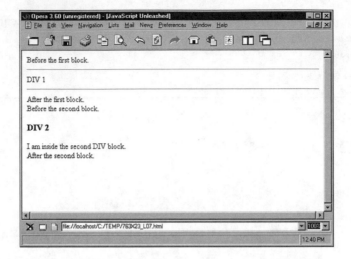

**LISTING 23.8**   Applying Style Sheets and Position to Your `<div>` Blocks

```html
<html>
<head>
  <title>JavaScript Unleashed</title>
  <style type="text/css">
  <!--
    #first{
    background-color: green;
    height: 100;
    left: 275;
    position: absolute;
    top: 40;
    width: 100;
    }

    #second{
    background-color: red;
    height: 100;
    left: 100;
    position: absolute;
    top: 55;
    width: 100;
    }
  -->
  </style>
</head>
<body>
```

**LISTING 23.8**    continued

```
Before the first block.
<div name="layer1" id="first">
  <hr>
  DIV 1
  <hr>
</div>
After the first block.
<br>
Before the second block.
<div name="layer2" id="second">
  <h3>
    DIV 2
  </h3>
  <p>
    I am inside the second DIV block.
  </p>
</div>
After the second block.
</body>
</html>
```

**FIGURE 23.8**

*Positioning blocks of data.*

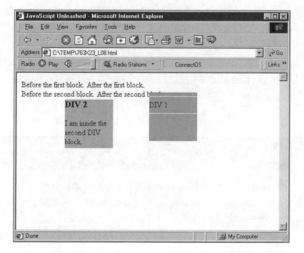

## Manipulating with JavaScript

Now that we have had a primer in creating layers and specifying their characteristics, we can start to add the power of JavaScript to the mix. In this section, we are going to introduce you to the JavaScript capability to change dynamically the presentation of layers and move them.

> **Note**
>
> The main focus of this chapter is to introduce you to layers. If you have a full understanding of how to create layers and access them in JavaScript, you may want to proceed to Chapter 24 for more detail on the use of these two technologies.

The first thing you need to understand in accessing layers in JavaScript is the syntax that should be used. Because of the differences in implementation between Internet Explorer and Navigator, you will have to access layers using different methods.

In Navigator browsers, you access them via the `layers` array. Because you have the `name` attribute set in the `<div>` tag, you are able to specify the name of the layer. From our previous example, the following line of code could be used to access the first layer:

```
document.layers['layer']
```

Internet Explorer is a bit different, in that you access layers through the `all` array. The value you pass to specify the layer you are accessing is not held in the `name` attribute of the `<div>` tag, but in the `id` attribute. For the previous example, use the following line of code to access the first layer. Notice that I used `first` here. This is the value of the `id` attribute:

```
document.all['first']
```

> **Note**
>
> This is not the only way to access layers with JavaScript. However, it is the best way to do so across Navigator and Internet Explorer because it reduces the amount of coding needed.

In the Navigator world, you can access the properties of a layer immediately after the `document.layers['layerName']` declaration. For Internet Explorer, however, you access it through the `style` array, which means your syntax will be something such as `document.all['`*`layerName`*`']style`. An example will help explain.

Let's assume that `isNav` means that the browser is a Navigator browser and that `isIE` is an Internet Explorer browser. In the following `if` conditional statement, we will hide the first layer in Listing 23.8.

```
if(isIE){
  document.all['first'].style.visibility = "hidden";
}else if(isNav)[
  document.layers['layer1'].visibility = "hidden";
}
```

When creating scripts to run in both browsers we want to use the same value for both `name` and `id` in the `<div>` tag. The next thing is to store the reference to the array we want to access in a variable. We can do the same for Internet Explorer's style requirement. The following pseudo-code will take care of these issues.

```
var layer = new String();
var style = new String();

if(isIE){
  layer = ".all";
  style = "style";
}else if(isNav){
  layer = ".layers";
  style = "";
}
```

We have all the information we need at this point to build a cross-browser function that will handle layers. However, there is one last step that involves the user of the `eval()` method. This method will take a string and evaluate it as if it were a JavaScript call. We can "build" the proper call to access and change a property of a layer, such as `visibility`.

In Listing 23.9, all of this is pulled together. As you will see, I have created a single layer that appears under two buttons, through some CSS-P properties. After the page loads, the `checkBrowser()` function is called, which specifies if the browser is Internet Explorer or Navigator. It also stores the proper array to access the layers in a `layer` variable.

Each of the buttons makes a call to a `changeState()` function, passing it a value and a layer reference. The value tells the function whether it should show the layer that was passed. This function then takes the parameters passed and uses the `eval()` method to change the state of the layer. Figure 23.9 shows what the page looks like before the Hide button is pressed. This example works in both Internet Explorer and Navigator.

LISTING 23.9  Accessing Layers with JavaScript

```
<html>
<head>
  <title>JavaScript Unleashed</title>
  <style type="text/css">
  <!--
    #layer1{
    background-color: green;
    height: 100;
    left: 10;
    position: absolute;
    top: 50;
    width: 100;
    }
  -->
  </style>
  <script type="text/javascript" language="JavaScript1.2">
  <!--
    // Create global variables for browser type
    var layer = new String();
    var style = new String();

    // Determine if the browser is Internet Explorer, Navigator,
    // or other. Also, set the layer variable depending on the
    // type of access it needs.
    function checkBrowser(){
      if(navigator.userAgent.indexOf("MSIE") != -1){
        layer = ".all";
        style = ".style";
      }else if(navigator.userAgent.indexOf("Nav") != -1){
        layer = ".layers";
        style = "";
      }
    }

    // Take the state passed in, and change it.
    function changeState(layerRef, state){
      eval("document" + layer + "['" + layerRef + "']" + style +
➥        ".visibility = '" + state + "'");
    }
  //-->
  </script>
</head>
```

LISTING 23.9    continued

```
<body onload="checkBrowser()">
  <div name="layer1" id="layer1">
    DIV 1
  </div>
  <form name="form1">
    <input type="button" value="Hide"
➥      onclick="changeState('layer1','hidden')">
    <input type="button" value="Show"
➥      onclick="changeState('layer1','visible')">
  <form>
</body>
</html>
```

FIGURE 23.9

*The contents of the page before a button is pressed.*

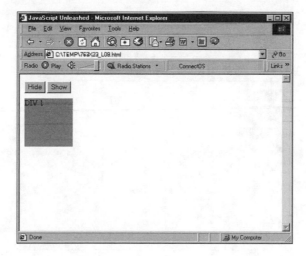

# Pulling in External Files

Using the <iframe> tag, you are able to pull in external files. This allows you to manage your content better and provides a mechanism to include content from a different location.

> **Caution**
>
> Even though the <iframe> tag is part of the HTML 4 Recommendation, it is not currently supported by Navigator browsers. However, support for this tag will be added in Navigator 5 (*aka* Mozilla), the open source browser from Mozilla.org. To

simulate the functionality of this tag until then, you can use the `<ilayer>` tag for Navigator 4.x browsers.

A good example of the use of this tag would be a Current News section on your site. Suppose you want to change the news daily, but you don't want to update every page on which it appears every day. Using the `<iframe>` tag, you can reference a single page that contains the news for that day. This allows you to make the change in a single location and effect the change on all of your pages.

To clarify, let's take an example. As you see in Listing 23.10, we will call in an external page called `news.html` (Listing 23.11). The tag will reference this page using its `src` attribute and apply other attributes. In Figure 23.10, I have given `<iframe>` a border so that you can see it more easily. Also, Table 23.4 lists the attributes of the `<iframe>` tag.

**FIGURE 23.10**
*The result of loading Listing 23.10 in Internet Explorer.*

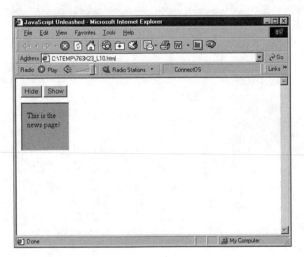

**LISTING 23.10**   Using the `<iframe>` Tag to Load External Files

```html
<html>
<head>
  <title>JavaScript Unleashed</title>
  <style type="text/css">
  <!--
    #layer1{
    height: 100;
    left: 10;
    position: absolute;
```

**LISTING 23.10** continued

```
    top: 50;
    width: 100;
    }
  -->
  </style>
  <script type="text/javascript" language="JavaScript1.2">
  <!--
    // Create global variables for browser type
    var isIE = new Boolean(false);
    var isNav = new Boolean(false);
    var unSupported = new Boolean(false);
    var layer = new String();
    var style = new String();

    // Determine if the browser is Internet Explorer, Navigator,
    // or other. Also, set the layer variable depending on the
    // type of access it needs.
    function checkBrowser(){
      if(navigator.userAgent.indexOf("MSIE") != -1){
        isIE = true;
        layer = ".all";
        style = ".style";
      }else if(navigator.userAgent.indexOf("Nav") != -1){
        isNav = true;
        layer = ".layers";
        style = "";
      }else{
        unSupported = true;
      }
    }

    // Take the state passed in, and change it.
    function changeState(layerRef, state){
      eval("document" + layer + "['" + layerRef + "']" + style
          + ".visibility = '" + state + "'");
    }
  //-->
  </script>
</head>
<body onload="checkBrowser()">
```

23

Layers

LISTING 23.10    continued

```
<iframe name="layer1" id="layer1" src="news.html" frameborder="1"
    noresize scrolling="no"></iframe>
<form name="form1">
  <input type="button" value="Hide"
      onclick="changeState('layer1','hidden')">
  <input type="button" value="Show"
      onclick="changeState('layer1','visible')">
<form>
</body>
</html>
```

LISTING 23.11    The Contents of the External File

```
<html>
<head>
  <title>JavaScript Unleashed</title>
</head>
<body bgcolor="red">
  <p>
    This is the news page!
  </p>
</body>
</html>
```

TABLE 23.4    Attributes of the `<iframe>` Tag

| Value | Description |
| --- | --- |
| align | Used to align the data inside the `<iframe>` tag. Takes values of left, right, top, middle, and bottom. Deprecated in favor of CSS. |
| class | A comma-separated list of style classes that instantiate the tag as an instance of the defined classes. |
| frameborder | Takes a value of 0 or 1 to determine if a border should be drawn around the frame. |
| height | Specifies the height of the `<iframe>`. |
| id | Often used by style sheets to define the style that should be applied to the data in the tag. |
| longdesc | Links to a longer description of the contents of the tag. |
| marginheight | The number of pixels between the content of the frame and the top and bottom borders. |

**TABLE 23.4** continued

| Value | Description |
|---|---|
| marginwidth | The number of pixels between the content of the frame and the right and left borders. |
| name | Used to give the block a name. This can be used by JavaScript to manipulate the layers. |
| noresize | When present, prevents the user from resizing the frame. |
| scrolling | Takes the value of auto, yes, or no to determine if scrollbars are to be shown. |
| src | Specifies the URL containing the content of the `<iframe>`. |
| style | Allows you to specify a style definition within the tag, rather than outside in a style sheet. |
| title | Allows you to provide a more informative title for the `<iframe>` than does the `<title>` tag, which applies to the whole document. |
| width | Specifies the width of the `<iframe>`. |

As you can see, this capability and being able to control layers through the use of JavaScript can be very powerful. However, as we mentioned earlier, there are some inconsistencies across the major browsers. Internet Explorer more closely implements the HTML 4 and ECMAScript standards, and Navigator has created some new tags for handling layers. They will support the HTML 4 Recommendation with the next release, but until then you may need to use the `<layer>` and `<ilayer>` tags in your DHTML.

In the last section of this chapter we will look at these tags and how they can be used. Because we have already addressed the primary principles, however, we will not go into a lot of detail on how to build DHTML with these tags.

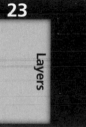

# `<layer>` and `<ilayer>`

Layers can be defined in Navigator using the `<layer>` and `<ilayer>` tags. `<layer>` elements let you precisely position a layer on a page, and `<ilayer>` elements appear wherever the flow of the document places them. The properties of the `<layer>` and `<ilayer>` tags are in Table 23.5.

**TABLE 23.5** `<layer>` and `<ilayer>` Tag Properties

| Property | Description |
|---|---|
| above | A Layer object higher in z-order of all layers in the document (null if the layer is topmost). |
| background | The URL of an image to use as the background for the layer. |
| below | A Layer object lower in z-order of all layers in the document (null if the layer is lowest). |

**TABLE 23.5** continued

| Property | Description |
|----------|-------------|
| bgcolor | The background color for the layer. |
| clip | Defines the clipping rectangle, which is the visible region of the layer. Anything outside of this rectangle is clipped from view. |
| height | The height in pixels of the layer. |
| left | The x-axis position in pixels of the layer, relative to the origin of its parent layer. |
| name | The name of the layer. |
| src | The URL for the layer's content source. |
| top | The y-axis position in pixels of the layer, relative to the origin of its parent layer. |
| visibility | Defines the layer's visibility attributes. show displays the layer, hide hides the layer, and inherit causes the layer to inherit the visibility of its parent layer. |
| width | The width in pixels of the layer. |
| z-index | The relative z-order of the layer, relative to its siblings and parent. |

As you can see, these tags have many of the same attributes as the other tags used in creating DHTML. Unlike other elements, however, a layer has its own JavaScript object in Navigator browsers: the Layer object.

**Note**

Because we documented and described this object in Chapter 9, "Client-Side Objects," we will not go into the details of its methods and properties here.

## A Tabbed Example

To give you a better understanding of how the <layer> and <ilayer> tags work, we are going to step through some examples. For this example, four GIF images are used to display charts within a tabbed page control. You can see the image showing the 1997 chart in Figure 23.11. Each of these images is assigned to a separate layer within our HTML document. The <layer> elements are given the same left and top parameters so that they will be aligned with each other.

**FIGURE 23.11**
*The GIF image used in the example.*

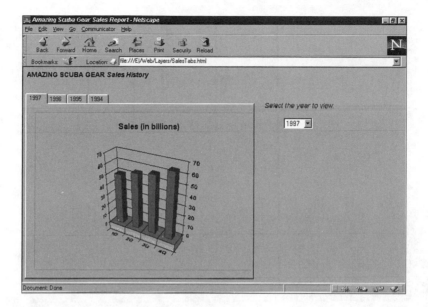

```
<layer name="tab3" left=5 top=55>
  <img src="./1994tab.gif">
</layer>
<layer name="tab2" left=5 top=55>
  <img src="./1995tab.gif">
</layer>
<layer name="tab1" left=5 top=55>
  <img src="./1996tab.gif">
</layer>
<layer name="tab0" left=5 top=55>
  <img src="./1997tab.gif">
</layer>
```

> **Note**
>
> Layers use the concept of "the last shall be first" (or, at least "highest"). In the preceding code, notice that the 1997 tab was defined last in the sequence of the HTML file. The final layer element defined is considered the highest and will be on top of the others.

In order to provide some user interaction, we can define another layer containing a form with a select list. The user can then select a tab from the list to view. We can define an onChange event handler to execute a function called showTab() and send the selected option as its parameter. Here is the code:

```
<layer name="select" left="500" top="55" width="150">
  <center>
    <p>
      <i>
        Select the year to view:
      </i>
    </p>
    <form name="selectForm">
      <select name="pickYear" size="1"
        onchange="showTab(this.selectedIndex); return false;">
        <option selected>1997</option>
        <option>1996</option>
        <option>1995</option>
        <option>1994</option>
      </select>
    </form>
  </center>
</layer>
```

### Note

Optimally, you would like an imagemap defined for the tab boundaries of the images. By associating an onClick event handler with these areas, you can simulate the feel of a typical tabbed page control.

Now we can create the showTab() function, which is used to display the selected tab. To do this, first we need to hide all layers, and then we can make the selected layer visible. The following code uses the document.layers array to step through each layer in the document, hiding each of the layers except the Select form layer. Next, the selected tab is assigned the inherit value to make it visible.

```
function showTab(idx){
  for (var i = 1; i < document.layers.length; i++){
    if(document.layers[i].name != 'Select'){
      document.layers[i].visibility = 'hide';
    }
  }
```

```
    document.layers["tab"+idx].visibility = 'inherit';
}
```

When we view and test the code, we can select a year from the Select list to display the corresponding tab. Figure 23.12 shows the result of the 1996 option's being selected from the Select list.

Listing 23.12 provides the complete source code for this example.

**LISTING 23.12**   Using Layers to Simulate Tabs on a Web Page

```
<html>
<head>
<title>JavaScript Unleashed</title>
  <script type="text/javascript" language="JavaScript1.2">
  <!--
    function showTab(idx){
      for (var i = 1; i < document.layers.length; i++){
        if(document.layers[i].name != 'Select'){
          document.layers[i].visibility = 'hide';
        }
      }
      document.layers["tab"+idx].visibility = 'inherit';
    }
  //-->
  </script>
</head>
<body bgcolor="Silver">
  <h4>
    AMAZING SCUBA GEAR
    <i>
      Sales History
    </i>
  </h4>

  <layer name="tab3" left=5 top=55>
    <img src="./1994tab.gif">
  </layer>
  <layer name="tab2" left=5 top=55>
    <img src="./1995tab.gif">
  </layer>
  <layer name="tab1" left=5 top=55>
    <img src="./1996tab.gif">
  </layer>
```

23

Layers

LISTING 23.12    continued

```
<layer name="tab0" left=5 top=55>
  <img src="./1997tab.gif">
</layer>
<layer name="select" left="500" top="55" width="150">
  <center>
    <p>
      <i>
        Select the year to view:
      </i>
    </p>
    <form name="selectForm">
      <select name="pickYear" size="1"
          onchange="showTab(this.selectedIndex); return false;">
      <option selected>1997</option>
      <option>1996</option>
      <option>1995</option>
      <option>1994</option>
      </select>
    </form>
  </center>
</layer>
</body>
</html>
```

## A Bouncing Ball Example

For a second example, we will create some animation. To create a bouncing-ball effect, we can use three different GIF images to represent a green ball, a red ball, and a multicolored ball. We want to enclose each ball in a separate <layer> element:

```
<layer name="greenball" width="13" height="13" left="5" top="1">
  <img src="./grnball.gif">
</layer>
<layer name="redball" width="13" height="13" left="25" top="135">
  <img src="./redball.gif">
</layer>
<layer name="colorball" width="13" height="13" left="255" top="115">
  <img src="./clrball.gif">
</layer>
```

FIGURE **23.12**
*The 1996 layer
is made visible.*

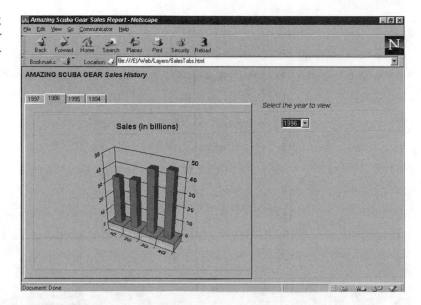

The width and height parameters of the <layer> elements have the same dimensions as the GIF images. The left and top parameters are random numbers positioned within a "canvas" that we will arbitrarily define as 400 pixels wide by 200 pixels high. These are the coordinates from which the balls will start.

After adding a <script> element within the <head> section of the document, we can define some global variables used throughout our animation routines. For each of the balls, we will be using the Layer object's offset() method, which lets you change the layer's position by applying a range, or *delta*, of x,y values. With that in mind, we want to have a pair of x,y delta values for each ball:

```
var grnX = 2;
var grnY = 2.5;

var redX = 2;
var redY = -2;

var colorX = 2;
var colorY = 3;
```

Therefore, when applied in offset(), these variables call for the green ball to move to the left 2 pixels and down 2.5 pixels, the red ball to move left 2 pixels and up 2 pixels, and the multicolored ball to move left 2 pixels and down 3 pixels.

We also want to specify within this script for a new property of the Window object called flickerFree to be set to true. This property helps provide smoother animation effects:

```
window.flickerFree = true;
```

Before working with the `<layer>` elements in our JavaScript code, we need to reference each layer and assign it to a variable. Within the `<body>` section of the document, add a new `<script>` element and place the following code in it:

```
<script type="text/javascript" language="JavaScript1.2">
<!--
  var green = document.layers["greenball"];
  var red = document.layers['redball'];
  var color = document.layers['colorball'];
//-->
</script>
```

Using the `document.layers` array, we can access each of the layers by name and assign variables to represent them in the script.

> **Note**
>
> Unlike the number variables defined earlier, you can't place this Layer object assignment code in the `<head>` script, because it references elements that are defined later in the `<body>`. Therefore, this assignment code must be processed after the `<layer>` elements have been defined.

## Defining the Animator Functions

The next step is to create the script to actually perform the animation. Our purpose is rather simple to start: Set each ball in motion based on its `offset()` value specified earlier. However, in reality, there is much to do around the periphery of this core functionality.

We need to monitor the x,y position of each ball before each call to `offset()`. If we don't, the balls will quickly move beyond the boundaries of the $400 \times 200$ canvas and beyond the HTML document itself. Therefore, if the Layer object's `left` property is between 0 and 400 and its `top` property is between 0 and 200, the `offset()` method should be executed. But if the layer fails in that boundary check, send it in a reverse direction, giving the appearance of a ricochet.

Let's look at how this logic is implemented in our script. We are using two functions:

- `startTheBallRolling()` is the main recursive function, and it's responsible for calling each ball to animate. It also performs necessary correction of the offset values when the ball tries to move beyond the canvas.

- `moveBall()` is in charge of moving the ball within the canvas boundaries. It analyzes the `top` and `left` properties of the ball and performs an `offset()` action if they pass the test. If the check fails, this function tells `startTheBallRolling()` which boundary is being violated.

While `moveBall()` is invoked by `startTheBallRolling()`, perhaps it makes the most sense to look at `moveBall()` first and then work our way back to `startTheBallRolling()`. The `moveBall()` function has three parameters: a reference to a ball object, and its x and y offset values. Performing the logic discussed earlier, it checks the ball's `left` and `top` properties and does one of the following:

- Performs the `offset()` and returns a value of `'ok'` to `startTheBallRolling()`.

- Returns a value of `'topBoundary'` to the calling function, denoting that the `top` property is being violated.

- Returns a value of `'leftBoundary'` to the calling function, denoting that the `left` property is being violated.

The code is as follows:

```
function moveBall(ball, offsetX, offsetY){
  if((ball.left < 400) && (ball.left > 0)){
    if((ball.top < 200) && (ball.top > 0)){
      ball.offset(offsetX, offsetY);
      return 'ok';
    }else{
      return 'topBoundary';
    }
  }else{
    return 'leftBoundary';
  }
}
```

Now let's look at the function that calls `moveBall()`. For each of the three ball objects, `startTheBallRolling()` calls `moveBall()` and then analyzes the success or failure of the attempt. For the green ball, the code is as follows:

```
if (moveBall(green, grnX, grnY) == 'topBoundary'){
  grnY = 0 - grnY;
  green.offset(grnX, grnY);
}else{
```

```
    if(moveBall(green, grnX, grnY) == 'leftBoundary'){
        grnX = 0 - grnX;
        green.offset(grnX, grnY);
    }
}
```

If moveBall() is successful and returns an 'ok' value, the script moves on. However, if 'topBoundary' (or 'leftBoundary') is returned, we know we need to correct the y (or x) offset value. To do this, we assign a new value to the offending offset value, making it equal to zero minus its current value. An offset() action is then performed, setting the ball on its way in the inverse direction. This same code is duplicated for the red ball and the multicolored ball:

```
if(moveBall(red, redX, redY) == 'topBoundary'){
    redY = 0 - redY;
    red.offset(redX, redY);
}else{
    if(moveBall(red, redX, redY) == 'leftBoundary'){
        redX = 0 - redX;
        red.offset(redX, redY);
    }
}

if(moveBall(color, colorX, colorY) == 'topBoundary'){
    colorY = 0 - colorY;
    color.offset( colorX, colorY );
}else{
    if(moveBall( color, colorX, colorY) == 'leftBoundary'){
        colorX = 0 - colorX;
        color.offset( colorX, colorY);
    }
}
```

Finally, setTimeout() is called to make this entire process recursive:

```
setTimeout("startTheBallRolling()", 2);
```

The final step is to actually start the ball rolling by assigning startTheBallRolling() to serve as the event handler for the window's onLoad event:

```
<body onload="startTheBallRolling()">
```

After defining the animator functions, the final step is to view and test the code. Figures 23.13 and 23.14 show the animated action.

Listing 23.13 provides the entire source file for the BallsGoneWild demo.

**Figure 23.13**

*The balls in motion.*

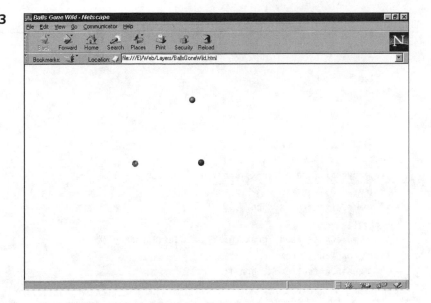

**Listing 23.13**    Animating Images on Your Web Page

```
<html>
<head>
<title>JavaScript Unleashed</title>
  <script type="text/javascript" language="JavaScript1.2">
  <!--
    // Global variables
    var grnX = 2;
    var grnY = 2.5;

    var redX = 2;
    var redY = -2;

    var colorX = 2;
    var colorY = 3;

    // Smooth animation effects
    window.flickerFree = true;

    function moveBall(ball, offsetX, offsetY){
      if((ball.left < 400) && (ball.left > 0)){
        if((ball.top < 200) && (ball.top > 0)){
          ball.offset(offsetX, offsetY);
          return 'ok';
        }else{
```

LISTING 23.13    continued

```
        return 'topBoundary';
      }
    }else{
      return 'leftBoundary';
    }
  }

  function startTheBallRolling() {
    if (moveBall(green, grnX, grnY) == 'topBoundary'){
      grnY = 0 - grnY;
      green.offset(grnX, grnY);
    }else{
      if(moveBall(green, grnX, grnY) == 'leftBoundary'){
        grnX = 0 - grnX;
        green.offset(grnX, grnY);
      }
    }

    if(moveBall(red, redX, redY) == 'topBoundary'){
      redY = 0 - redY;
      red.offset(redX, redY);
    }else{
      if(moveBall(red, redX, redY) == 'leftBoundary'){
        redX = 0 - redX;
        red.offset(redX, redY);
      }
    }

    if(moveBall(color, colorX, colorY) == 'topBoundary'){
      colorY = 0 - colorY;
      color.offset( colorX, colorY );
    }else{
      if(moveBall( color, colorX, colorY) == 'leftBoundary'){
        colorX = 0 - colorX;
        color.offset( colorX, colorY);
      }
    }
    setTimeout("startTheBallRolling()", 2);
  }
  //-->
  </script>
</head>
```

**LISTING 23.13**    continued

```html
<body onload="startTheBallRolling()">

  <layer name="greenball" width="13" height="13" left="5" top="1">
    <img src="./grnball.gif">
  </layer>
  <layer name="redball" width="13" height="13" left="25" top="135">
    <img src="./redball.gif">
  </layer>
  <layer name="colorball" width="13" height="13" left="255" top="115">
    <img src="./clrball.gif">
  </layer>

  <script type="text/javascript" language="JavaScript1.2">
  <!--
    var green = document.layers["greenball"];
    var red = document.layers['redball'];
    var color = document.layers['colorball'];
  //-->
  </script>

</body>
</html>
```

**23**

**Layers**

**FIGURE 23.14**
*Continued action.*

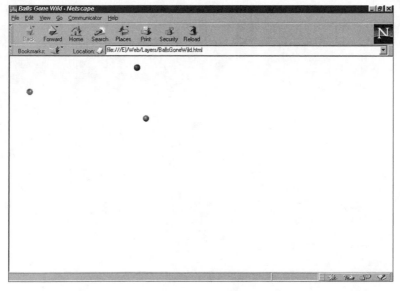

# Summary

Layers are potentially one of the most significant advancements in HTML over the past few years. They let you move beyond the sequential word processor — like world of HTML and into the world of graphical layout and design. JavaScript significantly adds to the power of layers by giving the developer full control over their behavior. The results can be powerful and stunning.

# CHAPTER 24

# DHTML Menus and Toolbars

Knowing how to program in JavaScript and knowing how to apply your programming skills are two completely different things. Many people are able to pick up a programming language and learn how to use its syntax and understand its semantics. However, few truly learn the art of applying what they have learned and know in real-world applications.

Dynamic HTML (DHTML) first came on the scene with the fourth versions of both Internet Explorer and Netscape Navigator. Both of these browsers had support for the JavaScript, layering, and style sheets necessary for designing pages whose full set of dynamic properties resided in the original Web page. It was this capability that gave birth to DHTML, and since then many sites have begun to adopt these technologies to add flash and functionality.

In this chapter, we are going to take a look at two examples of DHTML applications. The first is a menu, and the second is a toolbar. In a very real-world manner, we are going to decide what browsers to support and code around any differences in browser implementations for our examples.

# Initial Considerations

When you start a DHTML project, there are several questions that you want to ask yourself. Some of these we touched on in Chapter 23, "Layers," but we will restate them here:

- What browsers do you want to support? Remember that only Navigator 4+ and Internet Explorer 4+ currently have all the functionality you need to create DHTML applications.

- Do you want to accommodate non-supporting browsers?

- How gracefully do you want to fail in non-supporting browsers?

We have discussed these questions before, so I will not go into detail here. Just remember that picking your supporting browsers is a very big decision, and in doing so you must select and design not only for current releases but for future releases as well.

In addition to these questions, you should also ask yourself the following:

- Can you do it?

- How do you plan for the future?

- Is there a better way?

# Making Sure It Is Possible

This question is often one that is overlooked. JavaScript is perceived as a simple language that anyone can learn. This might have been true in version 1.0 or 1.1, but 1.2 brought a whole new beast to the table. Since its release, JavaScript has truly stepped up by providing even more objects to support the Document Object Model (DOM) as well as the corresponding XML technology. Creating a DHTML application is not as easy as you would think, and different browser implementations can make it a very tedious task.

# Planning for the Future

Another considerationis planning for the future. Netscape and Microsoft are releasing browsers every year or so, which means you may have to update your code often.

In planning for the future, you should consider everything from upcoming standards to new browser releases. You should also try to stay on top of the technologies you are working with, so that you will be exposed to any bugs or issues with the various implementations. Designing DHTML applications can be tough, but the payoff can be seen as soon as you get it working.

# Considering APIs

A final thing to think about is using a JavaScript Application Programming Interface (API). When creating your DHTML, you are going to come to a point at which you say, "There has to be an easier way to do this; someone else has to have done this before."

You are probably right. The great thing about JavaScript being an Internet programming language is that if you search around a bit, you will find that several individuals have created functions that you want to use—such as moving layers. You will also find that many of these developers have created their own objects, such as a cascading menu or a graphing object.

If you find that someone has done this and made the code available, do not reinvent the wheel—learn from the code and use it on your site.

**24**

**DHTML Menus and Toolbars**

---

**Tip**

See Appendix A, "Top Ten JavaScript Resources on the Web," for some good sites to check for JavaScript APIs.

# Designing Menus

When you design your DHTML menu, there are obvious questions such as what menus and items you want to appear and what overall functionality you are trying to provide. Additionally, you need to decide what look-and-feel you want. What are the colors and dimensions of your menus? How tall do you want the menu bar to be, and where would you like the menu to appear?

These are all things you need to ask yourself so that you can apply the appropriate formatting and styles to create the look you desire. For our menu, we have the following design objectives:

- Work with Internet Explorer only.

- Gray menu bar at the top of the browser window.

- Two menu options: Go and Help.

- The Go menu will have three links to popular developer sites for Netscape and Microsoft.

- The Help menu will have a single item, About, that when selected will pop up a dialog box with information about the menu.

- The About dialog box will contain an image and a close button.

## Defining Layers

The first thing we are going to do in creating our menu is define our layers and the menu bar itself. For this, we are going to use a combination of HTML and CSS. Within the HTML, we will use <div> tags to define the layers and a <table> for a dialog box. We will also make use of the <a> tag to handle click events on the items in the menu. You can see the code for the entire <body> section of our menu in Listing 24.1.

**LISTING 24.1  HTML Defining Our Layers**

```
<body bgcolor="#ffffff" link="#000000" vlink="#000000" alink="#000000"
    onload="checkBrowser()">

  <div name="menubar" id="menubar"></div>

  <div name="go" id="go">
    <a href="javascript:void(0)"
      onmousedown="changeState('helpmenu','hidden');
    changeState('gomenu','visible')">
```

**LISTING 24.1**    continued

```
      Go</a>
  </div>

  <div name="help" id="help">
    <a href="javascript:void(0)"
      onmousedown="changeState('gomenu','hidden');
➥changeState('helpmenu','visible')">
      Help</a>
  </div>

  <div name="gomenu" id="gomenu">
    <a href="http://developer.netscape.com">
      DevEdge</a>
    <hr size="1">
    <a href="http://www.mozilla.org">
      Mozilla.org</a>
    <hr size="1">
    <a href="http://msdn.microsoft.com">
      MSDN</a>
  </div>

  <div name="helpmenu" id="helpmenu">

    <a href="javascript:void(0)"
➥       onclick="changeState('helpmenu','hidden');
➥    changeState('about','visible')">
      About...</a>
  </div>
  <div name="about" id="about">
    <table border="0">
      <tr>
        <td>
          <img src="info-icon.gif" width="32" height="32">
        </td>
        <td>
          This DHTML Menu was created by R. Allen Wyke for JavaScript
          Unleashed.
        </td>
      </tr>
      <tr>
        <td colspan="2" align="right">
          <form name="form1">
```

24

DHTML Menus
and Toolbars

LISTING 24.1    continued

```
            <input type="button" value="Close"
➥       onclick="changeState('about','hidden')">
        <form>
    </tr>
  </table>
 </div>
</body>
```

Because one of the important steps in creating any JavaScript application is code reuse, we are going to reuse some of the code from Chapter 23 in this example. You are going to see some familiar function names and functionality. Because our menu is only supported in Internet Explorer, I have trimmed down the browser detection part of the code, so if you want to try and add support for Navigator, then you should replace the function in this example with the one used in Listing 23.9 in Chapter 23.

As you can see in Listing 24.1, each of the layers has an id and a name. This allows us to apply styles so that we can control the look and exposure of these layers. For our styles we need several definitions. The following is a description of what we have to define:

- No underlining of <a> tags.
- Coloring and positioning of the menu bar.
- Coloring and positioning of Go and Help elements on the menu bar.
- Coloring, positioning, and hiding of Go and Help menus.
- Coloring, positioning, and hiding of the About dialog box.

Listing 24.2 contains the style sheet definitions that we will need for this formatting.

LISTING 24.2    Style Definitions for the Menu

```
<style type="text/css">
<!--
  /* Global styles */
  a{
    text-decoration: none;
  }

  /* Properties that sets the background of entire menu */
  #menubar{
    background-color: #c0c0c0;
    left: 0;
```

**LISTING 24.2** continued

```
    position: absolute;
    top: 0;
    width: 100%;
}


/* Properties of the menus on the menubar */
#help{
    background-color: #c0c0c0;
    position: absolute;
    right: 0;
    top: 0;
}


#go{
    background-color: #c0c0c0;
    left: 0;
    position: absolute;
    top: 0;
}


/* Properties of the actual menus that are hidden until clicked */
#gomenu{
    background-color: #c0c0c0;
    left: 10;
    position: absolute;
    top: 20;
    visibility: hidden;
    width: 80;
}


#helpmenu{
    background-color: #c0c0c0;
    right: 10;
    position: absolute;
    top: 20;
    visibility: hidden;
    width: 80;
}


/* Properties of About Dialog box */
#about{
    background-color: gray;
```

LISTING 24.2   continued

```
      border: 2px solid black;
      height: 50;
      left: 100;
      position: absolute;
      top: 50;
      visibility: hidden;
      vertical-align: left;
      width:  200;
  }
-->
</style>
```

Now that everything has been laid out and layers have been defined, it is time to put the *D* in *DHTML*.

## Handling Actions

The first thing we need to do in the script portion of our menu is check to see if the browser making the request is actually an Internet Explorer browser. For this, I have defined a short if statement that will pop up a message for non-Internet Explorer browsers. This code is as follows:

```
if(navigator.userAgent.indexOf("MSIE") == -1){
  alert("This menu is supported in Internet Explorer");
  window.back();
}
```

As you can see, if the browser is not Internet Explorer, we pop up a quick message then direct the user back to the page he came from.

Like the code in Chapter 23, we declare some global String variables to hold our layer and style settings for Internet Explorer browsers. The values of these variables are set after the page loads using the checkBrowser() function, which looks like this:

```
var layer = new String();
var style = new String();

function checkBrowser(){
  layer = ".all";
  style = ".style";
}
```

The last piece of coding we need handles the hiding and showing of layers. If you look closely, you will see that it is the same code we used in Chapter 23, but simplified.

```
function changeState(layerRef, state){
  eval("document" + layer + "['" + layerRef + "']" + style +
➥           ".visibility = '" + state + "'");
}
```

This completes the <script> portion of our menu. The entire piece can be seen in Listing 24.3.

**LISTING 24.3**  Code for the Menu

```
<script type="text/javascript" language="JavaScript1.2">
  <!--
  // Declare global variables
  var layer = new String();
  var style = new String();

  // Check to see if this is a Navigator brower
  if(navigator.userAgent.indexOf("Nav") != -1){
    alert("This menu is not supported in Navigator");
    window.back();
  }

  // Set the layer and style variables.
  function checkBrowser(){
    layer = ".all";
    style = ".style";
  }

  // Take the state passed in, and change it.
  function changeState(layerRef, state){
    eval("document" + layer + "['" + layerRef + "']" + style +
➥           ".visibility = '" + state + "'");
  }

//-->
</script>
```

**24**

**DHTML Menus and Toolbars**

# Using the Menu

Once you have completed the menu (Listing 24.4), you are ready to load it into a browser for testing. The menu at this point should look like the one in Figure 24.1. As you can see in the figure, CSS allows us to place the menu items at the very top of the browser window and keep the links from being underlined. You will also notice that by defining the menubar item, we allow the user to resize and still have the proper distribution of the gray menu background.

LISTING 24.4    Complete Source Code for the Menu

```html
<html>
<head>
  <title>JavaScript Unleashed</title>
  <script type="text/javascript" language="JavaScript1.2">
  <!--
    // Check to see if this is a Navigator browser
    if(navigator.userAgent.indexOf("MSIE") == -1){
      alert("This menu is supported in Internet Explorer");
      window.back();
    }

    // Declare global variables
    var layer = new String();
    var style = new String();

    // Set the layer and style variables.
    function checkBrowser(){
      layer = ".all";
      style = ".style";
    }

    // Take the state passed in, and change it.
    function changeState(layerRef, state){
      eval("document" + layer + "['" + layerRef + "']" + style +
        ".visibility = '" + state + "'");
    }

  //-->
  </script>
  <style type="text/css">
  <!--
    /* Global styles */
```

**LISTING 24.4**  continued

```
a{
  text-decoration: none;
}

/* Properties that sets the background of entire menu */
#menubar{
  background-color: #c0c0c0;
  left: 0;
  position: absolute;
  top: 0;
  width: 100%;
}

/* Properties of the menus on the menubar */
#help{
  background-color: #c0c0c0;
  position: absolute;
  right: 0;
  top: 0;
}

#go{
  background-color: #c0c0c0;
  left: 0;
  position: absolute;
  top: 0;
}

/* Properties of the actual menus that are hidden until clicked */
#gomenu{
  background-color: #c0c0c0;
  left: 10;
  position: absolute;
  top: 20;
  visibility: hidden;
  width: 80;
}

#helpmenu{
  background-color:  #c0c0c0;
  right: 10;
  position: absolute;
```

LISTING 24.4    continued

```
      top: 20;
      visibility: hidden;
      width: 80;
    }

    /* Properties of About Dialog box */
    #about{
      background-color: gray;
      border: 2px solid black;
      height: 50;
      left: 100;
      position: absolute;
      top: 50;
      visibility: hidden;
      vertical-align: left;
      width: 200;
    }
  -->
  </style>
</head>
<body bgcolor="#ffffff" link="#000000" vlink="#000000" alink="#000000"
  onload="checkBrowser()">

  <div name="menubar" id="menubar"></div>

  <div name="go" id="go">
    <a href="javascript:void(0)"
      onmousedown="changeState('helpmenu','hidden');
➡changeState('gomenu','visible')">
      Go</a>
  </div>

  <div name="help" id="help">
    <a href="javascript:void(0)"
      onmousedown="changeState('gomenu','hidden');
➡changeState('helpmenu', 'visible')">
      Help</a>
  </div>

  <div name="gomenu" id="gomenu">
    <a href="http://developer.netscape.com">
      DevEdge</a>
```

**LISTING 24.4** continued

```
    <hr size="1">
    <a href="http://www.mozilla.org">
      Mozilla.org</a>
    <hr size="1">
    <a href="http://msdn.microsoft.com">
      MSDN</a>
  </div>

  <div name="helpmenu" id="helpmenu">

    <a href="javascript:void(0)"  onclick="changeState('helpmenu','hidden');
➥changeState('about','visible')">
      About...</a>
  </div>
  <div name="about" id="about">
    <table border="0">
      <tr>
        <td>
          <img src="info-icon.gif" width="32" height="32">
        </td>
        <td>
          This DHTML Menu was created by R. Allen Wyke for JavaScript
          Unleashed.
        </td>
      </tr>
      <tr>
        <td colspan="2" align="right">
          <form name="form1">
            <input type="button" value="Close"
➥onclick="changeState('about','hidden')">
          <form>
      </tr>
    </table>
  </div>
</body>
</html>
```

If you click on the Go menu in the upper-left corner, the menu of sites is exposed. As you can see in Figure 24.2, the URL of the link is still displayed in the browser's status bar.

The final menu item thatwe created was a Help item. If you click on it, you will see the About option, which you can select to display the dialog shown in Figure 24.3.

FIGURE **24.1**
*The menu, loaded in a browser.*

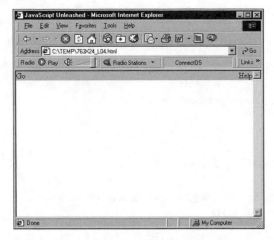

FIGURE **24.2**
*Accessing the Go menu.*

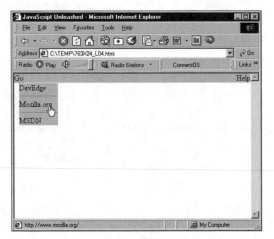

# Exploring Other Things You Can Do

Now that we have built our menu, I am sure that you want to extend it to do more. The following is a quick list of things to implement to get a better feel for building your own DHTML menus. You also can check out Netscape's DevEdge site (http://developer.netscape.com) for a free Menu object.

- Supporting the Navigator browser.

- Clicking outside the currently expanded menu closes it.

- Repositioning of the About dialog box.

- Creating cascading menus.

**Figure 24.3**

*The About dialog box.*

# Building Toolbars

Building a toolbar is one of the coolest things you can learn to do in DHTML. You may have to tap all your skills to make a toolbar work and interact with other toolbars the way you want. Building a toolbar requires not only the use of JavaScript but CSS and layers as well. The key thing is to determine what you want the toolbar to look like and how you want it to work. Then you can work backward and design the layout, code, and style you want.

## Applying Events

The first thing you need to become familiar with in designing toolbars is the events you will use. In an everyday application such as your browser, if you watch the buttons as you press and roll over them, you will see that these events trigger changes in the state of the button.

We are going create a toolbar that is similar to a browser toolbar. The one we are going to create will look and function like the newer toolbars, such as on Internet Explorer 3+ and Navigator 4+.

## What Should Happen?

The first thing we need to do is document what should happen in the toolbar. Open your browser and watch how the state of the buttons changes as you roll over them and press them. Figures 24.4 through 24.6 show how the button state changes on Navigator 4 browsers.

**FIGURE 24.4**
*A normal toolbar.*

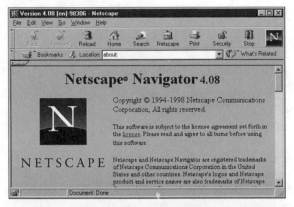

**FIGURE 24.5**
*Rolling over a button with the mouse.*

**FIGURE 24.6**
*Pressing a toolbar button.*

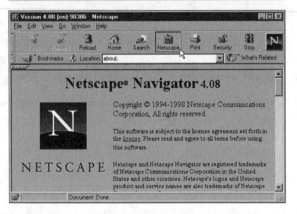

As you can see, there are three states that we must simulate. When the user allows the mouse button to come up, we should invoke an event to perform a certain task. Additionally, we should restore the state of the button when the user's mouse moves off the button and a click is not occurring.

# What Can Happen?

Looking at this from a Web-development perspective, all of the necessary functionality for our toolbar can be created. There are events for the mouse rolling over and off an element and for pressing and releasing a button. In conjunction with the `Image.src` property, which can replace an image on the page with another image, we will be able to simulate rolling over and pressing a button. This takes care of the visual effects.

We also need for these buttons to perform a task. For this we will use the `onClick` event in an `<a>` tag. If the user presses a button, we can capture that click and process it. The following lists the buttons we will use and what they will do.

- **Back**   This button will simulate the Back or Previous button on a browser. We will use different methods to accomplish this for Internet Explorer and Navigator to demonstrate how you can program around instances when browser support differs.

- **Forward**   This button will simulate the Forward or Next button. We will use different methods to accomplish this for Internet Explorer and Navigator to demonstrate how you can program around instances when browser support differs.

- **Home**   This button will simulate the Home button on Navigator browsers. Internet Explorer does not support this method.

- **Reload/Refresh**   This button will simulate the Reload or Refresh button on a browser to reprocess and render the current page. We will include a call to the `Date.getTime()` method on the page so you can see that it has been reloaded.

- **Find**   This button will simulate the Edit, Find menu option, which lets you search the text in the browser window. Internet Explorer does not support this method.

- **Print**   This button will simulate the Print button on a browser to bring up the Print dialog box for printing the current page.

In addition to these six buttons, we will also have a form with a text field that allows the user to enter a URL and press a Go button to load the URL in the browser window.

Now that we know our requirements, let's build the application. We will look at designing the images and writing the code as well.

# Considering Design Issues

Before you start writing any code, you need to make some decisions about how you want to actually write and store your code. Most of the functionality of the menu could be included with the HTML tags themselves—it is not a lot of code. However, the functionality that our example represents could be used elsewhere, so we want to use a more modular approach.

## Code Storage

Before we start building our application, we need to decide where the code will be stored. You will have to decide this based on what it is you are building. For our application, we will store all the code within the HTML document. If you take this example and implement it on your site in multiple locations, you should consider storing the code in an external JavaScript source file (.js).

## Modular Programming

We are going to plan this application to be as modular as possible. We want the code to be useable elsewhere if needed. To accomplish this, we are going to create as many functions as necessary to process information.

For our application, there are three different sets of functionality that will be occurring. These are listed and described in the following list:

- **Image State Change**  This function, which we will call rollImage(), will be responsible for changing the image when it is rolled over or pressed.

- **Button Processing**  This function, which we will call process(), will perform the button's tasks. When a user clicks a button, this function will react appropriately.

- **URL Handling**  This function, which we will call takeBrowser(), will take the data entered on the form and direct the browser to that location.

## Designing Images

Unlike other applications, with a Web-based application you have to provide most of the components that make up any kind of interface. Other than the sub-objects of the Form object, you will have to provide all of your own images and interface components. Because of the nature of your task, you will also have to provide versions for when the mouse is over the image and when it is pressed.

Earlier we said that a button on a toolbar should change state when the user rolls his mouse over it and when it is pressed. For our example to work properly, we will need the following images:

- **Normal:** The default image.

- **Rollover:** The default image with a 1-pixel white border on the left and top and 1-pixel gray border on the right and bottom.

- **Pressed:** The default image with a 1-pixel gray border on the left and top, and a 1-pixel white border on the right and bottom.

# Designing the HTML

The first thing we are going to design is the HTML that will contain the layout of our toolbar. There are several components to the toolbar interface we are going to design, which can be seen in Figure 24.7.

**FIGURE 24.7**

*The interface we are going to build.*

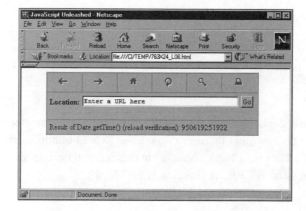

For simplicity we are going to use tables to hold and arrange our buttons. There will be three rows in our table, with six cells in the top row and a single cell in the second and third rows. The background of the table will be gray with the actual document having a white background.

The first row of the table will contain the images that make up our toolbar. Each image will be surrounded by <a> tags so that we can apply mouse events. Currently, Navigator does not allow you to apply these events to <img> tags, even though Internet Explorer does, so we must wrap the image. The following is an example of what an individual image cell will look like.

```
<td align="center">
  <a href="javascript:process('back')"
    onmouseup="rollImage('0','up')"
    onmousedown="rollImage('0','down')"
    onmouseout="rollImage('0','out')"
    onmouseover="rollImage('0','over')">
  <img border="0" src="back.gif" width="24" height="24" alt="Back"></a>
</td>
```

In the second row of our toolbar, we have a text box in which the user enters a URL. When the user presses the Go button, the browser will attempt to load the URL. The HTML for this is a fairly straightforward use of the <form> tag. The button makes use of the

24

DHTML Menus and Toolbars

`onclick()` event handler to call a function that will redirect the browser. You will also see that we used the `colspan` attribute to properly implement a cell all the way across the width of the table. The HTML for this is as follows:

```
<td colspan="6">
  <form name="netsite">
    <b>
     Location:
    </b>
    <input type="text" size="40" value="Enter a URL here" name="where">
    <input type="button" value="Go" onclick="takeBrowser(this.form)">
  </form>
</td>
```

The last row simply contains the result of calling the `getTime()` method of an instance of the `Date` object. This is so that the user can see the Reload button work. When the user presses Reload, the numerical value displayed in this cell will change, confirming the actual reload of the page. The HTML for this row is as follows:

```
<td colspan="6">
  Result of Date.getTime() (reload verification):
  <script type="text/javascript" language="JavaScript1.2">
  <!--
    document.write((new Date()).getTime());
  //-->
  </script>
</td>
```

These three rows, in combination with the `<body>` tag, make up the entire interface part of the toolbar. Listing 24.5 shows what we have at this point.

**LISTING 24.5**   HTML Portion of Our Toolbar

```
<body bgcolor="#ffffff">
  <table border="1" cellpadding="5" cellspacing="0" align="center"
          bgcolor="#c0c0c0">
    <tr>
      <td align="center">
        <a href="javascript:process('back')"
            onmouseup="rollImage('0','up')"
            onmousedown="rollImage('0','down')"
            onmouseout="rollImage('0','out')"
            onmouseover="rollImage('0','over')">
          <img border="0" src="back.gif" width="24" height="24"
                alt="Back"></a>
```

**LISTING 24.5** continued

```
          </td>
          <td align="center">
            <a href="javascript:process('forward')"
                onmouseup="rollImage('1','up')"
                onmousedown="rollImage('1','down')"
                onmouseout="rollImage('1','out')"
                onmouseover="rollImage('1','over')">
              <img border="0" src="forward.gif" width="24" height="24"
➥                    alt="Forward"></a>
          </td>
          <td align="center">
            <a href="javascript:process('home')"
                onmouseup="rollImage('2','up')"
                onmousedown="rollImage('2','down')"
                onmouseout="rollImage('2','out')"
                onmouseover="rollImage('2','over')">
              <img border="0" src="home.gif" width="24" height="24"
➥                    alt="Home"></a>
          </td>
          <td align="center">
            <a href="javascript:document.location.reload()"
                onmouseup="rollImage('3','up')"
                onmousedown="rollImage('3','down')"
                onmouseout="rollImage('3','out')"
                onmouseover="rollImage('3','over')">
              <img border="0" src="reload.gif" width="24" height="24"
➥                    alt="Reload"></a>
          </td>
          <td align="center">
            <a href="javascript:process('find')"
                onmouseup="rollImage('4','up')"
                onmousedown="rollImage('4','down')"
                onmouseout="rollImage('4','out')"
                onmouseover="rollImage('4','over')">
              <img border="0" src="search.gif" width="24" height="24"
➥                    alt="Search"></a>
          </td>
          <td align="center">
            <a href="javascript:process('print')"
                onmouseup="rollImage('5','up')"
                onmousedown="rollImage('5','down')"
                onmouseout="rollImage('5','out')"
```

LISTING 24.5   continued

```
                      onmouseover="rollImage('5','over')">
             <img border="0" src="print.gif" width="24" height="24"
                         alt="Print"></a>
        </td>
      </tr>
      <tr>
        <td colspan="6">
          <form name="netsite">
            <b>
              Location:
            </b>
              <input type="text" size="40" value="Enter a URL here" name="where">
              <input type="button" value="Go" onclick="takeBrowser(this.form)">
          </form>
        </td>
      </tr>
      <tr>
        <td colspan="6">
          Result of Date.getTime() (reload verification):
          <script type="text/javascript" language="JavaScript1.2">
          <!--
            document.write((new Date()).getTime());
          //-->
          </script>
        </td>
      </tr>
    </table>
</body>
```

# Implementing Image Rollovers

To get the image rollovers working properly, we are going to make use of the Image object, which restricts our application to JavaScript 1.1 browsers. We are primarily interested in the src property, which will allow us to change the image. As you saw in the HTML in Listing 24.5, each of the <a> tags around our images calls a rollImage() function, which we will define here.

In building image rollovers, first we need to declare the images we are going to use. Because there are various states, the best way is to store them in an array. This allows us to access the images in the array and in the document with the same index numbers. For instance, the first image in the document can be referenced through the document.images array with this code:

```
document.images[0]
```

If we store the "over" and "pressed" versions of our images in two different arrays in the same indexed position, [0], then we are able to pass a single position variable to the function to perform image swapping. Because we will also need to return the image to its previous state, the default, we need three arrays. The following shows the code you use to create these arrays and store images in them:

```
// Create arrays to hold the "over" images
    var overImg = new Array();
    overImg[0] = new Image(24,24);
    overImg[1] = new Image(24,24);
    overImg[2] = new Image(24,24);
    overImg[3] = new Image(24,24);
    overImg[4] = new Image(24,24);
    overImg[5] = new Image(24,24);

    // Create arrays to hold the "down" images
    var downImg = new Array();
    downImg[0] = new Image(24,24);
    downImg[1] = new Image(24,24);
    downImg[2] = new Image(24,24);
    downImg[3] = new Image(24,24);
    downImg[4] = new Image(24,24);
    downImg[5] = new Image(24,24);

    // Create arrays to hold the default images
    var defaultImg = new Array();
    defaultImg[0] = new Image(24,24);
    defaultImg[1] = new Image(24,24);
    defaultImg[2] = new Image(24,24);
    defaultImg[3] = new Image(24,24);
    defaultImg[4] = new Image(24,24);
    defaultImg[5] = new Image(24,24);

    // Preload "over" images in the array
    overImg[0].src = "back-over.gif";
    overImg[1].src = "forward-over.gif";
    overImg[2].src = "home-over.gif";
    overImg[3].src = "reload-over.gif";
    overImg[4].src = "search-over.gif";
```

24

DHTML Menus
and Toolbars

```
overImg[5].src = "print-over.gif";

// Preload "down" images in the array
downImg[0].src = "back-down.gif";
downImg[1].src = "forward-down.gif";
downImg[2].src = "home-down.gif";
downImg[3].src = "reload-down.gif";
downImg[4].src = "search-down.gif";
downImg[5].src = "print-down.gif";

// Preload default images in the array
defaultImg[0].src = "back.gif";
defaultImg[1].src = "forward.gif";
defaultImg[2].src = "home.gif";
defaultImg[3].src = "reload.gif";
defaultImg[4].src = "search.gif";
defaultImg[5].src = "print.gif";
```

Next we need to define the function. This is easier than you might expect. The function will take two parameters. The first parameter is the index number of the image we are processing. The function call, which is contained in the <a> tag, will pass a numerical value that represents its location in the document. For instance, the first image will pass 0, the second will pass 1, and so on. Remember that this is a zero-based list, so the first image is 0.

The second parameter is the type of rollover that is occurring. For our purposes, there are four types: over, out, up, and down. Based on what is passed, we will use a switch statement to evaluate the value and perform the proper swapping of images. This is done by accessing the src property of instances of the Image object—both in the document and in the arrays. The entire function definition will look like the following:

```
function rollImage(img,type){
  switch(type){
    case "over":
      document.images[img].src = overImg[img].src;
      break;
    case "out":
      document.images[img].src = defaultImg[img].src;
      break;
    case "up":
      document.images[img].src = defaultImg[img].src;
      break;
    case "down":
      document.images[img].src = downImg[img].src;
```

```
        break;
    }
}
```

This completes the rollover functionality we need.

## Implementing a Location Field

On the second row of our toolbar is a text area that will allow the user to enter a URL then press Go to redirect the browser. As you saw in the HTML, this button calls a `takeBrowser()` function, passing it the `this.form` object. Once the function is invoked, it will use the `Form` object reference that was passed, assign it to a variable, and access the value of the text field. Then it uses the `location.href` property to change the page currently loaded in the browser, thereby redirecting it to the URL that the user entered.

This function does not perform error checking so, if the user enters an incorrect value, the browser will simply complain that it cannot load the page. You will also see in the code, which follows, that it accesses the value of the text field through the name of the field, which is specified by the `name` attribute.

```
function takeBrowser(ref){
    var form = ref;
    location.href = form.where.value;
}
```

## Processing Button Events

The last function to write will take care of the processing. This function, which we will call `process()`, will take a single parameter. We will evaluate this parameter using a `switch` statement for the six possible buttons.

The Find and Home buttons do not work in Internet Explorer, so we have to return an alert dialog informing the user. There are also some other functions that are implemented differently in Navigator and Internet Explorer browsers, so we have to work around them as well. To do this, we include a variable that tells us if the browser is an Internet Explorer browser. This Boolean value is stored in the `isIE` variable that is tested on the first line in the function. (Because of limitations on how long a line of code can be in this book, the `isIE` variable actually appears on the second code line, which is a continuation of the first line.) The code for this function looks like the following:

```
function process(item){
➡        var isIE = new Boolean(navigator.userAgent.indexOf("MSIE") != -1);

    switch(item){
```

```
        case "find":
          if(isIE){
            alert("Internet Explorer does not support this method");
          }else{
            window.find();
          }
          break;
        case "print":
          window.print();
          break;
        case "home":
          if(isIE){
            alert("Internet Explorer does not support this method");
          }else{
            window.home();
          }
          break;
        case "reload":
          document.location.reload();
          break;
        case "forward":
          if(isIE){
            history.forward();
          }else{
            window.forward();
          }
          break;
        case "back":
          if(isIE){
            history.back();
          }else{
            window.back();
          }
          break;
    }
  }
```

# Examining the Result

We have stepped through the HTML and all of the JavaScript, so now we can test our application. The final code is in Listing 24.6, and Figures 24.8 and 24.9 show the position of the buttons when moused over and down. As you test the program, watch the time string change as you hit the Reload button. The result of clicking the Find and Print buttons is obvious, because a dialog box pops up. If you want to test the Forward and Back buttons, you will need to load several pages into your browser so that you have something to go forward and back to.

**LISTING 24.6**  The Complete Source of the Toolbar

```html
<html>
<head>
  <title>JavaScript Unleashed</title>
  <script type="text/javascript" language="JavaScript1.2">
  <!--

    // Create arrays to hold images
    var overImg = new Array();
    overImg[0] = new Image(24,24);
    overImg[1] = new Image(24,24);
    overImg[2] = new Image(24,24);
    overImg[3] = new Image(24,24);
    overImg[4] = new Image(24,24);
    overImg[5] = new Image(24,24);

    var downImg = new Array();
    downImg[0] = new Image(24,24);
    downImg[1] = new Image(24,24);
    downImg[2] = new Image(24,24);
    downImg[3] = new Image(24,24);
    downImg[4] = new Image(24,24);
    downImg[5] = new Image(24,24);

    var defaultImg = new Array();
    defaultImg[0] = new Image(24,24);
    defaultImg[1] = new Image(24,24);
    defaultImg[2] = new Image(24,24);
    defaultImg[3] = new Image(24,24);
    defaultImg[4] = new Image(24,24);
    defaultImg[5] = new Image(24,24);
```

**24**

**DHTML Menus and Toolbars**

LISTING 24.6   continued

```
// Preload images in the array
overImg[0].src = "back-over.gif";
overImg[1].src = "forward-over.gif";
overImg[2].src = "home-over.gif";
overImg[3].src = "reload-over.gif";
overImg[4].src = "search-over.gif";
overImg[5].src = "print-over.gif";

downImg[0].src = "back-down.gif";
downImg[1].src = "forward-down.gif";
downImg[2].src = "home-down.gif";
downImg[3].src = "reload-down.gif";
downImg[4].src = "search-down.gif";
downImg[5].src = "print-down.gif";

defaultImg[0].src = "back.gif";
defaultImg[1].src = "forward.gif";
defaultImg[2].src = "home.gif";
defaultImg[3].src = "reload.gif";
defaultImg[4].src = "search.gif";
defaultImg[5].src = "print.gif";

// Change the state of image depending on the event that fired.
function rollImage(img,type){
  switch(type){
    case "over":
      document.images[img].src = overImg[img].src;
      break;
    case "out":
      document.images[img].src = defaultImg[img].src;
      break;
    case "up":
      document.images[img].src = defaultImg[img].src;
      break;
    case "down":
      document.images[img].src = downImg[img].src;
      break;
  }
}

// Process the URL that was entered in the text box
function takeBrowser(ref){
```

LISTING 24.6   continued

```
    var form = ref;
    location.href = form.where.value;
}

// Process the buttons as they are pressed
function process(item){
    var isIE = new Boolean(navigator.userAgent.indexOf("MSIE") != -1);

    switch(item){
        case "find":
            if(isIE){
                alert("Internet Explorer does not support this method");
            }else{
                window.find();
            }
            break;
        case "print":
            window.print();
            break;
        case "home":
            if(isIE){
                alert("Internet Explorer does not support this method");
            }else{
                window.home();
            }
            break;
        case "reload":
            document.location.reload();
            break;
        case "forward":
            if(isIE){
                history.forward();
            }else{
                window.forward();
            }
            break;
        case "back":
            if(isIE){
                history.back();
            }else{
                window.back();
            }
```

**LISTING 24.6**    continued

```
          break;
      }
    }
  //-->
  </script>
</head>
<body bgcolor="#ffffff">
  <table border="1" cellpadding="5" cellspacing="0" align="center"
           bgcolor="#c0c0c0">
    <tr>
      <td align="center">
        <a href="javascript:process('back')"
            onmouseup="rollImage('0','up')"
            onmousedown="rollImage('0','down')"
            onmouseout="rollImage('0','out')"
            onmouseover="rollImage('0','over')">
          <img border="0" src="back.gif" width="24" height="24" alt="Back">
                    </a>
      </td>
      <td align="center">
        <a href="javascript:process('forward')"
            onmouseup="rollImage('1','up')"
            onmousedown="rollImage('1','down')"
            onmouseout="rollImage('1','out')"
            onmouseover="rollImage('1','over')">
          <img border="0" src="forward.gif" width="24" height="24"
                    alt="Forward"></a>
      </td>
      <td align="center">
        <a href="javascript:process('home')"
            onmouseup="rollImage('2','up')"
            onmousedown="rollImage('2','down')"
            onmouseout="rollImage('2','out')"
            onmouseover="rollImage('2','over')">
          <img border="0" src="home.gif" width="24" height="24"
                    alt="Home"></a>
      </td>
      <td align="center">
        <a href="javascript:process('reload')"
            onmouseup="rollImage('3','up')"
            onmousedown="rollImage('3','down')"
            onmouseout="rollImage('3','out')"
```

**LISTING 24.6** continued

```
                onmouseover="rollImage('3','over')">
            <img border="0" src="reload.gif" width="24" height="24"
➥                   alt="Reload"></a>
    </td>
    <td align="center">
      <a href="javascript:process('find')"
          onmouseup="rollImage('4','up')"
          onmousedown="rollImage('4','down')"
          onmouseout="rollImage('4','out')"
          onmouseover="rollImage('4','over')">
        <img border="0" src="search.gif" width="24" height="24"
➥                   alt="Search"></a>
    </td>
    <td align="center">
      <a href="javascript:process('print')"
          onmouseup="rollImage('5','up')"
          onmousedown="rollImage('5','down')"
          onmouseout="rollImage('5','out')"
          onmouseover="rollImage('5','over')">
        <img border="0" src="print.gif" width="24" height="24"
➥                   alt="Print"></a>
    </td>
  </tr>
  <tr>
    <td colspan="6">
      <form name="netsite">
        <b>
          Location:
        </b>
          <input type="text" size="40" value="Enter a URL here" name="where">
          <input type="button" value="Go" onclick="takeBrowser(this.form)">
      </form>
    </td>
  </tr>
  <tr>
    <td colspan="6">
      Result of Date.getTime() (reload verification):
      <script type="text/javascript" language="JavaScript1.2">
      <!--
        document.write((new Date()).getTime());
      //-->
      </script>
```

**24**

**DHTML Menus
and Toolbars**

**LISTING 24.6**   continued

```
        </td>
      </tr>
   </table>
</body>
</html>
```

**FIGURE 24.8**
*Rolling over a button with the mouse.*

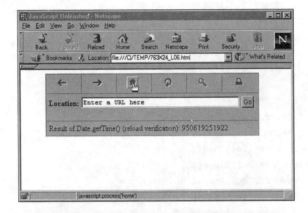

**FIGURE 24.9**
*Pressing a tool-bar button.*

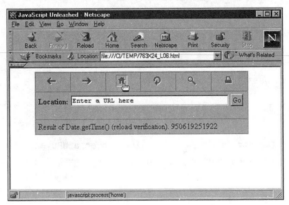

# Summary

In this chapter we have covered a lot of details on implementing DHTML on your site. Using what you have learned here and in Chapter 20, "Rollovers," Chapter 22, "Cascading Style Sheets," and Chapter 23, you should be well on your way to implementing dynamic pages using not only JavaScript but other HTML elements and CSS as well.

**24**

**DHTML Menus and Toolbars**

# Interacting with Other Technologies

It doesn't matter if you are new to JavaScript or a long time programmer, because more than likely you have not tapped all the power of the language. As Web developers know, there are many other technologies out there, such as Java applets and ActiveX controls, that can be used to enhance your user's Web experience.

This chapter talks about some of those technologies and how they can be used in conjunction with JavaScript. Some of the technologies are specific to certain browsers, but they are valid nonetheless.

# Browser Plug-Ins

Current Internet browsers natively support content from only a few file formats, such as text (this would include HTML) and images. In order to do their work outside the Web browser, however, people regularly use many other file formats to perform different tasks.

For instance, most word processing applications have their own native file formats (such as Microsoft Word's .doc file format), as do spreadsheet applications, presentation applications, multimedia applications, and so on. If the Web browser supports these various file formats, you can make a great deal of content readily available for communication on the Web, not to mention opening up the Internet to new and exciting ways of presenting information.

For Netscape (or any other company) to build native support into its browser for all the useful file formats, however, would be impractical because of the costs, time, and expertise that would be involved. So most of these browsers support another solution: plug-ins.

> **Note**
>
> Although this chapter will focus on the various technologies that JavaScript can interact with, it will not focus on how to embed these technologies in your pages. For example, it will not go into detail on how to use the `<applet>`, `<object>`, and `<embed>` tags or the attributes of those tags. For more information on this subject, check out Microsoft's Developer Network (`http://msdn.microsoft.com`), Netscape's DevEdge (`http://developer.netscape.com`), and the World Wide Web Consortium (`http://www.w3.org`).

# Introducing Plug-Ins and MIME Types

Plug-ins rely on MIME (multipurpose Internet mail extensions) types to identify the data type being passed to them. By identifying the data type, the plug-in can figure out how to handle the data.

MIME is an Internet standard that defines how file formats (other than plain text) can be passed in Internet mail messages. (See Internet Requests For Comment (RFCs) 1521 and 1522, for complete details.) The impetus for this standard came from the fact that people wanted to exchange more than just plain text documents through email. MIME now allows Internet email applications to view formatted text, attachment files, and various other file types that can help enhance the message. The MIME standard can handle any file format created so far, including text, PostScript, image, sound, video, and compressed files.

MIME types define the content type and the specific subtype of different file formats. This can be best explained with an example.

The MIME type for `.wav` (Microsoft audio) files is defined as `audio/x-wav`. `audio` describes the broader content type or category of files supported. `x-wav` describes the specific file type (or subtype) supported, as required by the browser to interpret `.wav` files.

When the browser is started, it scans its installed plug-ins and assigns a given MIME type to an appropriate plug-in that can read it. Once a MIME type is encountered in the user's browsing, the browser loads the assigned (or registered) plug-in into memory, and the MIME type is handled by the plug-in. The MIME type may be displayed in one of three ways:

- Inline: It appears on the page along with other content. The specific size of the plug-in is determined from values of the preset `height` and `width` parameters of the tag used to load the plug-in.

- Full: The plug-in covers the entire browser window, excluding the toolbars.

- Hidden: The plug-in runs in the background (as with some audio plug-ins).

# Determining Installed Plug-Ins

Being able to determine what plug-ins are installed and which MIME types are supported on a client browser opens up a number of doors to a Web page developer in terms of controlling the content passed down to the user. For instance, one development scenario might be, "If the user does have the plug-in, show the page with all the relevant MIME types, or else show alternate (more basic) content." In most browsers (not Internet Explorer, however), JavaScript can help you accomplish this.

**25**

Interacting with Other Technologies

The supporting browsers have two built-in objects that reveal very useful information about the plug-ins and MIME types that a client browser supports:

- navigator.plugins: This object, which is a property of the Navigator object, is an array of all the plug-ins currently installed on the client. The array is actually a subobject of the Navigator object, so it has the following properties:

  - name: The name of the plug-in (for example, shockwave).
  - filename: The name of the plug-in file.
  - description: A description of the plug-in (supplied by its vendor).
  - length: The number of elements in the array.
  - [...]: An array of mimeTypes objects that the plug-in can read.

- navigator.mimeTypes: This property, which is also a subobject of the Navigator object, is an array of all the mimeTypes supported on the client. This subobject has the following properties:

  - type: The name of the MIME type (such as audio/x-wav).
  - description: A description of the MIME type (supplied by its vendor).
  - enabledPlugin: Plug-ins that can be read by this MIME type.
  - suffixes: The filename extensions that the MIME type is identified by (such as .wav for MIME type audio/x-wav). Multiple suffixes are separated by commas.

## The Plugins Object

Using these objects with JavaScript, you can quickly determine if a plug-in has been installed and how to proceed from there. The following is an example that checks to see if Macromedia's Shockwave plug-in has been installed. If so, the plug-in loads and displays the file. If not, it displays alternative information:

```
var DesiredPlugin = navigator.plugins["shockwave"];

// refers to name property of plug-ins object
if (DesiredPlugin) {
  document.write('<embed src="mymovie.dir" height="240" width="320">');
}else{
  document.write('<img src="movietitle.jpg" height="240" width="320">');
}
```

The navigator.plugins object also has a method called refresh(). This method causes the browser to look for any newly installed plug-ins and update itself accordingly. If the argument true is used with the refresh() method (such as navigator.plugin.

refresh(true)), the presence of a new plug-in will be registered without the need to exit and restart the browser.

**Tip**

If `navigator.plugins.refresh(true)` is used, the browser will reload only pages that might change as a result of a plug-in update. However, by default (if the `refresh()` method isn't used), the browser reloads all pages that contain any plug-in file types.

## The `MimeTypes` Object

Using the new `navigator.mimeTypes` object, you can also determine quickly whether a client supports a particular MIME type. The following example checks to see if the browser supports the `application/x-director` (for Macromedia Director Shockwave movies) MIME type. Once that determination is made, it follows logic similar to that of the previous example:

```
var DesiredMimetype = navigator.mimeType["application/x-director"];
if (DesiredMimetype){
  document.write('<embed src="mymovie.dir" height="240" width="320">');
}else{
  document.write('<img src="movietitle.jpg" height="240" width="320">');
}
```

You can also use a simple JavaScript loop to display all MIME types supported on the client. Try this code:

```
for (var i = 0; i < navigator.mimeTypes.length; i++){
  document.write(navigator.mimeTypes[i].type + "<br>");
}
```

**Tip**

For more information on these objects, see their respective sections in Chapter 9, "Client-Side Objects."

**25**

**Interacting with Other Technologies**

# ActiveX Controls

Microsoft's ActiveX technology also provides a means of embedding controls (Microsoft OLE in this case) within HTML documents. An OLE control thus embedded is referred to as an ActiveX control. These controls are recognized by Microsoft Internet Explorer 3+ and by Netscape Navigator equipped with an ActiveX plug-in.

> **Note**
>
> Currently, these controls are supported only on the Windows platform. However, Microsoft is supposedly working on a method of deploying ActiveX controls to its supported browser platforms, which include MacOS, Solaris, and HP-UX.

If such a browser loads an HTML document with an ActiveX control that isn't already present on the browser's host machine, the browser loads that control from the server. Naturally, because these controls are really OLE objects, they can execute only in a browser on an OLE-capable platform such as Microsoft Windows. This creates a portability issue for browser users who want to access such a document.

## Understanding ActiveX Controls

If *ActiveX* is a new term for you, let me try to draw two comparisons. Depending on your background, one will probably be more applicable than the other. If you have a Web or Java background, ActiveX controls are Microsoft's answer to Java applets, the mini-applications that can run inside a browser window. Or, if you're from a Windows database development background, think of them as the Web equivalent to VBXs (Visual Basic controls), VCLs (Delphi components), or OCXs (OLE controls). As you will see, the actual tie with OCXs is far closer than a simple comparison.

Before Microsoft decided that ActiveX was a much better marketing term, essentially the same controls were called OCXs. ActiveX controls are built on top of OLE technology that has been available for several years. However, it should be noted that ActiveX controls have less overhead than a standard OLE control. Because an ActiveX control is never linked or embedded in the same way a Word document is, part of the OLE technology is removed from an ActiveX control. The result is a component that is quicker and has less of a footprint.

Java's principal reason for being is portability across all operating environments. In contrast, the primary selling point for ActiveX controls is compatibility with the dominant desktop operating system in the market—Windows 9x, NT, and now 2000. This compatibility is demonstrated in that the same ActiveX controls that you use in a Web page can be used by any Windows application or development tool that can work with OCXs. The rationale is that because most Web users are already using Windows, ActiveX controls are a natural extension from their desktop on the Web.

The following is an example of the HTML code for embedding an OLE control (in this case, an OLE `ButtonCtrl` object) in an HTML document:

```
<object id="MyButton" width="83" height="27"
  classid="CLSID:3472D900-5A27-11CF-8B11-00AA00C00903">
  <param name="ExtentX" VALUE="2196">
  <param name="ExtentY" VALUE="714">
</object>
```

The string given for the `classid` attribute is the value of the `CLSID` entry of the `ButtonCtl` OLE control type as it appears in the Windows System Registry. Fortunately, it isn't necessary to generate this code manually. The code in this example was created by the ActiveX Control Pad application from Microsoft. The ActiveX Control Pad, in addition to enabling manual text editing of HTML documents, provides semi-automated placement and scripting of ActiveX controls. When using the ActiveX Control Pad application to place an ActiveX control within an HTML document, a list of all OLE controls currently known to the System Registry can be summoned. All such OLE controls are available for use by HTML document authors.

### Resource

Going into the details of the ActiveX control pad is beyond the scope of this book. Although it can be hard to find, the ActiveX Control Pad can be downloaded from Microsoft's Developer Network Online. At last check, you could find this application at `http://msdn.microsoft.com/workshop/components/dtctrl/setupdcp.exe`.

An ActiveX control has a set of events, each of which can be associated with a piece of JavaScript, or rather JScript, code. For example, the `ButtonCtl` control has an `onClick` event similar to that of button-type input in an HTML form. ActiveX controls can be arbitrarily complex, however; for example, the Calendar control has the following events that can be scripted: `AfterUpdate`, `BeforeUpdate`, `Click`, `DblClick`, `KeyDown`, `KeyPress`,

**25**

*Interacting with Other Technologies*

KeyUp, NewMonth, and NewYear. The following is an example of the code for scripting an event for an ActiveX control:

```
<script type="text/javascript" for="MyButton" event="onClick()">
<!--
  alert('hello universe');
//-->
</script>
```

## Implementing Security

ActiveX has the concept of digital signing built into its components. A component developer can then "brand" a digital signature onto an ActiveX control to ensure users of the origin of the software itself. This digital signature is displayed by Internet Explorer as the control is downloaded. After seeing the signature, the user chooses to download or not download. For controls with no digital signature, users are informed that the control is from an unknown origin and are prompted to confirm or decline the download.

> **Note**
>
> You can set up an "auto-approval" process with a vendor you trust so that all components from that source are automatically approved.

## Accessing with JScript

Once the ActiveX control is embedded in your document, you can add JScript code and work with it like any other JScript object. You can set properties, respond to events, or call methods of an ActiveX control.

Once you start working with ActiveX controls, you will see that there's nothing magical about attaching JScript code to them. As long as you know the properties and methods of the control, you can use your normal JScript editor to create your scripts. Listing 25.1 shows an example of the JScript code for responding to the Command button's Click method.

LISTING 25.1   Using JScript to Interact with ActiveX Controls

```
<html>
<head>
  <title>JavaScript Unleashed</title>
  <script type="text/javascript">
```

**LISTING 25.1** continued

```
  <!--
    function loadBox() {
      alert("The Great Question");
}
  //-->
  </script>
  <script type="text/javascript" for="CommandButton1" event="Click()">
  <!--
    var msg = "She loves me";
    var altMsg = "She loves me not";
    if(CommandButton1.Caption == msg){
      CommandButton1.Caption = altMsg;
      window.defaultStatus = altMsg;
    }else{
      if(CommandButton1.Caption == altMsg){
        CommandButton1.Caption = msg;
        window.defaultStatus = msg;
      }
    }
  //-->
  </script>
</head>
<body onload="loadBox()">
  <object id="CommandButton1" width="98" height="32"
    classid="CLSID:D7053240-CE69-11CD-A777-00DD01143C57">
    <param name="VariousPropertyBits" value="268435483">
    <param name="Caption" value="She loves me">
    <param name="Size" value="2096;678">
    <param name="FontCharSet" value="0">
    <param name="FontPitchAndFamily" value="2">
    <param name="ParagraphAlign" value="3">
    <param name="FontWeight"  value="0">
  </object>
</body>
</html>
```

Because the `<object>` tag doesn't allow you to add event handlers as parameters, you're forced to use an alternative event-handling syntax of Microsoft's that uses expanded `<script>` tag syntax to add the `for` and `event` parameters. This tells JScript what the object and event the code within the `<script>` tags is designed for. The script that performs this task in Listing 25.1 looks like this:

```
<script type="text/javascript" for="CommandButton1" event="Click()">
<!--
  var msg = "She loves me";
  var altMsg = "She loves me not";
  if(CommandButton1.Caption == msg){
    CommandButton1.Caption = altMsg;
    window.defaultStatus = altMsg;
  }else{
    if(CommandButton1.Caption == altMsg){
      CommandButton1.Caption = msg;
      window.defaultStatus = msg;
    }
  }
//-->
</script>
```

# Java Applets

One of JavaScript's most powerful features is its capability to interact with Java applets. JavaScript scripts may invoke Java methods, examine and modify Java variables, and control Java applets. Java applets, in turn, may access JavaScript methods, properties, and data structures.

### Note

This method of accessing Java applets is referred to as LiveConnect and is supported only by Navigator browsers.

## Accessing Java from JavaScript

JavaScript scripts communicate with Java applets running in an HTML page by accessing members (methods and fields) of the Java objects associated with those applets. Any Java method declared with the public modifier is available to be called from JavaScript, and any Java field declared as public is available to be examined or modified. The first step in communicating with a Java applet from JavaScript is to obtain a reference to the applet. Once that's accomplished, you can directly access any of the applet's public members.

> **Note**
>
> LiveConnect is a Netscape client-side technology that promises seamless manipulation of data between Navigator's three main client-side development environments—plug-ins, Java, and JavaScript. You can find additional information on LiveConnect at Netscape's DevEdge site at `http://developer.netscape.com`.

The LiveConnect technology allows JavaScript to communicate with Java in the following ways:

- Direct calls to Java methods
- Control over Java applets
- Control over Java plug-ins

## Referencing Applets

Applets running in a document are reflected in JavaScript within the `document.applets` array. For example, the first applet defined in the current document could be referenced from JavaScript as `document.applets[0]`. The same applet could also be referenced by name as `document.applets["appletName"]`, or simply `document.appletName` if its name was specified in the `<applet>` tag. An applet's name can be specified in the `<applet>` tag by giving a value to the `name` attribute. For example, this tag

```
<applet name="myApplet" code="testApplet.class" width="100" height="100"
➡  mayscript></applet>
```

would create an applet of class `testApplet` named `myApplet`. If it also happened to be the first applet on the page, it could be referenced by `document.applets[0]`, `document.applets["myApplet"]`, or `document.myApplet`.

JavaScript scripts may also reference Java applets running in other frames in the same browser window. For example, if a Java applet were running in a frame called `frame1`, it could be referenced from a sibling frame as `parent.frame1.document.myApplet`.

## Java Plug-Ins

JavaScript regards each plug-in on a Web page as an item in an `embeds` array. For instance, `document.embeds[0]` represents the first embedded object on the page.

If the plug-in is associated with the Java class `netscape.plugin.Plugin`, its static variables and methods can be accessed in the same way I showed you in the preceding section for accessing the Java applet's variables, methods, and properties.

**25**

*Interacting with Other Technologies*

# Accessing JavaScript from Java

To access JavaScript methods, properties, and data structures from a Java applet, you must first import the Netscape `javascript` package. This is done with the following syntax:

```
import netscape.javascript.*
```

`netscape.javascript` defines the `JSObject` class and the `JSException` exception object. You must allow an applet to access JavaScript by declaring the `mayscript` attribute (with no arguments) for the `<applet>` tag. This prevents an applet from accessing JavaScript on a page without the developer's knowledge. An error occurs if the `mayscript` attribute hasn't been declared.

> ### Tip
>
> Before you can access JavaScript, you must get a handle for the Navigator window. Use the `getWindow` method of the class `netscape.javascript.JSObject` to get a window handle. For example
>
> ```
> winHandle = JSObject.getWindow(this)
> ```
>
> `winHandle` is a variable of the type `JSObject`.

To access JavaScript objects and properties, you need to use the `getMember` method of the class `netscape.javascript.JSObject`. This is done by calling `getMember` to access each contained JavaScript object in turn. You must make sure to get a handle for the JavaScript window first, however (use the `getWindow` method).

You can use the `call` and `eval` methods of the `netscape.javascript.JSObject` class to call JavaScript methods. Again, use `getWindow` to get a handle for the JavaScript window, and then use `call` or `eval` to access a JavaScript method. You can use the following syntax:

- `JSObject.getWindow().call("methodName", arguments)`

    *methodName* is the name of the called JavaScript method, and *arguments* is an array of arguments to pass to the method.

- `JSObject.getWindow().eval("expression")`

    *expression* is a JavaScript expression that evaluates to a JavaScript method.

## Working with `JSObjects`

Because complex JavaScript objects such as arrays and `Window` objects are reflected in Java as objects of type `JSObject`, it's important to know how to manipulate these objects and extract information from them. When a JSObject represents a JavaScript array, it's useful to be able to examine the individual array elements, and when a JSObject represents a JavaScript Window, Document, History, or similar object, it's useful to be able to examine its properties.

It might seem tempting at first to avoid the whole issue by dissecting objects on the JavaScript side and breaking them into sets of simpler objects. Once broken apart, the elements could be sent to Java as sets of simple objects that would be translated into Java String, Double, and Boolean objects.

The major drawback to that approach, other than being a lot of extra work, is that it leaves no way to handle objects of variable size. If it wasn't known, in advance, how many elements an array might have, there would be no way to pass each individual element to a Java method, because Java methods take a number of arguments that is fixed at compile time. It's probably a better idea to simply pass complex JavaScript objects into Java "as is" and learn how to deal with them there.

> **Note**
>
> Be sure to include the mayscript attribute in the <applet> tag of any applet you want to operate on JSObjects. Without it, an applet doesn't have access to JavaScript objects and properties. This safeguard was designed to let HTML authors include untrusted Java applets on their pages without having to worry that those applets might have access to potentially sensitive information available only in JavaScript.

As a concrete example, suppose that you wanted to use JavaScript as a GUI for a Java point-plotting applet. With the following variable and function declarations

```
<script type="text/javascript">
<!--
  var xvals = new Array();
  var yvals = new Array();

  function addPoint(x, y){
    xvals[xvals.length] = x;
    yvals[yvals.length] = y;
  }

  function plotPoints(){
    document.myApplet.plotPoints(xvals, yvals);
```

```
  }
</script>
```

and the following HTML form augmented with event handlers

```
<form>
  <input type=text name="xval">
  <input type=text name="yval">
  <br>
  <input type=button value="Add Point"
    onclick="addPoint(form.xval.value, form.yval.value)">
  <br>
  <input type=button value="Plot Points" onclick="plotPoints()">
</form>
```

you could collect (x,y) coordinate pairs using the two text input fields and the addPoint()
function and then send them to the applet in one big batch using the plotPoints()
function.

That would allow you to send an arbitrary number of points to the applet to be plotted but
would require dissection of the point arrays from within Java. This example's
plotPoints() Java method is a good representation of what you can do with JSObjects.
The code might look something like this:

```
public void plotPoints(JSObject xvals, JSObject yvals){
  Double length = (Double) xvals.getMember("length");
  int n = Math.round(length.doubleValue());
  for (int i = 0; i < n; i++){
    try{
      String sx = (String) xvals.getSlot(i);
      String sy = (String) yvals.getSlot(i);
      Double x = new Double(sx);
      Double y = new Double(sy);
      doPlot(x, y);
    }catch(NumberFormatException e)
      System.err.println("Illegal point specification");
  }
}
```

Let's take a closer look at the relevant parts of this program, line by line.

```
public void plotPoints(JSObject xvals, JSObject yvals)
```

This method is expecting two JSObjects, an array of x-coordinates, and an array of y-
coordinates. Note that JavaScript arrays, even numeric ones, don't show up in Java as

arrays of one of Java's built-in numeric types. If the function had instead been written with the signature

```
public void plotPoints(double[] xvals, double[] yvals)
```

or something similar, any attempt to call it from JavaScript would have failed. You're stuck with the JSObjects, then, instead of the numeric arrays you might have preferred.

```
Double length = (Double) xvals.getMember("length");
```

This call to getMember() is the first step in converting the arguments from the form in which they were passed to a more useable form. The getMember() method is used to obtain the length property of one of the array objects (the two arrays have the same length). getMember() returns a generic Java Object (the base class for all Java objects), so you need to cast it to a more appropriate and useful type. You know that the length property of JavaScript arrays is a numeric property, and you should recall that JavaScript numbers are reflected in Java as Doubles, so the object returned by getMember() is cast to a Double object.

Note that there is no flexibility in the type chosen here; numbers obtained from JSObjects *must* be cast to Double. It is only when JavaScript numeric values are passed directly to Java as function arguments that they can initially appear as Java types other than Double.

```
int n = Math.round(length.doubleValue());
```

Although this statement doesn't directly involve any JSObjects, it does demonstrate a useful idiom for converting JavaScript numbers into useful Java numeric types. Programmers often find themselves in possession of Double objects when they're more interested in other types, so it can become necessary to convert them. In this case, the Double object's doubleValue() method is used to extract the actual numeric value, and the Math package's round() method is used to obtain the integer closest to that value.

```
String sx = (String) x.getSlot(i);
String sy = (String) y.getSlot(i);
```

Inside the loop, you need a way to obtain the numeric value of each element of the JSObjects representing the xvals and yvals arrays. Here the getSlot() method is used to extract the individual element at a given array index. getSlot() takes an integer argument and returns the JavaScript object located at that index. getSlot(), like getMember(), returns a generic Java Object, so again it needs to be cast to a more useful type. You know that the xvals and yvals arrays are populated with JavaScript strings, so Java Strings are the correct type to use in this case.

It may seem counterintuitive at first, because you've been thinking of the array elements as numbers, but String really is the correct cast to make. Remember that the values with

**25**

Interacting with
Other
Technologies

which the arrays are populated were originally obtained from text input fields in an HTML form. In JavaScript, just because a string happens to look like a number (consisting entirely of digits) doesn't automatically mean that it is a number.

```
Double x = new Double(sx);
Double y = new Double(sy);
```

You need a way to convert strings that look like numbers into actual numbers, and this `Double` constructor fits the bill nicely. It takes a `String` as an argument, and returns a `Double` object corresponding to the double-precision floating-point value represented by the `String`. If the `String` doesn't represent a numeric value, a `NumberFormatException` is thrown, which is why these statements are wrapped in a `try` block. If an exception is thrown, the attempt to plot this point is aborted, and the next iteration of the loop begins.

```
doPlot(x, y);
```

This is where, having extracted the useful (x,y) coordinate values from the `JSObjects`, the call is made to the hypothetical low-level point-plotting method.

Although an exhaustive explanation of the `JSObject` class is beyond the scope of this book, one more example should help demonstrate a few more of its methods. Suppose that you want to add a method to the applet that plots all the points the user has typed into the form so far, without waiting for the user to explicitly click the Plot Points button. A method such as the following would allow the applet to venture out into the JavaScript world and inspect the relevant JavaScript objects whenever it wanted:

```
private void getPoints(){

  // Get the window and the document.
  JSObject window = JSObject.getWindow(this);
  JSObject document = (JSObject) window.getMember("document");

  // Get the point arrays.
  JSObject xvals = (JSObject) document.getMember("xvals");
  JSObject yvals = (JSObject) document.getMember("yvals");

  // Now, just call plotPoints()
  plotPoints(xvals, yvals);
}
```

Let's take a closer look at the lines that introduce new methods or concepts not found in the preceding example.

```
private void getPoints()
```

Notice that this method is `private`—it isn't intended to be called from JavaScript. Notice also that it takes no arguments, because all the information necessary to complete its task is contained within JavaScript. The whole point of this exercise is that Java applets are free to seek objects and properties from JavaScript without waiting for some user action on the JavaScript side to start the ball rolling.

```
JSObject window = JSObject.getWindow(this);
```

The `JSObject` class has a static method called `getWindow()`, which can be used by an applet to obtain the JavaScript `Window` object corresponding to the window that contains the applet. The object returned is simply the same object denoted by `Window` in JavaScript. `getWindow()` is a particularly important and useful method, because it is the only way a Java applet can obtain a "new" `JSObject` (that is, one not derived from another, pre-existing `JSObject`) without being passed one explicitly from JavaScript; the `JSObject` class has no public constructors. The argument to `getWindow()` is the applet object itself.

```
JSObject document = (JSObject) window.getMember("document");
```

Once the `Window` object is obtained, the `getMember()` method is used to extract a property by name. In this case, that property is the window's `Document` object, the object denoted by `window.document` in JavaScript. The reason for this is that the variables `xvals` and `yvals`, like all variables defined at "top level" scope in a JavaScript script, are properties of the `Document` object. Complex JavaScript objects such as `Document` are reflected in Java as `JSObjects`, so the `Object` returned by `getMember()` is cast to that type.

```
JSObject xvals = (JSObject) document.getMember("xvals");
JSObject yvals = (JSObject) document.getMember("yvals");
```

Once you have the `Document` object, you can begin to extract the variables you're looking for. The `getMember()` method can once again be used for this purpose. The `xvals` and `yvals` objects are JavaScript arrays, which are reflected in Java as `JSObjects`, so the `Objects` returned by `getMember()` are again cast to that type.

```
plotPoints(xvals, yvals);
```

Now that you've obtained the `JSObjects` representing the `xvals` and `yvals` arrays, you can call the `plotPoints()` method from within Java, exactly as you would have called it from JavaScript.

Two other noteworthy methods of the `JSObject` class are `call()` and `eval()`, which have the following prototypes:

```
public Object call(String methodName, Object args[]);
public Object eval(String s);
```

**25**

*Interacting with Other Technologies*

`call()` calls its object's *methodName* method with arguments given by the `args` array. It is equivalent to calling

```
this.methodName(arg[0], arg[1], ...);
```

from within JavaScript. For example, the following within an applet

```
JSObject window = JSObject.getWindow(this);
Object args[] = { "Hello, world!" };
window.call("alert", args);
```

is equivalent to the following JavaScript:

```
alert("Hello, world! ");
```

An object's `eval()` method evaluates its argument string as a JavaScript expression. Evaluation occurs within the context of the object. Replacing the last line in the preceding example with

```
window.eval("alert('Hello, world! ')");
```

yields the same result. Note the use of single quotes inside the double quotes.

## Translating Data Types

One of the most difficult and confusing aspects of calling Java methods from JavaScript can be getting the types of the arguments you pass to Java to match up with the types of the arguments the Java method is looking for. If the two sets of arguments don't match exactly, the attempted function call fails, and you get an error message saying that JavaScript couldn't find a Java method that was expecting the arguments you tried to pass.

Java is a strongly typed language (meaning that every variable has a specific, declared type), and all Java methods must declare in advance how many arguments they are expecting, of what type, and in what order. Within a Java program, any attempt to invoke a method with an argument sequence that doesn't exactly match the method's declared argument sequence, type for type, results in a compile-time error.

JavaScript, in contrast, has much more relaxed typing and, as an interpreted language, must do all its checking at runtime anyway. JavaScript variables don't have a declared type; in fact, they don't have to be declared at all, because they can simply come into existence by being referenced. The same JavaScript variable can be assigned a string in one statement, an integer in the next statement, and an array in the next.

How are JavaScript objects converted into Java objects when they're passed to Java methods? How does Java know how to find a Java type that matches exactly the JavaScript object's structure? The short answer is that, in general, it doesn't. There probably is no such object. Unless the object happens to fall into one of certain exceptional cases, Java won't necessarily have a class that exactly mirrors the object's JavaScript type, so it simply assigns it a default type, `JSObject`, specifically designed to represent JavaScript objects in Java.

Fortunately, the aforementioned exceptional cases encompass some of the most common and useful data types, including JavaScript's three basic data types: `strings`, `numbers`, and `booleans`. JavaScript strings (that is, string constants and variables that have most recently been assigned strings) appear in Java as instances of the Java `String` type. JavaScript numbers (numeric constants and variables most recently assigned integer or real numeric values) are converted to Java `Double` objects. JavaScript Boolean values (`true` and `false`) become Java `Boolean` objects.

One other special case concerns JavaScript objects that are wrappers around Java objects. Such objects are simply "unwrapped" and converted to their original Java types. Although this fact is currently undocumented, there is additional flexibility in passing JavaScript numbers directly to Java methods. An attempt to make a call such as

```
document.myApplet.setNumber(3.7);
```

would succeed if the `myApplet` applet had a method with a signature of

```
public void setNumber(type x);
```

where *type* is one of the following: `Double`, `double`, `float`, `long`, `int`, `short`, `char`, or `byte`, although the documentation implies that only `Double` ought to be acceptable. In cases where the applet has more than one overloaded method expecting one of these types, the first such method (the method closest to the top of the Java source file) is chosen. Tie-breaking by lexicographic location is probably not the best way to resolve conflicts between overloaded methods, and it is very likely that some other mechanism will be devised.

Suppose you wrote a `setText()` method to be picky about acceptable values for `theText`, and you wanted a way to find out if a given call to `setText()` had resulted in `theText()` being successfully set. If you designed the new function to return a Boolean flag indicating success or failure, it might look something like this:

```
public boolean setText(String s){
  if (s.equals("Hello world!")){

    // I'm sick of that string; don't accept it.
```

```
    return false;
  }else{
    theText = s;
    return true;
  }
}
```

If you wrote a JavaScript script that included this line

```
var changed = document.myApplet.setText("Hello world!")
```

the value returned by setText() would be stored in changed. The question remains, though: Exactly how will the Java Boolean value returned by setText() be converted into a JavaScript object? In this particular case, the answer is simple and intuitive: Java Boolean values become JavaScript boolean values when they're returned to JavaScript.

Passing Java objects to JavaScript isn't always quite so simple—a number of rules govern the exact translation for a given object. The good news is that things often work out just the way you might hope. Java arrays become JavaScript arrays, Java numeric types become JavaScript numbers, Java Boolean values become JavaScript boolean values, and Java Strings become JavaScript Strings. For completeness, here is the entire set of rules used to govern the conversion:

- Java numeric types (byte, char, double, float, int, long, short) become JavaScript numbers.

- Java Boolean values become JavaScript boolean values.

- Java JSObjects are converted back to their original JavaScript objects.

- Java arrays become JavaScript Array objects.

- All other Java objects are converted to JavaScript wrapper objects that can be used to access the original Java members.

When an attempt is made to convert a JavaScript wrapper into a JavaScript string, number, or Boolean, the original Java object's toString(), doubleValue(), or booleanValue() method is called, if it exists, and the value of the converted object is the value returned by the corresponding method. If the corresponding method doesn't exist, the conversion fails. Note that Java strings work as expected in JavaScript, even though they are technically passed to JavaScript as wrapper objects. Any attempt to use one in a context where a JavaScript string is expected causes the correct conversion to be applied.

# Delving into the Details of Java Applets

Up to this point, we have looked at how JavaScript-to-Java interaction takes place. You should now have a pretty good idea of what can be done and to some degree how it works. Now we are going to look at some of the finer details of what actually goes on when you are calling or accessing these methods and properties across environments.

## Calling to Java Methods

Assuming that LiveConnect is enabled, you can use the following syntax to access a Java method:

```
Packages.packageName.className.methodName
```

where *packageName* and *className* are properties of the object `Packages`. The name `Packages` can be omitted from the JavaScript call with default Java, Sun, or Netscape packages that are shipped with Navigator. For instance, the Java class `java.lang.System` can be referred to as either `java.lang.System` or `Packages.java.lang.System`.

Take a look at this example to get a better idea of how this works. In the following code, the JavaScript code uses its access to Java to print a message to the Java console:

```
<script type="text/javascript">
<!--
  java.lang.System.out.println("Greetings from JavaScript");
//-->
</script>
```

## Setting Java Properties

Although it's usually not good programming style for Java classes to expose their data members (also called *properties* or *fields*) to direct outside access by declaring them `public`, occasionally situations arise in which it can be useful to do so. When Java applets have public fields, JavaScript scripts have the power to modify them directly, just as they have the power to invoke public Java methods. For example, consider the following fragment of a Java applet:

```
public String theText;

public void setText(String s){
  theText = s;
}
```

It is probably better programming practice to set the text as follows:

```
document.myApplet.setText("Hello world!");
```

It would be equally possible to just write

```
document.myApplet.theText = "Hello world!";
```

The same rules that govern translation of JavaScript objects into Java objects during function calls also apply here. This implies, by the way, that only the Java String, Double, Boolean, JSObject, and primitive numeric types can be directly set in this way, because all JavaScript variables are initially reflected in Java as one of those types.

## Using Java Packages

JavaScript's capability to interact with Java isn't limited to applets. JavaScript scripts also have direct access to static methods and fields of core Java packages, and they can even construct new Java objects. Java packages are available in JavaScript within the containing document's Packages array. For example, Java's java.lang.System package, which can be used for console I/O, can be referenced in JavaScript as Packages.java.lang.System, and Java's java.lang.Math package can be referenced as Packages.java.lang.Math. As a result, to write the value of pi to the Java console, you could use the following:

```
var pi = Packages.java.lang.Math.PI;
Packages.java.lang.System.out.println("pi is: " + pi);
```

As a special shorthand, references to three default packages—java, sun, and netscape—may safely omit the Packages keyword. That is, within a JavaScript Document object, java, sun, and netscape are aliases for Packages.java, Packages.sun, and Packages.netscape, respectively. Using those aliases, it is possible to rewrite the pi example as follows:

```
var pi = java.lang.Math.PI;
java.lang.System.out.println("pi is: " + pi);
```

It's also possible to construct new Java objects dynamically, using the new operator. This is a handy way to access some of Java's powerful built-in utility classes—hash tables, stacks, vectors, dates, and more—without having to write an entire Java applet. In the following JavaScript example, two Java Date objects are constructed, and they are compared using the after method of the Date class to see if the current date is after the deadline.

```
var theDate = new java.util.Date(); // the current date
var deadline = new java.util.Date(00, 6, 26); // July 26, 2000
if (theDate.after(deadline)){
  alert("I missed my deadline!");
}else{
  alert("Made it!");
}
```

# Controlling Applets

Once a reference to an applet has been obtained, the next step is to communicate with it by invoking one of its methods. For example, if the applet had a public method called `hello()` that took no arguments, that method could be called like this:

```
document.myApplet.hello();
```

Making that call from within JavaScript has precisely the same effect as calling the applet object's `hello()` method from within Java. As another example, suppose you have a Java applet with an audio soundtrack, and you want to turn the sound on and off from JavaScript. If the applet provided methods such as the following, you could call those methods from JavaScript to control the applet's soundtrack:

```
public void soundtrackOn();
public void soundtrackOff();
```

If you wanted to make toggling the soundtrack on and off as simple as clicking a mouse button, you could use JavaScript as "wiring" to hook up radio buttons in an HTML form to the Java applet. The following example shows how a `form` element's `onclick` method can be used to communicate with the applet:

```
<form>
  <input type="radio" checked="true" name="sound"
    onclick="document.myApplet.soundtrackOn()">
  On
  <br>
  <input type="radio" name="sound"
    onclick="document.myApplet.soundtrackOff()">
  Off
</form>
```

The values for the `onclick` event handlers specify that the `soundtrackOn()` or `soundtrackOff()` method of the applet named `myApplet` is called whenever the corresponding radio button is clicked. As a slightly more complicated example (which illustrates passing arguments to Java methods), suppose the applet also has a method with a prototype of

```
public void changeText(String s);
```

which, when called, changes the text displayed by the applet to the value specified by string s. If the following elements were added to the form

```
<input type="text" name="newtext">
<input type="button" value="Change Text"
➡     onclick="document.myApplet.changeText(form.newtext.value)">
```

users could enter new strings into the text input field and have them reflected in the applet. When the Change Text button is clicked, the text field's value is extracted, converted to a Java `String`, and passed as the argument to the applet's `changeText()` method. This is a powerful tool. The capability to pass JavaScript objects to Java methods makes it possible to quickly and easily build attractive GUIs out of standard HTML forms augmented with JavaScript event handlers and to use them to control Java applets.

# LiveAudio

LiveAudio is an integral part of the Netscape Navigator Web browser—a built-in plug-in that allows Navigator to play sound files natively. LiveAudio, in essence, extends Navigator to accept a brand new type of content. This means that, if an audio-capable computer is used, a majority of Web users can painlessly receive and hear audio files. This, in turn, opens up a whole new world of opportunities for the Web developer—the capability to deliver information and entertainment through audio.

LiveAudio is tightly integrated into the Navigator environment and can easily be manipulated with JavaScript and LiveConnect. These advantages, along with LiveAudio's wide availability, warrant a detailed discussion of LiveAudio. This chapter shows some examples of LiveAudio and discusses how you can use JavaScript to manipulate it.

> ### Warning
>
> This edition of the book will probably be the last that will offer information on LiveAudio. The industry is widely moving toward embedded players, such as Real's G2 Player and Microsoft's Windows Media Player, for handling audio and video files.

According to Netscape's Web site, "LiveAudio is LiveConnect-aware." This means that you can take advantage of the LiveConnect framework and JavaScript to control embedded (or inline) LiveAudio elements. Via LiveConnect, JavaScript can interact with LiveAudio to allow you to accomplish the following programmatically:

- Create alternative sound control interfaces.

- Defer the loading of an audio file until a user interaction occurs (for example, clicking a Play button).

- Create interface buttons that make clicking noises.

- Provide audio enhancement to user interaction. For instance, set an object to say what it's doing when the user clicks it or moves the mouse cursor over it.

# Using JavaScript Methods

JavaScript provides several control methods for LiveAudio to help a developer easily manipulate audio files embedded as inline objects on a Web page. For these methods to be available to JavaScript, however, you must embed a LiveAudio console somewhere on your page.

Here are the methods available to you to control LiveAudio through JavaScript:

- `play()`: Starts playing the sound. You can specify a loop value, similar to the `loop` attribute value, followed by an optional URL for the sound if the original URL isn't used.

- `stop()`: Stops the sound if it is playing.

- `pause()`: Pauses the sound at the current position. You can use the `play()` method, or the `pause()` method again, to continue the playback.

- `start_time()` and `end_time()`: Allow you to override the start and end times. Specify the value in seconds.

- `start_at_beginning()` and `stop_at_end()`: Reset the start and stop times to the beginning and end of the sound file.

- `setvol()`: Sets the sound's volume between 0% and 100%.

- `fade_to()`: Sets the volume but fades from the current value.

- `fade_from_to()`: Allows you to specify two values and fades from one to the other.

- `IsReady()`: Returns `true` if the sound is loaded and ready to play.

- `IsPlaying()`: Returns `true` if the sound is playing.

- `IsPaused()`: Returns `true` if the sound is paused.

- `GetVolume()`: Returns the current volume.

These methods are provided to you through the `document.embeds` property, which is an array of `<embeds>` on a given page. To apply one of these methods, simply access it through the following format:

```
document.embedName.method();
```

**25**

**Interacting with Other Technologies**

For example, if you want to invoke the `play()` method on an embedded player named `myRadio`, do the following:

```
document.myRadio.play();
```

## Playing Sounds on JavaScript Events

As I mentioned earlier, you can use JavaScript to invoke sounds at any place within your site. Often, though, the most appropriate place to use sound to enhance a user's experience is with the "on" events. The following example demonstrates this concept by showing you how to invoke several sounds on your page using JavaScript event handlers to capture and handle the `onLoad`, `onUnLoad`, and `onClick` events.

In this example, which you can see in Listing 25.2, a keyboard-typing sound (`type.wav`) is played when the page is loaded. To demonstrate the `onClick` event, when the user clicks the hyperlink, he hears the sound of a cash register, and clicking the button will result in the sound of a gunshot. Also, on unloading the page, the user hears glass shattering. The resulting browser window is in Figure 25.1.

**LISTING 25.2**   Controlling Sounds with JavaScript

```html
<html>
<head>
  <title>JavaScript Unleashed</title>
  <script type="text/javascript">
<!--
    function playSound(sfile) {

      // load a sound and play it
      window.location.href=sfile;
    }
//-->
  </script>
</head>
<body onLoad="playSound('Type.wav')" onUnLoad="playSound('Glass.wav')">
  <h2>
    Sounds on JS Events
  </h2>
  <hr>
  The following are examples of JS event handlers used to play sounds.
  <hr>
  <a href="#" onClick="playSound('Cashreg.wav')">
    Click here for sound
  </a>
```

LISTING 25.2    continued

```
<p>
  <form name="form1">
    <input type="button" value="Play" onClick="playSound('Gunshot.wav')">
  </form>
</p>
</body>
</html>
```

**FIGURE 25.1**
*Examples of invoking sounds on JavaScript events.*

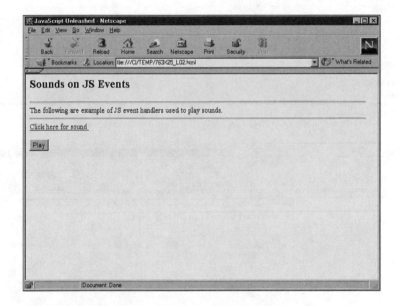

The following example demonstrates how you can use some of the built-in JavaScript methods to control your sound files. The code shown in Listing 25.3 lets you load a sound and then control it using several buttons. Also, note the use of a hidden console to invoke LiveAudio initially. Figure 25.2 shows the resulting page in the browser.

**LISTING 25.3    Controlling Embedded Sounds with JavaScript**

```
<html>
<head>
  <title>JavaScript Unleashed</title>
</head>
<body>
  <h2>
    Embedded Sounds in JavaScript
```

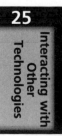

**25**

**Interacting with Other Technologies**

**LISTING 25.3    continued**

```
</h1>
<embed mastersound name="sound1" src="test.wav" volume="100" hidden="true"
  autostart="false">
<hr>
This document includes a hidden embedded sound, which is loaded after
the page is loaded. You can use the JavaScript buttons below to control
the sound.
<hr>
<form name="form1">
  <input type="button" value="Play" onclick="document.sound1.play(true)">
  <input type="button" value="Pause" onclick="document.sound1.pause()">
  <input type="button" value="Stop" onclick="document.sound1.stop()">
</form>
</body>
</html>
```

**FIGURE 25.2**

*Controlling embedded sounds in JavaScript.*

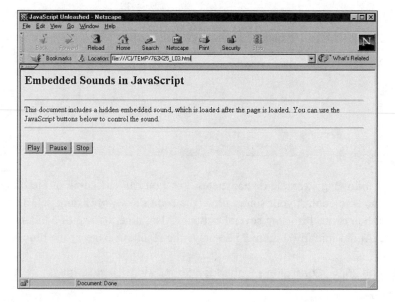

# Summary

This chapter described some of the ways JavaScript can communicate with other technologies. It introduced you to Netscape's plug-in technology and explained the distinctions between plug-ins, helper applications, and MIME types.

We also discussed how ActiveX controls can be tightly integrated with JScript. We looked at what ActiveX technology is and how you can use it in your scripts. We also covered connecting to Java applets via LiveConnect.

We concluded the chapter by talking about the use of JavaScript event handlers to invoke sounds within an HTML page, as well as how to set up external audio players as helper applications to hear the files.

# Essential Programming Techniques

# PART V

# Guaranteeing Your Scripts Work in Netscape and Microsoft Browsers

JavaScript has gone through quite a few changes since its conception, as do all computer languages. A large number of changes occurred in versions 1.1 and 1.2. During these versions the core functionality was constantly changing, making it hard for programmers to write JavaScript code that would work on different browsers. Normally this problem is handled simply by avoiding the features that have compatibility problems, but JavaScript's problems were in its core functionality!

To further confuse the problem, Microsoft reverse-engineered JavaScript to avoid having to purchase licensing. The result was Microsoft's own flavor of JavaScript, called JScript. These events caused JavaScript to be viewed as very unstable.

Fortunately, Netscape and Microsoft recognized that a JavaScript "Tower of Babel" served no one. They submitted the language to a standardization committee called the ECMA (European Computer Manufacturers Association), which put together ECMAScript 1.0 (ECMA-262). The standard was quickly adopted by both Netscape and Microsoft.

After this point, the core functionality of JavaScript began to stabilize with JavaScript 1.3 and JScript 3.0. This stability is continuing today in JavaScript 1.4 and JScript 5.0. The problem areas today are no longer core JavaScript but rather the integration of new Web technologies such as cascading style sheets (CSS) into JavaScript.

As you can see, JavaScript has undergone quite a few changes since its conception that still affect the way you write scripts today. In this chapter, you will learn what browser versions support JavaScript functionality.

# Language Version Versus Browser Version

At this point you are probably a bit confused with the version numbers associated with JavaScript and JScript as well as the version numbers associated with Netscape and Microsoft browsers. Table 26.1 matches browser versions to language versions.

**TABLE 26.1**  Language Version Versus Browser Version

| Browser | Version | Language |
|---|---|---|
| Netscape Navigator | 2.0 | JavaScript 1.0 |
| | 3.0 | JavaScript 1.1 |
| | 4.0 – 4.05 | JavaScript 1.2 |
| | 4.06 – 4.7x | JavaScript 1.3 |
| | 6.0 | JavaScript 1.4 & 1.5 |
| Microsoft Internet Explorer | 3.0 | JScript 1.0 |
| | 4.0 – 4.5 | JScript 3.0 |

**TABLE 26.1** continued

| Browser | Version | Language |
|---------|---------|----------|
|         | 5.0     | JScript 5.0 |
|         | 5.5     | JScript 5.5 |

From this chart you can see why it is so important to know what browsers your customers will be using to view your Web pages. By deciding up front what browsers your Web pages will support, you can save a lot of development time. On the other hand, if there is some particular JavaScript functionality that you really want to use in your Web pages, you will need to choose your browser support based on the JavaScript version that supports the desired functionality or use a detection technique, covered in Chapter 27, "Browser Detection Techniques."

# JavaScript Dialect Comparisons

JavaScript was the child of Sun Microsystems. Netscape's Navigator was the first browser to interpret the language and to push JavaScript beyond its core functionality by interacting with plug-ins and the Java runtime environment. Microsoft soon entered the game with JScript. As mentioned in the introduction, JavaScript went through many changes during its first few years of existence. Only now are we starting to see JavaScript's core functionality stabilize and the language expand into other Web technologies. Although the current version of JavaScript is fairly stable, you may want to support older browsers, so it is important that you know when each functionality was introduced or changed. Even more importantly, you will probably want your scripts to run on both Netscape and Microsoft browsers. Therefore, we need to look at what the various dialects of JavaScript are and which browsers provide support for them.

## Netscape's JavaScript

This section is broken into five subsections, one for each version of JavaScript. Each subsection details all the objects, properties, methods, event handlers, built-in functions, operators, and statements that are new for a particular version.

**Tip**

Check Netscape's Web site at the following URL for the most recent information on the newest versions of JavaScript.

`http://devedge.netscape.com/tech/javascript/index.html`

# JavaScript 1.0

The base language specification, JavaScript 1.0, was first supported in Netscape Navigator 2.0. The following lists show the original object, function, operator, and statement functionality.

## Objects

| | | | |
|---|---|---|---|
| Button | Form | Location | Reset |
| Checkbox | Frame | Math | Select |
| Date | Function | Navigator | Submit |
| Document | Hidden | Option | Text |
| FileUpLoad | History | Password | Textarea |
| Embed | Link | Radio | Window |

## Functions

| | |
|---|---|
| escape | parseIn |
| eval | unescape |
| parseFloat | |

## Operators

| | | | | | | | |
|---|---|---|---|---|---|---|---|
| - | _ | ! | != | % | %= | & | && |
| &= | * | *= | , | / | /**/ | // | /= |
| ?: | ^ | ^= | \| | \|\| | \|= | ~ | + |
| ++ | += | < | << | <<= | <= | = | - = |
| == | > | >= | >> | >>= | >>> | >>>= | new |

## Statements

| | | |
|---|---|---|
| delete | for...in | return |
| do...while | function | while |
| for | if...else | with |

Tables 26.2 through 26.4 show the original properties, methods, and event handlers.

**TABLE 26.2**    Properties Supported in JavaScript 1.0 and Higher

| Property | Object |
|---|---|
| action | Form |
| aLinkColor | Document |
| appCodeName | Navigator |
| appName | Navigator |
| appVersion | Navigator |
| bgColor | Document |
| checked | Checkbox, Radio |
| cookie | Document |
| defaultChecked | Checkbox, Radio |
| defaultStatus | Window |
| defaultValue | Password, Text, Textarea |
| document | Frame, Window |
| E | Math |
| elements | Form |
| encoding | Form |
| fgColor | Document |
| form | Checkbox, FileUpload, Hidden, Password, Radio, Reset, Select, Submit, Text, Textarea |
| frames | Frame, Window |
| hash | Link, Location |
| host | Link, Location |
| hostname | Link, Location |
| href | Link, Location |
| lastModified | Document |
| length | Form, Frame, History, Select, String, Window |
| linkColor | Document |
| links | Document |
| LN10 | Math |
| LN2 | Math |
| location | Document, Window |
| LOG10E | Math |
| LOG2E | Math |
| method | Form |
| name | Button, Checkbox, FileUpload, Form, Frame, Hidden, Password, Radio, Reset, Submit, Text, Textarea, Window |
| options | Select |
| parent | Frame, Window |

**TABLE 26.2** continued

| Property | Object |
|----------|--------|
| pathname | Link, Location |
| PI | Math |
| port | Link, Location |
| protocol | Link, Location |
| selectedIndex | Select |
| self | Window |
| search | Link |
| SQRT1_2 | Math |
| SQRT2 | Math |
| Status | Window |
| previous | History |
| prototype | Date |
| referrer | Document |
| search | Location |
| selected | Option |
| self | Frame |
| target | Form, Link |
| text | Option |
| title | Document |
| top | Frame, Window |
| userAgent | Navigator |
| URL | Document |
| vlinkColor | Document |
| value | Button, Checkbox, FileUpload, Hidden, Option, Password, Radio, Reset, Submit, Text, Textarea |
| window | Frame |

**TABLE 26.3** Methods Supported in JavaScript 1.0 and Higher

| Method | Object |
|--------|--------|
| abs | Math |
| acos | Math |
| alert | Window |
| anchor | String |
| asin | Math |
| atan | Math |
| atan2 | Math |
| back | History |
| big | String |

*Guaranteeing Your Scripts Work in Netscape and Microsoft Browsers*

**CHAPTER 26**

711

26

Guaranteeing
Your Scripts
Work

**TABLE 26.3**  continued

| Method | Object |
| --- | --- |
| blink | String |
| bold | String |
| blur | Password, Reset, Select, Text, Textarea |
| ceil | Math |
| charAt | String |
| charCodeAt | String |
| clearTimeout | Window |
| click | Button, Reset, Submit |
| close | Document, Window |
| concat | String |
| confirm | Window |
| cos | Math |
| exp | Math |
| fixed | String |
| floor | Math |
| focus | Checkbox, Password, Reset, Select, Text, Textarea |
| fontColor | String |
| fontSize | String |
| forward | History |
| fromCharCode | String |
| getDate | Date |
| getDay | Date |
| getHours | Date |
| getMinutes | Date |
| getMonth | Date |
| getSeconds | Date |
| getTime | Date |
| getTimezoneOffset | Date |
| getYear | Date |
| go | History |
| handleEvent | Password, Select |
| indexOf | String |
| italics | String |
| lastIndexOf | String |
| link | String |
| log | Math |
| match | String |
| max | Math |

**TABLE 26.3** continued

| Method | Object |
| --- | --- |
| min | Math |
| open | Document, Window |
| parse | Date |
| pow | Math |
| prompt | Window |
| random | Math |
| round | Math |
| select | FileUpLoad, Text, Textarea |
| setDate | Date |
| setHours | Date |
| setMinutes | Date |
| setSeconds | Date |
| setTime | Date |
| setTimeout | Frame, Window |
| setYear | Date |
| sin | Math |
| small | String |
| sqrt | Math |
| strike | String |
| sub | String |
| submit | Form |
| substring | String |
| sup | String |
| tan | Math |
| toGMTString | Date |
| toLocaleString | Date |
| toLowerCase | String |
| toSource | Math |
| toString | Date, Math |
| toUpperCase | String |
| UTC | Date |
| write | Document |
| writeln | Document |

**TABLE 26.4** Event Handlers Supported in JavaScript 1.0 and Higher

| Event Handler | Object |
|---|---|
| onBlur | Password, Radio, Reset, Select, Text, Textarea |
| onChange | Select, Text, Textarea |
| onClick | Button, Document, Radio, Reset, Submit, Text |
| onDblClick | Document |
| onFocus | Password, Radio, Reset, Select, Text, Textarea |
| onKeyDown | Document |
| onKeyPress | Document |
| onKeyUp | Document |
| onLoad | Window |
| onUnLoad | Window |
| onMouseDown | Button, Document |
| onMouseOver | Link |
| onMouseUp | Button, Document |
| onSelect | Textarea |
| onSubmit | Form |

# JavaScript 1.1

JavaScript 1.1 is supported in Netscape Navigator 3. The following lists are the object, functions, operators, statements, tag enhancements, and capability changes since the previous JavaScript versions.

**Objects**

| | | |
|---|---|---|
| Applet | Function | Object |
| Area | Image | Package |
| Array | MimeType | Plugin |
| Boolean | Number | String |

**Functions**

| | |
|---|---|
| taint | untaint |

**Operators**

| | |
|---|---|
| typeof | void |

**Statement**

continue

**Tag Enhancements**

- SRC attribute for <SCRIPT> added.

- LANGUAGE attribute for <SCRIPT> can specify language version.

- <NOSCRIPT> tag added.

- JavaScript entities (such as &{myVar};) supported.

**Capabilities**

- Added LiveConnect, the capability for Java and JavaScript to communicate.

- Added capability to detect available plug-ins.

- Added object prototypes, the capability to create properties to be shared by all objects of the same type.

- Added capability for Select objects to be modified dynamically.

- Added capability to pass strings between scripts in separate windows or frames.

- Changed the way in which you can index Object properties. If you define a property by name, you must always reference it by name. Similarly, if you define a property by an index value, you must always reference it by that index.

- Changed eval() from a built-in function to a method of every object.

- Added the capability to print and save the dynamic HTML generated by the write() and writeln() methods by using the File menu commands.

- Improved behavior of three built-in functions: isNaN, parseFloat, and parseInt, each of which now performs similarly across platforms.

- Added the capability to delete an object by setting its reference equal to null.

- Added the capability to reset event handlers dynamically.

- Added support of data tainting.

- Added the capability to index arrays using strings.

Tables 26.5 through 26.7 list the property, method, and event handler enhancements added in JavaScript 1.1.

**TABLE 26.5**   Properties Supported in JavaScript 1.1 and Higher

| *Property* | *Object* |
|------------|----------|
| applets    | Document |
| arguments  | Function |

**TABLE 26.5** continued

| Property | Object |
|----------|--------|
| border | Image |
| caller | Function |
| closed | Window |
| complete | Image |
| constructor | Object |
| current | History |
| defaultSelected | Option |
| description | MimeType, Plugin |
| domain | Document |
| embeds | Document |
| enabledPlugin | MimeType |
| filename | Plugin |
| formName | Document |
| forms | Document |
| hash | Area |
| height | Image |
| history | Window |
| host | Area |
| hostname | Area |
| href | Area |
| hspace | Image |
| images | Document |
| java | Packages |
| length | Array, Plugin |
| lowsrc | Image |
| MAX_VALUE | Number |
| mimeTypes | Navigator |
| MIN_VALUE | Number |
| NaN | Number |
| NEGATIVE_INFINITY | Number |
| name | Image, Plugin |
| netscape | Packages |
| next | History |
| opener | Window |
| pathname | Area |
| plugins | Document, Navigator |
| port | Area |
| POSITIVE_INFINITY | Number |

**TABLE 26.5** continued

| Property | Object |
|----------|--------|
| previous | History |
| protocol | Area |
| prototype | Boolean, Function, Image, Number, Object |
| search | Area |
| src | Image |
| suffixes | MimeType |
| sun | Packages |
| target | Area |
| type | Button, Checkbox, FileUpload, Hidden, MimeType, Password, Radio, Reset, Select, Submit, Text, Textarea |
| vspace | Image |
| width | Image |

**TABLE 26.6** Methods Supported in JavaScript 1.1 and Higher

| Method | Object |
|--------|--------|
| blur | Button, Checkbox, FileUpload, Frame, Submit, Window |
| click | Checkbox |
| eval | Object |
| focus | Button, FileUpload, Frame, Submit, Window |
| javaEnabled | Navigator |
| join | Array |
| refresh | Plugins |
| reload | Location |
| replace | Location |
| reset | Form, Reset |
| reverse | Array |
| scroll | Window |
| sort | Array |
| split | String |
| taintEnabled | Navigator |
| toSource | Array, Boolean |
| toString | Array, Boolean, Number, Object |
| valueOf | Object |

TABLE 26.7   Event Handlers Supported in JavaScript 1.1 and Higher

| Event Handler | Object |
|---|---|
| onAbort | Window, Image |
| onBlur | Button, Checkbox, FileUpload, Frame, Submit, Window |
| onChange | FileUpload |
| onClick | Checkbox |
| onError | Window, Image |
| onFocus | Button, Checkbox, FileUpload, Frame, Submit, Window |
| onLoad | Image |
| onMouseOut | Area, Link |
| onMouseOver | Area |
| onReset | Form |

## JavaScript 1.2

JavaScript 1.2 is supported in Netscape Navigator 4.0 through 4.05. The following lists include object, statement, and capability enhancements added in JavaScript 1.2 that previous versions don't support.

**Objects**

| | |
|---|---|
| Anchor | RegExp |
| Event | Screen |
| Layer | |

**Statements**

| | |
|---|---|
| export | labeled |
| import | switch |

**Capabilities**

- Added capability to manipulate layers.

- Added capability to programmatically control cascading style sheets.

- Added additional parameters to the window open() method to allow for additional customization of the opening window.

- If the <SCRIPT> tag's LANGUAGE parameter is JavaScript1.2, the equality operators (== and !=) compare only like-typed operands.

Tables 26.8 through 26.10 list the property, method, and event handler enhancements added in JavaScript 1.2.

TABLE 26.8   Properties Supported in JavaScript 1.2 and Higher

| Property | Object |
|---|---|
| above | Layer |
| anchors | Document |
| arity | Function |
| background | Layer |
| below | Layer |
| bgColor | Layer |
| data | Event |
| document | Layer |
| height | Document, Event |
| innerHeight | Window |
| innerWidth | Window |
| language | Navigator |
| layers | Document |
| layerX | Event |
| layerY | Event |
| left | Layer |
| locationBar | Window |
| menuBar | Window |
| modifiers | Event |
| name | Anchor, Layer |
| outerHeight | Window |
| outerWidth | Window |
| pageX | Event, Layer |
| pageXOffset | Window |
| pageY | Event, Layer |
| pageYOffset | Window |
| parentLayer | Layer |
| personalbar | Window |
| platform | Navigator |
| screenX | Event |
| screenY | Event |
| scrollbars | Window |
| siblingAbove | Layer |
| siblingBelow | Layer |
| src | Layer |
| statusbar | Window |
| target | Event |

*Guaranteeing Your Scripts Work in Netscape and Microsoft Browsers*

**CHAPTER 26**

719

26

Guaranteeing
Your Scripts
Work

**TABLE 26.8** continued

| Property | Object |
|----------|--------|
| text | Anchor, Link |
| top | Layer |
| toolbar | Window |
| type | Event |
| visibility | Layer |
| which | Event |
| width | Document, Event |
| x | Anchor |
| y | Anchor |
| zIndex | Layer |

In addition, all properties associated with RegExp and Screen objects are supported.

**TABLE 26.9** Methods Supported in JavaScript 1.2 and Higher

| Method | Object |
|--------|--------|
| back | Window |
| captureEvents | Document, Layer, Window |
| clearInterval | Frame, Window |
| clearTimeout | Frame |
| compile | RegExp |
| concat | Array, String |
| disableExternalCapture | Window |
| enableExternalCapture | Windwow |
| exec | RegExp |
| find | Window |
| forward | Window |
| getFullYear | Date |
| getMilliseconds | Date |
| getSelection | Document |
| getUTCDate | Date |
| getUTCDay | Date |
| getUTCFullYear | Date |
| getUTCHours | Date |
| getUTCMilliseconds | Date |
| getUTCMinutes | Date |
| getUTCMonth | Date |
| getUTCSeconds | Date |

**TABLE 26.9** continued

| Method | Object |
| --- | --- |
| handleEvent | Area, Button, Checkbox, Document, Form, Image, Layer, Link, Password, Radio, Reset, Select, Submit, Text, Textarea, Window |
| home | Window |
| load | Layer |
| match | String |
| moveAbove | Layer |
| moveBelow | Layer |
| moveBy | Layer, Window |
| moveTo | Layer, Window |
| moveToAbsolute | Layer |
| pop | Array |
| print | Frame, Window |
| push | Array |
| releaseEvents | Document, Layer, Window |
| replace | String |
| resizeBy | Layer, Window |
| resizeTo | Layer, Window |
| routeEvents | Document, Layer, Window |
| scrollBy | Window |
| scrollTo | Window |
| search | String |
| setFullYear | Date |
| setInterval | Window |
| setMilliseconds | Date |
| setUTCDate | Date |
| setUTCFullYear | Date |
| setUTCHours | Date |
| setUTCMilliseconds | Date |
| setUTCMinutes | Date |
| setUTCMonth | Date |
| setUTCSeconds | Date |
| setInterval | Frame |
| shift | Array |
| slice | Array, String |
| splice | Array |
| stop | Window |
| substr | String |

**TABLE 26.9** continued

| Method | Object |
|---|---|
| test | RegExp |
| toSource | Array |
| toUTCString | Date |
| unshift | Array |
| unwatch | Object |
| watch | Object |

**TABLE 26.10** Event Handlers Supported in JavaScript 1.2 and Higher

| Event Handler | Object |
|---|---|
| onBlur | Layer |
| onDblClick | Link |
| onDragDrop | Window |
| onFocus | Layer |
| onKeyDown | Image, Link, Textarea |
| onKeyPress | Image, Link, Textarea |
| onKeyUp | Image, Link, Textarea |
| onLoad | Layer |
| onMouseDown | Link |
| onMouseOut | Layer |
| onMouseOver | Layer |
| onMove | Frame, Window |
| onResize | Frame, Window |

## JavaScript 1.3

JavaScript 1.3 is supported in Netscape Navigator 4.06 through 4.7x. The following lists are the function and capability enhancements added in JavaScript 1.3 that previous versions don't support.

**Functions**

IsFinite        isNaN

**Capabilities**

- Compliance with ECMAScript 1.0.

- Unicode support.

- New strict equality operators === and !==.

- Changes to the equality operators == and !=.

- Simple assignment should not be performed in a conditional statement such as if (x = y).

- Any object whose value is neither undefined nor null (including a Boolean object that is false) evaluates to true when passed into a conditional statement.

Table 26.11 lists the method enhancements added in JavaScript 1.3.

**TABLE 26.11**    Methods Supported in JavaScript 1.3 and Higher

| Method | Object |
| --- | --- |
| apply | Function |
| call | Function |
| toSource | Array, Date, Function, Number, Object, String |
| toString | String |

# JavaScript 1.4

Netscape never introduced a browser during the time JavaScript 1.4 was introduced. The new functionality that appeared in 1.4 was passed along to JavaScript 1.5 and is supported in Netscape Navigator 6.0. The following lists are the operator and statement enhancements added in JavaScript 1.4 that previous versions don't support.

**Operators**

in        instanceof

**Statements**

catch        throw        try

# JavaScript 1.5

JavaScript 1.5 is the latest Netscape implementation and is supported in Netscape Navigator 6.0. The following list is the capability enhancements added in JavaScript 1.5 that previous versions don't support.

**Capabilities**

- Compliance with ECMAScript 3.0.

- Runtime errors are reported as exceptions.

- Enhancements to Regular Expressions.

Table 26.12 lists the method enhancements added in JavaScript 1.5.

**TABLE 26.12**  Methods Supported in JavaScript 1.5 and Higher

| Method | Object |
| --- | --- |
| toFixed | Number |
| toExponential | Number |

# Microsoft's JScript

This section is broken into three subsections, one for each version of JScript. Each subsection details all the objects, properties, methods, event handlers, built-in functions, operators, and statements that are new for that particular version.

> **Tip**
>
> Check Microsoft's Web site at `http://msdn.microsoft.com/scripting/jscript/default.htm` for the most recent details of the newest versions of JScript.

## JScript 1.0

JScript 1.0 is supported in Microsoft Internet Explorer 3.0. The following lists include the core object, function, operator, and statement functionality.

**Objects**

| | | |
| --- | --- | --- |
| Area | Function | Radio |
| Button | Hidden | Reset |
| Checkbox | History | Select |
| Date | Link | String |
| Document | Location | Submit |
| Embed | Math | Text |
| FileUpLoad | Navigator | Textarea |

| | | |
|---|---|---|
| Form | Option | Window |
| Frame | Password | |

**Functions**

| | |
|---|---|
| escape | parseInt |
| eval | unescape |
| parseFloat | |

**Operators**

| | | | | | | | |
|---|---|---|---|---|---|---|---|
| - | _ | ! | != | % | %= | & | && |
| &= | * | *= | , | / | /**/ | // | /= |
| ?: | ^ | ^= | \| | \|\| | \|= | ~ | + |
| ++ | += | < | << | <<= | <= | = | -= |
| == | > | >= | >> | >>= | >>> | >>>= | new |

**Statements**

| | |
|---|---|
| For | return |
| for...in | while |
| function | with |
| if...else | |

Tables 26.13 through 26.15 show the core properties, methods, and event handlers.

**TABLE 26.13** Properties Supported in JScript 1.0 and Higher

| Property | Object |
|---|---|
| action | Form |
| aLinkColor | Document |
| appCodeName | Navigator |
| applets | Document |
| appName | Navigator |
| appVersion | Navigator |
| bgColor | Document |
| checked | Radio |
| cookie | Document |
| defaultChecked | Radio |
| defaultStatus | Window |
| defaultValue | Password, Text, Textarea |
| document | Frame, Window |
| E | Math |
| elements | Form |

TABLE 26.13   continued

| Property | Object |
|---|---|
| encoding | Form |
| fgColor | Document |
| form | Button, FileUpload, Hidden, Password, Radio, Reset, Select, Submit, Text, Textarea |
| form | Reset, Select, Submit |
| frames | Frame, Window |
| hash | Area, Link, Location |
| host | Area, Link, Location |
| hostname | Area, Link, Location |
| href | Area, Link, Location |
| lastModified | Document |
| length | Form, Frame, History, Select, String |
| linkColor | Document |
| links | Document |
| LN10 | Math |
| LN2 | Math |
| location | Document, Window |
| LOG10E | Math |
| LOG2E | Math |
| method | Form |
| name | Button, FileUpload, Form, Frame, Hidden, Password, Radio, Reset, Select, Submit, Text, Textarea, Window |
| options | Select |
| parent | Frame, Window |
| pathname | Area, Link, Location |
| PI | Math |
| port | Area, Link, Location |
| protocol | Area, Link, Location |
| previous | History |
| referrer | Document |
| search | Area, Link, Location |
| selected | Option |
| selectedIndex | Select |
| self | Frame, Window |
| SQRT1_2 | Math |
| SQRT2 | Math |
| status | Window |
| target | Area, Form, Link |

**TABLE 26.13**  continued

| Property | Object |
|----------|--------|
| text | Option |
| title | Document |
| top | Frame, Window |
| type | Button |
| userAgent | Navigator |
| URL | Document |
| vlinkColor | Document |
| value | Button, FileUpload, Hidden, Option, Password, Radio, Reset, Submit, Text, Textarea |
| window | Frame |

**TABLE 26.14**  Methods Supported in JScript 1.0 and Higher

| Method | Object |
|--------|--------|
| abs | Math |
| acos | Math |
| alert | Window |
| anchor | String |
| asin | Math |
| atan | Math |
| atan2 | Math |
| back | History |
| big | String |
| blink | String |
| bold | String |
| blur | Button, Checkbox, Password, Radio, Reset, Select, Text, Textarea |
| ceil | Math |
| charAt | String |
| charCodeAt | String |
| clearTimeout | Window |
| click | Button, Radio, Reset, Submit |
| close | Document, Window |
| confirm | Window |
| cos | Math |
| exp | Math |
| fixed | String |
| floor | Math |
| focus | Button, Password, Radio, Reset, Select, Text, Textarea |
| fontColor | String |

**26**

**TABLE 26.14** continued

| Method | Object |
| --- | --- |
| fontSize | String |
| forward | History |
| fromCharCode | String |
| getDate | Date |
| getDay | Date |
| getHours | Date |
| getMinutes | Date |
| getMonth | Date |
| getSeconds | Date |
| getTime | Date |
| getTimezoneOffset | Date |
| getYear | Date |
| go | History |
| indexOf | String |
| italics | String |
| lastIndexOf | String |
| link | String |
| log | Math |
| max | Math |
| min | Math |
| open | Document, Window |
| parse | Date |
| pow | Math |
| prompt | Window |
| random | Math |
| round | Math |
| select | FileUpLoad, Password, Text, Textarea |
| setDate | Date |
| setHours | Date |
| setMinutes | Date |
| setMonth | Date |
| setSeconds | Date |
| setTime | Date |
| setTimeout | Frame, Window |
| setYear | Date |
| sin | Math |
| sqrt | Math |
| strike | String |

**TABLE 26.14** continued

| Method | Object |
|--------|--------|
| sub | String |
| submit | Form |
| substring | String |
| sup | String |
| tan | Math |
| toGMTString | Date |
| toLocaleString | Date |
| toLowerCase | String |
| toSource | Math |
| toString | Date, Math |
| toUpperCase | String |
| UTC | Date |
| write | Document |
| writeln | Document |

**TABLE 26.15** Event Handlers Supported in JScript 1.0 and Higher

| Event Handler | Object |
|---------------|--------|
| onBlur | Password, Radio, Reset, Select, Text, Textarea |
| onChange | Select, Text, Textarea |
| onClick | Button, Document, Radio, Reset, Submit, Text |
| onDblClick | Document |
| onFocus | Password, Radio, Reset, Select, Text, Textarea |
| onKeyDown | Document |
| onKeyPress | Document |
| onKeyUp | Document |
| onLoad | Window |
| onUnLoad | Window |
| onMouseDown | Button, Document |
| onMouseOver | Link |
| onMouseUp | Button, Document |
| onSelect | Textarea |
| onSubmit | Form |

# JScript 3.0

JScript 3.0 is supported in Microsoft Internet Explorer 4.0 through 4.5. The following lists are the object, operator, and statement enhancements added in JScript 3.0 that previous versions don't support.

*Guaranteeing Your Scripts Work in Netscape and Microsoft Browsers*

**CHAPTER 26**

729

26

Guaranteeing
Your Scripts
Work

**Objects**

| | |
|---|---|
| Applet | Number |
| Array | Object |
| Boolean | Plugin |
| Event | RegExp |
| Image | Screen |
| MimeType | |

**Operators**

| | |
|---|---|
| typeof | void |

**Statements**

| | | | |
|---|---|---|---|
| continue | do...while | import | switch |
| delete | export | labeled | |

Tables 26.16 through 26.18 show the properties, methods, and event handlers added in JScript 3.0.

**TABLE 26.16**  Properties Supported in JScript 3.0 and Higher

| Properties | Object |
|---|---|
| $* | RegExp |
| $& | RegExp |
| $_ | RegExp |
| $ ` | RegExp |
| $' | RegExp |
| $+ | RegExp |
| $1, $2,...$9 | RegExp |
| all | Document |
| anchors | Document |
| arguments | Function |
| arity | Function |
| availHeight | Screen |
| availWidth | Screen |
| border | Image |
| caller | Function |
| checked | Checkbox |
| closed | Window |
| colorDepth | Screen |
| complete | Image |
| constructor | Object |

TABLE **26.16** continued

| Properties | Object |
| --- | --- |
| current | History |
| data | Event |
| defaultChecked | Checkbox |
| defaultSelected | Option |
| description | MimeType, Plugin |
| domain | Document |
| embeds | Document |
| enabledPlugin | MimeType |
| filename | Plugin |
| form | Checkbox |
| formName | Document |
| forms | Document |
| global | RegExp |
| height | Event, Image, Screen |
| history | Window |
| hspace | Image |
| ignoreCase | RegExp |
| images | Document |
| innerHeight | Window |
| innerWidth | Window |
| input | RegExp |
| language | Navigator |
| lastIndex | RegExp |
| lastMatch | RegExp |
| lastParen | RegExp |
| layerX | Event |
| layerY | Event |
| leftContext | RegExp |
| length | Plugin, Window |
| locationbar | Window |
| lowsrc | Image |
| MAX_VALUE | Number |
| Menubar | Window |
| MIN_VALUE | Number |
| mimeTypes | Navigator |
| modifiers | Event |
| multiline | RegExp |
| name | Anchor, Checkbox, Image, Plugin |

*Guaranteeing Your Scripts Work in Netscape and Microsoft Browsers*

**CHAPTER 26**

731

26

Guaranteeing
Your Scripts
Work

**TABLE 26.16** continued

| Properties | Object |
|---|---|
| NaN | Number |
| NEGATIVE_INFINITY | Number |
| next | History |
| opener | Window |
| outerHeight | Window |
| outerWidth | Window |
| pageX | Event |
| pageXOffset | Window |
| pageY | Event |
| pageYOffset | Window |
| personalbar | Window |
| platform | Navigator |
| plugins | Document, Navigator |
| POSITIVE_INFINITY | Number |
| length | Array |
| prototype | Boolean, Date, Function, Image, Number, Object, String |
| rightContext | RegExp |
| screenX | Event |
| screenY | Event |
| scrollbars | Window |
| source | RegExp |
| src | Image |
| statusbar | Window |
| stop | Window |
| suffixes | MimeType |
| target | Event |
| text | Link |
| toolbar | Window |
| type | Checkbox, Event, FileUpload, Hidden, MimeType, Password, Radio, Reset, Select, Submit, Text, Textarea |
| value | Checkbox |
| vspace | Image |
| which | Event |
| width | Event, Image, Screen |

**TABLE 26.17** Methods Supported in JScript 3.0 and Higher

| Method | Object |
|---|---|
| back | Window |
| blur | FileUpload, Frame, Submit, Window |
| captureEvents | Window |
| clearInterval | Frame, Window |
| clearTimeout | Frame |
| click | Checkbox |
| compile | RegExp |
| concat | Array, String |
| eval | Object |
| exec | RegExp |
| find | Window |
| focus | Checkbox, FileUpload, Frame, Submit, Window |
| forward | Window |
| getFullYear | Date |
| getMilliseconds | Date |
| getUTCDate | Date |
| getUTCDay | Date |
| getUTCFullYear | Date |
| getUTCHours | Date |
| getUTCMilliseconds | Date |
| getUTCMinutes | Date |
| getUTCMonth | Date |
| getUTCSeconds | Date |
| handleEvent | Area, Button, Checkbox, FileUpload, Form, Image, Link, Password, Radio, Reset, Select, Submit, Text, Textarea, Window |
| home | Window |
| javaEnabled | Navigator |
| join | Array |
| match | String |
| moveBy | Window |
| moveTo | Window |
| open | Window |
| preference | Navigator |
| print | Frame, Window |
| releaseEvents | Window |
| reload | Location |
| replace | Location, String |

**TABLE 26.17** continued

| Method | Object |
|--------|--------|
| reset | Form |
| resizeBy | Window |
| resizeTo | Window |
| reverse | Array |
| routeEvent | Window |
| scroll | Window |
| scrollBy | Window |
| scrollTo | Window |
| search | String |
| setFullYear | Date |
| setInterval | Frame, Window |
| setMilliseconds | Date |
| setUTCDate | Date |
| setUTCFullYear | Date |
| setUTCHours | Date |
| setUTCMilliseconds | Date |
| setUTCMinutes | Date |
| setUTCMonth | Date |
| setUTCSeconds | Date |
| slice | Array, String |
| small | String |
| sort | Array |
| split | String |
| stop | Window |
| substr | String |
| test | RegExp |
| toSource | Array, Boolean, Date, Function, Number, Object, String |
| toString | Array, Boolean, Function, Number, Object, String |
| toUTCString | Date |
| unwatch | Object |
| valueOf | Object |
| watch | Object |

TABLE **26.18** Event Handlers Supported in JScript 3.0 and Higher

| Event Handler | Object |
|---|---|
| onBlur | Checkbox, Submit, Window |
| onClick | Checkbox |
| onDragDrop | Window |
| onError | Window |
| onFocus | Checkbox, Submit, Window |
| onKeyDown | Textarea |
| onKeyPress | Textarea |
| onKeyUp | Textarea |
| onMove | Window |
| onResize | Window |

## JScript 5.0

JScript 5.0 is supported in Microsoft Internet Explorer 5.0. The following lists are the function, operator, and statement enhancements added in JScript 5.0 that previous versions don't support.

**Functions**

isFinite     isNaN

**Operators**

in           instanceof

**Statements**

catch        try          throw

Table 26.19 shows the method enhancements added in JScript 5.0 and higher.

TABLE **26.19** Methods Supported in JScript 5.0 and Higher

| Method | Object |
|---|---|
| Apply | Function |
| Call | Function |

# Bugs

Every new version of JavaScript or JScript requires Netscape or Microsoft to provide a new version of its browser to support the newest JavaScript functionality. As we all know, no piece of software is 100% perfect, and a browser is no exception. Each version of Netscape Navigator and Microsoft Internet Explorer has its own set of bugs.

For the JavaScript developer, this means that some JavaScript functionality does not work quite like it was intended or does not work at all. It is important that you know what bugs exist in all the different browser versions so that you can design your scripts accordingly. Depending on what browser versions your scripts support, you may choose to work around the bug, using a detection technique covered in Chapter 27, or avoid the problem area altogether.

Because browser bugs vary greatly between browsers and browser versions, I will not attempt to address each one. Rather, I will encourage you to take browser bugs seriously by first deciding what browsers and browser versions your scripts are to support. Once you have decided that, take some time to review the bugs associated with those browsers. Make sure your scripts do not fail because of those bugs.

Netscape has done an excellent job of providing access to a complete list of all the JavaScript-related bugs associated with its browsers. This list of bugs can be found at `http://devedge.netscape.com/support/bugs/known/javascript.html`.

Microsoft, on the other hand, does not provide an easily accessible list of JScript-related bugs, so you will have to spend some time searching its site (`msdn.microsoft.com`) to find bugs.

# Summary

In this chapter, we looked at JavaScript as it is implemented in Netscape and Microsoft browsers. JavaScript had some problems in its early years but is finally beginning to stabilize, thanks to the efforts of Netscape, Microsoft, and the ECMA. Although JavaScript is stabilizing, not everyone is using the newest browsers. For this reason, it is important that you know what JavaScript functionality is supported in the various browser versions as well as what bugs plague each browser. Armed with the information in this chapter, you will be on your way to guaranteeing that your scripts work in Netscape and Microsoft browsers.

# Browser Detection Techniques

To help introduce this chapter's topic, I want to you meet Joe. Joe is a Web developer who wants to enliven his Web site by using JavaScript for special effects, easier site navigation, animation buttons, and data validation. After spending considerable energy getting everything to work properly, he remembered that he should at least confirm that everything he developed under the current Netscape Navigator works with Microsoft Internet Explorer, as well as older versions of the Netscape browser. That's when everything broke down. His special effects relied on `Layer` objects, which aren't universally supported, and his code used a lot of `Array` objects, which fizzle under Navigator 2.0. The end result was that his site was usable only by those who had the same version of the browser he did.

Although Joe is fictional, this same sad story is often repeated by developers. If you have written much JavaScript code at all, you have undoubtedly encountered similar woes.

Given the varying degrees of compatibility across JavaScript dialects, it's critical that you account for incompatibility during script development. After all, a primary objective of using JavaScript is to enhance your Web site. If you ignore the compatibility issues, users running browsers that don't support your variation of JavaScript will be disappointed. Therefore, as you design Web pages, your goal should be to develop "safe" scripts—those that maximize the capabilities of later versions of JavaScript but that account for browsers offering lesser support. In this chapter, we will look at two techniques you can employ, depending on the context, to detect the type of browser a client is using.

# The "All or Nothing" Approach

The first technique is what I call the "all or nothing" approach, which determines whether an entire script is run or ignored completely by the browser. To use this technique, specify the desired language dialect you're using in the `<script>` tag's `language` parameter. Statements within a `<script>` tag are ignored if the browser doesn't have the same level of JavaScript support specified.

The advantage of using this technique is that you can be confident that if the browser understands the `language` parameter, it will provide full support for the JavaScript dialect in use. The disadvantage is that unsupporting browsers will be forced to ignore the entire script.

# The "In-Place Detection" Approach

An alternative to the all or nothing approach is the "in-place detection" method (sometimes referred to as "browser sniffing"), a technique that requires determining the appropriate browser version within a script before making a risky, dialect-specific programming call.

Although this technique is slightly more complicated, the advantage of using it is that you can provide alternative functionality based on the level of JavaScript support you encounter. There are four useful pieces of browser-related information that you can extract from the `Navigator` object in JavaScript.

# Browser Type

The `appName` property of the `Navigator` object provides your script with the name of the client's browser. The two most popular are Netscape and Microsoft Internet Explorer. The following line of code displays the browser name on the screen:

```
document.write(navigator.appName);
```

If you need to be able to identify other browser types, you will need to use the `userAgent` property of the `Navigator` object. This property contains a lot of information, but by searching for a specific string with the `indexOf()` method, you can identify the browser name. Because this value is a string, it is a good idea to convert it to all lowercase to make comparisons easier. Table 27.1 lists some of the more common values assigned to the `userAgent` property and the browsers they represent.

**TABLE 27.1**   Values of the `userAgent` Property

| Value | Browser |
| --- | --- |
| mozilla | Netscape Navigator |
| msie | Microsoft Internet Explorer |
| opera | Opera |
| webtv | Web TV |

The following code segment tests for various browser types using the `userAgent` property:

```
var browserType = navigator.userAgent.toLowerCase();

If (browserType.indexOf('mozilla')
    document.write("Netscape Navigator");
else if (browserType.indexOf('msie')
    document.write("Microsoft Internet Explorer");
else if (browserType.indexOf('opera')
    document.write("Opera");
else if (browserType.indexOf('webtv')
    document.write("Web TV");
```

> **Tip**
>
> For more information on the userAgent string, check out the Web site:
> `http://www.it97.de/JavaScript/JS_tutorial/bstat/navobj.html`

## Browser Version

The appVersion property of the Navigator object provides your script with the version of the client's browser. The following line of code displays the browser version on the screen:

```
document.write(navigator.appVersion);
```

If you convert this property into a floating number (non-integer) with the parseFloat() method, you can do simple mathematical comparisons, rather than having to compare specific strings. You will see that this is especially handy in the next section when you are trying to determine the JavaScript version. The following line of code demonstrates how to create this floating value:

```
var browserVersion = parseFloat(navigator.appVersion);
```

## JavaScript Version

Using your knowledge about JavaScript dialects from Chapter 26, "Guaranteeing Your Scripts Work in Netscape and Microsoft Browsers," you can determine which version of JavaScript you are using from the browser type and version information that was discussed earlier. Table 27.2 shows how to match browser type and version information to the JavaScript version.

**TABLE 27.2**   JavaScript Versions

| JavaScript Version | Browser | Browser Version |
|---|---|---|
| 1.0 | Navigator | 2.0 |
| 1.0 | Internet Explorer | 3.0 |
| 1.1 | Navigator | 3.0 |
| 1.2 | Navigator | 4.0-4.05 |
| 1.2 | Internet Explorer | 4.0 |
| 1.3 | Navigator | 4.06-4.5 |
| 1.4 | Navigator | 5.0 |
| 1.4 | Internet Explorer | 5.0 |

## Operating System Platform

The `platform` property of the `Navigator` object provides your script with the client's operating system platform. The following line of code displays the operating system platform:

```
document.write(navigator.platform);
```

You will need this information if, for example, you are on a Macintosh, trying to workaround a bug that exists only in Netscape Navigator. In most cases you will not need this information but, should you need it, you will know how to get it.

## Dynamic Positioning Example

Now that you know a number of ways to retrieve information about the client's browser and operating system, let's work through an example using this information.

One of the biggest differences plaguing Navigator and Internet Explorer today is the use of dynamic positioning. Netscape originally implemented dynamic positioning using its `Layer` object, Microsoft using the HTML `<div>` tag. To perform dynamic positioning that will work on both Netscape and Microsoft browsers, you will need JavaScript to determine what browser the client is using.

Listing 27.1 creates two layers (one red and another plain text) using either `<div>` tags or `<layer>` tags. The red box contains buttons that will move the box around the browser window. The red box also has a button that will make the text box disappear and reappear, as shown in Figure 27.1. The actual motion is accomplished by changing the value of the layer's properties in the case of Netscape layers or cascading style sheet properties in the case of a `<div>` block. For more information on using layers and the `<div>` tag, see Chapter 23, "Layers."

**LISTING 27.1**   Detecting Navigator and Internet Explorer

```
<html>
<body>

<script language="JavaScript">
<!--

//Create a layer tag if netscape
if(navigator.appName.indexOf("Netscape") != -1)
  document.write('<layer id="redBox" ');

//Create a div tag if Microsoft
```

**LISTING 27.1** continued

```javascript
if(navigator.appName.indexOf("Microsoft") != -1)
  document.write("<div id='redBox' ");

//Set the style used for the red box
document.write('style="position:absolute; ');
document.write('left:150px; ');
document.write('top:150px; ');
document.write('background-color:red;">');

//-->
</script>


This is a block of moving buttons
<form>
<input type="button"
       value="UP"
       onClick="moveUp()">
<input type="button"
       value="DOWN"
       onCLick="moveDown()">
<input type="button"
       value="LEFT"
       onClick="moveLeft()">
<input type="button"
       value="RIGHT"
       onClick="moveRight()"><BR>
<input type="button"
       value="SHOW/HIDE Text Box"
       onClick="showHide()">
</form>

<script language="JavaScript">
<!--
//If Netscape close the layer tag
if(navigator.appName.indexOf("Netscape") != -1)
  document.write("</layer>");

//If Microsoft close div tag
if(navigator.appName.indexOf("Microsoft") != -1)
  document.write("</div>");
//-->
```

**LISTING 27.1**    continued

```
</script>

<script language="JavaScript">
<!--
//If Netscape create a text layer using layer tag
if(navigator.appName.indexOf("Netscape") != -1)
{
  document.write('<layer id="textBox" >');
  document.write("Here is some text defined as a block");
  document.write("</layer>");
}

//If Microsoft create a text block using div tag
if(navigator.appName.indexOf("Microsoft") != -1)
{
  document.write("</div>");
  document.write("<div id='textBox'>");
  document.write("Here is some text defined as a block");
  document.write("</div>");
}
//-->
</script>


<script language="JavaScript">
<!--

var isNetscape = 0;
var isMicrosoft = 0;

//Determine if this is a Netscape or Microsoft browser
if(navigator.appName.indexOf("Netscape") != -1)
  isNetscape = 1;
if(navigator.appName.indexOf("Microsoft") != -1)
  isMicrosoft = 1;

//Move the red box up 20 pixels
function moveUp()
{
  if(isNetscape)
    document.layers.redBox.pageY+=(-20);
  if(isMicrosoft)
```

**LISTING 27.1**    continued

```
      document.all.redBox.style.pixelTop+=(-20);
}


//Move the red box down 20 pixels
function moveDown()
{
  if(isNetscape)
    document.layers.redBox.pageY+=20;
  if(isMicrosoft)
    document.all.redBox.style.pixelTop+=20;
}


//Move the red box to the left 20 pixels
function moveLeft()
{
  if(isNetscape)
    document.layers.redBox.pageX+=(-20);
  if(isMicrosoft)
    document.all.redBox.style.pixelLeft+=(-20);
}


//Move the red box to the right 20 pixels.
function moveRight()
{
  if(isNetscape)
    document.layers.redBox.pageX+=20;
  if(isMicrosoft)
    document.all.redBox.style.pixelLeft+=20;
}


//Hide or show the text box
function showHide()
{
  if(isNetscape)
  {
    //If text box is currently hidden then make it visible
    if(document.layers.textBox.visibility == "hide")
      document.layers.textBox.visibility="inherit";
    else
      document.layers.textBox.visibility="hide";
  }
  if(isMicrosoft)
```

**LISTING 27.1** continued

```
  {
    //If text box is currently hidden then make it visible
    if(document.all.textBox.style.visibility == "hidden")
      document.all.textBox.style.visibility="visible";
    else
      document.all.textBox.style.visibility="hidden";
  }
}

//-->
</script>

</body>
</html>
```

**FIGURE 27.1**

*Detecting Navigator and Internet Explorer.*

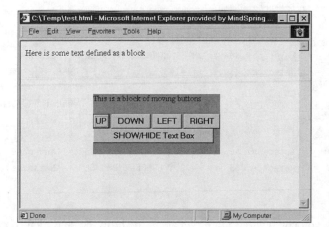

> **Warning**
>
> In Netscape Navigator, you will notice that, when the buttons move, the text associated with the buttons will sometimes get jumbled. This is because Netscape does not refresh the entire screen when a `layer` property is changed. Internet Explorer does a much better job of refreshing the screen when the style sheet properties are changed. In addition, you will also notice that Netscape sporadically colors the layer background red.

In this example, the indexOf() method was used to search for the string "Netscape" or "Microsoft" in the appName property of the Navigator object. Depending on which string is found, the isNetscape or isMicrosoft variable is set to true. These variables are then used throughout the script to determine which functionality should be used.

If you need more browser granularity in your script, you might find it useful to create a function that determines both the browser type and version. For example, the determineCurrentBrowser() function shown in the following code examines the Navigator object's appName and appVersion properties and then assigns a value to a global variable called CURRENT_BROWSER:

```
/* Global variable */
var CURRENT_BROWSER = new String();


/* ------------------------------------------------------------ */
determineCurrentBrowser() {

    var bwr = navigator.appName;
    var ver = parseFloat(navigator.appVersion);


    if ( bwr == "Netscape" && ver >= 5) CURRENT_BROWSER = "Netscape 5.0";
    if ( bwr == "Netscape" && ver >= 4.06 && ver <=4.5) CURRENT_BROWSER = "Netscape
    4.06 - 4.5";
    if ( bwr == "Netscape" && ver >= 4 && ver <= 4.05) CURRENT_BROWSER = "Netscape
    4.0 - 4.05";


    if ( bwr == "Netscape" && ver == 3 ) CURRENT_BROWSER = "Netscape 3.0";
    if ( bwr == "Netscape" && ver == 2 ) CURRENT_BROWSER = "Netscape 2.0";


}
```

Alternatively, you could choose to forget about the browsers and focus on the highest level of JavaScript support offered. The advantage of this method is that it is often easier for comparison purposes:

```
/* Global variable */
var JS_VERSION


/* -------------------------------------- */
function JSVersionCheck() {

    var bwr = navigator.appName;
    var ver = parseFloat(navigator.appVersion);
```

```
    if ( bwr == "Netscape" && ver >= 5) JS_VERSION = 1.4;
    if ( bwr == "Netscape" && ver >= 4.06 && ver <=4.5) JS_VERSION = 1.3;
    if ( bwr == "Netscape" && ver >= 4 && ver <= 4.05) JS_VERSION = 1.2;
    if ( bwr == "Netscape" && ver == 3 ) JS_VERSION = 1.1;
    if ( bwr == "Netscape" && ver == 2 ) JS_VERSION = 1.0;


}
```

# Summary

In this chapter, two techniques were examined that you can use to account for
incompatibility during script development. A primary objective of using JavaScript is to
enhance your Web site. If you ignore the compatibility issues, users running browsers that
don't support your variation of JavaScript will be disappointed. So use the two browser-
detection techniques to create scripts that maximize the capabilities of later versions of
JavaScript but account for browsers offering less support.

**27**

**Browser
Detection
Techniques**

# JavaScript-Based Site Navigation

# Exploring Navigation Techniques

JavaScript transfers much of the burden of content delivery and formatting to the browser rather than having the server deal with it. One of the benefits of this client-side control is improved navigation. Instead of merely providing static links that connect Web pages within a site, Webmasters can use JavaScript to control the display of a site's information.

Before frames were available, it was difficult to add navigational aids to a Web page without limiting the site's layout and its content in several ways. For example, displaying a map showing a view of your site at all times could only be done by adding it to each page. The map would need to be small enough to not distract the user. If the page being viewed was too long, the map would often be unavailable as the user scrolled through the page. Limiting your Web site to one-page documents may not have been an option, and a site map that was available only part of the time looked unprofessional.

Frames can solve this problem. Splitting the browser into more than one window lets you keep a site map visible at all times while the user scrolls through the many pages of an HTML document. Using links on the site map, a new page can be displayed in the other frame. It doesn't take JavaScript to do this. Simply use the `target` attribute of the anchor tag to point to any frame you want. However, what if the page currently being displayed contains a data entry form and needs to be submitted before moving on to another page? Submitting the form using a submit button is fine, but it brings the user to a new page, leaving him somewhere off the map. In some cases, it may be ideal to allow the user to move throughout the site entering data without requiring him to click a submit button on each page. This can be done using JavaScript by submitting the forms across frames.

If your site map is rather large, you may prefer to display only part of the map at a time. Updating the map then becomes necessary. How do you update a map, submit a form, display the resulting document, and keep track of where the user is with one click? Using JavaScript is the easiest way. The navigation techniques in this chapter demonstrate how to create and use a dynamic toolbar as well as how to use the JavaScript `History` object.

# Scripting a Dynamic Toolbar

A toolbar is a common user interface used to navigate through any software program. Relative to JavaScript, a *dynamic* toolbar is one that can change when the user interacts with it. As an example, I have written a toolbar that controls a simple slide show. Four buttons on the toolbar are used to move forward or backward through an array of slides. Two other buttons are used to start or stop an automatic cycle through all of the slides. One logical way to program this is to create two custom objects—a `Button` object and a `Toolbar` object.

# Writing a Custom `Toolbar` Object

A toolbar can be thought of as a set of buttons, so I have named the `Toolbar` object `buttonSet`. Listing 28.1 shows the `buttonSet` constructor used to set up all of the properties and methods available to a toolbar.

**LISTING 28.1**  The `buttonSet` Object Constructor

```
function buttonSet(name)
{
    /*
    * Description: button object constructor.
    * Arguments: name - The variable name of the buttonSet.
    */

    // Properties
    this.name = name;
    this.startIndex = 7;
    this.length = 7;
    this.isBusy = false;

    // Methods
    this.addBtn = addBtn;
    this.print = print;
    this.clear = clear;
    return this;
}
```

The `addBtn` method creates and adds a new `Button` object to the `buttonSet`. The `print` method writes the `buttonSet` to an HTML document. The `clear` method resets all buttons contained within the `buttonSet` to their original states, either disabled or enabled. These methods are described in detail in the following sections.

## Using the `Button` Object

The `buttonSet` object is used to keep track of one or more `Button` objects. Each `Button` object holds the information needed for when it is clicked or displayed as an HTML `<img>` element. Listing 28.2 shows the two functions used to create a new `Button` object.

**LISTING 28.2**  The `Button` Object's `click` Method and Constructor

```
function click()
{
    /*
```

LISTING 28.2   continued

```
 * Description: Method of button. Executes command for this button.
 * Arguments: None.
 */

  eval(this.command);
}

function button(name, file, alt, url, spacer, condition, command)
{
  /*
   * Description: button object.
   * Arguments:
   *   name - The name used as this button's HTML element name.
   *   file - The button image's source url.
   *   alt  - The alt attribute for the button.
   *   url - The url which can reference(across frames) the
   *         buttonSet that holds this button.
   *   spacer - number of pixels of horizontal spacing used
   *            after the button being added.
   *   condition - conditional statement that determines
   *               whether or not to display this button.
   *   commmand - The command to be executed by this button.
   */

  // Properties
  this.name = name;
  this.file = file;
  this.alt = alt;
  this.url = url;
  this.spacer = spacer;
  this.condition = condition;
  this.command = command;

  // Methods
  this.click = click;
  return this;
}
```

The name property becomes its HTML name. The button's `file` property is the source URL for the button's image. The `alt` property is used as the HTML `alt` attribute. The `url` property is used as the HREF property of the anchor associated with the button's image.

Using a transparent graphic file, the spacer property specifies how much space to leave before placing another button image to the right of this one. This allows you to create different sections within the toolbar or compensate for button images with different widths. A Button will be displayed only if its conditional expression evaluates to true. This is the key to knowing which buttons are displayed and available to the user. Whenever a buttonSet object is written to an HTML page, it looks at each Button's conditional expression to determine if the Button is enabled. If it is enabled and the user clicks it, the command is executed. The command string can be any JavaScript statement, as long as it can be executed from the document where the buttonSet is created.

## Instantiating a Toolbar

Using the following lines of code, the slide show program creates a new buttonSet object and resets its current state.

```
Toolbar = new buttonSet("Toolbar");
Toolbar.clear();
```

It is important when creating a new buttonSet that the argument passed to the constructor be equal to the variable name of the object being created. This allows the buttonSet object to create JavaScript commands using its own name. The clear() method is used to set or reset the global variables used by the buttonSet to determine which of its buttons are enabled. Listing 28.3 shows the clear() method that was written for the Slide Show application.

**LISTING 28.3**   The clear() Method of the buttonSet() Object

```
function clear()
{
   /*
   * Description: Method of buttonSet object. Used to reset any global
   *              variables on which any buttons in the buttonSet rely
   *              on for their condition statements.
   * Arguments: None.
   */

   gIsRunning=false;
}
```

Once the new buttonSet has been created, the Slide Show application creates each button by using the addBtn() method. The first button created is shown in the following code:

```
Toolbar.addBtn("First","graphics/first.gif","First Picture",0,"true",
   "changeSlide('first')");
```

Listing 28.4 shows the complete addBtn() method, which simply creates a new Button object and then adds it to the buttonSet.

**LISTING 28.4**   The addBtn() Method of the buttonSet Object

```
function addBtn(name,file,alt,spacer,condition,command)
{
  /*
   *  Description: Method of the buttonSet object used to add a new button to
   *               the end of the button set.
   *  Arguments: name - (string) The name used as this button's HTML
⮞ element name.
   *             file - (string) The button image's source url.
   *             alt  - (string) The alt attribute for the button.
   *             spacer - (integer) number of pixels of horizontal spacing used
   *                      after the button being added.
   *             condition - (string) conditional statement determines
   *                         whether or not to display the button.
   *             commmand - (string) The command to be executed.
   */

  var i = this.length;
  this[i] = new button(name,file,alt,
            "javascript:parent."+this.name+"["+i+"]"+".click()",
            spacer,condition,command);
  this.length++;
}
```

The url argument specified for the button constructor in Listing 28.4 is worth noting. This string will be used as the HREF property of the button's image. The following example is the HTML generated for the first Slide Show button:

```
<a href="javascript:parent.Toolbar[7].click()">
<img src="graphics/first.gif" alt="First Picture" width="24"
⮞ height="24" border=0>
</a>
```

When the user clicks this image, the click() method of the seventh property of the Toolbar object is called. The seventh item in the Toolbar object (essentially an array) is where the first Button object was stored using the addBtn() method. This is the best way to call the click() method across frames while working in both Netscape and Microsoft browsers. The buttonSet object is set up in such a way that the programmer using it doesn't need to keep track of how the buttons are indexed.

## Displaying the Toolbar

The global variable `gIsRunning` is `true` when the slide show is automatically stepping through each slide; otherwise, it is `false`. This variable is used by four `Button` objects to display two buttons at a time. One is for an active state, and the other is for its disabled state (its face is grayed out). The following examples show two buttons that depend on `gIsRunning`:

```
Toolbar.addBtn("Start", "graphics/auto.gif", "Start Slideshow", 0,
               "gIsRunning==false", "changeSlide('start')");
Toolbar.addBtn("StartGrey", "graphics/autoGrey.gif", "Start Slideshow", 0,
               "gIsRunning==true", "");
```

The `StartGrey` button will be displayed only if `gIsRunning` is equal to `true`. On the other hand, if `gIsRunning` is equal to `false`, the `Start` button will be displayed. If the `Start` button is enabled and the user clicks it, the following code is executed within the `changeSlide()` function:

```
if(command == "start") {
    gIsRunning = true;
    Toolbar.print(window.frames[2].document);
    gTimer = window.setTimeout("startAuto()",1500);
}
```

`gIsRunning` is set to `true`, and the toolbar is printed to the `Document` object specified. The current toolbar is eliminated, and a new HTML page is created containing a new toolbar, which then takes into account the new state of `gIsRunning`. This means that the `StartGrey` button will be enabled, while the `Start` button is never even written into the new page. This gives the illusion of graying out the `Start` button when, in fact, it is a different button. Listing 28.5 shows the `print()` method, which is responsible for writing the new HTML page.

**LISTING 28.5** The `print()` Method of the `buttonSet` Object

```
function print(dObj)
{
    /*
    * Description: Method of buttonSet object.
    * Arguments: dObj - document object receiving buttonSet.
    */
    this.isBusy = true;
    var spaceInt;
    var DQUOTE = '\"';
    var topBase = "";
    var basePath = ""+window.location.pathname;
```

**LISTING 28.5** continued

```
var baseDir = "";
var baseFile = basePath.substring(basePath.length-10,basePath.length);

baseDir = basePath.substring(0,basePath.length-12);
topBase=window.location.protocol+"//"+window.location.host+baseDir;

dObj.open();
dObj.bgColor = parent.frames[0].document.bgColor;
dObj.writeln('<!DOCTYPE HTML PUBLIC "-//IETF//DTD HTML//EN">');
dObj.writeln('<html><head>');
dObj.writeln('<title>Toolbar</title>');
dObj.writeln('<base href = '+DQUOTE+topBase+DQUOTE+'>');
dObj.writeln('<script language="JavaScript">');
dObj.writeln('</script>');
dObj.writeln('</head>');
dObj.writeln('<body bgcolor="'+
    parent.frames[0].document.bgColor.toUpperCase()+'">');
dObj.writeln('<center>');
dObj.writeln('<table width="100%" border="0">');
dObj.writeln('<tr><td align="center">');

//Print each button. Start at property index i.
for(var i = this.startIndex; this.length > i; i++)
{
    if(eval(this[i].condition))
    {
        dObj.write('<A HREF = "'+this[i].url+'">');
        dObj.write('<img src="'+this[i].file+'" alt="'+this[i].alt+
            '" width="24" height="24" border=0>');
        dObj.write('</A>');
        // Add space if specified.
        spaceInt = 0 + this[i].spacer;
        if(spaceInt != 0)
        {
            dObj.write('<img src="graphics/space.gif" width='+spaceInt+
                ' height=24 border=0>');
        }
    }
}
dObj.writeln('</td></tr></table>');
dObj.writeln('</center>');
dObj.writeln('</body></html>');
```

**LISTING 28.5**   continued

```
    dObj.close();
    this.isBusy = false;
}
```

The print() method begins by setting the isBusy flag to true to prevent the user from clicking other buttons while the toolbar is refreshing. Next, a base URL is formed that is equal to the base URL of the current window. This is stored in the topBase variable and is used to generate a <base> tag for the new toolbar document. This assumes that the filename for the frameset HTML document is 12 characters long, as is the case with SlideShw.htm. This is to accommodate Netscape Navigator versions prior to 3.0.

> **Warning**
>
> If you fail to specify a base URL for a JavaScript-generated HTML document, Netscape Navigator versions prior to 3.0 will not correctly resolve unqualified URLs.

The print() method continues by opening access to the destination document. It then writes each line of HTML required to build a Web page that looks like a toolbar. I use a table to center all the buttons. A for loop is used to print each button that is stored within the buttonSet. If a space was specified, a blank graphic will be inserted and "stretched" to the designated number of pixels. Finally, the document is closed, and the browser window is refreshed.

## Refreshing the Toolbar

As you can see, refreshing the toolbar is as easy as calling its print() method. Simply set the global variables on which the buttons depend, and call print(). Documents within other frames can also refresh the toolbar. For example, you can modify the Slide Show application so that the user cannot start the slide show from the last slide. To do this, add a new global variable called gCanStart to the clear() method, and set it equal to false. Modify the addBtn calls for the Start and StartGrey buttons to take gCanStart into account. The new code would look like this:

```
Toolbar.addBtn("Start", "graphics/auto.gif", "Start Slideshow", 0,
    "gIsRunning==false && gCanStart==true", "changeSlide('auto')");
Toolbar.addBtn("StartGrey", "graphics/autoGrey.gif", "Start Slideshow", 0,
    "gIsRunning==true || gCanStart==false", "");
```

Then insert the following script into the <head> block of the last slide document:

```
<script language="JavaScript">
<!--
var savedState;
savedState = parent.gCanStart;
parent.gCanStart=false;
parent.Toolbar.print(parent.frames[2].document);
parent.gCanStart=savedState;
//-->
</script>
```

Next, add another call to Toolbar's print() method when the document unloads. This would look like the following:

```
<body onUnload="parent.Toolbar.print(parent.frames[2].document)">
```

This will return the toolbar to its previous state after moving to another slide.

If you have every slide set the global variables and reset the toolbar, you can eliminate the need to refresh the toolbar using the onUnload event handler. Using this approach, you can have every document specify which buttons to display, knowing that it will be reset the next time a different document is loaded.

## Using the Slide Show Application

On the CD-ROM included with this book, you will find a directory containing all the files needed for the Slide Show application. Simply load slideshow.htm into the browser to activate the frameset. The toolbar is used to move through each slide and its corresponding description. Figure 28.1 shows what the Slide Show application looks like when loaded into the browser.

Five slides are included with the program. You can use the toolbar to advance or move back by one slide using the third and second buttons, respectively. You can also use the first and fourth buttons to move to the first and last slides, respectively, in the slide show. The last two buttons on the right will start and stop the program from stepping through each slide for you. Notice how the last button is grayed out. This is the StartGrey button. After the Start button, shown as a right-pointing arrow followed by an ellipse, is clicked, the slide show begins to cycle through each pair of HTML documents. Figure 28.2 shows a snapshot of the browser during the show. Notice how the stop button is enabled while the show is running, and the Start button is grayed out.

**FIGURE 28.1**
*A toolbar used with the Slide Show application.*

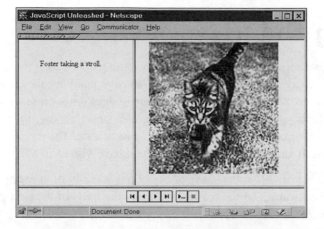

**FIGURE 28.2**
*A snapshot of the slide show in progress.*

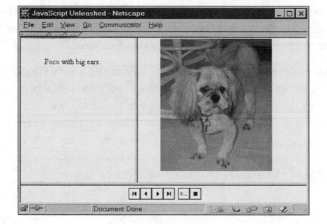

## Examining the Extra Features

The core `buttonSet` object could be altered even more. For example, it could be modified to support vertical toolbars instead of horizontal ones, or even both. Simply modify the `print()` method to add the `<br>` tag after each button. You could create the toolbar in a separate browser window. It could be used as a navigation tool or even a help menu. No modifications would be necessary. Simply pass the `Document` object of the new window to the `print()` method.

# Using the `History` Object

So far you have seen how to navigate through some predefined Web pages. What if you want to provide navigation controls on your Web page that have the same functionality as those found on your browser's toolbar? Fortunately, JavaScript provides a special `History` object that allows you to navigate through the Web sites that your browser has already displayed. This includes Web pages that you did not create. The `History` object is able to do this because it stores all of the URLs that you have visited in a list.

To utilize this list of URLs, the `History` object has some built-in methods for navigating forward and backward. The `back()` method loads the URL of the next previously visited Web site. The `forward()` method loads the next URL from the History list.

In addition, the `History` object has another method and some properties. Unfortunately, for security reasons, many browsers do not let you use the additional method and properties. This is not really a big drawback, because most of the usefulness of the `History` object comes from the `back()` and `forward()` methods.

To demonstrate the use of the `History` object, let's create a very simple page that contains two buttons for navigating. One button will take you back to the previous URL in the History list while the other button will take you to the next URL in the History list. These buttons will use their `onClick` event handlers to call on the two `History` methods discussed earlier. The code for this Web page is shown in Listing 28.6.

**LISTING 28.6**  Using the `History` Object to Navigate

```
<html>
<head>
<title>Using the History object</title>
</head>

<body>
<center>
<h1>Navigating with the History object</h1>

Press one of the following buttons to navigate.
<hr>

<form>
  <input type="button"
         value="Back"
         onClick="window.history.back()">
  <input type="button"
```

**LISTING 28.6**     continued

```
            value="Forward"
            onClick="window.history.forward()">
</form>
</center>
</body>
</html>
```

In order to see how the buttons work, begin by loading one of your favorite Web sites. Once the Web site is loaded, type in the URL used in Listing 28.6. Then enter the URL of another favorite site that is different from the first site you loaded. Now press the Back button on your browser. At this point you should see a Web page like the one shown in Figure 28.3. Now you can use the navigation buttons to navigate to either of the Web sites you just visited.

**FIGURE 28.3**
*Navigating with the* History *object.*

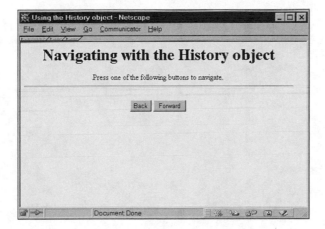

# Summary

With JavaScript's capability to perform many actions at once, it's possible to create more sophisticated navigation aids. With one click from the user, JavaScript can validate data, submit a form, regenerate a frame, and change the contents of another frame.

The toolbar example showed how to refresh an HTML page in order to give the illusion that buttons are being disabled or enabled as the user interacts with them. A method for changing the contents of three frames with one button click was also shown. The buttonSet object can easily be used in other page designs with little modification.

The History object allows you to provide the functionality of your Web browser's Forward and Back buttons in your Web pages. This can be very useful if you create a window that does not have the normal browser toolbars but needs the capability to load pages that have already been visited.

# Forms and Data Validation

## In This Chapter

**29**

**CHAPTER**

When HTML 2.0 was released, it contained a new capability that allowed Web page developers to create online forms. The HTML forms capability had several advantages as a mechanism for creating online forms:

- Client/server model: The Web browser supplies a generic graphical user interface (GUI) driven by the specific HTML script. Domain-specific processing is handled on the server side through the CGI program.

- Platform independence: Web browsers run on multiple platforms. The developer need not be concerned about platform-specific issues when developing forms.

- Network transparency: Network communications are built into the Web browser/Web server pair and implemented through the HTTP protocol.

- Standardized GUI: Forms were standardized with HTML 2.0. A user who is familiar with form elements can apply that knowledge to any form on the World Wide Web or corporate intranet.

The HTML forms interface in itself has a few deficiencies:

- Dynamic user feedback: HTML forms have no means of providing dynamic information on required input on a per-form-element basis.

- Client-side form validation: HTML forms can't validate a form element, a group of elements, or an entire form on the client side.

- Dialog boxes: HTML forms can't alert the user dynamically about an input error or request additional input.

- User confirmations: The forms have no way to ask for confirmation before taking irrevocable types of action.

- Interactivity among form or window elements: In HTML forms, the interactivity is limited to CGI processing on the server side.

The JavaScript language addresses each of these deficiencies. JavaScript builds on the basic capabilities of HTML and produces a more powerful client-side GUI interface. In this chapter, you will learn how to implement these additional capabilities in JavaScript. The chapter ends with an application written in JavaScript that makes use of these capabilities to implement a tool for choosing combinations of text and background colors.

I make extensive use of JavaScript event handlers in this chapter. You can view event handlers as callbacks associated with a form or form element. They are explicitly specified as part of a form or form element tag. Event handlers are called when a user-triggered event occurs and, in turn, they call an appropriate JavaScript code fragment or function. Table 29.1 contains a summary of JavaScript event handlers.

**TABLE 29.1**    JavaScript Event Handlers

| Event Handler | Associated Object(s) | Triggering Event |
|---|---|---|
| onBlur | Button, Checkbox, Radio, Select, Submit, Text, Textarea | Form object loses input focus. |
| onChange | Select, Text, Textarea | Value of Form object is modified. |
| onClick | Button, Checkbox, Radio, Link, Reset, Submit | Form object is clicked. |
| onFocus | Button, Checkbox, Radio, Select, Submit, Text, Textarea | Form object gains input focus. |
| OnKeyDown | Textarea | Key is pressed within Form object. |
| OnKeyPress | Textarea | Key is pressed and released within Form object. |
| OnKeyUp | Textarea | Key is released in Form object. |
| onLoad | Window | Web browser finishes loading Window object. |
| OnMouseDown | Button | Mouse button is pressed within Form object. |
| onMouseOver | Link | User moves cursor over link. |
| OnMouseUp | Button | Mouse button is released within Form object. |
| OnReset | Form | Form has been reset. |
| onSelect | Text, Textarea | User selects text within Form object. |
| onSubmit | Form | Form has been submitted. |
| onUnload | Window | Window is terminated by user. |

# Gathering User Feedback

With a well-designed form, the user should be able to determine rapidly what information is required. In very simple forms, you can accomplish this with well-thought-out labels adjacent to each form element. In complex forms, you should include a help facility that offers a detailed explanation of how to fill out the form. With JavaScript, you can add user prompting on a per-field basis. This allows you to supply additional information about the requirements or function of a form element at the moment that the information is needed. By doing so, you can reduce the amount of text required in the form element label and simplify the form's appearance.

User prompting is implemented with JavaScript's event-handling capability and the browser's status bar. You can use the onFocus event handler to execute a user-defined function when a given Form object receives input focus. Similarly, you can use the onMouseOver event handler to execute a user-defined function whenever the cursor is placed over a link. You can use these event handlers to call a function that displays a user prompt on the browser's status bar.

## Creating an Example Form for User Feedback

The following example illustrates how to provide user feedback on the browser status bar using JavaScript. Imagine for a moment that you are creating an HTML form interface to a very advanced automated toaster. The goal is to produce an interface so easy to use that the most naive user can instruct it to produce savory toasted bread. Figure 29.1 shows the interface.

**FIGURE 29.1**
*The automated toaster form.*

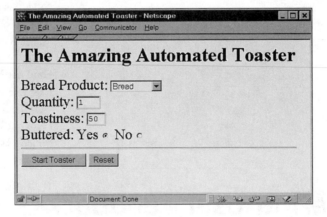

The user can set the values of four input objects:

- A Selection object representing the type of bread
- A Text object representing the quantity of toasted bread desired
- A Text object indicating the amount of toasting (as a numeric quantity)
- A pair of radio buttons indicating whether the bread should be buttered

Each of the Selection and Text objects has associated onFocus and onBlur event handlers. These handlers display and remove appropriate user prompts associated with a given input object. The onClick event handler is used to associate user feedback with the radio buttons.

The window.defaultStatus property is set to display a default greeting message when no other messages are present.

The code for the toaster example is shown in Listing 29.1. Because you don't really have an automated toaster, the code sends mail once the form is filled in. In this listing, you need to substitute your actual email address for the text *your_mail_ID*. In general, any time you see a segment of code in italic, you need to substitute user- or site-dependent information.

**LISTING 29.1**    toaster.htm

```
<!-- Web Page for controlling an automated toaster
  -- Note: Since we don't really have an automated toaster
  ..      mail the results back to the developer -->
<html>
<head>
<title>The Amazing Automated Toaster</title>

<script language="JavaScript">
<!-- script start
function setStatus(str)
{
    window.status = str;
    return true;
}

var greeting="Hello! How about some nice toasted bread products!";
window.defaultStatus = greeting;
// script end -->
</script>
</head>

<body>
<h1>The Amazing Automated Toaster</h1>

<form action="mailto:your_mail_ID" method="post">

<font size=5>Bread Product:</font>
<select name="product"
    onFocus="setStatus('Select desired bread product from list.')"
```

**29**

Forms and Data
Validation

LISTING 29.1    continued

```
        onBlur="setStatus('')">
<option>Bread
<option>Waffle
<option>Bagel
<option>Roll
<option>Muffin
<option>Croissant
<option>Scone
</select>
<br>

<font size=5>Quantity:</font>
<input type="text" name="quantity" value="1" size=4 maxlength=4
    onFocus="setStatus(
        'Enter quantity of bread products desired (1-1000).')"
    onBlur="setStatus('')">
<br>

<font size=5>Toastiness:</font>
<input type="text" name="toastiness" value="50" size=3 maxlength=3
    onFocus="setStatus(
'Enter degree of toastiness from 0-100 (0=untoasted 100=burnt).')"
    onBlur="setStatus('')">
<br>

<font size=5>Buttered:</font>
<font size=5>Yes</font>
<input type="radio" name="buttered" value="yes" checked
    onClick="setStatus(
        'Do you want butter on the bread product?')">
<font size=5>No</font>
<input type="radio" name="buttered" value="no"
    onClick="setStatus(
        'Do you want butter on the bread product?')">

<hr>
<input type="submit" value="Start Toaster">
<input type="reset">

</form>
</body>
</html>
```

# Testing a User Form

You would usually write a CGI program to process data submitted through a form. However, you might need to develop a form before the CGI program is available. Perhaps you want to debug the form without actually calling the real CGI program. There are several simple methods for testing a form, independent of the CGI program:

- For forms that use the get method, a standard CGI program called test-cgi is available at most sites. Use the following form tag:

```
<form action=http://your_site_name/cgi-bin/test-cgi method="get">
```

  When you submit your form, you will receive a page containing, among other things, the values of the form elements from the submitted page. Although the test-cgi CGI file is provided with most servers, its availability and exact location could be site dependent. Contact your Web site administrator for details.

- For forms that use the post method, a standard CGI program called post-query is available at most sites. Use the following form tag:

```
<form action=http://your_site_name/cgi-bin/post-query method="post">
```

  When you submit your form, you will receive a page containing, among other things, the name/value pairs corresponding to the form elements from the submitted page. Although post-query is provided with most servers, its availability and exact location might be site dependent. Contact your Web site administrator for details.

- For forms that use the post method, you can specify that form results should be mailed to your account. Use the following form tag:

```
<form action="mailto:your_mail_ID" method="post">
```

  When you submit your form, you will receive an email message containing name/value pairs corresponding to the form elements from the submitted page. (With Netscape Navigator and Microsoft Internet Explorer, the user will receive a warning when submitting a form by email. This is not an error; it is a security feature designed to warn the user that the recipient of the form will be able to view the user's email address in the mail header. In other words, form submission by email is not anonymous.)

**29**

**Forms and Data
Validation**

# Displaying Message Boxes

JavaScript supports several methods for communicating with the user through pop-up alert messages and two types of dialog windows. You can use these methods to communicate important information to the user, confirm a choice made by the user, or request additional information. You can use alert messages as aids in debugging as well.

You use the `alert()` method to pop up a short message to the user. It is a method of the `Window` object. You need not specify the `Window` object to invoke it. You can use the `alert()` method to inform the user of an input error, as shown in the following code:

```
alert("Error: value outside valid range of 0 to 240 volts.");
```

Using this code line displays the message shown in 29.2.

**FIGURE 29.2**
*An alert message.*

You can also use the `alert()` method as a debugging aid. Use it to display a string containing debugging information:

```
var dbgstr = "Value of 'wattage' = " + wattage;
alert(dbgstr);
```

You can use it to do tracing within your JavaScript program:

```
function CalculateWattage(volts,amps)
{
    var dbgstr = "CalculateWattage(" + volts + "," + amps + ")";
    alert(dbgstr);
. . .
}
```

Every time the function `CalculateWattage()` is called, an alert pops up, showing the call and the calling arguments. When you finish debugging the program, you can remove or comment out the debugging code. See Chapter 34, "Debugging," for more information on how to use the alert box for debugging your JavaScript code.

The `confirm()` method is similar to `alert()`, but it lets the user respond to the message. The responses are limited to OK and Cancel. The `confirm()` method returns `true` if the user selects OK and `false` if the user selects Cancel, as shown in the following code:

```
function submitCallback()
{
    if (selfDestructSelected == true)
        return confirm(
            "Invoke self-destruct mechanism in 60 seconds?");
    else return true;
}
...
<form ... onSubmit="return submitCallback()">
```

This code produces the pop-up confirmation dialog window shown in Figure 29.3.

**FIGURE 29.3**

*The confirmation dialog box.*

Clicking OK allows the submit to proceed. Clicking Cancel returns `false`, which in turn returns `false` to the `Form` object, preventing the form from being submitted.

The `prompt()` method is another `Window` method. It allows you to prompt the user for an arbitrary value, as shown in the following code line:

```
var favColor = prompt("What\'s your favorite color?");
```

You can supply an optional second argument to be used as a default value:

```
var duration = prompt("Enter duration in months:",6);
```

This code line produces the dialog box shown in Figure 29.4.

**FIGURE 29.4**

*The prompt dialog box.*

You usually ask the user for information through a form input element, but you can use the prompt dialog box when there is an infrequent need to query the user based on other input information. The following sample code asks for the user's email address only if the individual requests that specials be sent via email.

```
<html>
<script language="JavaScript">
```

```
<!--begin script>
function sendEmail(formObj)
{
  if(formObj.emailSpecials.checked)
  {
    ans = prompt("Please enter your email address.");
    formObj.email.value=ans;
  }
}
//end script-->
</script>

<center>
<h1>Bob's Music Store</h1>
To recieve our free catalog by mail please enter your email address below.
<form name="addressForm" onSubmit="sendEmail(this)">
<table>
  <tr>
    <td>Name:</td>
    <td><input type="text" name="name"></td>
  </tr>
  <tr>
    <td>Address</td>
    <td><input type="text" name="address"></td>
  </tr>
  <tr>
    <td>City</td>
    <td><input type="text" name="city"></td>
  </tr>
  <tr>
    <td>State</td>
    <td><input type="text" name="state"></td>
  </tr>
  <tr>
    <td>Zip</td>
    <td><input type="text" name="zip"></td>
  </tr>
  <tr>
    <td colspan=2><input type="checkbox" name="emailSpecials">
    Please email me about special deals!</td>
  <tr>
</table>
```

```
<input type="hidden" name="email" value="">
<input type="submit" name="submit" value="Submit">
</form>

</center>
</html>
```

> **Tip**
>
> When a message or dialog box pops up, the user is distracted from his task and must focus attention on the pop-up window and respond appropriately. Therefore, alert messages and dialog boxes should be used sparingly.

## Using Status Messages

Another way to give the user feedback while data is being entered is to use status messages. Status messages are the phrases you see in the status bar at the bottom of a window. JavaScript lets you modify what is displayed in this bar, giving you the ability to send messages to the user while he interacts with the HTML form. I find that messages displayed in the status bar are less distracting than dialog windows, but they are not always noticed. Listing 29.2 gives an example of how to give the user extra help while he is entering data into a form.

**LISTING 29.2**   Displaying Status Messages

```
<html>
<head>
<title>JavaScript Unleashed</title>
<script language= "JavaScript">
<!--
function statusMsg(msgType) {
   var message = "";
   if(msgType == "string") {
      message = "Any characters can be used here.";
   }
   if(msgType == "integer") {
      message = "Please enter a whole number here.";
   }
   else if(msgType == "dollar") {
      message = "Please enter a dollar amount here. (e.g. 19.99)";
   }
```

LISTING 29.2    continued

```
   else if(msgType == "credit") {
      message = "Please enter a credit card number here. Do not use dashes.";
   }
   window.defaultStatus = message;
   window.status = message;
}
//-->
</script>
</head>
<body onFocus="statusMsg('')">
<form name="form1" action="#" method="post"><br>
First Name <input type="text"
           size=20
           maxlength=20
           name="Integer"
           onFocus="statusMsg('string')"><br>
 Last Name <input type="text"
           size=20
           maxlength=20
           name="Integer"
           onFocus="statusMsg('string')"><br>
Age <input type="text"
    size=5
    maxlength=5
    name="Integer"
    onFocus="statusMsg('integer')"><br>
Amount <input type="text"
       size=6
       maxlength=6
       name="Dollar"
       onFocus="statusMsg('dollar')"><br>
Card # <input type="text"
       size=16
       maxlength=16
       name="Credit"
       onFocus="statusMsg('credit')"><br>
<br>
<input type="submit" value="Submit">
</form>
</body>
</html>
```

When the user moves the cursor to a field or the browser automatically moves the cursor to a field, the onFocus event handler calls the function statusMsg(). The requested type of message is then displayed in the status bar by setting the status property of the Window object. The statusMsg() function also enables you to clear out the status bar by passing it an empty string. This is demonstrated when you click the browser window anywhere outside of the text elements. This triggers the onFocus event handler for the document, which clears the status message.

> **Tip**
>
> It is a good idea to set the defaultStatus property of the window to display the same status message. This ensures that your message will not easily disappear as the user moves the mouse pointer around the screen. This is most useful when you're using frames and you want the message to "stick" even though the user moves the mouse pointer to a different frame.

# Validating User Input

Prior to the advent of JavaScript, form validation was handled by a CGI program. This approach was effective but required that the entire form be completed by the user and transmitted to the server prior to validation. In some environments, such as low-speed connections to the World Wide Web, a noticeable lag can occur between the time the form is submitted and the time a validation error is returned to the user. Furthermore, by waiting until the form is submitted for validation, the user doesn't receive feedback until after the entire form is completed. Immediate feedback is desirable because the user has just entered information and can place the feedback in the appropriate context. Immediate feedback might influence later behavior and reduce user errors in responding to subsequent form elements. Finally, conventional CGI programming reports input errors in a new Web page. The user must back up to the form to make changes, which interrupts the flow of the form-entry task.

## Validating Free Form Input

You can use two event handlers to validate text and textarea form elements. The onBlur event handler is called when a text or textarea form element loses input focus. The onChange event handler is called when the content of a text or textarea form element is modified.

A form element is said to *have focus* when any user input will be directed to that element. When a text or textarea form element has focus, a text cursor appears in that element. When the user switches to another element (using the mouse or the Tab key), the original element is said to *lose focus*.

The onBlur handler is called any time the input field loses focus. The user may or may not have changed the data in the field. The event handler could call the validation code for unchanged data or the default values in the field. You should design the validation code to deal with this possibility.

The onChange event handler is called only when the content of the field is modified. If the user momentarily selects the field (perhaps to view feedback in the status bar) and then chooses another field, the user-defined callback code is not invoked. Although this is more efficient, there is a downside. Suppose that you warn a user about erroneous data in a field. If he clicks the field and then declines to modify it, or if he retypes the same erroneous data, this is not considered a change. The onChange event handler is not triggered. For this reason, if you choose to use onChange, you should also validate the input at the time of submission (through the onSubmit or onClick event handler).

The next example provides a text field for the user to input the quantity of an item. Valid values are 100 to 1000. The onBlur event handler is used to call a validation function. The text input object is passed to the event handler. If the input is invalid, the following occurs:

- An alert box pops up to inform the user.

- Input focus is returned to the text field.

- The text is selected (and highlighted) so that it can be easily modified.

Note that the onFocus event handler is used to provide user feedback for the text field—perhaps to inform the user about minimum and maximum orders:

```
function validateQuantity(quantObj)
{
    if (quantObj.value < 100) {
        alert("Minimum order is 100 units.");
        quantObj.focus();
        quantObj.select();
    }
    else if (quantObj.value > 1000) {
        alert("Quantities greater than 1000 "
            + "units require special order.");
        quantObj.focus();
        quantObj.select();
    }
```

```
      return;
}

...

<h2>Enter number of units:</h2>
<input type="text" name="quantity" value="100" length=4
    maxlength=4 onFocus="quantFeedback()"
    onBlur="validateQuantity(this)">
```

## Ensuring Consistency

Sometimes there are dependencies between several input fields. Figure 29.5 illustrates part of a form used by a business for entering a department budget. The user is prompted to enter a total budget and then allocate portions of that budget to three different categories.

**FIGURE 29.5**

*A form for entering a budget.*

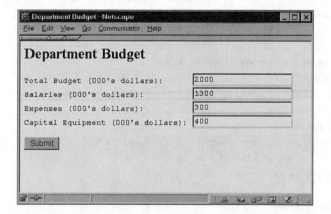

The sum of the three categories should add up to the total budget. Prior to JavaScript, the sum wouldn't have been verified until after the form was submitted and processed by a CGI program. Using JavaScript, the data can be validated prior to submission, saving the user time and preserving context (that is, the same Web page is present before and after validation). The following code segment is an implementation of the budget entry form:

```
<form name="myform" method="post" action="actionURL"
    onSubmit="return validateBudget(myform)">
<h2>Department Budget</h2>

<pre>
Total Budget (000's dollars):      <input type="text"
    name="totalBudget" value="0" onBlur="validateNumeric(this)">
```

```
Salaries (000's dollars):              <input type="text"
    name="salaries" value="0" onBlur="validateNumeric(this)">
Expenses (000's dollars):              <input type="text"
    name="expenses" value="0" onBlur="validateNumeric(this)">
Capital Equipment (000's dollars): <input type="text"
    name="capital" value="0" onBlur="validateNumeric(this)">
</pre>

...

<input type="submit" name="submit" value="Submit">
</form>
```

onBlur event handlers call a user-supplied validation routine that will ensure the user enters valid numeric input in each field. You must supply the following function to verify that the sum of the allocations adds up to the total amount budgeted:

```
function validateBudget(formObj)
{
    var calcBudget = parseInt(formObj.salaries.value,10)
        + parseInt(formObj.expenses.value,10)
        + parseInt(formObj.capital.value,10);
    var totalBudget = parseInt(formObj.totalBudget.value,10);

    if (calcBudget != totalBudget) {
        alert("Error: total budget is not equal to "
            + "sum of allocations.");
        return false;
    }
    else return true;
}
```

This function pops up an alert box in the event of an error and prevents the submit from being processed.

> **Caution**
>
> HTML is still an evolving language. In most cases, Web browsers ignore unknown tags or keywords, which could be changed in standard HTML or vendor-supplied HTML enhancements. This is good for users of Web browsers, because you don't want your browser to crash every time it encounters an unknown tag or keyword.
>
> However, this is a problem for JavaScript programmers. If you misspell the name of an event handler or any other keyword within an HTML tag, your program won't function properly, and your browser won't flag the error. When using JavaScript event handlers in forms, it is prudent to visually inspect your code for typographical errors.

## Enforcing Policy Statements

Policies associated with a form should be indicated to the user through explanatory text within the form, a separate help document (appropriately linked to the form), or both. You can use JavaScript to verify that user input conforms to these policies.

Suppose the form allows the user to specify a ship date but contains a policy statement that orders can't be shipped on the weekend. You can use JavaScript code to verify that the ship date is not on a weekend, thus enforcing the policy. The following code segment implements these policies:

```
// Compute ship date from
//    user input.  Returns
//    date object
function calcShipDate(formObj)
{
    var day = parseInt(formObj.shipDay.value);
    var month = parseInt(formObj.shipMonth.value);
    var year = parseInt(formObj.shipYear.value);
    var hrs = 0;
    var min = 0;
    var sec = 0;
    shipDate = new Date(year,month,day,hrs,min,sec);
    return shipDate;
}


// Validate shipping policy - don't
//    ship on weekends.  Make sure
//    date is not in past or current date
```

29

**Forms and Data Validation**

```
function shippingPolicy(formObj)
{
    var shipDate = calcShipDate(formObj);
    var day = shipDate.getDay();
    var currentDate = new Date();

    if (shipDate.getTime() < currentDate.getTime()) {
        alert("Error: ship date must be future date.");
        formObj.shipDay.focus();
        formObj.shipDay.select();
        return false;
    }

    if (day == 0) {
        alert("Sorry, we cannot ship on Sunday.");
        formObj.shipDay.focus();
        formObj.shipDay.select();
        return false;
    }
    else if (day == 6) {
        alert("Sorry, we cannot ship on Saturday.");
        formObj.shipDay.focus();
        formObj.shipDay.select();
        return false;
    }
    else return true;
}

...

<form name="myform" method="post" action="actionURL"
    onSubmit="return shippingPolicy(myform)">
```

If the user enters a date corresponding to a Saturday or Sunday, he is reminded of the shipping policy, focus and selection are set to the date input field, and the form is not submitted. The code also enforces the implicit policy of disallowing same-day shipping.

**Note**

When processing dates using JavaScript, be aware that the date and time are based on the setting of the user's computer. It's likely that the client software and server software are running in different time zones. It's also possible that the time setting on the client side is incorrect, perhaps due to the user setting the wrong time and date on his computer.

## Ensuring Completeness

Forms frequently consist of a set of mandatory and optional fields. The form can't be properly processed if the mandatory fields aren't supplied. Again, you can use JavaScript to ensure that they are present.

The next example is a form requesting customer contact information (see Figure 29.6). The name, address, and home phone number are considered mandatory fields. All other fields are optional.

**FIGURE 29.6**

*The contact information form.*

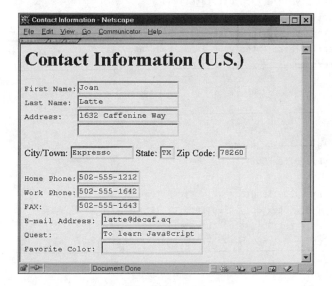

When the form is submitted, a validation function is called. If any of the mandatory fields are empty, the user is notified, and the form is not submitted. The code for the contact information form is shown in Listing 29.3.

**LISTING 29.3**    `contact.htm`

```html
<html>
<head>
<title>Contact Information</title>
<script language="JavaScript">
<!-- script start
// Ensure that mandatory fields of
// form have been completed
function validateComplete(formObj)
{
    if (emptyField(formObj.firstName))
        alert("Please enter your first name.");
    else if (emptyField(formObj.lastName))
        alert("Please enter your last name.");
    else if (emptyField(formObj.address1)
        && emptyField(formObj.address2))
        alert("Please enter your address.");
    else if (emptyField(formObj.city))
        alert("Please enter your city or town.");
    else if (emptyField(formObj.state))
        alert("Please enter your state.");
    else if (emptyField(formObj.email))
        alert("Please enter your E-mail address.");
    else return true;

    return false;
}

// Check to see if field is empty
function emptyField(textObj)
{
    if (textObj.value.length == 0) return true;
    for (var i=0; i<textObj.value.length; ++i) {
        var ch = textObj.value.charAt(i);
        if (ch != ' ' && ch != '\t') return false;
    }
    return true;
}

// script end -->
</script>
</head>
<body>
```

**LISTING 29.3** continued

```html
<h1>Contact Information (U.S.)</h1>
<form name="myform" action="actionURL" method="post"
 onSubmit="return validateComplete(document.myform)">
<pre>
First Name:<input type="text" name="firstName">
Last Name: <input type="text" name="lastName">
Address:   <input type="text" name="address1">
           <input type="text" name="address2">
</pre>

City/Town:
<input type="text" name="city" size=12>
State:
<input type="text" name="state" size=2>
Zip Code:
<input type="text" name="zip" size=5>

<pre>
Home Phone:<input type="text" name="homePhone" size=12>
Work Phone:<input type="text" name="workPhone" size=12>
FAX:       <input type="text" name="FAX" size=12>
E-mail Address: <input type="text" name="email">
Quest:          <input type="text" name="quest">
Favorite Color: <input type="text" name="favColor">
</pre>
<hr>
<input type="submit" name="submit" value="Submit">
</form>
<body>
<html>
```

The code performs a very basic validation—a field is present if it is not blank. No attempt is made to determine whether the fields contain reasonable data or gibberish. You could include some additional, simple validation. For example, you could validate that the state is a two-letter abbreviation or that the phone number contains the correct number of digits. In general, you should perform simple validations on the client side and more complex validations on the server side.

**29**

**Forms and Data Validation**

> **Note**
>
> The preceding example is a contact form for English-speaking users in the United States. The Internet is a worldwide network. In some countries, the family name precedes the given name, states are not a political subdivision, ZIP Codes don't exist, and the user's language is not English. People still have a favorite color, however. The issue of internationalization is well beyond the scope of this book; nevertheless, you should be cognizant of the potential user base when designing forms.

# Creating Interactive Forms

Prior to JavaScript, even the simplest interactive form required interaction with a CGI program on the server. With JavaScript, you can create interactive forms in which the interaction is handled entirely on the client side without requiring a round trip to the server.

Interactive programming in JavaScript does have a few limitations. It would be useful to be able to change any individual element of a page dynamically. Newer versions of Netscape and Microsoft browsers are able to change page content dynamically without going back to the server, thanks to DHTML and cascading style sheets (CCS). Unfortunately, these standards are still being ironed out and are only implemented to varying degrees. Unless you want to limit the browser versions on which your HTML files will run, you should assume for now that once a Web browser renders a page and the elements are formatted, they cannot be modified by JavaScript code.

If you can't change the formatting of a page once it is written, what can you do? JavaScript allows you to create interactions between the following items:

- Form elements on the same page

- Form elements and another window

- Form elements and another frame

You can use any of the techniques described earlier in this chapter—user feedback, message boxes, and input validation—to enhance a form. You can alter the entire page by completely rewriting it. In that case, the browser erases the current page and reformats an entire new page from scratch. You can also change the background color of the page (a Document property) but not the foreground color. The page text has already been rendered in the foreground color, so it can't be changed.

# Using Calculated Fields

The next example, shown in Figure 29.7, is a different implementation of the budgeting example from earlier in this chapter. This example has a new text field named `remainder`. Although you can't update regular text or graphics on a page once it's written, you can update a form element. In this case, you update the `remainder` text element based on the values in the other elements. As the user enters the total budget and allocations, the `remainder` text field shows the amount of money left after the allocations are subtracted from the total budget.

**FIGURE 29.7**
*The calculated budget example.*

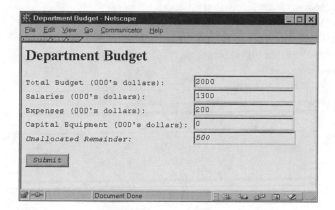

This example uses the `onChange` event handler to update the `remainder` field whenever one of the values of the other text fields is modified. When the user submits the form, the script recalculates the remainder. If it is zero, the form is submitted; otherwise, an alert dialog box is displayed. The code for this interactive budget is shown in Listing 29.4.

**LISTING 29.4**   Department Budget Tool

```
<html>
<head>
<title>Department Budget</title>

<script language="JavaScript">
<!-- script start
function calcRemainder(formObj)
{
    var calcBudget = parseInt(formObj.salaries.value,10)
        + parseInt(formObj.expenses.value,10)
        + parseInt(formObj.capital.value,10);
```

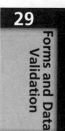

29

Forms and Data
Validation

**Listing 29.4**    continued

```
    var totalBudget = parseInt(formObj.totalBudget.value);

    var unalloc = totalBudget - calcBudget;
    formObj.remainder.value = unalloc;
}

function validateBudget(formObj)
{
    calcRemainder(formObj);
    var unalloc = formObj.remainder.value;
    if (unalloc != 0) {
        alert("Error: Total budget is not equal "
            + "to sum of allocations.");
        return false;
    }
    return true;
}
// script end -->
</script>
</head>

<body>
<form name="myform" method="post" action="actionURL"
    onSubmit="return validateBudget(myform)">
<h2>Department Budget</h2>

<pre>
Total Budget (000's dollars):      <input type="text"
    name="totalBudget" value="0"
    onChange="calcRemainder(myform)">
Salaries (000's dollars):          <input type="text"
    name="salaries" value="0" onChange="calcRemainder(myform)">
Expenses (000's dollars):          <input type="text"
    name="expenses" value="0" onChange="calcRemainder(myform)">
Capital Equipment (000's dollars): <input type="text"
    name="capital" value="0" onChange="calcRemainder(myform)">
<em>Unallocated Remainder:<em>                <input type="text"
    name="remainder" value="0">
</pre>

<input type="submit" name="submit" value="Submit">
</form>
```

**LISTING 29.4    continued**

```
</body>
</html>
```

You can use JavaScript to write small interactive applications where all the processing is done on the client side. Listing 29.5 calculates the future value of an investment. The user supplies the initial amount, an interest rate, and the number of years that the investment is compounded. Figure 29.8 shows the screen after the script has been loaded into the browser. Note that the output of the JavaScript `calculate()` function is displayed through text input objects, as described earlier.

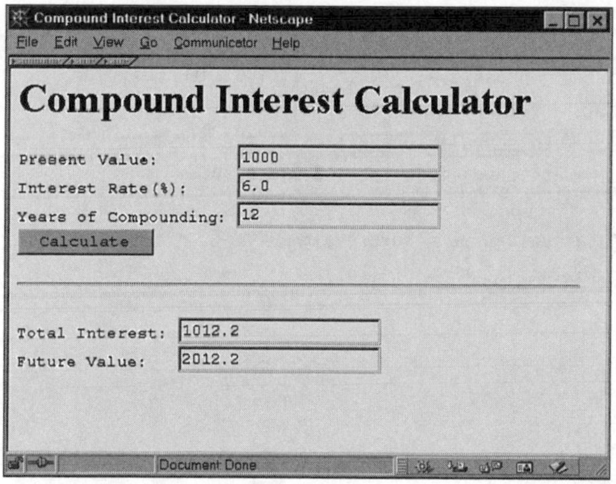

**FIGURE 29.8**
*The compound interest form.*

No CGI program is required, because all processing is done on the client side. Note that instead of using a `Submit` input object, the form uses a `Button` object. Also, instead of using an `onSubmit` event handler, the script uses an `onClick` event handler. The `Submit` object and `onSubmit` event-handler semantics are used when the Web browser transmits a form to the server side. Because you want to do the processing on the client side, you use the `onClick` event handler and the `calculate()` function when the button is pressed. The button was labeled Calculate for clarity but could have been labeled Submit. Unless the user views the source code for the page, it will be indistinguishable from a page that uses HTML on the client side and a CGI script on the server side. The code for the compound interest form is shown in Listing 29.5.

**29**

**Forms and Data Validation**

**LISTING 29.5**  Compound Interest Calculator

```html
<html>
<head>
<title>Compound Interest Calculator</title>
<script language="JavaScript">
<!-- script start

// script end -->
function calculate(formObj)
{
    var presentVal = parseFloat(formObj.presentVal.value);
    var intRate = parseFloat(formObj.intRate.value)/100.;
    var years = parseFloat(formObj.years.value);

    var futureVal = presentVal * Math.pow((1.0+intRate),years);
    var totalInt = futureVal - presentVal;
    futureVal = Math.round(futureVal*100.0)/100.0;
    totalInt  = Math.round(totalInt*100.0)/100.0;

    formObj.futureVal.value = futureVal;
    formObj.totalInt.value = totalInt;

    return;
}
</script>
</head>

<body>
<h1>Compound Interest Calculator</h1>
<form name="myform">
<pre>
Present Value:         <input type="text" name="presentVal">
Interest Rate(%):      <input type="text" name="intRate">
Years of Compounding: <input type="text" name="years">
<input type="button" name="calc" value="Calculate"
    onclick="calculate(myform)">
</pre>
<hr>
<pre>
Total Interest: <input type="text" name="totalInt">
Future Value:   <input type="text" name="futureVal">
<pre>
</form>
```

LISTING **29.5** continued

```
</body>
<html>
```

# Creating Reusable Validation Code

The following sections demonstrate ways to validate the most common types of data asked for over the Internet. The examples are especially easy to use in a code library that is stored in a separate file or in the frameset parent document. All examples accept a text element object as one of their arguments. This allows you to update the text field during data validation when necessary. For more specific data validation, incorporate JavaScript *Regular Expressions*, which are covered in Chapter 31, "Pattern Matching Using Regular Expressions," into the techniques discussed in this section.

## Integer

Listing 29.6 is used to ensure that only whole numbers are accepted as input. The script is called when the user clicks the Validate button. The result, either `true` or `false`, is then displayed in the Result text field. This specifies whether the data passed the validation process.

LISTING **29.6** Integer Validation

```
<html>
<head>
<title>Integer Validation</title>
<script language="JavaScript">
<!--begin script
function isInt(textObj) {
   var newValue = textObj.value;
   var newLength = newValue.length;
   for(var i = 0; i != newLength; i++) {
      aChar = newValue.substring(i,i+1);
      if(aChar < "0" || aChar > "9") {
         return false;
      }
   }
   return true;
}
// end script-->
</script>
```

29

Forms and Data
Validation

LISTING 29.6    continued

```
</head>

<body>
<h1>Integer Validation</h1>
<form name="form1">
<input type="text"
   size=16
   maxlength=16
   name="data">
<input type="button"
   name="CheckButton"
   value="Validate"
   onClick="document.form1.result.value = '' +
    isInt(document.form1.data)">
<br>
Result <input type="text"
   size=16
   maxlength=16
   name="result">
</form>
</body>
</html>
```

# String

Listing 29.7 shows how to ensure that the user has entered a string of allowable characters, which means alphabetic characters and a few others. The others are specified with the extraChars variable. If the user enters any character that is not in the alphabet or the extraChars variable, the function returns false. Listing 29.7 might be used to validate names, because some names contain periods, spaces, hyphens, and commas.

LISTING 29.7    String Validation

```
<html>
<head>
<title>String Validation</title>
<script language="JavaScript">
<!--begin script
function isString(textObj) {
   var newValue = textObj.value;
   var newLength = newValue.length;
   var extraChars=". -,";
```

**LISTING 29.7**    continued

```
   var search;
   for(var i = 0; i != newLength; i++) {
      aChar = newValue.substring(i,i+1);
      aChar = aChar.toUpperCase();
      search = extraChars.indexOf(aChar);
      if(search == -1 && (aChar < "A" || aChar > "Z") ) {
         return false;
      }
   }
   return true;
}
// end script-->
</script>
</head>

<body>
<h1>String Validation</h1>
<form name="form1">
<input type="text"
   size=16
   maxlength=16
   name="data">
<input type="button"
   name="CheckButton"
   value="Validate"
   onClick="document.form1.result.value = '' +
    isString(document.form1.data)">
<br>
Result <input type="text"
   size=16
   maxlength=16
   name="result">
</form>
</body>
</html>
```

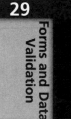

# Dollar

Listing 29.8 uses a technique that is somewhat different from the integer and string validation examples. Instead of performing a straightforward validation, it formats a value to be displayed as an amount of money to two decimal places. This is also an example of how the function uses the Text object it was given to update the object's value. If the function can't convert the data it was given into money, it defaults to an amount of 0.

**LISTING 29.8**  Money Format

```html
<html>
<head>
<title>Money Format</title>
<script language= "JavaScript">
<!--begin script
function moneyFormat(textObj) {
   var newValue = textObj.value;
   var decAmount = "";
   var dolAmount = "";
   var decFlag = false;
   var aChar = "";

   // ignore all but digits and decimal points.
   for(i=0; i < newValue.length; i++) {
     aChar = newValue.substring(i,i+1);
     if(aChar >= "0" && aChar <= "9") {
        if(decFlag) {
           decAmount = "" + decAmount + aChar;
        }
        else {
           dolAmount = "" + dolAmount + aChar;
        }
     }
     if(aChar == ".") {
        if(decFlag) {
           dolAmount = "";
           break;
        }
        decFlag=true;
     }
   }
}

   // Ensure that at least a zero appears for the dollar amount.
```

**LISTING 29.8    continued**

```
if(dolAmount == "") {
   dolAmount = "0";
}
// Strip leading zeros.
if(dolAmount.length > 1) {
   while(dolAmount.length > 1 && dolAmount.substring(0,1) == "0") {
       dolAmount = dolAmount.substring(1,dolAmount.length);
   }
}


// Round the decimal amount.
if(decAmount.length > 2) {
   if(decAmount.substring(2,3) > "4") {
       decAmount = parseInt(decAmount.substring(0,2)) + 1;
       if(decAmount < 10) {
          decAmount = "0" + decAmount;
       }
       else {
          decAmount = "" + decAmount;
       }
   }
   else {
       decAmount = decAmount.substring(0,2);
   }
   if (decAmount == 100) {
      decAmount = "00";
      dolAmount = parseInt(dolAmount) + 1;
   }
}


// Pad right side of decAmount
if(decAmount.length == 1) {
   decAmount = decAmount + "0";
}
if(decAmount.length == 0) {
   decAmount = decAmount + "00";
}


// Check for negative values and reset textObj
if(newValue.substring(0,1) != '-' ||
     (dolAmount == "0" && decAmount == "00")) {
   textObj.value = dolAmount + "." + decAmount;
```

---

LISTING 29.8    continued

```
   }
   else{
      textObj.value = '-' + dolAmount + "." + decAmount;
   }
}
// end script-->
</script>
</head>

<body>
<h1>Money Format</h1>
<form name="form1">
<input type="text"
   size=16
   maxlength=16
   name="data">
<input type="button"
   name="CheckButton"
   value="Format"
   onClick="moneyFormat(document.form1.data)">
</form>
</body>
</html>
```

---

# Credit Cards

Accepting credit card orders is an important aspect of doing business over the Web. With JavaScript, you can run a preliminary check on a credit card number before it's stored on the server for final validation. Listing 29.9 demonstrates how you can run this test on credit card numbers to ensure that the card number follows the basic rules set by credit card companies. If the card number fails this validation, you can inform the user that he may have entered the wrong number and should check again. If the user chooses not to update the card number, you can still accept it and perform the final check on the server side using an electronic commerce service.

> **Warning**
>
> Listing 29.9 should only be used as a preliminary check for credit card validation. Using an electronic commerce service on the server side is the only way to properly validate credit cards at this time.

The isCreditCard function begins by ignoring any dashes that the user entered. It then runs the number through an algorithm that calculates a code, known as a checksum, for the credit card number. If the checksum is equal to the last digit of the credit card number, the number is valid. However, passing this test doesn't necessarily mean that an account exists for the number or that the account hasn't expired. It simply means that the number follows the rules for being a credit card number.

> **Resource**
>
> If you would like more details on how credit card checksums are calculated, you can find an excellent description at `http://www.websitter.com/cardtype.html`.

**LISTING 29.9**   Credit Card Validation

```html
<html>
<head>
<title>Credit Card Validation</title>
<script language="JavaScript">
<!--begin script
function isCreditCard(textObj) {
 /*
  *  This function validates a credit card entry.
  *  If the checksum is ok, the function returns true.
  */
  var ccNum;
  var odd = 1;
  var even = 2;
  var calcCard = 0;
  var calcs = 0;
  var ccNum2 = "";
  var aChar = '';
  var cc;
  var r;

  ccNum = textObj.value;
  for(var i = 0; i != ccNum.length; i++) {
     aChar = ccNum.substring(i,i+1);
     if(aChar == '-') {
        continue;
     }
```

LISTING 29.9 continued

```
      ccNum2 = ccNum2 + aChar;
   }

   cc = parseInt(ccNum2);
   if(cc == 0) {
      return false;
   }
   r = ccNum.length / 2;
   if(ccNum.length - (parseInt(r)*2) == 0) {
      odd = 2;
      even = 1;
   }

   for(var x = ccNum.length - 1; x > 0; x--) {
      r = x / 2;
      if(r < 1) {
         r++;
      }
      if(x - (parseInt(r) * 2) != 0) {
         calcs = (parseInt(ccNum.charAt(x - 1))) * odd;
      }
      else {
         calcs = (parseInt(ccNum.charAt(x - 1))) * even;
      }
      if(calcs >= 10) {
         calcs = calcs - 10 + 1;
      }
      calcCard = calcCard + calcs;
   }

   calcs = 10 - (calcCard % 10);
   if(calcs == 10) {
      calcs = 0;
   }

   if(calcs == (parseInt(ccNum.charAt(ccNum.length - 1)))) {
      return true;
   }
   else {
      return false;
   }
}
```

**LISTING 29.9**    continued

```
// end script-->
</script>
</head>

<BODY>
<h1>Credit Card Validation</h1>
<form name="form1">
<input type="text"
    size=16
    maxlength=16
    name="data">
<input type="button"
    name="CheckButton"
    value="Validate"
    onClick="document.form1.result.value = '' +
     isCreditCard(document.form1.data)">
<br>
Result <input type="text"
    size=16
    maxlength=16
    name="result">
</form>
</body>
</html>
```

# Example: The JavaScript Color Checker

The next example, shown in Figure 29.9, uses the capabilities described in this chapter to implement a color checker. One of the challenges in designing an HTML form is choosing a background color and a text color that are aesthetically pleasing as well as legible. An enormous number of combinations fulfill those criteria—and an enormous number don't. The JavaScript color checker lets the user specify two colors and view what the combination looks like in a separate window. The window contains the HTML code for specifying the color combination. The user can then cut and paste the specification directly into his HTML code.

**FIGURE 29.9**
*The color checker.*

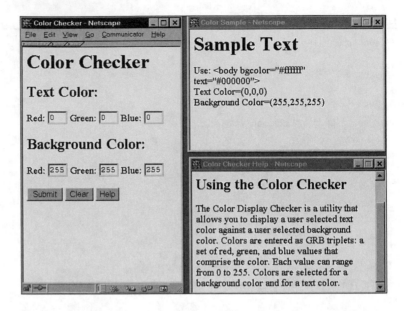

You specify color values by supplying an RGB triplet. The RGB triplet consists of three values representing the red, green, and blue components of the color. These values range from 0 to 255. For instance, the triplet (255,0,0) specifies pure red. Table 29.2 shows a few RGB color values.

**TABLE 29.2  RGB Color Values**

| RGB Value | Color |
| --- | --- |
| (0,0,0) | Black |
| (255,0,0) | Red |
| (255,255,0) | Yellow |
| (255,0,255) | Magenta |
| (0,255,0) | Green |
| (0,255,255) | Cyan |
| (0,0,255) | Blue |
| (128,128,128) | Dark gray |
| (200,200,200) | Light gray |
| (255,255,255) | White |

As with the earlier interactive forms, all processing is done on the client side. The program defines a constructor for Color objects that hold an RGB triplet. The Color objects have a method called setColor() that sets the RGB triplet and computes an equivalent hexadecimal string that can be used to set colors in conjunction with an HTML <body> tag. The program uses two instances of the Color object: one for the text color, and one for the background color. The onBlur event handler calls a validation routine, validateRGB(), whenever one of the six color-component text input fields loses focus.

Although the program doesn't have a Submit input object, it does have a Button object labeled Submit. The onClick method calls the processForm() function, which does something new. It creates a window for output that is separate from the color checker program. The window is referenced by a handle named popWin. The processForm() function checks to see if popWin is null (its initial value). If it is, processForm() creates a separate Color Sample window using the Windowopen() method.

Next, things get a little tricky; the user might close the Color Sample window. The only way to detect this is to examine the value of popWin.document. If popWin is not null, but popWin.document is null, the Color Sample window was closed. If this is the case, you have to re-create the Color Sample window. The processForm() function calls the doSample() function, which generates the content of the Color Sample window.

In the <body> tag, you'll see an instance of the onUnload event handler, which is called when the main window is terminated. It calls the closePopWin() function, which terminates the Color Sample window and the Help window if they exist. Finally, note the button named HelpButton. When the user clicks this button, the program creates a new window containing help text. Listing 29.10 contains the complete source code for the Color Checker tool.

**LISTING 29.10**   Color Checker Tool

```
<html>
<head>
<title>Color Checker</title>

<script language="JavaScript">
<!-- script start
// Constructor for color object
function color(r,g,b){
  this.setColor = setColor;
  this.setColor(r,g,b);
}

// Color object set method
function setColor(r,g,b){
  this.red = r;
  this.green = g;
  this.blue = b;
```

LISTING 29.10    continued

```javascript
  this.hex = rgb2hex(r,g,b);
}

// Convert RGB triplet to hexadecimal string
function rgb2hex(r,g,b){
  var str = '"#' + num2hex(r) + num2hex(g)+ num2hex + '"';
  return(str);
}

// Convert numeric string to hexadecimal string
function num2hex(n){
  var str = "";
  var hexstring = "0123456789abcdef";
  while(true) {
    digit = hexstring.substring((n%16),((n%16)+1));
    str = digit + str;
    n = n >> 4;
    if (n == 0) break;
  }
  // Pad string if necessary
  if (str.length < 2) {
    str = '0' + str;
  }
  return(str);
}

// Validate RGB component values
function validateRGB(textObj){
  var str = textObj.value;
  if (str.length == 0) {
    userAlert(textObj);
    return false;
  }

  for (var i = 0; i < str.length; ++i) {
    var ch = str.charAt(i);
    if (ch < "0" || ch > "9") {
      userAlert(textObj);
      return false;
    }
  }
```

LISTING 29.10    continued

```
  var value = parseInt(str,10);
  if (value < 0 || value > 255) {
    userAlert(textObj);
    return false;
  }
  else {
    return true;
  }
}


// Alert user on input error
function userAlert(textObj){
  alert("Please enter a value between 0 and 255.");
  textObj.focus();
  textObj.select();
}


// Write sample frame
function doSample(doc,tc,bc){
  var mytext="<h1>Sample Text</h1>";
  doc.open();
  doc.write("<html><head><title>Color Sample</title></head>");
  doc.write('<body bgcolor=' + bc.hex + ' text=' + tc.hex + '>');
  doc.write(mytext);
  doc.write('Use: &lt;body bgcolor=' + bc.hex + ' text='+ tc.hex + '&gt;');
  doc.write("<br>Text Color=(",tc.red,",",tc.green,",",tc.blue,")");
  doc.write("<br>Background Color=(",bc.red,",",bc.green,",",bc.blue,")");
  doc.write("</body></html>");
  doc.close();
}


// Process submitted form
function processForm(myform){
  var winFeatures = "scrollbars,width=400,height=250";
  if ((validateRGB(myform.redtxt) &&
       validateRGB(myform.grntxt) &&
       validateRGB(myform.blutxt) &&
       validateRGB(myform.redbg) &&
       validateRGB(myform.grnbg) &&
       validateRGB(myform.blubg)) == false){
    return false;
  }
```

**29**

**Forms and Data Validation**

**LISTING 29.10** continued

```javascript
    var textColor = new color(myform.redtxt.value,myform.grntxt.value,
                              myform.blutxt.value);
    var backColor = new color(myform.redbg.value,myform.grnbg.value,
                              myform.blubg.value);
    if (popWin == null)
      popWin = window.open("","PopWindow",winFeatures);
    else {
      if (popWin.document == null){
        popWin = window.open("","PopWindow",winFeatures);
      }
      doSample(popWin.document,textColor,backColor);
      popWin.focus();
      return true;
    }
}


// Reset form to initial values
function resetForm(myform){
  myform.redtxt.value = 0;
  myform.grntxt.value = 0;
  myform.blutxt.value = 0;
  myform.redbg.value = 255;
  myform.grnbg.value = 255;
  myform.blubg.value = 255;
  processForm(myform);
}


// Prompt for valid user input
function setPrompt(){
  window.status="Please enter a value between 0 and 255.";
  return true;
}


// Close Pop-up Windows
function closePopWin(){
  if (popWin != null && popWin.document != null)
    popWin.close();
  if (helpWin != null && helpWin.document != null)
    helpWin.close();
}


// Clear prompt
```

**LISTING 29.10**    continued

```
function clearPrompt(){
  window.status="";
  return true;
}

//Display help page
function displayHelp() {
  var winFeatures = "scrollbars,width=400,height=250";
  if (helpWin == null)
    helpWin = window.open("","HelpWindow",winFeatures);
  else if (helpWin.document == null)
    helpWin = window.open("","HelpWindow",winFeatures);

  helpWin.document.open();
  helpWin.document.write("<html><head><title>Color Checker Help
➥</title></head>");
  helpWin.document.write("<body bgcolor=ffffff>");
  helpWin.document.write("<h1>Color Checker Help</h1>");
  helpWin.document.write("<h2>Using the Color Checker</h2>");
  helpWin.document.write("The Color Display Checker is a utility that ");
  helpWin.document.write("allows you to display a user selected text ");
  helpWin.document.write("color against a user selected background color. ");
  helpWin.document.write("Colors are entered as GRB triplets: a set of ");
  helpWin.document.write("red, green, and blue values that comprise the ");
  helpWin.document.write("color.  Each value can range from 0 to 255. ");
  helpWin.document.write("Colors are selected for a background color ");
  helpWin.document.write("and for a text color. ");
  helpWin.document.write("</body></html>");
  helpWin.document.close();
  helpWin.focus();
  return true;
}

// Initialization
var popWin = null;
var helpWin = null;

// script end -->
</script>
</head>

<body bgcolor="#ffffff" text="#000000" onUnload="closePopWin()">
```

29

Forms and Data
Validation

**LISTING 29.10** continued

```
<h1>Color Checker</h1>
<form name="myform">
<h2>Text Color:</h2>
Red: <input type="text"
            size=3
            maxlength=3
            name="redtxt"
            value="0"
            onChange="validateRGB(this)"
            onFocus="setPrompt()"
            onBlur="clearPrompt()">
Green: <input type="text"
            size=3
            maxlength=3
            name="grntxt"
            value="0"
            onChange="validateRGB(this)"
            onFocus="setPrompt()"
            onBlur="clearPrompt()">
Blue:  <input type="text"
            size=3
            maxlength=3
            name="blutxt"
            value="0"
            onChange="validateRGB(this)"
            onFocus="setPrompt()"
            onBlur="clearPrompt()">

<h2>Background Color:</h2>
Red: <input type="text"
            size=3
            maxlength=3
            name="redbg"
            value="255"
            onChange="validateRGB(this)"
            onFocus="setPrompt()"
            onBlur="clearPrompt()">
Green: <input type="text"
            size=3
            maxlength=3
            name="grnbg"
            value="255"
```

LISTING 29.10    continued

```
                    onChange="validateRGB(this)"
                    onFocus="setPrompt()"
                    onBlur="clearPrompt()">
Blue: <input type="text"
              size=3
              maxlength=3
              name="blubg"
              value="255"
              onChange="validateRGB(this)"
              onFocus="setPrompt()"
              onBlur="clearPrompt()">
<br><br>
<input type="button"
       value="Submit"
       onClick="processForm(document.myform)">
<input type="reset"
       value="Clear"
       onClick="resetForm(document.myform)">
<input type="button"
       value="Help"
       name="HelpButton"
       onClick="displayHelp()">
</form>
</body>
</html>
```

# Summary

JavaScript greatly enhances the basic form capability of HTML. Much of the processing that can be performed on the server can be done on the client side using JavaScript. The capabilities can be summarized as follows:

- User feedback: JavaScript lets you provide feedback to the form user through a combination of event handlers and control of the browser's status bar contents.

- Message boxes: By using JavaScript alert and dialog boxes, you can display a pop-up message to the user, request confirmation prior to submitting a form, and query the user for additional information.

- Validating user input: You can validate input fields, groups of fields, or the entire form by using event handlers and JavaScript functions. Users can receive feedback in the context of the current form (that is, the page is not replaced by a new page with an error message).

- You can build interactive forms in which part or even all of the processing is performed on the client side.

You can use JavaScript to create forms that are easier to use and less prone to error. In turn, you can create forms that respond far more quickly than server-oriented programs, particularly when the user has a low bandwidth connection to the server.

# Personalization and Dynamic Pages

If you have spent any time surfing the Internet, you know that more and more sites are trying to become a one-stop shop for everyone's Internet-related needs. To keep those who use the Internet from being overwhelmed with every piece of news and information from around the world, sites are personalized to match each individual's particular interests. A Web site knows that a certain individual wants to read only the sports page, see certain stock prices, and order groceries online. Today's Web page wants to be everyone's best friend, grocer, or personal financial advisor. Gone are the days of cold, static Web pages. Today's Web pages are dynamic!

When an individual goes to his favorite online bookstore, he is not presented with just a list of books; he is referred to other books that he might like, based on his past purchases. Although many online stores and Web site portals use massive server-side databases to keep track of an individual's personal interests and buying history, so as to provide a personalized and dynamic experience, there are a number of things you, as a Web designer, can do with JavaScript to make your Web site warm and inviting.

In this chapter, I am going to show you how to use JavaScript to manipulate cookies, URL query string parameters, and hidden form variables to make your site more dynamic and personal. To better understand how to make Web pages dynamic, let's take a moment to understand why Web pages are static by nature.

# Understanding the Static Web Page

Web servers have very short memories. When you request a page, the server doesn't really know who you are, what you entered on a form three pages ago, or whether this is your first visit to the site or your seventy-fifth. One of the challenges of using the Hypertext Transfer Protocol (HTTP) is that it doesn't track the *state* of your interactions with the server. *State* refers to any information about you or your visit to a Web site. It's maintained as you move from page to page within the site, and it may be used by the Web server or a JavaScript program (or both) to customize your experience at the site. With this information in hand, you can set user preferences, fill in default form values, track visit counts, and do many other things that make browsing easier for users and give you more information about how your pages are used.

There are a number of ways to maintain state information:

- Store it in cookies.

- Encode it in URL links.

- Send it in hidden form variables.

- Store it in variables in other frames.

- Store it on the Web server.

There are some technical challenges regarding state maintenance. While browsing a site, a user might suddenly zoom off to another Web site and return minutes, hours, or days later, only to find that any saved state information is out of date or has been erased. He might return by clicking his browser's Back button, by using a bookmark, or by typing in the URL directly, causing state information encoded in the URL to be overwritten or lost.

The Web developer must maintain state information regardless of whether the user navigates through the site using buttons on a form or a URL link on a page. This could mean adding information to both hidden form variables and every URL <a href...> tag that appears on the page.

With all these difficulties to overcome, these state maintenance mechanisms had better be useful. Luckily, they are. There are many advantages to maintaining state, both within a single site visit and from one visit to the next. Consider the following scenarios:

- A shopping cart application: A user browses through the site selecting items and adding them to a virtual shopping cart. At any time, the user can view the items in the cart, change the contents of his cart, or take the cart to the checkout counter to purchase. Keeping track of which user owns which shopping cart is essential.

- Personalized portals: Many Web sites provide portals where the user can customize what he sees when he arrives. After the user chooses a layout, a color scheme, news setting, and so on, the preferences are stored on the user's computer through the use of cookies. The user can return to the site any time and get his previously configured page.

- Frequent visitor bonuses: By storing information on the client computer, an application can track how many times a browser has hit a particular page. When the user reaches a certain level of hits, he gets access to more or better services.

- Change banners: Change graphic banners and text each time the user hits a page. This technique is often used to cycle through a list of advertisements.

- Bookmarks: Track where a user was when he last visited the site. Was he reading a story, filling out a questionnaire, or playing a game? Let him pick up where he left off.

- Games: Remember current or high scores. Present new challenges based on past answers and performance.

# Introducing Cookies

Cookies let you store information on the client browser's computer for later retrieval. Although they have drawbacks, cookies are the most powerful technique available for maintaining state on the client side.

> **Note**
>
> Netscape came up with the original cookie specification. Although they are called *cookies*, there doesn't seem to be any good reason why Netscape chose that particular name. The cookie specification page admits that "the state object is called a cookie for no compelling reason."

In their simplest form, cookies store data in the form of name=value pairs. You can pick any name and value combination you want. More advanced cookie features include the capability to set an expiration date and to specify what Web pages may see the cookie information.

## Advantages of Cookies

One of the most powerful aspects of cookies is their persistence. When a cookie is set on the user's browser, it may persist for days, months, or even years. This makes it easy to save visit information and user preferences and have them available every time the user returns to your site.

Cookies are especially helpful when used in conjunction with JavaScript. Since JavaScript has functions for reading, adding, and editing cookies, your JavaScript programs can use them to store global information about a user as he surfs through your Web site.

## Limitations and Disadvantages of Cookies

Some limitations of cookies could prove problematic. Cookies are stored on the user's computer, usually in a special cookie file. As with all files, this cookie file might be accidentally (or purposefully) deleted, taking all the browser's cookie information with it. The cookie file could be write-protected, thus preventing cookies from being stored there. Browser software may impose limitations on the size and number of cookies that may be stored, and newer cookies may overwrite older ones.

Because cookies are associated with a particular browser, problems come up if a user switches from one browser to another. If you use Netscape Navigator and have a collection of cookies, they will no longer be available if you switch to Microsoft Internet Explorer.

Finally, if several people use the same computer and browser, they might find themselves using cookies that belong to someone else. The reason for this is that cookie information is stored in a file on the computer, and the browser has no way to distinguish between multiple users.

There are also some problems, both real and imagined, concerning the use of cookies. Because many browsers store their cookie information in an unencrypted text file, sensitive information, such as a password, should never be stored in a cookie. Anyone with access to the computer could read it.

Some Web browsers have a feature that alerts the user when an attempt is made to set a cookie. The browser can even be configured to prevent cookies from being set at all. This sometimes results in confusion on the user's part when a dialog box informs him that something is happening involving something called a "cookie." If cookies are disabled, your carefully designed Web application might not run at all.

You cannot set an infinite number of cookies on every Web browser that visits your site. Here are the number of cookies you can set and how large they can be:

- Cookies per server or domain: 20

- Total cookies per browser: 300

- Largest cookie: 4KB (including both the `name` and `value` parameters)

If these limits are exceeded, the browser might attempt to discard older cookies by tossing the least recently used cookies first.

## Cookie Myths

The biggest problem with cookies might be psychological. Some Web users believe that cookies are a tool used by "Big Brother" in order to discover their innermost secrets. Perhaps I exaggerate a bit. However, considering that cookies are capable of storing information about pages the user has visited on a Web site and how many times he has been there, what advertising banners he has viewed, and what he has selected and entered on forms, some people think that their privacy is being invaded whenever a cookie gets on their computers.

In reality, cookies are seldom used for these purposes. Although technically these things are possible, there are now better and easier ways of getting the same information without using cookies. I guess this means that you can still be paranoid—just not about cookies.

Another user might complain about Web sites writing information to his computer and taking up space on his hard drive. This is a legitimate concern. Web browser software limits the total size of the cookies stored to 1.2MB, with no more than 80KB going to any one Web site. Consider, though, that this number is small when compared to the size of the pages and graphic images that a Web browser routinely stores in its page cache.

Other users are concerned that cookies set by one Web site might be read by other sites. This is completely untrue. Your Web browser software prevents this from happening by making a cookie available only to the site that created it.

If your users understand the usefulness of cookies, this "cookie backlash" shouldn't be a problem.

### Resource

Netscape came up with the original cookie specification. You can find more information on the Netscape Web site at `http://www.netscape.com/newsref/std/cookie_spec.html`.

# Using Cookies

By now you have considered the pros and cons of cookies and have decided that they are just what you need to make your JavaScript application a success. In this section, you will find a number of handy functions for reading and setting cookies, which will help you make your Web sites dynamic and more personal. Also included in this section are Internet references for finding additional information concerning cookies.

## Retrieving Cookie Values

Cookie names and values are stored and set using the `cookie` property of the `Document` object. To store the raw `cookie` string in a variable, you would use a JavaScript command such as this:

```
var myCookie = document.cookie;
```

To display it on a Web page, use the following command:

```
document.write ("Raw Cookies: " + document.cookie + "<br>");
```

JavaScript stores cookies in the following format:

```
name1=value1; name2=value2; name3=value3
```

Individual `name=value` pairs are separated by a semicolon and a blank space. There is no semicolon after the final value. To make it easier to retrieve a cookie, you should use a JavaScript routine such as the one in Listing 30.1.

**LISTING 30.1**   The `GetCookie` Function

```
function GetCookie (name) {
  var result = null;
  var myCookie = " " + document.cookie + ";";
  var searchName = " " + name + "=";
  var startOfCookie = myCookie.indexOf(searchName);
  var endOfCookie;
  if (startOfCookie != -1) {
    startOfCookie += searchName.length; // skip past cookie name
    endOfCookie = myCookie.indexOf(";", startOfCookie);
    result = unescape(myCookie.substring(startOfCookie, endOfCookie));
  }
  return result;
}
```

In Listing 30.1, the `myCookie` string helps avoid annoying boundary conditions by making sure all cookie string names start with a space and end with a semicolon. From there, it's easy to find the start of the `name=` portion of the string, skip it, and retrieve everything between that point and the next semicolon.

## Setting Cookie Values

The *name=value* combination is the minimum amount of information you need to set up a cookie. However, there is more to a cookie than that. Here is the complete list of parameters used to specify a cookie:

- *name=value*
- expires=*date*
- path=*path*
- domain=*domainname*
- secure

## Cookie Names and Values

The *name* and *value* can be anything you choose. In some cases, you might want it to be explanatory, such as `FavoriteColor=Blue`. In other cases, it could just be code that the JavaScript program interprets, such as `CurStat=1:2:1:0:0:1:0:3:1:1`.

In its simplest form, a routine to set a cookie looks like this:

```
function SetCookieEZ (name, value) {
  document.cookie = name + "=" + escape(value);
}
```

Notice that the value is encoded using the `escape()` function. If there were a semicolon in the string, it might prevent you from achieving the expected result. Using the `escape()` function eliminates this problem.

Also notice that the `document.cookie` property works rather differently from most properties. In most cases, using the assignment operator (=) causes the existing property value to be completely overwritten with the new value. This isn't the case with the `cookie` property. With cookies, each new *name* you assign is added to the active list of cookies. If you assign the same *name* twice, the first assignment is replaced by the second.

There are some exceptions to this last statement. These are explained in the `path` section, later in this chapter.

## Expiration Date

The `expires=`*date* parameter tells the browser how long the cookie will last. The cookie specification page at Netscape states that dates are in the form of

```
Wdy, DD-Mon-YY HH:MM:SS GMT
```

Here's an example:

```
Mon, 08-Jul-96 03:18:20 GMT
```

This format is based on Internet RFC 822, which you can find at `http://www.w3.org/hypertext/WWW/Protocols/rfc822/#z28`.

The only difference between RFC 822 and the Netscape implementation is that in Netscape Navigator the expiration date must end with GMT (Greenwich Mean Time). Happily, the JavaScript language provides a function to do just that. Using the `toGMTString()` function, you can set a cookie to expire in the near or distant future.

> **Tip**
>
> Even though the date produced by the `toGMTString()` function doesn't match the Netscape specification, it still works under JavaScript.

If the expiration date isn't specified, the cookie remains in effect until the browser is shut down. This code segment sets a cookie to expire in one week:

```
var name="foo";
var value="bar";
var oneWeek = 7 * 24 * 60 * 60 * 1000;
var expDate = new Date();
expDate.setTime (expDate.getTime() + oneWeek);
document.cookie = name + "=" + escape(value) +
    "; expires=" + expDate.toGMTString();
```

## path

By default, cookies are available to other Web pages within the same directory as the page on which they were created. The `path` parameter allows a cookie to be made available to pages in other directories. If the value of the `path` parameter is a sub-string of a page's URL, cookies created with that `path` are available to that page. For example, you could create a cookie with the following command:

```
document.cookie = "foo=bar1; path=/javascript";
```

This would make the cookie `foo` available to every page in the `javascript` directory and those directories beneath it. If the command looked like this

```
document.cookie = "foo=bar2; path=/javascript/sam";
```

the cookie would be available only to pages in the `/javascript/sam` directory and those beneath it but would not be available to pages in the `/javascript` directory.

Finally, to make the cookie available to everyone on your server, use the following command:

```
document.cookie = "foo=bar3; path=/";
```

What happens when a browser has multiple cookies on different paths but with the same name? Which one wins?

Actually, they all do. In this situation, it's possible to have two or more cookies with the same name but different values. For example, if a page issued all the commands listed previously, its `cookie` string would look like this:

```
foo=bar3; foo=bar2; foo=bar1
```

To stay aware of this situation, you might want to write a routine to count the number of cookie values associated with a cookie name, as shown in Listing 30.2.

**LISTING 30.2** The `GetCookieCount` Function

```
function GetCookieCount (name) {
  var result = 0;
  var myCookie = " " + document.cookie + ";";
  var searchName = " " + name + "=";
  var nameLength = searchName.length;
  var startOfCookie = myCookie.indexOf(searchName);
  while (startOfCookie != -1) {
    result += 1;
    startOfCookie = myCookie.indexOf(searchName, startOfCookie + nameLength);
  }
  return result;
}
```

Of course, if there is a `GetCookieCount` function, there would need to be a `GetCookieNum` function to retrieve a particular instance of a cookie. That function would look like Listing 30.3.

**LISTING 30.3** The `GetCookieNum` Function

```
function GetCookieNum (name, cookieNum) {
  var result = null;
  if (cookieNum >= 1) {
    var myCookie = " " + document.cookie + ";";
    var searchName = " " + name + "=";
    var nameLength = searchName.length;
    var startOfCookie = myCookie.indexOf(searchName);
    var cntr = 0;
    for (cntr = 1; cntr < cookieNum; cntr++)
      startOfCookie = myCookie.indexOf(searchName, startOfCookie + nameLength);
    if (startOfCookie != -1) {
      startOfCookie += nameLength; // skip past cookie name
      var endOfCookie = myCookie.indexOf(";", startOfCookie);
      result = unescape(myCookie.substring(startOfCookie, endOfCookie));
    }
  }
  return result;
}
```

To delete a cookie, the name and the path must match the original name and path used when the cookie was set.

## domain

After a page on a particular server creates a cookie, that cookie is usually accessible only to other pages on that server. Just as the `path` parameter makes a cookie available outside its home path, the `domain` parameter makes it available to other Web servers at the same site.

You can't create a cookie that anyone on the Internet can see. You can only set a path that falls inside your own domain. This is because the use of the `domain` parameter dictates that you must use at least two periods if your domain ends in `.com`, `.edu`, `.net`, `.org`, `.gov`, `.mil`, or `.int` (for example, `.mydomain.com`). Otherwise, it must have at least three periods (`.mydomain.ma.us`). Your `domain` parameter string must match the tail of your server's domain name.

## secure

The final cookie parameter tells your browser that this cookie should be sent only under a secure connection with the Web server. This means that the server and the browser must support HTTPS security. (HTTPS is a protocol for transferring encrypted information over the Internet)

If the `secure` parameter is not present, it means that cookies are sent unencrypted over the network.

Now that you have seen all the cookie parameters, it would be helpful to have a JavaScript routine set cookies with all the parameters. Such a routine might look like Listing 30.4.

LISTING 30.4   The `SetCookie` Function

```
function SetCookie (name, value, expires, path, domain, secure) {
  var expString =
            ((expires == null) ? "" : ("; expires=" + expires.toGMTString()));
  var pathString = ((path == null) ? "" : ("; path=" + path));
  var domainString = ((domain == null) ? "" : ("; domain=" + domain));
  var secureString = ((secure == true) ? "; secure" : "");
  document.cookie = name + "=" + escape (value) +
                  expString + pathString + domainString + secureString;
}
```

To use this routine, you call it with whatever parameters you want to set and use `null` in place of parameters that don't matter.

# Deleting a Cookie

To delete a cookie, set the expiration date to some time in the past; how far in the past doesn't generally matter. To be on the safe side, a few days should work. Listing 30.5 shows the ClearCookie routine that is used to delete a cookie.

**LISTING 30.5**   The ClearCookie Function

```
function ClearCookie (name) {
  var ThreeDays = 3 * 24 * 60 * 60 * 1000;
  var expDate = new Date();
  expDate.setTime (expDate.getTime() - ThreeDays);
  document.cookie = name + "=ImOutOfHere; expires=" + expDate.toGMTString();
}
```

When deleting cookies, it doesn't matter what you use for the cookie value. Any value will do.

**Caution**

Some versions of Netscape do a poor job of converting time to GMT. Some common JavaScript functions for deleting a cookie consider the past to be one millisecond behind the current time. Although this is true, it doesn't work on all platforms. To be on the safe side, use a few days in the past to expire cookies.

# A Cookie Example

The JavaScript program in Listing 30.6 provides an example of cookies in use. This program allows the user to create a personalized "News-of-the-Day" page containing links to sites of general interest in a number of different categories. The user's favorite links are stored in cookies. Figure 30.1, which follows the listing, shows what the Favorites page looks like.

**Warning**

In IE 3.0 the JavaScript cookie property works only if the pages that use the cookie property are pulled from a Web server.

**LISTING 30.6** The Favorites Script

```
<html>
<head>
<script language="JavaScript">
<!-- Comment out script from browsers that don't know JavaScript


//================================================================
// Here are our standard Cookie routines
//================================================================
//----------------------------------------------------------------
// GetCookie - Returns the value of the specified cookie or null
//             if the cookie doesn't exist
//----------------------------------------------------------------
function GetCookie(name)
{
  var result = null;
  var myCookie = " " + document.cookie + ";";
  var searchName = " " + name + "=";
  var startOfCookie = myCookie.indexOf(searchName);
  var endOfCookie;
  if (startOfCookie != -1)
  {
    startOfCookie += searchName.length;
    // skip past cookie name
    endOfCookie = myCookie.indexOf(";", startOfCookie);
    result = unescape(myCookie.substring(startOfCookie,endOfCookie));
  }
  return result;
}


//----------------------------------------------------------------
// SetCookieEZ - Quickly sets a cookie which will last until the
//               user shuts down his browser
//----------------------------------------------------------------
function SetCookieEZ(name, value)
{
  document.cookie = name + "=" + escape(value);
}


//----------------------------------------------------------------
// SetCookie - Adds or replaces a cookie. Use null for parameters
//             that you don't care about
//----------------------------------------------------------------
```

30

Personalization
and Dynamic
Pages

LISTING 30.6    continued

```
function SetCookie(name, value, expires, path, domain, secure)
{
  var expString = ((expires == null)? "" : ("; expires=" +
➥expires.toGMTString()));
  var pathString = ((path == null) ? "" : ("; path=" + path));
  var domainString = ((domain == null)? "" : ("; domain=" + domain));
  var secureString = ((secure == true) ? "; secure" : ""));
  document.cookie = name + "=" + escape(value)+ expString + pathString +
➥domainString+ secureString;
}


//----------------------------------------------------------------
// ClearCookie  - Removes a cookie by setting an expiration date
//                   three days in the past
//----------------------------------------------------------------
function ClearCookie(name)
{
  var ThreeDays = 3 * 24 * 60 * 60 * 1000;
  var expDate = new Date();
  expDate.setTime (expDate.getTime() - ThreeDays);
  document.cookie = name + "=ImOutOfHere; expires="+ expDate.toGMTString();
}


//================================================================
// Here are the object and the routines for our Favorites app
//================================================================
//----------------------------------------------------------------
/* Here is our "favorite" object.
   Properties: fullName - The full descriptive name
               cook     - The code used for the cookie
               urlpath  - The full url (http://...) to the site
       Methods: Enabled - Returns true if the link's cookie is
                            turned on
               Checked  - Returns the word "CHECKED" if the
                            link's cookie is turned on
               WriteAsCheckBox - Sends text to the document in a
                                   checkbox control format
               WriteAsWebLink  - Sends text to the document in a
                                   <a href...> format
------------------------------------------------------------*/
function favorite(fullName, cook, urlpath)
{
```

**LISTING 30.6** continued

```javascript
  this.fullName = fullName;
  this.cook    = cook;
  this.urlpath  = urlpath;
  this.Enabled = Enabled;
  this.Checked = Checked;
  this.WriteAsCheckBox = WriteAsCheckBox;
  this.WriteAsWebLink = WriteAsWebLink;
}


//----------------------------------------------------------------
// Enabled - Checks to see if the cookie exists
// returns - true if the cookie exists
//           false if it doesn't
//----------------------------------------------------------------
function Enabled()
{
  var result = false;
  var FaveCookie = GetCookie("Favorites");
  if (FaveCookie != null)
  {
    var searchFor = "<" + this.cook + ">";
    var startOfCookie = FaveCookie.indexOf(searchFor);
    if (startOfCookie != -1)
      result = true;
  }
  return result;
}


//----------------------------------------------------------------
// Checked - Checks to see if the cookie exists (using Enabled)
// returns - 'CHECKED ' if the cookie exists
//           "" if it doesn't
//----------------------------------------------------------------
function Checked ()
{
  if (this.Enabled())
    return "CHECKED ";
  return "";
}
//----------------------------------------------------------------
// WriteAsCheckBox - The favorite may be either a regular URL or
//                   a section title.  If the urlpath is an empty
```

**LISTING 30.6** continued

```
//                    string, then the favorite is a section title.
//                    The links will appear within a definition
//                    list, and are formatted appropriately.
//-----------------------------------------------------------------
function WriteAsCheckBox ()
{
  // Check to see if it's a title or regular link
  if (this.urlpath == "")
  {
    // It's a section title
    result = '<dt><strong>' + this.fullName + '</strong>';
  }
  else
  {
    // It's a regular link
    result = '<dd><input type="checkbox" name="'+ this.cook + '" '+
➡this.Checked()+ 'onClick="SetFavoriteEnabled(this.name,
➡this.checked);">'+ this.fullName;
  }
  document.write(result);
}


//-----------------------------------------------------------------
// Global Variable:
// NextHeading - Sometimes we only want to print a heading if one
//               its favorites is turned on.  The NextHeading
//               variable helps us to do this. See WriteAsWebLink
//-----------------------------------------------------------------
var NextHeading = "";


//-----------------------------------------------------------------
// WriteAsWebLink - The favorite may be either a regular URL or
//                  a section title.  If the urlpath is an empty
//                  string, then the favorite is a section title.
//                  The links will appear within a definition
//                  list, and are formatted appropriately.
//-----------------------------------------------------------------
function WriteAsWebLink()
{
  var result = '';
  if (this.urlpath == "")
  {
```

**LISTING 30.6** continued

```
    NextHeading = this.fullName;    // It's must be a Title
  }
  else
  {
    if (this.Enabled() || (GetCookie("ViewAll") == "T"))
    {
      if (NextHeading != "")
      {
        result = '<p><dt><strong>' + NextHeading+ '</strong>';
        NextHeading = "";
      }
      result = result + '<dd><a href="' + this.urlpath + '">'+ this.fullName +
➥ '</a>';
    }
  }
  document.write(result);
}


//=================================================================
// Global Variables
//■■■■■■■■■■■■■■■■■■■■■■■■■■■■■■■■■■■■■■■■■■■■■■■■■■■■■■■■■■■■■■■■■■■■■
/*----------------------------------------------------------------
FaveList will be a list of all favorite objects, which are
then declared below.  favorites with an empty urlpath property
are section headings
----------------------------------------------------------------*/
var FaveList = new Array();
// Comics Section ------------------
FaveList[1] = new favorite("Comics", "", "");
FaveList[2] = new favorite("Dilbert", "cdilb",
➥"http://www.unitedmedia.com/comics/dilbert/");
FaveList[3] = new favorite("Doonesbury", "cdoon",
➥"http://www.uexpress.com/cgi-bin/ups/mainindex.cgi?code=db");
FaveList[4] = new favorite("Mr. Boffo", "cboff",
➥"http://www.uexpress.com/cgi-bin/ups/new_mainindex.cgi?code=mb");
// General News Section -------------
FaveList[5] = new favorite("General News", "", "");
FaveList[6] = new favorite("CNN", "ncnn", "http://www.cnn.com/");
FaveList[7] = new favorite("NPR", "nnpr","http://www.npr.org/news/");
FaveList[8] = new favorite("Boston Globe", "nbos","http://www.boston.com/");
// Computer Industry Section --------
FaveList[9] = new favorite("Computer Industry", "", "");
```

**LISTING 30.6**    continued

```
FaveList[10] = new favorite("PC Week", "ipcw","http://www.pcweek.com/");
FaveList[11] = new favorite("TechWeb", "icmp",
➡"http://www.techWeb.com/wire/wire.html");
FaveList[12] = new favorite("Netscape", "ntsc","http://devedge.netscape.com/");
FaveList[13] = new favorite("Microsoft", "micr","http://msdn.microsoft.com/");
// Search Engines Section ----------
FaveList[14] = new favorite("Search Engines", "", "");
FaveList[15] = new favorite("Yahoo!", "syah","http://www.yahoo.com/");
FaveList[16] = new favorite("Alta Vista", "sav","http://www.altavista.com/");
FaveList[17] = new favorite("Excite", "sexc","http://www.excite.com/");
// Auction Section -----------------
FaveList[18] = new favorite("Auctions", "", "");
FaveList[19] = new favorite("ebay", "ebay","http://www.ebay.com/");
FaveList[20] = new favorite("Yahoo Auctions", "yhac",
➡"http://auctions.yahoo.com/");
// Misc. Section -------------------
FaveList[21] = new favorite("Misc.", "", "");
FaveList[22] = new favorite("Today in History", "mtih",
➡"http://www.thehistorynet.com/today/today.htm");
FaveList[23] = new favorite("Merriam-Webster's Word of the Day","mwod",
➡"http://www.m-w.com/cgi-bin/mwwod.pl");
FaveList[24] = new favorite("Quotes of the Day", "mquot",
➡"http://www.starlingtech.com/quotes/qotd.html");


//================================================================
// Page Writing Routines
//================================================================
//----------------------------------------------------------------
// SendOptionsPage - Writes a page allowing the user to select
//                   her favorite preferences
//----------------------------------------------------------------
function SendOptionsPage()
{
  document.write('<h1>Select Favorites</h1>');
  document.write('<form method=post>');
  // Here's the button for viewing the Favorites page
  document.write('<input type=button value="Show Favorites" '+ 'onClick="'+
➡'ReloadPage()'+';">');
  // The links will look nicer inside a definition listdocument.write('<dl>');
  for (var i = 1; i < FaveList.length; i++)
    FaveList[i].WriteAsCheckBox();
  // Write each checkbox
```

**LISTING 30.6**    continued

```
  document.write('</dl><p>');
  ClearCookie("ViewAll");
  document.write('</form>');
}


//----------------------------------------------------------------
// LoadOptions - Sets the ShowOptions cookie, which makes the
//               option selection page appear when the page is
//               then reloaded.
//----------------------------------------------------------------
function LoadOptions()
{
  SetCookieEZ("ShowOptions", "T");
  window.open(document.location.href, "_top", "");
}


//----------------------------------------------------------------
// ToggleView - Toggles ViewAll mode on and off.  When on, all
//              links will be displayed.  When off, only the
//              user's favorite selections will be displayed.
//----------------------------------------------------------------
function ToggleView()
{
  if (GetCookie("ViewAll") == "T")
  {
    ClearCookie("ViewAll");
  }
  else
  {
    var fiveYears = 5 * 365 * 24 * 60 * 60 * 1000;
    var expDate = new Date();
    expDate.setTime (expDate.getTime() + fiveYears );
    SetCookie("ViewAll", "T", expDate, null, null, false);
  }
  window.open(document.location.href, "_top", "");
}


//----------------------------------------------------------------
// SendPersonalPage - Writes a page showing the categories and
//                    links which the user prefers. Only shows a
//                    heading if one of its favorites is enabled
//----------------------------------------------------------------
```

**LISTING 30.6    continued**

```
function SendPersonalPage()
{
  if (GetCookie("ViewAll") != "T")
    document.write('<h1>Your Favorites:</h1>');
  else
    document.write('<h1>Links:</h1>');
  // Here are the buttons for viewing the options or
  // "View All" pages
  document.write('<form method=post>');
  if (GetCookie("ViewAll") == "T")
  {
    document.write('<input type=button value="View Favorites"
➥ '+'onClick="ToggleView();">');
  }
  else
  {
    document.write('<input type=button value="View All" '+'onClick=
➥"ToggleView();">');
  }
  document.write('<input type=button '+ 'value="Select Personal Favorites"
➥ '+ 'onClick="LoadOptions();">');
  document.write('</form>');
  // The links will look nicer inside a definition list
  document.write('<dl>');
  for (var i = 1; i < FaveList.length; i++)
    FaveList[i].WriteAsWebLink();    // Write each link
  document.write('</dl><p>');
}


//=================================================================
// Helper Functions
//=================================================================
//-----------------------------------------------------------------
// isEnabled - Returns True if the favorite identified by the
//             name parameter is enabled.
//-----------------------------------------------------------------
function isEnabled(name)
{
  var result = false;
  var FaveCookie = GetCookie("Favorites");
  if (FaveCookie != null)
  {
```

**LISTING 30.6**   continued

```
    var searchFor = "<" + name + ">";
    var startOfCookie = FaveCookie.indexOf(searchFor);
    if (startOfCookie != -1)
      result = true;
  }
  return result;
}


//---------------------------------------------------------------
// AddFavorite- Enables the favorite identified by the name
//              parameter.
//---------------------------------------------------------------
function AddFavorite(name)
{
  if (!isEnabled(name))
  {
    var fiveYears = 5 * 365 * 24 * 60 * 60 * 1000;
    var expDate = new Date();
    expDate.setTime (expDate.getTime() + fiveYears );
    SetCookie("Favorites", GetCookie("Favorites")+ "<" + name +
➥">", expDate, null, null, false);
  }
}


//---------------------------------------------------------------
// ClearFavorite- Disables the favorite identified by the name
//                parameter.
//---------------------------------------------------------------
function ClearFavorite(name)
{
  if (isEnabled(name))
  {
    var FaveCookie = GetCookie("Favorites");
    var searchFor = "<" + name + ">";
    var startOfCookie = FaveCookie.indexOf(searchFor);
    var NewFaves = FaveCookie.substring(0, startOfCookie)+
FaveCookie.substring(startOfCookie+searchFor.length,FaveCookie.length);
    var fiveYears = 5 * 365 * 24 * 60 * 60 * 1000;
    var expDate = new Date();
    expDate.setTime (expDate.getTime() + fiveYears );
    SetCookie("Favorites", NewFaves, expDate, null, null, false);
  }
```

**30**

**Personalization and Dynamic Pages**

LISTING 30.6   continued

```
}

//-------------------------------------------------------------
// SetFavoriteEnabled - Turns the favorite identified by the name
//                      parameter on (SetOn=true) or off
//                      (SetOn=false).
//-------------------------------------------------------------
function SetFavoriteEnabled(name, SetOn)
{
  if (SetOn)
    AddFavorite(name);
  else
    ClearFavorite(name);
}


//-------------------------------------------------------------
// ReloadPage - Reloads the page
//-------------------------------------------------------------
function ReloadPage()
{
  window.open(document.location.href, "_top", "");
}


// End Commented Script -->
</script>
</head>
<body>
<script language="JavaScript">
<!-- Comment out script from browsers that don't know JavaScript
/*-------------------------------------------------------------
Here's where we select the page to send.  Normally we send the
personalized favorites page (by calling SendPersonalPage). However,
If the cookie ShowOptions is set, we'll send the options selection
page instead (by calling SendOptionsPage).
-------------------------------------------------------------*/
if (GetCookie("ShowOptions") == "T")
{
  ClearCookie("ShowOptions");
  SendOptionsPage();
}
else
{
```

**LISTING 30.6**    continued

```
  SendPersonalPage();
}
// End Commented Script -->
</script>
<center>
This is a very dull page unless you have a JavaScript
enabled browser.<br>
</center>
</body>
</html>
```

**FIGURE 30.1**
*The Favorites page.*

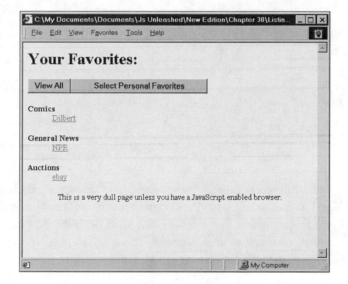

Without JavaScript, a task like this would have been handled at the server. Each hit would have involved having the server run some type of script or program to read the user's cookies and generate his page on-the-fly. With JavaScript, all this processing takes place on the client's browser; the server just downloads the static page. It might not even do that, because the page might come from the client's local cache. When the page is loaded, all the links, selected or not, are sent. With the help of cookies and JavaScript, the client decides which ones to show the user.

This program makes use of three different cookies. The Favorites cookie contains a unique code for each favored link. The ViewAll cookie toggles between showing the user's favorites and all possible links. The program may also display either of two pages: one for

**30**

Personalization and Dynamic Pages

the selected links and the other for changing the configuration and options. When the ShowOptions cookie is set, the Options selection page is displayed. Otherwise, the regular page is shown. Figure 30.2 shows what the configuration page looks like.

**FIGURE 30.2**

*The Favorites configuration page.*

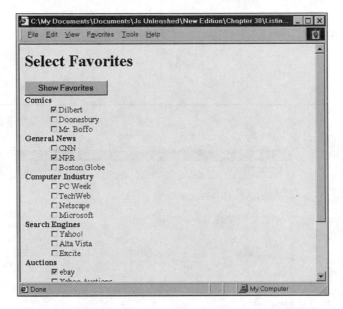

The program creates objects called—you guessed it—"favorites." Each favorite is, in essence, a Web link to another page. The favorite contains information on the link's URL, a user-friendly page description, and the code that identifies it in the Favorites cookie string. The favorite also knows how to print itself on a Web page as a regular link for the Favorites page or in a check box format for the Options page.

# Which Servers and Browsers Support Cookies?

Although other ways of Web programming, such as CGI and special server interfaces, require that the server and the browser understand cookies, only the browser matters to JavaScript. This means that you can use JavaScript with impunity as long as you know your clients are JavaScript capable.

However, many JavaScript Web applications probably mix the language with other development tools, which requires the server to understand cookies. Because new servers and browsers are coming to the Net so quickly, it's impossible for a printed book to keep up with the latest software.

---

**Resources**

You can find cookie information on the Web at the following locations:

Netscape cookie specification page: `http://www.netscape.com/newsref/std/cookie_spec.html`

Browsers supporting cookies: `http://www.research.digital.com/nsl/formtest/stats-by-test/NetscapeCookie.html`

Cookie Central: `http://www.cookiecentral.com/`

Web browsers that support cookies from Digital: `http://www.research.digital.com/nsl/formtest/stats-by-test/NetscapeCookie.html`

Robert Brooks' Cookie Taste Test: `http://www.geocities.com/SoHo/4535/cookie.html`

---

# Using Other State Maintenance Options

As mentioned earlier in this chapter, there are a few drawbacks to using cookies. Perhaps you would rather just avoid the controversy and find some other way to maintain state from one page to the next. There are two ways of doing this. Which one you use depends on how you will have users get from one page of your site to the next.

The main limitation of these methods is that they work only from one page to the page immediately following. If state information is to be maintained throughout a series of pages, these mechanisms must be used on every page.

## Query String

If most of your navigation is done through hypertext links embedded in your pages, you need to add extra information to the end of the URL. This is usually done by adding a question mark (?) to the end of your Web page URL, followed by information in an

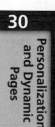

encoded form, such as that returned by the escape() method. To separate one piece of information from another, place an ampersand (&) between them.

For example, if you want to send with your link the parameters color=blue and size=extra large, use a link like the following:

```
<a href=''/mypage.html?color=blue&size=extra+large''>XL Blue</a>
```

This format is the same as the format used when submitting forms with the get method. A succeeding page can read this information by using the search property of the Location object. This property is called search because many Internet search engines use this part of the URL to store their search criteria.

The following is an example of how to use the location.search property. In this example, the name of the current page is sent as a parameter in a link to another page. The other page reads this property through the search property and states where the browser came from.

Listing 30.7 shows the first page that contains the link.

**LISTING 30.7**  Where1.html

```html
<html>
<head>
<title>Where Was I? - Page 1</title>
</head>
<body>
<h1>Where Was I? - Demonstration</h1>
This page sets information which will allow the page it is linked
to  out where it came from. It uses values embedded in the link
URL in order to do this
<p>
We'll assume that any URL parameters are separated by an ampersand.
<p>
Notice that there doesn't need to be any JavaScript code in this page.
<p>
And now,
<a href="where2.html?camefrom=Where1.html&more=needless+stuff">
Let's go to Page 2.</a>
</body>
</html>
```

Listing 30.8 shows the second page, demonstrating how to use location.search to find where the browser came from.

**LISTING 30.8**   Where2.html

```html
<html>
<title>Where Was I? - Page 2</title>
<head>
</head>
<body>
<h1>Where Was I? - Demontration</h1>
This page reads information which allows it to  out where it came from.
<P>
<script language="javascript">
<!-- begin script
// WhereWasI
// Reads the search string to  out what link brought it here
function WhereWasI() {
  // Start by storing our search string in a handy place (so we don't
  // need to type as much)
  var handyString = window.location.search;
  // Find the beginning of our special URL variable
  var startOfSource = handyString.indexOf("camefrom=");
  // If it's there, find the end of it
  if (startOfSource != -1) {
    var endOfSource = handyString.indexOf("&", startOfSource+9);
    var result = handyString.substring(startOfSource+9, endOfSource);
  }
  else
    var result = "Source Unknown"; // Could not find the "camefrom" string
  return result;
}
if (WhereWasI() != "Source Unknown")
  document.write ("You just came from <b>" + WhereWasI() + "</b>.<br>")
else
  document.write ("Unfortunately, we don't know where you came from.<br>");
// end script -->
</script>
</body>
</html>
```

# Hidden Form Variables

The method used in the preceding section works as long as the user navigates from one page to another using links. In order to do the same thing with forms, you can use hidden form variables instead of the location.search parameter.

Hidden form variables have the following format:

```
<input type="hidden" name="HiddenFieldName" value="HiddenFieldValue">
```

You can specify whatever you like for *HiddenFieldName* and *HiddenFieldValue*. The value parameter is optional.

Using hidden fields doesn't necessarily require the use of JavaScript code. They are defined instead in the <input> tag of normal HTML documents. However, you do need some sort of server-based script, such as a CGI program or a server API program, in order to read the values of these hidden fields.

The form containing the hidden variables is submitted to a server script or even a JavaScript function, which spills out everything it knows about your browser onto a single Web page, including the form's field information. You find your hidden field information listed at the bottom of the page. It looks like this:

```
Form Post Data:
Raw Form Data String: camefrom=where3.htm&otherStuff=I+don%27t+care
camefrom=where3.htm
otherStuff=I don't care
```

# Summary

In this chapter, you learned a number of ways to make your Web pages more dynamic and personal by maintaining state between pages of a Web application. Of all the ways we looked at, cookies are the most powerful method.

Cookies allow you to store information on the client computer and use it from within your Internet application to store values and other critical information. Because of the nature of cookies, they can be used for everything from the simplest form of name=value pairs to the more advanced forms.

Although cookies represent the most powerful method of accomplishing state maintenance, other approaches are available, such as URL query string parameters and hidden fields.

# Pattern Matching Using Regular Expressions

One of the most powerful attributes of JavaScript is its capability to perform pattern matching. In fact, JavaScript's implementation of pattern matching, called Regular Expressions, was taken directly from one of the best pattern-matching languages available today—Perl. Pattern matching allows you to find complex patterns in strings with just a line or two of code. To implement some of the simplest pattern-matching expressions without Regular Expressions would require many lines of code. In this chapter, you will learn the syntax used to create Regular Expressions and try your hand at creating a couple of JavaScript programs that make use of Regular Expressions.

# Creating Regular Expressions

Although Regular Expressions may seem like a mystical power, you, as a JavaScript developer, will see them as little more than strings that contain letters, numbers, and symbols. You just create the pattern and JavaScript does the work. To make Regular Expressions easy to work with, they are conveniently contained in their own JavaScript object called RegExp. Creating Regular Expressions is very similar to creating strings in that Regular Expressions can be created with an object constructor or with just an assignment operator (=).

## RegExp() Constructor

Since a Regular Expression is an object in JavaScript, you can simply pass in your pattern as an argument to a RegExp() constructor and then assign the resulting RegExp object to a variable. For example, the following line of code creates a RegExp object called firstName that contains the pattern John.

```
var firstName = new RegExp("John");
```

Do not worry about what the pattern means (that will be discussed shortly), but rather focus on the syntax used to create the RegExp object.

## Assignment Operator

The second way to create a Regular Expression is to assign the pattern directly to a variable and let JavaScript determine that the variable should be a RegExp object. The following line of code also creates a RegExp object called firstName that contains the pattern John.

```
var firstName = /John/;
```

At this point, you may be wondering how JavaScript knows that you want firstName to be a RegExp object rather than a String object. The difference is that strings are enclosed in single or double quotes, while patterns are enclosed in forward slashes (/). Notice that the

forward slashes (/) are not needed in the RegExp() constructor because it can be distinguished from the String() constructor.

# Regular Expression Syntax

Now that you know how to create a Regular Expression object, the next step is to understand the syntax used to create the actual pattern. As mentioned earlier, the pattern syntax is taken directly from Perl. If you have used Perl before, this will look familiar. Table 31.1 lists all of the special pattern-matching characters.

TABLE 31.1   Pattern-Matching Characters

| Character | Description |
| --- | --- |
| \w | Matches any word character (alphanumeric). |
| \W | Matches any non-word character. |
| \s | Matches any whitespace character (tab, newline, carriage return, form feed, vertical tab). |
| \S | Matches any non-whitespace character. |
| \d | Matches any numerical digit. |
| \D | Matches any character that is not a number. |
| [\b] | Matches a backspace. |
| . | Matches any character except a newline. |
| [...] | Matches any one character within the brackets. |
| [^...] | Matches any one character not within the brackets. |
| [x-y] | Matches any character in the range x to y. |
| [^x-y] | Matches any character not in the range x to y. |
| {x,y} | Matches the previous item at least x times but not to exceed y times. |
| {x,} | Matches the previous item at least x times. |
| {x} | Matches the previous item exactly x times. |
| ? | Matches the previous item once or not at all. |
| + | Matches the previous item at least once. |
| * | Matches the previous item any number of times or not at all. |
| \| | Matches the expression to the left or the right of the \| character. |
| (...) | Groups everything inside parentheses into a sub-pattern. |
| \x | Matches the same characters that resulted from the sub-pattern in group number x. Groups that are designated with parentheses are numbered from left to right. |
| ^ | Matches the beginning of the string or beginning of a line in multiline matches. |
| $ | Matches the end of the string or the end of a line in multiline matches. |

**TABLE 31.1** continued

| Character | Description |
|---|---|
| \b | Matches the position between a word character and a non-word character. |
| \B | Matches the position that is not between a word character and a non-word character. |

Some of the characters listed in the table are fairly straightforward, while others are bit cryptic. The following sections examine each one.

## \w and \W

The lowercase w (\w) matches any word character. A word character is alphanumeric, which means it can be either an alphabetic character (a-z) or a number (0-9). The uppercase W (\W) is the opposite of its little brother (\w) in that it matches any non-word character. For example, the search pattern

```
var pattern = /\w\W/;
```

would find b? in a search string but would not find ?b because the first character must be a letter or a number, and the second character cannot be a letter or a number.

## \s and \S

The lowercase s (\s) matches any whitespace character. A whitespace character is a tab, newline, carriage return, form feed, or vertical tab. The uppercase S (\S) is the opposite of its little brother (\s) in that it matches any non-whitespace character. For example, the search pattern

```
var pattern = /\s\S/;
```

would find a carriage return character that is followed by the letter g but would not find the letter g followed by a carriage return.

## \d and \D

The lowercase d (\d) matches any number between zero (0) and nine (9). The uppercase D (\D) is the opposite of its little brother (\d) in that it matches any character that is not a number. For example, the search pattern

```
var pattern = /\d\D/;
```

would find 4p in a search string but would not find p4 because the first character must be a number, and the second character cannot be a number.

*Pattern Matching Using Regular Expressions*

**CHAPTER 31**

839

31

Pattern
Matching Using
Regular
Expressions

## [\b]

A lowercase b in brackets ([\b]) is used to match the backspace character. There are not very many instances when you would want to search for a backspace character, but if you do, this is the search pattern syntax to use.

# The Period

A period (.) by itself is used to match any character except a newline character.

# [...] and [^...]

Brackets are used to match any one character that appears within the brackets. If a caret (^) appears directly after the left bracket, any characters that do not appear within the brackets are matched. For example, the search pattern

```
var pattern = /[abc][^def]/;
```

would find ag in a search string but would not find ge because the first character must be either a, b, or c, and the second character cannot be d, e, or f.

# [x-y] and [^x-y]

A dash can be used within the bracket syntax to specify a range rather than having to type a long list of characters. Any character in the range *x* to *y* that appears in the search string, where *x* and *y* are characters that you specify, will result in a positive match. If a caret (^) appears directly after the left bracket but before the range, any characters that are not in the range specified are matched. For example, the previous bracket example could have been written as

```
var pattern = /[a-c][^d-f]/;
```

This pattern would find ag in a search string but would not find ge because the first character must be either a, b, or c, and the second character cannot be d, e, or f.

# {x,y}, {x,}, and {x}

There are a few variations of the curly braces syntax, but all are associated with the repetition of the character preceding the left curly brace. In this syntax, *x* and *y* represent numbers. If both *x* and *y* are used in the syntax, the preceding character is matched at least *x* times but not to exceed *y* times. If only *x* is provided followed by a comma, the preceding character is matched at least *x* times. Finally, if *x* is provided by itself (without a comma), the preceding character is matched exactly *x* times. For example, the search pattern

```
var pattern = /cho{1,2}se/;
```

would find chose or choose in a search string but would not find chooose because the character o must be matched at least 1 time but not exceed 2 times.

## ?, +, and *

There are three operators that perform some specific tasks associated with the curly braces. They are the question mark (?), the plus sign (+), and the asterisk (*). The question mark (?) matches the preceding character once or not at all. The plus sign (+) matches the preceding character at least once. Finally, the asterisk (*) matches the preceding character any number of times or not at all. For example, the search pattern

```
var pattern = /ab?c/;
```

would find abc or ac in a search string but would not find abbc because the character "b" can be matched once or not at all.

## Logical OR (|)

The vertical bar character ( | ) acts like a logical OR by matching the character on either the left or right of the vertical bar ( | ). For example, the search pattern

```
var pattern = /cat|dog/;
```

would find cat or dog in a search string.

## ( . . . )

Parentheses allow you to sub-nest search patterns inside other search patterns. For example, the search pattern

```
var pattern = /f(a|o)r/;
```

would find far or for in a search string.

## \x

You can use the \x in conjunction with parentheses to match the same characters that resulted from the sub-pattern in group number x. Groups are designated with parentheses and are numbered from left to right. For example, the search pattern

```
var pattern = /f(a|o)r\1/;
```

would find fara or foro in a search string but would not find faro or fora.

When the caret character (^) is placed in front of text, a match will only be found if the text appears at the beginning of a search string or the beginning of a line in multiline matches. For example, the search pattern

```
var pattern = /^The/;
```

would find the word The only if it appeared at the beginning of a line or the beginning of the string that is being searched.

## $

The dollar sign ($) is the opposite of the caret character (^) in that when it is placed in front of some text, a match will only be found if the text appears at the end of a search string or the end of a line, in multiline matches. For example, the search pattern

```
var pattern = /^home/;
```

would find the word home only if it appeared at the end of a line or the end of the string that is being searched.

## \b and \B

The lowercase b (\b) matches a position between a word character and a non-word character. Keep in mind that a word character is alphanumeric, which means it can be either an alphabetic character (a-z) or a number (0-9). The uppercase B (\B) is the opposite of its little brother (\b) in that it matches the position that is not between a word character and a non-word character. For example, the search pattern

```
var pattern = /cat\b/;
```

would find the word cat but not the word catch in the search string Please catch the cat if you can because the word "cat" is followed by a space, which is a non-word character.

Maybe you are starting to ask yourself, "What if I want to match a character that has special meaning such as a dollar sign?" All the characters that have special meaning to the Regular Expression object can be used literally (escaped) by using a backslash (\) followed by the character in question. Table 31.2 lists all the characters that conflict with pattern-matching symbols.

**TABLE 31.2** Escaped Characters

| Character | Description |
| --- | --- |
| \f | Form feed |
| \n | Newline |
| \r | Carriage return |

**TABLE 31.2** continued

| Character | Description |
|-----------|-------------|
| \t | Tab |
| \v | Vertical tab |
| \/ | Forward slash (/) |
| \\ | Backward slash (\) |
| \. | Period (.) |
| \* | Asterisk (*) |
| \+ | Plus (+) |
| \? | Question mark (?) |
| \| | Vertical bar ( \| ) |
| \( | Left parenthesis (() |
| \) | Right parenthesis ()) |
| \[ | Left bracket ([) |
| \] | Right bracket (]) |
| \{ | Left curly brace ({) |
| \} | Right curly brace (}) |
| \XXX | ASCII character represented by the octal number *XXX* |
| \xHH | ASCII character represented by the hexadecimal number *HH* |
| \cX | The control character represented by *X* |

There is one final piece of syntax that allows you to set some attributes associated with the Regular Expression. The attributes are shown in Table 31.3.

**TABLE 31.3** Pattern-Matching Attributes

| Character | Description |
|-----------|-------------|
| g | Global match. Find all possible matches. |
| i | Make matching case-insensitive |

Unlike the syntax covered so far, these attributes are set outside the forward slashes that define the pattern when creating a Regular Expression with just an assignment operator. For example, a Regular Expression that is to search globally for the word "bear" would look like the following:

```
var animalSearch = /bear/g;
```

If you are creating a Regular Expression using the RegExp() constructor, store the attributes as a string and pass the string in as the second argument of the constructor. For example, a Regular Expression that is to perform a case-insensitive search for the word "bear" would look like the following:

```
var animalSearch = new RegExp("bear","i");
```

*Pattern Matching Using Regular Expressions*

CHAPTER 31

843

31

Pattern
Matching Using
Regular
Expressions

# Using Regular Expressions

Now that you have this really useful pattern assigned to a RegExp object, what do you do with it? There are two ways to utilize Regular Expressions. One way is through methods provided by the RegExp object, and the other is through methods provided by the String object. After all, the whole point of Regular Expressions is to have the ability to search for patterns within strings. The pattern-matching methods provided by the RegExp object are shown in Table 31.4. Notice that these methods require that the String object to be searched be passed in as an argument.

**TABLE 31.4**  Pattern-Matching Methods in the RegExp Object

| Method | Description |
| --- | --- |
| exec(str) | Searches for pattern in *str* and returns result |
| test(str) | Searches for pattern in *str* and returns true if match found; otherwise, false is returned |
| (str) | Same as exec(str) method |

The pattern-matching methods provided by the String object are shown in Table 31.5. Notice that these methods require that the RegExp object for which you are searching be passed in as an argument.

**TABLE 31.5**  Pattern-Matching Methods in the String Object

| Method | Description |
| --- | --- |
| match(regExpObj) | Searches for *regExpObj* pattern in string and returns result. |
| replace(reqExpObj,str) | Replaces all occurrences of the *regExpObj* pattern with *str*. |
| search(reqExpObj) | Returns the position of matching *regExpObj* pattern within the string. |
| split(regExpObj,max) | The string is split everywhere there is a matching *regExpObj* pattern up to *max* splits. The substrings are returned in an array. |

> **Note**
>
> The methods listed in Tables 31.4 and 31.5 are not the only methods associated with RegExp and String objects. Only the more commonly used methods for search and replace functionality are shown.

# Regular Expression Tester

The cryptic syntax used to create patterns for Regular Expressions can be a bit confusing, especially when you begin to mix and match functionality to create a complex search pattern. For this reason, this chapter includes a program for testing Regular Expressions. This program will not only help you learn how to create Regular Expressions using the RegExp() constructor, it is also a great utility for creating and testing your own search patterns.

The utility performs either a search or a replace on the search string, replace string, and pattern that you enter, as shown in Figure 31.1. The power of this utility is that you can create a search string and a pattern, and then quickly verify that your pattern works as you intended. The code for the program is shown in Listing 31.1.

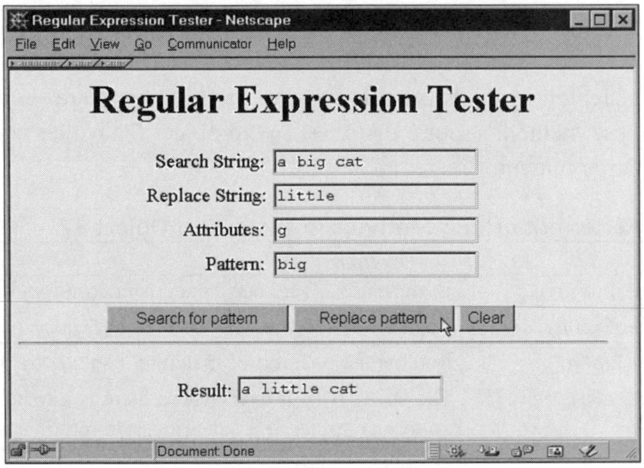

**FIGURE 31.1**
*The Regular Expression Tester.*

**LISTING 31.1**   The Regular Expression Tester

```
<html>
<head>
<title>Regular Expression Tester</title>

<script language="JavaScript">
<!-- begin script


// The function searches for the pattern in searchStr
function searchForPattern(searchStr,pattern,REattributes,theResult)
{
```

**LISTING 31.1** continued

```
  //Create Regular Expression Object
  var regExpObj = new RegExp(pattern,REattributes);

  //Populate the result field with the result of the search
  theResult.value = regExpObj.exec(searchStr);
}

// This function replaces all occurances of the pattern in
// searchStr with replaceStr
function replacePattern(searchStr,replaceStr,pattern,REattributes,theResult)
{
  //Create Regular Expression Object
  var regExpObj = new RegExp(pattern,REattributes);

  //Populate the result field with the result of the search
  theResult.value = searchStr.replace(regExpObj,replaceStr);
}

// This function clears all the fields in the page
function clearFields(field1, field2, field3, field4, field5)
{
  field1.value = "";
  field2.value = "";
  field3.value = "";
  field4.value = "";
  field5.value = "";
}

// end script -->
</script>
</head>

<body>
<center>
<h1>Regular Expression Tester</h1>
<form name="myForm"">
<table board=0>
  <tr align=right>
    <td>Search String:</td>
    <td><input type="text" name="searchString"></td>
  </tr>
  <tr align=right>
```

**LISTING 31.1** continued

```html
    <td>Replace String:</td>
    <td><input type="text" name="replaceString"></td>
  </tr>
  <tr align=right>
    <td>Attributes:</td>
    <td><input type="text" name="REattributes"></td>
  </tr>
  <tr align=right>
    <td>Pattern:</td>
    <td><input type="text" name="pattern"></td>
  </tr>
</table>
<br>
<input type="button"
       value="Search for pattern"
       onClick="searchForPattern(searchString.value,
                                 pattern.value,
                                 REattributes.value,
                                 result)">
<input type="button"
       value="Replace pattern"
       onClick="replacePattern(searchString.value,
                                replaceString.value,
                                pattern.value,
                                REattributes.value,
                                result)">
<input type="button"
       value="Clear"
       onClick="clearFields(searchString,
                            replaceString,
                            pattern,
                            REattributes,
                            result)">
<br><hr><br>
Result: <input type="text" name="result">

</center>
</body>
</html>
```

*Pattern Matching Using Regular Expressions*
CHAPTER 31

847

31

Pattern
Matching Using
Regular
Expressions

The Regular Expression Tester can be broken down into four major parts: user interface, search function, replace function, and clear fields function.

# User Interface

The user interface for the Regular Expression Tester consists of a form with five text boxes and three buttons. The searchString text box provides a place for you to enter the string that is to be searched for the specified pattern. The replaceString text box provides a place for you to enter the string that is to be used to replace parts of searchString where a pattern match is found. This field is only used when the Replace Pattern button is clicked. Pattern-matching attributes, such as global search/replace and case-insensitivity, are placed in the attributes text box. The pattern text box provides a place for you to enter the Regular Expression search pattern that is to be searched for in the searchString. When the Search for Pattern or Replace Pattern button is clicked, the result of the search or replace is inserted into the result text box.

# Search Function

When the Search for Pattern button is clicked, the onClick event handler calls the searchForPattern() function. This function passes the pattern and attributes information entered in the HTML form into the RegExp() constructor to create a RegExp object called regExpObj. The RegExpexec() method is then used to search for the pattern in the search string that was entered in the form. The result of the search is then placed into the result text box. If no match was found, the result text box will be empty.

# Replace Function

When the Replace Pattern button is clicked, the onClick event handler calls the replacePattern() function. This function passes the pattern and attributes information entered in the HTML form into the RegExp() constructor to create a RegExp object called regExpObj. The replace() method of the searchStr object is then used to replace occurrences of the pattern in the searchStr with the replaceStr. The result of the search and replace is then put into the result text box. If no match was found, the searchStr will be placed into the result text box.

# Clear Function

When the Clear button is clicked, the onClick event handler calls the clearFields() function. This function simply clears all of the text boxes.

# Example: Phone Number Validation Program

So far, I have introduced Regular Expressions and discussed how to create them, as well as provided a program for helping you create your own search patterns. But how would you use Regular Expressions in a real-life programming situation? With e-commerce becoming more prevalent on the Internet today, it is important that phone numbers, addresses, and credit card numbers be validated before allowing a customer to place an order. Some validations, such as credit cards, must be processed on the server side, but other relatively static information can be validated on the client side. One such piece of information that lends itself to client-side validation is area codes. Since they do not change that often, area codes can be placed into Web pages and validated using the searching capability of JavaScript's Regular Expressions.

In this section, you will see how Regular Expressions can be used to validate area codes before allowing a customer to proceed. For the sake of this example, assume that you are building a Web site for a North Carolina—based company that sells widgets. Before you process a customer's online order, you want to make sure that the company has a valid North Carolina phone number, so that you do not have to make an out-of-state call should there be shipping problems.

Obviously, it would not be reasonable to put every North Carolina phone number into your Web page to validate phone numbers, but you can check to see if the customer's area code is a valid North Carolina area code. If it is not valid, you want to alert the user that he must enter a North Carolina phone number. If the area code is valid, you want to proceed with the order.

By creating a search pattern for North Carolina phone numbers, you could quickly determine if the phone number entered by the customer is valid. Given that all phone numbers have a 3-digit area code, followed by a 3-digit prefix, followed by a 4-digit extension, you see a pattern that looks like this: ###-###-####. Since the # characters represent digits, you could use the Regular Expression syntax \d to search for just numbers in these positions. At this point, the search pattern would look like the following:

```
/\d\d\d-\d\d\d-\d\d\d\d/
```

Notice that forward slashes (/) were used to represent the beginning and end of the pattern. Since you know there are currently only six valid area codes for North Carolina (828, 252, 704, 919, 910, 336), you can add this to your search pattern as follows:

```
/(828|252|704|919|910|336)-\d\d\d-\d\d\d\d/
```

You add a sub-search to the search pattern by placing all the possible area codes inside parenthesis and separating each area code with a vertical bar character ( | ). The vertical bar tells the Regular Expression to try to match the number to the left or the right of the | character. This is essentially a logical OR operation. If the customer enters an area code that is specified in the sub-search, a positive match will be made.

Now that you have a search pattern for North Carolina phone numbers, all you have to do is create a user interface and test the pattern against phone numbers that customers enter. If you search for the search pattern in a string containing a valid phone number, the matching phone number will be returned. On the other hand, if you search for the search pattern in a string that does not contain a valid phone number, NULL will be returned. By testing for NULL, you can determine if the customer's phone number is valid. The following JavaScript function will perform the logic that was just described.

```
function validatePhone(areaCode,prefix,extension)
{
  //Assemble phone number
  var phoneNum = new String(areaCode + "-" + prefix + "-" + extension);

  //Create a regular expression pattern that searches for
  //phone numbers with an area code of: 828, 252, 704,919, 910, or 336
  var regExpObj = /(828|252|704|919|910|336)-\d\d\d-\d\d\d\d/;

  if(regExpObj.exec(phoneNum) == null)
  {
    alert(phoneNum + " does not contain a valid North Carolina area code!");
  }
  else
  {
    alert("Thank you for your order!");
  }
}
```

By adding some additional HTML code to accept the customer's phone number to this function, you can create a full-blown phone number validation program. Listing 31.2 shows the completed phone number validation program.

**LISTING 31.2**  Phone Number Validation

```
<html>
<head>
<title>Phone Number Validation</title>
<script language="JavaScript">
<!-- begin script
```

LISTING 31.2    continued

```
function validatePhone(areaCode,prefix,extension)
{
  //Assemble phone number
  var phoneNum = new String(areaCode + "-" + prefix + "-" + extension);

  //Create a regular expression pattern that searches for
  //phone numbers with an area code of: 828, 252, 704,919, 910, or 336
  var regExpObj = /(828|252|704|919|910|336)-\d\d\d-\d\d\d\d/;

  if(regExpObj.exec(phoneNum) == null)
  {
    alert(phoneNum + " does not contain a valid North Carolina area code!");
  }
  else
  {
    alert("Thank you for your order!");
  }
}
// end script-->
</script>
</head>

<body>
<center>
<h1>NC Sales Company</h1>

Thanks for your order.  Please provide us with your North
Carolina phone number so we can contact you if there are
any problems shipping your order.

<form name="form1">
Phone Number: <input type="text"
                     size=3
                     maxlength=3
                     name="area">-
             <input type="text"
                     size=3
                     maxlength=3
                     name="prefix">-
             <input type="text"
                     size=4
                     maxlength=4
```

*Pattern Matching Using Regular Expressions*

CHAPTER 31

851

31

Pattern
Matching Using
Regular
Expressions

**LISTING 31.2**  continued

```
                        name="extension">
<br><br>
<input type="button"
       value="Submit"
       onClick="validatePhone(area.value,
                              prefix.value,
                              extension.value)">
</form>
</center>
</body>
</html>
```

Now that the program is complete, give it a try. If you enter a valid phone number, such as 919-293-4444, and click the Submit button, you are presented with an alert box that tells you that your order is being processed. If you enter an invalid area code, such as 918-293-4444, and click the Submit button, the search fails and you are presented with the error message shown in Figure 31.2.

**FIGURE 31.2**
*The Phone Num-*
*ber Validation*
*Program.*

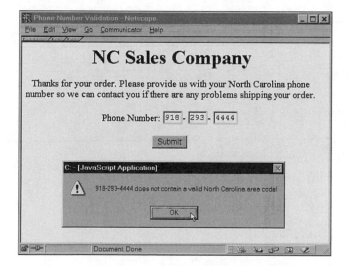

# Summary

In this chapter, you were introduced to the JavaScript Regular Expression object. You learned how to create search patterns and the RegExp objects that hold them. You also learned how to use the patterns you create to perform text searches using methods built into the RegExp and String objects.

To show you how to work with Regular Expressions in JavaScript, a Regular Expression Testing utility was outlined. This tool is especially handy in helping you create and test your own complex search patterns. Finally, a phone number validation program was created to demonstrate how Regular Expressions can be used in real-life programming situations.

# CHAPTER 32

# Client-Side Data Techniques

The Web offers a revolutionary approach to database applications with the capability to access remote data via a Web browser and return the results to you in HTML format. Although this is now common practice with CGI scripts, you can also use JavaScript to access data as well.

When you think of Web database access, you typically think of letting the data reside on the server. However, JavaScript also lets you work with data on the client side. In this chapter, I look at how you can work with data on the client side using JavaScript and when and how these can be alternatives to CGI and server-based solutions.

# Determining the Data Source: Client or Server?

Before we look at how to work with client-side data in JavaScript, it is essential to discuss when using client-side data makes sense. Although client-side data can be any kind of data, we are going to approach it in this chapter as if it were a database table. For example, you might want to take data from a relational database and convert it to a structured JavaScript dataset that can be stored in an HTML file on the client computer. Because we are approaching this chapter from a database perspective, I will refer to the JavaScript dataset as the *client-side table*.

Client-side tables have two major limitations. First, the database must be read-only. Because the data is actually embedded in your HTML source, you can't allow users to add or modify and save this data on the client side. Theoretically, you could develop a process to update the same data on the server as needed, reloading the client database when a change occurs. Generally speaking, unless you jump through a lot of hoops, a client-side table is read only.

Second, the database must be relatively small. Because the data is stored in the HTML file, it is downloaded in its entirety when the user accesses the Web page. You would obviously never want to embed a 100,000-record database in your file (or anywhere close to that size). Even for users with direct Internet connections, the download time would be very annoying.

The maximum size of a dataset really depends on the context. If you create a client-side table that will be accessed over a 28.8Kbps to 56Kbps modem, you might want to limit the size of the table to no more than 1,000 records. However, if you're creating an intranet solution in which all users have high-speed connections, you might want to push the envelope and allow more than that.

Given these limitations, why would you ever want to use a client-side table when there are software solutions designed to work with just about every database? There are two reasons. First, for some purposes, a client-side table can provide a much simpler solution than dealing with CGI scripts or other processes on the Web server, when a dataset is relatively small and static. Second, because everything resides on the client—data, searching mechanism, and user interface—you avoid the need to access the server at all. The result is that the search process is much quicker; you avoid the added load on the server to process a search and eliminate two transmissions between the client and server.

You might argue that even though the data is moved to the client for processing, the data still has to pass through the server when the page is downloaded. Of course, that's true, but the server isn't required to process a CGI search—it just sends an HTML file to a client who requests it.

As corporations roll out intranets, many small LAN-based applications will be ported to the Web. Because many of these are database-centric, it's likely that corporate Web servers' traffic will increase just to support these applications. In some cases, client-side tables could help minimize the load on the server. One such example is a company phone list application. What company doesn't have such a list, at least on paper? In this chapter, I use the phone list application as a practical and useful example for using client-side data to meet a business need.

# What Is a Client-Side Table?

As a Web developer, when I hear the term *table*, I think of HTML tables that are created with the HTML `<table>` tags. This is not what we are talking about in this chapter. As a database application developer, when I hear the term *table,* I immediately envision a table of columns and rows in a relational database format. For example, Figure 32.1 shows a typical database table. You can manipulate or search this data in a variety of ways, depending on the capabilities of the database management software itself. In this section the term *table* will be interpreted as a table in a database.

Unfortunately, although you can work with relational tables on the server side by accessing a database, you can't do the same using the capabilities of client-side JavaScript. You're forced to convert a database table into a structured format that your JavaScript code can use. In JavaScript, the basic organizing structure you want to use is an array. You can access each element of a JavaScript array and evaluate it—just as a relational database evaluates each record in a table during a query. Figure 32.2 shows the parallel between data in a relational table and that in an array.

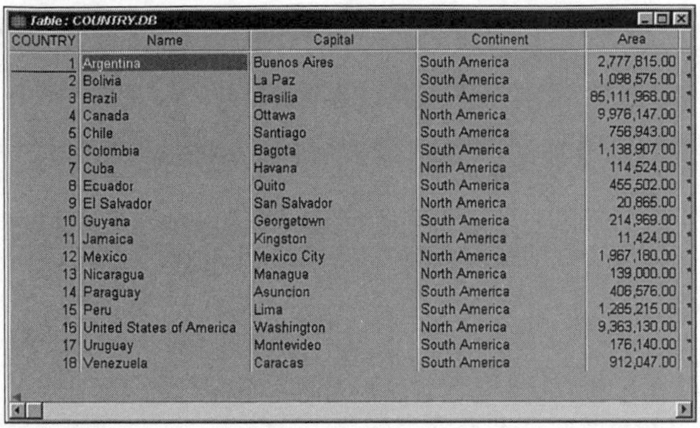

Table : COUNTRY.DB

| COUNTRY | Name | Capital | Continent | Area |
|---|---|---|---|---|
| 1 | Argentina | Buenos Aires | South America | 2,777,815.00 |
| 2 | Bolivia | La Paz | South America | 1,098,575.00 |
| 3 | Brazil | Brasilia | South America | 85,111,968.00 |
| 4 | Canada | Ottawa | North America | 9,976,147.00 |
| 5 | Chile | Santiago | South America | 756,943.00 |
| 6 | Colombia | Bagota | South America | 1,138,907.00 |
| 7 | Cuba | Havana | North America | 114,524.00 |
| 8 | Ecuador | Quito | South America | 455,502.00 |
| 9 | El Salvador | San Salvador | North America | 20,865.00 |
| 10 | Guyana | Georgetown | South America | 214,969.00 |
| 11 | Jamaica | Kingston | North America | 11,424.00 |
| 12 | Mexico | Mexico City | North America | 1,967,180.00 |
| 13 | Nicaragua | Managua | North America | 139,000.00 |
| 14 | Paraguay | Asuncion | South America | 406,576.00 |
| 15 | Peru | Lima | South America | 1,285,215.00 |
| 16 | United States of America | Washington | North America | 9,363,130.00 |
| 17 | Uruguay | Montevideo | South America | 176,140.00 |
| 18 | Venezuela | Caracas | South America | 912,047.00 |

**FIGURE 32.1**
*A relational database table.*

**FIGURE 32.2**
*You can work with tabular sets of data differently, depending on the context.*

**Ordered Set of Tabular Data**

**Relational Table**

| **Best Movies** |
|---|
| Casablanca |
| Chariots of Fire |
| African Queen |
| A Room With a View |
| Beauty and the Beast |
| Dances With Wolves |
| Forrest Gump |

**JavaScript Array**

```
bestMovies = new Array(7)
bestMovies[1] = "Casablanca"
bestMovies[2] = "Chariots of Fire"
bestMovies[3] = "African Queen"
bestMovies[4] = "A Room With a View"
bestMovies[5] = "Beauty and the Beast"
bestMovies[6] = "Dances With Wolves"
bestMovies[7] = "Forrest Gump"
```

# Creating a Lookup Table

The first step in using a client-side table in JavaScript is creating the table itself. A client-side table can't be an external file, so all the data must be embedded in the HTML file. However, in order for that information to be useful, you need to structure it so that the data can be searched and retrieved as desired.

As shown earlier, one option for structuring client-side data is to use a one-dimensional array. For example, if you want to put an entire list of employee names in an array, it will look something like this:

```
var employees = new Array(10)
employees[1] = "Richard"
employees[2] = "David"
employees[3] = "Rachel"
employees[4] = "Mark"
employees[5] = "Mellon"
employees[6] = "Margo"
employees[7] = "Darius"
employees[8] = "Dan"
employees[9] = "Dave"
employees[10] = "Pepe"
```

You could then use this array and search for individual elements within it, based on what you learned in the array discussion in Chapter 11, "Creating Custom JavaScript Objects." However, a one-dimensional array is not too helpful in this context, because most lookup tables have multiple columns of data to track. In the phone list example, suppose you want to track an employee's name, title, department, phone extension, and email address.

A more useful option is to create a custom object called `employee` and then group these employee records in a one-dimensional array. Doing this lets you store multiple columns of data in an object but also work with the `employee` objects as a collective group.

To define the `employee` object, you must first create a constructor method, as shown here:

```
function employee(FirstName, LastName, Title, Department, PhoneExt,
        EmailAddress) {
    this.FirstName = FirstName;
    this.LastName = LastName;
    this.Title = Title;
    this.Department = Department;
    this.PhoneExt = PhoneExt;
    this.EmailAddress = EmailAddress;
}
```

The next steps after creating the object constructor method are to create the `employee` objects themselves and place them in the container array called `empList`. You can do this with a single line of code for each employee. The first five employees in our complete list of 105 are shown here:

```
empList[1] = new employee("Richard", "Wagner", "Chief Technology Officer",
➥"R&D", "400", "rwagner@acadians.com");
empList[2] = new employee("Grady", "Anderson", "Programmer", "R&D", "198",
➥"grady@acadians.com");
empList[3] = new employee("Thomas", "Sprat", "Marketing Manager", "Marketing",
➥"656", "tsprat@acadians.com ");
```

```
empList[4] = new employee("William", "Cleyball", "Marketing Manager",
➥"Marketing", "651", "wcal@acadians.com ");
empList[5] = new employee("Fred", "Tortallini", "Marketing Manager",
➥"Marketing", "404", "tort@acadians.com ");
```

You now have the employee data captured in a structured format that is useful in client-side JavaScript.

> **Note**
>
> Don't get discouraged as you think of the work that is required to migrate data stored in relational databases to a JavaScript array or object. You have many options in creating this information, apart from actually typing the text every time you want to use the data. If the data changes often, you could create a CGI script or another backend process that generates this code automatically upon exporting a database table.

# Creating the Search User Interface

The manner in which you want the users of the application to work with the client-side table will depend, of course, on the exact context of your application. This example calls for a user interface in which the user can search for employees based on text he enters. Because you have several fields in the table, you also might want to give the user the flexibility to search on the four primary searchable fields of the table: FirstName, LastName, Title, and Department.

Suppose you want the results to be presented in an HTML document upon searching. To display both the search definition and results at the same time, you could use a multiframe window. With that in mind, the phone list example uses the following files:

- employeeInfo.html is the parent frameset window and contains the employee database and other global information.
- searchfrm.html is the topmost frame and provides a user interface for entering a search request.
- result.html is the bottom frame and displays the search results. It is blank by default.

Figure 32.3 shows the multiframe window setup for the application.

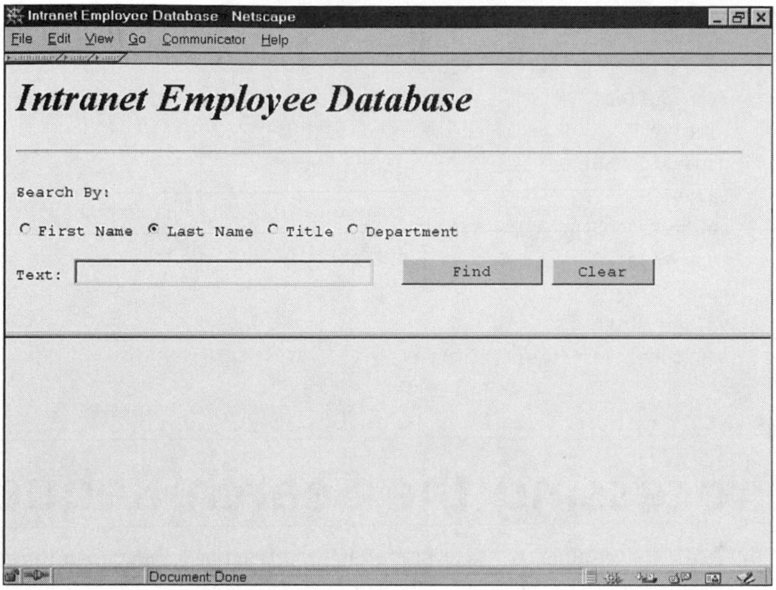

**FIGURE 32.3**

*The database
search user inter-
face.*

The only part of the user interface that the user will interact with is the search window
(searchfrm.html). The following segment shows the HTML source for the search
definition form inside the window:

```
<body>
<form method="POST" name="form">
<pre>Search By: </pre>
<pre><input
    type=radio
    name="searchBy"
    value="FirstName">First Name <input
    type=radio
    checked
    name="searchBy"
    value="LastName">Last Name <input
    type=radio
    name="searchBy"
    value="Title">Title <input
    type=radio
    name="searchBy"
    value="Department">Department</pre>
<pre>Text: <input
    type=text
    size=30
```

```
        maxlength=30
        name="searchByText">    <input
        type=button
        size=20
        name="findButton"
        value="   Find    "
        onClick="doSearch()"> <input
        type=reset
        name="Clear"
        value=" Clear "
        onClick="clearForm()"></pre>
</form>
</body>
```

# Processing the Search Request

The heart of an application based on a client-side table is the capability to search the data. In the employee phone list example, you need to determine the field on which the search should be conducted and then pass that information, along with the actual search request, to the search processing method.

Search processing is done in two locations in this example. The doSearch() method in the searchForm frame prepares the search and then passes the information to the findEmployee() method of the parent window.

To do this, assign the doSearch() method to the event handler for the Find button. In this function, check to see which of the radio buttons is checked and assign the searchField variable a string value based on the result. Next, after checking to ensure that a value has been entered in the searchByText field, call the parent window's findEmployee() method using the searchField variable and the value of the searchByText field as its parameters:

```
function doSearch() {
    var searchField = ""

    if (document.form.searchBy[0].checked) {
        searchField = "FirstName" }
    else {
        if (document.form.searchBy[1].checked) {
            searchField = "LastName" }
        else { if (document.form.searchBy[2].checked) {
                searchField = "Title" }
            else { if (document.form.searchBy[3].checked) {
                searchField = "Department" }
```

```
            }
        }
    }

    if (document.form.searchByText.value == null ||
        document.form.searchByText.value == "") {
alert("Please enter your search criteria before continuing.") }
    else {
        parent.findEmployee(searchField, document.form.searchByText.value)
    }
}
```

In the parent window (employeeInfo.html), the findEmployee() method takes these two parameters and uses them to evaluate the array of employee objects. A for loop is used to traverse the array of employee objects, checking the value of the search request (the searchWord parameter) with the specified property (the searchField parameter), using the string object's indexOf() method.

Before you get into the actual code, it's helpful to look at a more basic but equivalent example. If you wanted to search for the value of Richard in the FirstName property of all the employee objects, your code would look like this:

```
for (var i=1; i<empList.length; i++) {
if (empList[i].FirstName.indexOf('Richard') != -1) {
        empList[I].show() }
```

The for loop evaluates each object and returns a value greater than or equal to zero if the text is contained within the value of an employee object's FirstName property. If a match is found, the employee object's show() method is performed. Don't concern yourself with this method yet; it's covered in the section "Displaying the Search Results," later in this chapter.

Following the same logic, look again at the phone list application. You have to take care of a problem first: Because you want to use the searchField parameter to represent an object property name and not a string value, you need to use the built-in eval() method. The eval() method interprets a string value and evaluates it as a JavaScript expression. If you convert the JavaScript code to a single string, it can be evaluated using the eval() method:

```
function findEmployee(searchField, searchWord) {
    var str = "";

    // formatting code will go here

    for (var i=1; i<empList.length; i++) {
```

```
        str = "if (empList[" + i + "]." + searchField +
           ".indexOf('" + searchWord +
           "') != -1) { empList[" + i + "].show() }";
        eval(str);
    }


    // formatting code will go here
}
```

# Displaying the Search Results

The final step in the search process is to present the results of the search to the user. Use the bottom frame (resultForm) to display this information. You can enhance the findEmployee() method you looked at in the preceding section to perform this process.

Because you want to generate HTML on-the-fly, you want to use the resultForm's Document object as a "canvas" to write on. You first need to prepare the document canvas to accept input by using the Documentopen() method. Next, to display results in a table format, you can create an HTML table using the <table> tag and set up the table header:

```
window.resultForm.document.open();
window.resultForm.document.write("<h2>Matches:</h2>");
window.resultForm.document.write("<table border=1>");
window.resultForm.document.
➡write("<tr><td width=10%><strong>First Name</strong></td>");
window.resultForm.document.write("<td width=15%><strong>Last Name
➡</strong></td>");
window.resultForm.document.write("<td width=20%><strong>Title</strong></td>");
window.resultForm.document.write("<td width=15%><strong>Department
➡</strong></td>");
window.resultForm.document.write("<td width=5%><strong>Ext.</strong></td>");
window.resultForm.document.write("<td width=15%><strong>Email</strong>
➡</td></tr>");
```

Now that the initial preparation of the resultForm is complete, you're ready to process the search as specified earlier. As you recall, each matching employee is called to execute a show() method. This method is used to display the employee information as a single record in the table. You therefore need to add a show() method to the employee object constructor:

```
function employee(FirstName, LastName, Title, Department, PhoneExt,
    EmailAddress) {
    this.FirstName = FirstName;
    this.LastName = LastName;
    this.Title = Title;
```

```
    this.Department = Department;
    this.PhoneExt = PhoneExt;
    this.EmailAddress = EmailAddress;
    this.show = emp_show;
}
```

When an `employee` object's `show()` method is called, the `emp_show()` method is triggered. This method provides the location in which to place code for formatting and displaying the current employee's information. Using the `write()` method, you can place the values of each of the object's properties in separate table cells. Here is the code:

```
function emp_show() {
    window.resultForm.document.write("<tr><td width=10%>" +
        this.FirstName + "</td>");
    window.resultForm.document.write("<td width=15%>" +
        this.LastName + "</td>");
window.resultForm.document.write("<td width=20%>" + this.Title + "</td>")
    window.resultForm.document.write("<td width=15%>" + this.Department +
        "</td>");
    window.resultForm.document.write("<td width=5%>" + this.PhoneExt +
        "</td>");
window.resultForm.document.write("<td width=15%>" + "<a href='mailto:" +
        this.EmailAddress + "'>" + this.EmailAddress + "</td></tr>");
}
```

Notice that a link is defined for the employee's email address. A user can then click the employee's email address in the table to send a message to him.

The final formatting code you need to write is in the `findEmployee()` method. After each of the employee records is processed, a `write()` method ends the table definition by sending a `</table>` tag. Finally, the canvas is closed to additional input when a `close()` method is issued. Here is the complete `findEmployee()` method:

```
function findEmployee(searchField, searchWord) {
    var str = "";

    window.resultForm.document.open();
    window.resultForm.document.write("<h2>Matches:</h2>");
    window.resultForm.document.write("<table border=1>");
    window.resultForm.document.write("<tr><td width=10%><strong>First Name
➥</strong></td>");
    window.resultForm.document.write("<td width=15%><strong>Last Name
➥</strong></td>");
    window.resultForm.document.write("<td width=20%><strong>Title
➥</strong></td>");
```

```
    window.resultForm.document.write("<td width=15%><strong>Department
➡</strong></td>");
    window.resultForm.document.write("<td width=5%><strong>Ext.</strong>
➡</td>");
    window.resultForm.document.write("<td width=15%><strong>Email</strong>
➡</td></tr>");
    for (var i=1; i<=empList.length-1; i++) {
        str = "if (empList[" + i + "]." + searchField + ".indexOf('"
        + searchWord + "') != -1) { empList[" + i + "].show() }";

        eval(str);
    }
    window.resultForm.document.write("</table>");
    window.resultForm. document.close();
}
```

# Running the Application

You are now ready to test the application by opening the employeeInfo.html file in your browser. Suppose you want to search for Grady Anderson. Enter **Anderson** in the text field, keep the Last Name radio button selected, and click the Find button. Figure 32.4 shows the result. You can clear both the search form and the result frame by clicking the Clear button.

**FIGURE 32.4**
*Search results displayed in a table.*

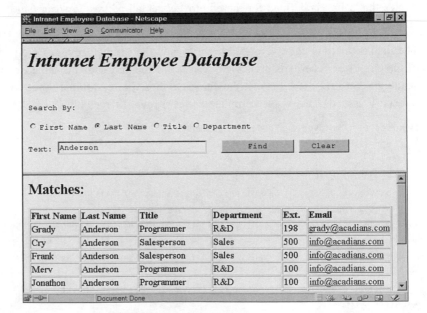

Listing 32.1 provides the complete source code for the `employeeInfo.html` parent window, and Listing 32.2 contains the JavaScript source for the `searchfrm.html` window.

**LISTING 32.1**   `employeeInfo.html`

```
<html>
<head>
<title>Intranet Employee Database</title>
<script language="JavaScript">

    // Intranet Employee Database


    // Global variables
    var i = 1;
    var n = 1;

    // Create Array objects
    var empList = new Array();

    // show() - employee object method
    function emp_show() {
        window.resultForm.document.write("<tr><td width=10%>" +
            this.FirstName + "</td>");


        window.resultForm.document.write("<td width=15%>" + this.LastName
            + "</td>");
        window.resultForm.document.write("<td width=20%>" + this.Title
            + "</td>");
        window.resultForm.document.write("<td width=15%>" + this.Department
            + "</td>");
        window.resultForm.document.write("<td width=5%>" +this.PhoneExt
            + "</td>");
        window.resultForm.document.write("<td width=15%>" +
            "<a href='mailto:"
            + this.EmailAddress + "'>" + this.EmailAddress + "</td></tr>");
    }

    // Employee object constructor
    function employee(FirstName, LastName, Title, Department,
        PhoneExt, EmailAddress) {
        this.FirstName = FirstName;
```

LISTING 32.1    continued

```
            this.LastName = LastName;
            this.Title = Title;
            this.Department = Department;
            this.PhoneExt = PhoneExt;
            this.EmailAddress = EmailAddress;
            this.show = emp_show;
        }


        // Search for employee based on field and word
        function findEmployee(searchField, searchWord) {
            var str = "";


            window.resultForm.document.open();
            window.resultForm.document.write("<h2>Matches:</h2>");
            window.resultForm.document.write("<table border=1>");
            window.resultForm.document.write("<tr><td width=10%>
➥<strong>First Name</strong></td>");
            window.resultForm.document.write("<td width=15%>
➥<strong>Last Name</strong></td>");
            window.resultForm.document.write("<td width=20%><strong>
➥Title</strong></td>");
            window.resultForm.document.write("<td width=15%><strong>
➥Department</strong></td>");
            window.resultForm.document.write("<td width=5%>
➥<strong>Ext.</strong></td>");
            window.resultForm.document.write("<td width=15%><strong>
➥Email</strong></td></tr>");


            for (var i=1; i<=empList.length-1; i++) {
                str = "if (empList[" + i + "]." + searchField + ".indexOf('"
                + searchWord +"') != -1) { empList[" + i + "].show() }";
                eval(str);
            }
            window.resultForm.document.write("</table>");
            window.resultForm.document.close();
        }


// Create employee objects on start up
empList[1] = new employee(
"Richard", "Wagner", "Chief Technology Officer", "R&D", "400",
    "rwagner@acadians.com");
```

**LISTING 32.1**    continued

```
empList[2] = new employee(
"Grady", "Anderson", "Programmer", "R&D", "198", "grady@acadians.com");
empList[3] = new employee(
"Thomas", "Sprat", "Marketing Manager", "Marketing", "656",
    "tspratt@acadians.com ");
empList[4] = new employee(
"William", "Cleyball", "Marketing Manager", "Marketing", "651",
    "wcal@acadians.com ");
empList[5] = new employee(
"Fred", "Tortallini", "Marketing Manager", "Marketing", "404",
    "tort@acadians.com ");
empList[6] = new employee(
"Smack", "Hopkins", "Marketing Manager", "Marketing", "606",
    "smack@acadians.com ");
empList[7] = new employee(
"Luey", "Gentry", "Marketing Manager", "Marketing", "450", "luey@acadians.com ");
empList[8] = new employee(
"Erwin", "Waltham", "Marketing Manager", "Marketing", "545", "ew@acadians.com");
empList[9] = new employee(
"Dallas", "Spanner", "Marketing Manager", "Marketing", "656",
    "dallas@acadians.com");
empList[10] = new employee(
"Spill", "Hopkins", "Marketing Manager", "Marketing", "120",
    "spill@acadians.com ");
empList[11] = new employee(
"Huey", "Wagner", "Marketing Asst", "Marketing", "854", "huey@acadians.com ");
empList[12] = new employee(
"Tom", "Longly", "Marketing Asst", "Marketing", "512", "info@acadians.com ");
empList[13] = new employee(
"Huck", "Starback", "Marketing Asst","Marketing", "212", "info@acadians.com ");
empList[14] = new employee(
"Crazy", "Lags", "Marketing Asst","Marketing", "122", "info@acadians.com ");
empList[15] = new employee(
"Bart", "Simpson", "Salesperson", "Sales", "500", "info@acadians.com");
empList[16] = new employee(
"Bill", "O'Reilly", "Salesperson", "Sales", "500", "info@acadians.com");
empList[17] = new employee(
"Sally", "Smatterhorn", "Salesperson", "Sales", "500", "info@acadians.com");
empList[18] = new employee(
"Kim", "Pakki", "Salesperson", "Sales", "500", "info@acadians.com");
empList[19] = new employee(
"Jacob", "Ladder", "Salesperson", "Sales", "500", "info@acadians.com");
```

**LISTING 32.1**   continued

```
empList[20] = new employee(
"Jared", "Gaspe", "Salesperson", "Sales", "500", "info@acadians.com");
empList[21] = new employee(
"Justus", "Argon", "Salesperson", "Sales", "500", "info@acadians.com");
empList[22] = new employee(
"Jordan", "Basker", "Salesperson", "Sales", "500", "info@acadians.com");
empList[23] = new employee(
"Lisa", "Smith", "Salesperson", "Sales", "500", "info@acadians.com");
empList[24] = new employee(
"Cry", "Anderson", "Salesperson", "Sales", "500", "info@acadians.com");
empList[25] = new employee(
"Ollie", "Ryder", "Salesperson", "Sales", "500", "info@acadians.com");
empList[26] = new employee(
"Polly", "Potts", "Salesperson", "Sales", "500", "info@acadians.com");
empList[27] = new employee(
"Xerxes", "Smith", "Salesperson", "Sales", "500", "info@acadians.com");
empList[28] = new employee(
"Sally Rae", "Smith", "Salesperson", "Sales", "500", "info@acadians.com");
empList[29] = new employee(
"Golden", "Driscoll", "Salesperson", "Sales", "500", "info@acadians.com");
empList[30] = new employee(
"Frank", "Anderson", "Salesperson", "Sales", "500", "info@acadians.com");
empList[31] = new employee(
"Merv", "Anderson", "Programmer", "R&D", "100", "info@acadians.com");
empList[32] = new employee(
"Manu", "Waver", "Programmer", "R&D", "100", "info@acadians.com");
empList[33] = new employee(
"Jason", "Driscoll", "Programmer", "R&D", "100", "info@acadians.com");
empList[34] = new employee(
"Ardent", "Matthews", "Programmer", "R&D", "100", "info@acadians.com");
empList[35] = new employee(
"Ortho", "Dontal", "Programmer", "R&D", "100", "info@acadians.com");
empList[36] = new employee(
"Troy", "Smith", "Programmer", "R&D", "100", "info@acadians.com");
empList[37] = new employee(
"Fred", "Barker", "Programmer", "R&D", "100", "info@acadians.com");
empList[38] = new employee(
"Richini", "Barker", "Programmer", "R&D", "100", "info@acadians.com");
empList[39] = new employee(
"Ricardo", "Bollinger", "Programmer", "R&D", "100", "info@acadians.com");
empList[40] = new employee(
"Ron", "Bollinger", "Programmer", "R&D", "100", "info@acadians.com");
```

**LISTING 32.1** continued

```
empList[41] = new employee(
"Ronald", "Barker", "Programmer", "R&D", "100", "info@acadians.com");
empList[42] = new employee(
"Browser", "Tyler", "Programmer", "R&D", "100", "info@acadians.com");
empList[43] = new employee(
"Serf", "Tyler", "Programmer", "R&D", "100", "info@acadians.com");
empList[44] = new employee(
"Bill", "Tyler", "Programmer", "R&D", "100", "info@acadians.com");
empList[45] = new employee(
"William", "Smith", "Programmer", "R&D", "100", "info@acadians.com");
empList[46] = new employee(
"Billy", "Barker", "Programmer", "R&D", "100", "info@acadians.com");
empList[47] = new employee(
"Kurt", "Barker", "Programmer", "R&D", "100", "info@acadians.com");
empList[48] = new employee(
"John", "Barker", "Programmer", "R&D", "100", "info@acadians.com");
empList[49] = new employee(
"Jonathon", "Anderson", "Programmer", "R&D", "100", "info@acadians.com");
empList[50] = new employee(
"Frederick", "Barker", "Programmer", "R&D", "100", "info@acadians.com");
empList[51] = new employee(
"Smitty", "Tyler", "Programmer", "R&D", "100", "info@acadians.com");
empList[52] = new employee(
"Sargent", "Anderson", "Programmer", "R&D", "100", "info@acadians.com");
empList[53] = new employee(
"Pepe", "Potts", "Programmer", "R&D", "100", "info@acadians.com");
empList[54] = new employee(
"Leo", "Godfrey", "Programmer", "R&D", "100", "info@acadians.com");
empList[55] = new employee(
"Geo", "Stewart", "Programmer", "R&D", "100", "info@acadians.com");
empList[56] = new employee(
"Meo", "Anderson", "Programmer", "R&D", "100", "info@acadians.com");
empList[57] = new employee(
"Oeo", "Orefo", "Programmer", "R&D", "100", "info@acadians.com");
empList[58] = new employee(
"Jack", "Wagner", "Chief Entertainment Officer", "Exec", "300",
    "jwagner@acadians.com");
empList[59] = new employee(
"Brady", "Smith", "Programmer", "R&D", "100", "info@acadians.com");
empList[60] = new employee(
"Tristin", "Ryder", "Programmer", "R&D", "100", "info@acadians.com");
empList[61] = new employee(
```

**LISTING 32.1** continued

```
"James", "Tyler", "Programmer", "R&D", "100", "info@acadians.com");
empList[62] = new employee(
"Charles", "Potts", "Programmer", "R&D", "100", "info@acadians.com");
empList[63] = new employee(
"Bill", "Potts", "Senior Manager", "Management", "200", "info@acadians.com");
empList[64] = new employee(
"Bart", "Anderson", "Senior Manager", "Management", "200", "info@acadians.com");
empList[65] = new employee(
"Ian", "Potts", "Senior Manager", "Management", "200", "info@acadians.com");
empList[66] = new employee(
"Woody", "Smith", "Senior Manager", "Management", "200", "info@acadians.com");
empList[67] = new employee(
"Mark", "Tyler", "Senior Manager", "Management", "200", "info@acadians.com");
empList[68] = new employee(
"Andrew", "Driscoll", "Senior Manager", "Management", "200", "info@acadians.com");
empList[69] = new employee(
"Andy", "Potts", "Senior Manager", "Management", "200", "info@acadians.com");
empList[70] = new employee(
"Dandy", "Driscoll", "Senior Manager", "Management", "200", "info@acadians.com");
empList[71] = new employee(
"Candy", "Potts", "Senior Manager", "Management", "200", "info@acadians.com");
empList[72] = new employee(
"Spander", "Smith", "Senior Manager", "Management", "200", "info@acadians.com");
empList[73] = new employee(
"Landry", "Potts", "Senior Manager", "Management", "200", "info@acadians.com");
empList[74] = new employee(
"Permy", "Smith", "Senior Manager", "Management", "200", "info@acadians.com");
empList[75] = new employee(
"Jostin", "Driscoll", "Senior Manager", "Management", "200", "info@acadians.com");
empList[76] = new employee(
"Justin", "Ryder", "Senior Manager", "Management", "200", "info@acadians.com");
empList[77] = new employee(
"Braxel", "Anderson", "Senior Manager", "Management", "200", "info@acadians.com");
empList[78] = new employee(
"Opene", "Smith", "Senior Manager", "Management", "200", "info@acadians.com");
empList[79] = new employee(
"Juan", "Barker", "Senior Manager", "Management", "200", "info@acadians.com");
empList[80] = new employee(
"Julios", "Driscoll", "Senior Manager", "Management", "200", "info@acadians.com");
empList[81] = new employee(
"Andre", "Barker", "Senior Manager", "Management", "200", "info@acadians.com");
empList[82] = new employee(
```

**LISTING 32.1** continued

```
"Bernard", "Smith", "Senior Manager", "Management", "200", "info@acadians.com");
empList[83] = new employee(
"Susan", "Ryder", "Senior Manager", "Management", "200", "info@acadians.com");
empList[84] = new employee(
"Susanne", "Anderson", "Senior Manager", "Management", "200", "info@acadians.com");
empList[85] = new employee(
"Chelsey", "Barker", "Senior Manager", "Management", "200", "info@acadians.com");
empList[86] = new employee(
"Cosmo", "Krammer", "Senior Manager", "Management", "200", "info@acadians.com");
empList[87] = new employee(
"Kirby", "Tipple", "Senior Manager", "Management", "200", "info@acadians.com");
empList[88] = new employee(
"George", "Allen", "Senior Manager", "Management", "200", "info@acadians.com");
empList[89] = new employee(
"Boy", "Goeria", "Senior Manager", "Management", "200", "info@acadians.com");
empList[90] = new employee(
"Teddy", "Washington", "Senior Manager", "Management", "200", "info@acadians.com");
empList[91] = new employee(
"Tut", "Kingman", "Senior Manager", "Management", "200", "info@acadians.com");
empList[92] = new employee(
"Oil", "Larenzo", "Secretary", "Company", "800", "info@acadians.com");
empList[93] = new employee(
"Susie", "Que", "Secretary", "Company", "800", "info@acadians.com");
empList[94] = new employee(
"Trista", "Wagner", "Secretary", "Company", "800", "info@acadians.com");
empList[95] = new employee(
"Kimberly", "Smith", "Secretary", "Company", "800", "info@acadians.com");
empList[96] = new employee(
"Rachel", "McDonald", "Secretary", "Company", "800", "info@acadians.com");
empList[97] = new employee(
"Reena", "Smiles", "Secretary", "Company", "800", "info@acadians.com");
empList[98] = new employee(
"Treena", "Miles", "Secretary", "Company", "800", "info@acadians.com");
empList[99] = new employee(
"Corrina", "Triles", "Secretary", "Company", "800", "info@acadians.com");
empList[100] = new employee(
"Rosemarie", "Barlington", "Secretary", "Company", "800", "info@acadians.com");
empList[101] = new employee(
"Il", "Plage", "HR Manager", "Recruiting", "900", "info@acadians.com");
empList[102] = new employee(
"Url", "Page", "HR Manager", "Recruiting", "900", "info@acadians.com");
empList[103] = new employee(
```

**LISTING 32.1** continued

```
"Youri", "Basto", "HR Manager", "Recruiting", "900", "info@acadians.com");
empList[104] = new employee(
"Pri", "Opeo", "HR Manager", "Recruiting", "900", "info@acadians.com");
empList[105] = new employee(
"Tikki", "Rodrequez", "HR Manager", "Recruiting", "900", "info@acadians.com");
</script>

</head>
<frameset rows="35%,65%">
  <frame src="searchfrm.html" name="searchForm" marginwidth="10"
marginheight="10">
<frame name="resultForm" marginwidth="10" marginheight="10">
<noframes>
Sorry, your browser does not support frames.
</noframes>
</frameset>
<body>
</body>
</html>
```

**LISTING 32.2** searchfrm.html

```
<html>
<head>
<title>Search Form</title>
<script language="JavaScript">

    // Intranet Employee Database

    function doSearch() {
        var searchField = "";

        if (document.form.searchBy[0].checked) {
            searchField = "FirstName"; }
        else {
            if (document.form.searchBy[1].checked) {
                searchField = "LastName"; }
            else { if (document.form.searchBy[2].checked) {
                    searchField = "Title"; }
                else { if (document.form.searchBy[3].checked) {
                    searchField = "Department"; }
```

**LISTING 32.2** continued

```
                }
            }
        }

        if (document.form.searchByText.value == null ||
            document.form.searchByText.value == "") {
              alert("Please enter your search criteria before continuing."); }
        else {
              parent.findEmployee(searchField,
               document.form. searchByText.value);
}
    }

    function clearForm() {
        parent.resultForm.document.open();
        parent.resultForm.document.close();


    }
</script><h1><font color="#000000"><em>Intranet Employee Database</em></font>
</h1>
</head>

<hr>
<body bgcolor="#FFFFFF">
<form method="POST" name="form">
<pre>Search By: </pre>
<pre><input
    type=radio
    name="searchBy"
    value="FirstName">First Name <input
    type=radio
    checked
    name="searchBy"
    value="LastName">Last Name <input
    type=radio
    name="searchBy"
    value="Title">Title <input
    type=radio
    name="searchBy"
    value="Department">Department</pre>
<pre>Text: <input
```

**LISTING 32.2**   continued

```
    type=text
    size=30
    maxlength=30
    name="searchByText">   <input
    type=button
    size=20
    name="findButton"
    value="   Find   "
    onClick="doSearch()"> <input
    type=reset
    name="Clear"
    value=" Clear "
    onClick="clearForm ()"></pre>
</form>
</body>
</html>
```

# Summary

Client-side databases are neither a replacement for larger scale SQL servers nor a means of data entry. However, although they are limited in scope, databases embedded in JavaScript code offer an innovative means of offloading some database processing that would usually take place on the server. A client can then be responsible for the entire database search and presentation process.

This chapter looked at how client-side data can be used as a database and explained when this should be done. We also discussed how to use JavaScript arrays as database containers that can be searched using JavaScript's built-in language constructs. A key part of the chapter was a practical example of where a client-side table would be ideal.

# Error Handling

**CHAPTER**

**33**

Error handling in general is a combination of preventive controls (identifying and fixing errors before execution), detective controls (identifying errors during execution), and corrective controls (fixing errors found during execution). JavaScript—or, more accurately, the JavaScript interpreter built into JavaScript-compliant browsers—provides automated detective error control in the form of dialog boxes that display information about the error. The introduction of new JavaScript scripting and debugging tools helps the developer take advantage of more automated preventive and—to a lesser extent—corrective controls. This chapter discusses methods of identifying, fixing, and testing your JavaScript, as well as techniques for writing solid and maintainable code.

# Types of Errors

JavaScript errors are identified by the JavaScript-compatible browser as the HTML page is loaded and can be classified in the following three types:

- Syntax errors
- Runtime errors
- Logical errors

## Caution

The JavaScript interpreter doesn't identify logical errors. You must test the functionality of your code to identify potential errors in your program logic. For example, running your JavaScript code will result in a logical error if you perform an arithmetic expression on a string variable (this is described in more detail later—see Figure 33.1).

## Syntax Errors

Syntax errors, which stem from incorrectly constructed code, are often caused by typographical errors, spelling mistakes, missing punctuation, and unmatched brackets. The following example demonstrates several common syntax errors:

```
fuction errorProne() {    // "function" is misspelled
var i = o;    // should be initialized to zero "0"--not letter "o"
for (i >= 0; I =< 10; i++) {
            // variable "I" is not defined (should be small "i")
    document.write("The square of " + i + " is " + (i*i) + "<br>")
            // missing semicolon ";"
```

```
    document.write("The cube of " + i + " is ' + (i*i*i) + "<hr>");
            // double quote expected
}
// missing closing braces to end function
```

---

**Caution**

JavaScript is case sensitive, so be careful of capitalization. In particular, when you're using JavaScript's built-in objects—and their properties, methods, and events—be sure to look up the exact syntax from the *JavaScript Language Reference Guide*.

---

Syntax errors are the most commonly made and easiest-to-correct errors in JavaScript. The JavaScript interpreter often does a good job of identifying the exact source of these errors in your code, and the resolution generally requires no more than a simple edit.

---

**Note**

Because JavaScript is interpreted and doesn't currently offer a syntax debugging tool, you identify syntax errors by running the code—loading the HTML page containing JavaScript into a JavaScript-compatible browser.

---

**33**

Error Handling

## Runtime Errors

Runtime errors occur when a syntactically correct statement attempts to do a task that is impossible to perform. Common runtime errors include invalid function calls, mismatched data types, undeclared variable assignment, and arithmetic impossibilities (such as division by zero).

Runtime errors are reported by the browser much like syntax errors are reported; however, their resolution often requires a more thorough investigation of the code. The following example demonstrates a runtime error caused by a division by zero:

```
function mismatched() {
var i = 10;
for (i <=10; i >= 0; i--) {
        // this loop will cause a division by zero and unpredictable results
document.write(i + " divided by twice its square (" +
(i*i*2) + ") = " + (i/(i*i*2)) + "<br>");
```

```
      }
}
```

# Logical Errors

Logical (or logic) errors occur when an application or function doesn't perform the way its users or designers intended. In other words, an application that has syntactically good code and is free of runtime errors but still produces incorrect results has logical errors. Logical errors are the hardest type to identify and fix and usually demand a thorough test of the application, analysis of the result, and a review of the design. Many logical errors are propagated from a poor understanding of the requirements, bad design, and subsequent incorrect code. The following example demonstrates a logical error caused by evaluation of mismatched data types:

```javascript
function mismatched() {
var Constant = "10";
var i = 10;
for (i <=10; i > 0; i--) {
    document.write(i + " + " + Constant + " = " + (i + Constant) + "<br>");
    }
}
```

You can see in Figure 33.1 that the results displayed are clearly incorrect, even though the code ran successfully. In this case, JavaScript evaluates the result of the expression (i + Constant) as a string and concatenates the two operands.

**FIGURE 33.1**

*An example of a logical error.*

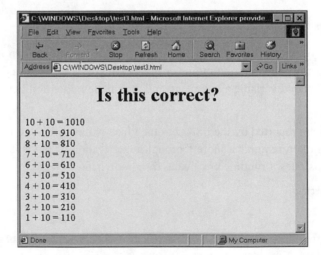

# Interpreting Error Messages

Once the browser recognizes an error (syntax or runtime), it displays a large dialog box, as shown in Figure 33.2. The information contained in this dialog box helps identify the approximate source and location of the error. The dialog box contains the following information:

- The URL or filename where the error occurred.

- The line number in the file where the error occurred. This is a sequential line count from the beginning of the HTML (or JS) file—not just the JavaScript code. Don't rely too heavily on this information, because the source of the error might well be at a different place.

- A description of the error. This is valuable information in identifying the type of fix required.

- The actual code that contains the error. This is also not always reliable information, because the source of the error might well occur before this line.

- A pointer indicating where on the line the error occurred. Again, don't rely on this too heavily; try to follow the flow of nearby code.

**FIGURE 33.2**
*A JavaScript error message reporting a syntax error.*

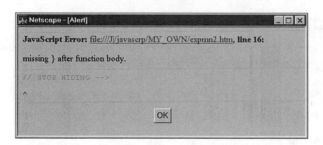

Table 33.1 summarizes the most common JavaScript error messages and their potential causes.

**TABLE 33.1** Common JavaScript Error Messages

| JavaScript Error Message | Potential Causes |
| --- | --- |
| `item` is not defined | Named variable is not defined. Variable is misspelled. Named function is not defined. Unterminated string (regarded as an undefined variable by JavaScript). |
| `item` is not a function | Function is not defined. Function is misspelled. Other errors exist before function definition. |

**33**

**Error Handling**

TABLE **33.1**  continued

| JavaScript Error Message | Potential Causes |
|---|---|
| `item cannot be converted to a function` | Variable is misstated as a called function. Function (or a built-in object's method) is misspelled. |
| `item has no properties` | Object property is referenced incorrectly. Array is referenced incorrectly. |
| `item is not a numeric literal` | Variable does not contain numeric data. Other errors exist before variable assignment. |
| `unterminated string literal` | Missing quotes (around string). String value has more than 250 characters. String values include a line break. |
| `missing ) after argument list (and similar error messages)` | Missing parenthesis, brace, or semicolon. |

# Fixing Your Code

Even though JavaScript's error messages are helpful in identifying many program bugs, you usually need to do more investigative work yourself to fix all the errors—especially logical ones. This section outlines some common things to do to make your investigative work both easier and a little more systematic. In Chapter 34, "Debugging." I will discuss how Netscape JavaScript Debugger can help you fix your code.

## Check the HTML

Because JavaScript commonly interacts with HTML code, you must first make sure that the file has no HTML errors. Use the following list as a guideline:

- Check for starting and ending `<script>` tags.

- Check for the attribute `language = "JavaScript"` inside the `<script>` tag.

- Check for missing or misspelled HTML tags.

- Check for angle brackets (`<>`) to open and close a tag.

- Check for matching pairs of tags (for example, `<script>...</script>`).

- Check for correct use of the HTML comment tags (`<!-...->`) to hide your JavaScript.

- Make sure the form and frame names called in your JavaScript code match the names defined in the HTML files.

> **Caution**
>
> If you need to insert JavaScript code inside an HTML table, do not place the `<script>` tags inside table cells (`<td>...</td>`); this is a known bug in JavaScript that usually causes browsers to lock up. Instead, place `<script>` tags inside the desired table row definitions (`<tr>...</tr>`) and create the HTML cell definition (`<td>...</td>`) using the JavaScript `document.write()` method.

## Use Comments to Identify Problems

You can use comments to systematically block out various lines (and functionality) in your code to identify and fix source of errors. This is an iterative process. The following list outlines the steps involved:

1. Comment out one or more lines from your code.
2. Save the code.
3. Reload the page in the browser.
4. Note the effect.
5. Modify the code or comment out more lines.
6. Repeat until you've fixed the error.

## Use the `alert()` Method to Trace Your Code's Progress

To identify some runtime and many logical errors in your code, you must be able to follow the flow of the code and imagine how it processes its data. Many debugging tools let you step into your code, execute it one line at a time, and in a side window (called the *debugging window*) see the result of the executed code. You can use JavaScript's `alert()` method to simulate a similar debugging environment. `alert()` displays a dialog box that you can easily program to show various useful messages and values that help trace your code's progress. In Chapter 34, I work through a complete debugging exercise using just `alert()` methods. Here are some techniques for using `alert()`:

- Use something such as `alert("Starting Check")` to identify the starting point for debugging. As you progress and fix errors, you can move this down in the code.

- Use alert() to display values of variables, arrays, and function returns. By running some simple test scenarios, you can quickly determine whether the values displayed are what you expect.

- Use alert() to display the results of expressions. This is particularly helpful for tracking logical errors, because many of them come from using expressions incorrectly.

# Testing Your Code

Traditionally, testing code means that you are preparing your application for production. This concept is equally true when it comes to publishing JavaScript-enhanced Web pages on the Internet—except that your "production" is now a worldwide stage with many potential users on a variety of platforms. With that as a premise, you can use many common testing techniques to help test your JavaScript code. You need to make some modifications to cater to the special world of JavaScript and the Internet, but not many. JavaScript is a programming language capable of producing sophisticated applications that, like applications in traditional programming languages, demand solid testing.

> **Note**
>
> Testing is different from debugging. Testing is a means of finding errors. Debugging is a means of determining the source of errors and correcting them.

When you test your code, you should assume that you will find errors. If you believe there are no errors at all, you will probably not find any! In practice, even the most thorough tests can never prove the absence of errors (you would have to run an infinite number of test cases to do that); you can only prove their existence.

To help test your code, you should write a formal test plan—one that contains both a checklist (a one-page list of all high-level testing activities) and detailed test-case scenarios to test the code with. Test-case scenarios should list specific and systematic test steps that you can perform on the application, along with expected results. Consider the following items when devising test scenarios:

- Application requirements: Tests to make sure the application satisfies the original functional requirements. Tests should include getting user (or customer) feedback on how closely the application functions to their original requirements. Users' knowledge of the underlying model for the application should lead to identification and correction of many logical errors caused by the implementation of incorrect business rules.

- Design requirements: Tests to make sure the application conforms to its proposed design. These tests should include getting feedback from the application designers on how closely the application follows their design. These tests can also identify potential flaws in the design.

- Data flow patterns: Tests to check the validity of data flow in the system, especially with respect to the design. These tests should validate the integrity of the data that is processed by your application. You need to sketch the data flow in application from input through processing to output and trace how data is affected at each phase.

- Functions: You should test each function in the application for correct functionality. These tests should validate the functionality of individual functions, irrespective of the rest of the code. The success of these tests often depends on how modular (single-focused in purpose, with zero dependencies) the functions are. (Modular programming is explained in more detail later in this chapter, in the section "Writing Modular Code.")

- Lines of code: You should test each line of code in the application for correct functionality. This can be done by stepping through each line of code and checking the result (for example, by using comments to isolate code).

- Bad data: Tests to see how the application performs when it receives bad data (for example, too little data, too much data, the wrong type of data, and the wrong size of data). These tests should also test for application behavior when required or optional data is missing (for instance, blank data entry fields on a form). Tests should confirm the existence of error-handling techniques to deal with these situations.

- Boundary analysis: Tests to see how the application performs at boundaries of data types, loops, and iterative function calls. These tests should ensure that the application can correctly cope with minimum and maximum values of variable ranges, and that error handling is built for the values that the application can't handle.

- Common values: Tests to see how the application performs when given information commonly entered by the user. These tests should ensure that the application works flawlessly for common data, because its failure to do so will affect the majority of users.

- Common errors: Tests common or previously occurring errors to ensure they have been corrected. Tests must be run to ensure that bugs that were corrected earlier (through further development) don't reappear in a later version of the code. The most common potential cause of this type of errors is poor change management (or version control), which may require follow-up tests of those procedures to identify and correct the root cause.

- Different platforms: Tests the application on various hardware and software platforms. The Internet consists of many users working on many different hardware systems (such as Intel, Macintosh, and Sun) and operating systems (such as Windows 95, Windows 98, Windows NT, and different flavors of UNIX and Linux). Your code should be tested on as many different platforms as possible so you can understand its behavior and, if necessary, modify it.

- Minimum configurations: Tests the application on minimum configuration client desktops. Again, users will have different resources to access the Internet. You should test to see how much demand your application puts on a client machine (for example, in terms of memory, bandwidth, processing power). This should help you understand what is the minimum configuration of each hardware and software platform on which your application will run successfully. The test should be developed to check how the code will perform under the recommended minimum configurations and how error handling for users with less than minimum configuration is handled.

- Different browsers: Tests the application on different JavaScript-compatible browsers. These tests should help you identify how each browser handles your code and whether the code performs consistently. If the code doesn't perform consistently, you may need to modify your code or write some error-handling code.

- HTML compatibility with old browsers: Tests theapplication to ensure that the HTML file can be read by older (non-JavaScript-compatible) browsers. You should test your code with text-only or older browsers to see how the lack of JavaScript compatibility affects the user's environment—for instance, if the browser locks up or crashes, or if the page simply fails to load. Test for whether an alternative way of reading your content is available and how effective and reliable it is.

**Tip**

In many cases, because of the functionality desired, it makes sense to consciously design and implement a site around a specific base (or minimum) browser level. For instance, you may decide that the user must have at least Navigator 4.7 or Internet Explorer 4.0 in order to effectively use your application. In such a case, you must inform the users about these requirements before they enter the site and include hyperlinks to where they can download the appropriate browsers. Alternatively, you can write some JavaScript to detect the user's browser type and, if it doesn't conform to the minimum standards, display a warning message or have the user automatically hyperlinked to an appropriate browser download site. See Chapters 26, "Guaranteeing Your Scripts Work in Netscape and Microsoft Browsers," and 27, "Browser Detection Techniques," for more details and an example of this JavaScript code.

- Reloading: Tests application behavior when the HTML page is reloaded. These tests make sure that your code doesn't crash or behave oddly if the page is reloaded. If reloading affects the code, tests should confirm the existence of error-handling code and instructions to help the user avoid the problem.

- Resizing: Tests application behavior when the browser window is resized. These tests confirm that your code doesn't crash or behave oddly if the page is resized. If there is an effect, your tests should confirm the existence of error-handling code and instructions to help the user avoid the problem.

**33**

**Error Handling**

**Note**

When you resize a Netscape Navigator window, the current Web page is reloaded. Microsoft Internet Explorer just resizes the window when reloading the current Web page.

- Stress testing: Tests application behavior when many people use it at the same time. These tests can be done either by having several users running your code following a specific and detailed script or by setting up some type of automatic site launcher. You should monitor, record, and analyze the results of all tests (including response times and behavior glitches). You should also make note of how your code affects the rest of your site. If necessary, modify your code, and re-test the affected code.

- Lost connections: Tests application behavior when the Internet connection is lost or the page is stopped. Users commonly lose connection to a site or manually force a halt in data transmission. Your code must be able to cope with this and exit gracefully (without locking up or crashing the browser) when needed. You should test for this functionality.

### Tip

Netscape Navigator has a built-in URL that you can use to test lines of JavaScript code quickly. In Navigator's location box, enter `javascript: JavaScript code`. (`mocha: JavaScriptcode` performs the same test.)

For example, entering `javascript: alert("Hello World!")` displays the string `Hello World` in an `alert()` dialog box.

# Programming Using Solid Techniques

Like any other programmers, JavaScript authors can benefit greatly from learning and using solid programming techniques to code their applications. Even though JavaScript is still too immature to have a wealth of its own material on solid coding practices, you can adopt a good set of general guidelines from proven techniques used in other (particularly object-oriented) programming languages. The following list shows some of the techniques adopted for JavaScript:

- Building code from a high-level and detailed design
- Writing modular code
- Writing strongly cohesive code
- Writing loosely coupled code
- Writing reusable code
- Writing error-handling code
- Using strong naming conventions

- Using comments

- Declaring and initializing variables

Each of the techniques listed here is explained briefly in the following sections. Be warned, however: Consistently performing such techniques involves a stiff learning curve, not only because of the level of discipline required, but also because you might need to forget some previous bad habits and learn some new good ones!

# Building Code from a High-Level and Detailed Design

Building code from a high-level and detailed design is the first step in constructing good code. A high-level design should help you identify the types of functionality required across different functions in the application. A detailed design should help you identify and name individual functions and sketch out their processes.

Good detailed design (especially if written in pseudo-code) can be transformed into code and comments without too much difficulty. You should at least be able to write function and variable declarations straight from the design. Following that, you should be able to iteratively break down the rest of the detailed design and convert each section into code.

# Writing Modular Code

Writing modular code means dividing your application into several individual functions (or modules), where each function performs only one task and communicates with the other functions through function calls. You gain several benefits from such modular coding:

- Reduced complexity: Each module focuses on only one task, so most modules remain simple.

- Reduced duplication: If one type of functionality occurs in several different places, the code to make that happen needs to be written only once (in a function).

- Reduced effect of change: You can change a commonly used functionality in only one place (the function where it resides) instead of several places.

- Increased process hiding: Implementation details of functions are hidden from other functions. This means that you can change the way a function works without changing the rest of your code (by maintaining the same interface to the function).

- Increased code reusability: You can reuse individual functions in other programs requiring the same type of functionality.

- Improved readability: Modular programming leads to simpler and more focused components in a program, which in turn makes the program more readable and easier to maintain.

# Writing Strongly Cohesive Code

Cohesion relates to how closely activities in a function are related. A strongly cohesive code means that the function is almost entirely dedicated to just one purpose. The goal is to do only one thing and do it well. An example of a perfectly cohesive function is JavaScript's Math.sqrt(*value*) function. This function simply performs the square root of the value it receives as an argument and returns the result.

Strong cohesion leads to high reliability because the scope of each function is very narrowly defined and the number of tasks it performs is extremely limited.

# Writing Loosely Coupled Code

Coupling relates to how closely two functions are related. Loosely coupled code means that the relationship between two functions is small, visible, and direct. This provides flexibility for either function to call the other but not depend on the other for much of its own functionality.

# Writing Reusable Code

Modular programming, alongwith strong cohesion and loose coupling, provides the ideal recipe for creating reusable code. You can essentially plug this code (or function) into any other code to provide a known functionality. Writing reusable code has many benefits:

- High reliability: Reusable functions are proven and tested many times.

- Low cost: There's no need to write a new function.

- Portability: You can make code available to other platforms more easily.

- Information hiding: The code's internal operations are hidden from calling objects.

# Writing Error-Handling Code

A good program must be able not only to anticipate uncommon and erroneous events (for example, bad input data, unusual user behavior, and interruption of transfer) but also to deal with them all gracefully. This is where writing good error-handling code becomes a vital issue. Error handling should be built into your code to perform at least some of the following tasks:

- Check the values of all data input from external sources: You should check for the validity of the data, including data types, value ranges, and completeness. If an error occurs, the program should discard the current data and request a new submission.

- Check the value of all function parameters: You should check the validity of data coming from other functions. In case of error, the receiving function should discard the erroneous data and send a new request to the sending function.

- Perform exception handling: Exceptions should be noted by the program and logged in an exceptions log. If no solution exists, the function should exit gracefully.

- Check for other important errors: If possible, the error-handling code should prevent errors from occurring.

- Perform graceful exits: If your code crashes or the user stops the file transmission before the page is completely loaded, the browser should remain intact (that is, not lock up or crash). This can be performed by writing an error-handling routine to check if the page is successfully loaded or by opening a new browser window for your application, so that if it crashes it brings down only its own window.

**33**

**Error Handling**

# Using Strong Naming Conventions

Using strong naming conventions refers to using appropriate, consistent, and meaningful names for all the declarations (for example, objects, properties, methods, and variables) in your code. Strong naming conventions help to reduce your code maintenance, improve readability, increase understanding, and eliminate confusing name proliferation (calling the same thing by two different names).

You can use many variations to develop a strong naming convention in your code. Here is a suggested list of things to identify distinctly in your code:

- Global variables

- Local variables

- Named constants

- Function names

- Function arguments

> **Tip**
>
> Use formatted compound words to enhance the meaning and readability of your names. For example, use `MaximumWeight= 200` for a variable or `findHeightInMeters(Height) { ...` for a function.

# Using Comments

Comments can be a very effective form of source code communication from a programmer to the rest of the world, including other programmers who might maintain the code later. As much as good comments help increase a program's readability, bad comments can be wasteful and misleading. A certain amount of care and attention is required to write useful comments. Here are some guidelines for writing good comments:

- Include important and general program information with the source code (for example, author, date of last update, purpose of the function, and last changes). It might be the only source of documentation that is readily available or up-to-date.

- Write comments about the code that the source code itself can't (easily) explain. Comments should add value so the user can understand more than what is already apparent.

- Write comments at the level of intent of the code to explain why something is done. This means writing comments in an appropriate location (for example, right before or after a line of code) to explain the purpose of code, and not just how the code does its processing.

- Comment on global variables. What do they contain? When are they updated?

- Comment on unusual or hard-to-follow pieces of code. What do they do? Why are they used?

- Keep in mind that those who load your Web page can see the JavaScript comments by simply viewing the HTML source from their browsers, so do not put information in JavaScript comments that you do not want others to see.

## Declaring and Initializing Variables

Even though JavaScript lets you use undeclared and uninitialized variables in your code, it is good programming practice to consistently declare and initialize your variables. Declaring variables in one common place (usually at the beginning of a function or global area) makes tracking and maintaining them relatively easy. Initializing variables assures that the variables contain the correct data type throughout the remainder of the program. (For example, if var Counter = 0;, the variable Counter is set to a numeric data type.)

> **Caution**
>
> Don't use JavaScript's reserved keywords as variable names—this results in errors. Check JavaScript's reference guide for a list of reserved keywords.

# Bulletproofing Your Code

JavaScript, like other programming languages, has nuances—including language bugs, obscure features, and strange behavior—that you need to recognize to write really solid code. You also need to be aware of the differences between JavaScript, as implemented in Netscape Navigator, and JScript (the Microsoft implementation of JavaScript), as implemented in Microsoft Internet Explorer. Even though they are fundamentally identical, each has functionality that the other does not have. Rather than spend page after page listing bugs, obscure features, and strange behaviors of various browsers only to find out that they were fixed in the last release of the code, I will just emphasize that JavaScript (and consequently JScript) is still an evolving language. This means that you should know the level of the browser(s) you choose for your base (or minimum) site requirement and how those browsers differ from other browser versions.

To view a list of the most currently known JavaScript bugs and potential workarounds, go to Netscape's JavaScript Known Bugs page at

`http://developer.netscape.com/support/bugs/known/`

To read the latest information about JScript, visit the Scripting Technologies page at

`http://msdn.microsoft.com/scripting/default.htm?/scripting/jscript/`

If you cannot find the information you need from one of these sites, participate in a JavaScript discussion group (such as Usenet's `comp.lang.javascript` newsgroup). Finally, to significantly improve your chance of writing code that works on both browsers, you must be sure to test your code thoroughly on both browsers and avoid JavaScript that seems to work in one but not the other.

# Summary

This chapter introduced you to the three types of JavaScript errors—syntax, runtime, and logic—and described common JavaScript error messages and their possible causes. You also looked at ways to fix your code and identify errors—including specific things, places, and techniques to look for to help you do so. In addition, I discussed a systematic approach for testing your code, consisting of a test plan and detailed test scenarios, including specific items to consider in creating detailed test scenarios.

I showed you ways to build more preventive control into your code (so that you can spend less time debugging) with proven techniques for writing solid and maintainable code. These techniques will save you many hours of work in the long run and will help you write better code.

To wrap up, this chapter briefly covered some of the current bugs of JavaScript and how you can avoid them to bulletproof your code.

# Debugging

## IN THIS CHAPTER

**34**

**CHAPTER**

Although it is sometimes underestimated as a programming activity, debugging source code is a fundamental element of developing applications in any programming language. JavaScript is no exception.

Now that JavaScript is finding its place in the coding community, we are finally seeing support of a native and comprehensive third-party scripting and debugging environment that is similar to mature programming languages (such as C++, Visual Basic, and Java). I like to think of these new tools falling into one of the following three categories:

- Integrated Development Environment (IDE) Tools: These help you quickly construct rich and dynamic Web sites, including JavaScript-enabled pages.

- JavaScript Scripting Tools: These help you more efficiently develop JavaScript-enabled pages through the use of intuitive visual interface and editing techniques. One example of these scripting tools is Acadia's Infuse.

- JavaScript Debugging Tools: These help you more effectively debug, fix, and test your code with the use of a graphical interface and commonly practiced debugging techniques (such as breakpoints and stepping into or out of code). An example of such tools is Netscape's JavaScript Debugger.

The introduction of new JavaScript scripting and debugging tools helps the developer take advantage of more automated preventive and, to a lesser extent, corrective controls. When you do not have access to JavaScript debugging tools, or the debugging job is very small, a simple JavaScript alert box can work as a debugging tool. In this chapter, you will examine three free JavaScript debugging options that are at your disposal.

# Using the Microsoft Script Debugger

The Microsoft Script Debugger (MSSD) is a freely downloadable script debugging tool that works as an integrated part of Internet Explorer (version 3.01 and later). You can use MSSD to write and, more importantly, debug your JavaScript (known as JScript with the Microsoft implementation) or Visual Basic Script (VBScript) code. MSSD has the advantage of being able to handle the debugging demands of ActiveX, Java, JScript, and VBScript. (You can download it from `http://msdn.microsoft.com/scripting/`.)

## An Overview of Microsoft Script Debugger Features

The following are the main features of the Microsoft Script Debugger:

- A dynamic view of HTML structure: As you can see from Figure 34.1, MSSD lets you view the whole structure of your page from the Project Explorer window and view the individual HTML files (for example, in a frameset) within their own windows.

**FIGURE 34.1**

*Viewing HTML files in the Microsoft Script Debugger.*

- Multiple language integration: You can seamlessly debug JavaScript, VBScript, and Java within the same document.

- Code coloring: MSSD displays your code with standard debugging color coding to help you better identify the composition of your code and ease debugging.

- Breakpoints: You can set breakpoints anywhere in your script to stop the debugger from executing at that point.

- Stepping into code: MSSD allows you to step (execute and pause) through your code one line at a time.

- Stepping over code: This lets you step into your code, but it executes procedure calls as one unit (rather than stepping into them) and returns to the next statement.

- Stepping out of code: As opposed to stepping over, this allows you to execute the remaining lines (from the point of execution) of a called procedure, and then it returns you to the next statement after the procedure call.

**34**

**Debugging**

- Integrated call stack: MSSD seamlessly integrates the call stack from both VBScript and JScript in your code into a single call stack.

- Immediate expression window: This allows you to immediately evaluate an expression within the call stack or test new code. The result from executing the line of code is displayed in the immediate window.

# Using the Microsoft Script Debugger to Debug a File

We will now walk through the steps of a sample debugging session using MSSD. During this exercise, we will be more concerned about the features of MSSD and their application than the content or functionality of the sample files. The remainder of this section assumes that you are using Microsoft Internet Explorer (version 3.01 or later) as your current browser and that you have already successfully downloaded and installed MSSD.

## Starting the Microsoft Script Debugger

The only way to start MSSD is to first open Internet Explorer and load the desired HTML source file. Then you can activate MSSD by choosing View, Source.

> **Note**
>
> If MSSD isn't installed, viewing the source will open the source file in the Notepad editor.

To start the debugging process, choose Edit, Break at Next Statement from Internet Explorer, or choose Debug, Break at Next Statement from MSSD, and execute the script. This starts the debugger and stops it at the first statement in the current script.

## Using the Break at Next Statement Command

The Break at Next Statement command (which appears on the Script Debugger option of the View menu of Internet Explorer and the Debug menu of MSSD) is similar to a step command, in which the debugger executes the next statement in the script and then breaks, except that you can also use it when you aren't currently running the script.

This is an important debugging feature of MSSD, because a lot of JavaScript code is commonly declared in the header (or <HEAD>) section of an HTML file, and this command is the only way to debug that code. This is because the code in the header of the file has already been executed by the time the HTML file is loaded (remember that JavaScript is interpreted). Also, any breakpoints set after the HTML file has been loaded are lost if you reload the page.

## Evaluating Expressions

An expression can be evaluated with the aid of MSSD's immediate window and the following two methods:

- `Debug.write(string)`: This method writes a specified string—commonly, the value of a variable—to the immediate window, with no intervening spaces or characters between each string.

- `Debug.writeln([string])`: This method is identical to the preceding method, except that a newline character is inserted after each string. Also, the string argument is optional. If it's omitted, only a newline character is written to the immediate window.

Figure 34.2 shows an example of using the immediate window to evaluate expressions (or values of variables).

**FIGURE 34.2**
*Using the immediate window to evaluate expressions.*

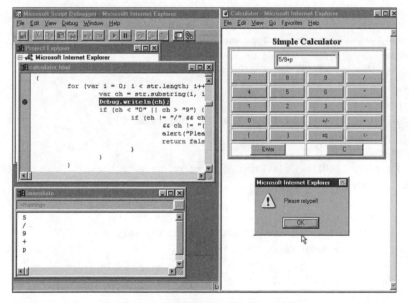

34

Debugging

## Walking Through a Complete Example

To better understand the capabilities of MSSD, you should practice using it to debug your code. The following exercise should provide you with a good starting point:

1. Open Internet Explorer.

2. Select Edit, Break at Next Statement.

3. Open the HTML file that contains Listing 34.1. You can type its URL, drag and drop the file into the browser window, or use File, Open. The content of this file is shown in Listing 34.1 (note that you should replace the names of the WAV files mentioned with the names and paths of sound files that you have available on your system):

**LISTING 34.1**  Using JavaScript Events to Play Sounds

```html
<html>
<head>
<title>Sound on JS events</title>
<script language="javascript">
<!-- Hide from old browsers

function playSound(sfile) {
// load a sound and play it
    window.location.href=sfile;
}
// Stop hiding -->
</script>
<body onLoad="playSound('Type.wav');"
onUnLoad="playSound('Glass.wav');">
<font size=+2>Sounds on JS Events</font>
<br>
<hr>
The following are example of JS event handlers used
to play sounds.
<hr>
<a href="#" onClick="playSound('Cashreg.wav');">
Click here for sound</a>
<br><br>
<form name="form1">
<input type="button" value="Press Button to play a sound"
onClick="playSound('Gunshot.wav');">
</form>
</body>
</html>
```

4. As the file is opened, MSSD is simultaneously activated, and a break occurs after the first statement is executed, as shown in Figure 34.3.

FIGURE **34.3**
*MSSD breaks after reading the first statement.*

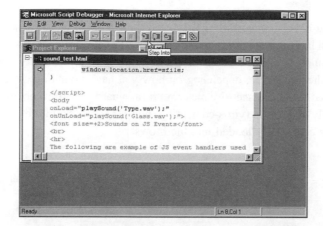

5. You can now step through your code to see the next sequence of program flow activities. Use the Step Into, Step Over, and Step Out toolbar icons to step through your code. Figure 34.4 shows the next line of code that is executed after you click the Step Into button.

FIGURE **34.4**
*Stepping into code using the MSSD toolbar icon.*

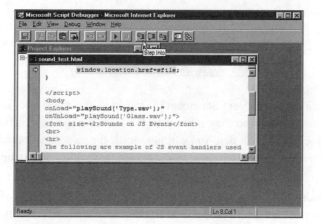

**34**

Debugging

### Tip

You can view the names of the icons on the MSSD toolbar by holding the mouse pointer—but not clicking—over any icon for a second or so. You can also read more detailed descriptions of all the icons and features of MSSD on the online help menu.

6. Once you have stepped through (or used the Continue icon) to where the `onLoad` event call has been completed, you should hear a sound file played by your system (if your computer has audio capabilities). You may need to explicitly permit the browser to open the sound file, depending on how you have your Internet Explorer browser configured. This is a security measure to safeguard you from opening unknown and potentially dangerous (virus-containing) non-HTML files. Figure 34.5 shows the file after it is completely loaded into the browser.

**FIGURE 34.5**
*The result of loading Listing 34.1.*

7. Select Edit, Break at Next Statement to stop code execution after the next statement. Click Press a Button to Play a Song on the HTML page. The debugger will stop at the `onClick` event handler. You can now track the executing procedure calls by opening the Call Stack window, as shown in Figure 34.6, and stepping through your code.

8. You can also view the value of expressions or an appropriate line of code (that is, not blank lines or comment lines, and so on) in your script using the immediate window:

    1. From MSSD, click inside the `playSound` function in your code (this is the first function declared in the header).

    2. If you attempt to type anything inside the function, MSSD brings up a panel asking if you want to edit the document. Click Yes, and type **`Debug.writeln(sfile);`** just before the curly bracket (}) to close the function.

    3. Save the edited file by selecting File, Save (or by clicking the Save toolbar icon).

**FIGURE 34.6**
*Using the Call Stack window to see active procedure calls.*

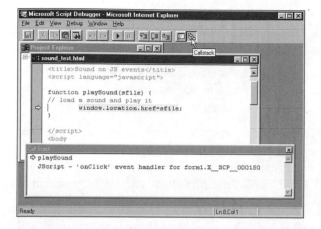

4. You can also set a manual breakpoint at the Debug line. Press F9 to set (or toggle) the breakpoint. (The breakpoint line will be highlighted in red and will have a red dot next to it in the left margin.)

5. Now switch over to your browser and refresh (reload) your HTML file. (Remember that you will lose your set breakpoints after refreshing the file, so if you want to break the code at a particular line, press F9 to set the breakpoint in MSSD.)

9. As the file starts execution, open MSSD's immediate window to view the current content of the Debug expression. As you continue to step through your code, you should see that the content of the immediate window is updated every time the Debug.writeln function is called, as shown in Figure 34.7.

**FIGURE 34.7**
*Using the Debug.writeln method and evaluating an expression in the immediate window.*

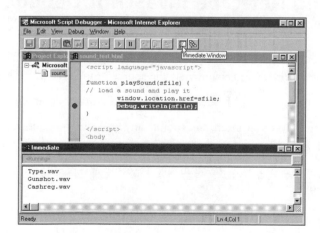

## A Final Word on the Microsoft Script Debugger

The Microsoft Script Debugger provides a very helpful environment for you to kick-start your JavaScript debugging and testing. The tools provided in MSSD are much like tools usually found in full-blown programming language environments such as Visual Basic and C++. Also, MSSD's interface, setup, and installation are all very user friendly and intuitive.

However, MSSD has some limitations in that you need to switch frequently between Internet Explorer and MSSD to conduct debugging, and that you can't print source code. If you want more functionality than what MSSD offers, you may want to consider Microsoft's Visual InterDev 6.0. This product offers all the script-debugging features listed here, plus a full-blown Web developing environment.

At the least, MSSD is certainly a good tool to have in your arsenal, and it's a great value to boot because it's free. However, it can't take the place of writing solid code and systematically testing it.

# Using the Netscape JavaScript Debugger

Like the Microsoft Script Debugger, the Netscape JavaScript Debugger is a freely downloadable JavaScript debugging tool that works as an integrated part of Netscape Navigator. (You can download it from `http://devedge.netscape.com/software/tools/index.html`.)

## Examining Netscape JavaScript Debugger Features

The following are the main features of the Netscape JavaScript Debugger:

- Source View window: Lets you view the source of the HTML page being debugged.

- Interrupt: Lets you stop the debugger from executing code at any time.

- Breakpoints: Lets you insert breakpoints anywhere in your script to stop the debugger from executing at that point.

- Stepping into code: Allows you to step (execute and pause) through your code one line at a time.

- Stepping over code: Lets you step into your code, but executes function calls as one unit (rather than stepping into them) and returns to the next statement.

- Stepping out of code: Allows you to execute the remaining lines (from the point of execution) of a called function, and then returns you to the next statement after the procedure call.

- Console window: Provides an area for evaluating JavaScript expressions on-the-fly in the context of the currently active frame.

- Object inspector: Allows you to inspect and work with the property values of an object.

- Watches window: Allows you to monitor expressions each time the interpreter stops and activates the debugger.

- Call stack: Displays the current execution location.

- Error Reporter dialog: Displays information about syntax errors and runtime errors in your JavaScript code.

# Using the Netscape JavaScript Debugger to Debug a File

We will now walk through a sample debugging session using the Netscape JavaScript Debugger. The remainder of this section assumes that you are using Netscape Navigator as your current browser and that you have already successfully downloaded and installed the Netscape JavaScript Debugger.

## Starting the Netscape JavaScript Debugger

To open an HTML source file for debugging in the Netscape JavaScript Debugger, follow these steps:

1. Begin by loading the `JSDebugger.html` page, located in the `Netscape\ Communicator\Program\JSDebug` directory, and select the link to start the debugger.

2. In Navigator, open the page you want to debug in Netscape Navigator.

3. Use the Open button on the Debugger toolbar to select the page from a list of the pages you have opened in Navigator since starting the debugger. The page will be displayed in the Source View window.

4. In the debugger, set breakpoints in the code where you want the debugger to stop.

5. Select the Reload button in Netscape Navigator to start debugging the page.

> **Note**
>
> Any time you stop the Netscape JavaScript Debugger, you cannot use Netscape
> Navigator to browse Web pages.

## Walking Through an Example

To better understand the capabilities of the Netscape JavaScript Debugger, you should
practice using it to debug your code. The following exercise should provide you with a
good starting point:

1. Open the HTML file that contains Listing 34.2 by typing its URL in Netscape
   Navigator. Open the same file in the Netscape JavaScript Debugger.

**LISTING 34.2**    Problem Code

```
<html>
<title>vehicle_test.html</title>
<body>

<script language="JavaScript">

//Create two global variables used to describe the vehicles
var vehicleColor;
var vehicleType;

//Set the type of vehicle
function setType()
{
  return(vehicleType="truck");
}

//Set the color of the vehicle
function setColor()
{
  return(vehicleColor="blue");
}

//If the vehicle type and color were not properly set the alert the user.
if(setType() || setColor())
  document.write("The " + vehicleType + " is " + vehicleColor);
else
```

**LISTING 34.2**    continued

```
  alert("The vehicle type and color could not be set");

</script>

</body>
</html>
```

2. Once the file is open and executed, the resulting Web page should look similar to Figure 34.8. One look at the result and you can see something went wrong. The script was supposed to set the vehicle type to `truck` with the `setType()` function and the vehicle color to `blue` with the `setColor()` function. If these two functions had worked properly, a string would be written to the screen; otherwise, an alert message would be displayed to let you know one of the assignment operations failed. No alert message was displayed, yet the variable representing the vehicle's color was never set to `blue`.

**FIGURE 34.8**
*The result of loading Listing 34.2.*

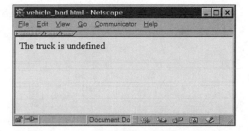

3. Because you are concerned with the values of the `vehicleType` and `vehicleColor` variables, you should add these two variables to the watch list in the debugger.

4. To start debugging, pause the debugger by pressing the Interrupt icon. Refresh the Netscape Navigator window to start debugging.

5. Begin stepping through the code line by line by pressing the Into icon. As each line is executed, keep an eye on the value of the two variables that are being watched in the Console window. Before the `if` statement is reached, notice that both variables are undefined as you would expect. When the `if` statement is reached, the debugger will step into the `setType()` function as you continue to press the Into icon. After you have stepped through the `setType()` function, `vehicleType` is properly set to `truck`. At this point, you would expect to step into the `setColor()` function, but instead you step into the `document.write()` method, as you see in Figure 34.9. What caused the `if` statement to not call the `setColor()` function? A closer look at the `if` statement reveals that if the first argument in a logical `OR` operation evaluates to `true`, then the

second argument is never evaluated. Because the setType() function returned true, the setColor() function was never executed. To correct the problem, simply change the logical OR operator to a logical AND operator. The correct version of the script is shown in Listing 34.3. The result of executing the file is shown in Figure 34.10.

**LISTING 34.3    Corrected Code**

```
<html>
<title>vehicle_correct.html</title>
<body>

<script language="JavaScript">

//Create two global variables used to describe the vehicles
var vehicleColor;
var vehicleType;

//Set the type of vehicle
function setType()
{
  return(vehicleType="truck");
}

//Set the color of the vehicle
function setColor()
{
  return(vehicleColor="blue");
}

//If the vehicle type and color were not properly set the alert the user.
if(setType() && setColor())
{
  document.write("The " + vehicleType + " is " + vehicleColor);
}
else
{
  alert("The vehicle type and color could not be set");
}

</script>

</body>
</html>
```

**FIGURE 34.9**
*The Netscape JavaScript Debugger after an action.*

**FIGURE 34.10**
*The result of loading Listing 34.3.*

## A Final Word on the Netscape JavaScript Debugger

The Netscape JavaScript Debugger provides a very helpful environment for you to kick-start your JavaScript debugging and testing. The tools provided in the Netscape JavaScript Debugger are much like tools usually found in full-blown programming language environments such as Visual Basic and C++. Also, the debugger's interface, setup, and installation are all very user friendly and intuitive.

However, the Netscape JavaScript Debugger has some limitations. Among the most noticeable are that you need to switch frequently between Netscape Navigator (the browser) and the debugger to conduct debugging, and that you cannot create, modify, or print source code.

34

Debugging

# Using the `alert()` Method

When you cannot get your hands on a full-featured JavaScript debugger or you are short on time and don't want to fire up a JavaScript debugger to solve a simple functionality problem, there is hope. If you have coded in any language for any length of time, you know that one of the simplest and quickest ways to debug functionality problems is to display the content of important variables at various stages of your program's execution. By doing so, you can determine if your code is executing as you intended.

JavaScript has a handy method called `alert()` that lends itself well to stopping the execution of your script to see a value of a variable. With a little thought and proper placement of this method, you can quickly track down functionality problems in scripts.

## Walking Through an Example

To illustrate how to use the `alert()` method to debug JavaScript code, the same script that was used in the Netscape JavaScript Debugger example (see Listing 34.3) will be used again so that you can compare the two methods.

1. Open a JavaScript-enabled browser.

2. Open the HTML file that contains Listing 34.2 by typing its URL in Netscape Navigator.

3. When the file is open and executes, the resulting Web page should look similar to Figure 34.8, earlier in the chapter. One look at the result and you can see something went wrong. The script was supposed to set the vehicle type to `truck` with the `setType()` function and the vehicle color to `blue` with the `setColor()` function. If these two functions had worked properly, a string would be written to the screen; otherwise, an alert message would be displayed to let you know that one of the assignment operations failed. No alert message was displayed, but the variable representing the vehicle's color was never set to `blue`.

4. Because you are concerned with the values of the `vehicleType` and `vehicleColor` variables, you should display their values in `alert()` methods. You should carefully place these `alert()` methods at points in the code that will help you pinpoint the problem area. For example, an `alert()` method in each of the variable-setting functions will let you know that each function is being executed. An `alert()` method before and after the `if` statement will tell you how the conditional evaluates. Listing 34.4 contains these extra `alert()` methods and can be opened by typing its URL into the browser.

**LISTING 34.4** Debugging Using `alert()` Methods

```html
<html>
<title>vehicle_debug.html</title>
<body>

<script language="JavaScript">

//Create two global variables used to describe the vehicles
var vehicleColor;
var vehicleType;

//Set the type of vehicle
function setType()
{
  alert("Inside the setType function.");  //Debug statement
  return(vehicleType="truck");
}

//Set the color of the vehicle
function setColor()
{
  alert("Inside the setColor function.");  //Debug statement
  return(vehicleColor="blue");
}

//Debug statement
alert("Before if statement: type="+vehicleType+" color="+vehicleColor);

//If the vehicle type and color were not properly set the alert the user.
if(setType() || setColor())
{
  //Debug statement
  alert("After if statement: type="+vehicleType+" color="+vehicleColor);

  document.write("The " + vehicleType + " is " + vehicleColor);
}
else
  alert("The vehicle type and color could not be set");

</script>

</body>
</html>
```

**34**

**Debugging**

**Tip**

Make sure that you include enough information in each `alert()` method so that you can tell where you are in the code just by reading the text in the alert box.

5. Once the file is open and executes, notice which alert boxes are displayed and which ones are not, as well as the variable values at each stage. The first alert box that is displayed shows that both variables are undefined before the execution of the `if` statement, as you would expect. The next alert box shows that the `setType()` function was executed. The final alert box shows the vehicle type set to `truck`, but the color is still undefined after the `if` statement, as you can see in Figure 34.12. What happened to the `setColor()` function? The `alert()` method in the `setColor()` function was never executed, which tells you that the `setColor()` function was never called from within the `if` statement. There is something wrong with the `if` statement.

**FIGURE 34.11**
*The result of loading Listing 34.4.*

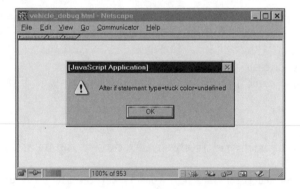

6. A closer look at the `if` statement reveals that if the first argument in a logical OR operation evaluates to `true`, then the second argument is never evaluated. Because the `setType()` function returned `true`, the `setColor()` function was never executed. To correct the problem, simply change the logical OR operator to a logical AND operator. Don't forget to remove the `alert()` methods that you added for debugging. The working version of the script is shown in Listing 34.3, which appeared earlier in this chapter. The result of executing the file is shown in Figure 34.10, which appeared earlier in the chapter.

**Caution**

Don't forget to remove the `alert()` methods that you added for debugging.

## A Final Word on Using the `alert()` method

As you have seen from the example, the `alert()` method can be a handy debugging tool for quickly solving small functionality problems. If you are debugging complex functionality problems or syntax problems, the `alert()` method will be more of a hindrance than a time saver. Although useful, the `alert()` method should not be considered a replacement for a full-featured debugging tool such as Netscape's JavaScript Debugger.

# Summary

This chapter introduced you to three debugging tools that you can use to debug your JavaScript code. The Microsoft Script Debugger and the Netscape JavaScript Debugger allow you debug complex JavaScript code. Both tools are good to have in your arsenal and, because they are free, they are great values to boot. Although not covered in this chapter, there are a number of full-blown development tools on the market that handle debugging, but they often come with a steep price tag. The last part of the chapter focused on using the alert box as an alternate debugging tool when you don't have access to a debugging tool such as Netscape's or Microsoft's. Even with these new tools, thoroughly testing and debugging JavaScript code is still the responsibility of the developer. However, none of the debugging tools discussed in this chapter can take the place of writing solid code and systematically testing it.

**34**

Debugging

# 35

# CHAPTER

# JavaScript and Web Security

## IN THIS CHAPTER

JavaScript gives the Web site developer the capability to extend static HTML pages with a dynamic, event-driven programming language. The JavaScript-enhanced Web page provides interactive client-side functionality by executing JavaScript code fragments inside the client's Web browser. The inclusion of JavaScript code fragments in the document page raises fundamental security concerns about the code integrity of the browser's script interpreter as well as about the script itself. Viewing a JavaScript-enabled page exposes the user to a greater possibility of damage than the rendering of a pure HTML document, due to the fact that the executing code fragments place another layer of complexity on top of the browser application.

With traditional desktop software, there is a well-defined covenant between the user and the software. Installing and using the programs requires explicit actions and decisions by users. JavaScript code doesn't conform to accepted conventions. Script code is loaded from a remote source and executed without user confirmation. Execution of untrusted code from a remote source is analogous to receiving an apple in the mail from an unknown return address and eating it. Verifications and limitations must be placed on the use of JavaScript code in order to safeguard the user's computer from malicious or unintentional attacks on valuable information and applications. No user wants to "pull the wire" between his computer and the outside world, so knowledge of the capability for JavaScript code to attack and damage a client or server machine is necessary.

The Web was designed as an open system for publishing graphical hypertext content over the Internet. Site developers have embraced the opportunity to extend the static HTML document with dynamic, interactive capabilities through the inclusion of scripting languages in Web documents. The scripting languages are either executed on the server machine or downloaded to a client machine and executed as remote code. Security is becoming a fundamental concern, because JavaScript and Java are becoming more prevalent, thereby making them more attractive targets for attack.

Security in a connected computer network can be evaluated in terms of the "level of confidence" in a transmission. The receiving party wants to trust that the original transmission was indeed sent by the expected sender. Also, the message should not have been altered en route. In a heterogeneous computer network such as the Internet, such confidence currently can't be absolute. The Internet was designed as a distributed system whereby network traffic must pass through many different machines to reach its intended destination. The flow of the traffic through multiple host machines exposes the traffic to modification or replacement at many points. Also, the sender's return address is designated by an address, which can be spoofed (mimicked). Although the global reach and electronic structure of unsecured transmissions defy accountability, encryption, digital signatures, and source code verification are attempts to raise the barrier against attack.

The user must trust that the application code will behave in a proper manner and not damage the user's system. In a typical desktop environment, code residing on the local hard drive is considered trusted, while code received from network resources—remote code—is given a lower level of trust, based on the source (a corporate LAN or the site of a virus hacker). The trust engendered in the past has commonly been based on the source of the application code. The security risk taken by installing a shrink-wrapped package purchased off the shelf of a retail store and produced by a well-known software publisher is perceived to be minimal when compared to downloading the latest freeware game from the Internet. Adoption of electronic distribution channels for applications (JavaScript and Java code) requires the adoption of new technology and procedures, as well as education of the expected consumer.

The computer industry is moving toward assigning digital signatures to developers and creating signed applets as a way to define accountability for JavaScript code. The identity of the JavaScript developer will likely be broadcast to the Web browser through a digital signature appended to the script file. Users, in conjunction with newer browsers, can determine whether to accept a code download from a site based on the signature received. Figure 35.1 shows a sample dialog box displaying the information contained in a digital certificate.

**FIGURE 35.1**

*A sample view of a digital certificate.*

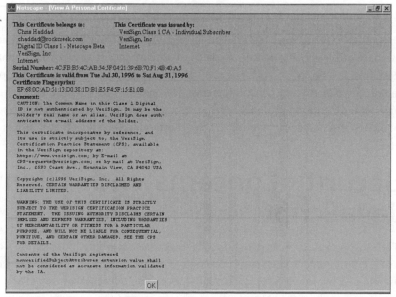

**35**

**JavaScript and Web Security**

Encryption is used to prevent modification of the data transmission while en route. The browser encryption protocols, Secure Sockets Layer (SSL), and Secure Hypertext Transport Protocol (SHTTP) work together to ensure that JavaScript code fragments aren't altered during transit. Finally, verification of the source code is critical to providing a secure environment. Virus checkers are extended to verify that JavaScript code doesn't contain any dangerous routines.

The cost and complexity of the security measures implemented to protect a user's computer system must be balanced with the hardships imposed by their existence. The following list describes the client machine's areas of vulnerability when executing scripting code:

- Altering the file system

- Reading/writing to a file

- Reading/writing system memory

- Sending private information over the network

- Communicating with other network resources

- Executing/closing programs on the local computer or an external host

- Using excessive system resources (Denial of Service attacks)

- Crashing the host program (Web browser)

Programming languages are created to give the developer tools to build an application. Because of the security concerns related to executing code on network clients, Netscape has designed JavaScript without many of the functions present in traditional programming languages. The missing capabilities give Web surfers a level of protection against attack but hamper the creation of compelling application content. This chapter describes the capability of JavaScript and Java code to breach security and the steps that you can take to prevent attacks.

# Security Concerns with Client-Side JavaScript

The most prevalent security risk to local machines accessing the Internet is currently related to executing remote JavaScript code on the client. The use of client-side JavaScript can be ascertained by viewing the document source. The existence of an HTML `<SCRIPT>` tag signifies that the page contains client-side code, and the optional tag attribute `LANGUAGE="JAVASCRIPT"` specifies that the page contains code conforming to the JavaScript language.

The JavaScript code may be inline with the HTML source document or in a separate file referenced by the use of another optional <SCRIPT> tag attribute, SRC="*javafile.JS*". If JavaScript execution has been enabled for the Web browser, the script can run immediately after the page has downloaded and has been processed by the script interpreter or JIT (Just-In-Time) compiler. Some browsers have the option of warning the user before a script is about to execute and offering the user the capability to select certain *trusted* sites from which code will be allowed to execute.

When viewed from the perspective of traditional desktop programmers, the implementation of client-side JavaScript currently handles security in a Draconian fashion. The following security restrictions are imposed on JavaScript code when executed by Netscape Navigator:

- There is no capability to read or write files.

- There is no access to file system information.

- JavaScript can't execute programs or system commands.

- JavaScript can't make network connections to other computers except to the machine from which the applet was downloaded.

- There are restrictions on the access of <FORM> data.

JavaScript applications can't save user session information to the local hard drive, except through the cookie mechanism, communication with a plug-in, and one code trick. The trick relies on piping the information to a helper application. If a user has defined a helper application for a MIME type, the JavaScript code can open a message window and output the information to the helper application. The user can then explicitly save the information to the client machine through the helper application's File, Save option. Figure 35.2 shows what happens after data is piped to notepad.exe via the test_stream code example. The following code describes the functions necessary to perform this operation:

```
function test_stream()
{
msgwindow = window.open("","hiwin","");
msgwindow.document.open("text/plain");   // or text/sams to define a new MIME type
msgwindow.document.write("JavaScript data, save to sick drive \nA, 100, 35\n");
    // write some text
msgwindow.document.write("Choose File¦Save to create a data file");
msgwindow.document.close();
msgwindow.close();
}
```

**FIGURE 35.2**
*Downloading data to the client from JavaScript.*

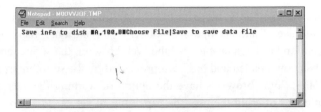

> **Caution**
>
> If the document.open command is passed a parameter (mime-type) defined as Ask User or Save in the Helper tab, the script doesn't save any information and generates an Out of Memory error.
>
> Because document.write currently can't write nulls (\0) to the data stream, this example has limited use for binary files.

Access to information about the user's browser environment by the script code is critical to properly understanding the client limitations that might affect the operation of the script. The script can query the navigator class to ascertain the system platform as well as the browser version and type. Also, a list of registered mime-types and plug-ins can be enumerated. The navigator properties are read-only and therefore aren't a security concern. The system properties that can be acquired through access to the navigator class are listed in Table 35.1.

**TABLE 35.1**   navigator Class Properties

| Property Name | Description |
| --- | --- |
| navigator.appCodeName | Browser code name |
| navigator.appName | Browser application |
| navigator.appVersion | Browser version |
| navigator.mimeTypes[] | Mime-types available |
| navigator.plugins[] | Plug-ins installed |
| navigator.userAgent | HTTP agent string |

> **Note**
>
> The HTTP agent string is sent to the server during HTTP requests. Both Netscape Navigator and Microsoft Internet Explorer provide access to the navigator class.

JavaScript shouldn't be used to create applications that are responsible for access control. Because the user can view all JavaScript code in the document (or frame) source window, the security algorithm can be deduced easily. Even files loaded by means of the optional source tag are available for the user to download and decipher.

# Denial of Service Attacks

Because a user can't terminate executing JavaScript code, Denial of Service attacks can perform the most damage. Service attacks have the capability to lock up the user interface and require the user to terminate the browser application. Common attacks include

- Stack overflow

- Infinite loops

- Infinite modal dialogs

- Using all available memory

## Stack Overflow

The stack overflow condition is the easiest Denial of Service attack to prevent and is properly trapped by all browser implementations. A JavaScript error window displays the message Out of Stack Space or Stack overflow in function_x, as shown in Figure 35.3. The following code demonstrates how to create a stack overflow by repeatedly calling a recursive function:

```
<HTML><HEAD>
<TITLE> Create Recursive Function Call Condition</TITLE>
<!-- File lockstack.htm -->
<SCRIPT>
function stack_lockup(){
stack_lockup();}
</SCRIPT></HEAD><BODY>
Entering Recursive Function Call
<SCRIPT LANGUAGE="JavaScript">
//<!-- comment so that Javascript is not displayed by non-JS browsers

stack_lockup();//this line executes immediately after the document downloads
// don't forget to JS_comment the start/end of the HTML comment -->

</SCRIPT></BODY></HTML>
```

**35**

**JavaScript and Web Security**

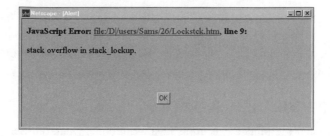

**FIGURE 35.3**
*The Netscape Navigator error window on stack overflow.*

## Infinite Loops

Infinite loops are the bane of all programmers, and JavaScript coders don't escape their curse. The following code fragment locks up the browser:

```
for(var i=0;;i++)
    document.write("End this message");
```

> **Caution**
>
> JavaScript code that executes infinite loops locks up all browser windows, including windows that are downloading files. According to Netscape, JavaScript code should terminate after 100,000 branches, and the user should be able to click the Stop button. However, I was unable to verify that the browser met the second specification.

## Infinite Modal Dialogs

JavaScript code that displays alert boxes repeatedly is an example of an infinite modal dialog box attack. The following fragment will lock up the browser's user interface:

```
for(var i=0;;i++)
    alert("Why can't i kill this script");
```

## Using All Available Memory

Netscape Navigator doesn't limit the amount of memory that JavaScript can allocate. This attack eventually swamps the virtual memory storage and slows the machine to a crawl:

```
for(var i=0;;i++)
    str = str + "why doesn't everyone play nice";
```

A majority of these attacks are obvious and could be stopped if the user had the capability to terminate an executing script (a feature currently being investigated by Netscape). The more insidious attack is based on degradation of service. The rogue JavaScript code doesn't take over the machine, but it hoards resources to the point that other browser windows appear sluggish.

## Netscape Navigator 2.0 Issues

> **Note**
>
> Because Netscape 2.0 and Internet Explorer 3.0 are no longer very popular, much of the following information is outdated.

The Netscape Navigator 2.0 browser implementation takes a conservative approach toward balancing the needs of the developer with the necessity of protecting a user from security concerns. Because many security holes have been eliminated in later revisions of Netscape Navigator, valid JavaScript code developed for version 2.x doesn't often run properly on later versions.

The balance between private and public access to JavaScript information in Navigator 2.0 was fairly clear. Navigator automatically prevented scripts from one server from accessing properties of documents residing on a different server. These security restrictions prevented a script from fetching private information that the user wouldn't want made public. Since the release of Navigator 2.0, there has been a low-level rewrite of the code related to security issues. Most importantly, the rule related to cooperation between scripts from different servers has been relaxed and codified as a new methodology—data tainting.

You should be aware of outstanding bugs in the Netscape Navigator 2.x versions and update your browser with the latest patches. Netscape has fixed numerous bugs in the 2.01 and 2.02 releases. Most bug fixes were patches to security holes in the Java implementation. I suggest that users and developers update to the latest final release version of Netscape Navigator as soon as it is available.

## Later Navigator Versions

A major rewrite of the JavaScript interpreter has changed the definition of valid code compared to earlier versions. The security measures taken by the Netscape browser are currently in a state of flux as the development community determines the correct balance between language capabilities and user privacy.

The operation of the `document` calls has been changed to ensure that JavaScript code doesn't overwrite the original script. The presence of the `document.open` or `document.write` function call outside of `<BODY>` tags that don't reference a new window results in a code error. Here is an example of an invalid script:

```
<SCRIPT LANGUAGE="Javascript">
var i;
function initialize_app()
{
i = "1";
}

function setup()
{
document.open();
document.write("My test app equals",i);
initialize_app();
document.close();
}
</SCRIPT>
<BODY onload="setup()"></BODY>
```

The browser creates a new document context and flushes out the old JavaScript. The result is the error message `initialize app is not defined`, because the JavaScript interpreter can no longer access the function. The correct workaround to this security restriction is to either write all the text after the `onload` function has finished or write the new document into another frame. The following example demonstrates the first workaround:

```
<SCRIPT>
function setup()
{
initialize_app();
}
</SCRIPT>
<BODY onload="setup()">
</BODY>
<SCRIPT>
document.write("My test app equals",i);
</SCRIPT>
```

# Data Tainting

The concept of data tainting has been added to the language as a mechanism for windows originating from different servers to cooperate and share data. You enable data tainting by setting the environment variable NS_ENABLE_TAINT to any value.

When data tainting is enabled, all JavaScript objects and properties are public and accessible. The feature is necessary for windows to share information across servers. Windows can pull foreign form information from other accessible windows but, when the foreign information is posted to the server, a confirming dialog pops up, allowing the user to cancel or confirm the post operation. If the environment variable isn't set, references to form data on other servers generate the error message access disallowed from scripts at *URL1*.htm to documents at *URL2*.htm.

> **Tip**
>
> Even when data tainting is disabled, windows have the capability to call functions loaded in other windows from other servers. For instance, frame1 loaded from server1 can call a frame2 function loaded from server2.

JavaScript provides functions that let the programmer set or remove tainting on objects. The function taint() returns a tainted reference to a property, and untaint() returns a copy that is untainted. For instance, the following code returns a copy of the private data that can be sent over a URL or form post operation to a server:

```
unmarked = untaint(document.forms[0].element[0].value);
```

> **Caution**
>
> When the NS_ENABLE_TAINT environment variable is set, JavaScript code in one window can view all document properties in other windows, including private data and session history information.

The tainting mechanism currently contains many security bugs and should be used with care. Many developers have demonstrated code that circumvents the protection mechanism by laundering the data through a sequence of data manipulations.

# Internet Explorer 3.x

Because the capability to execute JavaScript and Java applets has just recently been included in Microsoft's Internet Explorer, an extensive security review hasn't been performed by independent third parties. Review of the software's application interface reveals a well-thought-out approach to security. Privacy measures and applet logging have been built into the browser and work with the user to ensure that information is transmitted to servers only explicitly. Figure 35.4 shows a dialog box that details the privacy options available in Internet Explorer.

**FIGURE 35.4**

*Microsoft Internet Explorer security options.*

The application interface also includes the capability to restrict code downloads to only those servers deemed trustworthy. This feature relies on the use of security certificates by the server to identify trusted sites while browsing. Internet Explorer has a dialog box that will display the sites that are trusted by the client browser, as shown in Figure 35.5.

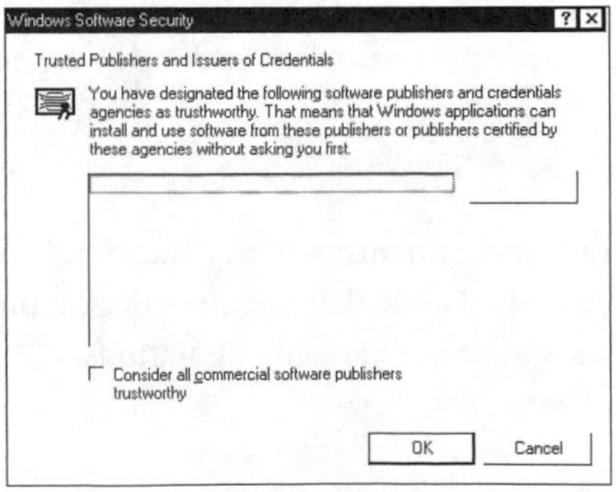

**FIGURE 35.5**

*The Windows Software Security dialog box.*

# Maximizing Security Protection

Before you surf into uncharted waters, you can take steps to reduce the exposure to security attacks due to renegade JavaScript or Java code. You can determine which level of protection to use by seeing how much trust is given to the source of the Web pages visited. When visiting new sites (or visiting those listed after a query for virus hackers), it's advisable to totally remove the capability for the browser to execute scripting languages. Also, the network administrator can take a top-down security approach to disable execution of Java classes obtained from the Internet. The firewall can be configured to remove the capability of Java class files to pass through a proxy server into the internal network. If you keep up with the latest security bulletins and advisories, you should have a clear understanding of the risks involved during trips outside the firewall.

## Secure Sessions and Digital Signatures

As I mentioned earlier, secure sessions are initiated by the browser and establish an encrypted transmission stream between the server and the browser. The encryption is based on a digital certificate stored on the server. Further protection is achieved by digitally signing each file downloaded to the client. Verification authorities such as Verisign are working in conjunction with browser developers to create a framework for appending digital signatures for applets and script files. Later versions of Netscape Navigator and Internet Explorer will provide information about the current security level of the document or frame in addition to onscreen visual cues.

To view the security level of a document (or frame) in Netscape Navigator, choose View, Page Info (Document Info in older versions) or View, Frame Info. The Security line gives the current security level. Figure 35.6 shows Netscape Navigator security information.

To view the security level of a document in Microsoft Internet Explorer, select File, Properties and then choose the Security tab or click on the Certificates button, depending on the version of Internet Explorer you are using. Figure 35.7 shows Internet Explorer security information.

## Disabling Scripting Languages in the Browser

At the individual client level, the most effective way to protect the user from damaging code fragments is simply to remove the browser's capability to execute scripting code. The drawback of this approach is that many exciting capabilities are then removed from a Web site, and the Web site might not operate as intended. You should use these options when you visit untrusted sites of questionable intent.

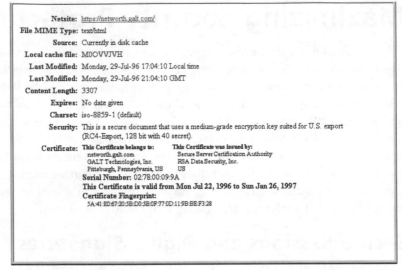

## JavaScript

To disable JavaScript in Netscape Navigator 2.01, select Options, Security Preferences and choose the General tab. Check the Disable JavaScript box, and then click the OK button.

**Note**

Netscape Navigator 2.0 doesn't give you the option of disabling JavaScript.

To disable JavaScript in later versions of Netscape Navigator, select Edit, Preferences (see Figure 35.8) and choose the Advanced option. Remove the check mark from the Enable JavaScript box, and then click OK.

**FIGURE 35.8**
*Disabling Java-Script in later versions of Netscape Navigator.*

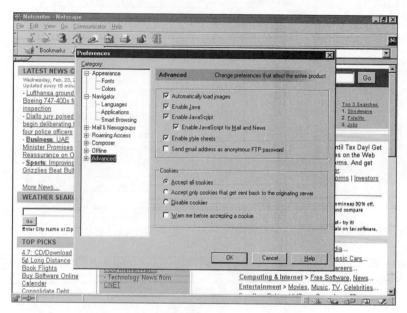

To disable JavaScript in Internet Explorer 4 or later, select Tools, Internet Options and click the Security tab. Click the Custom Level button, scroll down to Active Scripting (see Figure 35.9), and click Disable.

Internet Explorer 3 doesn't have the capability to disable JavaScript.

## Java

To disable Java in Netscape Navigator 2.01, select Options, Security Preferences and choose the General tab. Check the Disable Java box, and click OK.

To disable Java in later versions of Netscape Navigator, select Edit, Preferences and choose the Advanced option. Remove the check mark from the Enable Java box, and click OK.

To disable Java in Internet Explorer, select Tools, Internet Options and choose the Security tab. Select Custom Level and scroll down to Java. Click Disable, and click the OK button. Figure 35.10 shows the Internet Explorer dialog box used to disable Java programs.

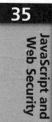

**35**
**JavaScript and Web Security**

**FIGURE 35.9**
*Disabling Java-
Script in Internet
Explorer.*

**FIGURE 35.9**
*Disabling Java-
Script in Internet
Explorer.*

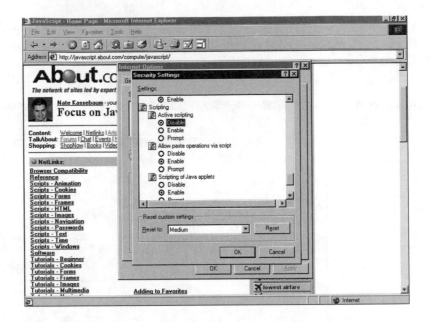

**FIGURE 35.10**
*Disabling Java in
Internet Explorer.*

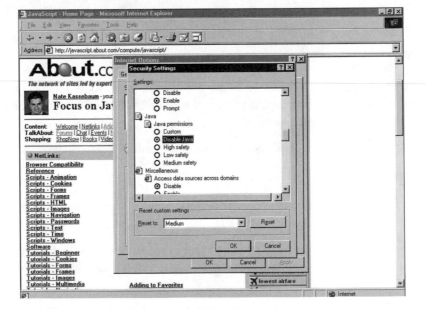

# Firewall Filtering

Firewalls and proxy servers are commonly the first line of defense between the Internet and an internal network (WAN, LAN, or remote machine). Network administrators can configure firewall routers to filter network traffic based on various parameters and thereby ensure that a user can't download a file that could cause a security breach. However, the level of filtering should be determined by balancing the benefits achieved through higher security against the cost involved to implement a solution. Router or proxy server-based high security solutions are generally expensive to implement, either from a resource or monetary standpoint, and you must be sure not to over-engineer the security wall.

HTTP requests are used by the client browser to request Java and JavaScript code fragments. Because HTTP is also used for normal Web browser functionality, the proxy server can't just deny access to all HTTP requests, because that would result in no access to the Web by the browser. A filtering methodology (that can be used to remove Java downloads) is to filter URL HTTP requests to block all files that have a .class or .cla extension. Filtering JavaScript code is more difficult because the source files may legally use any extension and because code fragments may be embedded inside Web pages.

# Security Information Resources on JavaScript and Java Security

The Internet contains many sites devoted to information about security issues. Keeping informed of the latest security bulletins is a good start for making an informed decision about the risks involved in using the latest technology.

The most accurate, up-to-date information can be found at the following Web sites:

Netscape: `http://developer.netscape.com/docs/manuals/index.html`

*Information related to Netscape products*: Sun at `http://java.javasoft.com/sfaq/`

*Information related to Java*: CERT at `http://www.cert.org`

*Nonpartisan advisories about current security breaches*: CERT FTP at `ftp://info.cert.org/pub/cert_advisories/`

*Search directory for files containing the name Java:* Safe Internet Programming at `http://www.cs.princeton.edu/sip/`. This site is run by a research group at Princeton University that is investigating Internet scripting extensions. They are responsible for discovering the latest Java security holes.

# Security Concerns for Server-Side JavaScript

The functionality of Web servers can be extended through the execution of JavaScript and Java routines as either CGI programs or server modules. Server-Side JavaScript uses existing knowledge of the JavaScript language to create applications that can reference databases and other resources residing on the server. The capability to execute Server-Side JavaScript in a Netscape server is currently described as LiveWire technology, and it's enabled through the server administration manager. Figure 35.11 shows the Enterprise server screen that is used to activate Server-Side JavaScript (LiveWire).

**FIGURE 35.11**
*Activating Server-Side JavaScript.*

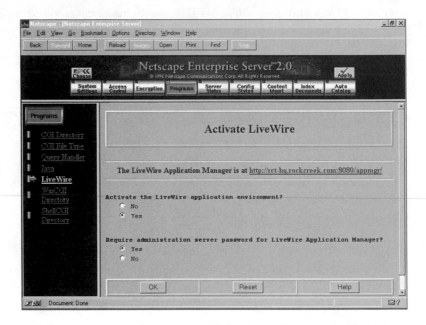

It's important to recognize that the Server-Side JavaScript capability must then be mapped to specific directories on the server. The necessity of authorizing server directories capable of executing Server-Side JavaScript helps protect the server by isolating the areas that could cause a security breach. Figure 35.12 shows the server screen that is used to activate LiveWire for a particular server subdirectory.

**FIGURE 35.12**
*Activating
LiveWire direc-
tories to execute
JavaScript.*

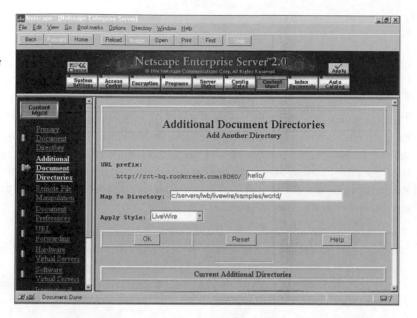

The LiveWire technology exposes four new JavaScript objects for use on the server:
`request`, `client`, `project`, and `server`. The `request` object has a property, `request.ip`,
that lets the server determine the IP address that originated the client request. This object
member can be used to verify trusted clients who can be given access to confidential
information. The global application data object, `project`, should be locked before data
variable values are changed; otherwise, the integrity of application variables and counters
isn't synchronized between the client processes.

The most significant security concern is the capability for Server-Side JavaScript to read
and write directly to the hard drive. Improperly formatted data can often crash programs
that read or write files. The server script code should check extensively to ensure that the
user data is in a valid format before writing it to disk. Also, it's imperative that Server-Side
JavaScript code be constructed with file-locking mechanisms to take into account that
multiple processes execute on the host server. The simplest locking mechanism is to
rename the file before opening it for file I/O. On all operating systems, the `rename`
command is expected to be an atomic operation on any platform. The following code
illustrates this principle:

```
while(rename(filename,lockname))      // rename filename to the lock filename
    ;                     // block on access to file
```

**35**

**JavaScript and
Web Security**

```
else
    {
// perform file i/o
rename(lockname,oldname);        // rename file to original name
}
```

The server-side code shouldn't write to disk files in public directories that have execution capability. It's a common hacker trick to use a trusted server-side program to create a file on the server that can be used for attack later. For instance, a CGI program that uploads text files from the client to the server can be used to create a script file that can be executed. When the uploaded file is accessed by the attacker via the Web browser, the server-side code executes and can attack the server machine.

Web site administrators and code developers should be aware that Server-Side JavaScript can crash the production server. Excessive use of system memory, improperly locking objects, infinite loops, and improper file I/O can bring the server to a halt. All script code should be fully tested on a development server before going live. Furthermore, code should be empirically evaluated for possible deadlock conditions to verify that server-side scripts won't infinitely block a resource.

### Caution

Client-side JavaScript can attempt to access any port on the originating server. A security check should be performed to ensure that a proper firewall is in place between the server and the Internet.

The Java interpreter must be explicitly activated for server directories. The server application manager is used to specify directories that can execute Java modules. Figure 35.13 shows the application manager screen used to activate Java for a particular server subdirectory.

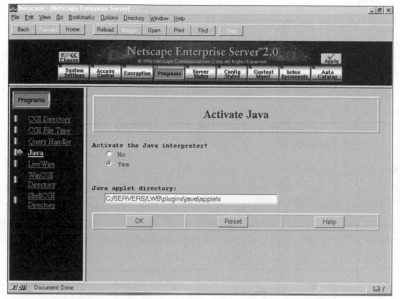

**FIGURE 35.13**

*Activating Java
directories on the
server.*

# Java and Security

The Java language offers many more capabilities than JavaScript. The later versions of Netscape let the developer write a mix of Java and JavaScript code inside Java applets (LiveConnect technology). Also, JavaScript can call Java applet functions directly, passing parameters and receiving return values. The two languages can be used in tandem to create comprehensive remote client solutions.

Knowledge of Java's history is important for putting in perspective security issues related to its current implementation. The language mirrors C++ in many respects—it has common language syntax, similar keywords, and support for object-oriented programming, including inheritance. Java diverges from C++ in ways that add flexibility to the language and attempt to create a more secure environment: The code can't forge pointers, garbage collection of objects is handled automatically, and only single inheritance is implemented. The machine-independent structure of Java attempts to insulate the programmer from the target machine's operating system. Basic programming building blocks are extended with prebuilt packages capable of targeting either server or client systems.

Java was originally designed to be a language for creating embedded applications on personal appliances (desktop TV boxes, personal communicators, hand-held computers, and so on). The possibility of attack on these closed systems is much lower than it is when connecting to the largest public network with open standards.

The application programming interface proposed by Sun Microsystems for the Java language during its public alpha test phase was robust enough to handle a majority of the tasks required by traditional desktop computer applications. The goal was to allow a trusted browser or trusted Java environment to run untrusted Java class components. Java's current implementation falls short of that mandate, because its security mechanisms don't follow basic industry security standards for trusted systems. The Java language as a standalone definition can't be considered a secure language, because it doesn't define the most basic components of a secure architecture.

Java doesn't contain basic security mechanisms such as an audit capability in the class loader to document the modules loaded during an attack. Because applets can exist beyond the scope of the Web document that loaded them, a rogue applet can mount an attack without the user's drawing a correlation to its existence. A user-defined audit policy should be available that allows the logging of applet execution, applet originating network address, and applet bytecode.

Also, the implementations of Java haven't proven to be a secure language as envisioned by its creators. Many subsystems have security bugs that haven't been entirely fixed, leading to recurring security alerts. Table 35.2 details the most important of these, which are documented by Sun Microsystems in the Applet Security FAQ (`http://java.sun.com/sfaq/`).

**TABLE 35.2    Some Java Security Bugs**

| Date | Problem | Status |
| --- | --- | --- |
| March 26, 1999 | Unverified Code | Fixed in JDK 1.1.8 |
| July 22, 1998 | Princeton class loader attack | Fixed in JDK 1.2 |
| June 2, 1996 | Illegal type cast attack | Fixed in JDK 1.1 |
| May 18, 1996 | New version of previous class loader attack | Fixed in Netscape 3.0b4 |
| April 1996 | URL name resolution attack | Fixed in Netscape 3.0b4 |
| March 1996 | Verifier implementation bug | Fixed in Netscape 2.02 |
| March 1996 | Class loader implementation bug | Fixed in Netscape 2.01 |
| February 1996 | DNS attack | Fixed in Netscape 2.01 |

The researchers who discovered these security bugs have publicly stated that Java might have to be radically altered to meet their definition of a secure environment. The illegal type cast attack successfully circumvents the safe-type cast mechanism in Java. Successful attacks on the type cast mechanism allow Java objects to masquerade as other types. The capability of hackers to develop a rogue class loader means that untrusted application code could potentially be loaded and executed from an untrusted source without the browser's knowledge.

# Security Components

The security mechanisms to control Java objects are written in Java itself. When the browser runtime system starts, no security restrictions are in place. The class that monitors security, `SecurityManager`, is loaded from the directory contained in the client's `CLASSPATH` environment variable. These trusted class files (`MOZxxx.ZIP` in Netscape Navigator 2.0 and `JAVxxx.ZIP` in Netscape Navigator 3.x) should be protected by frequent virus checks and marked as read-only.

## Bytecode Verifier

Once a Java class is downloaded from the remote host, the code is checked by a bytecode verifier. This important step ensures that the Java code conforms to known language opcodes and that the operand stack isn't subjected to overflows or underflows. All class object accesses are checked for adherence to the protection mechanism defined for the object members (private, protected, public). Furthermore, the code is verified to ensure that no illegal data conversions are present. After the verifier performs its job, the code is converted by the Java runtime compiler into machine code.

## Security Manager

The `SecurityManager` class is used by the Java runtime system to access control authorization of Java classes. Because the `SecurityManager` is implemented as a Java object, when the runtime initially starts, the security manager is protected by the Java type system. If the type system has proven impenetrable and the file system hasn't been compromised, `SecurityManager` is considered a trusted class.

The Java compilers are responsible for compiling the Java source code (a `.java` file) into a machine-independent bytecode (a `.class` file). The bytecode is transmitted over the network to the local machine and interpreted or compiled into native code by the Java runtime system. Verifying the Java bytecode is a critical step in determining the integrity of a Java applet. Just as current virus-checking programs search for illegal processor and operating system calls, bytecode should be verified to not contain any security attacks. The bytecodes must be evaluated in the context of their types. For example, the `SecurityManager` type should have fewer restrictions than a user-defined type.

The lack of a formal definition for the Java type system and the need to thoroughly analyze all program execution sequences render this evaluation by current verifiers complicated and unreliable.

Security between applet methods is enforced by a concept of *named space*. Every Java applet should have a unique name, depending on the location from which it was downloaded. The Java documentation states that the named space of system-level objects has the capability to be shared by all other named spaces (applets), and that the runtime class loader always searches the list of system-named spaces to prevent downloaded code from overwriting a system class. Yet forging named space hashes that inadvertently replace vital system class components like the class loader has been one of the first security bugs found in Java. Class loader bugs have been extensively documented by the researchers at Princeton University.

## Security Restrictions

The basic Java language is extended by many valuable class packages that save the programmer from reinventing basic interfaces. The implementation of a package can shield the programmer from platform-specific issues, but it can restrict access to certain low-level components as well. Basic access to the machine subsystems responsible for network communications, file I/O, memory access, and system resources is affected by the particular implementation of Java being used. Currently, server-side Java code has fewer security restrictions than those imposed on the client.

> **Tip**
>
> In Java code, error messages that include the term `SecurityException` indicate that a security restriction has been violated.

## Network Communications

To *sandbox* is to restrict the capability of the applet code to communicate with other machines. A sandboxed applet can communicate only with the server from which it originated. The restriction that the code will only "play in its sandbox" is the primary line of defense against rogue applets. The security manager subjects networking calls to the restriction that they can only open communication channels between the client and the applet's originating DNS address. Because the methodology relies on the DNS subsystem to provide address verification, compromises to the DNS address server in turn invalidate the security mechanism.

According to the documentation, applets can open communication channels back to the server on any port. In reality, the Netscape Java implementation places undocumented restrictions on which ports are available.

> **Tip**
>
> Having an applet in the toolchest that queries all socket ports and returns possible communication channels saves a great deal of time when you're determining the ports that your Java implementation supports.

## File I/O

Current implementations of client-side Java don't permit reading or writing to the client's hard disk. On a client machine, calls to open, read, write, and close files generate a `SecurityExceptions` or `IOExceptions` notification. Sun Microsystems' Applet Viewer application uses an access control file to grant read and write permissions to the client's disk drive. It's likely that some derivation of that scheme will be adopted in the future by the Netscape browser. As I mentioned earlier in this chapter, server-side Java can access the host hard drive to perform file operations.

## Memory Access

In Java, source code doesn't have the concept of memory pointers. This simplifies the implementation of language by the programmer and reduces code errors. Because data structures aren't referenced by pointers, many proponents of Java envision it to be a more secure language than C++. Also, Java programmers should be unable to forge pointers to functions.

## System Resources

The capability to lock system resources is a security risk in Java. For example, in the Netscape implementation, locking the `java.net.InetAddress` class results in blocking all new network connections.

Both Java and JavaScript are revolutionary languages that help the Web site developer create interactive content. However, the capability to run remote code on client machines must be considered from the perspective of potential damage to the user's operating environment.

The goal of the Internet vendor community is the creation of a trusted environment in which users don't have to worry that an action will have damaging consequences. Ideally, the user would also know that an operation was about to occur and would be able to prevent it.

**35**

**JavaScript and Web Security**

Mechanisms are still being developed for creating a safe networked environment that is intuitive to the end user. The security measures encapsulating JavaScript code might not be ready for mission-critical environments, but the fast growth of Internet technologies deserves a close watch for tomorrow's solutions.

# Summary

As computer users reach beyond their desktops and communicate with business partners and friends all over the world, issues related to computer security and privacy are becoming paramount concerns. This chapter provided an introduction to the client areas that should be protected from malicious tampering and showed how users can safeguard their machines when running JavaScript and Java programs. The security methodologies are currently in a state of flux. The execution of remote code on client machines is severely restricted in the current implementations, as the needs of the user and the developer are balanced against concern for potential misuse. Knowledge of the limitations and features present in current technology is critical when establishing a proper level of trust and proliferating dynamic and compelling applications and content throughout the Internet community.

# Appendix

# Part VI

## IN THIS PART

# APPENDIX

# Top Ten JavaScript Resources on the Web

# Netscape DevEdge Online

`http://developer.netscape.com`

This is Netscape's central Web site for all of its developer technologies. Here you can find Netscape's official JavaScript documentation, as well as articles and newsletters to keep you abreast of what Netscape is doing in the JavaScript world. It includes the following highlights:

> JavaScript Authoring Guide at `http://developer.netscape.com/docs/manuals/communicator/jsguide4/index.htm`
>
> JavaScript Developer Central at `http://developer.netscape.com/tech/javascript/index.html`
>
> Official JavaScript Language Specification (PostScript format) at `ftp://ftp.netscape.com/pub/review/jsspec.ps.gz`

# Microsoft Scripting Technologies

`http://msdn.microsoft.com/scripting/default.htm`

This is Microsoft's main Web site for JScript and VBScript information. Here you can download the newest version of the Microsoft scripting engine, as well as find documentation and examples for JScript and VBScript. It includes the following highlights:

> JScript Language Reference at `http://msdn.microsoft.com/scripting/jscript/doc/jstoc.htm`
>
> JScript FAQ at `http://msdn.microsoft.com/scripting/jscript/techinfo/jsfaq.htm`
>
> JScript Samples at `http://msdn.microsoft.com/scripting/jscript/samples/jssamp.htm`

# Voodoo's Introduction to JavaScript

`http://rummelplatz.uni-mannheim.de/~skoch/js/script.htm`

Voodoo's Introduction to JavaScript is a 12-part tutorial covering all the popular aspects of JavaScript. This tutorial is fit for beginners and experts. Part 1 explains the basics of what JavaScript is and how it is used, and the later parts explain how to use layers and advanced Dynamic HTML.

# Irt.org

`http://www.irt.org/articles/script.htm`

Irt.org (Internet Related Technologies) contains a huge collection of high quality articles on all kinds of topics, including ASP, HTML, Dynamic HTML, VBScript, CSS, XML, JavaScript, and more. The URL above links directly to the JavaScript section, where you'll find many useful articles in a well-organized directory.

# Focus on JavaScript

`http://javascript.about.com`

This site is maintained by Nate Kassebaum, one of the authors of this book. Here you will find weekly articles about JavaScript, as well as links to the most current information on other sites. Highlights include the following:

> About.com JavaScript Tutorial at `http://javascript.about.com/library/bl_tutorial.htm`

> Focus on JavaScript Newsletter at `http://javascript.about.com/gi/pages/mmail.htm`

# SuperScripter

`http://www.builder.com/Programming/Scripter/`

This is the JavaScript section of C|NET's Builder.com. Each week, Builder.com's JavaScript guru writes an article demonstrating an aspect of JavaScript. The archive here contains some of the best articles and examples available online.

# JavaScripts.com

`http://www.javascripts.com`

JavaScripts.com contains thousands of cut-and-paste JavaScript code examples for you to use in your own Web pages. The site is for members only, but membership is free and all that is required is your email address.

# The JavaScript Source

`http://javascript.internet.com`

The JavaScript Source is primarily a library of JavaScript code samples, but it also features a discussion forum and a section on JavaScript-related books. The code library is very good, with nearly 500 high quality scripts at the time of this writing.

# WebCoder.com

`http://www.webcoder.com`

WebCoder.com contains script examples, how-to articles, a JavaScript and Dynamic HTML reference, and demo pages for many popular and new JavaScript applications.

# Website Abstraction

`http://www.wsabstract.com`

Website Abstraction is a large directory of free JavaScript code and JavaScript tutorials. The site also contains information and samples of other Web building technologies, such as Java and Dynamic HTML.

# INDEX

# F

**fade from to( ) method, 697**
**fade to( ) method, 697**
**fading color (Web pages), 572**
  bgColor property, 572
  code example, 573-574
  JSFade( ) function, 572-573
**favorites, cookie code example (Favorites script), 818-830**
**features**
  MSSD
    *breakpoints, 895*
    *code coloring, 895*
    *HTML structure view, 895*
    *immediate expression window, 896*
    *integrated call stack, 896*
    *multiple language integration, 895*
    *stepping into code, 895*
    *stepping out of code, 895*
    *stepping over code, 895*
  Netscape JavaScript Debugger
    *breakpoints, 902*
    *call stack, 903*
    *console window, 903*
    *error reporter dialog, 903*
    *interrupt, 902*
    *object inspector, 903*
    *source view window, 902*
    *stepping into code, 902*
    *stepping out of code, 903*
    *stepping over code, 902*
    *watches window, 903*
**feedback (forms), 765-775**
  alert messages, 770
  alert( ) method, 770
  automated toaster form example, 766-768
  confirm( ) method, 770
  message boxes, displaying, 770-773

  prompt( ) method, 771
  status messages, 773-775
  testing user forms, 769
**fields**
  calculated fields (interactive forms), 785-789
  location, DHTML (Dynamic HTML) toolbars, 663
  remainder text field, 785
**file I/O, Java security, 937**
**File menu commands, New Browser, 394**
**file object, 343-346**
  methods, 343-344
  open( ) method parameters, 344
  properties, 344
**file sizes, cookies, 321**
**filename property, 676**
**files**
  employeeInfo.html, 858
  GIF
    *billboards, 565*
    *DOM, 546*
    *Paint Shop Pro, 546*
    *pushbuttons, 574*
  image, caching, 504-505
  Image object, caching, 504-505
  JavaScript library, 324, 328
  .js, 51
  loading, iframe tag, 621-625
  result.html, 858
  searchfrm.html, 858
  source
    *creating, 323-324*
    *HTML documents, 324*
    *JavaScript library files, 324*
  .wav, 675
**fileupload object, 244**
  methods, 244
  properties, 244
**filtering, firewalls, 929**
**Find button, 655, 663-665, 864**

**findEmployee( ) method, 860**
  code, 863-864
  code to call, 860-861
**findText parameter, 259**
**firewall filtering, 929**
**fixed( ) method, 255**
**flickerFree property, Window object, 631**
**floating-point numbers, 99**
**floor( ) method, 286**
**focus, 776**
  direct, browser windows, 408
  event, 372
  indirect, browser windows, 407
  onBlur event handler, losing, 375-376
  onFocus event handler, receiving, 372-374
  removing, browser windows, 408
**Focus on JavaScript Newsletter Web site, 943**
**Focus on JavaScript Web site, 943**
**fontcolor( ) method, 255**
**fontsize( ) method, 255**
**for loops, 156**
**for...in loops, 159**
**form elements**
  focus, 776
  text, 775
  textarea, 775
**form object, 237, 448**
  checking form elements, 453-454
  defining, 448-449
  methods, 237
  properties, 237-238, 449-453
  submitting forms, 449-452
**form tags, 44, 657, 769**
**formatting**
  hypertext, String object, 267
  String object with tag, source code, 267-269
  strings, 262-269

# I

# What's on the CD-ROM

The companion CD-ROM contains many useful third-party tools and utilities, plus the source code and JavaScript samples from the book.

# Macintosh Installation Instructions

1. Insert the CD into the CD-ROM drive.

2. When an icon for the CD appears on your desktop, open the CD by double-clicking its icon.

3. Double-click the icon named Guide to the CD-ROM, and follow the directions that appear.

# Technical Support from Macmillan

We can't help you with Windows or Macintosh problems or software from third parties, but we can assist you if a problem arises with the CD-ROM itself.

Email support: Send email to support@mcp.com.

CompuServe: GO SAMS to reach the Macmillan USA forum. Leave us a message addressed to SYSOP. If you want the message to be private, address it to *SYSOP.

Telephone: (317) 581-3833

Fax: (317) 581-4773

Mail:     Macmillan USA
          Attention: Support Department
          201 West 103rd Street
          Indianapolis, IN 46290-1093

Here's how to reach us on the Internet:

World Wide Web (The Macmillan Information SuperLibrary)

http://www.mcp.com/sams

# Windows 98 Installation Instructions

1. Insert the CD into the CD-ROM drive.
2. From the Windows 98 desktop, double-click the My Computer icon.
3. Double-click the icon representing your CD-ROM drive.
4. Double-click the icon called `SETUP.EXE` to run the installation program.
5. Installation creates a program group named JavaScript Unleashed 3. This group will contain icons you can use to browse the CD-ROM.

**Note**

If Windows 98 is installed on your computer and you have the AutoPlay feature enabled, the `SETUP.EXE` program starts automatically whenever you insert the CD into the CD-ROM drive.

# Windows NT Installation Instructions

1. Insert the CD into the CD-ROM drive.
2. From File Manager or Program Manager, choose File, Run.
3. Type *drive*`\SETUP.EXE` and press Enter, where *drive* corresponds to the drive letter of your CD-ROM. For example, if your CD-ROM is drive D:, type `D:\SETUP.EXE` and press Enter.
4. Installation creates a program group named JavaScript Unleashed 3. This group will contain icons you can use to browse the CD-ROM.